South America
on a Shoestring

South America on a Shoestring

Published by
  Lonely Planet Publications
  PO Box 88, South Yarra
  Victoria 3141, Australia

Typeset by
  Lonely Planet Productions (thank you Margaret & Andy)

Printed by
  Colorcraft, Hong Kong

Illustrations by
  Peter Campbell

Design by
  Andrena Millen

First Published
  January 1980

National Library of Australia
Cataloguing in Publication Data

Crowther, Geoff.
  South America on a Shoestring.

  ISBN 0 908086 08 3

  1. South America — Description and travel —
  Guide-books. I. Campbell, Peter, Illus.
  II. Title.

918'.04

DISTRIBUTION

Ask your local bookshop to order Lonely Planet travel guides from one of our distributors below. If you have any trouble write to us directly in Australia — we'll rush copies to you as fast as the mail can carry them:

Canada — Milestone Publications Box 445, Victoria, British Colombia, V8W 2N8 — **Hong Kong** — Hong Kong University Press, 94 Bonham Road, Hong Kong — **India** — UBS Distributors, 5 Ansari Rd, New Delhi — **Japan** — Intercontinental Marketing Corporation, PO Box 5056, Tokyo 100-31 — **Malaysia** — see Singapore — **Nepal** — see India — **Netherlands** — Nilsonn & Lamm bv, Pampuslaan 212, Weesp, Postbus 195 — **New Zealand** — Caveman Press, Box 1458, Dunedin — **Papua New Guinea** — Robert Brown and Associates, Box 3395, Port Moresby — **Philippines** — see Singapore — **Singapore** — Apa Productions, Suite 1021, International Plaza, Anson Rd, Singapore — **Thailand** — Chalermnit Bookshop, 1-2 Erawan Arcade, Bangkok — **UK** — Roger Lascelles, 16 Holland Park Gardens, London W14 8DY — **USA** — Bookpeople, 2940 Seventh St, Berkeley CA 94710 — Hippocrene Books, 171 Madison Ave, New York, NY 10016

Lonely Planet Travel Guides
Other Lonely Planet travel guides include *Kathmandu & the Kingdom of Nepal* — "the best little modern guide to the mountain kingdom". *Trekking in the Himalayas* — now including day-by-day route reports of all the major treks. *Papua New Guinea* — *a travel survival kit* — explore the "last unknown". *New Zealand* — *a travel survival kit* — both islands of the "land of the long white cloud". *Africa on the Cheap* — even the countries to avoid. *Australia* — *a travel survival kit* — the

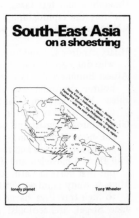

complete guide to down-under. *Hong Kong & Macau* — so much more than duty free shopping. *South-East Asia on a Shoestring* — the number one guide to the region. *Across Asia on the Cheap* — with a "bad news on Iran & Afghanistan" supplement. *Burma* — *a travel survival kit* — one of the most fascinating countries in the region. *Europe* — *a travel survival kit* — this one is available only in Australasia. Coming soon — *Sri Lanka* — *a travel survival kit.*

Geoff was born in Yorkshire, England and started his travelling days as a teenage hitch-hiker. Later, after many short trips around Europe, two years "on the road" in Asia and Africa, spells in the overgrown fishing village of Hull and on the bleak and beautiful Cumberland fells with a happy band of long-haired lunatics and mystics Geoff got involved with the London underground information centre BIT. He helped put together their first, tatty, duplicated *Overland to India* guide and later their *Overland through Africa* guide. Geoff's first guide for Lonely Planet was *Africa on the Cheap* and in 1981 he'll be out there travelling for us again to research another all new guide.

MANY THANKS...........

This guide represents not only my own maniacal flair for composing railway timetables and bus fares, sussing out seedy hotels in the back of beyond and wielding the rapidograph, but also the efforts of the following people, without whose support and help I would by now be unbearable, etc, etc. They are:

Hilary Andrews, hand-loom weaver, sub-aquarist and lover from Hull, England who did a great deal of the research and collation and came along on the trip.

Alison Sommerville, lawyer and ex-BIT Information Service worker from Melbourne, Australia, who also helped with research and came along on the trip.

Eileen Mills, astrologist and masseuse, formerly of Hull, England and now c/o Central Railway Station, Sydney, Australia, who also helped with research.

Glen Kinross, dentist and beverage hall connoisseur from somewhere in Australia (he never did tell me just where) who is still out there in Bolivia as these words are written and regularly sending back more info.

Phil Davies, musician and TEFL teacher of London, England, who put us on to our first hosts in Latin America and encouraged me to go with tales of Mexico.

Mike & Andy Godfrey, TEFL teachers of Guildford, England, who welcomed us to their travellers' haven in Mexico City.

Jane Siegel, archaeologist and dreamer from New York, USA, who travelled through Peru with me.

David Stanley & Mark Robertson, from Toronto, Canada and Melbourne, Australia respectively, two more intrepid South American explorers.

Thanks a million.

AND A REQUEST

Travel guides are only kept up to date by people who travel. It's impossible to retrace every step for each new edition but you can help us, and your fellow travellers by writing and telling us what you've found along the way. The best letters score a free copy of the next edition — or any other Lonely Planet guide.

Contents

Contents

Introduction

Until fairly recently South America was a mysterious continent — even a dream — to most Europeans and Australasians (though less so to North Americans) if only because of the expense of getting there but, with the advent of cheaper fares to the US and a lowering of air fares in general, it no longer is so. It's now possible to get to Central America from Europe for well under £100 (US$200) or to South America for around £160 (US$320). From Australia you can make it for under A$500 return. How much still depends to a large extent on your own initiative and what you're prepared to be satisfied with but this guide has been written to help you make the most of it.

Some guides try to be too comprehensive and end up containing so much information that it takes you longer to read through the lists of hotels and decide which ones suit your pocket and preferences than it would to find one from scratch. Others skimp and pad out the hard information with waffle leaving you clueless outside the main cities and tourist sites. We've tried to steer a middle course in this guide and to indicate sufficient possibilities without at the same time turning it into an *Encylopaedia Britannica*, but we haven't missed out the "musts" where the character of a place, its people, crafts, ancient ruins or spectacular views demanded inclusion. Use it as you see fit but beware of allowing it (or indeed any guide) to become a leaning post. Even if it contained a complete cross-referenced list of all possible means of transport, hotels and places to see so that you got the impression you could plan a trip right down to the last detail, things still wouldn't work out that way in practice. Hotels change, timetables change, transport gets delayed, sometimes for days rather than hours, so nothing is essentially lost if you don't know the exact departure times or prices. Try to take things a lot more loosely than you would do at home. If you try to rush around at the speed of light you'll miss out on a great deal, lay yourself wide open to overcharging and theft and possibly end up tearing your hair out with exasperation.

We've assumed you're going to be reasonably flexible about your route and that the chances are you'll meet other travellers and local people who will persuade you to go to places you hadn't previously planned on visiting. With this in mind we've avoided putting forward a hard and fast "gringo trail" to be followed religiously — though such trails do exist particularly in the Andean countries where they are largely dictated by geography and communication networks. We've also avoided pre-empting your impressions unnecessarily by cluttering the guide with long descriptive passages based on personal experience since each person will have his or her own priorities and will in any case experience the same event/people/place in a uniquely different way.

Learn some Spanish (and Portuguese if you're going to Brazil) before you go. Presumably, if you want to see a country you also want to meet its people, talk with them and spend some time with them as well as mingle with your fellow travellers and go sight-seeing. Very few Latin Americans speak English (why should they?) and you'll feel isolated unless you have at least a working knowledge of their language. Remember too that they are a very gregarious people and that the streets and markets are as much a part of the social scene as their individual houses so if you want something — even something as simple as asking the direction — a greeting, a joke, a few minutes conversation, before making

7

your request makes all the difference. Otherwise you're just another "yanqui turista". This seems obvious but you'd be amazed how many travellers don't apparently give it a thought or go around with their heads inside guide books talking only to people from their own country. Yet no matter how fluent you are in Spanish you still won't be able to speak with a great many Indian people since they still have their own languages and don't speak Spanish.

North American influence is very strong expecially in cities and its tentacles stretch far and wide — Coca Cola, Colonel Sanders, McDonalds, American cars and attitudes are all here — you'll have to go a long way to miss it completely. Nevertheless, the culture brought by the Spanish conquistadores and later developed into what it is today by the Mestizo populations is still very much alive. So are the Indian cultures inherited from the days of the Aztec, Maya, Chibcha and Inca civilizations in those countries which have large pure Indian populations concentrated in certain areas. But there's a good deal of prejudice against them, except where they can be turned into convenient tourist attractions — a strange attitude to take to such a rich common heritage (though probably no stranger than the widespread acceptance that anything "modern" was preferable to anything "old" so common in the affluent countries during the '50s and '60s and even today in some places). There have been many bungling attempts based on this sort of prejudice to bring the Indians into the "mainstream" of economic and social life but they have generally been recognised for what they really are — a thinly disguised attempt to get the Indian to abandon his culture, accept that of the Mestizo and then be exploited for his labour and lands.

Partly because of this uneasy co-existence between separate cultures and Latin America's history of exploitation, first by Imperial Spain and later by Western nations, many countries are going through profound political and social changes. There is an enormous gap between the rich and the millions of poor who lead a desparate hand-to-mouth existence. There are also some very heavy military regimes propped up by US money and arms who use torture systematically to stifle opposition, prevent even a modest redistribution of wealth and thus maintain the status quo. This sort of stuff is the bread and butter of the press and if newspapers were your only source of information you could well imagine that Latin America was just a forbidding miasma of political instability, rampant inflation and violence. It's not — but then good news is no news. Don't be put off going there, most ordinary people are open, friendly and eager to talk to you, especially when it's clear you have at least a little time to pass with them. It's an amazing continent with a million and one different contrasts. You won't regret going. The hardest part is making the decision to go.

PAPERWORK

The essential documents are a passport and an International Vaccination Certificate. If you're taking your own vehicle you will also need an International Driving Permit and a Carnet de Passage (Triptique) for your vehicle. An International Driving Permit is also essential if you're not taking your own vehicle but are thinking of making use of the "drive-away" schemes as a means of getting across the States cheaply — see under *Getting There* for further details. Whoever supplies you with your vaccinations will provide you with the International Vaccination Certificate which must then be counter-stamped by the local health authority. Any national motoring organization will fix you up with an International Driving Licence (assuming you have a driving licence for your own country) and a Carnet de Passage.

In addition it's useful to have an International Student Card and, if you're going to use hostels, an International Youth Hostel Card. If you're carrying a Student Card it's an idea to also have a letter on appropriately headed notepaper confirming that you are a student at the place mentioned on your card, but remember that Student Cards are of limited use in Latin America unlike Africa, the Middle East and Asia where they can save you a small fortune. Unless you're going to Peru and intent on visiting quite a few archaeological sites they are probably not worth the hassle and expense of acquiring unless you're a "genuine" student and can therefore get one free or almost free from your student travel service. If you're intent on getting hold of one and are not a "genuine" student try one of the following ways: befriend someone who issues them/has access to them; temporarily enroll on some full-time course; try some of the less reputable charter flight companies; write to any of the Eastern European student organizations who dispense cards like confetti (any slight evidence of student status will suffice); contact BIT Information Service, 97A Talbot Rd, London W11, England; buy a fake card. Wherever travellers congregate someone will be selling student cards (average price US$5) but the quality of them varies, so inspect carefully before buying.

International Youth Hostel Cards are obtainable from your national Youth Hostel organization though you generally have to be an ordinary member in the first instance before they will isssue an International Card (for a further charge).

VISAS

Visas are stamped into blank pages in your passport and are obtained from the embassy or consulate of the appropriate country either before you set out or along the way. It's best to get them along the way expecially if your travel plans are not fixed. Details of visa requirements are noted in the main text under the appropriate country. Very few, if any, visas are required by nationals of most West European countries and Japan. North American and Australasian nationals are unlucky in this respect as they still need quite a few. British nationals need only one — for Guatemala. Don't turn up at borders without a visa unless you know one is not needed or can be obtained at the border, or you'll find yourself tramping back to the nearest consulate to get one before you're allowed across. A cache of passport-size photographs is useful if you're going to have to apply for visas (24 should see you through).

There's usually no hassle getting a visa whatever your appearance though they may ask you, either verbally or on the application form, how much money you're carrying. In some cases they may ask to see it but this is rare. The hassle, if any, comes at the border or the airport where you may very well be asked to show how much money you have. If the official who is dealing with you "decides" — for relevant or irrelevant reasons — that you haven't "sufficient" then your permitted length of stay may be limited. This is generally no sweat, since if you want to stay longer you can always renew the visa at an Immigration Office inside the country by showing, if necessary, your own and someone else's travellers' cheques artfully combined. I've never seen them scrutinize the signatures. But the biggest bugbear is when entry is dependent on you having an onward ticket (ie they won't let you in without an air, bus, rail or boat ticket out of the country). This requirement is strictly enforced in the following countries: Costa Rica, Panama, Colombia, Peru, the three Guianas, Venezuela and (possibly) Chile.

Here are two alternatives to the onward ticket problem: Deposit, say, US$500 in a bank and then ask the manager for a letter confirming that you have those funds available to draw on for a return ticket should the need arise (make a Spanish translation of the letter). You can always withdraw the money once you have the letter. This might work with some countries but it certainly doesn't work for Peru. It's probably only useful as a back-up for your funds. Buy a Miscellaneous Charges Order for, say, US$50 or 100 from an airline which does flights to most Latin American countries — eg *Braniff*, *Pan Am*, etc. They are rather like having a deposit account with an airline and look like an airline ticket although they're not for any specific flight. They can be refunded in full or exchanged for a specific flight ticket with any IATA airline. This is usually, but not always, acceptable by border/airport officials.

In general the only countries which are any real hassle are Colombia and Venezuela (and the Caribbean islands of Trinidad and Barbados — if you're flying in that way from Europe). For these countries it's best to have a specific, but undated, flight ticket out of the country. Again, these tickets are refundable (minus a small percentage) or transferable to any other IATA airline. Try, if possible, to buy MCOs or any airline tickets outside Latin America because many countries have high sales taxes (3 to 8%) on airline tickets bought within the country. If you haven't got this together before you arrive remember that transport companies and their agencies are well aware of this requirement and, because they don't want to have to provide you with a free return journey to the point where you boarded their transport, they often won't sell you a ticket unless you already have an onward ticket or will insist that you buy a return ticket. This applies to air tickets bought in Costa Rica or Panama for destinations in Colombia. It also applies to bus tickets bought for journeys from Nicaragua to Costa Rica (but not vice versa) and to or from Costa Rica and Panama. Further details are in the main text plus what you can do, if anything, about getting a refund on the return half of the ticket if you're not coming back that way.

Peru is perhaps a special case. If you turn up without an onward ticket at the border the officials will send you next door to the *Morales Moralitos* bus office where you will be offered a selection of overpriced bus tickets either out of the country or almost out of the country. Which one you choose will obviously depend on which way you're planning to go but the cheapest ticket is the Cuzco to Puno one at 1200 soles (US$6). There are others for Puno to La Paz (Bolivia) for 2000 soles, Lima to Tumbes for 4000 soles, etc. *Morales Moralitos* bus line has a bad reputation with travellers so it's fair to balance the record by saying that I bought a Cuzco-Puno ticket at the border and was later able to exchange it without loss for a ticket from Arequipa to Puno and Puno to Yunguyo on the Bolivian border.

CUSTOMS

These vary considerably from country to country and between different entry points to any one particular country. Some can be really obstreperous, others hardly look at you. It's said that a great deal depends on your appearance but, as far as hair goes, I doubt this. I have "long" hair and a beard and not once was a thorough search made of my luggage or my guitar case and I was never subjected to a body search. Draw what conclusions you like from this but don't take it as an invitation to be careless or reckless if you're carrying anything which could get you ten years in a two by three metre rat-infested, windowless hole somewhere. Undoubtedly a great deal depends on your attitude, whether you can speak Spanish/Portuguese, which country you come from (there's considerable "Yanqui" prejudice in many Latin American countries), what time of day it is, what side of the bed the official got out of that morning, how many other people are crossing the border at the same time and what sort of transport you're on etc.

Borders where many people cross daily are usually okay — they can't possibly check everyone — and, smuggling being a long-established Latin American tradition, they're probably after bigger fish than you. But, again, don't assume that customs officials are naive or that you can be careless. There's often one set of laws for the local people and another for the travellers and it's often not unconnected with the fact that substantial bribes can be extracted from unwary travellers. Airport arrivals and departures are usually checked more thoroughly because of hijackings and drug smuggling. If they're using X-rays to screen people for arms make sure all your exposed and unexposed film is held well out of the way otherwise it will fog.

The only countries where a black market currency scene operates these days is in Peru and Argentina but there are no longer any Currency Declaration Forms to fill in and import of local currency is unrestricted in practice. In theory Peru has a limit of 1000 soles (about US$5) but I've never heard of anyone having any hassles through having more than this. Some borders are highly bureaucratic and crossing the border can take hours. If you lose your patience it will simply take longer. Take small comfort in the fact that you're providing someone with a job. Ho, ho. The only border where we had any hassle was the Honduras/El Salvador border where they took exception to my beard and hair (and, after several hours of hassling in Spanish, to my rucksack as well) and refused entry. We came back a couple of days later on the through *TICA* bus to Tegucigalpa and were hardly given a glance. Call it a compulsory Spanish conversation lesson if you like! At some land borders they don't even demand an onward ticket even though officially you have to have one. This applies at the Boa Vista/Santa Helena border going into Venezuela from Brazil. At the Venezuela/Colombia border on the road from Maracaibo to Santa Marta the Colombians asked to see the onward ticket, but as soon as we flashed an *Aerocondor* ticket folder they waved us on. With this in mind it might be a good idea to hang on to one or two airline ticket stubs as it may well be the border officials have never been on a flight and are unsure what a valid ticket looks like.

If you're thinking of getting involved in dope smuggling, if only for your own personal consumption, we suggest you first read two booklets produced by Release, 1 Elgin Avenue, London, W9, UK — *The Truckers Bible* and *Just Another Truckstop* — which contain some very sobering information. It's finally up to you of course but remember that it is *very* big business particularly in Colombia, Peru, Bolivia and Brazil and if you're at the bottom of the pile you'll be the first one to be shopped.

TRANSPORT

Road transport, especially by bus, is very well developed throughout Latin America and even the smallest places are accessible. The state of the roads and

the quality of the buses is, however, another story. The two combined would provide any novelist with enough material to fill a hundred books and you'll certainly never be short of things to write home to your friends about. Virtually all the major roads and many of the minor ones throughout Central America are paved and in good repair; buses are generally quick, comfortable and reliable and, at least in the major cities and towns, all buses arrive and depart from a centralized terminal. All the various bus companies maintain ticket offices at these terminals and have information boards posted where you can see at a glance which routes they cover, departure times, prices and whether the bus is a direct one or otherwise. Where this is not the case, the addresses of the various bus stations have been given under the appropriate town and their location marked on the town plans. Seats on buses are numbered and booked in advance but, except on major routes between large cities, it's unlikely that a bus will be fully booked up to within an hour of departure.

TICA bus and *Sirca* run international buses between the capital cities of the various Central American republics and so are convenient if you need to get somewhere quickly and with the minimum of chasing about. *TICA*, for example, will take you from Guatemala City to Panama City for US$35.50 with an overnight stop in each of the capital cities. Taking these buses is, however, a relatively expensive way of getting from A to B (not to mention boring and insulated) and, as with anywhere else in the world, it's cheaper and much more fun to take a local bus to the border, walk across the border and then catch another local bus on the far side. The only way in which they score over local buses is *if* there's going to be any hassle at the border, you don't get it on one of these buses.

The only exceptions you're likely to come across regarding what's been said about Central American road and bus conditions are to be found in northern Guatemala, Nicaragua north of the lakes and rural Costa Rica. In Guatemala the roads from the Belize border to Tikal, Tikal to Flores and Flores to Puerto Barrios are atrocious and the buses look like retired 18th century tanks. The journey from Flores to Guatemala City can take 18 hours so it's not surprising that many travellers go for the soft option of the US$20 flight as opposed to the bus at half the price. In Nicaragua and Costa Rica bad road conditions are generally due to the rainy season when roads and sometimes bridges get washed out. In the dry season they're generally okay after repair even when unsurfaced. There is still no road connection between Central America and South America through the Darien jungle on the border between Panama and Colombia. The Pan American Highway comes to an end about 80 km beyond Panama City and doesn't start again until you're well inside Colombia. This means that, unless you're planning on hacking your way through the jungle (a 10-day trek in good conditions), you'll have to take a plane or a boat to Colombia. Details of all the various possibilities appear under *Costa Rica* and *Panama*.

Generalizing about bus and road conditions in South America is much more difficult if only because it's such a vast area with such a wide range of geographical and climatic conditions. Certainly some of the worst roads are to be found in the highlands of Peru (average height 3500 metres) where in places the only thing which distinguishes a river bed from a road is the absence of water. Buses are stripped to their bare essentials, tyres have rarely seen a tread for years and the whole thing seems to be held together by the double set of springs at the back which makes the suspension rock-hard and ensures that each and every bump is transmitted directly to your backside. Seats are numbered — after a fashion — and bookable in advance but that's just the start. When the seats are taken the corridor is packed to capacity and beyond, and the roof is loaded with cargo to at least half the height of the bus and topped by the occasional goat. You start to have serious doubts whether you'll ever get there with moments of sheer panic when you hit a pot-hole or a section of road with the wrong camber and the whole caboose lurches alarmingly over to one side. But somehow, 18 hours or so later, after enduring this fetid human sardine can, you're spat out onto the pavement feeling like a jellied mixture of death warmed up and super-tenderized steak. However, after a shower and a long rest punctuated by vivid recollections, you wake up and start laughing about it, remembering how beautiful the mountains and valleys were even through your bleary eyes, and ready for the next leg of the journey. Well, almost!

Similar stretches of road can be found in parts of Colombia and Bolivia and again in the Brazilian jungle where roads are characterized more by vast seas of red dust (or yawning oceans of thick mud after rain) rather than pot-holes or boulders. Overtaking from behind a dust-storm where visibility rarely exceeds a few metres and with trucks carrying umpteen tonnes of lumber coming the other way can be a hazardous business. One fondly hopes and eventually comes to believe that the Brazilians have some mysterious sixth sense about these things. You better believe it, otherwise you might end up adding a touch of colour to the end of a mahogany log. Elsewhere on the sub-continent there's a mixture of good paved and unpaved roads and other unpaved roads in need of either minor or extensive repair. Occasionally you come across six-lane superhighways like the ones around Caracas and the main Brazilian cities.

In some countries (eg Venezuela, Brazil, Bolivia and Argentina), the bus terminals are centralized as they are in Central America but in others the various bus companies maintain their own bus stations. Details are in the main text. Buses vary from the super de-luxe Mercedes-Benz coaches found in Brazil, Venezuela and parts of Bolivia to sardine tins indistinguishable from the ones which ply the Peruvian highlands. Obviously much depends on the condition of the road. Sometimes the same company will run a mixture of new and geriatric buses on the same route and there's no way of knowing which you're going to get until it turns up, so don't make the mistake of assuming that because you see a company running new buses along a certain route that you'll necessarily get one too. In Peru the long-distance coastal routes and the international routes are served by two main companies: *TEPSA* and *Roggero*. If possible choose *Roggero*. They tend to be booked further up in advance but their buses are much better, don't serve as milk-runs when they've told you it's "rapido" and are more reliable. *TEPSA*, especially on the northern routes, can be a pain in the ass. Another Peruvian company with a bad reputation among travellers is *Morales Moralitos*. Whether they've altered their ways somewhat as a result of all the flak they must have collected over the years I don't know (unlikely), but I've tried to put the record straight in the last paragraph under *Visas* as a result of my own experiences with them.

HITCHING

It's possible to hitch all over Central and South America but if you're looking for free lifts you'll be there a *long* time. Free lifts are the exception rather than the rule as hitching is a recognized form of public transport, especially among the poor people and in the highlands where buses can be infrequent. There are more or less fixed fares over certain routes (just ask the other people what they're paying) and these are generally less than what the bus fare would be but can be as high in some places. You get a better view from the top of a lorry and people tend to be more friendly but if you're hitching on the altiplano in the Andean countries take some warm clothing with you. Once the sun goes down or is obscured by mountains it gets *very* cold. There's no need to stand at the side of the road waiting for a lift unless this happens to be convenient for you. Virtually every town has its central lorry park often located near to or in the market. Ask around here for a lorry going in the direction you want to take and how much it will cost and be there about half an hour before the driver says he's going. If the driver has as many passengers as he wants then you'll leave more or less on time. If not it's probable that you'll get a brief guided tour of the town as the driver hunts for more passengers.

In some places, if you're intent on keeping moving the same or the next day, you'll have no alternative but to hitch since the buses will be booked up days in advance. This is particularly true of Potosi and one or two other places in Bolivia. It's also true of parts of the Peruvian and Brazilian jungles where there may not be any buses. One other notable place where this applies is if you're going north from Boa Vista, in the extreme north of Brazil, to either Guyana or Venezuela. If you're going to Guyana then you have to find a lorry in Boa Vista itself as there are no buses to the border or, for that matter, on the other side of the border either. If you're going to Venezuela there's a bus to Santa Helena just over the border in Venezuela but none there to El Dorado or Tumeremo. We eventually got a (free) lift from there after two days at the side of the road when a rally car from Uruguay broke down right opposite where we were standing and had to be hoisted onto the back of a truck and taken to Caracas for repairs. The alternative was to have chartered a car along with a few other people who wanted to go that way — somewhat expensive.

RAILWAYS
Where these occur they're invariably cheaper (even in first class) than buses but also slower. They cover some of the most spectacular routes in the world. Some that you should not miss if you're going that way include:

Chihuahua-Los Mochis on the Pacific coast (Mexico) via the Barranca del Cobre — comparable to the Grand Canyon in the US.

Santa Marta-Bogota (Colombia) — slow rise from sea level to the capital at about 2600 metres.

Quito-Guayaquil (Ecuador) — precipitous drop from about 3000 metres to sea level via a number of ingenious switchbacks with incredible mountain scenery.

Lima-Huancayo (Peru) — rapid rise from sea level to the Andean altiplano at about 3200 metres, via the 4600 metre Croya pass. It is one of the highest railways in the world.

Puno/Juliaca-Arequipa (Peru) — similar to the last and including another 4600 metre pass.

La Paz-Antofagasta (Bolivia-Chile) — 4000 metres down to sea level. It is a two day journey, often booked up weeks in advance — spectacular lunar-type landscapes and extinct volcanoes.

Santiago-Mendoza (Chile-Argentina) — a spectacular journey up one side of the Andes and down the other.

Many railways were not built primarily to carry passengers but to serve the needs of mining concerns and banana or coffee plantations and so are of limited or no use to travellers. There are quite a few such lines in the Central American republics and Chile.

In South America there are generally three types of trains:

Ferrobus — this is a relatively fast, diesel-powered single car which caters for passengers going from A to B but not intermediate stations. It stops only for meal breaks. You must book in advance (a day or so will be adequate). Cost is about the same as first class.

Ordinary passenger train — these lower trains with two or more classes are cheaper than the ferrobus where there is one. They stop at all intermediate stations.

Mixed passenger/freight trains — these are even slower. It is possible you might be able to travel in empty freight wagons free so negotiate with the guards. Remember though that they really are *very* slow.

FLIGHTS

Because of the vast distances between centres of population and the barriers imposed on overland communications by geography, South America was one of the first places to develop internal air services. There is an extensive pattern of internal flights especially in the Andean countries and prices are surprisingly low — often little more than twice the bus fare. After several 18 hour-plus bus journeys across the mountains over atrocious roads you may decide here and there, as many travellers do, that you just can't face another and take a flight. Some of the world's most amazing mountain views can be had from such flights. There are one or two points you should bear in mind, relating especially to Peru and Bolivia, however. First planes rarely depart on time and can be up to half a day late. Second the concept of queueing for a boarding pass is virtually unknown. In practice, if your baggage is on the scales, you get served. Watch the locals: you'll soon suss out the "system". Third Aeroperu are notorious for cancelling planes at a moment's notice and so a backlog of passengers builds up, all of whom are intent on getting on the next flight. This is clearly impossible but that doesn't deter them so it's bedlam at the check-in counter. The most aggressive, most devious and those with least baggage are the ones who come out of this ordeal smiling, unless the airline lays on an additional plane, again without warning. The most notorious spot for this is Ayacucho which is perhaps fortunate as it's a pleasant place to stay in for a few days (but a disaster if you're going to Lima to catch a connecting international flight).

Internal flights in Brazil and Venezuela tend to be considerably more expensive, but in Brazil and Argentina it is possible to get free flights with the armed forces sometimes. Whether you score or not depends on quite a few factors one of which is luck. Ideally you need a letter on some appropriately headed notepaper saying you're a student of, for instance, biology/geography/sociology/etc and requesting a free flight. In Cuiaba, Brazil, I talked my way through to the guy in charge of armed forces transport planes (*FAB*) and he promised my companions and I a free lift from there to Porto Velho. The only drawback was the plane had left two hours earlier and there wouldn't be another for about 15 days. You'll hear a few stories like this from other travellers along the way. You might also be lucky.

For details about international flights and onward-ticket hassles see under *Getting There*, *Costa Rica*, *Panama* and *Colombia*. In the US write to *Taking Off*, Education Cooperative Travel Service, Dept LA, 176 West Adams St, Suite 2121, Chicago Ill 60603, enclosing US$2.

Organised Overland Trips

If you're interested in one of these organised tours around Central/South America it's a good idea to first get hold of a copy of the magazine *Trailfinders* (the magazine for overlanders) published by Trailrovers, 46 Earls Court Rd, London W8, England (tel 01 937 9631). This is put out three times a year (March, June and December). Subscription is £1.50 (UK) or £3.50 (elsewhere). These people will send you at the same time a reasonable selection of overland tour company brochures if you ask them. Here is a precis of what is available:

Central & South America

Duration	Basic Cost	Extras not included	Route	Transport	Company
28 days	£625	meals & hotels	Lima-La Paz-Cuzco-Lima	public	Trailrovers

42 days	£725	meals & hotels	Lima-La Paz-Potosi-Sucre-Riberalta-Puerto-Maldonado-Cuzco-Lima	public	as above

prices of these two trips inclusive of return London-Lima airfare

36 days	£455	food & accom, connecting travel	Bogota-Santiago	expedition coach	Treasure Treks
36 days	£455	as above	Santiago-Bogota	as above	as above
36 days	£395	as above	Santiago-Rio & vv	as above	as above
74 days	£830	as above	Bogota-Rio & vv	as above	as above
3 months	£630	food, half accom, side trips, connecting travel	alternate directions around the continent	bus & riverboat	Aardvark
1 month	£260	food, half accom, connecting travel	Cuzco-Rio & vv	bus	as above
35 to 82 days	$485 to $1100	food, accom, connecting travel	Bogota-Rio & vv	expedition coach	Bustrek
1 month	£260	food, half accom, connecting travel	Caribbean-Amazonia-Rio	bus & riverboat	Aardvark
22 days	£895	meals	High Andes/Lake Titicaca	coach, air, boat & rail	Pennworld
28 days	£490	meals, connecting travel	Mexico-Lima & vv	minibus	as above
36 days	£435	meals, hotels, connecting travel	Rio-Lima	minibus	as above
36 days	£495	as above	Lima-Rio	coach	as above
15 weeks	£1180	connecting travel	Barranquilla-Rio	expedition vehicle	Encounter Overland
16 weeks	£1280	as above	Barranquilla-Rio & vv	as above	as above
84 days	£695	food, accom, connecting travel	Bogota-Rio	expedition	Capricorn/Goway
50 days	£400	as above	Bogota-Santiago	as above	Capricorn/Goway
16 weeks	£1220/1380	connecting travel	Barranquilla-Rio	expedition coach	Sun-downers
23 days	£173/183	accom, entry fees	Mexico & Guatemala	coach	Trek America

Addresses of the overland companies are:

Trailrovers 46 Earls Court Rd, London W8, England
Treasure Treks 3rd floor, Panton House, 25 Haymarket, London SW1, England
        40-42 Willis St, Wellington, New Zealand
        15 Hunter St, Sydney 2000, Australia
        3 Manchester Lane, Melbourne 3000, Australia
Aardvark 14 Coleridge Rd, London N8, England
        516 Rathdowne St, North Carlton, Vic 3054, Australia
        Adventure Centre, 5540 College Ave, Oakland, CA 94618, USA
Pennworld 122 Knightsbridge, London SW1, England
        Tower Building, Australia Square, Sydney 2000, Australia
        177 Collins St, Melbourne 3000, Australia
Encounter Overland 271 Old Brompton Rd, London SW5, England
        369 Pine St, San Francisco, CA 94104, USA
Capricorn 21 Ebury Bridge Rd, London SW1, England
Trek America 62 Kenway Rd, London SW5, England
Bustrek c/o Educational Co-op Travel Service, Dept LA, 176 West Adams St, Chicago, Ill 60603, USA

"Connecting travel" in the above list means the cost of getting to the point where the tour starts. If you want to spend any length of time in South America — the longest trek is approximately four months — then you'll have to think in terms of at least £1500 ($3000). This is considerably more than it would cost you to go under your own steam but that's the price of having someone to organise it for you.

SOMEONE TO TRAVEL WITH

It's a fact of travelling life that overlanding is rarely a solo activity and this is particularly true of the "Gringo Trail" — an endearing term for the route which most travellers take through Central America and then down the Andes to Tierra del Fuego. Even if you start out by yourself, you'll inevitably meet other people along the road heading in the same or a similar direction with whom you can team up for a while if the mood takes you or you like each other's company. The most likely places are hotels where many travellers congregate, beaches, buses, trains, archaeological sites, cafes and fiestas — in other words, just about everywhere along the main route.

Travellers get thin on the ground in Argentina, Brazil, the Guianas and Venezuela not just because the former two are so large but because there are innumerable ways to travel through them. All the same, collections of them can be found in Buenos Aires, Sao Paulo, Rio de Janeiro and Manaus. In Manaus they can be particularly useful if you're looking for information on river trips along the Amazon and its tributaries.

If you'd prefer to set off with someone, student travel notice boards are particularly good places to keep an eye on. The same goes for Youth Hostel office notice boards in large cities. If you're in London, try the BIT Information Service's notice board (free) at 97A Talbot Road, London, WII (telephone 01 229 8219/8210); newsagents' noticeboards around Earls Court; and Trailfinders noticeboard, also in Earls Court, at 46 Earls Court Road, London, W8. There are also two magazines which usually contain plenty of advertisements for travelling companions: *Time Out* in London (weekly) and *Nation Review* in Australia. In New York try the New York Student Centre, Hotel Empire, Broadway and 63rd Street (telephone 212 695 0291).

TAKING YOUR OWN VEHICLE

If you're considering doing this from anywhere other than North America and intent on bringing it back, make sure you're rich first. It's easy enough to take one through Central America as far as Panama but from there on your problems start. It will cost you at least US$500 (plus US$90 for each passenger) to ship a car from Panama to Colombia not to mention the bureaucratic hassles and paperwork at either end which are designed to try the patience of a saint. We wouldn't like to discourage you if you're determined. But a few words from a friend of mine who spent 3½ years driving around the world in a VW Kombi might help:

"Costs. Astronomical however you look at it!...... The whole process is rife with problems and is the worst part of any overland trip. If you try to sell the van instead of shipping it and then buy another one on the other side, you will have equal hassles with carnet rules and regulations, and fitting out another vehicle as a home-on-wheels is likely to be difficult except in the USA or in Australia, where camping is an industry on its own... Wherever you land your car, you will find that there are hidden extras such as landing, port and unloading charges (we averaged around US$100 per shipping on top of freight costs...) Thieves abound in profusion on every dock. Stay with your vehicle the entire time, *day and night*. If you ignore this almost certainly something(s) will be stolen... If you're shipping your van with all your belongings in it (a) remove everything 'removable' from the exterior — horns, hubcaps, wipers, wing mirrors, etc. If you don't someone else will. (b) seal the living room area from the driving cab... (c) draw all curtains in the living room area so that no-one can see in (d) remove everything from the driver's cab — mirrors, fan, cassette player, ashtray, compass, contents of glove compartment. (e) Double-lock living area doors, having padlocked all interior cupboards...All this may sound excessive. It isn't. During our entire journey we did not meet a single traveller who had not had something stolen — usually while shipping."

He's written an excellent little guide book packed with information which you should get hold of if you're thinking of taking a vehicle down into South America — *Overland and Beyond* by Jonathan Hewat. You can get a copy from him at 106 West St, Corfe Castle, Dorset, England.

Another good guide to get hold of which is more orientated towards people taking their own vehicles than this guide is: *Latin American Travel Guide* and *Pan American Highway Guide*, Compsco Publishing Company, 663 Fifth Ave. New York, NY 10022. Air mail prices: US$12.70 (USA); US$12.70 (Western Hemisphere): US$15.70 (Australia and Far East).

SHELTER/ACCOMMODATION

In most Latin American countries it is usually possible to find a roof over your head for around US$1 to 2 per night. Obviously a great deal depends on what you're prepared to be satisfied with in terms of comfort, facilities, services, cleanliness, etc; how much searching you're prepared to do, particularly after a long journey, and whether you're in a city or a small rural town. The larger your group, the less, proportionally, you will pay per person for accommodation since it's likely you'll be sharing a room. By giving brief selective lists of cheap accommodation we've tried in this guide to cut down to a bare minimum the amount of chasing about you will have to do on arrival in a town or city. Where cheap accommodation tends to be clustered together in one particular area, we've located this on the town plans in case specific places are full or you don't happen to like any of the ones we've mentioned.

The cheapest places are "hospedajes" or "casas de huéspedes". They're usually very basic, providing only a bed and sometimes a table and chair in an otherwise bare room. Sometimes blanket and sheets are provided, sometimes only a sheet, sometimes nothing at all. Showers and toilets are shared with everyone else in the place. Standards of cleanliness vary widely, I've stayed in some spotless hospedajes with sheets and blankets provided for only US$1. On the other hand I've paid double that in some places and then spent the next week wondering what nasty scrofulous diseases I might have picked up there — yet not once in nearly a year did I pick up any unwanted travelling companions (fleas, lice, athlete's foot, etc). Hospedajes and casas de huéspedes generally don't provide or cater for meals. In cities they're often used by families and so can be noisy. As they're frequently located in old Spanish-type houses the bareness of the rooms is often redeemed by a beautiful enclosed courtyard containing trees and other plants. Slightly more expensive are the "pensiones" (average price US$1.50-3). The distinction between a "hospedaje" and a "pension" is often academic, but in the more expensive ones the facilities and services tend to be of a slightly higher standard and it's possible to find rooms with their own shower and/or toilet.

After that there are the hotels. What you get obviously depends *almost* entirely on what you pay for a room but until you get beyond the US$4 per night range it's unlikely you'll get substantially better accommodation than you would do in a cheaper pension or hospedaje. The exception is that, if you're paying US$3-4/night, it's likely you'll have your own private shower and toilet and clean sheets. Most hotels are fairly modern, concrete, buildings and don't have the benefit of a peaceful courtyard to relax in and talk to other guests in the evenings. One spartan, concrete box after the next does eventually get you yearning for something with a little more character even if there is the odd roach scurrying about. Where they score over the other types of accommodation is in the provision of a fan where the climate justifies it. By positioning your bed under the fan you can keep mosquitoes at bay all night. In cities you need to choose carefully between hotels because, in some, rooms are partially subdivided by hardboard partitions. The noise kicked up by the adjacent occupants combined with the blaring garbage of a TV set in the foyer can make sleep a fond memory. Others double as whore-houses. You'll perhaps become inured to all-night sighs, cries and giggles, doors banging and toilets flushing. On the other hand, if you've just completed a long and exhausting journey, you might not.

The exceptions to the general rule of being able to find accommodation for US$1-2/night are Brazil and Venezuela. You'll be lucky to find anything under US$4 per night anywhere in Venezuela and for that price you're right at the bottom of the market. It's a *very* expensive country. In Brazil reckon at least US$3 and you'll be lucky at that. Another notable exception is Panama City where the minimum is US$3.

Wherever you go in Latin America one thing you should bear in mind is that people have little or no concept of noise pollution. They'll rave, shout and bawl all night. TVs will be on full blast. Car horns will cave-in your ear drums night and day. Bus radios and cassette players will drive you to the frontiers of insanity. It *does* have its negative aspects and can really grate on your nerves if all you want to do is get some rest, but it also has many positive aspects. It's part of their natural spontanaeity and will probably ensure that the deadening aspects of industrial discipline as it's understood in the affluent countries never takes too much root here. It's also obvious whom the streets belong to. But if you're the sort of person who can't handle noise when you're tired, bear this in mind.

HEALTH

Useful books to study are *The Traveller's Health Guide* by Dr A.C. Turner, published by Roger Lascelles or *The Preservation of Personal Health in Warm Climates* published by the Ross Institute of Tropical Hygiene, London. Both tell you all you need to know.

Vaccinations Officially, before you're allowed to enter most countries in Latin America you're required to have a valid International Health Certificate as proof that you're not the carrier of any of the old favourites which used to decimate populations in the days of yore. The essential vaccinations are cholera, smallpox and yellow fever. In addition to these compulsory ones, you're strongly advised to be vaccinated against typhoid, paratyphoid, tetanus, polio and tuberculosis. Some people also take in a jab for hepatitis. At no border or airport anywhere in Latin America was I asked for the Certificate but you'd be ill-advised to neglect vaccination on account of this. If you've been living all your life in a western country you're probably already protected against polio and tuberculosis since it's likely you were vaccinated at school. Typhoid, paratyphoid and tetanus are often given in the one jab as a "cocktail" called TABT but this practice is being discontinued and they're reverting to single jabs for each. You need to plan ahead at least a month as not only can they not all be given at the same time but typhoid and tenanus both need second injections two to four weeks after the first. The effect of the vaccines vary with different people and with the skill of the doctor or nurse. Typhoid and cholera often leave you with a stiff arm if you've not had them before. The others have little or no effect.

The International Vaccination Certificate covers smallpox, cholera, yellow fever and typhoid. Their validity is as follows: cholera, six months; smallpox, three years; yellow fever, 10 years; typhoid/paratyphoid, one year. Tetanus, polio, tuberculosis and hepatitis are not included since they are not compulsory. Their effectiveness is as follows: tetanus, variable, usually about two years; polio and tuberculosis, for life; hepatitis, up to six months but effectiveness varies — some medics say it's not worth it at all.

It's unlikely you'll be asked, but if you turn up at borders/airports with expired Certificates they may insist on you having the relevant jab before being allowed to enter. Don't count on a brand-new needle if this happens to you. It's likely it will have been used on successive travellers with the resultant danger of you contracting serum hepatitis — the variety which needle freaks get through using dirty needles.

General Health Get your teeth checked and treated if necessary before you set out. Dentists are few and far between and treatment is expensive.

The two main things which are likely to affect your general health while abroad are diet and climate. Cheap food bought in cafes and street stands tends to be over-cooked, very starchy (mainly corn or maize) and lacking in protein, vitamins and calcium. Over a period of time the latter two, when combined with a lack of exercise for the gums, can seriously affect the health of your teeth. Make sure you supplement the cooked food you buy with milk or yoghurt (where available and pasteurized) and fresh fruit. Read up a little on dietary requirements before you set off. Give your gums some exercise by chewing a stick of liquorice root or any twig. Carrying cooking utensils around can be impractical though in some cases unavoidable (eg if you're going to walk the Inca Trail). Avoid untreated milk and milk products — in many countries herds are not screened for brucellosis or tuberculosis. Fortunately, in many countries it's possible to buy refrigerated cartons of pasteurized milk and in Mexico the dairy business is being actively promoted.

In hot climates you sweat a great deal and so lose a lot of water and salt. Make sure you drink sufficient liquid and have enough salt in your food to make good the losses (a tea-spoon of salt a day is sufficient). If you don't make good these losses you run the risk of suffering from heat exhaustion and cramps. Heat can make you impatient and irritable especially if you're a speedy person. Try to take things at a slower pace. Hot dry air will make your hair brittle and may cause it to thin out. Oil it frequently with refined coconut oil. Your skin will also benefit from the occasional oiling. Keep your skin clean to minimize the risk of infection and allow you to sweat freely. Even the most basic hospedajes have showers. A good pair of sunglasses are a virtual necessity. If you arrive without a pair or lose/break the pair you have, they're sold all over the continent. Bargain for them from street sellers. US$3-4 should buy you an excellent pair. Take great care of cuts, grazes or skin infections otherwise they tend to persist and get worse. If they're wet, bandage them up. Open sores attract flies and there are plenty of those. Change bandages daily and use antiseptic cream if necessary. A troublesome, though temporary, skin condition that many people from temperate climates come across initially is prickly heat. Many tiny, itchy blisters form on one or more parts of your body — usually where your skin is thickest, as on your hands. They are sweat droplets which are trapped under the skin because your pores aren't large enough or haven't opened up sufficiently to cope with the greater volume of sweat. Anything which promotes sweating — exercise, a lot of tea, coffee, alcohol — makes it worse. Keep your skin aired and dry. Reduce clothing to a loose fitting minimum and keep out of direct sunlight. The use of calamine lotion or zinc oxide based talcum powder helps to soothe the skin. Apart from that there isn't much else you can do about it. It's just an acclimatization problem that usually doesn't persist. Other than on a beach, avoid walking around on bare feet as you could pick up hookworm which is widespread in some areas. If swimming on a rocky beach keep an eye out for sea-urchins.

Remember that adjustment to the outlook, habits, social customs, etc of different people can be a strain depending on your own outlook, prejudices and temperament. Many travellers suffer from some degree of culture shock — something you can get on returning too if you've been away a long time. Heat tends to exaggerate petty irritations that would pass unnoticed in a more temperate climate. Exhausting all-night, all-day bus journeys over bad roads don't help if you're feeling this way. Make sure you get enough sleep.

Mountain Sickness (Soroche) Some people suffer from this on the altiplano of Ecuador, Peru and Bolivia (average height 2600-4000 metres). Rapid ascent from sea level, over-exertion and lack of physical fitness can bring on the symtoms which include headache, dizziness, lack of appetite, nausea and vomiting. Breathlessness and heart pounding are quite normal at these altitudes due to the lack of oxygen and are not part of mountain sickness. Acclimatization can take up to six months and during this period it's normal to feel relatively breathless on exertion. If you do get mountain sickness the best treatment is quite simple, get down to a lower altitude. A pain-killer for headache and an anti-emetic for vomiting will also help. Oxygen will give relief and you can sometimes find it in first class railway compartments and the more expensive hotels but you're unlikely to find it in second class compartments or in cheaper accommodation.

An excellent remedy for both soroche and the normal breathlessness and heart pounding is "mate de coca" — tea made from coca leaves — which you can get in most cafes in Peru and Bolivia (but not in Ecuador, as this country has outlawed its cultivation). You can also buy the leaves legally in most tiendas (small general stores) throughout Peru and Bolivia for from US$4-5 per kilo or from herbal stalls which you can find in every market. The practice of chewing coca leaves goes back centuries and is still common among the Indians of the Andean altiplano. By dulling the pangs of hunger, cold, thirst and fatigue, coca will give you that extra stamina to take the altitude in your stride and enable you to do some serious walking in the mountains. If you've been reading any of the usual ill-informed gutter press shock-horror stories about the slippery slope, creeping addiction, mental and moral degeneration, etc relating to chewing coca leaves, forget them. Some people like nothing better than getting rich and famous by putting something down they know nothing about or have never personally experienced. More about coca leaves and how to use them is given in the Peru chapter.

Drinking Water Most cities have a decent, chlorinated water supply and you can drink from the tap but outside these areas avoid unboiled water or ice, especially during the rainy season. Rivers can be contaminated by communities living further up the valleys so if you're walking in the mountains get your supply from springs or small streams. Unboiled water is a major source of diarrhoea and hepatitis. The other major sources are salads that have been washed in contaminated water and eating unpeeled fruit that's been handled by someone who has one of these infections. Where possible stick to tea, mate, coffee, minerals drinks (carbonated — in Spanish *con gas*) or beer. Peel fruit before eating it. Your susceptibility to gut infections will depend to a large extent on the conditions you've been used to at home and the sort of food you eat.

If you have to use water and you're not sure about its purity use a water purifying tablet such as "Sterotabs". These are effective against most microorganisms but not against amoebic dysentery. To kill these you need an iodine-based sterilizer. The only trouble with the latter is that they make the water taste foul. The best way to purify water is, of course, to boil it for a little while.

Medical supplies, including most drugs, anti-biotics, etc are available without prescription at pharmacies all over the continent so there's little point in taking any quantities with you.

Diarrhoea and Dysentery (Montezuma's Revenge, The Inca Two-Step and other endearing terms). Sooner or later, unless you're quite exceptional, you'll get a bout of diarrhoea so accept it as inevitable and know how to deal with it. Diarrhoea doesn't always mean you've caught something — it can be merely the result of a change of food. If you've spent most of your life living out of plastic-wrapped packages and tins from the supermarket it's going to take time for you to adjust. Most gut infections (and hepatitis) are spread by one or another of the following: infected urine or faeces contaminating water supplies; people with dirty hands preparing food; droplet infection from sneezing, coughing or spitting; flies. Sanitary fitting and systems in Latin America are not built to take quantities of paper so instead of being flushed away it's thrown into the corner by the pan. When you've seen a few of these toilets, particularly the ones which aren't cleaned out regularly, you'll realise why flies are such a health hazard. In many places there aren't even any toilets so people use any convenient corner. But to maintain some balance I should point out that only once in nearly a year did I get diarrhoea although my travelling companions did get it a little more often. We were pretty fastidious but we ate in the cheapest cafes all along the line.

Avoid rushing off to the chemist and filling yourself with anti-biotics at the first sign of a loose gut. It's a harsh way to treat your body and, if misused, the bugs will build up a tolerance to the drugs. First try to starve them out and at the same time give your system a rest: take it easy, relax and avoid travelling. Here's how: The first way is to starve. Eat nothing. Drink plenty of liquid (tea or mate without sugar or milk). Many cafes in Latin America serve camomile tea which is excellent for this (called te de manzanilla). Otherwise drink aqua minerale — 24 to 48 hours should do the trick. If you really can't hack starving keep to a small diet of yoghurt, lemons, boiled vegetables and tea with no sugar or milk. If starving doesn't work or if you really have to move on and can't rest there are a whole range of drugs available. Lomotil is probably one of the best though it's come under fire recently in medical literature. Finally if all that fails try the anti-biotics, but remember that these will not only kill the bugs which are bothering you but also the beneficial ones which live normally within your gut and help in food digestion and the absorption of vitamins. The delicate balance of your internal ecology will be upset. After a severe bout of diarrhoea or dysentery you will be dehydrated. This often causes painful cramps. Relieve these by drinking fruit juices or tea into which a small spoonful of salt has been dissolved. Maintaining a correct salt balance in your blood stream is important.

If you are unfortunate enough to contract dysentery there are two types: bacillary, the most common, acute and rarely persistent; and amoebic, persistant and more difficult to treat. Both are characterized by very liquid shit containing blood and/or excessive amounts of mucus. It's painful and strained (ah, travellers' tales!). With bacillary dysentery an attack comes suddenly and is accompanied by fever, nausea and painful muscular spasms. It responds well to anti-biotics or other specific drugs. If you find blood in your shit get medical advice as soon as possible. Find a hotel, take it easy, drink plenty of liquid (no sugar or milk) and take salt to counteract cramps. Untreated dysentery will get worse and will result in a scarred intestine.

Hepatitis This is a liver disease similar to jaundice but, depending on what strain you pick up, can be more severe. There are several varieties, but the one you're most likely to come across is infectious hepatitis. It's a very contagious disease and you pick it up somewhere along the oral-faecal route by drinking water, eating food or using cutlery or crockery that's been contaminated by an infected person. Foods which might carry it are salads that have been washed with infected water or unwashed fruit that's been handled by someone with dirty hands.

Symptoms appear 15 to 50 days after infection (generally around 25 days) and consists of fever, loss of appetite, nausea, depression, complete lack of energy, pains around the bottom of your rib cage (the location of the liver). Your skin will turn progressively yellow and the whites of your eyes yellow to orange. The easiest way to keep an eye on the situation is to watch the colour of your eyes and urine. If you have it, the colour of your piss will be deep orange no matter how much liquid you've drunk — if you haven't drunk much liquid and/or you're sweating a lot don't jump to conclusions! Check it out by drinking a lot of liquid all at once. If it's still orange go somewhere where you won't mind convalescing for a few weeks. The severity varies considerably. Sometimes it lasts less than two weeks and gives you only a few bad days. I once had a bout in Africa which lasted six months and although I only had two bad weeks at the beginning I couldn't do anything that demanded any amount of energy for at least two months.

There's no cure as such but high vitamin B diets are said to help. Fat-free diets have gone out of medical fashion but you may find you can't handle grease at all for a while. If that's the case, cut it out until you find it palatable again. The more considerate you are to yourself in this respect the quicker it will clear up. Seeking medical attention is probably a waste of time and money. There's nothing they can do for you that you can't do for yourself other than tell you how bad it is, but then you don't need a weatherman to tell you which way the wind blows! Alcohol and tobacco are out — don't give your liver extra work to do detoxifying that lot. If you must use hash, eat it.

Area of Malaria Risk in South America

Malaria This is prevalent throughout most of Latin America except parts of Mexico, Costa Rica, Venezuela, Chile, Argentina and Uruguay (see map). It's spread by mosquitoes which transmit the parasite which causes the disease when the insect bites you. You only need to be bitten by one mosquito carrying the parasite to contract the disease. Avoid it by taking a malarial prophylactic which kills the parasites if they get into your bloodstream. There is no vaccination for malaria. You need to start taking anti-malarials about two weeks before you enter a malarial area and continue for about two weeks after leaving the area. Virtually any chemist will get you a supply without prescription in Latin America.

Yellow Fever Endemic in Panama,

Venezuela, Colombia, Ecuador, Peru, Bolivia, the Guianas and Brazil (see map). Again this is spread by mosquitoes which transmit the disease when they bite you. Make sure your yellow fever vaccination is up to date — it's valid for 10 years.

It's easy enough to protect yourself from malaria and yellow fever but mosquitoes themselves are another kettle of fish. There are several ways of keeping the little bastards at bay. One is to use an insect repellant which you apply to your skin every few hours or whenever necessary. Try to choose one which contains DET (diethyl toluamide) or DMP (dimethyl phthalate). One quite effective repell-

Area of Yellow Fever risk in South America

ant which you'll find all over Latin America is *Autan*. Another you might come across is called *Off*. You might have difficulty locating them in rural areas so stock up in cities. There is no need to take vast supplies with you when you set off. Another effective deterrent, particularly when you're asleep, is to position your bed under a fan, where there is one. Mosquitos don't like moving air currents and tend to stay on the walls.

If there are no large gaps into the room where you intend to sleep, an extermination campaign with a boot or rolled-up newspaper will reduce the chances of you being bitten. Don't forget under the bed or inside cupboards! Of course there's always at least one little sly bastard that will escape detection. If there's no fan, you'll hear its evil little whine shortly after the light goes out! Mosquito bites can be troublesome until your skin adjusts. It's probably useless to say but don't scratch them. You'll make them worse and if you open them up they stand the chance of being infected by something else. Not scratching is an excellent meditational endurance test. The same applies to bed bug bites should you be unlucky enough to come across these.

Rabies This is endemic in Mexico and much of South America. Avoid mad dogs but if you do get bitten it might be a good idea to see a doctor and get a course of injections.

Snakebites As a rule snakes don't like areas where there's a lot of human activity so unless you're thinking of doing a considerable amount of trekking in jungles or sparsely populated areas you might never even see one. With one or two exceptions they won't attack unless trodden on or cornered which seems fair enough. Only rarely is a snake bite from even the most venomous variety fatal as the snake seldom injects a full dose of venom.

If you do get bitten, first examine the bite marks. If there are two rows of continuous tooth marks then the snake was harmless. If there are two fang marks the snake may well have been venomous. (There may be only one fang mark or three or four depending on whether only one fang or reserve fangs as well have penetrated your skin.) Don't treat these bites casually. Keep still —

don't start running anywhere as this increases your blood circulation and therefore the absorption of the venom. Wash the wound with any liquid that's available — urine if there's nothing else. Don't rub the wound. Wrap a tourniquet (handkerchief, piece of cloth, anything handy) tightly around your limb higher up than the bite but not so tight that it stops the blood completely. Release this for one minute every half hour.

You'll probably get a severe headache and feel nauseous. If possible get to a doctor/hospital or get someone to carry you there for an injection of anti-venom. It's never too late to receive even if your breathing muscles have become paralysed. You'll recover quickly after the injection. Try to remember what the snake looked like. The time-honoured way of making a cut above the bite and sucking out the venom is useless unless done immediately and properly. Most bites happen on the legs or ankles so wear boots or shoes at night and cover your legs. Commercial snakebite kits are available but useful only if you use them for the specific type of snake for which they're designed.

Other things to bear in mind Small scorpions tend to drop out of tiled roofs around the onset of the rainy season. Keep an eye out for them and shake out your boots before putting them on in the morning. If you get head lice, wash your hair with a shampoo containing benzene hexachloride (eg "Lorexane"). Body lice are best dealt with by shaving off affected hair and throwing away whatever article of clothing was nearest your skin or washing it in the same type of shampoo you would use for your hair. Treat scabies with a lotion of benzoyl benzoate obtained from any chemist (go easy on the stuff around your genitals and asshole — it really stings there but nowhere else). Meat eaters remember that the flesh of pork and cattle may contain the encysted eggs of tapeworms. Make sure it's very well cooked.

If you're into herbal medicines you could supplement your Potter's and Culpepper's by keeping an eye out for booklets on Indian remedies such as: *Antiguo Formulario "Azteca" de Yerbas Medicinales* found in Mexico and Guatemala. Similar booklets can be found on Inca remedies in Peru — the best place is probably on Abancay in Lima.

Health Insurance Get some! You may never need it but if you do it's worth a million. There are a lot of travel insurance policies available and any travel agent will be able to recommend one. Get enough to cover any possible injury/illness and preferably one with a "fly-you-home" clause in case you've got to get home for treatment. Make sure it will cover you for any money you would lose on a booked flight ticket.

On the Road

FOOD

So long as you stick to food stalls and small cafes where local people go, you can generally eat a reasonable meal for US$1 or a little more. In Brazil and Venezuela, however, reckon on at least US$2-3. Most cafes put on a set budget meal both at lunch time (known as "comida corrida" or "almuerzo") and at dinner time (known as "comida" or "cena"). Breakfast ("desayuno") is rarely a set meal and you generally order whatever you feel like eating though in some places special stuffed and deep fried pasties ("empanadas") are prepared at this time of day. Two or three of those with a coffee should set you up for the morning. Lunch is the largest meal of the day. The only trouble with comida corrida/almuerzo and cena is that they tend to be almost exactly the same wherever you are in Latin America and so you quickly get bored with them. They also tend to be very starchy, maize being the staple diet of the vast majority of people. Before you get to the point where you never want to see another tortilla, try the variations on this theme such as "tostadas" (deep-fried tortillas served with a vegetable or meat-based chutney) and "enchilladas" (steamed and stuffed tortillas). There's very little variety in vegetables until you start paying considerably more for your food. If you're a vegetarian you'll have a hard time of it and may well have to put the bulk of your food together yourself — take a small portable stove and something to cook in. Every town has a market where a wide variety of fruit and vegetables can be bought from the market. Fruit, of course, will head the list. It's cheap and plentiful — bananas, coconuts, melons, guayabas, mangoes, peaches, pomegranates, prickly pears, apples, etc depending on season and location. Another thing you'll probably eat plenty of are avocado pears ("aguacate") — an excellent source of protein and vitamins.

One type of cafe which seems to be mushrooming at the present is Latin America's answer to Col Sanders' chicken and chip cafes. You'll see the *Pollo a la Brasa* signs in many places, particularly in Mexico, Peru and Venezuela. A meal generally costs more that a comida corrida and the chicken tends to be very greasy but they make a pleasant change if you're tired of looking at tortillas.

Most fizzy drinks (called "gaseosas" and "refrescos") seem to contain nauseaing amounts of sugar and after a while you may prefer to stick to "agua minerale" (carbonated mineral water). Two varieties which contain less sugar and more actual fruit juice are *Squirt* and *Boing* — found in Mexico, Guatemala and sometimes Nicaragua. Coca-Cola and Pepsi are, of course, ubiquitous, except in Peru where they have their own home-grown variety called *Inca Cola*. A suitable word to describe the taste of this stuff eludes me — boiled lollipops is a fair approximation. Bottled lager-type beers are sold in most cafes. Some of the better ones are: *Bohemia, XXX* and *Superior* in Mexico (you sometimes come across large bottles of *Ballena* too, *Tecate* we found had an unpleasant aftertaste but some people rave about it); *Antarctica* and *Brahma Chopp* in Brazil. Beer usually costs two times the price of a soft drink (between 70 cents and US$1). Spirits include tequila and mescal (Mexico), rum (Central America, Venezuela, Colombia, Ecuador and Peru), pisco and aguadiente (Peru and Bolivia). Wine is produced in Mexico, Chile, Peru and Argentina — a bottle of ordinaire in the latter three countires should cost you no more than 70 cents, if that. A bottle of spirits will set you back US$2-3. Go easy on spirits in the Andes otherwise you'll wake up with a sledge hammer embedded in the back of your head.

MONEY

If you're remaining fairly mobile and intent on seeing most of the countries a reasonable average would be US$7/day. This will include the cost of basic accommodation, food, drink, transport, visas and the occasional purchase of something in a market. It does not include the cost of flying to the American continent. Obviously your average daily expenses depend on many factors and it is possible to get by without any great hardship on US$5/day, particularly if you're a beach freak; if you stay for long periods of time in one place and can therefore suss out cheap long-term accommodation and cook your own food; and if you do a lot of hitch-hiking. Being able to speak fairly fluent Spanish and/or Portuguese makes a hell of a difference as it opens doors which would otherwise be closed to you. Be wary of making sweeping assumptions about others' hospitality. Most people are just too poor to be able to offer this sort of thing. You may personally have very little to do with the reasons why you are relatively affluent and they have experienced nothing but grinding poverty all their lives, but, at least initially, you're seen as a representative of a rich country and it's assumed therefore that you have money.

Two notable exceptions to what has been said above regarding your average daily expenses are to be found in Brazil and Venezuela. These are both relatively expensive countries — Venezuela more so than Brazil — and you should reckon on up to US$10/day. On the other side of the coin, Peru is probably the cheapest country of all (mainly because of the difference between the official and blackmarket exchange rates which can be up to 30 percent) and you'll easily be able to get by on US$5 or less.

As Peru, Chile and Argentina are the only countries where there's any significant difference between the official and blackmarket exchange rates (there's also a small one in Colombia), it's best to take the bulk of your money as travellers' cheques. Avoid taking obscure travellers' cheques from small banks as you may find them impossible to cash. American Express, Cooks, First National City Bank and Bank of America cheques are widely recognised and you'll have no difficulty cashing them. Don't take too many large denominations (have plenty of US$20s and 50s), otherwise you may find yourself with excess amounts of local currency which you can only change at a relatively poor rate in the next country. Keep a record of the cheque numbers and the original bill of sale for the cheques. The former is needed if your cheques are stolen or lost and they have to be replaced. The latter is sometimes demanded by banks when you're changing money and is also useful if your cheques are stolen. Contrary to popular belief, American Express' services are good, if not better, than any other large bank and they will replace stolen or lost cheques instantly as long as you contact them (by phone) as soon as the loss is discovered — if you don't know their number contact your nearest Embassy or Consulate and ask them to ring the nearest Amex office. Get hold of a copy of the leaflet *Directory of American Express Company Offices and Representatives* before you go. American Express also operate a poste restante service for clients which is probably better than the local post office.

You must, however, take some cash with you — up to US$200 if you'll be using the blackmarket, less if not — in the form of US dollar bills because it's not always possible to change traveller's cheques, especially in small places. In Cuiaba, Brazil, the main Banco do Brasil would not only not change American Express Traveller's Cheques but they wouldn't even change dollar bills! Avoid taking anything other than US dollars as cash since, outside of main bank branches, few people will have any idea what the exchange rate is. When changing money on the streets (blackmarket or otherwise) have the exact amount you want to change ready in your pocket — avoid pulling out large wads of notes. Be *very* wary about the notes one by one — don't let them do it for you and don't hand over your dollar bills until you're satisfied you have the agreed amount. Some operators are so sharp they'd have your shoe laces off you while you were tying them up. This applies particularly to Colombia — Cartagena being the blackest spot of all. The most common trick is to entice you into changing money by offering a very attractive rate. They hand you the agreed amount minus 10 or 15 pesos to make sure that when you've counted it out you'll complain that it's short. They take it back, count it out, "discover" the mistake, top it up and hand it back to you, spiriting away all but one of the largest bills in the process. As you've just counted it the temptation is to be satisfied with what you're handed back. Don't be. Count it out again. Don't be hustled about "danger", "police" or any of the other excuses. Other than tricks like this, changing on the street is okay.

Avoid buying Peruvian soles in Ecuador other than at the border town of Huaquillas. The street rate in Lima is generally higher than anywhere outside the country. In Huaquillas you'll see plenty of money changers wandering about looking for custom carrying black attache cases. The rate they offer you is the best outside Lima (in Lima when the official rate was 130 soles = US$1 the street rate was 170 soles = US$1 but don't take these figures as gospel as inflation alters both from one day to the next).

If you have one, a credit card can be very useful, especially for buying flight tickets. Most airlines accept them. The only "safe" way to carry money is in contact with your skin. The usual method is in a leather or cloth pouch hung around your neck and kept inside your shirt or dress. It's a good idea to incorporate a length of guitar wire into the thong around your neck so that it can't be cut without (hopefully) alerting you. Another method is to sew extra pockets inside your jeans. Get one large enough to take your passport as well — it's easy enough getting a replacement but the cost of chasing around can be quite considerable depending on where you are.

If you have money sent to you remember that only in Central America, Venezuela, Ecuador, Bolivia and Uruguay can you have it in dollars. In other countries you will be given cheques/cash in local currency. In Brazil you're allowed 30 percent of the money in dollars and the rest in cruzeiros. Plan ahead. Bank drafts and similar transactions can take up to two months and even then it's not foolproof. "Waiting for money" is a time-honoured pastime among travellers. Avoid it if you can; it gets incredibly frustrating. Know precisely which branch, which bank and which city the draft is being sent to. If possible get the bank which is sending the draft to confirm by letter that it's gone through and is waiting for you. Drafts/ letters of credit are generally kept on file at banks in alphabetical order. If they can't find yours, insist on them checking under the first letter of your Christian name and under "M" (for Mr, Mrs, Miss, Ms) and "S" (for Senor, Senora). You'd be surprised!

Try not to run out of money and keep a small stash (say US$50) totally separate from your other valuables so that if they get ripped off you'll have this to fall back on while you get your cheques replaced. If you do completely run out of money there are several possibilities: (1) Go to your nearest Embassy or Consulate and ask them to repatriate you. Generally, they take your passport off you and fly you home. Don't expect to be going anywhere else until you've repaid them — and they fly you back on full-fare tourist class. (2) Get a job teaching English/French/German. There are language schools all over Latin America. Wages vary a great deal but are best in Mexico. Further details are in the chapters on individual countries. (3) Put your faith in human nature. Tell people around you what your predicament is and something will usually turn up. It's amazing how many people have been bailed out by their fellow travellers. Selling things, electronic gadgets (eg calculators, cassette players, etc) and photographic film, are good for supplementing your budget. Buy them where you don't have to pay import duty/tax on them, eg Panama City, Colon.

If you're British and want to take out more than £500 for your journey (in cash or travellers' cheques) you first have to complete *Form T* obtainable from any bank and send it to the Bank of England for approval. When you get it back, duly rubber-stamped, take it with you to the place where you buy your travellers' cheques/change money. The form is valid for three months from the date of authorization. It's part of the Exchange Control Regulations and the old, old story of pretending to be poverty stricken.

BARGAINING

Probably the only things you'll have to bargain for are long-term (ie a week or over) accommodation and purchases from markets, particularly hand-crafted goods. Your best source of current information on prices are your fellow travellers but however well you bargain you'll never get things at the same prices as the local people do because, as a tourist, you represent money. Speaking fairly fluent Spanish/Portuguese helps a great deal. Retain your sense of humour while bargaining. Decide what you want to pay/can afford and then start off at a price approximately 50% less than this so that as your price rises and the trader's price falls you can both appear to be generous in the final agreement. You may have to walk away several times or even go back the next day before you get anywhere near the price you want (if indeed you manage to get that far). In some places it will be virtually impossible to get the shopkeeper/stall owner to lower his/her prices, especially when there are a lot of tourists passing through and they know that if you won't pay the price asked someone else will. A good idea if you're looking for crafts/weavings is to go to the houses of the individual craftspeople rather than a market.

BAGGAGE

Take the minimum possible — an overweight pack will become a nightmare especially when it's hot. Don't join that diminishing minority of travellers who stagger around in a pool of sweat, dwarfed by an enormous pack containing everything including the kitchen sink. A backpack is preferable to an overnight bag as the latter screws up your balance. Get hold of one which will take some rough handling — overland travel destroys packs rapidly. Make sure the straps and buckles are well sewn on and strengthen if necessary before you set off. Whether you take a pack with or without a frame is up to you but there are some excellent packs on the market with internal frames (eg *Berghaus*). Probably the best stockists in Britain are the YHA Adventure Centre, 14 Southampton Street, London, WC2 (telephone 01 836 8541). Take a strong plastic bag with you that will completely enclose your pack. Use it on dusty journeys whether your pack is in the luggage compartment or strapped onto the roof. If you don't you'll be shaking dust out of your belongings for the next week.

A sleeping bag is more or less essential. At 3000 metres and higher it gets very cold at night and not all hotels provide blankets or provide only one. You'll be glad of it too on long bus, train or truck journeys as a supplement to wooden benches and sacks of potatoes. A sheet sleeping bag is also useful when it's too hot to use a normal sleeping bag. It's cool and keeps the mosquitoes off.

Take clothes for both hot and cold climates and include at least one good sweater for use at night in the mountains. It probably won't be enough particularly on the altiplano but, rather than take an overcoat which you'll have to lug through Central America and Colombia unused, wait until you get to Ecuador or Peru and buy a poncho. You'll certainly need one of these to go through the mountains of Peru and Bolivia. Western type clothes are not cheap in most places so set off in clothes that will outlast the journey.

Some people take a small tent and portable stove but you can hire these things where mountain trekking is popular, eg Cuzco in Peru, though the returnable deposit is sometimes outrageously high. Don't forget the small essentials: a combination pocket knife or Swiss Army knife; needle and cotton and a small pair of scissors; towel; tooth brushes and paste; oral contraceptives (if used); tampons; a supply of anti-malarial pills; one or two good long novels. Toiletries (paper, tooth paste, shaving cream, shampoo, etc) are available in even the smallest places. A water bottle (fabric covered) is very useful where it's very hot or for walking in the mountains.

Theft is a big problem in some countries — notably Colombia and Peru. On buses and trains keep an eye on your baggage at all times. If you can't see what's happening to it at stops, get off and make sure. This is especially important at night. Don't fall asleep in a railway compartment unless a friend is watching your gear. You'll wake up with everything gone but your knickers. On the street, in markets and other crowded places use only the front pockets of your jeans — pickpockets are notorious in these places as too are people who slash shoulder bags. In bus terminals a thief needs only a half a minute of your inattention to be halfway down the street with all your gear. It's a lucky traveller who gets through South America without having had something stolen. With this in mind it's a good idea to take out Baggage Insurance before you set off. Remember that most such policies have clauses limiting the amount which can be claimed on any indivicual article unless separately declared on the proposal form — often between £70 (US$140) and £100 (US$200). This will affect such things as cameras, watches, musical instruments and possibly cassette players. Most companies won't insure "fragile" articles (eg musical instruments) against damage but they will insure them against theft. If you have anything stolen, inform the company by air letter and go to the local police for a "denunciacion" (statement). In most places this has to be done on "papel sellado" (stamped paper) which you buy beforehand from any stationers and some street stalls for a few cents. In some police stations you might be able to find someone who speaks English and so can act as a translator, but in most this won't be the case and you'll have to speak Spanish or provide your own translator. Have a list prepared, in Spanish, of the items you have had stolen and their respective values together with a brief summary of how, when and where it happened. A copy of this denunciacion is generally required by the insurers before they will settle a claim.

In Peru the procedure for reporting a theft/loss is slightly more complicated if it includes the loss of your passport and/or traveller's cheques. In such cases you need "papel sellosexto" or "sellado" from any stationers plus "forma copia certificado de guardia civil" — special paper available only from the Banco de la Nacion (costs 50 soles). Take both to the local PIP (investigative police). After your statement has been typed out onto the two pieces of special paper they both have to be rubber-stamped with various official seals and counter-signed by the superior officer. Until you get your passport and visa/tourist card replaced, these two forms are your only method of ID and proof of loss. If your theft or loss occurs on a weekend when it's impossible to buy the forma copia report it to the PIP and carry on with the rest on Monday. Remember that the guardia is organized on a regional basis and a denunciacion must be made at the place where the loss occurred. If you were on transport and don't know precisely where the loss occurred it's best to say it happened on arrival to avoid any complications.

It can be expensive replacing a stolen/lost passport. Other than cost of backtracking to the nearest Embassy or Consulate there will be telex charges to your home country to check on details of your previous passport plus the cost of a new passport. In Peru, for British passport holders, these last two charges total nearly 8000 soles (US$60 at the official rate).

MAIL

Have letters sent to you c/o Posta Restante, Oficina de Correos Central (central post office) in the cities you pass through. Alternatively use the mail-holding service operated by American Express offices and their agents if you're a client (cheques, credit card, etc). Most embassies no longer hold mail and will forward it to the nearest Posta Restante at the central post office. Plan ahead. Remember that it can take up to two weeks for a letter to arrive at/come from another place in the world.

Most Posta Restantes are pretty reliable and will hold mail for one month — sometimes longer — after which they'll return uncollected letters to the sender. The service is free in most places but in others there's a small charge (never more than a few cents). As a rule you need your passport as proof of identity to collect letters. In large places where there's a lot of traffic, letters are generally sorted into alphabetical order and occasionally even into separate male and female sections.— though how they distinguish the one from the other when they're not preceded by Mr, Mrs, Ms, Miss, Señor, Señorita one can only guess. In small places they're often all lumped together in one box. Sometimes you're allowed to sort them out yourself: in other places an employee will do the sorting in front of you. If you've not receiving expected letters ask them to check under every conceivable combination of your Christian name, surname and other initials and under "M" (for Mr, Ms, etc) and "S" (for Señor, Señora, etc). In Managua I collected three letters: the first I found under "C" (my surname); the second under "G" (my Christian name) and another under "S" (the person who wrote had put Señor on the envelope)! This sort of confusion isn't as widespread as many people believe though most travellers have a crazy story to tell about letters. It arises, if at all, because of the way Spanish-speaking people are named. If you were called Juan García Moreno, for example, Juan would be your Christian name, García your father's name and Moreno your mother's name. A letter addressed such would be filed under your father's name and you'd find it under "G" unlike in an English speaking country where you would expect to find it under "M". To avoid this kind of confusion address a letter in block capitals, leave out all titles (Mr, Ms, etc) and underline your surname.

Sending parcels can be a pain in the neck in some places — particularly in Mexico. You're supposed to have the contents checked by some sort of customs official who works in the post office before they'll tell you how much the parcel is going to cost and before they'll take it off you, but for some reason or another he's an elusive character. I eventually, out of frustration, stuck on a few stamps and dumped my parcel in the mail box. It did eventually arrive, intact. In Guatemala, if the contents are declared to be worth more than US$5, post office officials will insist on inspecting them before allowing you to seal up the parcel, though in places like Panajachel they're more flexible. Peru has some of the highest postal charges in Latin America. Bear this in mind if you're thinking of sending back a lot of postcards.

LANGUAGE

Spanish is the language of the vast majority of people in all of Latin America other than Brazil where it is Portuguese. To set off without, at the very least, a working knowledge of those languages is very short-sighted. You'll meet people all over the continent who will want to speak with you, exchange views, ask you what's happening where you come from, tell you what's happening where you are, or just have a light social evening laughing and joking about nothing in particular over a bottle of wine or a few beers. If you can't speak their language these exchanges will be limited to a few cliches and you'll start to feel trapped inside a cultural and linguistic bubble. All this is quite apart from the obvious practical value of speaking the language in order to find your way around, order things in restaurants, bargain for items in markets and get yourself out of potential hassles.

A few months before you go suss out an evening course in Spanish or Portuguese; buy a phrase book and grammar book and learn it from that, or, borrow a record/cassette course from your local library — buying them individually can be expensive (*Linguaphone* courses, for example, cost around US$140-160). Try to find someone who comes from Latin America and ask them if you can come and practice your Spanish/Portuguese with them once or twice a week. When you get there don't worry about making grammatical mistakes or using the wrong word. If people see you're trying, they'll help you out and you can both laugh about your occasionally unfortunate choice of words. It's a good idea to set yourself a target of learning a few new words each day since, when you know off by heart all the standard phrases for finding your way about, there's a temptation to be satisfied with that and get stuck in a rut.

Note that accent and pronunciation can vary considerably from one country to the next. In some places, eg Mexico, it's quite clear, in others, such as Nicaragua, it's spoken fairly lazily with all the "g"s being dropped so that *Managua*, the capital, becomes *Manawa*. The speed with which people talk also varies, Puerto Rican being virtually impossible to understand unless you come from there. Words used for the same item sometimes differ: in Mexico and much of Central America the word for "matches" is *cerillos*, but in South America it's the medieval Spanish word *fosforos*. The word used for "toilet" is generally *servicio* or *baño* but can also be *urinario, sanitario, retrete, excusado, hombres* or *señoras*. Remember that there are significant differences between the Spanish spoken in Spain and that spoken in South America: "z", and "c" before "e" are pronounced "th" in Spain but are all "s" or "c" in Spanish America. What is pretty standard throughout Spanish-speaking America is that personal pronouns (I, you, he, she, we, they) are rarely used, being implied in the verb, and that "ll" is pronounced as a "y" rather than the more correct "ly". It takes a little more time to get used to this vernacular.

You may hear it said that Portuguese is very similar to Spanish and so if you know the latter it's possible to get by in Brazil by using that language. Our own experience of this was that although it's more than likely a Portuguese speaker will understand someone speaking Spanish, you can't understand the response! Although there are similarities, they are different languages with different words, phrases and pronunciation.

Apart from Spanish and Portuguese, there are large areas where various Indian languages are spoken and others where Creole English is predominant. The main Indian languages are Yanqui (Northern Mexico), Nahuatl (Central Mexico), Maya (Yucatán Peninsula, Mexico and Guatemala), Chibcha (Colombia), Quechua (Ecuador and Peru) and Ayara (Southern Peru and Bolivia). Because many Indians never see the inside of a secondary school or even a primary school and remain largely isolated from the mainstream of life in many countries — particularly in Guatemala, Peru and Bolivia — they speak only their own language and cannot speak Spanish. When you realise that they comprise up to 50 percent of the population in some countries, it's as well to consider learning a little of one or two of their languages if you're thinking of spending any amount of time in predominantly, or exclusively, Indian areas. This might be difficult outside Latin America itself as phrase books/grammar books/courses will be very thin on the ground. Only in the last couple of years, despite a 50 percent Indian population, has Quechua been made an "official" language alongside Spanish in Peru. One neat little phrase book you'll come across in the Yucatan and Guatemala is *300 Phrases in Common Use in Mayan, English and Spanish* which costs six Mexican pesos. It's available in bookstores and hotels. If you can't find one it's published by Abelardo Fuente Vega, Calle 59 No 454, Merida, Mexico. Creole English is spoken by black people living on the Caribbean coasts of Belize, Honduras, Nicaragua, Costa Rica, Panama, Guyana and the Colombian islands of San Andres and Providencia, though many are bilingual (Spanish and English).

BIBLIOGRAPHY
Books Some books for background reading are listed below:

A History of Latin America by George Pendle (Penguin), 75p (UK) US$2.95 (USA) is a very readable account of the period from the Conquest to the present, containing some acute observations on the character of Latin American people. There are hardly any details on pre-Conquest history.

The Ancient Sun Kingdoms of the Americas by Victor Wolfgang von Hagen (Paladin), £1.50 (UK) US$4.50 (USA), is probably the most readable account of the Aztec, Maya and Inca civilizations to date. Packed with details of everyday life, architecture, religion, agriculture, trade, socio-political organisation, etc, it has plenty of black and white photographs and maps. The author has written several books on this theme.

The Maya by Michael D. Coe (Penguin), £1.25 (UK), is a very detailed account of the civilization of this people with some excellent black and white illustrations. The style is very dry and it's probably a book more for the specialist than the layperson.

The Aztecs of Mexico by George C. Vaillant (Penguin), is similar to the above.

If you're a specialist or looking for specialist information, the standard tomes on American Archaeology are Volumes I and II of *An Introduction to American Archaeology* by Gordon R Willey (1966, Prentice Hall). They contain information on all the known pre-Conquest civilizations of the Americas, with plenty of photographs, maps and other illustrations. Get it from the library as it's quite expensive. Another series concentrating on incividual civilizations is the *Library of Art and Civilization of Indian America*, edited by Michael D. Coe (Thames & Hudson); eg *The Mochica; a culture of Peru* by Elizabeth P. Benson. They contain both colour and black and white photographs and again they tend to be expensive, around £4.50 per book.

A History of the Conquest of Mexico by W.H. Prescott. This is the standard book on this subject. He's also written *History of the Conquest of Peru* though many people prefer John Hemmings' *Conquest of the Incas* (Harcourt-Brace-Jovanovich, 1970). The latter gives some amazing insights into the Spanish Conquest.

The Discovery and Conquest of Mexico by Bernal Diaz del Castillo, translated by A.P. Maudslay (New York, 1956), is the detailed diary kept by a Spanish friar between 1517 and 1521 during Cortes' conquest of Mexico.

Lost City of the Inca: the story of Macchu Picchu and its Builders (New York, 1948) and *Across South America* (New York, Houghton Mifflin, 1911) are two books written by Hiram Binham, the discoverer of Macchu Picchu.

The Caste War of the Yucatan by Nelso Reed (Stanford University Press, 1964) is an excellent history of the Mayan uprisings against the Spanish and then the Mexican rule.

Open Veins of Latin America: five centuries of the pillage of a continent by Eduardo Galeano (Monthly Review Press, New York and London, 1973) is an excellent and very readable account of the cultural, social and political struggles in Latin America. It's highly recommended so don't go without reading it! It's one of the best books ever written on Latin America.

Guatemala — Another Vietnam? by Thomas and Marjorie Melvill (Pelican, 1971) is written by two people who were once Roman Catholic missionaries in that country but who became identified with the cause of revolutionary land reform. They were eventually expelled from Guatemala and from the Catholic Church and narrowly missed assasination at the hands of the Guatemalan Secret Police in Mexico. It's well worth reading.

Revolution and Counter Revolution in Chile by Michel Raptis (Allison and Busby, 1974) is a brief and readable account of the development and over-throw of the Chilean Revolution with particular reference on worker' participation in the process.

Narcotic Plants: hallucinogens, stimulants, inebriants and hypnotics. Their origins and uses by William Emboden (Studio Vista, 1972), written by an ethno-botanist, contains some very interesting descriptions and information about this class of Latin American plants (coca, yage, marijuana, datura, etc) with some excellent colour illustrations.

The Heights of Macchu Picchu by Pablo Neruda, translated by N. Tarn (Jonathan Cape, 1966), writings of the Chilean poet.

Other Guides In a guide book of this size and scope we can't possibly cover every conceivable aspect of travel in Latin America, particularly if you're taking your own transport, nor many of the thousands of smaller places off the beaten track. So if you're thinking of spending a long time in Latin America, you might like to supplement this book with one or more of the following guides:

The South American Handbook edited by John Brooks (Trade and Travel Publications, Bath), £7 (UK). This is obtainable in Britain either from Trade & Travel, Parsonage Lane, Bath BA1 1EN or from bookshops. In the USA it's distributed to bookshops by Rand McNally or in Australia you can get it from Lonely Planet. It is also available in many bookshops in Latin America. This is *the* guide to Latin America containing the most amazing and comprehensive collection of information you will find anywhere ranging from the smallest villages to the largest cities. It's updated every year though, because they depend to a large extent on current information being sent in by travellers, you may find parts of it out of date by anything up to a few years. We used it ourselves and were very impressed by its contents. If you're going to be spending a long time in Latin America we'd recommend you to score a copy as a supplement to this guide but we did have one or two criticisms: it seriously lacks town plans and the ones which are provided often cover too small an area; the addresses of hotels and cafes are rarely given making this information of limited use or putting you at the mercy of taxi drivers; the collation/organization of the information is, in parts, somewhat uncoordinated, making it sometimes difficult to re-locate; because it caters for every type of traveller, from the jet-set to the Amazonian explorer, a fair amount of the information is of little or no use to budget travellers. It does contain excellent sections on history, geography, politics, the people, etc for each country. You'll never get tired of reading it on long buses/trains.

Backpacking Along Ancient Ways in Peru and Bolivia by George and Hilary Bradt (Boston, 1974) is a book for hiking freaks — it covers trails around Chimbote, Huaraz, Chavin, Shintuya, Cuzco, Puna and La Paz. It is the first of a series on South American hiking trails and is available from Trailfinders, 46 Earls Court Rd, London W8, England; from 409 Beacon St, Boston, Mass, USA or from Lonely Planet in Australia.

The Maya World is a 30-page booklet written by two budget travellers, US$1.95. It includes cheap places to stay, where to eat, transport and how to get off the beaten track, covering Mayan areas of Mexico, Guatemala, Belize and Honduras.

The People's Guide to Mexico by Carl Franz (John Muir Publications, Box 613, Santa Fe, New Mexico 87501, USA), US$9 plus postage, is a meaty 380-page guide to Mexico contianing everything you'd ever want to know about travelling (and living) in that country. It's extremely witty so even if you had no intention of going there I'd recommend you score a copy it's so good!

A Traveler's Guide to El Dorado & the Inca Empire: Colombia-Ecuador-Peru-Bolivia by Lynn Meisch was produced by Headlands Press, San Francisco and published by Penguin Books in 1977 at $8.95. It's more a complete cultural introduction to the Incas than simply a travel guide.

A Moneywise Guide to North America — Canada, USA, Mexico (Travelaid, London, 1979) £2.75 in the UK, A$7.95 in Australia, is a guide to budget travel throughout the North American continent. Available from Travelaid, 7a Belsize Park, London NW3, England or from Lonely Planet Publications in Australia.

Where to Stay: USA is an Arthur Frommer publication from CIEE (Council on International Educational Exchange, New York). It costs £2.75 in England and contains information on places to stay costing from 50c to US$14 for a single. CIEE also publish *The Student Guide to Latin America* (US$5.95).

Caribbean Island Hopping (Wilton House Gentry, London), £5.95 in England.

If you're going to take your own transport:

Overland and Beyond by Theresa and Jonathan Hewat is £2 from either T and J Hewat, 106 West Street, Corfe Castle, Dorset, UK or from Trailfinders (address above). Written by two people who went around the world for three and a half years in their own VW Kombi, their book is packed with information and is highly recommended.

Latin American Travel Guide and Pan American Highway Guide (Compsco Publishing Company, 663 Fifth Avenue, New York, NY 10022). Airmail prices are: US$12.70 (USA and Canada); US$14.15 (Western Hemisphere); US$15.70 (Asia, Australia and Far East). Outside the US either send a US$ Money Order or add US$4 bank service charge. It is updated regularly, "...for the fly-drive traveller and for the motorist who likes to drive the entire length of the Pan American Highway from Alaska to Tierra del Fuego...."

Periodicals

South American Explorer published in English and Spanish (by South American Explorers Club, Avenida Portugal 146, Brena, Lima, Peru, postal address SAEC, Casilla 3714, Lima 100, Peru) is quarterly with an annual subscription of US$10 plus US$3 for overseas mail. The magazine is free to members of the Club who pay an annual subscription of US$25. The Club provides services, support, and information to travellers, scientific researchers, mountaineers, explorers, etc. The magazine contains articles/info on a wide variety of topics covering the whole of South America. They also supply books, guides and maps dealing with South America.

ABC Guide to World Shipping published quarterly (ABC Travel Guides Ltd, 40 Bowling Green Lane, London EC1, England — 112 Albert St, Auckland, New Zealand — 3-13 Queen St, Chippendale, NSW 2008, Australia) is useful if you want to suss out a way of getting to Latin America by sea — but see under *Getting There* as it's not all that easy unless you have a seaman's ticket or don't mind spending more than a flight would cost you.

Maps One of the cheapest and most reasonable maps of South America is that published by Bartholomews (£1.25 or A$3.80) which is sold at most map stockists or from Bartholomews, Duncan Street, Edinburgh, UK. Another is published by Kummerly and Frey at £4 or US$8. Good maps of Central America are hard to find but luckily this doesn't matter too much because the Tourist Offices of Mexico, Guatemale, Nicaragua and Costa Rica provide excellent maps of their respective countries free of charge. If you're going to be driving through the states or hitching, Rand McNally produce some cheap maps: *Eastern States*, *Central United States* and *Western United States*. They also do one for *New York City* (about US$2). Otherwise Bartholomews publish a North America map for £1.25 and likewise Kummerly and Frey for £4.

Other Sources of Information Most Latin American countries maintain excellent Tourist Offices from which you can get armfuls of coloured brochures, maps, hotel, restaurant, bus and rail lists. Most are very friendly and eager to help you. More often than not there will be a Tourist Office in every city and town of any size.

Getting There

The cost of getting to the Americas (north or south) will depend largely on where you want to start your journey. If you're coming from Australia and want to keep your costs to a minimum, the choice is simple. If, on the other hand, you're coming from Europe, there are many possibilities.

Either way, the cost of a flight ticket, and therefore ultimately how much it costs you to get to and back from Central or South America, depends on the following factors: (1) Whether you go standby. (2) Whether you book in advance. (3) When you want to go/return. (4) Which airline you want to fly with. (5) Whether you want a direct flight to a Central or South American city or whether you're prepared to take a cheap flight to a convenient US city or Caribbean island and then make your way to Latin America by, respectively, land transport or boat.

Ships and boats to the Americas can largely be discounted for the following reasons: (1) If you're a fare-paying passenger, a boat ticket will cost substantially more than a flight ticket. (2) If you're hoping to work your passage on a ship it's more than likely that you'll need a seaman's ticket. (3) From Europe many boats go to Caribbean islands and you still have to get to the mainland from there. (4) Finding a cheap/free boat or one on which you can work your passage can take time (which equals money) and the outcome is uncertain. If time is no object or you live near a place where such enquiries could be made, there are one or two possibilities. First, every year yachts leave Mediterranean resorts around late September and early October and sail to the Caribbean for the winter, returning the following spring, and it's possible to arrange a free lift/work your passage on one of these. Try Antibes or Cannes (France) around this time. Ask yacht skippers in the harbours or try in the *Bar du Pont*, Antibes, where the English yachting fraternity hang out. Otherwise try yachting magazines, the personal columns of national newspapers or try at Cowes, Isle of Wight in England or in Gibraltar — though you'll have to join the queue in the latter place. The second possibility is to get a copy of the *ABC Guide to World Shipping* either from a library or travel agent and suss out likely looking banana boat companies. If you can't find a copy of this guide it can be bought from ABC Travel Guides — see the section on books and guides.

Air fare warning Due to the 1979 oil price increases all international air fares are expected to leap upwards about the time this book emerges. Take the following figures as a guide only.

DIRECT TO SOUTH AMERICA

Flying directly to Central or South America is not the cheapest way of getting there. There are no cheap direct flights, standby fares, budget fares, charter fares or all the other special goodies that make crossing the Atlantic, and now to a lesser extent the Pacific too, such a bargain. If you're trying to economise the cheapest ways to Latin America will be either via the US or, from Europe only, via the Caribbean. However, if money is not so important, you can fly direct:

From Australia or New Zealand There are actually no direct flights to South America from Australia or New Zealand. The only way of getting there is to

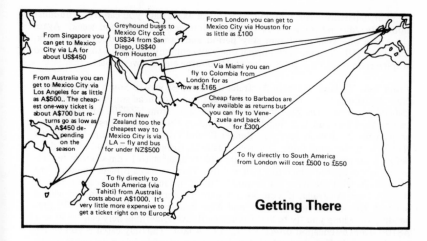

From Singapore you can get to Mexico City via LA for about US$450

Greyhound buses to Mexico City cost US$34 from San Diego, US$40 from Houston

From London you can get to Mexico City via Houston for as little as £100

From Australia you can get to Mexico City via Los Angeles for as little as A$500.. The cheapest one-way ticket is about A$700 but returns go as low as A$450 depending on the season

From New Zealand too the cheapest way to Mexico City is via LA — fly and bus for under NZ$500

Via Miami you can fly to Colombia from London for as low as £165

Cheap fares to Barbados are only available as returns but you can fly to Venezuela and back for £300

To fly directly to South America from London will cost £500 to £550

To fly directly to South America (via Tahiti) from Australia costs about A$1000. It's very little more expensive to get a ticket right on to Europe

Getting There

fly first of all to Tahiti from where you can fly with Lan Chile to Easter Island and then to Santiago in Chile. This is expensive: from Sydney the one-way fare to Santiago is around A$1050 although you do get to stopover in Tahiti and Easter Island on the way. However for very little more (less than A$50 at the last count) you could fly right on from Santiago to Madrid in Spain, making South America a stop on the way to Europe. Or you could include Buenos Aires and Rio de Janeiro into the route for a couple of hundred dollars. Or go to Europe via Miami from Santiago. There are also multi-stopover "Magic Circle" fares available from Australia — Sydney to Sydney fares with ten or more South American stopovers included range from about A$1600.

From Europe Regular one-way economy fares from London to South America are around £500 to Rio de Janeiro, £550 to Buenos Aires. If you compare that with the £100 or so which is all it can cost you to get to Central America (Mexico) you'll realise why the cheapest route to South America is not to fly directly to South America!

CHEAPEST FLIGHTS
From Australia You can fly to the US west coast from Sydney or Melbourne with either Qantas (to San Francisco only), Continental (between Sydney and Los Angeles only) or Pan Am. The cheapest fares are the APEX (Advance Purchase Excursion) fares and the Budget fares. From Melbourne to San Francisco APEX fares range from A$476 to A$946 return, depending on the dates you fly out and back. APEX fares must be booked and paid for at least 45 days before you depart. Once booked they cannot be altered either outbound or on return. There is no minimum stay period but the maximum stay is one year. Fares from Sydney are approximately A$40 cheaper.

Budget fares range from A$405 to A$778 again depending on when you fly out and back. On this fare you must nominate the week you wish to fly and pay for your ticket at least 21 days before the start of that week. Seven to 14 days prior to your departure week you will be told the exact date you can fly. You must nominate your return week at the same time as your outbound week. Again there is a one year maximum stay period and fares from Sydney are approximately A$40 cheaper. The normal one way economy fare point-to-point (ie no stopovers en route) is A$663 between Melbourne and the west coast.

From New Zealand As from Australia the cheapest way to South America from New Zealand is to fly to the US west coast and then head south to Mexico and Central America. The Epic Round Trip fare varies from NZ$702 to NZ$965 between Auckland and Los Angeles depending on the season. These tickets must be paid for 35 days in advance. Budget Round Trip fares vary from NZ$491 to NZ$804 on the same route. As from Australia, tickets must be paid for 21 days before your intended week of departure and then, seven to 14 days before departure, you will be told which day you will fly. There is also a Budget one-way fare of NZ$426 with the same restrictions. This is in fact also the cheapest way to the US from Australia, if you do not want a return ticket. Combined with a one-way ticket between Australia and New Zealand for A$153 to A$177 (depending on where you fly to and from) you'll save something between A$50 and A$100 over the cheapest direct Australia-USA fare. The only catch is you either have to arrive in New Zealand 21 days before departure to buy your ticket or get somebody (pick a travel agent from a NZ phone directory?) to buy it for you. Of course, if you were planning to stop off in NZ anyway.......... The regular economy one-way fare from Auckland to Los Angeles is NZ$707.

From Asia Yes here too the cheapest route is to fly to the US west coast and then head south. In Singapore or Bangkok travel agents will all have special cheap deals to get you that far at least at minimum cost.

From Europe London is by far the cheapest place to fly from — so much so that it's worth the cost of getting there from most places in Northern Europe in order to get a flight from London. There are bus/ferry deals between Paris and London and Brussels and London for £12 and £14 respectively. *National* buses cover these routes. If flying to the US, the city you choose as your arrival point should be determined by whether you want to see the US before going to Latin America. If you don't particularly want to see the US then a flight to Houston, Texas will work out cheaper than a flight to New York because of the extra accommodation, food and transport costs you will incur crossing the country. In any event, the London-New York and London-Houston fares differ by only about £5.

London-New York
(1) Laker "Supersaver Fares" vary from £89 to £165 return depending on your outward and return dates. There is an additional cost of £5 if you want a weekend rather than weekday flight and £3 airport tax. Flights must be booked through a travel agent or Laker Air Travel on the 23rd, 22nd or 21st day prior to departure. There's a one week minimum, one year maximum stay period. Once you're booked (bookings can be heavy) you're guaranteed a seat and there are about 17 flights per month. Laker flys from Gatwick.

(2) Jetsave "Latesave" scheme varies from £95 to £164 return. Basically similar scheme to the Laker Supersaver, booked through travel agents.

(3) Laker Skytrain costs £59 from London to New York, US$135 from New York to London. Flights depart daily and tickets can be purchased only on the day of departure but if that day's flight should already be sold out you can purchase a ticket for the next available flight so there's no need to queue more than once. Once you've bought a ticket your seat is guaranteed. In London tickets go on sale at 6.30 am at the Laker office at Victoria station or at Gatwick Airport from 4 am. In New York the main Laker office is at 95-25 Queens Blvd, Rego Park where tickets go on sale at 4 am. They're also available at the World Trade Center, at 1 East 59th St (at 5th Ave), at Newark Airport and at the Laker desk in the United Airlines Terminal at JFK Airport. They go on sale at 7 am at JFK. Going either way you may buy tickets for yourself and immediate family or for one friend who is travelling with you provided you have their valid passport and visa (if required) for each traveller. Laker have a phone number in London and New York with a recorded message advising you of the latest seat availability news.

(4) Standby on other airlines costs £70 London-New York and US$149 New York-London. British Airways, Pan Am, TWA, Air India, El Al, Iran Air and National all operate standby fares. Tickets are usually bought at the airlines' town terminal in London, at JFK Airport in New York, and are only sold on the day of departure. There are lots of flights daily but you only get on if there are seats available after full fare paying passengers have been accommodated and up to a maximum number of standby seats per week. For Pan Am, BA and TWA the weekly maximum is 1050 seats. In London it's best to phone around the airlines on the night before departure to check seat availability then get to the airline you choose in time for their terminal to open in the morning. In New York you might find it quicker to do the rounds of the ticket counters at JFK Airport but don't forget that JFK is a ridiculously badly planned airport and takes a long time to get around. Standby ticket sales stop three hours before flight departure time. Standby fares may be higher during the peak summer season.

(5) Budget fares cost £149 return and must be booked 21 days before your intended week of departure. Your flight date is notified 10 days before departure and also 10 days before return. Once you've booked you are guaranteed a seat but as for standby there are a limited number of seats per week.

(6) ABC Fares (Advance Booking Charter) vary from £126 to 139 in the low season and from £184 to 189 in the high season. You must book the flight 45 days before departure and there is also a 14 day minimum, 45 day maximum stay period but "long-stop holidays" are also available. Flights are charters from Gatwick.

(7) APEX fares (Advance Purchase Excursions) vary from £153 to 192.50 plus a £6 weekend supplement. Tickets must be booked and paid for 50 days in advance. Once booked your seat is guaranteed but at peak times the flights may be heavily booked.

London-Houston (Texas) If you don't want to go through the US then this is the cheapest route to Latin America (Mexico).

(1) British Caledonian Airways have standby fares from £69 to 89 depending on the season. Flights depart daily from Gatwick, ring British Caledonian the night before departure to check seat availability. All other details are the same as for London-New York standbys.

(2) Pan Am standby fares vary from £76 to 85, slightly more expensive from Houston back to London. Other details are the same as for London-New York standbys. Pan Am also offers London-Mexico City standby fares from £100 depending on the season, this involves a change of plane at New York and Houston.

(3) Braniff International standby fares vary from £76 to 116. These flights depart daily from Gatwick and involve a change of aircraft (and a six hour wait) in Dallas.

From Houston to Mexico there are the following possibilities in order of cheapness:

Greyhound Bus from Houston to Laredo (Mexican border) costs US$13.75, there are several buses daily and the trip takes 20 hours.
Greyhound Bus from Houston to Mexico City costs US$40.15.
Aeromexico will fly you from Houston to Mexico City on daily flights costing US$73. Aeromexico in London will confirm if this fare is still correct.
Braniff International will fly you Dallas-Mexico City for about US$148 return. This is an APEX fare and must be booked at least seven days in advance. The regular single fare is US$200!

Hence to get from London to the Mexican border (Laredo) it could cost you as little as £76 (US$152) on British Caledonian and Greyhound bus. From London to Mexico City could cost as little as £90 (US$178) by British Caledonian/Greyhound or £106 (US$211) on British Caledonian/Aeromexico. The last possibility works out at almost the same as flying on the cheapest possible standby flight from London to Los Angeles (£89) and then taking the Greyhound bus to Mexico City.

London-Los Angeles and London-San Francisco This is the second cheapest route to Latin America (Mexico).

(1) Laker "Supersaver Fares" vary from £169 to 249 depending on season. Fares are identical for Los Angeles or San Francisco but you must add an extra £10 for weekend departures. Flights usually operate to LA on Tuesday and Saturday (returns on Wednesday and Saturday) and to San Francisco on Sunday, returning on Monday. Other details are as for London-New York Supersaver fares.

(2) Jetsave "Latesave" fares vary from £196 to 245 return and are generally similar to the Laker Supersaver fares.

(3) Laker Skytrain standby fares to Los Angeles are £84, from Los Angeles to London the fare is US$199. In LA you can buy tickets at the airport or from a number of Laker sales desks in LA. Other details are as for Skytrain London-New York.

(4) Standby on other airlines to Los Angeles costs from £89 to 99 one way — fares vary with airline and season. Pan Am, British Airways and TWA operate this sector. Other details are as for standby flights London-New York. As in New York you can try the airline counters at LA International Airport — fortunately TWA, Pan Am and BA are all reasonably close together.

(5) Other special deals include Budget, ABC and APEX fares which must be booked in advance. See London-New York for details.

From Los Angeles to Mexico there are the following possibilities in order of cheapness:

Greyhound Bus from San Diego to Tijuana or Mexicali on the Mexican border. Cost is only a few dollars and there are several buses daily.
Greyhound Bus from San Diego to Mexico City operates once daily and costs US$33.70.
Aeromexico fly Los Angeles-Mexico City daily for US$116.

Hence to get from London to the Mexican border (Mexicali) it could cost as little as £95 (US$190) on Laker Skytrain and Greyhound Bus. To Mexico City could cost as little as £110 (US$220) by Laker/Greyhound

London-Mexico
(1) London-Laredo (Mexican border) — can be as little as £76 single.
(2) London-Mexico City — can be as little as £90 single. For full details on these see the London-Houston sections plus the paragraphs that follow.
(3) London-Merida (Mexico) — can be as little as £103 single. You can do this either by a standby flight with National Airlines or British Airways to Miami and change there for another flight to Merida or by direct standby flight with National. The minimum fare relates only to the low season, expect to pay approximately £10 more in the high season. Flights operate daily with either airline, this is also the first leg of the cheapest routes from London to both Central America and South America.

Many travel agents in London are offering deals similar to the above using a combination of standby and advanced booking to get you to Mexico, Central America and South America. Almost all of them initially put you on standby to either Houston, Texas or Miami, Florida. Check them out in *Time Out* in London. Some routes are heavily subscribed and they sometimes can't offer you anything for two months ahead. Plan ahead or do it under your own steam.

London-South America A word of caution: The cheapest countries to fly to — Colombia, Venezuela and the Caribbean islands of Barbados and Trinidad — all demand an onward ticket before they allow you in. Make sure you have this sorted out before you arrive by having either an MCO (Miscellaneous Charges Order) or a dated or undated ticket for a specific flight out of the country you intend to land in. Also make sure that the MCO or flight ticket is bought from an airline which is a member of IATA so that if you change your plans you can get a refund or have it transferred to any other airline which is a member of IATA (most are, but not COPA the Panamanian airline). This word of caution obviously only applies if you're travelling on a one-way ticket.

The cheapest route to South America by a very narrow margin (only a few pounds) is Laker from London to Barbados followed by British West Indian Airlines from there to Trinidad and Aero Postal from there to Maturin (Venezuela). This only applies in the low season and, as cheap one-way tickets and standbys are not available on the London-Barbados-London route, it's no good unless you plan to return that way. Furthermore the Laker flight also has a 120 day maximum — so it's no use if you're planning on a longer stay. The bulk of the alternatives involve flying standby to Miami (British Airways or National Airlines) and then changing onto a flight from there to one of the cities in Colombia or Venezuela.

(1) London-Barbados by Laker varies from £214 to 281 return but these flights are only available to residents of the UK and the Caribbean countries. You must book 45 days in advance and flights are once weekly.

From Barbados to the mainland (Venezuela) involves two flights. First you fly from Barbados to Port of Spain, Trinidad with British West Indian Airways. There are two flights daily, cost is approximately US$50 one-way and the flight takes 45 minutes. From there to Maturin, Venezuela there are flights with Aero Postal on Wednesday, Friday and Sunday. The flight takes half an hour and costs about US$30 one-way. Therefore the return fare London-Maturin-London works out at approximately £294 on Laker-BWIA-Aero Postal.

(2) London-Barranquilla (Colombia)/Bogota (Colombia)/Caracas (Venezuela) can cost (one-way in the low season) as little as £165 to Barranquilla, £171 to Bogota or £184 to Caracas.

Many travel agents *advertise* tickets at the above prices, plus or minus about £5, but by the time you've waded through the mire of supplements, surcharges and limitations on lengths of stay, the price of your ticket will work out to almost exactly the same as you would pay going under your own steam, with the possible exception of one or two of the return tickets. Most of the travel agents offering tickets at the above prices do so on the basis of a budget fare (booked 21 to 30 days in advance) or standby initially to Miami, followed by transfer to a scheduled flight from there on airlines like Air Panama, Aerocondor, Braniff International. For details of standby fares to Miami, see *London-Mexico* above.

From Miami to the South American mainland, two of the cheapest airlines are Air Panama and Aerocondor. Aerocondor fly to Barranquilla, Bogota and Caracas. Air Panama fly to Bogota and Caracas. The Air Panama schedule is:

From Miami:

to	depart	arrive	stops	days
Panama	18.00	19.30	0	Mo/Tu/Th
Panama	22.40	00.10	0	We/Fr/Sa/Su
Bogota	18.00	21.45	0	Tu/Th
Bogota	22.40	02.15	1	Su
Guayaquil	22.40	02.40	1	We/Sa
Caracas	18.00	23.40	1	Mo/Th
Caracas	22.40	04.00	1	We/Sa
Lima	18.00	23.25	1	Tu
Lima	22.40	05.00	2	We/Sa
Lima	22.40	03.55	1	Fr

From Bogota:

Miami	10.15	16.00	1	Mo
Miami	09.00	14.15	1	We/Fr

From Caracas:

Miami	10.45	16.00	1	Tu/Th
Miami	09.00	14.15	1	Fr/Su

Aerocondor fly daily from Miami to Barranquilla (direct) and daily from Miami to Bogota (and vice versa). They also fly twice weekly from both Barranquilla and Cartagena to Miami via San Andres Island (and vice versa). The latter flights are slightly more expensive than the direct flights (by about US$15 to 20) but allow you an unlimited stop-over on San Andres Island.

Approximate costs on either airline are: Miami-Bogota US$180 one-way or US$260 return, Miami-Barranquilla US$156 or US$250 return and Miami-Caracas US$204 or US$273 return.

(3) Luxembourg-Barbados with Caribbean Airways varies from £147 to 174 one-way or £294 to 348 return. Tickets are valid for one year and student discounts are also available on these flights. Get details from Caribbean Airways.

SOUTH AMERICA VIA BARBADOS
Visas Visas are not required but an onward ticket is essential. You will be refused entry without one. There may also be some discrimination against long-haired people and those with backpacks.

Currency

$$B\$1 = US\$0.51$$

The unit of currency is the Barbados dollar, sometimes called the Bajan dollar. All the major banks have offices here, banking hours are 8 am to 1 pm from Monday to Thursday and 8 am to 1 pm and 3 pm to 5.30 pm on Fridays. American Express is at Barbados International Travel Services (R), PO Box 6050, St Michael's Row, Bridgetown (tel 61622) and also at Queen St, Speightstown (tel 24182).

Consulates Venezuela, Brazil, Mexico and Trinidad & Tobago all have consular offices here.

Tourist Information Information can be obtained from Marine House, Hastings, Bridgetown and at Grantly Adams International Airport.

Transport Regular buses run between Bridgetown and the rest of the island. The main terminals are at Lower Green, Fairchild St and Princess Alice Highway. Fares are a fixed 35c. The return fare from the last scheduled stop to Bridgetown is 70c. Taxis are plentiful but expensive, Bridgetown-airport costs B$13, Bridgetown-Speightstown costs B$23. Bicycles can be hired from C V Chandler, Glenden Gardens, Garrison — B$5/day or B$25/week plus a returnable deposit of B$25, (tel 64983).

Accommodation Barbados lives off tourism therefore most accommodation is expensive, especially in the mid-December to mid-April high season. The *Youth Hostel* (also known as the Yoga Centre) is the cheapest on the island and under-cuts everybody else by 50%. It's situated behind the *Vista* cinema at Worthing (tel 87477) on the road from the airport to Bridgetown. If you ring them they'll come and collect you — US$2.70/night or US$8 for full board (three meals). It is situated in peaceful tropical gardens 100 metres from the sea. The post office is 100 metres away, as is a bank and it's "within staggering distance of the best pub". The building is an old colonial house, yoga lessons are free and all the food comes fresh from their own gardens or the sea. If it's full try the *YMCA* in Bridgetown.

Getting to Venezuela Boats are possibilities, ask around in the Careenage in the centre of Bridgetown and at the deep-water harbour. The snag is that visas are only issued by the Venezuelan Embassy if you have a letter from the ship's master saying that he will guarantee your removal from Venezuela within the period of the visa's validity (usually 45 days). If you can convince the captain that you won't be any hassle in this respect (ie you'll get yourself out within the period) then it shouldn't be too hard — and certainly cheaper than having to buy an onward ticket with an airline.

To Venezuela by air requires two flights — one from Barbados to Port of Spain, Trinidad and one from there to Maturin, Venezuela. See *London-South America* for full details and note that you must have an onward ticket from Trinidad in order to enter Trinidad — as well as the onward ticket from Venezuela.

GETTING THROUGH THE UNITED STATES

Hitching Hitching is pretty good, particularly on the interstate roads (in Europe they'd be motorways, autoroute, autopista, autobahnen or autostrade). As in Europe it's illegal to hitch on the interstates themselves — you must keep to the ramps/access roads. With luck it should take you four to five days to get from New York to the Mexican border or five to six days to cross from the east coast to the west.

The US is a society based on the use of the car. Even small towns are spread out for miles and the cheaper motels are often a long way from the centre of town. There are very few people on the streets after 6 pm except in large cities. As everyone (nearly) drives everywhere you will be an object of curiousity if you walk anywhere, especially at night. This of course can be an advantage or a dis-advantage depending where you are and what time it is. A lot of restaurants close early in the evening so if you want a decent cheap meal outside of a large city it might be best to get it at midday.

If New York, if you're looking for a lift, try the following:

Ride Bulletin Board, 130 West 24th St, (tel 212 989 0153). Shared cost lifts throughout the US.

People's Transit, (tel 1 800 547 0933). Matches up drivers and riders to all parts of the US.

New York Ride Center, 159 West 33rd St, (tel 99 279 3870). Shared expenses lifts; they also have offices in San Francisco, Los Angeles and Boston. Verging on the commerical, also known as Grey Rabbit Ride Center.

A Free Car, "Drive-Away" Schemes Car delivery is a well-known method of transport in the US for people without their own vehicle but with a driving licence. The way it works is that owners of a car who want it delivered from A to B but are unable to do it themselves, contact a drive-away agency who then arrange for someone else to do the driving. That's where you come in. There are drive-away agencies in all the major cities and they're usually fairly busy. To find a car which needs delivering in the direction you want to go all you have to do is tout around the various agencies until you find something suitable. The busiest routes are from east to west and vice versa and from north to south; for these routes it's possible to pick something up on the same day you contact the agency. For other routes you may have to wait around a few days and compromise on somewhere near to where you eventually want to go.

You need a full driving licence from your native country and preferably an International Driving Permit although this is not essential. They will also ask you for a reference from someone resident in the US, but this can be waived when you're a tourist and don't know anyone who lives there — if you're thinking of utilizing this method of transport it might be an idea to get your bank manager (or someone similar) to write a reference for you before you leave home, saying what a wonderful person you are. When they fix you up with a car you have to sign a contract which gives you a fixed number of days to deliver it, but you can renegotiate this time with the owners if they're willing. If the car breaks down you have to contact the owners or agency and they'll extend the time for delivery. A US$50 deposit is taken from you by the agency and is refundable on delivery. The first tankful of gas is provided free (owners often give you extra if they take a liking to you — we even got put up for the night as well!). After that it's up to you to do the driving and pay for any further petrol. Using this method of transport it cost each of us US$3 in fuel to get from New York to New Orleans; the owners gave use an extra US$20 for petrol and doubled the delivery time.

All drive-away agencies advertise in local papers, usually under the heading drive-away cars and they are listed im the phone books. Here are a few:

US Driveaway Inc, Suite 923, 152 West 42nd St, New York (tel 212 594 1122/ 594 1690/594 1238).

Dependable Car Inc, Suite 2002, 130 West 42nd St, New York (tel 212 WI7 5230). They are also at:
    237 23rd St, Miami Beach, Florida (tel 305 538 0516)
    162 Sunny Isle Boulevard, North Miami Beach, (tel 305 945 4104)
    8730 Wilshire Boulevard, Beverly Hills, California (tel 213 659 0951)
    802 East Walnut St, Garland, Texas (tel 214 494 5823)
    1405 Locust St, Suite 1123, Philadelphia (tel 215 PE5 8290)

Nationwide, 25 West 45th St, Room 1000, New York (tel 212 354 0170/ 354 0199)

Auto Delivery, 225 West 47th St, Pennsylvania Building, Suite 20001, New York (tel 947 9222/244 5240). They are also at:
    429 North Broad St, Elizabeth, New Jersey (tel 203 678 9307)

Buses Both Greyhound and Trailways run long-distance buses to just about everywhere imaginable in the US and also to Mexico City. They have their own large terminals in most places with cafes, bars, deposit lockers, etc. During the summer months they usually have special deals on offer and you should check these out before buying a ticket as you can save a lot of money. If you're in London you can ring the Greyhound office on 01 839 5591. Here are some Greyhound fares:

Houston, Texas-Laredo (Mexican border), US$13.75, 20 hours, several daily.
San Antonio, Texas-Mexico City, US$25.50, once daily.
Houston, Texas-Mexico City, US$40.15, once daily. This works out as cheap as taking a bus to the border and then Mexican buses from there.
Brownsville, Texas-Mexico City, US$12.70, once daily.
El Paso, New Mexico-Mexico City, US$21.70, once daily.
Nogales, Arizona-Mexico City, US$25.75, once daily.
San Diego, California-Mexico City, US$33.70, once daily.

Return fares are approximately five percent less than double the single fares.

NEW YORK CITY INFORMATION
Transport — from JFK Airport to Manhattan Carey buses run every 20 minutes from 6 am to 1.40 am between the airport and the East Side Airlines Terminal at 1st Avenue and 38th St. It costs US$4 and takes about 45 minutes. Regular local buses leave from the bus shelter opposite the main terminal every 15 minutes (ask the security guard to point it out to you). Take the bus to Kew Gardens, walk around the corner onto Queens Boulevard and from there take a Q60 bus into the centre of Manhattan. Last stop is at the junction of 2nd Avenue and 60th St. These buses cost 50c each, you must have the right change handy and the trip will take about an hour and a half. By bus and underground (subway) take the Q10 bus, which stops at each airline terminal, to Lefferts Boulevard/Liberty Avenue. From there take the subway train "A" to Columbus Circle (59th St and Broadway).

To/from La Guardia Airport Carey buses run to La Guardia every 20 minutes between 6 am and 1 am from the East Side Airlines Terminal. The 40 minute trip costs US$3. Take the IRT Number 7 subway train from 42nd St to 74th St and Broadway in Jackson Heights (direction: Queens), then take a Q33 bus from its terminal at 74th St and Roosevelt Avenue to La Guardia Airport.

General Details Buses run on every major avenue and cross street. There is a flat fare of 50c and you must have the exact change handy. A half-fare scheme is in operation from 6 pm on Saturdays until 1 am on Mondays. Also special US$1 tickets are available for unlimited travel in the mid-town shopping area at certain times and for unlimited travel anywhere in the city between 6 pm and 2 am.

There's a very extensive underground train (subway) network. There is a flat fare of 50c but you have to buy a token from the booth and deposit it in the turnstile. Free maps are available from the token sellers. Trains run all day and all night. Information is given out 24 hours a day by ringing 330 1234.

Yellow cabs are licensed and and charge 75c for the first seventh of a mile and 10c for each subsequent seventh of a mile. Tipping is 15% of the fare and, although this isn't obligatory, they may well bad-mouth you all down the street if you don't. Other cabs are not licensed but will take you to parts of the city that the yellow cabs won't go to — if they feel like it.

You can rent a bike from the *Town & Country Bike Shop* at the junction of Broadway and 61st St, US$1.50/hour or US$7.50/day or US$15/week. There's a refundable US$40 deposit to be paid.

Getting out of the city   For lifts see under *Hitching* in *Getting Through the States* above.   All buses to wherever you want to go leave from the enormous Port Authority Bus Terminal at 8th Avenue and 40th St.   Trains leave either from Grand Central Station at 42nd St and Vanderbilt Avenue or from Pennsylvania Station at 32nd St and 7th Avenue. If you need to go to New Jersey (Newark) take a Transport of New Jersey bus from Gate 35 on the upper level of the Port Authority Bus Terminal.   They go from 6.15 am to 1.15 am, take 30 minutes and cost US$1.75.

Accommodation

Hotel Rio, 132 West 47th St, US$13-18 for a double with bath, US$6-7 for a single without bath, US$21 for a triple with bath. It's warm, secure and just off Times Square. Probably one of the cheapest you will find.

YMCA (both sexes), 356 West 34th St. US$19 a double with bath, US$8.50 a single without bath.

New York Student Centre, *Hotel Empire*, Broadway and 63rd St, (tel 695 0291) costs US$20/double without bath, US$26/double with bath, US$28.50/ triple with bath. The information desk in the reception area has maps, timetables, etc. They also put out an information newspaper which is worth getting hold of and is free.

Pickwick Arms, 230 East 51st St costs US$19/double with bath, US$10-25/ single with bath.

Martha Washington, 30 East 30th St costs US$16-18/double with bath, US$8.50-9.50/single without bath.

Prince George Hotel, 14 East 28th St is US$8.50 a single if you have a Youth Hostel card.

Alternatively try the universities as they sometimes let cheap rooms during vacations for around US$5.

Eats   There are thousands of restaurants and cafes in New York, particularly along the Avenues and around Times Square and in Greenwich Village. It's possible to eat very cheaply and well by choosing your cafe. For breakfast the "diners" around Times Square are excellent value. Up until 10.30 am you can get a three-course breakfast of fresh fruit juice, two eggs done anyway you like, toast and jam, and as much coffee as you can handle for US$1-1.50. Service is quick, as you might expect in the High Court of Speed, and the food good.

Supermarkets are immense affairs and stock the largest range of products ever assembled under one roof, but you'll have difficulty locating the actual food from amongst the chemicals. Even the food itself is triple-wrapped and "deodorized" so that it all comes out tasting alike — bland. For real food try the very good delicatessen shops. Here are a few recommended places:

Kamehachi, 14 East 47th St and 150 West 4th St — very fresh Japanese sea food.
Chumleys, 86 Bedford St — cheap American-style food.
McSorleys Ale House, East 7th St.

Peacock Cafe, junction of Greenwich Avenue and 6th Avenue. A place to sit and relax with local characters.

Casa Verdi, Bleaker St, Greenwich Village, the *Cafe Borgia* and *Folk City* all attract people into folk music, cheap food and no hassles.

All State Cafe, 250 West 72nd St — a bar-come-cafe. Lunch of cheese and mushroom omelette is US$1.95.

Famous Dairy Restaurant, 222 West 72nd St. No meat but good rolls, pastries, soup for US$1.10.

Chik-Teri, between 71st and 72nd Sts — fast Japanese food, broiled chicken, rice and vegetables, Teriyaki style for US$1.99.

Places to Go at Night

Bottom Line, 15 West 4th St — well known jazz and rock bands.

The Tin Palace, 325 Bowery — singers and poetry readings.

Ones, 111 Hudson St — dancing every Wednesday to Sunday. On Wednesdays and Thursdays there's a live reggae band and on Fridays and Saturdays there's a disco. Sunday there's a rock band. Cover charge of US$2 every night except Sunday (free) and a minimum order of two drinks at the tables but no minimum at the bar.

CBGB Restaurant, 315 Bowery, between 1st and 2nd Sts — new wave bands. Admission varies between US$2-5, depending on the band. See the *Village Voice* for listings or ring 473 9763.

Max's Kansas City, 213 Park Avenue South between 17th and 18th Sts — rock music, reggae on Sundays. Entrance is US$4, (tel 777 7871).

Trudy Heller's Restaurant, 9th St and 6th Avenue — live music at 9.30 pm, 10.30 pm and 12.30 pm with disco in between. It's open seven days a week, the cover charge is US$3 with a minimum of two drinks at the tables.

Brownies Revenge — 31-piece jazz-rock band plays here every Monday night and everybody dances (tel 254 8346).

Mikell's Restaurant, 760 Colombus Avenue and 97th St — jazz seven nights a week at 10.30 pm, 12.30 pm and "am". Open till 4 am and entry is US$2, (tel 864 8832).

Useful Addresses

New York Convention and Visitor's Bureau, 90 East 42nd St, opposite Grand Central Station — free info, maps, calendars of events, etc.

Council for International Educational Exchange, 777 United Nations Plaza (tel 212 661 0310) — info, guide books, advice on flights, etc.

New York Student Center, Hotel Empire, Broadway and 63rd St, (tel 212 695 0291). It has relatively cheap accommodation, an information desk and a notice board (free) with maps, timetables, etc.

Times Square Information Center, Broadway and 43rd St — free maps & info.

Jefferson Book Shop, 16th St near Union Square.

Barnes & Noble Bookshop, 17th St and 5th Avenue.

Useful Publications

A newspaper put out by the New York Student Center (free) has information, addresses, tips, etc. Available from the center.

Insiders Manhattan Map is 50c from the Student Center.

Village Voice is available from from most news stands and bookshops, it has plenty of small ads about gigs, lifts, accommodation, cafes, etc.
New York Magazine Ticket Service (tel 989 5872) has information on theatres.

MIAMI INFORMATION

Miami International Airport A total of 63 airlines are represented here. National Airlines and British Airways are the only ones which do standby fares to London. Be prepared for a wait at peak times as there are many travellers returning both from the US, Central America and South America. You need to be at the ticket desk immediately they open at 9 am which means you start queueing with the other hopefuls at 3 am. The system works on a strictly first-come, first-served basis, so make sure you're somewhere near the head of the queue to be sure of a seat. Avoid weekends, holiday periods and Monday mornings if possible, as there can be quite a backlog. British Airways leave at 6 pm everyday; National Airlines leave at 7 pm. You won't be allocated a seat until 5 pm unless the plane is particularly empty. See under *Getting There* for full details of the flights. There is a Tourist Information booth in the airport lobby where you can get free maps, timetables, etc.

It's impossible to walk out of the airport — all sidewalks turn into sidewalkless freeways on which you'd end up decorating someone's front bumper or getting arrested. If you have time to kill take the normal bus service into town and spend the day on Miami Beach. The buses leave from outside the main entrance and cost 50c. Give the more frequent red-top buses a miss — they'll charge you US$4 for the privilege. Beware of the tar on the beach — there's more of that than sand! If you want something more exotic there's plenty to choose from: marinas, zoos, Disney World, etc — but be prepared to pay.

Accommodation The Hari Krishna mob, skilfully disguised as ordinary people, frequently beseige the ticket counter selling *Back to Godheads*. They'll put you up for the night if you adopt the "right" spiritual attitude and are prepared to be hassled for an hour or two in the evening. Agreeing with everything they say works wonders. Alternatively there's a *Serv-ur-Self Motor Lodge* at 5001 NW 36th St, Miami (tel 305 883 4700). US$16/single, US$19/double, US$22-26/four people. There are weekly discounts and they have a free courtesy bus to the airport. All the following hotels are in the $9-17/single, $12-19/double range:

Leamington, 307 NE 2nd St, Miami.
Lindsey Hopkins, 1410 NE 2nd St, Miami.
Paramount, 259 E Flagler St, Miami.
Park View, 250 NE 4th St, Miami.
Ponce de Leon, 231 E Flagler St, Miami.
Royalton, 131 SE 1st St, Miami.
Urmey, 34 SE 2nd Avenue, Miami.

Useful Telephone Numbers

Greyhound Buses, 374 7222
Trailways Bus Line, 373 6561

American Express, 432 4100
Johnson Bus Service, 891 7790

HOUSTON INFORMATION
Information Sources
Traveler's Aid Society, Houston International Airport (tel 443 0827); 5501 Austin St (tel 522 3846); 1410 Texas Avenue (tel 223 8946). It has information, assistance and medical and legal aid for travellers.

Greater Houston Convention and Visitor's Council, 1006 Main St, C&L Building has maps, brochures, timetables and restaurant information, (tel 658 9201).

Transport The International Airport is situated 33 km north of downtown Houston. The airport bus fare is US$4 to downtown areas, taxis cost US$15.

For bus information contact the following: Greyhound Buses, 1410 Texas, (tel 221 1161); Continental Trailways, 1114 McKinney, (tel 223 2101). Trains go from Southern Pacific Station, 902 Washington St, (tel 1 800 421 8320).

Accommodation All the following hotels are in the $9-17/single, $12-19/double range:

Ben Milam Hotel, 1521 Texas Avenue.
Center City Motor Inn, 1015 Texas Avenue.
Chief Motel, 9000 South Main.
Crestwood Motel, 9001 South Main.
Grant Motel, 8200 South Main.
Roadrunner Motel, 8500 South Main.

There are plenty of cheap cafes/bars around the Greyhound bus terminal.

SAN FRANCISCO INFORMATION
Information Sources San Francisco Convention and Visitors' Bureau, Hallidie Plaza, Power and Market Sts, open daily. Recorded information is on 391 2000.

Accommodation
The Bedford, near Union Square at 761 Post (tel 673 6040). It has 150 rooms, a dining room, coffee shop — modest rates.

Beverly Plaza Hotel, at the entrance to China Town between Grant Avenue and Bush (tel 781 3566).

Cecil Hotel, one and a half blocks from Union Square at 545 Post (tel 673 3733) — a European-type hotel.

Hotel David, between Geary and Taylor (tel 771 1600) — 54 rooms.

The King George Hotel, just off Union Square (tel 781 5050). This European-style hotel is family owned and operated and has modest prices.

Motel Capri, 2015 Greenwich (tel 346 4667) — 45 rooms, quiet.

Sutter Hotel, near Union Square on Sutter at the junction with Kearny (tel 227 4248 or toll free on 800 227 4248).

LOS ANGELES INFORMATION
Information Sources
Southern California Visitors' Council, 705 West 7th St (tel 213 628 3101). This is an information centre, open weekdays 9 am-5 pm. Maps, information on accommodation, events, etc, are all free.

Travelers' Aid Society, Los Angeles International Airport (tel 646 2270) and the Greyhound Bus Terminal (tel 625 2501). It helps with information and legal and medical problems.

Los Angeles Convention and Visitors' Bureau, 505 South Flower St (tel 488 9100).

In addition to these there are multilingual receptionists in red, white and blue uniforms available to help foreign visitors at the International Airport.

Accommodation All the following are in the $9-17/single, $12-19/double range.

> *Biola*, 536 South Hope St.
> *City Center Motel*, 1135 West 7th St.
> *Clark*, 426 South Hill St.
> *Holiday Lodge Motel*, 811 North Alvarado.
> *Hotel Figueroa*, 939 South Figueroa.
> *Kent Inn*, 920 South Figueroa St.
> *Hotel de Ville*, 1123 West 7th St.
> *Nutel Motel*, 1906 West 3rd St.
> *Oasis Motel*, 2200 West Olympic Boulevard.
> *San Carlos Hotel*, 507 West 5th St.

Eats Los Angeles is an excellent place to get into Mexican food before you actually get to Mexico but some of the best bargains in cheap eats can be found in the fine old cafeterias (some of them are kitsch works of art) in downtown LA.

Transport The international airport is 22½ km from downtown LA. The bus service costs $2.50. To Hollywood also $2.50; North Hollywood and the San Fernando Valley also $2.50; Riverside, San Bernadino, $6 — hourly departures. Buses go from the Greyhound Bus Terminal, 6th St and Los Angeles St (tel 620 1200) and Continental Trailways, 6th St and Main St (tel 626 3911). Trains from Los Angeles Union Station, 800 North Alameda St (tel 624 0171).

SAN DIEGO INFORMATION
Information Sources

Plaza Information Booth, Horton Plaza, 3rd and Broadway (tel 234 5191).
San Diego Convention and Visitors' Bureau, 1200 3rd Avenue, Suite 824 (tel 232 3101) will provide a hotel-motel guide giving information and rates on more than 200 hotels.

Transport The international airport is five minutes west of the downtown area by taxi. Otherwise there is an airport bus for 35c. There are three bus terminals:

> Greyhound Bus Terminal, 1st and Broadway (tel 234 4661).
> Continental Trailways, Union and C Sts (tel 232 2001).
> Mexicoach, 1050 Kettner Boulevard (tel 232 1227).

Mexico

Mexico has so many facets you could spend a long time here and still know only a small part of the whole. It's one of the largest Latin American countries with the second largest population — around 65 million and growing rapidly. Of this number a sizeable proportion — estimated at 25 million — are pure Indian people divided into numerous groups and sub-divisions each with their own language and cultural heritage, though the majority of the population are Mestizo (around 60%).

Mexico, like Mesopotamia, the Nile and Indus Valleys, was one of the ancient cradles of civilization with a history stretching back some 3000 years to the time when the large-scale migrations of the tribes had ceased, agriculture had become established and the first temple-cities started to make their appearance. One of the first tribes to make a lasting impression were the Olmecs (800 BC-600 AD) who inhabited the Vera Cruz, Tabasco, Oaxaca and highland Guatemala area. They were famous for their huge carved stone heads with characteristic flat noses, thick sensual lips and narrow slits for the eyes. Their influence can be seen on the very earliest relics at Monte Alban before the site was taken over and expanded into a ceremonial centre by the Zapotecs. This amazing artificially-flattened mountain-top centre just outside Oazaca has been influenced by virtually all the civilizations which have grown up on Mexican soil and was in more or less continuous use by one tribe or another for centuries before the arrival of the Spanish. Don't miss it.

Further north in the Valley of Anáhuac (present-day Mexico City) another tribe, the Toltecs, developed a civilization (200 BC-900 AD) which left one of the world's most impressive ancient monuments — the Pyramids of Teotihuacan. These form part of an immense ceremonial city covering 27 square km and include temples to Tlaloc (the rain god) and Quetzalcoatl (the plumed serpent god) among others. In common with their rivals at the time, the Toltecs possessed ideographic writing, tribal records, a type of paper book and a concept of time based on two calendars — the divinatory 260-day count plus the 360-day lunar calendar for everyday use, the two interlocked so as to coincide every 52 years. This centre declined around 900 AD and the Toltecs moved to other sites such as Tula (900-1116 AD) where the architecture resembles that at the late Mayan sites of Chichén Itzá and Uxmal, etc. Evidence has been found that the Toltecs did make such a trek to this part of the world in the 12th century. During this time also, the reclining idol of Chac-Mool came to the fore — the stone-carved figure into whose lap were placed human hearts torn out of living victims and which was to make its appearance from Yucatán to northern Mexico and play such an important part in Aztec religious ritual.

Sandwiched between the Olmec, Zapotec, Mayan and Toltec civilizations were others such as the Mixtecs and Totonacs, all of them contributing to the growth and development of a civilization to which the Aztecs were heirs by the time they made their appearance as an organized tribe around 1200 AD.

At this time the Aztecs took over several islands about five km out in the middle of lake Texacoco — a choice forced upon them because the land on the shores had already been settled, though no doubt, defence was another reason. They grew crops in "floating gardens" made out of reed-woven baskets about three metres in diameter filled with earth and anchored in the shallow waters. Roots penetrating the bottom of the baskets eventually fixed the basket in one place. They grew all their food by this method until conquest opened up more land for them on the mainland. The remains of this method of cultivation can still be seen in present-day Mexico City at Xochimilco. The basis of their society was similar to that of other neighbouring tribes and consisted of the farmer who was also part of the agrarian militia. Each person belonged to a calpulli or clan of which there were eventually 20 in number. Each clan had a tribal council and an elected leader. The oldest/wisest/most experienced members of these tribal councils were selected as advisors to the head of state (the "emperor") and electors of the next head of state. The head of state could be chosen from among the brothers of the previous ruler or, if he had no brothers, from amongst his nephews. He was, therefore, an elected leader, though the choice of candidates was limited. Their language was Nahuatl, a tongue which became the *lingua franca* throughout much of the region during their ascendency though many tribes spoke it and it wasn't their invention. It's still spoken today by many people in Mexico and was used by the Church during colonial times to propagate Catholicism.

They were superb weavers and sculptors, skills which the conquistadores commented on enthusiastically in their letters to Spain, but sadly no examples of the former and few of the latter remain, having been destroyed by the ravages of time, the Conquest and the demands for stone to build the Spanish cities and cathedrals which supplanted the indigenous centres.

Maize and its cultivation was at the very centre of their lives. All religion was based on it. The day began with maize and ended with it and much of the day was taken up in the time-consuming process of preparing tortillas. Unlike the Incas in South America who had the potato to rely on as well as maize and the Mayas who had a whole variety of forest products to fall back on, the Aztecs were entirely at the mercy of the maize harvest. Their agriculture, too, was not as developed as that of the Incas and they knew little about fertilizers or irrigation. A successful maize harvest depended on gaining the favour of the rain god, Tlaloc, which in turn demanded a constant supply of sacrificial victims whose hearts could be torn out and offered to the gods. The only way of assuring such a constant supply of victims was to wage constant war. Thus, in time, perpetual war became the Aztecs' assurance that life would continue and by the time the Spaniards arrived the scale on which they carried out these human sacrifices had become obsessional. Many of the 371 tribes and city-states from whom the Aztecs received tribute had become thoroughly alienated by these demands and willingly became allies of Cortés though little did they suspect they were merely exchanging one oppressor for another.

The Aztec capital — Tenochtitlán — was a wonder of city planning at the time and boasted fresh water and sanitation systems better than anything Europe was to experience until the 18th century. It covered an area of two square kilometres and was connected to the mainland by four causeways which served both to facilitate communication and to act as dykes in the event of a rapid rise in the level of the lake water (there was no outlet) or high winds which could raise huge waves that lapped up to and over the city. Like Venice, there were many interconnecting canals honeycombing the city. At the centre of the city, enclosed by walls, were the magnificent temples to Huitzilopochtli,

Tlaloc and Xipe, Moctezuma's palace, the ball court, the quarters of the Eagle Knights military order and the huge market. The temples were visible for miles around. There's an excellent reconstruction of the city in the Anthropology Museum in Mexico City. Nothing of the city remains — it was razed by Cortés and the stones used to build the Spanish city which rose on the same site. Very little, too, remains of Lake Texcoco which has been drained several times over the centuries since the Conquest.

Cortés was aided in his conquest by a prediction contained in an old legend surrounding the god Quetzalcoatl. According to this legend the god had once been ruler of a kingdom in Mexico, had lost it in a battle and had then sailed away across the Gulf vowing to return again on his birthday. According to the Aztec calendar this could only happen in the year "1-Reed" which corresponded, in the Christian calendar reckoning, with the years 1363, 1467 or 1519. Ever since Moctezuma had been elected leader in 1503 reports had been filtering back to Tenochtitlán about white men who continued to appear and disappear along the Gulf shores. When Cortés arrived on the coast in 1519, it was assumed he was the returning god Quetzalcoatl and one of the first gifts which Moctezuma sent to him was a magnificent headdress of quetzal plumes. One of the factors contributing to the obsessional sacrifice of human captives had been this appearance and disappearance of strange people on the Gulf shore and the Aztecs' attempts to get an answer from their gods as to what it implied.

Cortés' first entry into Tenochtitlán with his small force of just over 500 Spaniards was peaceful since Moctezuma believed him to be a god and treated him as an honoured guest but it was not long before the host was made a captive within his own palace. While Cortés was away on the coast dealing with a rival Spanish force which had been sent from Cuba to reassert royal control over the expedition, Alvarado, one of Cortés' lieutenants ordered the murder of some 200 Aztec nobles. On his return Cortés tried to stem the growing anger by having Moctezuma appeal for calm but the people stoned their ruler to death and elected a new leader, Cuitlahuac, who also died almost immediately, though this time of smallpox, a disease introduced by the Spaniards. His cousin, Cuauhtemoc, was named the new leader and the Spanish were besieged in the palace until they had to retreat back across one of the causeways to the mainland. Many were killed attempting this and most of the treasures they had stolen were lost in the lake. Before long, however, they were back with the help of their Indian allies. Boats were built on the lake and Tenochtitlan was blockaded for four months before Cuauhtemoc finally surrendered. Cortés had him tortured to find out where the treasure was hidden and later murdered him in Honduras.

Immediately after the Conquest the Spanish began an intensive campaign to eradicate the Indian way of life, religion, customs and to lay a complete Spanish veneer over the whole country with the aid of the Catholic church and the economic system they brought with them from Spain. Land was distributed in a lavish manner amongst the conquerors, and the Indians who lived on it used as virtual slaves. The Catholic religion was encouraged by every means possible. Saints and miracles were "discovered" in the most convenient situations in order to effect conversion by the million. But it was all very superficial and still is, even today, with pagan ritual interwoven with Catholicism and the Indian gods simply re-named to fit in with the Christian pantheon. The temples and palaces of Tenochtitlán and the Mayan cities in the Yucatán were torn down to provide building stone for the new Spanish cities and churches; Indian books and tribal records were burnt or destroyed, new plants and animals introduced and mines opened. Everything was designed in Spain, controlled by Spain and operated in a manner best suited to help the Spanish economy without regard to the effect this might have locally in Mexico.

The social order which developed was rigid and well-defined with the King of Spain and his administration at the peak of the pyramid. The King's representatives in the colony, who had to be people born in Spain itself (the Peninsulares), came next followed by the Criollos — local born whites — who were in control of much of the lucrative mining and trading business and who had equal pretentions to the Spanish-born but who were not allowed into the government. Next came the Mestizos, part European and part Indian, who could legally indulge in trade or the arts but who were looked down on by the whites until their numbers became so great they could not be ignored any more. At the bottom of the social pile were the Indians who were excluded from virtually everything except back-breaking labour and exploitation.

The colony was not allowed to trade with any nation except Spain and this was rigidly controlled so as to extract the maximum in taxes and benefit Spanish industry. Non-Spanish were not allowed to settle in the country. In this way a wall was effectively built around the colony cutting it off from the outside world and causing it to stagnate economically and preventing the new winds of thought, which were remaking Europe, from entering. Mexico still suffers from these centuries of exploitation and isolation.

But the Spanish didn't have everything all their own way. Because of the limitations on trade and the consequent high price of imported goods, a lively smuggling tradition grew up and flourished alongside the "legitimate" trade. This was particularly true of goods from China and the East Indies via the Spanish colony of the Philippines and goods from Britain, France and Holland via the West Indies.

During the colonial period the church became immensely rich expanding its property holdings in every direction until by 1850 it owned two-thirds of all the arable land in the country placing an incredible strain on the people who had to support all these wasters. Corruption was rife and though in theory there were laws against the exploitation of the Indians and others, in practice it took so long to refer matters back to Spain and get a ruling that it was impossible to control.

Even the end of the colonial period originated in Spain, following Napoleon's invasion and one of his brother's being placed on the throne of Spain. A movement for independence had been growing for some years, based on the arbitrary class distinctions which prevented Criollos from being involved in the government. These local born whites, who by the turn of the 19th century numbered almost two million, raised the standard of revolt and under the leadership of Father Hidalgo and Ignacio Allende, a captain in the army, almost made independence a reality in 1810. They lost their nerve at the last moment despite the fact they could easily have captured Mexico City. The leaders were subsequently arrested and executed as was Jose Morelos, another priest, who took over as rebel leader. The war dragged on until 1821 when Augustin Iturbide, commander of the Royalist troops, switched sides and the Spanish troops were withdrawn from the country. At independence the country stretched from Panama to Oregon.

The war left the country divided and economically at a standstill. Communications, even within the central part of the country, were primitive at best and with all central control disrupted it was virtually impossible to defend. Iturbide initially declared himself Emperor but was soon forced into exile. For the next 100 years the two main camps of political thought were to struggle against each other for power. On the one side were the conservatives representing the church, the large land-holders and the army. On the other were the liberals representing the intellectuals, the lower clergy and the small land-holders and businessmen. Following Iturbide's fall from power, Santa Ana, the leader of the conservatives, took over. It was during his corrupt and incompetent rule that the disastrous war was fought with the United States which started with the declaration of independence of the former Republic of Texas and ended with the Mexicans ceding almost two-thirds of their country to the States following the occupation of Mexico City in 1847.

Following the war with the United States, Santa Ana again declared himself dictator but was soon deposed and a period of reform began under the leadership of Benito Juárez, a pure blood Zapotec Indian from the town of Guelatao just outside Oaxaca. His programme of popular education, freedom of the press and of speech, civil marriage, the separation of state and church, and the redistribution of church lands and property was hotly contested by the conservatives. Civil war broke out and was to last for three years ending with victory for Juárez. During this war all church property was confiscated and redistributed. But Juárez' troubles were not over. Because the civil war had cost so much, Juárez was forced to suspend payment of the national debt. The creditor nations — Britain, Spain and France — landed troops at Vera Cruz to "protect their financial rights". A familiar tale. Britain and Spain soon withdrew their troops but the French pushed on to occupy Mexico City and to install Maximillian von Hapsburg, brother of the Austrian Emperor, as Emperor of Mexico. Juárez took to guerrilla warfare to oppose the French, but it was not until the United States' civil war had ended and Washington insisted that the French get out of Mexico that Juárez could resume leadership and get on with his programme of reform. Following the withdrawal of the French troops, Maximillian was captured at Querétaro, north of Mexico City, and shot along with his generals.

Juárez died a natural death five years later shortly after his re-election to the Presidency and was succeeded by another liberal, Lerdo de Tejada. He was very soon tricked out of the Presidency by Porfirio Díaz who was then to rule as dictator from 1876 until 1910. He instituted a programme of industrialization and modernization which included the construction of railways and roads and the opening of oil wells, but in doing this he handed out concessions to foreign capitalists, always with a rake-off for himself, in such abundance that by the time his regime ended foreigners owned almost everything in Mexico that was worth owning. Those living on the land became indentured serfs not even having the right to leave their employer without his permission. Company stores, where provisions cost double what they did off the hacienda, became common. Whole tribes were forced off the land they had held since Aztec times so that it could be added to the holdings of those who already owned vast tracts. Labour unions were banned, strikes made illegal, the press silenced and opposition suppressed by a brutal secret police. Throughout it all, Díaz and the upper classes grew richer while the illiterate and half-starved peasants grew more and more desperate. A social upheaval became imminent.

In 1910, Francisco Madero, a wealthy land-owner from Coahuila who stood for a programme of political and

social reform, opposed Díaz in the elections. According to the official Díaz count, Madero polled less than 200 votes. The latter escaped to Texas and declared the elections a farce, calling for an insurrection later that year. Some time later Pancho Villa defeated the federal forces in Chihuahua and rebellions arose all over the country. Díaz' forces evaporated and he himself left for exile in Europe. Meanwhile Madero re-entered Mexico to become President but he failed to purge the army of the old guard who soon found the backing they were looking for in the person of the United States Ambassador, Henry Lane Wilson. Madero, his brother and the Vice-President, Pino Suarez, were arrested and shot by the army chief, Victoriana Huerta, but his victory was to be short-lived. Carranza, the Governor of Coahuila, rose in rebellion and was soon joined by Obregón and the entire state of Sonora, Pancho Villa and the state of Chihuahua and Emiliano Zapata in the south. Huerta fled the country after a series of disastrous battles and Carranza became President but a power struggle between the various rebel leaders was to drag on for years. Both Villa and Zapata were assassinated during this period with some none-too-subtle help from the United States but, since Obregón followed Carranza as President, there has been relative calm in the country and a steady, though slow, consolidation of the Revolution. Large estates were divided into ejidos (communal lands) and irrigation, raising of wages, education and the nationalization of oil wells, railways, etc have been promoted.

One of the highlights of Mexico is the way its artists have made satirical and poignant comments on this turbulent history in monumental frescos on public buildings and the way in which Indian

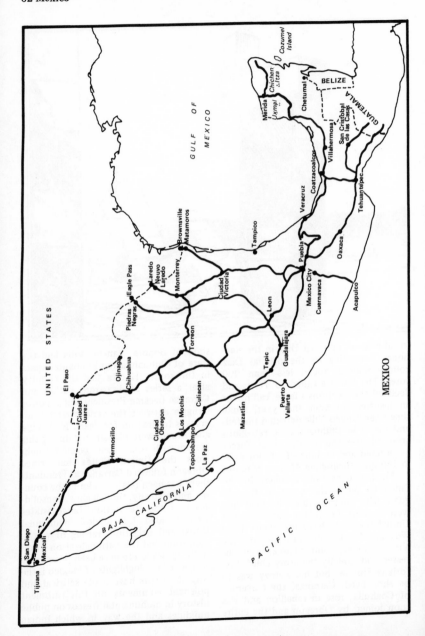

sculptural and architectural traditions have gelled with mediaeval Spanish ideas, particularly in the churches and cathedrals. Don't miss Orozco's work in the Government Palace and the Orphanage (Hospicio Cabañas) in Guadalajara or Diego Rivera's work in the National Palace in Mexico City. It's incredibly powerful stuff and as good as anything you'll find in the Sistine Chapel. Remember too that the Yucatán was the home of the second flowering of the Mayan civilization and that some of the most interesting ruins are to be found there particularly at Palenque, Uxmal, Chichén Itzá and Tulum. One place which will give you a superb overview of these various historical currents, but which won't overwhelm you with endless rows of display cases, is the Anthropology Museum in Mexico City — probably the best of its kind in the world. You could spend days there and still want to return. Don't miss it! And when you're tired of looking at ruins, churches and the inside of long-distance buses, there are hundreds of kilometres of superb beaches on the Pacific and Caribbean coasts and colourful highland Indian villages and towns like Oaxaca and San Cristobal de Las Casas where you can hang up your boots and pack for a while. Just call in to any Mexican Tourist office in one of the larger towns and cities and you can pick up a whole stack of literature and maps about places to go and see. They generally run a very good service.

VISAS

United States and Canadian nationals can enter Mexico without passports so long as they hold some proof of citizenship, eg birth certificate, voting card, etc. Canadians are allowed 90 days, US nationals 180 days. All other nationals require a passport and Tourist Card, the length of stay granted by the Tourist Card varying, depending on your nationality, from 30-90 days, but is extendable in all cases up to 90 days. Tourist Cards are free and can be obtained from Mexican Consulates, airline offices or at the border.

Extending your Tourist Card in Mexico City: Secretario de Gobernacion, 92 Juárez, Room 101 (first floor). Takes a few days.

CURRENCY

US$1 = 26 Pesos

The unit of currency is the Peso, (M$) = 100 centavos. The exchange rate fluctuates according to the international fortunes of the US$. There are no restrictions on the import or export of Mexican currency.

Changing travellers' cheques:

Banco Nacional de Mexico (BANAMEX) charge the smallest commission (1%) and give the highest exchange rate.

BANCOMER charge 1½% commission, give a lower rate than BANAMEX.

American Express don't charge commission but give the lowest exchange rate.

ACAPULCO

Accommodation If you're looking for anything "cheap" in Acapulco first paste your imagination over a length of elastic band and stretch it wide. It's a jet-set resort and finding anything "cheap" involves a good deal of effort. Having said that, there are "cheaper" places in the old part of town around the Zócalo, Quebrada, Juárez and the streets in between. Places nearer the beaches are generally more expensive, as you might expect. Out of season prices drop. Central hotels include:

El Faro, La Quebrada 83. M$120/single, M$180/double.
Hotel Norte, La Quebrada 73. M$80/single, M$120/double.

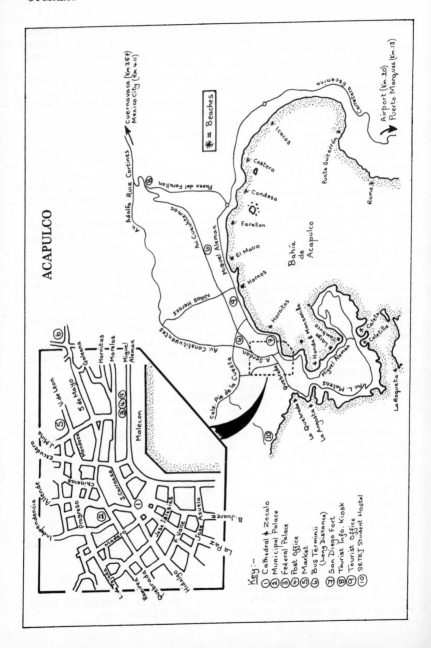

ACAPULCO

Key:-
① Cathedral & Zocalo
② Municipal Palace
③ Federal Palace
④ Post Office
⑤ Market
⑥ Bus Terminii
(Long Distance)
⑦ San Diego Fort
⑧ Tourist Info. Kiosk
⑨ Tourist Office
⑩ SETEJ Student Hostel

✳ = Beaches

Hotel Colimense, on Zócalo. M$100/single.

Hotel Acapulco, B. Juárez. M$130/single.

Amuebladas Crozco, near La Quebrada. M$91/single with shower — friendly.

Hotel Anorvel, two blocks off the Zócalo. M$195/double with shower.

Sutter. M$78/single.

Hotel Marsella, Villa Rocio. M$260/double.

Hotel Felmar. M$104/single.

Outside this area there is the SETEJ Student Hostel, *Casa SETEJ Acapulco*, Las Ardillas 121, Fraccionamiento Balcones al Mar, 6½ km along the highway to Pie de la Cuesta. M$40/night. They also do cheap meals: breakfast M$20, lunch and dinner M$30.

Another cheapie is *Quinta de las Rosas*, 196 Cuauntemoc Avenida, two blocks from *Estrella de Oro* bus terminal, opposite *Blanco* store. Cabins from M$85, M$120 with private bath and fan, M$130 with hot water and two meals (except in the high season). They pay your taxi from the bus station.

Eats Try *Picalagua*, Juárez 19. Seafood M$30 average for a meal. *Restaurante la Fuente*, Juárez 8. Comida corrida M$15. On Caletilla beach there's an open air cafe specializing in seafood, M$20 average for a meal.

Information Tourist Office is helpful in suggesting hotels in any price range. They have maps, literature, etc.

The first class bus terminal is at Avenida Cuauhtemoc 1490. A taxi from there to the Zócalo costs about M$47.

Places Nearby The Lagoons nearby are worth exploring if you're thinking of staying for some time — birds, water plants, tropical flowers. Suggested lagoons are: Laguna Coyuca (near Playa Pie de la Cuesta) and Laguna Tres Palos (near Puerto Marques). Don't miss the

divers at dawn and dusk who dive 40 metres into shallow water near La Quebrada.

CHETUMAL
Accommodation

Hotel Doris, Av. de los Heroes. M$150/four people, M$125/three people, three beds, toilet, shower, fan. If you're a tall person, tread with trepidation. My six foot six friend from Florida had the sink off the wall, his bed in several pieces and the metal bannister rail crumpled into a ghost of its former self amid an untidy pile of concrete rubble within minutes of arrival. I've seen shoddy workmanship before, but this was something else. As to who named the place....... But it's one of the cheapest in town and many travellers stay here. Step over the cockroaches.

Hotel Maria Isabel, Av. de los Heroes. M$300/four people, three beds, showers, toilet, etc.

Hotel Juan Carlos, Calle Gral. Plutarco Elias Calles. M$175/four people, similar to above.

Hotel Alcoces, Calle Lázaro Cárdenas, off Av. de los Heroes. M$180/four people, similar again.

There's another hotel (no name) on Calle Alvaro Obregón, off Ave. de los Heroes. M$175/two people.

Hotel Big Ben opposite *Doris* appeared to be closed but looked similar to the *Doris*. Give it a try if you don't fancy the *Doris*.

Undoubtedly the cheapest place in town (if you can get in) is the CREA Student Albergue between Gral Anaya and Alvaro Obregón, but it's dormitory accommodation. It has a 130-bed capacity with built in showers — M$40 a single.

Eats Probably the cheapest and best place is the *Hadad Restaurant* diagonally opposite the *Hotel Doris*. They

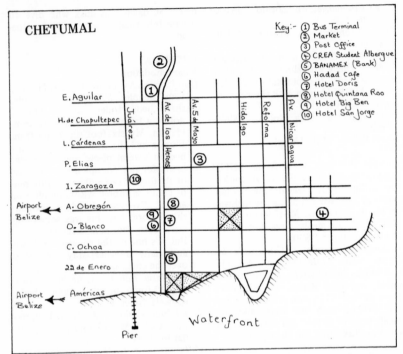

CHETUMAL

Key:-
1. Bus Terminal
2. Market
3. Post Office
4. CREA Student Albergue
5. BANAMEX (Bank)
6. Hadad Cafe
7. Hotel Doris
8. Hotel Quintana Roo
9. Hotel Big Ben
10. Hotel San Jorge

make excellent chicken enchiladas with cheese or avocado pear. Four enchiladas, cheese, salad, sauce and coffee M$30. Beers M$9.

There are several other cafes on the waterfront at the bottom of Av. de los Heroes which do a wider selection of food but their prices are considerably higher than the *Hadad*.

Things to Do/See Chetumal is a good place to buy hammocks. Try around the bus terminal and the market — there's always someone selling them there. Rumour has it they're made by prisoners in the local cooler. Just how much money gets back to them is anyone's guess but they're cheap.

Places Nearby If you're looking for a quiet, beautiful place to hang out for a while check out Cenote Azul about 20 km north of Chetumal where there's a 40 km long lake (Laguna Mariscal) with fantastic clear blue water and white sand. Ask around in the town for accommodation or camp out in a suitable place on the beach.

Other There are no boats from the pier in this town to Belize. You must catch the *Batty Bus* on Tuesdays, Thursdays or Saturdays. Or hitch a ride. You could even walk to the border — it's only about three km.

CHIHUAHUA
Accommodation
Hotel Plaza, behind the Cathedral. M$65/single — clean.
Hotel Maceyra. M$52/single with shower.

Hotel Reforma. M$65/single — good.

Other The train journey from here to Los Mochis is very spectacular. It includes 30 bridges, 10 tunnels and goes via the Barranca del Cobre which is comparable to the Grand Canyon in the USA. The train leaves five days a week. The autovía costs M$273/single, the vistatren is more expensive and equivalent to the first class fare. Book in advance and sit on the left-hand side of the carriage. There is a good dining car.

CUERNAVACA
Accommodation There are several cheap hotels on Calles León and Aragón:

Hotel Palacio, Dwight Morrow, 204. M$90/single, M$160/double.

Hotel Papagayo, Motolinia 13. M$50/single, M$80/double — swimming pool and gardens.

Eats *La Cueva*, Galeana 2. Comida Corrida M$30. *Viena Cafeteria*, Guerrero 104. Sandwiches M$15, coffee and pastries M$5. *Los Arcos*, on the Zócalo. Reasonable prices for its location.

Things to Do/See This is a country-cottage city of film stars, writers and the affluent of Mexico City. The climate is perfect. Aztec rulers, Cortés and Maximillian made it their summer retreat. The Palace of Cortés near the Zócalo was the State Legislature until 1967 and is now a museum — paleaontology to contemporary Indian culture with a Diego Rivera mural on the rear balcony depicting the Conquest of Mexico.

Places Nearby The village of Tepoztlán, 24 km away, is a village up in the mountains with a pyramid — a one hour strenuous climb but with magnificent views.

GUADALAJARA
Accommodation
Hotel Tapatia, M$90/triple.

Hotel San José, on 5 de Febrero opposite bus terminal. M$140/triple — clean, shower and toilet. It can be noisy, but then in this area you'd be lucky to find one which wasn't on occasions.

Hotel Santa Maria, Calle Estadio. M$75/single, M$100/double, M$120/triple, M$140/quadruple.

Pension Jalisco, Calle Balderas. M$35/single — clean, quiet, midnight curfew. Most rooms have three beds, a few have sinks, but most have a basin and jug. Share showers and toilet, which are clean and work. You can sit on the roof in the evening and watch the city. The manager is friendly.

Hotel Frances, Maestranza 35. M$60/single, M$80/double — bar and restaurant.

Also on Calle Estadio opposite the bus terminal are the following hotels: *Hotel Terminal*, *Hotel Consul* and *Hotel Canada* which are all about the same price as the *Santa Maria*. In addition there are many huespedes especially on Calles Balderas and Estadio, eg *La Colimense Felix*, *Pensión Valle*, *Pensión Marcel*, *Pensión Las Flores* and *Costematie*.

Eats Plenty of places around the bus terminal especially on Calles Estadio and 5 de Febrero where you can get a meal for M$18-25, but the food varies somewhat depending on the mood they're in. Find out what they're good at and stick to it. Food from the cafes around the Zócalo will be about double in price, though you can get surprisingly cheap meals (as a non-resident) from one or two of the hotels on Avenida Corona which connects the bus terminal and the Zócalo.

Information The Tourist Office is in the Palacio de Gobierno in the Plaza de Armas off Avenida Juárez. You can get free maps and there is an Orozco fresco.

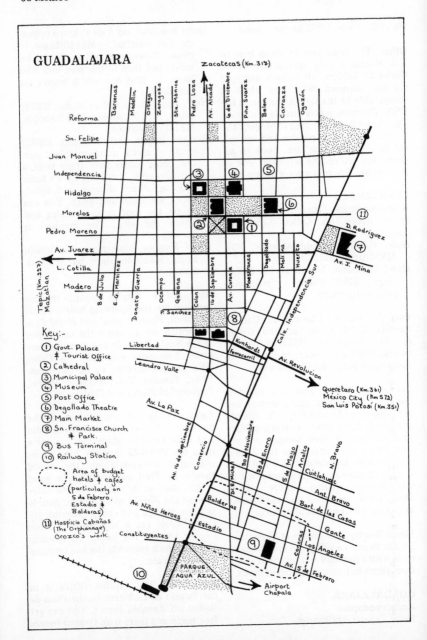

GUADALAJARA

Zacatecas (Km. 317)

Tepic (Km. 257) Mazatlán

Key:-
1 Govt. Palace & Tourist Office
2 Cathedral
3 Municipal Palace
4 Museum
5 Post Office
6 Degollado Theatre
7 Main Market
8 Sn. Francisco Church & Park.
9 Bus Terminal
10 Railway Station

Area of budget hotels & cafes (particularly on 5 de Febrero, Estadio & Balderas)

11 Hospicio Cabañas (The Orphanage). Orozco's work.

Querétaro (Km. 361)
Mexico City (Km. 572)
San Luis Potosí (Km. 351)

Airport Chapala

PARQUE AGUA AZUL

Another Orozco painting is in the Hospicio Cabañas near the central market (see map).

Things to Do/See The Parque Azul near the bus station costs 50 centavos to get in but it's worth a visit if you want to while away a drowsy afternoon or want an early morning walk — incredible flowering trees.

Other If you have your own transport and need any spares/work done, there are parts stockists and repair garages all the way down Calz. Independencia Sur.

ISLA MUJERES (Yucatán)

This island and the larger Cozumel are rapidly being developed into the overspill for Miami Beach, getting very pricey and high-risey. There are other unspoiled islands a little further north, such as Coba, where you could sleep undisturbed on the beach, though even this is still possible on the northern beach on Isla Mujeres.

Accommodation Hotels Zorro, Mesón del Pescador and Las Hamacas all range from M$52-78 per person. Alternatively you can camp on the northern beach where there are tents for hire and cooking and washing facilities. The northern beach is very spectacular with dazzling white sand and a turquoise sea.

Other Ferry boats to Isla Mujeres and Cozumel:
Puerto Juárez-Isla Mujeres. Departs 5 am, 9 am, noon, 2 pm, 3 pm, 6 pm and returns 2 am, 7 am, 10 am, noon, 2 pm, 4 pm, 6 pm — cost is M$10.
Punta Sam-Isla Mujeres. Departs 8.30 am, 11.30 am, 2.45 pm, 5 pm and returns 7.15 am, 10 am, 1.15 pm, 4 pm. M$5 per person, cars M$50. It takes 45 minutes and the bus from Merida stops at the ferry,
Playa del Carmen-Cozumel. Departs 6 am, noon, 6 pm and returns 4 am, 9.30 am, 4 pm. M$45.
Puerto Morelos-Cozumel. Departs 8 am and returns 11 am to noon. M$60 per person, M$250 for cars.

Buses from Puerto Juárez by ADO: to Merida 8 am, 10 am, noon, 3 pm, 5 pm, 7 pm. To Playa del Carmen (and Tulum) 4.30 am, 10 am, 3.30 pm.

LA PAZ (Baja California sur)
Accommodation
Yeneka M$78/single without food — clean, own shower.
Trailer Park, near the airport, M$56/single per day.
CREA Student Albergue, three km along the southern highway. M$79/night in dormitory accommodation (modern building) -- shared showers and toilets, sports facilities, cheap meals. It has 54 beds.

There are no cheap hotels further south at Cabo San Lucas — M$186/double is about the cheapest.

Other For the ferry schedule from here to Mazatlán and Los Mochis see Transport section. There are also ferries from Cabo San Lucas to Puerto Vallarta on Sundays and Wednesdays only.

LEÓN
Accommodation Rex Hotel, corner of Pino Suarez and 5 de Febrero, M$72/single, M$108/double, M$152/triple, M$192/quadruple. There is an attached restaurant and bar.

MAZATLÁN
A popular holiday resort for north Americans. If this is what you're looking for, here it is. If not, go further down the coast. '

Accommodation Cheapest places are around the market area:
Hotel Teresa, opposite the market. Cheap and friendly, can be noisy.

Pension Maria Luisa, nearby and similar.
Hotel Lerma, Calle Simon Bolivar at the
  beach. M$91/double — friendly.

Other The bus terminal is at Centro
Colonia. Local buses connect the
terminal with the centre of town. Taxis
are expensive. For ferries to Baja California (La Paz) see *Transport* section.

Places Nearby Nearby lagoons teem
with wild life, particularly birds —
worth a visit.

A cheaper place to stay might be the
Isla de la Piedra, a 20 centavos boat ride
(regular service) from the main docks —
east of the Armada naval station near
the brewery. There are rooms to rent or
you can have a string bed or straw mat
for about M$10/night, or you can hang
your own hammock up free under the
balconies of the cafes so long as you eat
there. The restaurant owners will lock
your gear up for you at night (not advisable to leave things around as they tend
to grow legs). Try *Juan y Maria's* cafe.
Avoid coming to the island on Sundays
or public holidays as people flock over
from the mainland.

MÉRIDA
Accommodation
Hotel Latino, Calle 66, No 505. M$104/
  double, M$154/triple — excellent. It
  is very clean (sheets and towels included); fan, toilet, shower, iced
  water, use of fridge, friendly management, cheap drinks (refrescos M$3,
  beers M$8).
Hotel Margarita, Calle 66 No. 506. Very
  similar to above but a little scruffier.
  Has small cafe in the foyer — good
  for snacks.
Hotel San Pablo, Calle 69 corner of
  Calle 70, costs are M$70/single,
  M$120/double.
Hotel San Jorge, Calle 69 opposite the
  first class bus terminal. M$110/
  single, M$150/double.

Hotel Rodriguez, Calle 69 near the
  market. M$104/double.

There are plenty of other hotels just in
front of the first class bus terminal and
along the streets which lead to it (see
map). They include: *Hotel Cayre*, *Hotel
San Fernando*, *Hotel Posada Angel*, *Casa
Bowen Hospedaje* (this latter with quiet
courtyard.
   Near Zócalo there's the *Gran Hotel*,
an old Spanish colonial building. It is a
nice place with good courtyard. M$60-
90/single, M$105-140/double. It is sit-
uated on Calle 60 No. 496.

Eats *Soberanis* on the Zócalo opposite
the Cathedral has excellent seafood/
sandwiches. Fillet of sole, chips, vegetables and sauce — M$40, a little expen-
sive no doubt but you get a lot of food
and it's well prepared. Avoid like the
plague, because if you don't you'll probably end up with it, *El Louvre* on the
corner of the Zócalo. The food is dis-
gusting — undercooked, cold, greasy,
live bugs crawling over the salad, eggs at
least a week old and excellent real
coffee (you need it after seeing the
food!). Good icecream available from
the place next to the Cathedral. There
are plenty of street stalls around the
first class bus terminal.

Information Tourist Office: you can
afford to give this one a miss. They have
little information, very poor city maps.
If you need a city plan buy one from a
bookshop on the Zócalo. They cost up
to M$7, depending on whether it's in
black and white or glorious technicolour.
   Local buses from railway station to
Zócalo or Post Office cost M$2.

Excursions to Chichén Itzá and Uxmal
Several buses every day go to both
places from the first class bus terminal.
Most are regular service buses which
pass these sites on their way to another

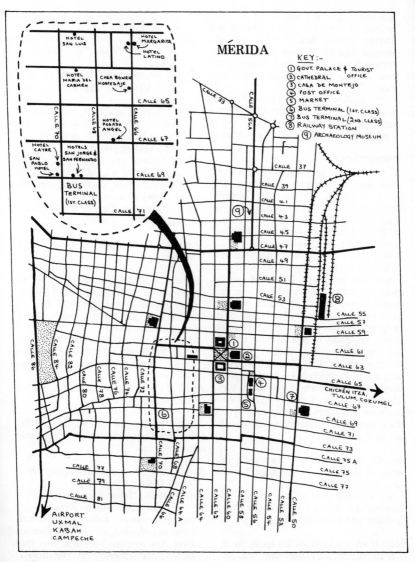

MÉRIDA

KEY:-
① GOVT. PALACE & TOURIST OFFICE
② CATHEDRAL
③ CASA DE MONTEJO
④ POST OFFICE
⑤ MARKET
⑥ BUS TERMINAL (1ST. CLASS)
⑦ BUS TERMINAL (2ND. CLASS)
⑧ RAILWAY STATION
⑨ ARCHAEOLOGY MUSEUM

town. If you're directed to a bus which just goes to the site, waits there while you look around and then returns, it's probably twice the price. Guided tours (strictly for the turkeys) can cost up to M$400 including lunch.

To Chichén Itzá: Depart at 6 am, 8.30

am and return at 3 pm, M$30 via Transportes de Oriente. This is the Mérida-Puerto Suarez bus. There are also second class buses from the appropriate terminal (see map) which depart every one to two hours, M$28. They stop more often than the others.

If possible avoid the expensive cafes near the site. Arrive early to avoid the guided tour crowds. It's open 6 am to 6 pm, entry is M$15 (M$10 on Sundays).

MEXICO CITY

It's one of the largest cities in the world and due to become *the* largest very soon. It's also, typically, very speedy. We suggest that before you set off you hunt around among your friends for the address of someone who lives there and write asking if they can put you up when you arrive. If not, don't despair. It's easy to meet people who may do when you get there. Thousands of expatriates of all nationalities live and work there, many of them teaching their language in one of the hundreds of language schools in this city. When you arrive, try going to one of these schools or institutions (eg British Council, Goethe Institut, US Information Office, etc) and asking likely-looking people if they know of anywhere you might stay. There are plenty of people around who welcome travellers, so long as they do their share of the domestics and contribute to expenses.

Accommodation If not, there are thousands of hotels — see the maps for the main concentrations.

On the top side of the Zócalo, the cheapest are located around the Plaza Garibaldi and Calle Allende:

Hotel Moderno, Calle de los Incas No. 9. M$80/single, M$110/double, M$140/triple, all rooms include shower and toilet. A lot of mariachis stay here (the musicians who play on the Plaza Garibaldi every night). It's a bit of a dismal place but has an easygoing management.

Hotel York, Av 5 de Mayo 31. M$80/single, M$150/double — dark and shabby.

Hotel Monte Carlo, Calle Uruguay 69. M$40-50/single, M$70-80/double — basic.

Hotel Patria, Calle Republica de El Salvador No 137, M$100/single or M$100-200/double, depending on what services you want.

Hotel Gillow, corner of I. la Catolica and 5 de Mayo. M$100-160/single, M$230/double, depending on what services you want again.

Hotel Guardiola, Madero No. 5. M$120/single, M$150/double.

Just below the Alameda, some of the cheapest are:

Hotel Conde, Pescaditos No. 15 on the corner of Revillagigedo. M$80/single.

Hotel Fleming, Revillagigedo No. 35. M$115/single, M$140/double. A restaurant is attached.

Hotel San Diego, Luis Moya No. 98. M$114/single, M$126/double. It has more expensive rooms with better services too.

Hotel Toledo, López No. 22. M$85/single, M$120/double.

Around Buenavista (the ADO, San Cristobal bus terminals and the train station) there are:

Hotel Royalty and *Hotel Jena*, Calle Jesus Terán.

Hotel Carlton, Miguel Ramas Arizpe.

Hotel Gilbert, Calle Amado Nervo.

Hotels Buenavista, *Estaciones*, *Bernal Diaz* and *Mexico*, all on Calle Bernal Diaz. On average they fall into the same price category as the hotels above.

Hotel Pontevedra, Insurgentes Norte No 226, M$90/single, M$105/double.

In the "Zona Rosa", hotels are on average at least 50% higher in price than the ones in the other areas with one notable exception: the SETEJ Student Hostel, *Casa SETEJ Mexico*, Cozumel No. 57, near the Sevilla Metro station. M$40/ dormitory accommodation. They also do cheap meals. Breakfast (two eggs, bread, butter, marmalade, coffee) M$20, lunch and dinner M$30. The cheapest deal in the city if you can handle dormitory accommodation. There are also the following:

Hotel Maria Angelo's, Lerma No. 11. M$120/single, M$150/double.
Bonampak Apartments, Mérida 81-A. M$100/single, M$150/double.
Hotel Compostela, corner of Sullivan and Sñ. Rendón. M$110/single, M$130/double.

Eats There are thousands of small cafes, but in order to eat cheaply you will naturally have to stay off the main drags (Insurgentes Juárez, Paseo de la Reforma, etc). It doesn't follow that the more you pay, the better you eat. In a cheap cafe, M$20-25 is about average for an almuerzo, comida corrida or cena. Try any of the back streets around the Zócalo, especially the Plaza Garibaldi, or, if on the other side of town, Maestro Antonio Caso. If you're around the Alameda, there's a good little cafe on the left hand side of the small square at the back of the Museo de Artes e Industrias Populares at Juárez 44. They do cheap and varied businessmen's lunches — highly recommended.

Information The Tourist Office booth at 92 Juárez has free maps of the country and city plans and coloured brochures. It also has free copies of *Una Semana en Mexico*, a publication with useful addresses, hotels, restaurants, buses, seedy bars, etc.

The main Tourist Office is now located at Presidente Masaryk No 172

between Hegel and Emerson in the Colonia Polanco at the back of Chapultepec Park. It's not really worth going there, as they have nothing which the booth at 92 Juárez doesn't have, and it appears to be just an exercise in marble and glass rather than an info centre.

To extend Tourist Cards, go to the Secretario de Gobierno, Room 101, 92 Juárez (first floor). Fill in a form, take it to another office in the same building and then come back in a few days.

For Student Cards, organized tours and trips to Cuba, the best place to go is SETEJ (Servicio Educativo de Turismo de los Estudiantes y la Juventud de Mexico), Hamburgo 273, Mexico 6 DF. These people organize a whole range of activities including internal and international charter flights. Their charter flights to Havana, Cuba, are probably some of the cheapest, but check with other airlines. With some proof of "status", they'll fit you up with an International Student Card. They're also the people who run the SETEJ Hostels in Mexico City and Acapulco. (tel 5 11 66 91 and 5 14 42 13).

American Express offices: Hamburgo 75 (tel 533 20.20).

Visas

Guatemalan: The consulate at Vallarta 1-501A issues them on the spot. You can get up to a three month stay depending on what you ask for on the form. Fees vary according to nationality, British US$5, for Australians US$3. There is no money showing, but two photos are needed.

Honduran: Consulate at Juárez 64-911 issues them on the spot, valid for a two month stay. There is no money showing. Fees US$3.

Cuban: Go to the Embassy at Francisco Marquez 160, Colonia Condesa.

Bus Terminals There are two main bus terminals in Mexico City:

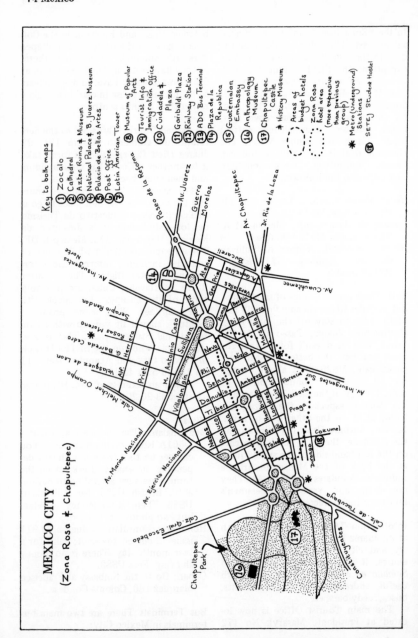

MEXICO CITY
(Zona Rosa & Chapultepec)

Key to both maps

1. Zocalo
2. Cathedral
3. Aztec Ruins & Museum
4. National Palace & B.Juarez Museum
5. Palacio de Bellas Artes
6. Post Office
7. Latin American Tower
8. Museum of Popular Arts
9. Tourist Info & Immigration Office
10. Cuidadela
11. Garibaldi Plaza
12. Railway Station
13. ADO Bus Terminal
14. Plaza de la Republica
15. Guatemalan Embassy
16. Anthropology Museum
17. Chapultepec Castle & History Museum

○ Areas of budget hotels
Zona Rosa hotel area (more expensive than previous group)

* Metro (Underground) Stations

18. SETEJ Student Hostel

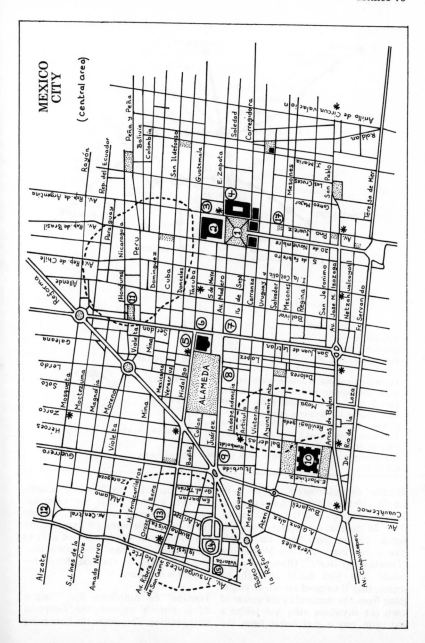

MEXICO CITY (central area)

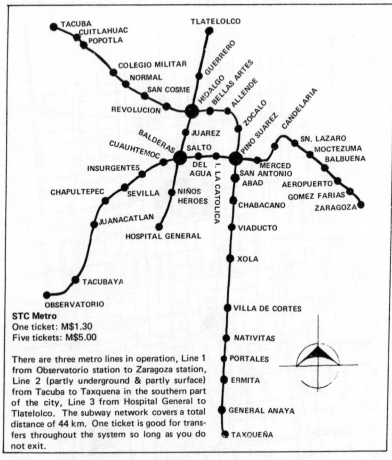

STC Metro
One ticket: M$1.30
Five tickets: M$5.00

There are three metro lines in operation, Line 1
from Observatorio station to Zaragoza station,
Line 2 (partly underground & partly surface)
from Tacuba to Taxquena in the southern part
of the city, Line 3 from Hospital General to
Tlatelolco. The subway network covers a total
distance of 44 km. One ticket is good for trans-
fers throughout the system so long as you do
not exit.

Terminal de Autobuses Norte, on Av de
los Cien Metros 4907, for buses going to
northern Mexico and the USA border.
Over 35 companies operate from this
depot. To get there from the Zócalo
take a bus marked "Cien Metros" or
"Terminal del Norte". Otherwise a taxi
should cost you M$30 (though, of
course, they'll demand more). If you're
going from the terminal to the centre of
town (or anywhere else) and taking a
taxi, you buy a taxi ticket from the

booth marked "Taxi" (sounds simple,
doesn't it, yet you'll see numerous
people wandering about lost, looking
for a taxi). The rates are fixed according to the map which is posted next to
the booth. You hand the token they
give you over to the taxi driver. No
tipping is necessary.

Terminal de Autobuses Sur, Tlalpan
2205, directly opposite the Taxqueña
Metro station. This serves the lines going

to and from Cuernavaca, Acapulco, Zihuantanejo areas. Taxi arrangements are the same as from the Terminal del Norte but it's *far* cheaper to use the Metro from here.

Other than these two main terminals, most of the bus companies operating from here to the south have their own terminals in the central area: Cristobal Colón is one block from San Lazaro Metro station on Calz Ignacio Zaragoza 38. ADO (Autobuses de Oriente) run from their terminal at Buenavista 9 near the Revolucion or Hidalgo Metro stations (ADO run first class buses only).

Things to Do/See

Zócalo. This is the oldest part of the city built over the ruins of the Aztec capital, Tenochtitlan. On one side is the *Cathedral*, the largest and oldest church in Latin America (building started 1525, finished 1813). The *Sagrario Metropolitano* is attached to one side of the Cathedral with its amazing Churrigueresque facade ("Churrigueresque" is a term almost as baroque as the Mexican roccoco it describes). On another side is the *Palacio Nacional* containing some mind-blowing frescoes by Diego Rivera which you shouldn't miss. Open daily (free). The Palacio also contains the *Juárez Museum* — objects, etc, from the life of Mexico's greatest reformer, Benito Juárez. Open daily 10 am-7 pm, Sundays 10 am-6 pm (free). On the corner between the Cathedral and the Palacio Nacional there are some Aztec ruins but don't get too excited, there's hardly anything there and there's some kind of reconstruction going on at the present so you have to peer through the proverbial hole in the fence.

Latin American Tower. If you want to have a good look at the city from its tallest building, there's an observatory at the top, open daily. Entry M$10, but you won't be able to see far for the smog.

Museums

Museo de las Culturas, Calle Moneda 13 (back of the Palacio Nacional). Open daily (except Fridays) 9 am - 6 pm. Entry M$6 (M$3 on Sunday).

Museo de Artes e Industrias Populares, Av Juárez 44. Open daily 10 am to 6 pm (free). There are things for sale too.

Museo de la Cuidad de Mexico, corner of Pino Suarez and the Republique del Salvador has one excellent exhibition on the history of Mexico City. Open daily 9 am-6 pm (free).

Museo Nacional de Antropología, Chapultepec Park, is probably the best museum in the world. Don't miss it and give yourself at least a day to see it. Unlike most other museums of a similar kind it doesn't saturate and bore you with mile after mile of glass showcases containing pottery fragments. It's also excellent if you want to get some idea of the best places to visit in Mexico. Open daily (except Mondays) 9 am-7 pm, Sundays 10 am-6 pm. Entry is M$15 (there are no student reductions anymore).

Galeria de Historia, Chapultepec Park, on the right in front of the castle, has a display of historical objects from the Conquest to the present. Open daily (except Tuesdays) 9 am-6 pm, Sundays 10 am-1.30 pm. Entry M$5 (Sunday M$3).

Museo de Arte Moderno, near the Anthropology Museum in Chapultepec Park. Open daily (except Mondays) 10 am-5 pm. Entry M$5.

Places Nearby

Pyramids of Teotihuacán. Pyramids of the Sun and Moon and the Temples of Tlaloc and Quetzalcoatl. An incredible place. Open daily, till 5 pm. Several buses go there from different places in the centre, all more or less for the same price (1¼ hours). Catch buses either from Terminal del Norte (see *Bus Terminals*), or from Calle Alarcon 19, which is two and a half blocks from the

Candelaria Metro station (first class buses, every 20 minutes), or from the bus station opposite Tlatelolco Metro station. The latter bus drops you at the far side of the Pyramid of the Sun whilst the former two take you to the main entrance. M$13.80 first class.

Entrance to site M$15 (Sunday M$10) with no student reductions. The small museum under the expensive restaurant on the site is free but looks run down. If you need a refresco on site or a little food, the cafe at the back of the Temple of the Butterflies near the Moon Pyramid is the cheapest (ie normal prices). There are plenty of hustlers on the site.

Xochimilco. The floating gardens are the remnants of what's left of the Aztec method of cultivation in Lake Texcoco. Take the Metro to Taxqueña and then catch a trolleybus to the market. Alternatively, take a bus from the Zócalo (Calle Mesones) to Ixtapalapa and Xochimilco, M$2.

There are a maze of canals which meander through flower and fruit gardens. Punts ply up and down. There is a good market on Saturdays and the place is very busy on Sundays with picnickers from the city. Canal-side cafes have music and dancing. If you're here on Holy Thursday, see the most spectacular

of the Mexican passion plays at Ixtapalapa. Good views from the nearby hills.

Sources of Information

The Gazer — El Miron is a weekly magazine in Spanish and English. Free from hotels, bars, restaurants, travel agencies. Has information on hotels, bars, airlines, banks, maps, sightseeing and useful addresses.

This Week — Una Semana is another weekly with a useful collection of hints, places to go, useful addresses, etc. Free from same places or from Tourist Information booth at Juárez 92 or from Calle Ramón Alcazar 8.

Guide to the Best of Everything in Mexico City by Rudi Robins (published by AMMEX Asociados SA, Lago Silverio 224, Mexico 17 DF) is available in most bookstores in the centre of town. In English, is has some very good suggestions and maps together with a fair amount of other stuff which would no doubt be way out of your budget and you probably wouldn't want to see anyway. Maybe just browse through it and pick out what interests you. Costs M$39.

The News masquerades as the English-language daily in Mexico City but there's precious little in it. You have to be desperate or totally unable to put half a dozen words of Spanish together, costs M$6.

Teaching English/German/French in Mexico City

There are thousands of expatriates here teaching their language though mostly it's teaching English. Many people stay here for a while to earn some money and learn Spanish before moving on. It's probably the best place in all Latin America to do it as far as wages are concerned so long as you can pick up sufficient private tuition.

Go to the various institutes and schools and ask the teachers if they know anyone wanting English tuition or whether there is a job vacant (there's always plenty of work). Try the Instituto Cultural Anglo-Mexicano (same building as the British Council), on Maestro Antonio Caso 127, the Cambridge school, or the Instituto de Norteamericano on Hamburgo 115. Some of the work which is offered is contract teaching (one to two years), but a lot of people are taken on casually or at a month's notice, etc. Go there and ask for an interview. If they need someone straight away, you more or less have yourself a job. The average wage is M$150-180/hour and there will be about 20-25 hours a week expected (maximum), three months' holiday per year. Income tax (!!) is about 25%. Private tuition depends on who wants it. Can be up to M$250-300/hour though you'd have to be a good teacher. Watch out for supply teaching posts with British and American schools, however, as they tend to exploit travellers passing through and the wages can be as low as M$50/hour.

Officially you need a college certificate, degree or TEFL certificate and/or experience but you can bluff this one with little effort. Sometimes they demand references — arrange for friends at home to have this one sewn up if they write. Work permits are arranged by employers — no hassle. Obviously you can avoid any of this hassle if you just take private work. There's other teaching-related work from British Council, eg marking exam papers, officiating at examinations, progress chasers for prospective examinees, etc. Ask for Frances King there.

If you're not into teaching, a friend of mine stayed in Mexico City for 18 months and supported himself playing music with a local band. There are occasionally other jobs with the media.

Flats are difficult to find (aren't they always in large cities). Ask around amongst those you work with. They range from M$2200/month (three rooms, kitchen, shower, bath, toilet) upwards. M$8000 per month would buy a palace (almost).

MONTERREY

Mexico's third largest city, after the capital and Guadalajara, Monterrey is a major industrial centre in the northeast of the country. Its climate is hot, dry and not too comfortable. Due to its proximity to the Texas border it is also quite expensive.

Accommodation There is nothing particularly cheap in the central Plaza Zaragoza area, you have to head about 20 blocks north to the Avenida Madera area where you'll find places like *Hotel Madero*, Madero Pte 428 or *Hotel Nuevo Leon* on Ave Naervo Norte near the bus station.

Eats Roast kid (cabrito) is the local speciality, sample it at *El Pastor*, Madero 1067 Poniente. Carta Blanca beer is brewed in the Cuauhtemoc Brewery off Route 83 — get there on a 14 bus for the free tours (followed by free beers) at 11 am, noon and 3 pm.

Other Around 9 pm on Thursdays, Saturdays and Sundays you can join the "paseo" in the Plaza Zaragoza — boys circulate counterclockwise, girls clockwise.

OAXACA

Accommodation

Hotel Rex, Calle de las Casas 308. M$40/single, M$80/double, M$120/ triple, the latter rooms have two double beds, shower and toilet. There are other rooms without private showers but with a handbasin. M$90/triple. Popular with travellers and the management are friendly.

Hotel Central, Calle 20 de Novienbre. M$72/double, M$90/triple, share showers and toilets.

Hotel El Tule, Calle de las Casas. M$60/ single, M$80/double, M$110-120/ triple — quiet courtyard.

Huéspedes Mixteca on Calle Aldeno. $50/double with shower. M$45/ double without shower.

Rivera Hotel, corner of Calle Aldama and San Juan de Dios, in the middle of the market area. M$50/double with one bed, M$70/double with two beds.

El Fortin Hotel, Díaz Ordaz 312. M$50-80/single, M$70-100/double, M$100-120/triple, M$120-140/quadruple, all without private shower or toilet. If you want your own shower the prices are: M$70-140/single, M$90-

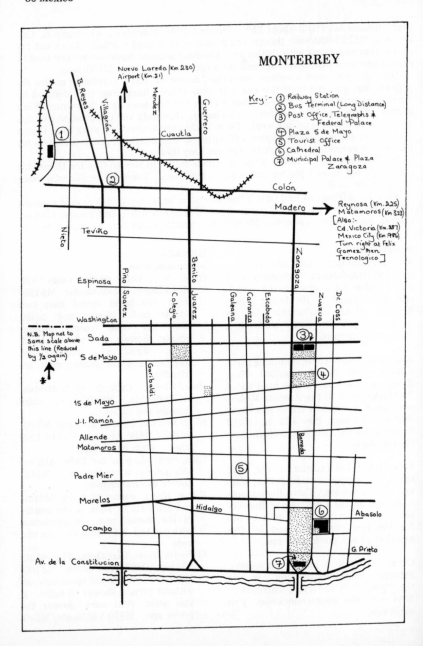

160/double, M$150-180/triple and M$170-200/quadruple.

Unmarked hospedaje, no doubt are very cheap at Calle J.P. Garcia 300. They are identified by looking for the note on the door which says, "Se renta Cuartos".

If you'd like something completely different and are tired of staying inside cheapo concrete boxes in this beautiful country, there's a delightful old colonial building with balconies overlooking the plaza in front of the Cathedral which is now a hotel, *Hotel Mote Albán*. There are two other quite expensive hotels very near the ADO bus terminal. You'll miss out on Oaxaca if you stay there.

Eats *Kiko Restaurant*, Av. Independencia 504, has very good meals and is a cheap pleasant, easy-going place. Steaks vary in quality, sometimes tough as old leather, sometimes tender, but they do excellent omelettes with chips, tomato, cucumber, bread. Steaks are M$20, beans M$3-3.50 depending on whether you want milk.

Gino's Pizzas opposite the *Kiko* are excellent but relatively expensive. M$11-15/slice, M$35-50/half tray, M$85-115/tray (latter sufficient for three people — just).

Avoid the *Montebello Restaurant* on Trujano. It masquerades as a cheap cafe but it's a rip-off in comparison with others (twice as expensive as the Kiko).

Things to Do/See The incredible market on Saturdays (which actually starts on Friday night and goes right through Sunday) has everything you ever imagined a market would sell, with fantastic weavings, clothes, flowers, food, herbs, jewellery, handicrafts. The streets around the permanent market hall are chock-a-block with stalls. Don't miss it!

At the same time as the market (on Saturdays) there's a collective of Zapotec weavers in the small square at the corner of 5 de Mayo and Calle Abasola.

The range of blankets, carpets and other stuff is incredible. They sit there and weave it — you can watch. Prices are high so don't expect anything cheap but it's the best weaving I've seen anywhere in Latin America. Many come from Teotitlán del Valle, which might be worth a visit if you're going to buy something.

Don't miss the amazing *Santo Domingo Church*. There is goldleaf everywhere in magnificent patterns. The museum next door in the old nunnery is also well worth a visit. There is a peaceful patio with fountain if you want to sit around and relax for a while. Open daily (except Mondays) 10 am-1 pm, 4 pm-7 pm. Entry M$10 (M$3 on Sundays and holidays).

Religious Museo de La Soledad is open noon-2 pm, 5 pm-7 pm (free). *Rufino Tamayo* Prehispanic Art Museum is open daily (except Tuesdays) 10 am-noon, 4 pm-7 pm. Entry M$4.

Places Nearby *Monte Albán* mentioned in the *Introduction* is an amazing artificially flattened mountain-top ceremonial centre which was in continuous use by various tribes from the days of the Olmec right up to the Conquest. Many civilizations left their mark on it though the Zapotecs perhaps gave it most. Give yourself all day — the views are magnificent and the site is huge. Entry M$10.

Buses from Autobuses Turisticos SA, Calle Trujano 607. M$16 return — rarely full. Depart 10 am, 12.30 pm, 4 pm and return 12 noon, 2 pm, 5.30 pm. The journey takes 30 minutes going, 15 minutes coming back. You can walk there — very pleasant in the early morning or late evening but avoid doing it in the middle of the day — it gets HOT. Takes about two hours to walk up, one hour down.

Mitla is another Zapotec city of palaces and ceremonial temples. The stone

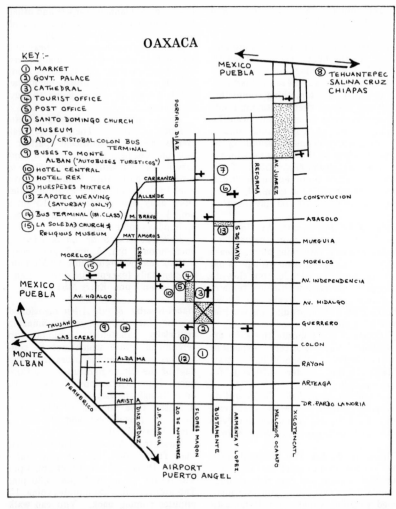

OAXACA

KEY :-
① MARKET
② GOVT. PALACE
③ CATHEDRAL
④ TOURIST OFFICE
⑤ POST OFFICE
⑥ SANTO DOMINGO CHURCH
⑦ MUSEUM
⑧ ADO/CRISTOBAL COLON BUS TERMINAL
⑨ BUSES TO MONTE ALBAN ("AUTOBUSES TURISTICOS")
⑩ HOTEL CENTRAL
⑪ HOTEL REX
⑫ HUESPEDES MIXTECA
⑬ ZAPOTEC WEAVING (SATURDAY ONLY)
⑭ BUS TERMINAL (1st CLASS)
⑮ LA SOLEDAD CHURCH & RELIGIOUS MUSEUM

sculpture is amazing and seems to have taken its inspiration from weaving patterns. Buses there from Fletes y Pasajes, Calle de las Casas and Mier y Terán are hourly. The journey takes 75 minutes. M$10. The bus goes via Santa Maria del Tule, a village with the world's largest tree — 49 metres in girth (!!), 51 metres high and estimated to be 3000 years old.

Other If you arrive in Oaxaca on the ADO bus, catch a local Circuito bus into the centre. M$1. Very frequent from the opposite side of the road to the bus terminal. The other first class bus terminal is nearer the centre. Immigration Police seem to be stationed permanently at the ADO terminal. They check gringos' Tourist Cards — nothing heavy, just routine and the guy can't keep his eyes off the ladies anyway.

PALENQUE
Accommodation

Casa Huéspedes León.   M$70/single, M$100/double, M$120/triple.   All rooms have own toilet, and there is a shower, fan and patio.   It is a bit scruffy but quite adequate — lot of travellers stay here.

Hotel Lacroix. M$75/single, M$125/double, M$145/triple, M$175/quadruple.   All rooms have their own toilet, shower and fan. It has modern Indian murals, friendly people, a large garden and is quiet.

Hotel Misol-Ha.   M$85/single, with toilet, shower and fan — modern building.

Hotel Palenque, probably overpriced at M$100/single, M$140/double. There is a restaurant and bar. ADO bus from Villa Hermosa stops here.

There are other hotels along the road to the ruins but they're even more expensive. If you want to be nearer to the ruins try *Mayabel Camping* about two km from the ruins where many gringos stay. Reasonable facilities and, if you're up early enough in the mornings, those magic mushrooms will bring a broad grin to your face.

Eats *Nicte-Ha Cafe* on the main square. Comida corrida M$40, ie considerably more than you'd pay in other Mexican towns but then this is Palenque and you do get vegetable soup, half a chicken and sauce (or beef with chips), beans, bread and coffee and sometimes tortillas as well. Beer M$10.

Places Nearby The Mayan ruins are about eight km from the village. There

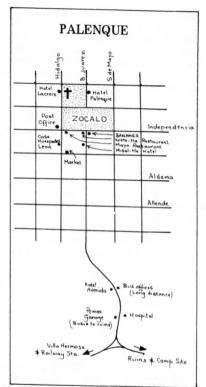

are buses every hour from the Pemex garage which cost M$4, but don't look at your watch too often. Last bus back from the ruins is at 5.30 pm. Entry to the ruins M$15 (M$10 on Sundays). It's an amazing site set in really fantastic jungle (cleared around the ruins just sufficiently for it not to get in the way).   There are thousands of beautifully coloured butterflies and dragon flies.

A visit to *Las Cascades* about two km back along the road to the village is recommended.   These are natural swimming pools in the stream which comes down from the site through the jungle.   There's a barely discernable path from the paved road between two enormous trees where horses are often tied up opposite a gate to a field and where the electricity lines cross the road. The stream goes under the road at this point. Follow the water pipe line up through the jungle for about 100 metres and there they are on the left. It's safe — no leeches and plenty of people use it, though there's rarely more than a few people there at any one time. Buses will pick you up from there — or hitch.

Other If you're catching the train to Merida or Mexico City, the station is about five km from the village. A taxi there costs M$10 per person and will take up to six people with luggage.

Palenque is an excellent place to buy hammocks and people come round to the hotel with a selection. They're cheap, even cheaper than Chetumal.

PUEBLA
Accommodation
Hotel Latino, next to the ADO bus terminal, M$78/double without bath — clean and good value.

Ritz, Calle 2 Norte, M$65 without bath, friendly.

Augusta, Calle 4 Poniente, M$65/double.

Hotel Espana, 5 de Mayo and Calle 8 Oriente is also recommended.

Eats Try the ADO bus terminal.

Places Nearby If you're interested in Indian handicrafts (cradles, embroidered fabrics, machetes, etc) try the Sunday market at Quetzalan nearby.

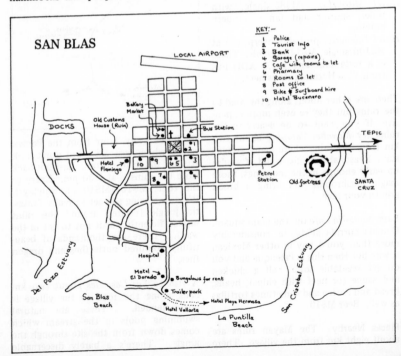

SAN BLAS

LOCAL AIRPORT

KEY:—
1 Police
2 Tourist Info
3 Bank
4 Garage (repairs)
5 Cafe with rooms to let
6 Pharmacy
7 Rooms to let
8 Post office
9 Bike & Surfboard hire
10 Hotel Bucenero

Bakery Market
Old Customs House (Ruin)
DOCKS
Bus Station
TEPIC
Hotel Flamingo
Petrol Station
Old fortress
SANTA CRUZ
Del Pozo Estuary
Hospital
Hotel El Dorado
Bungalows for rent
Trailer park
Hotel Playa Hermosa
San Blas Beach
Hotel Vallarta
La Puntilla Beach
San Cristobal Estuary

SAN BLAS (Pacific coast near Tepic)
Accommodation
Flamingo Hotel, M$80/single, M$110/ double. The showers are hot, the patio beautiful and it's quiet.
Bucanero Hotel, M$85/single, M$160/ double, M$220/triple. A bit flasher than the Flamingo, with more antiques but it has a cool, peaceful courtyard. You get free tequila if you eat at the *Torino Restaurant* (which is very pricey and you can rest assured they're not giving anything away by offering you "free" tequila).

Nearer the beach there are the following:
Hotel Vallarta, right on the beach, 27 rooms, hot water, simple and frugal.
Hotel Playa Hermosa, restaurant, bar, disco, swimming pool.
Trailer Park *Los Cocos*, 100 rooms, hot showers, restaurant, wash and dry nearby on the main road and bakery.
Motel El Dorado, Trailer Park — people camping there. It looks modern but has a tatty edge to it.
Also there are bungalows to rent from *El Alteno* cafe opposite the *El Dorado*. This cafe also does cheap comida corrida for M$30.

Don't expect anything really "cheap" here as the town is being developed as a resort for North American holiday makers, but it isn't spoilt. It's too small for that though no-doubt it gets chock-a-block during the college vacations.

Other Local buses to Tepic at 6.30 am, 9.30 am, 1 pm and 4 pm. To Guadalajara at 8.30 am and 5 pm. To Santa Cruz at 8.30 am, 11 am, 3.45 pm (approx) — M$15. Santa Cruz-San Blas at 7 am, 1 pm, 5 pm (very approx). Believe it or not the fare this way is M$13.
San Blas has a bank which will change travellers' cheques. There is no bank at Santa Cruz.

SANTA CRUZ (Pacific coast near Tepic)
Accommodation Has a pebble beach but there's a sandy stretch about a km away at Miramar. Because of this it's mellower than San Blas. Also there are no "hotels" as such. Best thing to do is to rent one of the many "palapas" (bamboo and thatch huts) available. Try *Rosalita* at the *Bakery*. M$15 a night including electricity, two string beds (one double), fireplace, use of washing facilities (tap and shower). Doesn't matter how many people share a hut. A very friendly lady and it is a peaceful place. Another place to try is *Irma Linda's* nearby. She has two palapas without electricity for M$80/week with two beds in each and another with electricity for M$100, also with two beds.
If you have no luck there ask at *Lupita* general store or at *Raoul's* cafe next door where many people meet in the evening to eat and drink and rap — or any gringo you see on the streets.
If you've still found nothing you could rent a room initially from the *Restaurant Belmont* on the plaza (ask for Francisco or Guadelupe) who have expensive rooms both at the restaurant and also down at the beach. At the restaurant they're M$50/night which gives you one double bed, electricity, no showers, no mosquito netting and share toilets. Down at the beach the accommodation is a tiny concrete, depressing little hovel again at M$50. No facilities at all — just planks and a tatty table. Avoid it if you can even though it's right on the beach.

Eats *Raoul's* enchillada place or the *Tropicana* bar are the best places. Otherwise there's the *Belmont* (relatively expensive) and another small cantina on the corner of the plaza opposite the Belmont. Outside the village at Miramar there are some excellent seafood restaurants but again they're not as cheap as the cafes first mentioned (again the food's excellent).

Other Post Office is at *Lupita* general store. They keep Poste Restante letters indefinitely. They also have most of the foods and requisites you might need.

At certain times of the day there are some vicious black-flies and midges (but not many mosquitoes) on the beaches around here. You'll need insect repellant if you're intent on staying there during these periods.

Local buses to San Blas at 7 am, 1 pm, 5 pm (very approx), M$13. From San Blas at 8.30 am, 11 am, 3.45 pm, for M$15.

SAN CRISTOBAL DE LAS CASAS
Accommodation
La Carpinteria, Avenida Gral. Utrillo and Calle Flavio A. Paniagua. Small pine-built cabins (beautiful smell) built around the carpenter's courtyard. M$41/double, hot shower extra. If you can't find the place ask at the Tienda Santo Domingo.
Los Baños, Calle 1 de Mayo. M$31/person, shared rooms. They also have cheap steam baths and meals — basic and friendly.
Casa de Huéspedes Margarita, Calle Real de Guadelupe, one and a half blocks from the Zócalo. M$65/single with hot water — clean.
Hotel San Francisco, Calle Insurgentes near the second class bus terminal. M$44/single.

Eats *Los Baños*, meal and steam bath M$31. *Casa Blanca*, Calle Real de Guadelupe, good cheap food. *Capri* two blocks from the Zocalo. Meal about M$31. The *Mercado* has cheap food stalls and jugos.

Things to Do/See There's a daily Indian market attended by people from various tribes in the area. It is in a different location from the mercado.

Places Nearby It's probably a good idea to remember that this area was the scene of Indian insurrections throughout much of the 19th century and during the first decade of the 20th. The Mexican government has been trying to integrate the Indians into the economic system for a long time but despite the programme, the area is still populated almost entirely by purebred Indians who speak their own languages and retain their own customs. For this reason it's best before visiting Indian villages to ask permission either at the Municipal offices in San Cristobal or the city hall (Cabildo).

San Juan Chamula, 10 km away. You can rent horses from Na Bolom at the corner of Calle Comitan & Avenida Vicente Guerrero. M$78 plus the same for a guide.
Tenejapa. Buses leave San Cristobal market at 7 am and 11 am for the Sunday market there — amazing weavings.
Amantengo de Valle, off the Pan-American Highway. Buses from San Cristobal or taxi which takes half an hour. It is good for pottery.

Other San Andrés — in all these places you can buy wares either from individual houses or the recently organised cooperatives which have been set up to give the craftspeople higher returns for their labour and cut down on the profit which the middle-men have traditionally taken. Ask for the cooperatives or go to the offices of FONARTE (Fomento Nacional en el Desarrollo de Artesania) which are at 42 Real de Mexicano, Barrio Mexicano.

Things bought in the stores or markets of San Cristobal tend to be higher priced and often of poorer quality. Remember that San Cristobal is a gringo hangout and there are occasionally spates of police surviellance.

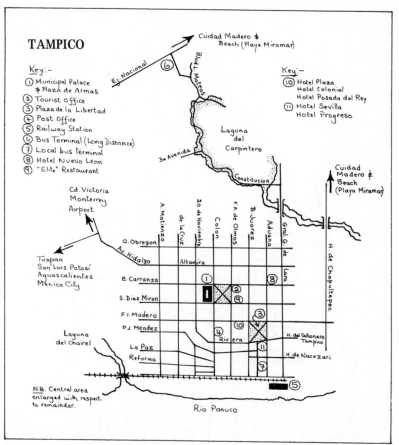

TAMPICO

Key:-
1. Municipal Palace & Plaza de Armas
2. Tourist office
3. Plaza de la Libertad
4. Post Office
5. Railway Station
6. Bus Terminal (Long Distance)
7. Local bus terminal
8. Hotel Nuevo Leon
9. "Elite" Restaurant

Key:-
10. Hotel Plaza, Hotel Colonial, Hotel Posada del Rey
11. Hotel Sevilla, Hotel Progreso

N.B. Central area enlarged with respect to remainder.

TAMPICO
Accommodation

Hotel Sevilla, Calle Rivera, right behind the local bus station and the train station. M$100/double — often full. It is a fairly new building.

Hotel Progreso, Calle Rivera. M$60/single, M$90/double, share showers — basic.

Hotel Nuevo León, Calle Aduana. M$120/double, will fit three people (two double beds).

Hotel Tampico Avenida Emile Carranza.

M$190/three people (two beds). 220 have bathrooms and toilets — middle range, older building.

Eats *Cafe y Nevería Elite* on S. Dias Mirón. A little expensive but open 24 hours and serves excellent food. Omlettes M$18-24, salads M$10, steaks M$28-60.

Things to Do/See If you've come here looking for that idyllic Gulf coast beach — too bad. You're 10 years

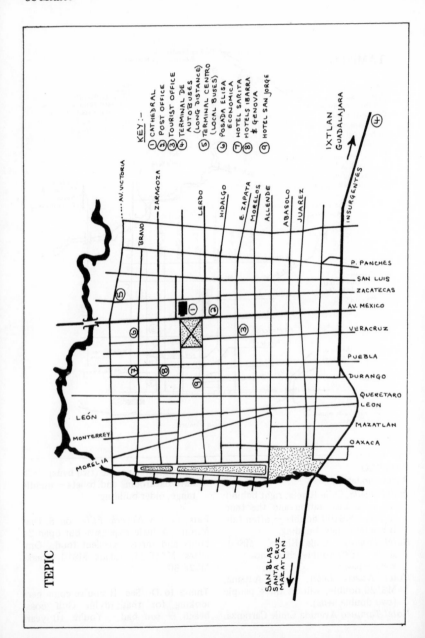

TEPIC

KEY:-
① CATHEDRAL
② POST OFFICE
③ TOURIST OFFICE
④ TERMINAL DE AUTOBUSES (LONG DISTANCE)
⑤ TERMINAL CENTRO (LOCAL BUSES)
⑥ POSADA ELISA ECONOMICA
⑦ HOTEL SARITA
⑧ HOTELS IBARRA & GENOVA
⑨ HOTEL SAN JORGE

too late. There's a huge, stinking, roaring oil refinery right to the beach and if that isn't enough to put you off, the beer cans, poly bags and bottles almost completely disguising the fact that sand is there, should clinch it. The tourist literature, of course, doesn't tell you this — just glorious technicolour shots of golden sunsets over mile after mile of deserted beach taken from a safe distance so the broken glass doesn't come into focus. You'll discover that the Mexicans have an ironic sense of humour.

Other The main bus terminal is on the outskirts of town (see map). Local buses run from the centre to the terminal. M$2.40. Taxis can cost up to M$50.

TEPIC
Accommodation
Hotel Sarita, 112 Calle Bravo Pte. M$120/triple with two double beds, toilet and shower. If you can avoid it, don't stay here. There are municipal sludge gobblers outside which will make you wonder whether Armageddon has arrived, and overgrown schoolboys inside who kick up one hell of a fuss so you'll be lucky to get much sleep — if the bed-bugs let you, that is.
Posada Elisa Economica, 14 Calle Bravo Pte is a quiet place set around a patio with trees. Undoubtedly the cheapest place in town but the lady wouldn't let us stay there as we were two women and a man, none of us married, etc etc and judging from the shocked expression on her face it must have said something about that in the bible somewhere.
Hotel Ibarra, corner of Calle Durango Norte and Calle Zaragoza Pte. The actual address is Calle Durango 297. M$155/triple.
Hotel Genova, Calle Zaragoza. M$160/triple.

Hotel San Jorge, Calle San Lerdo M$150/double. It is very comfortable judging from appearances but then it should be for that price.

Information Tourist Office, Calle Zapata Pte, has free city maps and other information. Their English is fine until you ask them a question but then you'll have learnt Spanish by now won't you..........

Other The local bus station for the Pacific coast villages of Santa Cruz, Miramar, Los Cochos, San Blas is on Avenida Victoria, one block from the Av. México. They depart at 8 am 1 pm, 3.30 pm, 5 pm. M$17 to Santa Cruz. It takes two hours and is a beautiful ride through tropical jungle and banana plantations.

The long-distance bus terminal (Terminal de Autobuses) is on Avenida Insurgentes which is 15-20 minutes walk from the centre. There are two hotels there where you can stay if you're just passing through and waiting for a connection.

VERA CRUZ
Accommodation
Hotel Imperio, Avenida Insurgentes Veracruzaños at Xicotencatl on the waterfront. Rooms with bath, some air-conditioned M$45-95/single and M$60-120/double. It has a bar, swimming pool, etc.
Hotel Castelán, Avila Camacho Boulevard. M$80/single, M$120/double. Air conditioning costs extra and a bar and restaurant are attached.
Hotel Vigo. US$6/double.
La Santilla, near main port area. US$6/double.

Eats Restaurant *La Concha*, Zamora 244. Comida corrida (seafood) M$25. *La Paella*. Zamora 138. Seafood specialities, comida corrida M$20.

TRANSPORT

Flights For international flights into Mexico from Europe and USA see the introductory section on Getting There.

Domestic flights are operated by the following companies (Aeromexico also service the international routes):

Aeromexico, Paseo de la Reforma 64, Mexico City, (tel 5 66 08 00). They have flights to Acapulco, Chihuahua, Cd Juarez, Cd Obregón, Cozumel, Culiacan, Guadalajara, Hermosillo, La Paz, Matamoros, Mazatlán, Mérida, Mexico DF, Monterrey, Oaxaca, Puerto Vallarta, Tijuana, Torreon, Reynosa, Poza Rica and Tampico.

Mexicana, Avenida Juárez and Balderas, Mexico DF, (tel 5 85 26 66). They have flights to Acapulco, Coatzalcoalcos, Cozumel, Cancun, Guadalajara, Hermosillo, Mazatlán, Mérida, Mexicali, Mexico DF, Minatitlan, Monterrey, Nuevo Laredo, Oaxaca, Puerto Vallarta, Tampico, Tuxtla, Gutierrez, Veracruz and Villahermosa.

Aerocaribe This airline only connects Cancun, Cozumel and Isla Mujeres on the Yucutan Peninsula.

If you're thinking of taking internal flights it might be well to check out SETEJ, Hamburgo 273, Zona Rosa, Mexico 6, D F, (the national student organisation). They charter flights to many places including Guatemala City and Havana, Cuba and so can often offer cheaper fares than you would get directly through the normal companies. They'll willingly send you full details of their current programme if you write to them. Here are some examples of the fares they offer on their weekly flights from Mexico City:

to Guatemala City	US$98 return
	US$60 one-way
to Havana, Cuba	US$140 return
	US$80 one-way
to Mérida	US$63 return
	US$35 one-way
to Guadalajara	US$30 return
	US$17 one-way
to Monterrey	US$46 return
	US$26 one-way
to Tijuana	US$143 return
	US$78 one-way

If you'd like to make a detour to Cuba, Mexico is the cheapest place to fly from. You can either fly from Mexico City or Mérida (latter is cheaper). Check out SETEJ and Cubana de Aviacion, Balderas and Juárez, Mexico City, (tel 5 85 26 66). There's a Cuban Consulate in Merida but at present they're only giving one-week visas.

Flight taxes in Mexico are M$100 for international flights and M$20 for internal flights.

To get into the centre from Mexico City airport either take the Metro (flat fare of M$1.30), bus No 12 to Avenida Juárez (M$12) or a taxi (government regulated fare is M$30).

Buses The bus network is extremely well developed and there are daily connections (often several buses per day) between all the major cities and towns in Mexico. Almost all the roads, even minor ones, are paved. There are two types of buses covering the long-distance routes: first and second class. The former are generally fairly new coaches, quite luxurious, somewhat faster and stop only occasionally. The latter are generally older buses, often crowded, more fun and stop more frequently to pick up and put down passengers. Which type you take will depend on what your priorities are since there's little difference in the fares. The average cost of first class buses is M$39 per 100 km; second class is approximately seven percent less.

Most cities and large towns have a modern bus terminal where all the first class buses and often many of the second class buses stop. Alternatively there may be two separate terminals. Local buses running to outlying towns and villages generally leave from their own terminal or, if there are separate terminals, then they leave from the second class terminal. This makes travelling by bus very convenient since all the various bus companies have ticket offices at the one terminus. Each one of these offices has a board detailing the routes which they cover, departure times, fares and the class of bus. Except on local buses and some second class buses, seats are numbered and it's best to book in advance although it's unlikely on most routes that buses will be fully booked up to within an hour of the departure time. The only major exceptions to the centralization scheme are to be found in Mexico City and towns in Southern Mexico where companies running first class buses generally have their own terminals. Where this applies the location of the various terminals has been indicated and they're also marked, where possible, on the appropriate maps.

There's no point in giving a comprehensive list of all possible routes, departure times and fares since connections are daily, often several times per day, between all the major centres. If you want to continue your journey the same day it's unlikely you'll have to wait more than a few hours so long as you don't arrive too late in the day. Some major routes:

Nuevo Laredo-Monterrey (Transportes del Norte), 2nd class, M$54, 3 hours.

Tampico-Guadalajara (Autobuses Verdes) 2nd class, M$174, 13 hours.

Guadalajara-Tepic (Autobuses Verdes), 2nd class, M$54.

Tepic-Mexico City 1st class, M$220, 15 hours.

Mexico City-Oaxaca (ADO), 1st class, M$135, 10 hours.

Oaxaca-Villahermosa (Cristobal Colon), 1st class, M$172, 13 hours.

Villahermosa-Palenque (ADO), 1st class, M$37, 2 hours.

Villahermosa-Mérida, 1st class, M$157.

Mexico City-Mérida, 1st class, M$157.

Campeche-Mérida, 1st class, M$48.

Veracruz-Mérida, 1st class, M$277.

Mérida-Chetumal, 1st class, M$111, 6 hours, (2nd class, M$104).

Chetumal-Belize (Batty Bus Co), M$60, 5 hours, only on Tuesdays, Thursdays and Saturdays at 10 am.

If you haven't much time are are in a hurry to get to Mexico City from the US, Greyhound run through buses from the border towns to Mexico City on a daily schedule:

from San Diego	US$33.70
from Nogales	US$25.75
from El Paso	US$21.70
from Laredo	US$13.75
from Houston	US$40.15
from San Antonio	US$25.50
from Brownsville	US$12.70

The return fares are approximately five percent less than double the single fares. Note that there's little difference between the above Greyhound fares and what it would cost you on the Mexican buses.

If you want a comprehensive list of bus routes, departures times, fares, etc. there's a monthly bus guide published which you can get for M$25 (representing a year's subscription) from "Guia de Autotransportes de Mexico", Apartado 8929, Mexico 1, DF.

Trains Trains are generally slower than buses but cheaper by a fair margin even in first class. For night or long-distance journeys they have the advantage of sleeping accommodation and dining cars. The first class is often barely half full so it's possible to stretch out over two seats and catch a good night's sleep.

From the USA border towns with railway connections are Mexicali/Calexico, Nogales/Nogales, Ciudad Juárez/El Paso, Ojinga/Presidio, Piedras Negras/Eagle Pass, Nuevo Laredo/Laredo and Matamoros/Brownsville. All except Matamoros and Piedras Negras have dining car and sleeping accommodation. If you're on a tight schedule and need to plan your journey through Mexico before setting off, Mexican National Railways have US offices in New York, Chicago, El Paso, Laredo and Washington. Otherwise contact Secretaría de Comunicaciones y Transportes, Oficina de Promoción y Pasajes Ferrocarriles, Pasaje Comercial A-1 Buenavista Station, Mexico 3, DF — tel 5 47 30 30 or 5 47 30 18.

Details of two lines you might well use follow:

Ferrocarril Chihuahua-Pacifico. The line runs between Ojinaga (opposite Presidio, Texas) and the Pacific port of Topolobampa/Los Mochis in Sinaloa state. That part of the route between Chihuahua and the coast is one of the most spectacular in the world and includes 30 bridges and 10 tunnels. It goes via the Barranca del Cobre which is comparable to the Grand Canyon in the USA. The train leaves five days a week. The autovia costs US$10.50/single. The vistatren is more expensive and equivalent to the first class fare. Book in advance and sit on the left-hand side of the carriage going from Chihuahua to the coast. There's a good dining car.

Ferrocarriles Unidos del Sureste. Line runs between Mexico City and Mérida via the northern part of the Tehunatepec Peninsula. Daily passenger train in both directions runs on the following schedule:

Mexico-Mérida	Stations	Mérida-Mexico
20.10	Mexico DF	9.15
23.00	Apizaco	6.21
0.40	Esperanza	4.46
2.20	Orizaba	2.58
3.20	Córdoba	1.55
5.30	Tierra Blanca	23.15
8.13	Rodriguez Clara	20.17
10.06	Medias Aguas	18.45
12.00	Coatzacoalcos	15.25
(two hour 15 minute wait)		(one hour 10 minute wait)
15.44	Tancochapa	14.17
17.12	Roberto Ayala	12.48
18.12	Juárez	11.47
18.41	Pichucalco	11.18
19.10	Teapa	10.50
20.21	Macuspana	9.39
21.01	Salto de Agua	9.04
22.00	Palenque	8.06
22.23	Lacandon	7.41
22.57	Zapata	7.08
23.20	Tenosique	6.25
0.03	Mactuan	5.59
0.34	San Pedro	5.26
0.53	El Triunfo	5.05
1.32	Candelaria	4.20
2.45	Escárcega	2.55
3.55	Carrillo Puerto	1.42
4.20	San Dimas	1.09
5.47	Campeche	23.05
(15 minute wait)		(15 minute wait)
7.21	Calkiní	21.46
9.05	Mérida	20.00

This is the train you catch if you're travelling from Palenque to Campeche or Mérida.

In addition to the above passenger train there is a daily mixed cargo/passenger train in both directions between Coatzacoalcos and Mérida and a daily (except Sundays) mixed cargo/passenger train in both directions between Campeche and Mérida. These latter two are much slower than the passenger train. They stop at all the stations above plus others. Their abbreviated schedules follow:

Coatzacoalcos-Mérida	Stations	Mérida-Coatzacoalcos
8.35	Coatzacoalcos	13.25
20.48	Palenque	1.37 (next
10.55 (next day)	Campeche	9.55 day)
(one hour 20 minute wait)		(one hour 40 minute wait)
17.10	Mérida	5.00

Campeche-Mérida	Stations	Mérida-Campeche
16.30	Campeche	3.40 (next
21.30	Mérida	23.00 day)

The fare on the passenger train from Palenque to Mérida is M$92 in first class (not very different from second class) but there are also pullman-type coaches which cost an extra M$12 (pay the difference on the train when the ticket inspector comes round). It's well worth taking the pullman since it's often nearly empty so you can stretch out over a couple of seats and sleep (pillows for hire if you've got a bad neck for M$5). The guard will keep an eye on your luggage throughout the night. The toilets are very clean with soap and toilet paper. This is luxury you can afford, etc! The same company also runs trains to Oaxaca from Mexico City. It is a daily service, M$54 in second class and takes 19 hours. Most of the people travelling on this train are Indians returning to their villages around the Oaxaca area.

Boats/Ferries

Mazatlán-La Paz (Baja California). Departs Mazatlán everyday (except Sunday) at 6 pm and departs La Paz everyday (except Monday) at 6 pm. The journey takes 16 hours. Salon class M$208, tourist class M$416, cabin M$832, cars from M$1248, car and trailer from M$2600.

Salon class has reclining chairs, cafeteria and movie theatre and the tourist class has cabins for two or four people, dining room, bar, lounge and swimming pool. Cabins fit two people and have twin beds and private bath. There's room for about 115 cars.

Puerto Vallarta-Cabo San Lucas (Baja California). Departs Puerto Vallarta on Tuesdays and Saturdays at 4 pm and departs Cabo San Lucas on Wednesdays and Sundays at 4 pm. The journey takes 18 hours. Salon class M$260, tourist class M$520, cabin M$1040, cars from M$1500, car and trailer from M$3120.

Guaymas-Santa Rosalía (Baja California).

Departs Guaymas on Tuesdays, Thursdays and Sundays at 12 noon and departs Santa Rosalia on Tuesdays, Thursdays and Sundays at 10 pm. The journey time takes six hours. Salon class M$125, tourist class M$229, car from M$832, car and trailer from M$1768.

Topolobampo/Los Mochis-La Paz (Baja California). Departs Topolobampo on Wednesdays and Fridays at 9 am and departs La Paz on Tuesdays and Thursdays at 8 pm. The journey takes eight hours. Salon class M$138, tourist class M$188, car from M$749, car and trailer from M$1400.

The addresses of the ticket and reservation offices are:

Mazatlán: Prolongación Calle Carnaval (tel 17020/17021 and 17022).

La Paz: Independencia 107-A, (tel 20109).

Puerto Vallarta: Muelle Maritimo, (tel 20476).

Cabo San Lucas: Muelle Maritimo.

Guayamas: Muelle Patio, (tel 22324).

Santa Rosalía: Muelle de la Aduana, (tel 20013 and 20014).

Topolobampo: reservations in Los Mochis at Naviera del Pacifico, Hidalgo 419 Poniente, (tel 21929).

For ferries to Isla Mujeres and Cosumel off the Yucatan coast see under Isla Mujeres.

Taking your own Vehicle Free maps, literature and information available from any of the following places:

Any Mexican Government Tourist Office.

Asociación Mexicana Automovilistica (AMA), Avenida Chapultepec 276, Mexico DF, (tel 5 11 68 73). They have offices in many Mexican cities.

Asociación Nacional Automovilistica (ANA), Miguel Shultz 140, Mexico DF, (tel 5 46 99 65).

Both AMA and ANA are members of the International Federation of Automobile Associations and extend reciprocal services to affiliate members. They can arrange insurance cover at the border for about US$2.50 per day, depending on the car and occupants. Watch out for police waving you through red lights and then demanding M$500

fine — or so I was told by someone who said it happened to them!

If you're thinking of taking a vehicle to Mexico, do yourself a favour and get hold of a copy of *The People's Guide to Mexico* (see the introductory section on books). It's particularly relevant for people taking vehicles and extremely witty.

OTHER INFORMATION

Fiestas As in other places in Latin America, a fiesta is a spontaneous folk expression based on a mixture of the culture brought by the Spanish and the various Indian cultures which had been developed before their arrival. It usually centres around the church and the main plaza which are often decorated for the occasion and can include fireworks and colourful folk dances in elaborate native costumes. Here is a selection:

January 6	Santos Reyes (Three Wise Men). All over Mexico.
January 17	San Antonio Abad. Blessing of the animals. All over Mexico.
January 18	Santa Prisca. At Tasco, Guerro. Fiesta of the town's patroness.
January 20	San Sebastian. At Chiapa de Corzo, Chiapas. Fair, folk dances. Also at Guanajuato and León, both in Guanajuato state.
Carnival (Variable date: February-March)	Acapulco, Guerrero; Huejotzingo, Puebla; Mazatlán, Sinaloa, Mérida, Yucatán; Tepozatlán, Morelos; Veracruz. These are perhaps the best but it takes place all over Mexico.
Holy Week (Variable Date)	Tasco, Guerrero and Pátzcuaro, Michoacán.
March-April 25	San Marcos. At Aguascalientes. Fair.
May 3	La Santa Cruz. At Milpa Alta, Federal District and Valle de Bravo, Mexico DF. Fair, folk dances.
Corpus Cristi (Variable date)	All over Mexico. At Papantla, Veracruz there's the dance of the flying bird men — a prehispanic ritual to the sun.
June 24	San Juan. All over Mexico.
July (usually the last two Mondays)	Oaxaca. Lunes del Cerro. Fiesta of the Guelaguetza. Folk dances.
August 15	Huamantla, Tlaxcala; Cholula, Puebla; Milpa Alta, DF.
September 7-8	Nativity of the Virgin Mary. At Tepoztlan, Morelos.
September 29	San Miguel. At San Miguel de Allende, Guanajuato. Bullfights, fireworks, concerts and folk dances.
October 4	San Francisco. At Cuetzalan, Puebla. Coffee growers fair and folk dances.

October 12	Guadalajara, Jalisco (festivals); Zapopan, Jalisco (religious celebrations.
November 1-2	All Soul's Day. At Mixquic, Michoacan; El Romerillo, Chis., etc. Candlelit all-night vigil at the cemetery graves decorated with offerings of flowers and food.
December 8	Nuestra Señora de la Salud. At Pátzcuaro, Michoacán. Fiesta to the town's patroness. Arts and crafts fair, folk dances, etc.
December 12	Our Lady of Guadalupe. Mexico's patroness. Fiestas all over the country.
December 16-25	Christmas season. All over the country. Parties, nativity plays, fireworks etc.
December 18	Nuestra Señora de la Soledad. At Oaxaca. The town's patroness. Folk dances.

Spanish Courses Many places offer these. They vary considerably in length and price. If you're interested one of the places you might like to check out is the student organization, SETEJ, Hamburgo 273, Mexico 6 DF. They hold courses in Cuernavaca and other places. The course costs M$7500 per week (20 hours tuition — four to five hours daily). They have rooms available for M$780/week including breakfast or M$1200/week including all meals.

Alternatively check out places in Guatemala where there are many similar courses on offer.

Central America

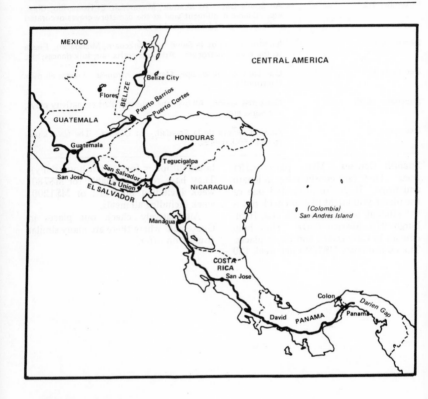

Guatemala

A beautiful and fascinating country of vast jungles, high mountains topped by a continuous string of volcanoes (some still active), lakes, ruins of incredible Mayan temples and ceremonial sites, old colonial cities, friendly Indian villages and colourful markets where some of the best woven fabrics in the whole of Latin America can be found. Because of its variety it's probably the favourite Central American country for travellers many of whom spend a lot of time here before moving on.

The early history of Guatemala is the history of the Mayan civilization which stretches in an unbroken line over 3500 years from around 2000 BC up until the Conquest by the Spanish in 1527, and even then it was not until 1697 that the last of the Mayan kingdoms centred on an island in Lake Petén Itzá (present day Flores) was conquered. The civilization was flourishing around 400 AD in the lowlands of Honduras, Guatemala and Belize and it was during this period that the great temple complexes of Copán (Honduras), Tikal (Guatemala) and Palenque (Mexico) were built. They are among the most impressive ruins you will find anywhere in the world. There are hundreds of others scattered throughout Guatemala though many are inaccessible, except on foot, being located in thick jungle a long way from any road, but there's still scope for discovery. Explorers still come across new sites from time to time.

No one has yet come up with a satisfactory explanation as to why there is no evidence of invasion, epidemics or exhaustion of the land — but around 800 AD these large population centres were more or less precipitously abandoned and there was a migration to the flat lands of northern Yucatán and the highlands of western Guatemala where a renaissance of their civilization took place, involving the introduction of Toltec motifs (a war-like tribe from the Valley of Mexico), a new architecture, new religious rituals, human sacrifice and the construction of raised causeways linking the highlands with the coast. The cities of Chichen Itza, Uxmal and Kabah, among others, were constructed at this time.

Unlike the highly centralized civilizations of the Aztec and Inca, the Maya had no empire but were a collection of fiercely independent tribes and city-states who shared a common culture, religion and language, and who traded extensively with each other. There was no political union and this lack of a precise centre or capital was the cause of the long and costly campaign the Spanish had to wage in their conquest of these people. Nevertheless, they created what was probably Central America's most advanced civilization. Their arts, crafts, mathematics, astronomy and sculpture were all highly developed and

they possessed an elaborate system of hieroglyphs and two interlocking calendars — known as the Long and the Short Counts — which were more accurate than the European Gregorian calendar. In common with other ancient civilizations, the Maya had a highly mystical explanation of nature and a pantheon of gods who were the guardians of natural events and human needs. The most important was Chac, the god of rain, since droughts were quite common — not because rainfall was deficient but because water was difficult to store in the porous rocks and they were ignorant of the concept of the wheel and its applications, which would have made raising sub-soil water for irrigating the fields a problem. Despite this, they were fortunate in living in a land which had such a rich variety of flora and fauna that it provided them with all they needed for food, clothing and medicine. In addition, the soil and climate were such that large surpluses of corn could be grown. This cereal was the mainstay of their agriculture and the basis of their diet, though sweet potatoes, black beans, chilis and cacao were also cultivated. They even bred a variety of stingless bee in hollow tree trunks in order to collect honey for sweetening and for making a fermented mead-like brew.

The Mayas were the only one of the three great American theocracies which were involved in trade both by sea and land. They had regular contact with peoples as far afield as Panama, the Caribbean Islands and Mexico. The wealth which this trade produced, together with the huge surpluses of corn, enabled them to support a non-producing priest and noble class and to construct their temples, cities and roads. War was more or less continuous, as it was between the Greek city-states, but was usually of short duration and apparently fought in a very ceremonial and ritualistic fashion. Its objects were the capture of prisoners, most of whom became slaves, while the headmen, who went into battle wearing enormous quetzal-feathered headdresses and painted gaudily from head to foot, were sacrificed. War was always subservient to the needs of agriculture and ceased entirely at planting and harvest time.

The organization of their society was based on the pyramid, with the priests and nobles at the top and the maize farmer at the bottom. Land was held in common and each family was assigned sufficient land to grow their food and pay their "taxes" (part of their harvest or a certain amount of labour on other projects). The priests were consulted before any new phase of activity was initiated and this involved elaborate rites, prayers, fasting and sacrifice in order to gain the favour of the gods and ensure a successful outcome. The building of houses, clearing of land and the planting and tending of crops were a communal activity.

This cultural heritage of the Maya remains largely intact despite 450 years of Spanish colonial and latterly Ladino rule. Pure-bred Maya still comprise about 50% of the population of Guatemala — the highest proportion of indigenous people in any Central American republic, including Mexico. The Spanish, in their zeal for conversion, baptized as many as they could get their hands on in the early days of the Conquest, but because of their numerical inferiority and the danger of insurrection recognized that much of this was mere window-dressing and allowed the Indians to continue practising their ancient pagan rites alongside those of Catholicism. This is still very much in evidence today. The Indians have retained their language (Quiché) and form a society within a society and, until recently, were virtually outside the money economy. They practise subsistence agriculture (mainly because they have been dispossessed of their lands over the centuries) and specialize in handicrafts

which they sell or exchange at markets and fairs. Family industry is important and they work hard but, unlike their Ladino compatriots, have little interest in making profits and growing rich — a factor which has caused a great deal of misunderstanding between the two groups. These handicrafts are what attract many travellers and tourists to the highlands of Guatemala and the markets which are held weekly and sometimes daily in many villages and towns throughout the area.

The Conquest (between 1527 and 1546) and its aftermath saw the gradual alienation of the Indian's lands as these were distributed among the Conquistadores and the Indians forced to work as unpaid labourers on the plantations in exchange for the loan of a small plot of land on which to grow food for themselves and their families. There was a good deal of brutality which, together with the diseases which the Spanish brought with them — mainly smallpox, respiratory diseases, syphilis — reduced the population of Central America from 14 to two million within 130 years according to one estimate. Bartolomé de las Casas, a Dominican friar, who went to this part of the world during the early days of the Conquest, made a big nuisance of himself with his campaigns for better treatment of and forebearance towards the Indians but succeeded in some small measure, though right up until the present the daily lot of the Indian has been one of poverty, malnutrition, sickness and illiteracy.

The plantation economy involved the large scale dislocation of highland people to the large land holdings on the Pacific coast, where they worked the coffee and cotton crops, which cannot be mechanized without affecting the quality of the crop and so require large seasonal work forces for harvesting. In order to ensure that sufficient numbers of labourers were available for this work, the Spanish, and latterly, the

Guatemalan Government, made sure that the Indians had insufficient of their own land on which to support themselves and thus would be forced to move and look for work (about one million Indians are in this position). On occasion, when the labour force has been deficient, the Army has been called in to round up more at the instigation of the latifundistas (the large land holders). This pattern of land ownership and the reliance on the exploitation of cheap labour (or unpaid labour) survives virtually intact and has been instrumental in preventing new and more productive methods of agriculture being introduced. Guatemala could be Central America's food basket yet nine-tenths of the population are still involved in subsistence agriculture using primitive implements — which, in effect, means maize and precious little else.

Illustrating the iniquitous distribution of land are recent figures which show that of those who own any land at all, the minifundista (small land owners) own 88.4% of the farms, constituting 14.3% of the land, with most of them insufficient to feed a family, while the latifundista (large land owners) own 2.1% of the farms, constituting 72.2% of the land. The USA based United Fruit Co until recently owned more land than 50% of the population of Guatemala. In addition, while the minifundista cultivate 80-95% of their land (much of it marginal), the latifundista keep large areas of their land idle — sometimes up to 60%.

Independence was declared from Spain on 15 September 1821. Along with the other Central American republics, Guatemala initially agreed to join Iturbide's Mexican empire but there was opposition and an army had to be dispatched south. When Iturbide abdicated they split off and formed a new federation with its capital at Guatemala City. The union was riven by internal dissension and suspicion between the Conserv-atives and the Liberals from its inception. Republic fought republic until Morazon, in command of the army of Honduras, eventually restored some semblance of order and moved the capital to San Salvador, but the peace didn't last long and there was an uprising of Indians in Guatemala led by Rafael Carrera, an illiterate Ladino but born leader. He gained control of Guatemala after defeating Morazon's armies and it was not long before the federation voted itself out of existence. Other attempts were made at various times during the 19th century to get the federation going again but there was too much suspicion of power motives for it ever to take off.

For the rest of the 19th century and well into the 20th, Guatemalan history followed the familiar Latin American pattern of strong-arm dictatorships alternating with periods of civilian government. Meanwhile the condition of the peasants continued to deteriorate and there were uprisings of the Indians in 1898 and 1943 — this last during the dictator Ubico's reign (1931-44).

In an effort to do the minimum necessary, Ubico abolished the system of debt-peonage (the arrangement whereby a landowner allowed a land-less peasant to cultivate a small patch of land in exchange for free labour on his plantation) but brought in a series of laws which were just as onerous. Then in 1944 the Revolutionary Party led by Juan José Arévalo won a landslide victory in the elections. Arevalo, an idol of the liberals, intellectuals, teachers, etc, instituted a series of radical land reform acts aimed at redistributing the land among the peasants. They included expropriating land given to Ubico's generals and supporters, the distribution of the National Fincas (large state-owned farms, 150 in number, most of which had been confiscated from German settlers during World War II after pressure from the USA), the setting up of agricultural cooperatives, labour unions, provision for education and medical care, a minimum wage (80 centavos a day for rural work, $1.25 a day for urban work) and the forced rental of uncultivated lands. His work was continued with even more vigour by his elected successor, Jacobo Arbenz, who, in addition, made a foray against the power and priviledges of private capital — particularly the United Fruit Co.

Both Presidents were branded as "communists" by the large landowners, the United Fruit Co, the Church and the USA — a popular rallying call for the forces of reaction and capitalist exploitation in those days. Colonel Castillo Armas, an exiled Guatemalan officer, was set up with money ($18m), arms and a training camp in Honduras by the USA, with the connivance of the Vatican, some of the Guatemalan army top brass and the latifundistas, to train an army for an invasion. When it was launched, Arbenz strangely resigned, though it was doubtful whether the invasion would have succeeded. Among the first of Armas' acts was the cancelling of the franchise of all illiterates (72% of the population), the banning of labour unions, the cancellation of the land reform programme and the return of all lands distributed to their former owners. In the melee which followed, many peasants, labour leaders and others were murdered, houses were burnt down and protestors shot or jailed.

Armas was assassinated in August 1957 and succeeded by General Miguel Ydígoras Fuentes who had himself elected fraudulently after making belligerent noises about a coup. His regime was thoroughly corrupt and much land was given to his friends and backers while the campaign of violence against peasants and labour leaders was maintained. He was not, however, popular with the Church or the USA, though they made their separate uneasy truces with him

after he bribed the Archbishop of Guatemala with money and forced a law through Congress allowing the Church once again to own land. He curried the favour of the USA by allowing them to set up a military training camp for anti-Castro guerrillas and assisting in the Bay of Pigs invasion. When things got worse he attempted to divert attention by instigating quarrels with Mexico, Belize and El Salvador so that, in the end, even the Armed Forces had had enough of him and he was overthrown in a coup led by Colonel Peralta.

Peralta's regime brought more repression of labour unions and ex-officials. In the face of such assaults the guerrilla movements in Zacapa and Izabel provinces drew more supporters and they started to make a series of daring raids. The army's answer was to make wholesale arrests of "suspects" — sometimes whole villages were arrested. Many were never seen again, no charges were brought, and months later news would leak out that they had been murdered. No investigations of these murders were ever carried out and indeed Peralta's last act before handing the country back to civilian rule was to pass a law exonerating "all members of the army, all policemen and all superiors for all the acts they committed in the repression of subversive activities".

Much to everyone's surprise, the Revolutionary Party, led now by Méndez Montenegro, won the elections but times had changed and the army was by then well entrenched. The new President found that he was little more than a puppet and had to constantly re-assure the army, the police and the latifundistas that there would be no return to the measures adopted by Arévalo and Arbenz. The only course of action which was open to him was a return to the disastrous colonization of the Petén schemes which had been tried before and failed through unsuitable soil, lack of finance, lack of communications, malaria, etc. Méndez' schemes were equally disastrous. During his Presidency the guerrilla movements became stronger and he was forced by the army to accept large USA loans for counterinsurgency measures. Meanwhile right-wing terrorist groups mushroomed and violence became widespread. Things have settled down a little since then but as the land-less are still in the same position they were in before and the population continues to expand at the rate of 100,000 a year, something has to give sooner or later.

If you'd like more detail on any of this, try the following books:

The Maya Michael D Coe (Penguin Books, 1971). Very comprehensive, full of photos, maps and drawings, but it gets a little too academic in parts and can be dry reading for anyone except perhaps an archaeologist.

The Ancient Sun Kingdoms of the Americas Victor W von Hagen (Paladin, 1977). Probably the most readable account you'll find of the Aztec, Maya and Inca civilizations — packed with photographs, recommended.

Tikal W R Coe (University of Pennsylvania, 9th edn, 1977, $4.50). History and maps, coloured plates and very useful on site. Can be found in Guatemala City bookshops and at the Tikal Museum.

Guatemala — Another Vietnam? by Thomas and Marjorie Melville (Penguin Books, 1971). An excellent, well-researched and well documented expose of Guatemalan politics, patterns of land ownership and attempts at land reform. Both authors lived and worked among the Indians of Guatemala for years before they were expelled.

Guatemalan Guide by Paul Glassman (Dallas, Texas, 1977). A guide book for tourist orientated interests but contains details you might find useful if you're either spending a lot of money (then why are you reading this!?) or if you're staying for a long time.

300 Phrases in Common Use in Mayan, English and Spanish A little phrase book you'll find for sale in the Yucatán and other parts of Mexico. (If you can't find it try: Abelardo Fuente Vega, Calle 59 No. 454, Merida, Yucatán. Costs M$6.)

VISAS

They are required by all except nationals of Western Europe (except Britain and Portugal), Central America (except Mexico), Argentina, Israel and Japan. If you need one, fees vary: US$5 British, US$3 Australians. Visas can be issued for a stay of up to three months so bear this in mind when you fill the form in. The same price applies for one month as two. USA and Canadian nationals do not even require a passport — merely some proof of identity.

Tourist Cards are issued to all those not requiring a visa, US$1, and are valid for a stay of up to three months. They are obtainable at the border, Guatemalan consulates or airlines flying into Guatemala. Ask for a multiple entry Tourist Card otherwise you will be issued with a single entry Card.

There is an Exit Tax of $1.50. Also, if you stay more than 30 days, you need an Exit Permit, $2.50, obtainable from Immigration or Police. There are Guatemalan Consulates in Tapachula, Comitán (Calle 1 Sur Poniente 42 in Mexico and Belize City, Benque Viejo in Belize. There is no trouble entering at the Belize/Guatemala frontier at Melchor de Mencos with friendly officials and no searches or money showing.

CURRENCY

US$1 = 1 Quetzal

The unit of currency is the Quetzal (Q) = 100 centavos.

Other Information

If you need medical attention the Croix Rouge, Calle 3, Ave. 8-9 in Guatemala City is recommended. It is not expensive.

GUATEMALA

ANTIGUA
Accommodation

Pensión Antiguanita, near main plaza. Q1.50/person — old and basic. Has good cheap food for 60-75 centavos.

Pensión Diaz, just off the main plaza. Q1.50-2.50/single — beautiful courtyard, old building.

Pensión El Arco, next to the arch (as you might expect). Q1.50/person — clean and friendly.

Hospedaje El Marne. Q1/person.

Posada Colonial. Q3/person including breakfast.

Other A beautiful old colonial town, Antigua is the old capital of Guatemala. The nearby volcano is active and earth tremors are frequent. The town has been damaged several times by earthquakes. Many travellers stay here to teach English (quite a few jobs available as a rule).

CHICHICASTENANGO
Accommodation If you can find it, there's a Baha'i house four blocks from the main plaza where you can sleep on the floor free. *Hotel Los Claveles* Q1.25/person. There is good food for 60 centavos and a bakery is attached.

For other cheap accommodation just ask the local lads — people rent out rooms for around Q1.50.

Eats *Comedor Cristobal* next to *El Tigre Tienda*, half a block from the post office. Comida Corriente Q1. Check out *Mayan Inn* to see if marimba musicians are playing on the patio in the evening. It's free to non-residents.

COBÁN
Accommodation *Pensión Continental*, on main plaza. Q1/person with own bedding or Q1.25 if you want sheets. *Pensión Familiar*. Q2/single with hot water — good.

Places Nearby The Lanquín Caves are supposed to be over 90 km long!! although only four km are open to the public. There are stalactites, an underground river (navigable for something like 75 km), a unique species of white, blind fish and Mayan altars, etc. Daily buses from the main plaza in Cobán to village of Lanquín costs Q1 but takes six hours over an unpaved, pot-holed road (75 km). There's a small pension opposite the police station for Q1 or you can camp near the entrance to the caves in a couple of lean-to shelters and build a fire. The camp site is down by the Lanquín River which emerges from the caves. Millions of bats fly out of the caves in the evening — go easy on the mushrooms.

EL ESTOR

A small ex-buccaneers' haunt on Lake Izabal where British pirates used to get their provisions. *Hospedaje El Milagro*. Q1.25/single.

FLORES
Accommodation

Pensión Universal. Q1/person for double. Rooms will fit three people as there are two single beds and hammock hooks in each room — scruffy, cold showers all day. Top two floors get insufferably hot in summer as they're constructed of concrete and act like storage heaters at night — many travellers.

Pensión Casablanca. Q1-1.50. You get beer and refresco from the scruffy, indifferent cafe downstairs, but the wooden structure probably means its cooler than the Universal at night. The cafe sometimes has mariachi bands belting away in there.

Hotel Santana. Q3/double — no single rooms but airy, friendly, clean and new. Has a good cafe which we nicknamed the "No hay cafe" because they never had anything you wanted until you discovered them

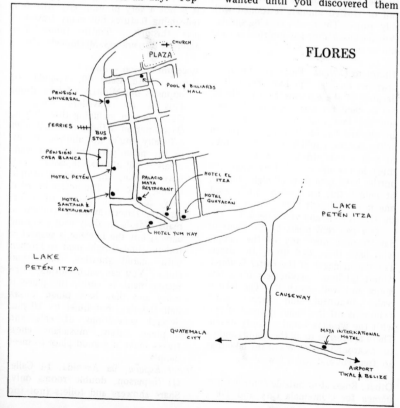

FLORES

serving it to the people at the adjacent table. But they're very friendly people. Scrambled eggs, rice, bread, two cups of coffee Q1, chicken, salad and rice Q1.50, fried fish, salad and rice Q2.25.

Hotel Petén. Q6/double with shower, Q5 without shower. Pretty comfortable, modern and there are pot plants everywhere.

Hotel Guayacan — old and scuffy. Try here if the other cheapies are full.

Eats Basically there are cafes: *Hotel Santana* (mentioned previously). *Palacio Maya* Restaurant has similar prices to the Santana but it's a weird place, full of stuffed animals festooned with silly props. The food's nothing special. *Pensión Casablanca* has indifferent food and service.

Things to Do/See Flores is a beautiful town on an island in Lake Peten Itza. Because of the extreme heat in Flores, the demand for scarce electrical power and the fact that beers and gaseosas are stacked outside before being placed in the fridges, you'll be extremely lucky to find a *cold* drink anywhere. First thing in the morning is best when the bottles have been there all night, though of course this isn't when you'll want one most — tough titty. Swimming in the lake is good and you'll need it.

You can rent boats by the hour or day from almost any of the people who have them tied up by the shore. Try the manager of the *Hotel Santana*. About Q1/hour, maybe less for a few hours and well worth it. The lake is really beautiful and there's good swimming off the island in front of you with the wireless aerial — sandy beach. There are ferries to all the islands and to towns around the shores of the lake that are frequent and cost a few cents.

Other Buses stop outside *Pensión Casablanca* for Guatemala City and Tikal.

If you're flying out of Flores remember that the airport is chaos. The ones who push hardest get the tickets and these are limited. What the Guatemalans do is collect as many passports as they can and hand them all in at once so suddenly there are only one or two tickets left. Get there early (6.30 am for the flight to Guatemala City) and don't leave your spot right in front of the ticket office otherwise you might find yourself staying in Flores longer than you calculated. There's always the bus of course. Further information under *Flights*.

GUATEMALA CITY

It is not a very pleasant city with few redeeming features but many travellers pass through. Traffic fumes, Col Sanders, Burgerkings, McDonalds, etc.

Accommodation — Zona 1

Pensión Mesa, Calle 10, Avenida 10, opposite old Ministry of Education. This is *the* travellers' hang-out. Q2.50/person including three meals, Q1.50/person without meals (though officially you're not allowed to stay in the main part unless you want meals — not always the case). They have double, triple and quadruple rooms — basic. The notice board is very good with plenty of information, letters awaiting collectors, maps. Meals are okay (not everyone agrees) but the hygiene is suspect — toilets situated right next to kitchen with shared showers, toilets and sinks. You can wash clothes. The management is surly, the place is noisy and they have piped musak half the day, but quiet by 10 pm. Several generations of cats and umpteen kittens, musicians, chess freaks make it a good place to meet people.

Hotel España, 9a Avenida, 14 Calle. Q1.75/person, double rooms only. Share showers and toilets (not too

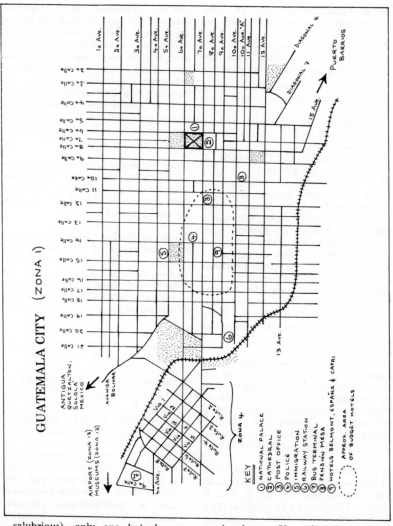

GUATEMALA CITY (ZONA 1)

AIRPORT (ZONA 13)
MUSEUMS (ZONA 13)

ANTIGUA,
QUETZALTEN,
SOLOLA,
MEXICO

PUERTO BARRIOS

KEY

① NATIONAL PALACE
② CATHEDRAL
③ POST OFFICE
④ POLICE
⑤ IMMIGRATION
⑥ RAILWAY STATION
⑦ BUS TERMINAL
⑧ PENSION MESA
⑨ HOTELS BELMONT, ESPAÑA & CAPRI
⌒⌒ APPROX. AREA OF BUDGET HOTELS

salubrious), only one hot shower, and there are no fans (heat can be stifling). A whore house which can be very noisy with the screams of adolescent males chasing equally daft females around the corridors. If you're well rested you might sur- vive here. If you're after a good night's sleep you'll need matchsticks for your eyes by morning. There is an indifferent cafe downstairs.

Hotel Belmont 1 and 2, next door to each other, 9a Avenida, 15 Calle, Q5/double — fairly plush, hot water.

Hotel Fénix, 7a Avenida, 16 Calle. Q3/single — quiet, easy going and together.

Hotel Leon, 9a Avenida, 13 Calle Q2.50/person including three meals — food indifferent, cold showers.

Hotel Capri, next door to the *Espana*. Q2.50/person without private showers.

Hotel Karen Inn, 17 Calle between Avenidas 8 and 9. Q1.50/person for good rooms.

Hotel Tikal, 21 Calle, Avenida 7. Q2.50/person — pleasant.

Hotel Chalet Suizo, 14 Calle, 6a Avenida. Pleasant, popular and right opposite the police station. They only have double rooms, Q4/double.

Hotel La Posada, 7a Avenida 5-41, across from the Palacio Nacional Q2.50/person — clean and pleasant.

Pensión Alzamora, 9a Avenida between Calles 9 and 10. Q2/person.

San Salvador, 8a Avenida between Calles 15 and 16. Stuffed birds are everywhere, a bit gloomy. There is a car park and the owners are friendly.

In *Zona 4* the following hotels are just opposite the main bus terminal on 7 Calle, Avenida 4 down a road named 4a Avenida "A" off 7 Calle. *Hotel Venezia*. Q6/double without bath, Q7 with bath — pretty flash. Cheaper places are *Posada Don Cesar*, *Pensión Jalisco*, *Hotel Izalco* and *Hotel Dorial*.

If you want to stay in the centre (Zona 1) after arriving at the above mentioned bus terminal, take bus no. 2, 5 or 6 from *El Triangulo* on 7a Avenida. This is a high-rise landmark containing offices (air-lines and Am-Ex) a few minutes walk from the terminal.

Eats There are a few local cafes, though you have to look quite hard for them, where you can get desayuno (breakfast) for around Q1 and almuerzo (lunch) and cena (dinner) for Q1.25. Standard plates of the day: eg breakfast can be eggs, bread, frijoles and coffee, almuerzo and cena will be chicken or beef, rice, frijoles, a small salad, tortillas and coffee. There are a few Chinese restaurants clustered together on Avenida 6 and 8 around Calle 12, Zona 1. They're pretty cheap, give you decent sized helpings and the food is good. A meal Q1.50-2. Eg *Fu Lu Sho*, 6a Avenida, Calle 12.

Other If arriving at the airport take bus no. 2 or 6 into the centre — goes down Avenida 7 to the Palacio Nacional. Poste Restante well organised. Charge 4½ cents per letter.

Things to Do/See Slide lectures on Maya civilization at Educational Programmes in Archaeology and the Natural Sciences (EPANS) Ltd, 4a Avenida 8-72, Zona 1 are every night except Saturdays. Donation requested Q1 acceptable.

Embassies

Colombia: 5a Avenida, 11-31, Zona 1, tel 86412. Open 8 am-noon, bus Nos 5 or 14.

El Salvador : Calle 3, 6-09, Zona 9. tel 65351/61054. Open 8 am-2 pm, bus No. 5.

Honduras: Calle 12, 6-14, Zona 9, tel 66220. Open 8 am-12.30 pm, bus No. 5.

Mexico: Calle 14, 6-12, Zona 1, Edificio Venezuela, Piso 50. Open 9 am-1 pm and 3 pm-5 pm, bus No. 5. There are Mexican Consulates also in Quetzaltenango (Pensión Bonifaz), Huehuetenango (Farmacia El Cid) and in Malacatán near the border (closed at 1 pm).

HUEHUETENANGO
Accommodation
Casa Viajero, Q1/person.
Hotel Central, block from main plaza.

Q1.25/person with hot water. Meals 75 centavos.

Palacio. Q1-1.50/person.

Posada Española. Q1/person.

Pensión Tikal, by the market. 75 centavos/person.

Information The Tourist Office in the government buildings on the main plaza has good maps. Go to the Mexican Consulate at Farmacia El Cid if you need a Tourist Card.

LIVINGSTONE

Accommodation Two places to stay are *Pension Rio Dulce* and *Pension Honduras*. There are also houses to rent fairly cheaply. Coconut bread, candy and banana bread sold here are excellent.

Things to Do/See This is a laid-back town on the Caribbean coast populated by black people of Jamaican origin who speak English. There are no roads into the town so you must get the ferry from Puerto Barrios or from Punta Gorda (Belize). There are beaches, coconut palms and palm leaf huts. Canoes can be rented for about Q1/day to visit Rio Blanco beach, straight in front of Livingstone or to paddle up the river.

PANAJACHEL

Accommodation A really beautiful place on the shores of Lake Atitlán and popular with travellers and, in season, Guatemalan weekenders. If you want the same beauty and tranquility without the tourists go and stay in one of the villages across the other side of the lake.

Unless you're just going to stay for a day or two (how could you!), the best thing to do is to find a house or part-house to rent. There are plenty available all over town — just ask around and visit a few to get an idea of what's available and the prices. There are some really beautiful places but note that at some times of the year (July-August and November-December) it can be tight. Prices depend on the type of place you want, its location, size, how long you're staying and what they think you'll pay. Can be Q5/week for part-house or one room in a house to Q20/week for whole house with four rooms, shower, toilet, kitchen, lounge, beds and beautiful garden complete with humming birds. Otherwise:

Casa de Viajero. Q2.50/double in cheapest room, otherwise Q2/single.

Hotel Panajachel. Q2/person — travellers' place.

Hotel Maya Kanek, Q2/person in the old wing with hot water, Q3-4 in new wing with private bath.

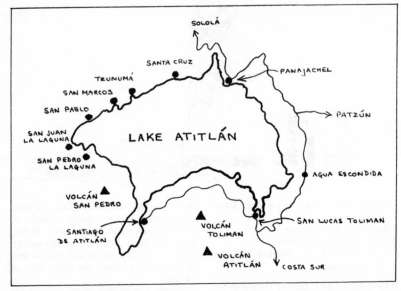

Pensión Buen Semaritano, no sign, next to tienda *La Miniatura*. 75 centavos/person — basic, provide your own bedding, cold water shower, but friendly people.

Hospedaje Posada. Q1/person central.

Eats Plenty of restaurants which serve good food and serve as evening meeting places for travellers.

Hsieh Vegetarian Restaurant, is probably the best deal in town on their good nights, but not always reliable in this respect. There are plenty of travellers and it is a good place to ask around for a house to rent. Cena (dinner) Q1.

La Cabaña Vegetarian and Typical Restaurant, next door to the *Hsieh* is very similar but has better breakfasts — excellent cheeseburgers, pancakes and coffee.

Maya Kanek does excellent food, especially fruit flans and pies (it's often known as the "Pie Shop").

A little more expensive than the other places but depends what you have.

Hamburguesa Restaurant, opposite the "Poco Loco". Excellent, clean little cafe run by a really friendly Indian lady and her family who really try hard to please. Comida, chicken, beef or fish plus salad and two vegetables, coffee, bread and butter, Q1.25.

There is another vegetarian restaurant just off the market (no name as yet) run by a friendly, overworked guy who speaks English. Possible to work there for food and a little money as he usually needs some help. Amazing soups and large, well-cooked, well-seasoned food Q1.25. Large fresh orange juice 30 centavos, lots of other things plus (of course!) muesli and yoghurt.

Mama's, across the river over the log footbridge and then second turning on the right past the football field, same road as the cemetery so take a

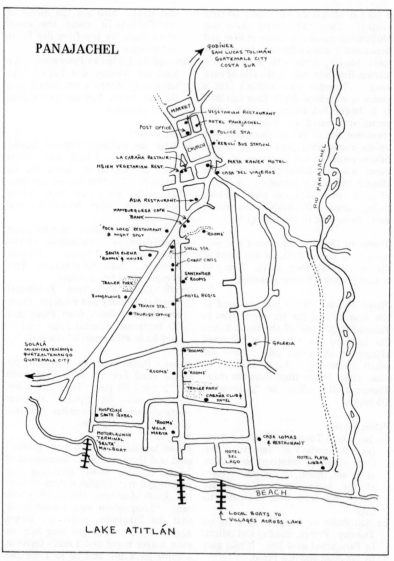

PANAJACHEL

GODÍNEZ
SAN LUCAS TOLIMÁN
GUATEMALA CITY
COSTA SUR

MARKET
VEGETARIAN RESTAURANT
HOTEL PANAJACHEL
POST OFFICE
POLICE STA.
CHURCH
REBULI BUS STATION.
LA CABAÑA RESTAUR.
MAYA KANEK HOTEL
HSIEH VEGETARIAN REST.
CASA DEL VIAJEROS

ASIA RESTAURANT
HAMBURGUESA CAFE
BANK
'POCO LOCO' RESTAURANT
& NIGHT SPOT
'ROOMS'
SHELL STA.
SANTA ELENA
'ROOMS' & HOUSE
CHEAP CAFÉS
SANTANDER
& ROOMS
TRAILER PARK
BUNGALOWS
HOTEL REGIS
TEXACO STA.
TOURIST OFFICE

SOLALÁ
CHICHICASTENANGO
QUETZALTENANGO
GUATEMALA CITY

GALERIA

'ROOMS'
'ROOMS'
'ROOMS'
'ROOMS'
TRAILER PARK
CABAÑA CLUB &
HOTEL
HOSPEDAJE
SANTA ISABEL
'ROOMS'
VILLA MARTA
CASA LOMAS
& RESTAURANT
MOTORLAUNCH
TERMINAL
'SELTA'
MAILBOAT
HOTEL
DEL
LAGO
HOTEL PLAYA
LINDA
RIO PANAJACHEL
BEACH
LOCAL BOATS TO
VILLAGES ACROSS LAKE

LAKE ATITLÁN

torch at night. It takes about 15 minutes from the centre of town. Cena (good spread) soup, choice of meat or fish, rice or chips, guaca-mole salad, tortillas and a desert, coffee extra.

"Night life" at the *Poco Loco*. Buying

a beer is obligatory but that's all (free crisps). They have corny third rate Hollywood movies, a stereo system and occasionally uncoordinated, out-of-tune local boogie bands who attempt disastrous live fade-outs at the end of each song. (Thought you couldn't play a guitar or were tone deaf? Hear this lot!) It is frequented by chess freaks, shirt gurus and bored or recently arrived travellers, but there's precious little else unless you're into yoga. One or two houses (more or less permanently) have gurus who pontificate and ply cider vinegar and honey remedies. A friend of mine came home one night stinking to high heaven after having been rubbed down from head to toe with garlic.

Things to Do/See Swimming and sunbathing in Lake Atitlán is like being at the sea only it's fresh water. Plenty of Indian women sell their weaving.

Places Nearby When you get tired of the tourists and the travellers' tales in Panajachel get one of the boats across the Lake to any number of the small villages on the other side. These are much mellower. Avoid the tourist boat which leaves from near the *Hotel Tzanjuyu* (it's called the "mailboat"). Q5 return.

Public Ferries

To San Lucas Tolimán at 7 am everyday (except Sunday) 50 centavos. Bus from there to Santiago de Atitlan at 9 am, noon, 3 pm and returns at the same times, 25 centavos direct bus from here to Guatemala City.

To San Pedro de Languna at 4 am on Tuesday, Friday, Sunday and returns to Panajachel at 4 pm. It also goes to San Juan and San Pablo.

To San Pedro from Santiago at 1 pm, 35 centavos. San Pedro to Panajachel, leaves early Friday morning (takes the Indians to the market on that day). Also ask the owner of the *Chi-Nim-Ya* about the canoe which does the trip from San Pedro to Santiago, 25 centavos.

Santiago de Atitlán to Panajachel. Mail boat on Tuesday and Friday. Alternatively there's a bus which goes via San Lucas Toliman or Godinas for 50 centavos.

Where to stay

Santiago de Atitlán: *Pensión Rosita*, near church. Q1.25 with sheets they do vegetarian meals for 50 centavos. *Chi-Nim-Ya*, on the lake. Q1 — they serve good food. There are a few other hospedajes and pensions.

San Pedro de Laguna: Several small hospedajes, eg *El Balineareo*, on the waterfront. Q1/room. *Pensión Mendez*. Meals 50 centavos. This is reputedly a brujo village.

Sololá: Eight km from Panajachel (market Tuesday and Friday): There are frequent buses from Panajachel 30 centavos. *Pensión Salas*. Q1 — very basic with meals 50 centavos.

Other Banco Agricola Mercantil, opposite *Poco Loco* is open 9 am-noon and 2 pm-4.30 pm. There are a few advertisements for Spanish language courses and not-too-cheap weaving courses in shop windows.

Police harassment: Two other guides I read said there was police harassment of freaks in this town, including one superb and very English statement from the *South American Handbook* which ran: "Long-haired men should know that the Panajachel police are biased against them". I've got long hair, an even longer beard and I don't travel in a three piece suit and tie so I decided to put this to the test by hanging around outside the police station playing a guitar. They didn't even come and throw five centavos into my hat.

PUERTO BARRIOS
Accommodation

Hotel Tivoli Q1 on the sea front. Q1 — basic. *El Dorado.* Q2.50/person — clean with bath and fans. *Hotel Espanol.* Q2.50-6, depending on what you want.

QUEZALTENANGO

The town is usually known by its Mayan name of *Xela* (pronounced "shela") or *Xelaju.* This is also how the buses are marked.

Accommodation

Pensión Altnese, Calle 9 Avenida 9, on the road out of town to the south. Q1/person — good and clean. Hot water extra 30 centavos.

Hotel Volta, Avenida 14, Calle 4. Q1.50/single. Evening meals with soup and coffee Q1.

Hotel Enrique, opposite *Rutas Limas*, off the main plaza. Q1/bed. Hot water extra 30 centavos.

Hotel Radar, Avenida 14 between Calles 3 and 4 near Parque Central Q1.50 including hot water.

Hotel Victoria, Calle 6, Avenida 14. Q2/person. Meals are served.

Canadá, on the main plaza. Q2.25/single. Somewhat expensive food Q2.

If these are full try *Hotel Exito, Hospedaje Central, El Quijote* (all Q1/single), the *Pensión Andina* (Q1.50), *Casa del Viajero. Casa Suiza* at Q2 has constant hot water, is clean and has good food for Q1.50.

Eats Try the market for cheap meals, otherwise *Capri* Restaurant on main

plaza has meals 75 centavos upwards. *Shanghai* Chinese Restaurant next to *Hotel Canadá*, good meals Q1. Also *Pájaro Azulón* on main plaza has good food Q1.50.

Outlying Indian Villages

San Francisco del Alto has a huge market on Fridays — one of the largest in Guatemala. Bus there leaves from the main plaza. 30 centavos.

Zunil is a beautiful, small Indian village nine km from Xela. You might also want to visit the thermal springs at Fuentes Georginas on the way there (entrance 50 centavos). The local idol is San Martín, a plastic tailor's dummy dressed in suit, shoes and hat and worshipped by local Indians who bring him drinks, cigarettes and other gifts. The statue is kept in a greenhouse on the far side of the river. There are lots of stories circulating about this character.

San Martín de Chile Verde is a small village near the sacred Mayan lake of Chicabal (situated in the crater of volcano and three hours walk from the village). Horses are available for hire — ask around. Ceremonies of brujo initiation held at the lake on May 2. Fiesta and Mayan religious ceremonies also held here around November 11. Accommodation next to *Centro de Salud* for Q1 (ask at the Centro) and a comedor opposite the church does food for 40-50 centavos.

TIKAL

Don't miss it! There's a Q1 entry fee to the National Park which is taken off you at the check-point on the road into Tikal. Keep the ticket as it's your entry ticket to the ruins. Also your passport is checked on entering Tikal village.

Accommodation All the hotels are expensive (as are drinks, too) but you can sling a hammock under a palapa at the camp site free. There's no water for washing, however, so you'll have to slide quickly into one of the hotels for this. In May (ie towards the end of the dry season), there are no mosquitoes so a net and repellant isn't necessary. This isn't the case at other times of the year so be prepared if you're sleeping out. Also, the hotels are often a little cheaper out-of-season.

Jungle Hotel. Q8/person in room with three single beds (no hammock hooks) for four people, or Q9/person for the same for three people. Included in the price is full board (3 meals a day), shared showers and toilets. Mosquito netting is on the windows. It has a large lounge, comfortable chairs and drinks — non-residents don't get hassled. Lights go off at 10 pm when the generator is turned off. You can change travellers' cheques here if you're paying for your stay with the cheque. Q4/person, without meals.

Jaguar Hotel. Q8/double without meals. There's one more smaller hotel. Q3/room with three small double beds.

Eats There are three small comedors in the village; two to the right of the runway and one to the left: *Comedor Florecita, Comedor Camping* and *Comedor Tikal.* They all do cheaper food and beer than the hotels (eg beers in the hotels 75 centavos in the cafes 50 centavos — gaseosas similar).

Other There's a serious lack of change in the village (and money for that matter). Difficult to change travellers' cheques unless you're paying your bill that way but cash US$ are interchangeable with Quetzales.

The Ruins These will take you a minimum of four hours to see. They're about one km from the village and plan to do most of your walking in the morning when it's still cool — it gets hot by mid-day. There are plenty of gaseosas sellers at the site. The guided tours arrive at about 10.30 am.

TRANSPORT
Flights
Guatemala City to Tikal (one hour). Daily at 7.30 am and returns at 3 pm. Q37.

Guatemala City to Flores (one hour). Daily at 11.30 am (except Sundays) and at 9.30 am. Q20. There are also daily flights (except Sundays) from Flores at noon and 7 am.

If you can't get on a flight because it's booked up (see under *Tikal* for hassles) there's *at least* one transport plane a day to Guatemala City (smaller aircraft) despite anything the airport officials tell you to the contrary, *but* you must arrange them from the *Maya International Hotel*. Ask to see Felipe Zotz — he runs the boutique across from the *Maya International*. Don't expect a reclining seat with a view, however.

Flores to Melchor de Mencos and Dos Langunas. Wednesdays at 8.30 am and returns Wednesdays — no fixed time but scheduled to arrive at 11 am so be there by about 9 am.

Flores to Uaxactun and Carmelita. Tuesdays, Thursdays and Saturdays at 8.30 am and returns same days — no fixed time but scheduled to arrive at 11 am so be there by about 9 am.

Flores to Paso Canallos and El Naranjo. Mondays and Fridays at 8.30 am and returns same days — no fixed schedule but due to arrive at 11 am so be there by about 9 am.

Mérida (Mexico) to Guatemala City and vice versa. Daily flights (except Mondays) at 3.50 pm. US$70.

There is a US$5 tax on international flights. Buses Nos. 2 and 6 go from Guatemala City airport to Centre (National Palace, Zona I).

Buses In Guatemala City many of the cheapest local and international buses arrive and depart from the Terminal on Avenida 4a, Calle 7 in Zona 4. City buses to and from this terminal are Nos 2, 5 and 6. They go from the Palacio Nacional and Avenida 7a (Zona 1) to El Triangulo in Zona 4 on Avenida 7a — three streets away parallel to the terminal. El Triangulo is a high-rise landmark — ask the way. There are plenty of other buses, often just as cheap, from various places in Zona 1.

Buses going west are:

Guatemala City-Antigua. *La Preciosa*, 15 Calle, 3-37, Zona 1. Monday to Friday every hour in both directions, first bus 7 am and last bus 8 pm. On Saturdays and Sundays every half hour in both directions. 45 centavos. *La Franciscana*, 18 Calle, 5-20, Zona 1 has the same schedule and prices.

Guatemala City-Sololá and Panajachel. *Transportes Rebulli*, 20 Calle, 3-42, Zona 1. Daily, every hour, first bus 6 am and last bus 5.50 pm and departs Panajachel on a similar schedule, first bus 4.45 am and last class bus from Panajachel daily at 11 am. Q2 and takes three and a half hours. *Transportes Higueros*, 17 Calle 6-25, Zona 1. Everyday at 4 am and 4 pm. Departs Panajachel daily at 5-5.30 pm. Q1.50. *Rutus Lima*, 8 Calle, 3-63, Zona 1. Daily at 7.45 am Calle, 3-63 Zona 1. Daily at 7.45 am. Departs Panajachel Mondays Tuesdays, Wednesdays and Fridays at 8 am and Thursdays and Sundays at 8 am, 3 pm. Q2.50.

Guatemala City-Santiago de Atitlán. *Transportes Rebulli*. Daily at 5 am, 8.30 am, 1.30 pm, 4.30 pm and departs Santiago at 3 am, 6 am, noon, 3 pm. Q1.50.

Guatemala City to Chichacastenango *Rutus Lima*. Daily at 7.45 am and departs Chichicastenango Mondays, Tuesdays, Wednesdays, Fridays and Saturdays at 8 am and Thursdays and Saturdays at 3 pm. Q2.50.

Guatemala City-Momostenango. *Veloz Momosteca*. Terminal in Zona 4. Daily every hour 5 am to 6 pm.

Guatemala City- Huehuetenango and La Mesilla (Mexican border) *Rutus Lima*. Daily at 8 pm and from La Mesilla at 11 am. Q3.75. *Transportes Condor*, 19 Calle, 2-01, Zona 1. Daily at 7.50 am, 9.50 am, 4.50 pm and departs La Mesilla at 6 am, 11 am. Q2.50 (Guatemala-Huehuetenango) Q1.50 (Huehuetenango-La Mesilla), Q3.50 (Guatemala-La Mesilla).

Guatemala City-Quetzaltenango (Xela). *Rutus Lima*. Daily at 7.45 am, 2.30 pm, 4.30 pm, 8 pm and departs Quetzaltenango at 5.30 am, 7.30 am, 2.30 pm, 8.30 pm. Q2.50. *Transportes Galgos*, Avenida 7a, 19-44, Zona 1. Daily at 5.30 am, 8.30 am, 2.30 pm, 5 pm, 9 pm and departs Quetzaltenango at 5 am, 8.30 am, 10.30 am, 3 pm, 5 pm. Q2.50. *Transportes Higueros*. Daily in both directions at 4 am and 4 pm. Q2.

Guatemala City-San Marcos. *Rutas Lima*. Daily at 7.30 am and 4.30 pm and departs San Marcos at 4 am and 6 pm. Q2.50.

Guatemala City-Mexico City. *Rutas Lima*. Daily at 8 pm. Q20. Takes 36 hours including a stop of four hours in Quetzaltenango. You can also catch this bus at the border at 1 pm everyday and go either to San Cristóbal de las Casas or to Mexico City. From here it takes 24 hours.

Buses going east are:

Guatemala City-Zacapa, Chiquimula and Esquipulas. *Rutas Orientalis*, 19 Calle, 8-18, Zona 1. Daily in both directions about every half hour from 5.30 am to 6.30 pm. *Transportes Sactíc*, Avenida 9, 18-38, Zona 1. Daily at 2 pm, 3 pm, 4 pm.

Guatemala City-Mixco Viejo. From Terminal in Zona 4. Take bus to San Juan Sacatepequez, then taxi to Mixco.

Guatemala City-Cobán. *La Cobanerita*, 9 Calle, 11-46, Zona 1. Departs daily at 7 am, 8 am, 11 am, 2 pm, 3.15 pm, 5 pm, 6 pm and departs Coban at 3 am, 4 am, 9 am, 1 pm, 5 pm, 6.30 pm and 8 pm. Q2.50.

Guatemala City-Copán (Honduras). It's probably easier to get to the Mayan ruins in Honduras from Guatemala City than it is from Tegucigalpa (capital of Honduras). Remember to have your visa arranged if you need one. There are no facilities for this at the border. *Transportes Guerra*, 19 Calle, 8-57, Zona 1. Bus to Chiquimula at 7.30 am then transfer to *Transportes Vasquez* and get to Copan at about 2 pm. Returning, there's a bus from Copán at 5 am then transfer at Chiquimula at 9.30 am. A second bus leaves Copán at 10 am, transfer in Chiquimula at 1.30 pm. Q1.50/single journey on both buses.

Guatemala City-Quirigua. *Transportes Union Pacifico* and *Las Patojas*, Avenida 9, 18-38, Zona 1. Daily every hour from 6 am to 7.30 pm. Q2. It takes four hours.

Guatemala City-Puerto Barrios. *Litegua*, Avenida 8, 15042, Zona 1. Daily in both directions at 7.30 am, 4 pm. Q3.50. It takes five hours. *Transportes Union Pacifico*. Daily in both directions at 5 am, 6 am, 7 am, 8 am, 9.30 am, 10.30 am, 11,30 am. Q3. It takes 6 hours.

Guatemala City-San Salvador (El Salvador). *Transportes Melva*, Terminal in Zona 4. Daily at 6.30 am, 8 am, noon, 2.30 pm and departs San Salvador at 5.45 am, 8 am, noon,

2.30 pm. Q2. It takes five and a half hours. There's no need to book — pay on the bus but beware of overcharging. We were quoted variously Q10, 5 and 3 before getting on. Even on the bus they tried Q2.50 but the locals erupted and it was reduced. The office will tell you the correct price. Bus arrives at the Terminal de Occident in San Salvador. Bus stops at Santa Ana (first major town in El Salvador) if you just want to go as far as there. There is a Guatemalan Exit Tax of Q1.50 at the border. *TICA-bus*, 14 Calle, Avenida 4 Zona 1. Daily to San Salvador (Q5), Tegucigalpa (Q10), Managua (Q17), San Jose (Q23) and Panama (Q35.50).

Buses going south are:
Guatemala City-Puerto San José and Iztapa. *Transportes Sactic*. Daily at 2 pm, 3 pm, 4 pm, 5.30 pm and departs Iztapa at 5 am, 6 am, 8 am, 9.30 am. Q1.
Buses going north are:
Guatemala City-Flores. *Fuente del Norte*. Daily at 2 am, 3 am, 4 am, 5 am, 7.30 am and departs Flores at 2 am, 3 am, 4 am, 8 am, 10.30 am. Q6. It takes at least 18 hours over what's left of a bone-shattering dirt-track until you hit the Guatemala City-Puerto Barrios Road. The company do the Flores-Melchor de Mencos route. Depart at 4 pm daily arriving 7 pm and departs Melchor at 4 am arriving at 7 am.

If you're coming from Belize and planning on going first to Tikal before Flores see *Belize* section for transport details, as it will probably involve getting a taxi with several others unless you want to wait many hours in Melchor.

Railways Other than the Guatemala City to Puerto Barrios train we can't recommend the railways as they're incredibly slow (the one to San Salvador takes two days!!).

Guatemala-Puerto Barrios. One train daily in both directions. Departs Guatemala City at 7.15 am. It takes 11 hours. Q5.90. The Railway Station is on Avenida 7a, Calle 18, Zona 1. No meals are served on the train but refreshments are available.

Boats and Ferries Probably the only boats which will interest you apart from possible river trips (for which you'll generally need a party of people to make them economical) are the following:

Puerto Barrios-Livingstone. Ferry everyday at 10 am, 6 pm and returns at 5 am, 2 pm. 50 centavos.
Livingstone-Lake Izabal, via Rio Dulce. Mailboat on Mondays and Fridays. If you want to explore the lake this is cheaper than renting a boat which will cost you about Q30.
Livingstone-Punta Gorda (Belize). Every two to three days. Q5. The name of the boat is *Mirtha*. There's also a motorized dorey (canoe) which plies this route. Leaves Livingstone Fridays and returns Wednesdays.
Livingstone-Belize City. The *Suyapa* plies this route but is very irregular enquire if interested but it's relatively expensive at Q20 and is described as "crowded with poor food".

Other trips To Sayaxché, south-west of Flores on the Rio de la Pasion (Mayan ruins, an agricultural colonization project and jungle river trips). You'll need plenty of time. Bus from Flores to Sayaxche and from here you can take a four to six day river trip to the vicinity of Coban further south. The trip involves frequent changes of boat and lots of bargaining and waiting. There are no "departure times" as such, people go when there's cargo or enough passengers. If these conditions apply you might do the trip for around Q5.

OTHER INFORMATION
Guatemalan Tourist Bureaux have good information including a map of the country indicating all the Mayan ruin sites. Address in Guatemala City is Avenida 6, 5-34, Zona 1.

American Express: Clark Tours, Edificio El Triángulo, Calle Mariscal Cruz and Avenida 7, Zona 4, Guatemala City.

PRINCIPAL MARKETS

Place	Speciality
Sundays	
Chichicastenango	
Huehuetenango	blankets
Momostenango	
Nahualá	
Panajachel	woven fabrics
Patzún	silk & wool; embroidered napkins, woven fabrics, striped red cotton cloth
San Lucas Tolimán	woven fabrics
Zunil	
Palin	textiles
San Martín Jilotepeque	weaving and huipiles
Quiché	palm hats
San Cristobal	textiles
San Juan Ostuncalco	sashes
Cantel	textiles
Sumpango	huipiles
Mondays	
Antigua	silverware
Comalapa	Indian costumes

Tuesdays	
San Pedro Carchá	pottery, textiles, wooden masks, silverware, woven fabrics
Sololá	woven fabrics
Patzún	
San Lucas Tolimán	
Sumpango	
Wednesdays	
Momostenango	
Patzicía	
Comalapa	
Sumpango	
Thursdays	
Chichicastenango	
Antigua	
Patzún	
Santa Cruz del Quiché	
Totonicapán	
Huehuetenango	
Sumpango	
San Martin Jilotepeque	
Fridays	
Sololá	
San Lucas Tolimán	
Santiago de Atitlán	
San Francisco el Alto	woolen blankets, woven & embroidered fabrics
Sumpango	
Comalapa	
Saturdays	
Patzicía	
Santo Tomás Chiche	
Sumpango	
Antigua	

Belize

A lush, richly forested, largely low-lying country of rivers and mangrove swamps with some sandy beaches, mountains rising in the west and south, cool evening sea breezes and a cosmopolitan population with a language (English), culture and temperament markedly different from its Latin neighbours.

From 15 to 60 km off-shore stretches an almost continuous chain of reefs and cays (small islands formed by the growth of coral) — the longest coral reef outside of Australia. They are very popular with travellers and campers. Most of the islands are very small and uninhabited though the larger ones support fishermen and skin-divers and some have been "developed" as tourist resorts. Many have beautiful beaches, the water is clear and swimming and snorkelling are recommended.

Over half the population of approximately 140,000, most of whom live in the towns, are Creoles — descendants of black slaves who were brought across from Jamaica during the 17th and 18th centuries. About 17 percent pure or almost pure Indian, mostly Mayas, the remainder being Kekchi (a sub-tribe of the Maya) and immigrant Waika Indians who are engaged in the lumber trade. Approximately 10 percent are indigenous Black Caribs who speak a distinct language of their own and are found mostly in the towns and villages of the southern coast. Various assorted European immigrants, the majority being German-speaking Mennonite farmers, and North Americans make up a further 10 percent. The remainder originate from the Middle East, China and neighbouring Spanish-speaking republics (many of the latter being political refugees). English is the majority language with Spanish speakers making up about 15 percent. Many people are bilingual and some trilingual.

The eastern part of the country, where the mountains rise to over 1000 metres, formed part of the lands occupied by the Old Maya civilization from the 4th to 9th centuries AD and there are a number of ruined temples and ceremonial sites which can be visited, some of which have been excavated. these include Altun Ha, 50 km north of Belize City; Xunantunich, near Benque Viejo, and Labantun in the far south. More details of this civilization are given under *Guatemala*.

The first non-American settlers were a motley collection of English ex-buccaneers, bankrupt planters and adventurers who came across from Jamaica with their black slaves in the 1640s to cut logwood, then a source of textile dyes. From time to time they would be driven out by Spanish forces but each time they returned. The threat of eviction by the Spaniards was finally removed in 1798 when a strong Spanish naval force was decisively beaten off St George's Cay. Even after this engagement Britain still made no claim to the territory, though in the past it had tried to protect the interests of the wood cutters by treaties with Spain, so that when Mexico and Guatemala declared their independence in 1821 they both laid claim to Belize on the grounds of being successors to Spain. The settlers, however, thought otherwise, maintaining that the territory had become British by conquest following the naval engagement off St George's Cay.

Years of protest and argument followed until Guatemala, spurred by fears of United States aggression, signed a convention with Britain whereby the boundaries of Belize were recognized in return for a contribution by Britain towards the cost of a road from Guatemala City to the sea near what was to become Belize City. Encouraged by this Britain declared the settlement a Colony in 1862 and a Crown Colony nine years later. Mexico renounced its claims to Belize by treaty in 1893, probably because it had enough trouble containing the various insurrections in Chiapas and the Yucatan Peninsula. Guatemala, however, renews its claims from time to time particularly when the government in power needs an external issue to divert attention from its internal problems. The most recent confrontation was in 1975 when abortive talks were held and diplomatic relations with Britain broken off.

The colony was granted internal self-government in 1964 and has been offered full independence any time it wants it. Because Belize is dependent on Britain for defence this is difficult to bring about, though it has received support from other Commonwealth countries, particularly in the Caribbean, and the United Nations. In a more recent attempt to settle the dispute Britain entered into semi-secret discussions with the Guatemalan Government, over the heads of the elected representatives in Belize, in which concessions were offered which would have involved re-drawing the borders of Belize and a considerable loss of territory. When details leaked out there was all hell to pay and the Belizean press was full of it for weeks — and still is. None but a small minority have any interest in becoming part of a repressive military dictatorship and a country in which most would effectively become second-class citizens, let alone the differences in culture and way of life. Ask anyone you meet. So it looks like the dispute will fester on for some time yet and units of the British Army will continue to enjoy a somewhat cushy overseas posting defending the borders of Belize, until cast-iron guarantees are forthcoming for the Belizeans' independence. If they're not, and the Army is with-

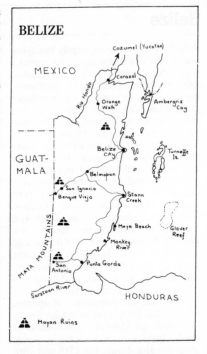

drawn, then the graffiti on the wall of the jail in Belize City may yet come true. It reads: "Because the Guats say so."

Although it's more expensive than neighbouring countries, you'll love Belize. It's one of the friendliest, most laid-back places you'll come across.

VISAS

They are not required by anyone. Ease of entry varies from time to time. Sometimes it's tight, othertimes easy. If you're getting the *Batty Bus* from Chetumal there's unlikely to be much hassle (strength in number?). We went through with a bus load of scruffy, sweating, bearded, long-haired yobos of assorted nationality, all with backpacks and no one had any trouble. They may ask how much money you have but rarely ask for proof (random check). Funds have, in the past, been the deciding factor as to whether they let you in or not, so it's perhaps a good idea to have enough — some have been asked for US$300 per person. The length of stay varies depending on what you ask for. Most people initially get six days but this is renewable in Belize City at Immigration or at any police station.

Consulates of USA, Guatemala, Mexico, Honduras, El Salvador and Nicaragua are in Belize City and there's also a Guatemalan Consulate in Benque Viejo near the border.

CURRENCY

US$1 = 2 Belizean Dollars

The unit of currency is the Belizean Dollar (B$) = 100 cents. The currency is tied to the US dollar. You may sometimes hear prices expressed in pre-decimal English terms, eg shilling (25c), and in American terms, eg nickel, dime and quarter.

Belizean money is virtually un-exchangeable outside the country except in Chetumal (Mexico).

OTHER INFORMATION

The Tourist Office next to the Court House, Regent Street, Belize, is of little use. They have a free booklet, *This Month in Belize* which is useful for addresses and other related stuff, plus a low-grade city map and country map. Many places sell good city maps for B$1 (eg *Mom's Restaurant*).

BELIZE CITY
Accommodation

Most travellers stay on Eve Street near the waterfront. There are several places:

Posada Tropicana, 55 Eve Street.

B$8-10/double (plus B$2 key deposit, returnable), a waterbed for the decadent costs a little extra — shared showers/toilets. In the common room you'll meet plenty of other travellers and there are maps, information board and cold drinks, automatic washer and drier (who needs the latter in Belize!!) for B$2 and B$1.50 respectively. Breakfast, lunch and dinner are available — midnight lock up. It's great if you like crowds.

Clark's Guest House, 64 Eve Street, opposite Tropicana. B$5/person. Ask for the rooms fronting onto the street with balconies. Shared shower and toilet, 11 pm lock up but you can get in after and drinks are available but no meals — really nice people. Tranquilo.

Mrs Haylock's Boarding House, 57 Eve Street. B$4/single — very friendly.

Freddie's, also on Eve Street though we couldn't find it. Reported to be $3/single.

Hotel Minerva, situated just by the swing bridge opposite *Mom's* Cafe. B$4/single. A noisy location especially during the day but interesting as it faces onto the market and Haulover Creek. Meals are available.

Visitors' Home, North Front Street. B$2/single.

Posada Mexicana, Freetown Road, B$2/single.

Belcove, 9 Regent Street. B$8/single, B$12/double.

Others include: *Anita's Boarding House* 28 North Front Street; *Sunshine Hotel*, North Front Street; *Crossroads Hotel*, corner of Mapp Street and Freetown Road.

There's also a Youth Hostel marked on the official city map on Racoon Street between Curassow Street and Dolphin Street but we have no details. Also a YWCA down Freetown Road but

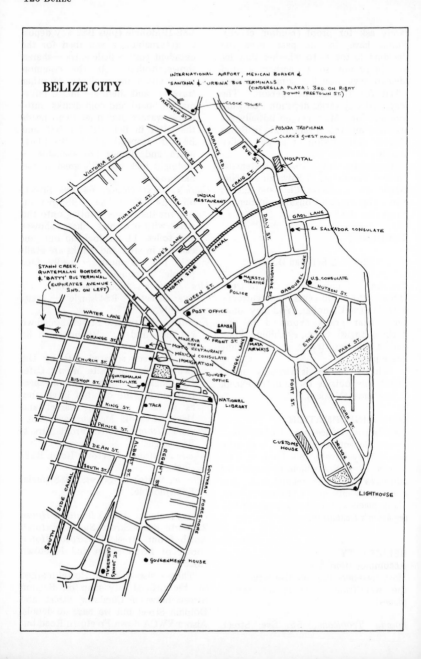

it's a long way from the centre. You can sleep on the beach free, seven km north of the city on Barracks Road. Take the first turning on the right — there's only one.

If you're coming into Belize City on the *Batty Bus* from Chetumal, the terminal is on Euphrates Avenue which is a quarter hour walk from Eve Street but it's *HOT* and very *HUMID*. If you're carrying 100 lb packs see a psychiatrist or take a taxi.

Eats

Mom's Restaurant, opposite the swing bridge. This is a travellers' hangout with English, American and local food, eg hamburgers, bacon, eggs, seafood, beer and the cheapest soft drinks of any restaurant in town. Open 6 am-10.30 pm. Roast beef, mash, salad, bread and gravy B$5, cheeseburger and chips B$2.60 and sandwiches B$1.50. There is a free notice board and huge city map: boats, buses, places for sale and sometimes rides to the Cays.

Maharaja Indian Restaurant, 69 Hyde's Lane. Kofta (meat balls and sauce for the uninitiated) B$3.50, vegetarian curry B$2.50, paratas B$1 each. They also have tandoori chicken, good yoghurt and seafood. The rice is free.

Golden Dragon Hotel and Restaurant, Majestic Theatre Yard. (Have air-conditioned rooms for B$10/single) Chinese food.

Jane's Restaurant, 64 Barracks Road. Chinese, American and local food.

China Inn, 74 Euphrates Avenue. Chinese food.

There are plenty of good local corner bars where you can drink beers and rap to local people. Try the *Democratic Bar* down Queen Street — reggae, dart board, bar billiards; friendly.

Local larger beers are Belikin and Charger 70 cents, soft drinks 30 cents, but there are often beer shortages — the brewery can't keep up. Guinness and Schlitz are also available but more expensive. English and American cigarettes B$1.25, but there are cheaper local varieties.

The *Continental Hotel* on the north side of town is where many travellers and British Army soldiers go for a drink and to hear live music. Sundays and Thursdays are busy with the army looking for girls (it's a pick-up joint). The army doctor is reputedly looking after their health but that doesn't mean you won't get a dose.

CORAZOL

Accommodation *Hotel Capri*, 4-4th Avenue, B$4 per person. *Caribbean Motel* has individual cabins. Or there's *Tony's Motel & Trailer Park*.

ORANGE WALK TOWN

Accommodation *La Favorita*, Lover's Lane, B$4.50/single. *Nueva Mi Amor*, 19 Northern Highway. *La Nueva Ola*, 73 Benque Otro.

Places Nearby There's a large Old Mayan ceremonial site in the area with enormous masonry slabs used in a stairway up to one of the pyramids.

SAN IGNACIO

Accommodation *Central Hotel*, B$4/single. *Golden Orange Hotel* B$24 (!!) including meals. Or *San Ignacio Hotel*.

Close by is the British Army's "Holdfast" camp (20 km from the border). There's a strong possibility the soldiers will put you up for the night — they like to see new faces. There's not much else for them to do except drink, rap and polish their boots. The road to the border passes right past the camp.

BENQUE VIEJO

Accommodation *Roxi*, B$2/double. *Frontier*, also B$2/double. *Border Hotel*, Church Street.

Eats There are meals at the *Riverside Restaurant* on the main square or in one of the huts.

Other There is a Guatemalan Consulate if you need a visa.

STANN CREEK
Accommodation *Riverside* at B$5/double. The *Hotel Catalina* is also cheap. Ask around for rooms in private houses. Unfurnished houses are rented out for B$30/month.

Eats The *Riverside* is said to be the best restaurant.

Places Nearby The small, quiet resort of Placencia can be reached by truck to Mango Creek (B$2) and then boat from there (B$4). There's a hotel there for B$5/double or you can sleep on the beach for free. Hotels include *Rum Point Inn*, *Sea Spray Hotel*, etc.

PUNTA GORDA
Accommodation *Foster's Hotel*, 19 Main Street; *Hotel Isabel*, Front Street; *Mira Mar Hotel*, 95 Front Street.

CAYO
Accommodation *Central Hotel*, 24 Burns Avenue.

CAY CAULKER
Accommodation Camping is possible at *Tony Vega's* — he rents out camping gear too. *Mrs Rivas* rents rooms for B$3 and does meals for B$1.50. Her husband will take you snorkelling if you're interested. *Frank Bazzell* also rents rooms. It's also possible to find houses to rent.

AMBERGRIS CAY
Accommodation Hotels are expensive — bed and shower for B$6/night and eat well for B$1.50 — but camping is possible.

Other There are a few British soldiers to get drunk with (rum for about B$4 a bottle). The reef is about 1½ km out. The local town, very small, is called San Pedro.

TRANSPORT
Hitching is okay and recommended.

Flights The International Airport is 15 km from the centre of Belize so hitch or get a taxi (B$7). The Municipal Airport is a short walk from the centre near the racecourse — for local flights.

The two local airlines are *Maya Corporation* and *Aero-Belize*. The former fly to 26 local runways. There's also *Chemicals Ltd* who arrange charters from Belize to outlying districts.

To Ambergris Cay: Daily by *Aero-Belize*, 8 am and 4.30 pm. B$20. Daily by *Maya Corp*, three flights/day. B$12.

International flights served by Belize Airways, TAN, SAHSA, TACA and Aeromexico. The Belize Airways office is at 34 Queen Street, Belize City.

To San Pedro Sula (Honduras). Tuesday, Thursday, Friday and Sunday at 3.30 pm (half an hour).

To San Salvador (El Salvador). Monday, Wednesday, Friday and Saturday at 3.30 pm (50 minutes).

Buses

Belize-Corazol, *Batty Bus*, daily at 10 am from Euphrates Avenue (four hours), B$3.

To Chetumal (Mexico) on Mondays, Wednesdays and Fridays, same time and same place (five hours), B$4. From Chetumal to Belize City on Tuesdays, Thursdays and Saturdays at 10 am. Cost is M$60.

Belize City-Orange Walk, *Santana* Bus Service. Daily at noon and 2 pm from Cinderalla Plaza. B$2, it takes three hours. *Urbina* Daily Bus Service, daily at 11 am, 1 pm and 2.30 pm from Cinderalla Plaza with the same price and journey time.

Belize-Belmopan-San Ignacio to Benque Viejo *Belizean Queen* Bus Service, Tuesdays to Fridays inclusive at 1 pm, 2 pm and 3 pm, Mondays and Saturdays at 1 pm, 2 pm, 2.30 pm, 3 pm and 3.30 pm. Sundays at 1 pm and 2 pm. It departs from Pound Yard Bridge. To Belmopan, B$1.25, two hours, 83 km. To San Ignacio, B$1.75, three and a half hours, 120 km. To Benque Viejo, B$2, four hours, 133 km. *Batty Bus* Service only goes to San Ignacio, Mondays to Fridays inclusive at 10 am, Saturdays and Sundays at 8 am and 10 am. It departs from Euphrates Avenue.

San Ignacio-Guatemalan Border Taxis

from here to the border will take six people at B$1.50 each. The border is easy-going either way (rumour has it that there's a US$3 fee for crossing the border at weekends and at any other time than between 8 am-noon and 2 pm-5 pm on weekdays, free otherwise). If you intend to catch a bus from the border to either Tikal or Flores you may well have to spend the night in Melchor de Mencos. There are daily buses to Flores at 6 am and 1 pm, B$3, taking three and a half hours. There's also a flight from Melchor to Flores on Wednesdays only in the morning with no fixed departure time, but you should be there by 9 am.

If you're going straight to Tikal from the border the bus leaves Melchor at 3.30 am arriving at about 10 am, which means that if you take the 10 am bus from Belize City to the border you've got a 13 hour wait. The alternative, unless your sanity is in question or you have a maiden aunt in Melchor, is to get a bunch of people together and hire a taxi. They cost US$30-35 per car to

either Tikal or Flores, will take six people plus luggage and take three hours. This is three times the price of the bus admittedly (US$1.50) but over that "road" at 3.30 in the morning.....

Belize-Dangriga (Stann Creek)-Punta Gorda by *Z Line* Bus Service, daily at 2 pm and 3 pm. *Southern Transport* Bus Service, Tuesdays and Fridays at 7 am. Both buses depart from the Pound Yard Bridge. To Dangriga, B$3.50, taking four hours, 175 km. To Punta Gorda, B$8, taking 10 hours, 350 km.

Boats to the Cays Look on the notice boards at *Mom's Restaurant* and the *Posada Tropicana*. Often cheaper trips go out — but they're irregular. Some ecologists work there — ask around in the same places.

To Cay Caulker & Cay Chapel, *MV Mermaid*, departs Belize Customs Wharf, Friday at 3 pm and Mondays at 2 pm; departs Cay Caulker, Fridays at 7 am and Sundays at 4 pm, B$8. Tickets from *Dee Jays*, 2 Queen Street, the *Posada Tropicana* and *Bel Air*, 87 North Front Street.

To Ambergris Cay, departs Belize and Amerbrgris Cay several times a week at 7.30 am, taking two hours, B$12. The ship is called the *Elsa P.* (see also the *Flight* section).

Connections between the Cays are irregular. It's often easier to go via Belize. The exception is between Ambergris, Caulker and Chapel Cays.

To Honduras

Once weekly cement boat goes to Puerto Cortes. US$10. Check at the docks for departure times. If you need a visa make sure you have it before getting the boat (Consulate in Belize City). The name of the boat is *Mirtha*. Another irregular boat doing this journey is the

Suyaps. It costs US$20 and the food is described as "poor" and the boat "crowded".

To Guatemala

Boat to Livingstone from Punta Gorda goes every two to three days. US$5. Also a motorised dorey (canoe) goes from Punta Gorda to Livingstone on Wednesdays, returning Fridays, US$5. There is a ferry from Livingstone to Puerto Barrios (twice daily for 50 centavos) from where you can get the train or the bus to Guatemala City.

PLACES TO SEE

Don't miss the Cays if you have time.

Mayan ruins Altun Ha, 50 km north of Belize City, is largely unexcavated but the head of a sun god make of jade and weighing three kg was found here in 1969 (largest piece of Mayan jade ever found). It's now sitting in the vaults of the Royal Bank of Canada in Belize City. (Maybe it underwrites the economy?)

The ruins of Xunantunich about seven km from Benque Viejo contain a spectacular main temple with a carved astronomical frieze. To get there walk for 10 minutes along the road to El Cayo from Benque Viejo, take the ferry across the river and on the far side turn right. If you take food you can stay in a palm hut at the ruins. The ruins are situated near the Pine Ridge Reserve (sightseeing, bird-watching and caves and one of the world's highest waterfalls — Hidden Valley — 550 metres).

For the ruins at Labantun, see below.

Indian Villages Try San Antonio and San Pedro Columbia on the extreme south of the country. The former is a mostly Mayan village with some Kekchi speakers and Mayan ruins. The latter is a Kekchi village. Both are very colourful and interesting and there are many religious festivals, the best one being on San Luis Rey Day (August 5). There are no buses there — contact a Mr Wagner for hire of pick-up in Stann Creek, or walk. The villages are in the foothills of the Maya Mountains.

The ruins of Labantun, excavated in 1970 but being overgrown fast, are situated two km after turning left just over the new bridge at San Pedro Columbia. There is local food at a hut and swimming in the river nearby.

OTHER INFORMATION

Weed (of variable quality) will cost you about B$40/ounce. Ordinary people have a very tolerant attitude to weed, after all, it's part of their culture. All the same — be discreet. You'll probably be offered "coke" on a few occasions. Unless things have changed quite radically remember that quinine crystals are a poor substitute for the real thing.

There's a rumour that the Government will sell you land at about US$2/hectare if you're willing to develop it. This also entitles you to residency.

20-30 year old fishing boats can be bought for around US$1000 made of solid mahognay.

El Salvador

One of the first things you'll notice coming into El Salvador is how intensively farmed the land is and how many more people there seem to be. Villages crop up every km or so along the road. In fact, El Salvador, although the smallest of the Central American republics, is the second most densely populated country in the Americas, Haiti being the first. Three quarters of the land is under cultivation, 80% of this being devoted to coffee, making El Salvador the world's third largest coffee producer after Brazil and Colombia. But it wasn't always like this.

Initially the Spanish ignored El Salvador for it contained neither mineral wealth nor regions of intensive agriculture. The early Spanish colonists mingled with the Indians and as late as the mid-19th century, after the various attempts at federation with the other Central American republics had failed, there were only a few hundred thousand people living there. Then, in the late 19th century, coffee was planted. The climate and soil, composed mainly of a deep layer of porous volcanic ash and lava, proved ideal for the crop and since there were good routes to take it to the coast, coffee growing expanded rapidly. Money poured into the country and the population increased by leaps and bounds until, by 1966, it stood at three million. Cotton is also grown and the country has the largest industrial base in Central America.

The wealth which these developments brought was not and is not evenly distributed of course. The usual oligarchy, here made up of a dozen or so ruling families, control all the coffee and the banking in the country and rule it through one military dictator after another. The result is low wages, high unemployment and the emigration of several hundred thousand Salvadoreños to the States and neighbouring republics, particularly to Honduras. The latter reacted badly to this influx and it was the main cause of the "Football War" fought between El Salvador and Honduras in 1969 (so called because it started as a riot at a football match between the two countries and quickly developed into a fully-fledged military conflict). Since that date there has been little trade or direct contact between the two and until recently their mutual land border was closed. It's now open again, but Salvadoreños going to Honduras need a visa and vice versa.

The wealth has, however, created Central America's best road system (nearly all roads are paved), good port facilities and a very modern and well-serviced capital, though out in the rural areas services leave much to be desired. Education is theoretically compulsory and free, but illiteracy remains at 50%.

Before the arrival of the Spanish the country was inhabited by the Pipil Indians who called their country "Cuscatlan" (Land of Precious Things) and had founded a civilization dating back to the 11th century. These people were farmers, potters, carpenters, masons, weavers and builders who had developed a system of hieroglyphics which have not yet been deciphered. The ruins of their temples and ceremonial centres are scattered throughout country and include the archeological sites of Cihuatan, Tehuacan and Quelepa. Pyramids of a pre-Mayan civilization have been discovered at San Andres and Tazumal which are 1400 years old. The descendants of the Pipil — the Panchos Indians — live in Panchimalco not far from San Salvador. Only 10% of the present day population are pure Indian, leaving a remainder of 80% mestizo and 10% of unmixed white ancestry.

El Salvador was one of the first countries to declare its independence from Spain when, in 1811, José Matías Delgado, a Creole priest and juror born in San Salvador, organised a revolt in conjunction with another priest, Manuel José Arce, and removed the Spanish officials from office. The Audienca in Guatemala suppressed the revolt and took Delgado prisoner back to Guatemala where he continued to agitate. Independence finally came in 1821 following Iturbide's example in Mexico. Along with the other Central American republics, El Salvador originally joined the Mexican Empire of Iturbide but this soon collapsed and was followed by various attempts at federation between the five Central American countries. The mutual hostility between Conservatives and Liberals, however, prevented anything coming of this and indeed at one time when federation was being discussed between representatives of the five countries in San Salvador, war broke out between San Salvador and Guatemala!

El Salvador has many volcanoes, one of which, Izalco, is still active and can be seen far out into the Pacific, though of late it seems to have become dormant. In addition, it has some beautiful beaches — some of black volcanic sand — and a number of lakes where you can find swimming, surfing and boating.

VISAS

Not required by anyone but the length of stay given at the border seems to vary according to some, as yet undeciphered, code of hieroglyphics. On our bus British were given five days, Australians 10 days and for a French couple, the man got five days while the woman 15! They're extendable anywhere in San Salvador.

The alternative is to get a Tourist Card entitling you to a stay of 90 days but there's apparently a charge of US$2 for this. There's an entry & exit fee of 1 Colón but they frequently forget about the former. Borders are easy going — no hassles, body or baggage searches.

Money changers can be found at all borders (usually at the official rate). Your bus driver will also, no doubt, make you an offer you cannot refuse. Pass over the ones who want 50c commission for changing small notes (anything below US$20). Tourist information (maps, etc) is available at borders but sometimes requires a little persistence.

There's a Nicaraguan Consulate at La Unión if you need a visa. Open everyday including Sundays.

CURRENCY

US$1 = 2.50 Colónes*

The unit of currency is the Colón = 100 centavos. Most banks take a small commission for changing travellers' cheques. One that doesn't is the Banco Comercio. *(Actually it's fractionally more than this but you won't get the fraction as it is less than one cent.)

PLACES TO VISIT

Izalco Volcano (over 1800 metres) It used to be very active, the smoke and flames could be seen far out to sea, but it's become quiescent again of late. To get there take a bus (1½ hours) or train (four hours) to Sonsonate then take local transport or hitch to Cerro Verde which has fine views down into the crater. There's a camping ground at nearly 2000 metres which overlooks the crater.

Also in Sonsonate there's the swimming pool of Atecozol situated in a beautiful park containing old mahogony trees, palms and balsam trees. From the latter the Indians extract a medicinal herb which used to be exported all over the world.

If you're visiting this area from June

17th to 25th or August 8th to 15th or on Christmas Eve, go to the Indian village of Asunción Izalco where amazing ceremonies are performed. A mixture of Christian and pagan rituals. The village is eight km from Sonsonate.

Lake Coatepeque Near to Santa Ana and close to the volcano of the same name. It's a favourite weekend resort for Salvadoreños — sailing, fishing and swimming. Local buses from Santa Ana. The surroundings are really beautiful. It's possible to stay free in the cabins (mattresses and showers) at Balneario Los Obreros — a workers' resort camp. Ideally you're supposed to get permission first from Sra Avelar, Departamento de Bienestar, Ministerio de Trabajo, 2a Avenida Norte, San Salvador. If you missed this try at the office at the Balneario when you get there. Otherwise there are hotels, like the *Lido*, US$4 or the *Casa Blanca*.

Lake Llopango Another lake resort near to the airport in San Salvador, situated in the crater of an extinct volcano. Again a popular resort for Salvadoreños with beautiful scenery. Bus No 15 (marked "Apulo") departs from Avenida Cuscatlán for the lake via the airport, costs 14c, takes 70 minutes. At the lake you can stay at the "Turicentro" camp site for 18c including showers and swimming facilities. The level of the lake has risen and fallen on occasion in the last 100 years due to geological disturbances.

Volcan San Salvador Reached from Santa Tecla, 13 km from the capital. Take bus (every 10 minutes) from 3a Avenida Norte near the junction with Calle Rubén Dario to Santa Tecla, costs 6c and from there a bus to Boquerón, costing 30c. From there it's a km and a half walk to the summit of the crater which is over a km wide and a km deep. The inner slopes are forested and at the bottom is a small cone left by an eruption earlier in the century. You can walk around the crater but it's rough going

and you should allow yourself four hours.

Puerta del Diablo & Los Planes de Renderos A short excursion from the capital for magnificent views. Take transport along Avenida Cuscutlán up to the new residential district, bus No 12 or 17. The area is crossed by Balboa Park and from there a road runs to the summit of Mount Chulul from where there are amazing views through the Puerta del Diablo — two enormous vertical rocks which frame the view.

SAN SALVADOR

Accommodation Many hotels are in the centre of town near the TICA Bus Terminal which is on Calle 1 Oriente, 531. If you come in on anything other than this bus the chances are you'll be put down at the Terminal de Occidente on Boulevard Roosevelt, some way from the centre. There are plenty of local buses from here to the centre.

Casa de Huéspedes Moderne, Avenida 8a Sur, No 125, 2.50 colónes — basic.

Hotel Bruno, Calle 1 Oriente, between Avenidas 8a and 10a. 5 colónes per person without private bath, 7.50 with bath — the communal bathroom is reasonably clean, hot water all day. Annexe is cheaper at 3.75 colónes per person — popular with travellers.

Hotel Custodio, 10a Avenida Sur, No 109. 6 colónes/single with bath — noisy.

Hotel San Carlos, 5 colones/single, 7.50 colónes/double.

There's also accommodation above the TICA bus offices in Apartado 166 for 4 colónes a night including hot showers. The above hotels are all near the TICA bus terminal.

Pensión Rosita, Calle Concepción, 4 Colónes a double, serves cheap meals.

Colonial Boarding House, next to Ramirez bus station, 6a Avenida Sur. 4.50 colónes, clean and quiet.

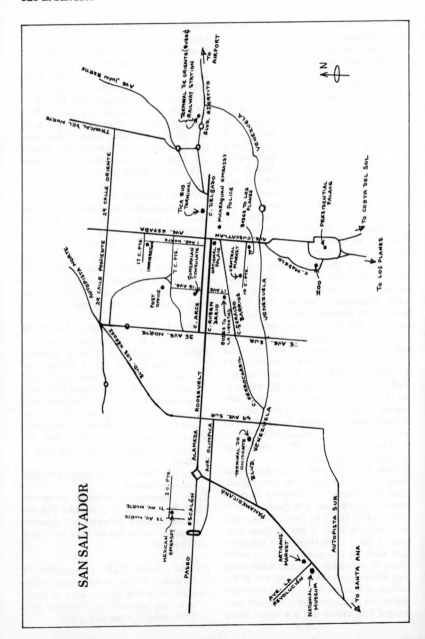

SAN SALVADOR

SAN SALVADOR.

KEY TO NUMBERING & NAMING OF AVENUES & STREETS.

Quadrant: Norte Poniente — Odd Streets — Odd Avenues	9a Av. Norte	7a	5a	3a	1a Av. Norte	AVENIDA ESPAÑA	2a Av. Norte	4a	6a	8a	Quadrant: Norte Oriente — Odd Streets (Calles) — Even Avenues (Avenidas)
9a Calle Poniente											9a Calle Oriente
7a " "											7a " "
5a " "											5a " "
3a " "											3a " "
1a Calle Poniente											1a Calle Oriente
CALLE ARCE											CALLE DELGADO
2a Calle Poniente											2a Calle Oriente
4a " "											4a " "
6a " "											6a " "
8a " "											8a " "
Quadrant: Sur Poniente — Even Streets — Odd Avenues	9a Av. Sur	7a	5a	3a	1a Av. Sur	AVENIDA CUSCATLÁN	2a Av. Sur	4a	6a	8a	Quadrant: Sur Oriente — Even Streets — Even Avenues

Internacional, 8a Avenida Sur, No 108, rooms without bath for 5 colónes.

Panamericano, opposite the Internacional, rooms for 5 colónes and meals for 2.50 colónes.

Hotel Aguilla, Paseo Independencia, opposite cinema. Rooms without windows for 3 colónes; with windows for 5 colónes.

Other hotels around 3a Avenida Norte and 3a Calle Poniente. They include the *Hospedaje Sonsonate* (4 colónes), *Hotel Roosevelt* (5 colones), *Hotel Lita* (2.50 colones), *Hospedaje Yucatán* (4 colones, very clean and an excellent restaurant downstairs). All prices are for singles.

If you're thinking of staying for a long time try *Josephines's*, 90-110 colónes per month; located through the green gates down the street opposite the park on Calle Rubén Dario, facing the IBM building.

If camping there's a site with swimming pool and picnic area for 1 colone per night at Los Chorros near Santa Tecla, just outside the city on the main road west.

For those tired of living or travelling there's the *American Guest House*, 17 Avenida Norte, 25 colónes/single; 45 colónes/double including bath.

Eats Central Market near Palacio Nacional has cheap food stalls. *Pension Rosita* comedor has been recommended above. On the corner of 3 Calle and Delgado, *King Kat* has meals and fruit juices for 1 colóne (gran-grande) or 75c (grande). *Comedor Izalco*, corner of 6a Avenida Norte and 7a Calle Oriente, has good cheap meals.

Things to do/see Excellent place to see movies — plenty of cheap cinemas with frequent programme changes. Mariachi musicians (free) play every night between 10 pm and 2 pm on 2a Avenida Norte and 3 Calle Oriente.

Information   Tourist Office is at Instituto Salvadoreño de Turismo, Calle Rubén Dario, No 619. They have a free map of the city but Texaco do a better one. Very helpful people.

Immigration Department is at 25 Avenida Norte, No 11-57. American Express reps are El Salvador Travel Service, Centre Commercial, La Mascota a Santa Tecla. Tel 23-0177.

Bus to the airport (13 km) No 29, costs 10c. A taxi costs about 5 colónes.

LA LIBERTAD

Accommodation   Hotels are very expensive here. Stay at the hotel attached to *La Mariscos Restaurant* — which has good seafood. Accommodation costs 2.50 colónes each in rooms which sleep two or three.

The resort is a surfers' Mecca.

LA UNIÓN

Accommodation   The unmarked hospedaje opposite the barracks (see map) costs 6 Colónes for three people, three beds — no fan (the place is HOT), share showers and toilet.   Interesting local fauna which includes rats, roaches the size of dinner plates and crabs which scratch their way up and down the drainpipes all night, but they only trouble your imagination.   A military band strikes up at 6 am and the washerwoman at 6.30 am so there's no chance of missing the ferry.   Other than that there's just the smell of dried fish, the owner who'll change travellers' cheques for a whacking commission and bored soldiers on night duty who'll bum cigarettes off you.   But everybody is very friendly.

Hospedaje Milagro, 3 Colónes/double, by the railway tracks.
Centroamérica, 3 colónes each with no extras, 6 colónes with fan or 10 colones with air-con.

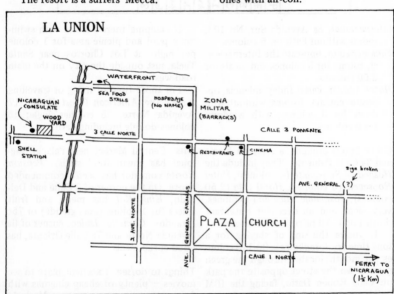

LA UNION

WATERFRONT

SEA FOOD STALLS

NICARAGUAN CONSULATE

WOOD YARD

SHELL STATION

HOSPEDAJE (NO NAME)

ZONA MILITAR (BARRACKS)

3 CALLE NORTE

CALLE 3 PONIENTE

RESTAURANTS

CINEMA

sign broken

AVE. GENERAL (?)

2. AVE. NORTE

AVE. GENERAL CABAÑAS

PLAZA

CHURCH

AVE.

CALLE 1 NORTE

FERRY TO NICARAGUA (1½ Km)

Hotel Miramar, costs 5 colónes/double and is "good".

Hospedaje Santa Marta, basic and friendly but my informant was suffering from amnesia as to other details.

Hotel San Carlos, opposite the railway station, 5 colónes/double. Good meals available.

Eats There are two very good cafes in the centre near the plaza — see the map. The one nearest the cinema often has mariachis strolling through.

Other If you need a visa for Nicaragua

there's a consulate here. Open all week including Sundays although there's an extra charge of 3 Colones on Sundays because they're officially not open, even though they are. The consul is an easy going guy and his wife speaks fluent English, nice people.

SANTA ANA
Accommodation

Pensión Monterrey, 5 colónes/double, near the bus station.

Pensión Lux, near the Monterrey.

Roosevelt, 6 colónes/single, 12.50 colónes/double. Serves good meals

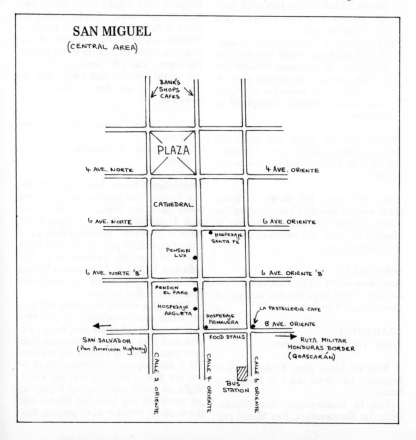

SAN MIGUEL
(CENTRAL AREA)

BANKS
SHOPS
CAFES

PLAZA

4 AVE. NORTE   4 AVE. ORIENTE

CATHEDRAL

6 AVE. NORTE   6 AVE. ORIENTE

HOSPEDAJE
SANTA FE

PENSION
LUX

6 AVE. NORTE 'B'   6 AVE. ORIENTE 'B'

PENSION
EL FARO

HOSPEDAJE   LA PASTELLERIA CAFE
ARGUETA   HOSPEDAJE
            PRIMAVERA   8 AVE. ORIENTE

SAN SALVADOR   RUTA MILITAR
(Pan American Highway)   FOOD STALLS   HONDURAS BORDER
                                       (GOASCARÁN)

CALLE 2 ORIENTE   CALLE 4 ORIENTE   CALLE 6 ORIENTE

BUS
STATION

for 2.50 colónes.

Florida, 10 colónes/room with bath. Good meals for around 5 colónes.

SAN MIGUEL
Accommodation

Hospedaje Argueta, 6 Colónes/three people — three single beds and hammock. The manager goes to a lot of trouble to make you welcome. Provides clean sheets and blankets. It's arranged around a quiet courtyard. Communal showers and toilets — clean.

Hospedaje Santa Fe, 1 Colón/three people. Rooms have two single beds and hammock — cold showers (and it's a whorehouse).

Pension Lux, 4 Colónes/three people. Rooms have one single bed and one hammock. If you want another bed it costs extra. Communal showers and toilet, built around a courtyard with trees. Strange atmosphere to the place.

There's also the clean and quiet *San Luis*, 3 colónes; the *Central*, 4 colones; the *Pensión El Faro* and the *Hospedaje Primavera*.

Eats Few cafes but plenty of street stalls where I wouldn't have touched the pieces of meat they had for a holiday in Majorca for two. All expenses paid. It was really filthy.

SONSONATE
Accommodation The *Hospedaje Taplan*, one block from the bus station, or the *Oriental*, 8 colónes.

TRANSPORT
Trains There are three lines:

West to Santa Ana, Sonsonate and Acajutla. One train per day, takes four hours.

East to Cojutepeque, San Vicente, Usulután, Zacatecoluca, San Miguel and La Unión. Daily from San Salvador to La Unión at 6.45 am, costs 4 Colónes and takes eight hours. Compares well with the bus.

West to Santa Ana (via Valle de Limoa), Ahuachapán, Guatemala and Puerto Barrios. Takes two days, spend a night in Zacapa. Passenger accommodation is primitive and you'll probably give it a miss even though the scenery is beautiful.

Local Buses Plenty to everywhere from the Terminal de Occidente on Boulevard Venezuela throughout the day — for example to San Miguel every thirty minutes to one hour. To La Unión five times a day. Buses are often small but friendly and good fun. They're "direct" but stop often to pick up and put down passengers, can get crowded. If you're out in the country and want a bus just flag the next one down. They'll stop anywhere.

To San Miguel: 4 Colónes, takes four hours.
To La Unión: 4 Colónes, takes nine hours.

International Buses Many buses do the run to and from Guatemala City several times daily (eg Transportes Melva: depart Guatemala City 6.30 am, 8 am, noon & 2.40 pm. Return at 5.45 am, 8 am, noon & 2.30 pm. Costs Q2 (US$2). They run from the terminal on 4a Avenida and 7 Calle in Guatemala City and Terminal de Occidente on Boulevard Roosevelt in San Salvador.

TICA Bus also do this route but they are much more expensive. If you have long hair, a beard or are carrying a rucksack and plan to go to Honduras from here you might be advised to take the TICA Bus however, otherwise the chances are that you'll be refused entry. Might be worth checking out if you can get the TICA bus from San Miguel near the border. Prices — to Guatemala City or Tegucigalpa US$5; Managua US$12; San José US$18; Panama US$30.50.

Note that TICA Bus have their own terminal in the centre: Calle 1 Oriente No 531.

To Honduras (taking local buses)

First go to San Miguel then catch a local bus to the border at Goascarán via Santa Rosa de Lima. Several buses and several companies do the run from San Miguel. Ask for Ruta 330 at the bus terminal. You can also get buses to anywhere from San Miguel on Avenida 8a Norte but they arrive packed and leave even fuller — best to get them from the terminal where they're initially empty. Last bus for the border leaves at 5.30 pm. Bus takes you right to the border, costs 1.25 Colónes (Santa Rosa), 1.75 Colones (Goascarán village), 2 Colones (Goascarán Bridge — the border). Takes about one to 1½ hours.

If refused entry, bypass Honduras by taking the ferry across the Gulf of Fonseca from La Unión to Nicaragua. Take the bus back along the road as far as the Shell station (a few km) and wait there for the bus to La Unión, costs 50 centavos. From the Shell station to La Unión costs 1 Colón, takes two hours.

To Nicaragua direct via Gulf of Fonseca

The daily ferry from La Unión to Potosí departs at 11 am but although it is frequently late you must be there by 10 am for customs and ticket formalities. The walk to the ferry pier takes about 20 minutes. The Migration Office is on the pier — not in town. The exit stamp and the Aduana (customs) stamp each cost 1 Colón. When you've paid these you buy your ticket which costs 7.20 Colónes. Your passport is taken from you and you get it back at the Nicaraguan customs on arrival at the other end. The ferry takes about five hours. Gaseosas and food are available on board.

Dolphins often lead the boat across the Gulf performing acrobatics.

Money changers hang around the pier but wait till you get to Nicaragua as they take commission whereas Nicaraguan customs and restaurants, etc, take cash dollars at the official rate of exchange (7 Córdobas = US$1).

By the time the ferry gets in the last bus will have already left for Chinandega so you're faced with either staying in Potosi where there's nothing except one food shack and one skuzzy hospedaje and plenty of mosquitoes or getting one of the many taxis which wait for the ferry — they're all collectivos. Charge 13 Córdobas each way to Chinandega, a beautiful 1½-1¾ hour drive. The bus would cost 10 Córdobas anyway. These taxis arrive in Chinandega in time to connect with the evening buses going to León and Managua if you don't want to stay in Chinandega. Bus to León costs 4 Córdobas and takes an hour.

If you're a glutton for punishment here's the bus schedule so you can stay in Potosi the night:

Transportes Ramon

depart		arrive	
Potosí	7.30	Chinandega	9.30
Chinandega	10.30	Potosí	12.30
Potosí	13.30	Chinandega	15.30
Chinandega	16.30	Potosí	18.30

See Nicaraguan section for customs details.

Odds & Sods There is a 10% tax on all airline tickets bought in or out of El Salvador for flights originating in the country.

Try the local food speciality "pupusa" — tortillas filled with cheese or pork rind. "Suprema" lager beer is probably the best. It's usually served free with hors d'oeuvres.

Honduras

A mountainous country of banana and coffee plantations, fields of cotton and sugar, rich mineral resources and extensive forest regions covering just under half of the total land area from which a good deal of the world's supply of fine wood, notably mahogany, is obtained. Although the second largest of the five Central American republics, it has a population of only two and a half million, most of whom live in the western part of the country. Only a small proportion (about one percent) of pure blooded Indians remain, concentrated in the area west of Santa Rosa de Copán to the Guatemalan border and along the area west of Santa Rosa de Copán to the Guatemalan border and along the Misquito coast — east of Trujillo to the Nicaraguan frontier. A large, black, English-speaking element predominates along the Caribbean coast and in the Bay Islands. Most of the population are Mestizos (about 90 percent). According to the Constitution, most of which is suspended under the military government, primary education is compulsory, but as there are so few schools over 60 percent remain illiterate. Honduras is one of the world's poorest and over-exploited countries in which the majority of peasants (over 65 percent) live a hand-to-mouth existence on small plots of land or as agricultural labourers on the large plantations. The military government is as corrupt as those found elsewhere in Latin America.

Like Guatemala and Belize, Honduras formed part of the lands occupied by the Mayas and the ruins of one of their major cultural centres can be seen at Copán in the extreme west of the country, near the Guatemalan border. The ruins were discovered by Stephens and Catherwood in 1839 when they were covered in jungle, but they were restored by the Carnegie Institute in the 1930s. Spread over many hectares and built on two levels, one of them on a cliff overlooking the river, they include courts, temples, the Hieroglyphic Stairway, ballcourts and stelae. The stone carving is magnificent and includes some of the best Mayan art to be seen anywhere outside of the British Museum and the Carnegie Institute (oh yes, they got their hands on this stuff as well).

Columbus first landed on the mainland here in 1502 and gave the country its present name — a name suggested by the deep waters to be found off the north coast (the Spanish word *honduras* means "depths"). Following the conquest of Mexico by Cortés, attempts at conquest and settlement were made but the Spaniards quarrelled among themselves and the settlements were in constant rivalry. In addition, they found little gold or silver to attract them. The Indians were not subdued until the late 1530s when the Indian chief Lempira who, with 30,000 of his followers, fought the Spanish until he was treacherously assassinated at a peace parley. Comayagua was founded in 1537 as the provincial capital and remained so until 1880 when it was transferred to Tegucigalpa. It provided a home for the first university in Central America in 1632 and is still an unspoiled colonial town of cobbled streets and white-washed one-storied houses.

Later on in the 16th century silver was discovered in the hills around Tegucigalpa and the growing economic importance of Honduras attracted French, British and Dutch buccaneers who frequently attacked the northern coast during the 16th and 17th centuries from their bases on the Bay Islands. These islands eventually passed into British hands and remained so for over a century along with the Misquito Coast, over which they declared a protectorate following an appeal by the Misquito Indians, who inhabited the area, for protection against the Spanish forces. The "Kingdom of Misquito" stretched east along the coast of Honduras and down the coast of Nicaragua to the border with Costa Rica on the Rio San Juan. During this time settlements of English and black people from other Caribbean islands were established at various points and are still very much in evidence today, particularly in the Bay Islands, Bluefields, the Corn Islands and San Juan del Norte (formerly Greytown) whose inhabitants are predominantly black, English-speaking and Protestant. The Kings of the Misquito Coast were crowned in the Protestant Cathedral in Bluefields. In 1859, however, Britain signed a treaty with Honduras relinquishing control of the Bay Islands and the Honduran section of the Misquito Coast, but the Nicaraguan section of the Miquito Kingdom continued until 1889.

On September 15, 1821, Honduras joined the other four Central American provinces comprising the Captaincy-General of Guatemala in declaring independence from Spain. All were annexed to the Mexican Empire of Agustín Iturbide in 1822-23. Upon the downfall of the Empire in 1823, Honduras joined the federation known as the United Provinces of Central America, whose first President was José Arce. Seven years later Francisco Morazán (the Honduran national hero) became the President. A liberal, Morazán introduced many social and economic reforms, but there was great rivalry between the Conservatives and Liberals and the Federation was soon to disintegrate, Honduras declaring its independence in 1838. Since then political control has been held successively by Liberals and Conservatives (the latter generally meaning a military dictatorship) for varying periods of time.

The last Liberal Government was voted into power following free elections in 1957 but following the all-too familiar pattern of politics in this part of the world, it was ousted by a military junta in 1963. The head of the junta became President in 1965 (General López Arellano). He was replaced by a civilian President in 1971 who lasted just under two years until he was ousted by Arellano. He resumed the Presidency until a major scandal broke out in 1975 involving him and the US company, United Brands. Arellano was accused of receiving US$1¼ million in bribes in exchange for substantial tax "allowances". But, of course, these people rarely ever come to trial and he's now living in comfortable exile in Miami.

The country's system of land ownership is still almost as feudal as when the Spanish left it. 0.3 percent of the population own 27.4 percent of the cultivatable land (remember that the eastern half of the country is virtually unpopulated, covered with thick forest and, in parts, unexplored) and the rest struggle on without two coins to rub together. There have been spontaneous peasant uprisings and there is guerrilla activity, particularly in the Juticalpa region, but the military usually side with the landowners, although in an unprecedented move 32,000 hectares of Standard Fruit, United Brands and several large landowners land was expropriated in 1975 and distributed to the peasants. Still it's not that much in a country where over one million earn less than US$30 per year.

VISAS

Required by all except nationals of Western Europe (excluding Eire, Austria and Portugal), Chile, Colombia, Costa Rica and Japan. They cost US$3 and are issued on the spot at Honduran Consulates. There is no money showing or requirement for onward tickets.

If you have long hair, a beard or are carrying a rucksack, you could well be refused entry at the Goascarán crossing from El Salvador. You can avoid these hassles by taking the through *TICA Bus* from San Salvador to Tegucigalpa. If you cross the border from El Salvador on Saturdays or Sundays there's a US$1 fee.

Tourist Cards are issued on entry, valid for a stay of 90 days. If you're likely to want to stay longer you must register within 48 hours of arrival at the Ministry of Foreign Affairs (Passport section) in Tegucigalpa and apply for an extension. A Certificate of Good Conduct will be required either from the Identification Department or from the Directorate of Public Security.

CURRENCY

US$1 = 2 Lempira

The unit of currency is the Lempira (Lem) = 100 centavos. Note the fractional names five centavos = cinquinto, 10 centavos = bufalo, 20 centavos = daime, 50 centavos = toston. Cash dollars can be used without difficulty and there's no restriction on import or export.

If crossing at Goascarán, there are plenty of money-changers on the Salvador side but they charge 50 cents commission for small bills (anything under US$20). Bank opening times are Monday to Saturday 8.30 am-noon and 2 pm-4.30 pm. On the northern coast they open half an hour later and close half an hour earlier and Saturday hours are 8 am-11 am.

TEGUCIGALPA
Accommodation
Hotel McArthur, 7a Avenida, between 5a and 6a Calles, No. 515. Lem 8-10/single, Lem 14/double. All rooms have private bath — friendly management.

Hotel Granada, 6a Avenida, No. 1330. Lem 5-7/single. It is run by the Peace Corps.

Hotel Las Américas, 6a Avenida, 5a Calle. Lem 6/single, Lem 8/double.

Boarding House Americano, opposite Presidential Palace. Lem 7/single with bath and food. Lem 5/single without bath.

Hospedaje América, 6a Avenida, No. 515. Lem 3/double — basic.

The ones above are in Tegucigalpa itself, the ones below in Comayaguela.

Hotel Bristol, 5a Calle, between Aveni-

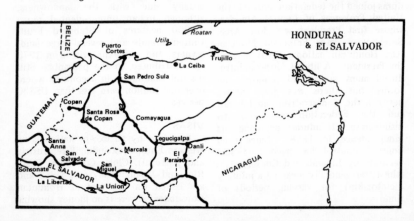

HONDURAS & EL SALVADOR

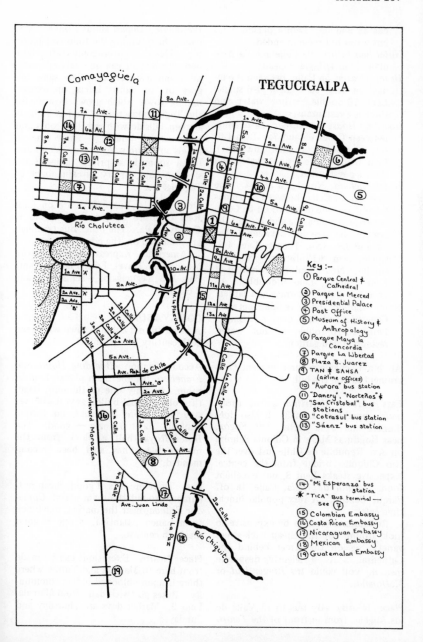

TEGUCIGALPA

Comayagüela

Río Choluteca

Boulevard Morazán

Río Chiquito

Key :-
① Parque Central & Cathedral
② Parque La Merced
③ Presidential Palace
④ Post Office
⑤ Museum of History & Anthropology
⑥ Parque Maya la Concordia
⑦ Parque La Libertad
⑧ Plaza B. Juarez
⑨ TAN & SAHSA (airline offices)
⑩ "Aurora" bus station
⑪ "Danery", "Norteños" & "San Cristobal" bus stations
⑫ "Cotrasul" bus station
⑬ "Sáenz" bus station

⑭ "Mi Esperanza" bus station
✳ "TICA" Bus terminal — see ⑦
⑮ Colombian Embassy
⑯ Costa Rican Embassy
⑰ Nicaraguan Embassy
⑱ Mexican Embassy
⑲ Guatemalan Embassy

das 4a and 5a. Lem 4/person — no hot water but recommended.

Hotel San Pedro, 9a Calle and 6a Avenida. Lem 4/single — clean.

Hotel Alcazar, 5a Calle, between Avenidas 4a and 5a. Lem 4-6/single, Lem 16/double — hot water and there is a restaurant.

Boarding House Hondureño, 2a Avenida between Calles 6a and 7a. Lem 4-8/ single (depends on what you want), Lem 6-10/double — hot water and there's a restaurant.

Hotel Richard, Nos 1,2,3 and 4. The first on 4a Calle, between Avenidas 6a and 7a; the next two on 5a Calle, between Avenidas 6a and 7a, and the last on 5a Avenida between Calles 5a and 6a. No. 1 costs Lem 4-6/ single, Lem 8-12/double. No. 2 is similar. Nos 3 and 4 are cheaper at Lem 3/single, Lem 6/double. All have hot water, a terrace and garden.

Hotel Jupiter, 6a Avenida, between Calles 5a and 6a. Lem 7-10/single, Lem 10-16/double — hot water, restaurant and garden.

All hotels charge a three percent Government tax on the bill.

Eats *Hotel McArthur* serves three-course breakfasts Lem 3. It also does dinners and a la carte. *El Fogon*, near Honduras Maya in Colonia Palmira on Ave Republic de Chile just over the Rio Chiquito bridge from the centre. Expensive steaks Lem 8, but excellent food. *Jardin de Italia*, Calle 4a off Parque Central. A very popular lunchtime cafe.

Restaurants tend to be expensive so look around for the cheap back-street variety, eg on the street behind the Cathedral. As a slightly desperate measure you could try *Burger Hut* or *McDonalds*.

Places Nearby By bus to El Valle de los Angeles from in front of the *Teatro Presidente*. Depart about 1 pm and stay overnight returning the following morning. There's a government craft school here where you can buy carvings, ceramics and leatherwork. The same bus goes on to Santo Lucia, an ex-gold mining town which grows flowers for the Tegucigalpa market and is built on a steep hillside with red-tiled roofs and whitewashed houses. There are no hotels so if you want to stay ask around for a room in a private house (take sleeping bag), or try hitching back to Tegucigalpa.

Other *TICA* Bus offices are on Calle Real opposite Parque La Libertad in Comayagüela. The other bus terminals are indicated on the city plan.

American Express representatives: Mundirama Travel, Edif. Fiallos, Planta Baja 123, Tegucigalpa. Tel 2 6979 and 2 6111.

COMAYAGUA

A beautiful old colonial town which the 20th century has left intact.

Accommodation *Boarding House San Francisco*, off the main plaza. Lem 5/ room. Possibly one of the most beautiful old colonial buildings you will ever stay in. *Hotel Libertad*, on Parque Central. Lem 3/single — good. The *Hotel Royal* half a block from the market plaza has also been recommended.

Eats There are lots of good, cheap restaurants around the main plaza. *Comedor Erlinda*, near the market, one block from Banco Atlantida, is one — good meals 75 centavos.

Places Nearby Excursions can be made from here to Marcala and Tutule where there is a pure-blooded Indian community. Buses go twice daily from Marcala. Lem 2. Market days are Thursday and Sunday.

COPÁN
Accommodation *Hotel Maya* Lem 6-8 in most rooms but it does have some cheaper ones for Lem 3. If you want meals the charge is Lem 2/day. *Hospedaje Hernandez*, at the entrance to town. Lem 2-3/single — recommended. Food is available. *Hotel Marina.* Lem 3-10/single, Lem 6-16/double. Meals are available for Lem 3.

Things to Do/See The Mayan ruins are set in beautiful mountain jungle beside the airstrip and the Río Copán, a pleasant one km walk east from the village. Entrance to ruins Lem 2.

LA CEIBA
An expensive, uninteresting place where you may have to stay on route to the Bay Islands.

Accommodation *Los Angeles*, Avenida La República No. 54. Lem 8-12/single. Lem 10-14/double. A restaurant is attached. *Royal Hotel.* Lem 7.50/single. *Casino*, 10a Calle, Avenida San Isidro. Lem 6/single, Lem 10-12/double — restaurant and hot water. The *San Carlos* has also been recommended.

SAN PEDRO SULA
A large industrial town where you might stay on the way to Copán.

Accommodation
Hotel Colombia Annexe. Lem 3/single. It is clean and friendly and the gringo senora there will help you with any information you might want.
Hotel Paris, 2a Avenida and 3a Calle. Lem 6/double with bath.
Hotel San Juan, 5a Avenida and 6a
Hotel San Juan, 5a Avenida and 6a Calle No. 33. Lem 6/single, Lem 10/double.
Hotel Nueva España, 3a Avenida 3a Calle SO. Lem 4/single or Lem 8/double.

Eats The *Napoli* is on the main plaza. *Hotel Roosevelt* does meals. Lem 2. The *El Mesón Español* does reasonable comida corrida.

SANTA ROSA DE COPAN
Accommodation *Hotel Maya*, Barrio El Carmen. Lem 4/single, Lem 8/double — hot water and cafe. *Hotel Eric.* Lem 6/single, Lem 12/double — basic.

TRUJILLO
Has an excellent beach and warm, friendly, relaxed Moreno people.

Accommodation *Central Hotel* (not recommended for single women) and the *Imperial* are the only, and poor, hotels in town. Lem 4/single. Ask around for a room in a private house.

Eats *Copa Pando* in Cristal, the Moreno part of town, does good large meals. Lem 2. *La Fonda* and *Dolly's* do good shrimps.

DANLÍ
Accommodation *Hotel Regis.* Lem 3/single.

Eats Good meals can be got at the *Central Boarding House.*

THE BAY ISLANDS
As mentioned in the introduction these three islands, Utila, Roatán and Guanaja, were once the haunt of British, French and Dutch buccaneers, including the infamous Henry Morgan. They were British possessions for over a century until 1859 when they were given to Honduras but English is still spoken and the black Caribbean way of life still predominates. · Roatán is the most expensive and developed of the islands, popular with rich weekend Hondurenos. Utila is the cheapest. Guanaja is not recommended because of its vicious sand fleas.

Accommodation On Utila and Roatán you can sleep on the beaches — in fact, on Roatán you'll have little choice in the matter, except at Coxen's Hole since hotel prices are outrageous.

Utila *Pensión Las Palmas.*
Roatán (Coxen's Hole) *Hotel Coral Lem* 4/single. It is run by the Mayor, clean and meals are served downstairs for Lem 3. Otherwise ask around for a room or hut. Not too difficult to come up with something cheap.
Sandy Bay The best beach on the island but the only accommodation is the *Hotel Los Paradisio* — a snip at Lem 70/double including meals.

TRANSPORT
Flights
Tegucigalpa-San Pedro Sula. Twice daily in both directions by *Sahsa*. Lem 25.
Tegucigalpa-Puerto Lempira. Lem 47.
San Pedro Sula-Roatán. Lem 32.
La Ceiba-Roatán. By *Sahsa*, daily. Lem 20.

There are daily services between San Pedro Sula and La Ceiba. Flights to Copán are irregular. Enquire if interested. The national airlines are *SAHSA*, *Aereos Servicios* and *LANSA*. There is a five percent sales tax on all international tickets purchased in Honduras and 2.5 percent sales tax on internal flight tickets. The airport tax is Lem 5.

Toncontin Airport in Tegucigalpa is six and a half km from the centre. A minibus to town costs 10 centavos and takes 20 minutes. La Mesa Airport in San Pedro Sula is 18 km from the centre. A bus costs 30 centavos or a taxi Lem 8.

Trains Most of the railways in Honduras runs between Puerto Cortés and San Pedro Sula and is probably the only one you might use daily service, taking four hours.

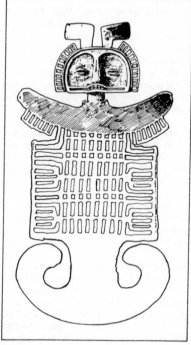

Buses
Tegucigalpa-San Pedro Sula. Plenty of mini-buses from the Comayagüela market all day. Take the four hour trip on a good paved road. Recommended bus lines are *Hedman y Alas* Lem 8 and *Empressa El Rey* Lem 6.
San Pedro Sula-Puerto Cortés. Leave every 20 minutes taking one and a half hours along a good paved road. 60 centavos. Recommended bus lines *Cital* and *Impala*.
Tegucigalpa-Copán. First go to San Pedro Sula, then take a bus from there to La Entrada. Lem 3. (*Copanecos*, *Impala* or *Torito* bus lines). From La Entrada, bus to Copán for Lem 3 — rough road, journey takes two hours. There are some direct buses from San Pedro

Sula but they're a little more expensive.

If you're thinking of going into Guatemala from Copán make sure you have your visa beforehand if you need one. There are no facilities on the border or at Copán. The Honduran Immigration Office is in Copán and you must get an exit stamp from the police checkpoint just outside of town before going on to the border.

The road from Tegucigalpa to Ocotal in Nicaragua via Danlí and El Paraíso is now paved and completed if you want to try a different way into Nicaragua. Buses ply along this road but no details are available as yet. Connecting buses for Managua are in Ocotal.

TICA Bus. Offices at Calle Real opposite Parque La Libertad in Comayaguela. Daily buses to Guatemala City, Lem 10; San Salvador, Lem 10; Managua, Lem 20; San Jose, Lem 30 and Panama, Lem 55.

Boats (to the Bay Islands)

To Utila A launch every Tuesday from La Ceiba, takes about five hours and costs Lem 10.

To Roatán Ferry from La Ceiba to Roatán (main town), Oak Ridge and French Harbour every day except Sunday. Lem 10. Returns from Oak Ridge at 6 am, calling at French Harbour (6.30 am), Roatán (7 am) and at Utila (9.30 am) next day. Roatán is known locally as Coxen's Hole. There are also irregular boats from Puerto Cortés to Roatán. Lem 10 plus 50 centavos dock tax for foreigners (ie backsheesh). The Suyapa also sails between Guanaja Island, La Ceiba and Puerto Cortés — enquire for times. This is the same Suyapa that does the Belize City, Punta Gorda and Puerto Barrios run. (See Belize or Guatemala section). Another boat, the Miss Sheila also plies this route. There are no paved roads on Roatan so you must either walk or take expensive Land-Rovers or jeeps.

Nicaragua

A hot, fertile, tropical country of sparsely populated rain forests, volcanoes, some of which are still active, earthquakes and the two largest lakes in Central America — Lakes Managua and Nicaragua. The latter was, until recent geological times, part of the sea but became isolated along with its fauna as a result of earth movements and volcanic activity so that over the course of centuries it became a fresh-water lake. Many of the different species of fish which were trapped when this occurred adjusted to the gradual change in salinity and today the lake boasts the only freshwater sharks in the world. Earthquakes are an ever-present threat in this country, the most recent and probably most devastating being the one that occurred in December 1972 when the capital, Managua, was almost completely destroyed — not the first time this has happened. It is now being rebuilt in the form of three satellite cities away from the old centre.

The bulk of the population, nearly half of which is urban, lives in the narrow strip of land between the Pacific Ocean and the two lakes, though with the introduction of coffee — the plant, not the drink — it has spread north along the Pan American Highway to the Matagalpa and Jinotega areas. The northern rain forests between the lakes, the Caribbean and the Honduran border have been "neglected" (as the prophets of never-ending economic growth are fond of saying) for centuries except by small bands of wood cutters during the 17th and 18th centuries, mainly British, and, more recently, by US-based banana companies. This failure to occupy the northern forests is the main reason for Nicaragua's unusual history — surely the most chequered of all the Central American republics. Though nominally

Spanish, the area, together with a large slice of the coast of Honduras, was, from 1780 to 1885, a British Protectorate known as the "Misquito Kingdom", though something of the sort had been declared as early as 1678 by the Governor of Jamaica. During their occupation of the area the British settled several colonies of Jamaicans (both white and black) along the coast, particularly at Bluefields and San Juan del Norte (formerly Greytown). Earlier in the 20th century the US-based United Fruit Company and others followed suit and brought in black people from Jamaica to work the banana plantations they had established in the Puerto Cabezas area, so that today there is a predominance of African blood along the coast. These people still speak English despite the ever present Spanish influences and remain (nominally) Protestant and maintain their own typically Black Caribbean life style. They make up nine percent of the total population. Pure Indians make up a further four percent the remainder being Mestizos together with a small proportion of Europeans of unmixed ancestry.

In 1522 when the Spaniards Andrés Niño and Gonzales Dávila were exploring the coast of Nicaragua from their base in Panama, the country was populated by two nomadic tribes of Indians — the Suma on the northern borders and the Misquito on the coast — and a settled tribe of agriculturalists on the southern shores of Lakes Managua and Nicaragua who had established a civilization of sorts. This latter group gave the Spaniards gifts of gold objects which of course brought them running back several years later in search of more. Granada and León were founded but the supply of gold soon dried up and most of the Spanish moved elsewhere. The two settlements were to jostle for supremacy from the start; the Liberals from their stronghold of Leon, and the Conservatives from their stronghold of Granada. When independence came neither could face the prospect of the other's city becoming the capital, so in 1858 a compromise of sorts was arranged and Managua, until then a small, unimportant village about half way between them, was chosen — an unfortunate choice in the light of subsequent natural disasters.

For the first 20 years or so following independence from Spain, Nicaragua's history followed closely that of the other Central American republics: annexation to Iturbide's Mexican Empire then various abortive attempts at federation between all or some of the republics. Early in the 20th century, Jose Santos Zelaya, dictator of Nicaragua between 1893 and 1909, attempted to unite Central America by force, but the war was brought to an end following intervention by Mexico and the US. Yet the idea of union lives on, the most recent attempt being in 1960 when the Central American Common Market was founded. Initially it went well though there was a feeling in Honduras and Nicaragua that they were doing least well out of the arrangement and it took a severe blow when the "Football War" broke out between El Salvador and Honduras.

In the middle of the 19th century the filibusterer William Walker, a doctor and lawyer born in Nashville, invaded Nicaragua at the head of a band of mercenaries — he not only had the obliging support of the US government but was backed by bankers Morgan and Garrison. They seized a steamer on Lake Nicaragua belonging to Cornelius Vandebilt's Accessory Transit Company — part of the link between the eastern US seaboard and the Pacific coast during the Californian gold rush — and attacked and partially sacked Granada and

took over the country. Rivas was installed as a puppet president with Walker as Commander of the Armed Forces. Vanderbilt's company was confiscated and handed over to Walker's friends. A little while later Walker had himself made President and, on the pretext of economic necessity and to gain the support of the southern US slave states, suspended the Nicaraguan laws against slavery. His government was formally recognised by the US in 1856 but a coalition of Central American states, backed by Vanderbilt, fought against him and eventually forced him to surrender to the US in order to avoid capture. He was welcomed back to the US as a national hero and before the year was out sailed once more for Nicaragua at the head of another band of thugs. He didn't get far and was arrested soon after landing at Greytown (San Juan del Norte) by the US Navy who returned him to the US. But he didn't give up and three years later sailed again. This time he was arrested by the British Navy and handed over to the Honduran authorities who shot him in Trujillo. He left an account of his expeditions called, *The War in Nicaragua*, if you're interested.

In 1912, US marines invaded Nicaragua to enforce the collection of customs dues which had been offered as collateral for a US loan the year before. They stayed until 1933 leaving Anastasio Somoza in command of the National Guard. From that day until mid-79 Nicaraguan affairs were completely dominated by the Somoza family from the Presidential seat to the paving stones which line the streets. They were either principal stockholder or outright owner of just about every industrial installation, distribution network, transport service, communications medium, agricultural product, bank and finance house of any size in the country. They amassed a vast fortune estimated at over US\$200 million, with a totally cynical disregard for anything and anyone other than their close friends and those whose support they bought. If you want to know what happended to the bulk of the disaster funds which flowed in following the destruction of Managua in the 1972 earthquake, for instance, you don't have to think too hard. The family was still charging rents for buildings which no longer existed years after the earthquake. If that wasn't enough they also controlled 25 percent of the available arable land.

Obviously they didn't maintain an empire like that without a great deal of violence and repression but in mid-79 they finally met their end. For years, following the invasion by the US Marines, Augusto César Sandino fought the National Guard and the Marines with whatever weapons were available with a small guerrilla army until he was treacherously assassinated in an ambush whilst on his way to meet Somoza in Managua for talks which had been arranged. Somoza claimed that the American Ambassador, Arthur Bliss Lane had ordered the execution but the guerrilla movement survived and named itself after its assassinated leader as the Sandinistas. In 1978 a series of daring raids and invasions included the capture of the National Palace and a substantial part of the country.

They were eventually temporarily driven out and pursued into neighbouring Costa Rica, provoking an international row in which Venezuela, for one, promised to send war planes to defend Costa Rica should it happen again. By this time the degree of support for the Sandinistas was unmistakable. Even the middle classes and businessmen had now turned against Somoza although it's probable that they would have preferred a more cosmetic change in government than the wholesale redistribution of land and wealth which the guerrillas have in mind. Anastasia Somoza Jr, who had succeed-

ed his brother Luis, who in turn had become President following the assassination of their father in 1956, retreated to his bomb-proof bunker in the National Guard HQ and ruled from there. In 1979 the struggle became increasingly bitter, the National Guard reached new depths of brutality and Somoza was reduced to bombing his own capital city in a futile attempt to drive out the guerrillas. Finally all neighbouring support dried up as every other Central American government abandoned Somoza. "Any form of government will be better than the present one," was a comment from the Costa Rican government. When the US, finally reading the writing on the wall, also withdrew its support Somoza soon scurried off to the US for what will no doubt be a comfortable and well-off retirement. Within days the National Guard had completely collapsed and the Sandinistas were in control.

VISAS

These are required by all except nationals of Belgium, Britain, Denmark, Luxembourg, Netherlands, Norway, Spain, Sweden and Switzerland, but they are free. US nationals need a Tourist Card. The length of stay is initially 30 days (renewable up to a total of 90 days). An entry fee of 10 Córdobas plus, if you're one of those people who need a visa, a further fee of 10.50 Córdobas are payable.

There are no hair, money or ticket hassles at the border or point of entry. In fact they're positively friendly. You might have a cursory baggage search — looking for arms.

Go to the Nicaraguan Consulate in La Unión, El Salvador, if you're planning on catching the daily ferry from there to Potosí. It's open everyday including Sundays (but there's a fee of 3 Colones on Sunday because they're officially not open).

HONDURAS

Ocotal

NICARAGUA

Potosí
Chinandega
Leon

Managua Granada

Penas Blancas

COSTA RICA

Little Corn Island

Rama

Bluefields

Great Corn Island

NICARAGUA

CURRENCY

US$1 = 7 Córdobas

The unit of currency is the Córdoba (Cor) = 100 Centavos. Travellers' cheques are sometimes a real hassle to change. The Banco de Nicaragua won't change them in Managua but will in Bluefields! The Banco de America sometimes will/sometimes won't and at other times asks for the original bill of sale for the cheques! Who the hell carries that around? The Banco de Centroamérica (a Somoza Concern) charges one percent.

Dollar bills are acceptable in many places including hotels and cafes (even small ones) and they'll give you 7 Córdobas to the dollar. Don't buy Córdobas in El Salvador. You'll get a bad rate.

CHINANDEGA
Accommodation
Pensión Cortés Cor 9.80/single — basic. *Salón Carlos*, Cor 21/person with breakfast — shared shower and toilet. *Hotel Glomar*, one block south from the Mercado Central, Cor 21/person — shared showers and toilets.

LEÓN
Accommodation
Pension Carmen. Cor 10.50/ single, but I couldn't find it nor could I find the *Hospedaje La Primavera*, Cor 8.40/single.

Hotel América, 2a Avenida Oriente between Calles 1 Sur and Central (also called Calle Rubén Dario). Cor 31.50/person. If you want three in a room they'll provide an extra bed for no extra charge. Rooms have a shower, toilet and fan. Air-conditioned rooms are about Cor 7. The management is friendly and there is a courtyard, colonial atmosphere. You can wash your clothes.

Hosteleria La Libertad, Cor 24.50 for a double. Rooms have single beds only so if there's two of you, you'd better be close (they have no doubles) — fan, shower, toilet, unfriendly management, cell-like rooms, no windows. It's a drive-in place where the road runs (literally) through the middle of the hotel. It is used as a whorehouse so all in all give it a miss if you can.

Eats There are excellent Chinese restaurants in town. Eg *Corona de Oro* has amazing Huevos rancheros (eggs) Cor 9.50 which consists of three eggs, two salads, rice, tomato sauce, bread. Hot tea with which you're served two whole limes which you can make into lemonade with the iced water, Cor 2 — your vitamin C ration for the week! The Chinese owner speaks English (and doubtless Chinese) but only a little Spanish. The waitresses speak Spanish. There's another excellent cafe on the corner of Parque Jérez, Calle Central and Avenida Central. Coffee for Cor 2, very good omelettes.

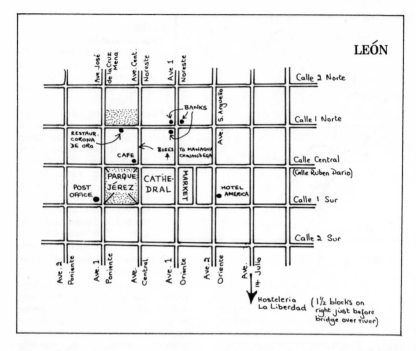

LEÓN

Ave. José de la Cruz Mena
Ave. Cent.
Noreste
Ave. 1
Noreste
S. Arguello

Calle 2 Norte

BANKS

Calle 1 Norte

RESTAUR. CORONA DE ORO

CAFE

BUSES

TO MANAGUA CHINANDEGA

Calle Central

(Calle Rubén Dario)

PARQUE JÉREZ

CATHE-DRAL

MARKET

POST OFFICE

HOTEL AMERICA

Calle 1 Sur

Calle 2 Sur

Ave. 2 Poniente
Ave. 1 Poniente
Ave. Central
Ave. 1 Oriente
Ave. 2 Oriente
Ave. Julio

Hostelería La Liberdad (1½ blocks on right just before bridge over river)

Other Bank of America changes travellers' cheques — no commission. Bank of London and America charges Cor 1 commission.

MANAGUA

This place can be very confusing unless you arrive by *TICA* Bus. The centre was almost completely destroyed in the 1972 earthquake and is now a vast collection of overgrown demolition plots with the odd ruin scattered here and there. The only buildings which survived are the National Palace, the Cathedral, the Post Office and a couple of banks. It's being rebuilt as a series of satellite towns which are spread out over many kilometres. There's no centre anymore as such. Make sure you know where you want to go if your bus puts you down anywhere other than the *TICA* bus terminal where most of the budget hotels are located. Getting into a taxi and asking for "El Centro" will put you down, bewildered, in the muddy streets of a shanty town/market area in what used to be the centre but where there's nowhere to stay. It's a 15 minute walk from there to the *TICA* bus terminal if you can't find a city bus going that way — a lot of them go along Calle Colon. If you get one going that way walk up the two streets from this street to the *TICA* bus terminal. Some people compare the centre with the aftermath of World War III. I wouldn't for a moment want to make light of the disastrous effect the earthquake must have had on people's lives but I found it really pleasant, full of flowers, saplings and butterflies, comparable with Mayan sites or perhaps Panama Viejo, except here it's lumps of concrete and steel rather than old stone.

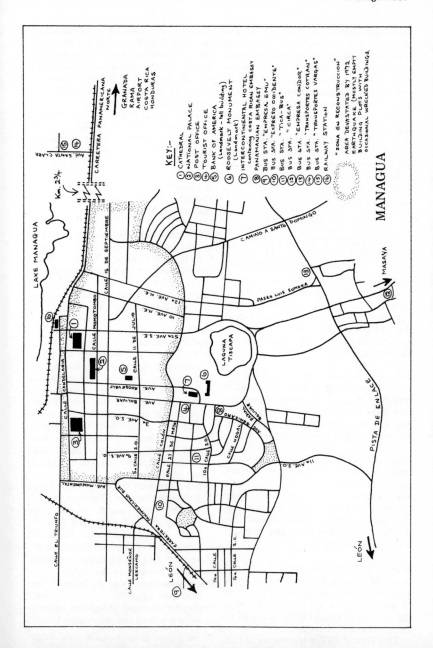

MANAGUA

KEY:-
1. CATHEDRAL
2. NATIONAL PALACE
3. POST OFFICE
4. TOURIST OFFICE
5. BANK OF AMERICA (Landmark - tall building)
6. ROOSEVELT MONUMENT (Landmark)
7. INTERCONTINENTAL HOTEL containing COSTA RICAN EMBASSY
8. PANAMANIAN EMBASSY
9. BUS STA. "EMPRESA EMU"
10. BUS STA. "EXPRESO OCCIDENTE"
11. BUS STA. "TICA-BUS"
12. BUS STA. "CIRCA"
13. BUS STA. "EMPRESA CONDOR"
14. BUS STA. "TRANSPORTES COTRAN"
15. BUS STA. "TRANSPORTES VARGAS"
16. RAILWAY STATION

◯ "ZONA EN RECONSTRUCCION" AREA DEVASTATED BY 1972 EARTHQUAKE (MOSTLY EMPTY BUILDING PLOTS WITH OCCASIONAL WRECKED BUILDINGS.

Accommodation The place where most travellers stay is an unmarked pensión in a private house about 100 metres on the right and across the street on the corner from the *TICA* bus terminal, Cor 10.50 per person (singles, doubles and triples) — basic, clean, friendly, good hot shower. There are meals in the evening — as good as you'll get out — meat, rice, beans, tortillas coke or coffee. Cor 8. Valuables are safe here despite appearances to the contrary. There is a notice board with information, but no fans.

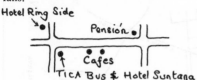

Hotel Ring Side

Pensión

Cafes

TICA Bus & Hotel Suntana

Hotel Sultana, at the *TICA* bus terminal same building). Cor 21/single. *Hotel Ring Side*, I was offered Cor 35/three people but someone else was quoted that per person when the *TICA* bus got in. It's very flash with TV, bathroom, air-con and sheets in each room.

Eats If you don't want to eat at the unmarked pensión or want to meet other travellers or go for a drink, there are two cafes between the *TICA* bus terminal and the pensión with good food. Travellers collect here in the evenings.

Information Poste Restante charges 35 centavos per letter. Ask them to check every conceivable initial of your name because they had got mine under three different headings despite the fact that they were printed in block capitals, the surname was underlined, and "Senor" used instead of "Mr".

Other If you're going to Rama and Bluefields, transport to *CONTRAN* bus terminal is by bus from Calle 27 de Mayo. Catch a No. 11. Taxi costs Cor 15 for the car. This bus also goes to the airport (Las Mercedes).

The Tourist Office has excellent free maps of the country and Managua — essential if you're going anywhere outside the central area. They also have details of the Managua-Bluefields trip though some of it is out of date and it's in Spanish, but then if you haven't learnt Spanish by now.......

Costa Rican Consulate is at Hotel Intercontinental, Apartado 753.

Changing money can be a problem if you only have travellers' cheques, see under *Currency*.

GRANADA
Probably the most pleasant city in Nicaragua after Bluefields.

Accommodation *Hotel Imperial* on the main square towards the waterfront — Cor 21/double, basic. *Pension Cabrera*, Cor 20/person with meals. *Pensión Vargas* is similar to the above. *Pensión Esfinge*, opposite the entrance to the main market, Cor 15.40/double.

RAMA
Accommodation
Hotel Amy. Cor 15/person. They only have double rooms containing two single beds — basic. Lots of insects but then you are in the middle of the jungle next to the river. There's netting at the windows but it would not stop a large butterfly the holes are so large. Reasonable food (often fish) but not cheap; salad tastes of disinfectant and the toilets are awash.

Pension opposite the Amy — the *Rama*, is cheaper at Cor 10/person, but it's unlikely they could persuade you to stay there if they paid you. It looks like Amnesty International's description of Nicaraguan jails!

Hotel Lee Cor 15.40/single. Probably slightly better than the *Amy*.

Hotel San José. Cor 7. Probably the best and cheapest.

Hospedaje Damasco If you can raise the owners out of bed, we couldn't.

There's one more pensión you might

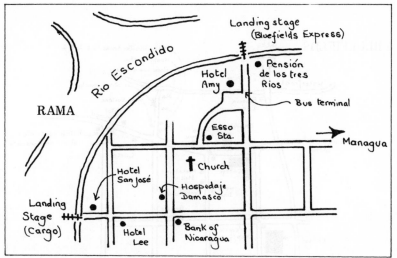

like to risk life and limb in, on the other side of the landing stage from the *Amy* called, *Pensión de los Tres Ríos*, which looks like it's about to plummet into the river at any time. Though, you could no-doubt stay there for a song. if you do, go to bed in a boat.

Other There are two petrol stations and a bank in town.

BLUEFIELDS
Accommodation

Hotel Dipp, Avenida Cabezas. Cor 40/ triple with three single beds (also have singles and doubles) — clean and basic, share shower and toilet. Some rooms have portable fans — if yours doesn't, ask for one (no extra charge). The management is friendly and it's a good place to meet people. Captains of boats going to the Corn Islands tout for passengers here. It has it's own restaurant: the food is nothing special, but cheap. There's a good balcony with chairs where you can have a smoke and watch the street.

Hospedaje Costeno y Comedor, in the market street. Cor 15/single, Cor 30/ double — basic.

Pensión Martha. Similar to Costeno. Cor 7/person.

Hotel Cueto. Pretentiously flash and overpriced since the chances are you'll get a room which is cell-like and has just as many cockroaches and mosquitos as a much cheaper place. It has its own restaurant which again isn't cheap. Cor 22/single, Cor 40/double, Cor 50/triple for rooms with a fan. Rooms with a fan and private shower are about double. Cor 55/single, Cor 100/double or Cor 115/triple for rooms with air-conditioning and private shower.

Hotel Hollywood, diagonally opposite the Cueto. Cor 20/double, Cor 15/ single — often full.

Other cheap and basic pensions indicated on the map are all around Cor 7/single. The local young people are very friendly so if you're planning on staying for a while they might make room for you in their houses.

Eats *Dipp Hotel* has been previously

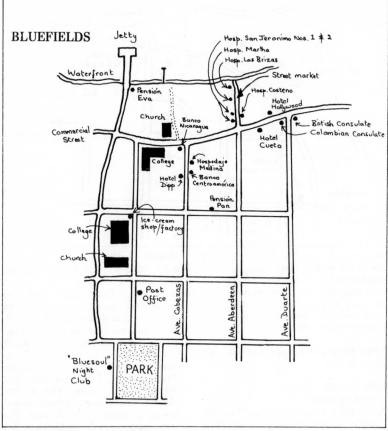

mentioned. *Hospedaje Medina* has a co-medor serving meals similar to the *Dipp.* The cheap comedors are in the market street. The Chinese restaurant next to the *Hollywood* opposite the *Cueto* has excellent food but, apart from the very filling soups, it's relatively expensive. Excellent ice-cream can be got from the shop next to the college — see street plan.

For night life the *Blue Soul* on the Park has a very cheap entry (reduction with student card!) and cheap drinks and is a friendly, laid-back place with dim lights, live bands (Nicaraguan reggae), open air (under cover). It goes on till late and is an excellent place for meeting local young people. The disco on Commercial Street between Avenidas Cabazas and Aberdeen is where the younger people go (15-19 year olds) — noisy, packed, bar, UV lights, etc.

Other The Banco de Centroamerica charges one percent commission on Travellers Cheques, the Banco de Nicaragua has no commission.

Colombian Consulate is open five days a week if you need a visa or tourist card. Visas are free, 90 day stay, two photographs. Friendly lady doesn't ask for onward ticket but this doesn't mean you won't need one on arrival — see under *Colombia*. The British Consulate is a couple of houses away. Open only on Fridays from 6pm.

Post Office is well organised and there are no fees for receipt of letters.

CORN ISLANDS (ISLAS MAÍZ)

Incredible beaches, white coral sand, tall coconut palms. Just what you'd expect, but get there soon. They were in the process of building an international airport so it won't be long before the high-rises go up and the weekend jet set from Miami arrive.

Accommodation Both food and accommodation is expensive, often outrageously so, unless you can find a place to rent privately for a week or two and cook your own food (easy to find). Ask around at any house for accommodation — everyone knows everyone else. Try around Wills Bowers fish freezer plant by the jetty or along the beach road in either direction. People will often go and live with their parents/friends for a week while they rent you their house.

We stayed at *Elry Morgan's* place along the beach toward's *Lundy's Island Hotel*, but ask for his mother Florence as he's often away fishing. They asked us for Cor 300/week initially but dropped it to Cor 150/week when we looked about to leave. For that three of us had a two room house with beds and sheets, a shack with cooking facilities, use of toilet and washing facilities. The people were very friendly and easygoing.

Just to give you some idea of the hotel prices: *Lundy's Island Hotel*, Cor 245/single including meals (per night!). *Hotel Morgan*, Cor 84/single including

meals. The others are *Hotel Playa Coco* and *Residencias Bryan*. The *Welcome Hotel* burnt down some time ago.

Eats If you're not cooking your own there's only one cafe as such and it's not cheap. Try to do your own and keep it simple. Coconuts are often free and can be found on the beach anyway. All food, just about, is flown in from Managua (!!) thus making it expensive.There are several good stores on the island, mostly Chinese. The largest are *Hooker's* and the *Boston*. Cheap fish can be got from Bower's Freezer plant where most of the boats from Bluefields land. Get insect repellant ("Autan") from *Boston* store.

Muy Muy restaurant and night spot is virtually the only place you'll find any action on the island (free entry) — live music (reggae bands), crowded, lots going on. It's a good place to meet people.

Other Post Office is a wooden shack just off the bottom end of the runway — but letters do get back despite all appearances!

The bank is at Pomarblue fishing jetty past *Lundy's* but they won't change travellers' cheques, only dollar bills (which everyone will accept anyway). *Lundy's* won't change unless you're staying there but the Chinese stores may change if you're buying provisions there.

The Island's electricity is run off generators which are turned off about 11 pm and occasionally break down for an hour or so here and there — have candles to hand.

TRANSPORT
Flights
Managua-Bluefields and Corn Islands. *Lanica.* Every Monday, Tuesday,

Thursday and Friday and returns to Managua, Monday, Wednesday, Friday and Saturday. Managua-Corn Islands. Cor 176. Bluefields-Corn Islands, Cor 56, taking 15 minutes.

Lanica also fly five times a week to Puerto Cabezas.

To Colombia by *SAM*. Their offices are at Edificio Policlinica Nicaragüense, Managua, tel 6615/26610.

There is a six percent sales tax on all tickets sold in the country plus a transportation tax of one percent. Airport tax is Cor 35 on international flights. No. 4 bus goes from the centre to Las Mercedes airport in Managua.

Buses

International buses *TICA* Bus has daily buses to San Jose (Costa Rica) at 6 am, 8 am and noon, and to Tegucigalpa (Honduras) twice daily. They will only sell you a *return* ticket (Cor 84) to San Jose and the return half is only refundable if you stay in Costa Rica for 10 or more days (ie you have to give them 10 days' notice). Your name is typed on the ticket making it difficult to sell the return half without access to some "Snopake" or something similar. The bus takes eight and a half hours and there are long delays at the border (bureaucracy), but otherwise there are no hassles about hair or money. The buses are air-conditioned and they get COLD — take a sweater.

Local buses Arriving by ferry at Potosí from La Unión (El Salvador). By the time the ferry arrives the last bus has gone to Chinandega and you will have to get a taxi. They cost Cor 13. (Cor 3 more than the bus) and take under two hours to Chinandega over a rough road in time to catch buses to León or Managua if you want to keep moving. The Transportes San Ramon Bus schedule from Chinandega-Potosí is: depart

Potosí 7.30 am, arrive Chinandega 9.30 am, depart Chinandega 10.30 am, arrive Potosí 12.30 pm, depart Potosí 1.30 pm, arrive Chinandega 3.30 pm, depart Chinandega 4.30 pm (stay the night).

Chinandega-León. Many companies do this route throughout the day and evening. Cor 4 and takes one hour.

León-Managua. Many different companies do the route throughout the day and evening. Buses vary in quality. Some are packed out (older ones) and others virtually empty. They have different terminals in Managua and takes just under two hours.

See the warning under *Managua* about knowing where you want to go when you arrive. The orange coloured buses from León will drop you a fair way out from the centre on Carretera Panamericana Sur on the western suburbs and you will have to get a bus or taxi from there to the *TICA* Bus terminal where the cheap hotels are.

Managua-Rama and Bluefields. See separate section at the end of this section.

Boats

Nicaragua (Potosí)-El Salvador (La Unión). Daily ferry at approximately 7 pm. Cor 21 and takes six hours. La Unión town centre is one and a half km from the jetty — walk, or bear this in mind when the taxi driver tells you it's half a day's journey.

Boats on Lake Nicaragua. *Las Isletas* are a big tourist attraction. Most are inhabited and very beautiful. Launches leave from Granada. The largest island — Isla de Ometepe — consists of two volcano cones, one of them over 1500 metres high. Two villages are on the island — Moyogalpa and Altagracia. The boat fare from Granada is Cor 7 and the one boat per day from Moyogalpa to San Jorge on the southern shore is 75 centavos. There are cheap pensions on the island.

The Río San Juan has interesting jungle boat rides. Launches run irregularly from San Carlos on the lakeside where the San Juan leaves the Lake. Also motorized dugouts from there to Los Chiles in Costa Rica for 50 centavos. Boats also run down to San Juan del Norte via El Castillo where there's an old Spanish fort. Boats go from Granada to San Carlos on Mondays, Wednesdays and Fridays. Cor 9, takes 12 hours.

Managua-Rama and Bluefields

Buses Managua-Rama. Several companies do the run, eg *Transportes Nicaragüense TRANICSA)*, all from Terminal Cotran on the Carretera Panamericano Norte on the way to the airport. Local bus No. 11 from the centre on Calle 27 de Mayo goes there or a taxi will cost Cor 15 for the car. Buses leave Managua at 3 am, 4.30 am, 5.30 am, 6 am, 6.30 am, 7 am, 7.15 am, 8.15 am and 12.30 am. The Directo is 6.30 am. Buses leave Rama at 5 am, 5.40 am, 6.30 am, 7 am, 8.50 am, 11.45 am, 12.30 pm, 1 pm, and 1.30 pm. The Directo is at 1 pm.

Unless you catch the Directo which takes five hours (300 km) and costs the same as the others, Cor 25, settle down for a long and frustrating (but beautiful) journey in a bus which stops and starts virtually every 100 metres to pick up and put down passengers and takes seven hours. The road is paved all the way. If you want to avoid staying in Rama overnight remember that the Bluefields Express leaves Rama daily at 1 pm so you'll have to catch an early bus.

Boats

The Bluefields Express. Daily costs Cor 35 and takes five and a half hours. It departs Rama at 1 pm and returns at 6 am. It is non-stop and goes through beautiful river and jungle scenery. Locals start gathering hours before it arrives in Rama at about 11.30 am because as far as seats are concerned it's first come first served and it's always chock-a-block, but so long as it doesn't rain you'll prefer to be in the prow anyway. It takes about one hour to load up and there is one hell of a hassle for seats and luggage space. They sell drinks on board (beers are Cor 4).

La Esperanza. Cor 20. It takes longer than the *Bluefields Express*. It leaves Bluefields on Mondays and Wednesdays at 3 pm and leaves Rama on Tuesdays and Fridays at 2 pm.

The following boats also do the run but, unless indicated, have no fixed schedule or departure times so you must ask around: *El Cairo* Rama-Bluefields on Tuesdays, Thursdays, Saturdays and Bluefields-Rama on Mondays, Wednesdays and Fridays. *El Porvenir* (Rama-Bluefields on Sundays, Wednesdays and Bluefields-Rama on Tuesdays, Saturdays). *San Martín. Johanna.* They all cost between Cor 15 and 20. Some very slow and make frequent calls along the riverside.

Bluefields-Corn Islands (Islas Maíz) The *Johanna* goes irregularly once every one to two weeks depending on cargo/passengers. Just ask at the jetty for the captain. Cor 25. The boat goes first to El Bluff across the bay where more cargo is loaded after which it waits there all day and sails at night arriving at the crack of dawn (six hours). If you don't fancy waiting all day in El Bluff get a launch across later in the day from Bluefields — plenty all day, usually costs Cor 7 but it's cheaper to get the "school boat" across with the schoolkids who live in El Bluff. This boat leaves around 4.30-5 pm. Sling your

hammock on the boat or crash on top of the cargo. All very informal and usually not too crowded. Take your own food and drink as there's none on the boat and things are quite expensive in El Bluff if you go off for a wander.

Other than the *Johanna* you can get free lifts on the fishing boats which go between Bluefields and the Corn Islands but they're easier to find in El Bluff. *Wills Bowers* and *Pomarblue* fishing companies are the ones to look for. Speak to the captains and then turn up about one hour before they're due off. It's quicker and more convenient than the *Johanna* but there's no shelter if it rains. Very occasionally boats go from Grand Corn Island to Little Corn Island, which is mellower still. You may have to wait around though for anything up to two weeks and spend days tracking one down. But they do go as people live there.

Costa Rica

One of the smallest of the Central American republics and the most prosperous, Costa Rica is unique in having a population composed almost entirely of Blancos — people of unmixed Spanish and other European origin. Only in the provinces of Limón and to a lesser extent Puntarenas are there sizeable minorities of people of a different origin — in Limón a steadily decreasing percentage (about 33%) of black people of Jamaican origin, brought in to work the banana plantations, and a very small (about 3%) pure Indian element. The reason for this is that the Indians who were living here when the Spanish arrived were almost completely wiped out by diseases which the latter brought with them. Other features which set it apart are the very high literacy rate and the lack of armed forces. The Army was abolished in 1948 though there is a very efficient para-military National Guard.

From the Conquest until fairly recent times it remained a poor and relatively isolated backwater populated only by a few Spanish settlers who farmed the lands of the Meseta Central but because of the almost total absence of an indigenous Indian population, who would have normally been exploited as free or cheap labour, the feudal latifundia/minifundia land distribution system so prevalent elsewhere never took root here.

Following independence, brief annexation to the Mexican Empire of Iturbide, and the various abortive attempts at Central American federation, the government looked around for a suitable cash crop which could be introduced to provide an income for exports. It found this in coffee which was introduced from Cuba at the beginning of the 19th century. Free land was offered to anyone who would grow coffee on it. The population began to grow more rapidly as more land was colonised and the income from the export of coffee increased gradually. Initially the growth of the industry was hampered by the lack of roads (only as late as 1846 was an ox-cart road constructed from the highlands to the Pacific port of Puntarenas) but picked up quickly after the construction of railways towards the end of the century from San José to Puerto Limón via Cartago and from San José to Puntarenas. Costa Rica is today one of the world's largest exporters of coffee.

About the time the railways were being constructed the US company,

United Fruit, acquired land in the Puerto Limón area and began to plant bananas, bringing in black labourers from Jamaica to clear the jungle and work the plantations — hence the concentration of black people on the Caribbean coast. The industry grew rapidly and by 1913 was providing 11 million bunches for export. But soon afterwards the plantations were attacked by the so-called Panama disease which progressively reduced the yields and forced the company to transfer to the lowlands of the Pacific coast from where the bulk of the bananas come from today.

This concentration on cash crops and transport networks which service them has, in many ways, stunted the growth of other crops which, because of Costa Rica's exceptionally fertile soil and climate, are grown in abundance on the farms of the Meseta Central but rarely ever reach a market in town because of the lack of roads and the profits absorbed by middle-men. Most of the transport in the rural highland areas is by carreta (ox-cart). They are very distinctive, no two being exactly alike, and all highly decorative. Aficionados claim they can tell which village the cart is from judging by the pattern on it, just as it's possible to tell the same of a Guatemalan Indian from the pattern of weaving in their clothing and of a Peruvian Indian from the style of the women's bowler hats.

Because of its somewhat uneventful history and limited settlement until recent times, Costa Rica is more a mecca for outdoor types, beach freaks and jungle lovers than those looking for ruins, Indian communities and colonial cities. But don't miss it. It's a fantastically beautiful country with volcanoes, some still active, plenty of ideal highland walking country, jungles packed with wild life and some of the best beaches in the world. Much of the country is still covered by forest.

Probably the best time to go walking is between December and May — the dry season — as, at other times, the roads are frequently turned into thick mud. The Atlantic side of the mountains and the Caribbean coast receive rain most of the year (on average 300 days a year) so take some waterproof clothing with you if you visit this area.

The capital, San Jose, is a very modern city, similar to a US west coast city, but very pleasant for all that. There is a large expatriate US community living here, many of them retired people, as Costa Rica is the only Central American republic which allows US citizens to own land.

VISAS

These are required by all except nationals of West European countries, Israel, Canada, Japan, Yugoslavia and Central American republics. Tourist Cards for those not listed above are obtainable from consulates for US$2 allowing a 30 day stay (extendable to six months).

You need an *onward ticket* to get into the country. There are several ways of fulfilling this requirement: First a miscellaneous charges order (MCO) from an airline which operates flights to and from Costa Rica. There are many but make sure you get one from an airline which is an IATA member. Note that COPA are not.

Second an airline ticket for a specified (though not necessarily dated) flight out of Costa Rica. But remember if the flight is to Panama or Colombia you will also need an onward ticket out of those countries too before being allowed in.

The third is a return bus ticket out of the country. Eg a return TICA bus ticket from Managua (Nicaragua) to San José. This is the one most travellers opt for. The ticket costs US$12 and in fact they won't sell you a single to San José anyway. But if you want a refund on the return half you have to give them 10

days notice. This means that if you're staying in Costa Rica less than 10 days you effectively lose US$6 unless you can sell the return half to someone further along the road — difficult since they type your name on the ticket!

An exit tax of US$2 is payable if you stay more than 48 hours in the country and an exit permit is required if you stay more than 30 days, US$2.25. Until recently there was a lot of hassle at the border (including refusal of entry) for anyone classifiable as a "hippy" — long hair, beard, rucksacks — but it seems to have been knocked on the head. They were very friendly at the border when I went through.

The Costa Rican Consulate in Managua is at Hotel Intercontinental, Apartado 753.

CURRENCY

US$1 = 8.60 Colónes

The unit of currency is the Colón (Col) which equals 100 centavos. The rate of exchange varies slightly according to the dollar's fortunes. There's no blackmarket. Bank opening hours are Monday to Friday, 8 am-11 am and 1.30 pm-3 pm. Some are open on Saturdays too.

SAN JOSÉ
Accommodation
Hotel Nicaragua Avenida 2 between Calles 11 and 13. Popular with travellers and can be full if you're late in.

Hotel Astoria, Avenida 7 between Calles 3 and 5. A friendly place that has lots of other travellers and plenty of room but no hot water. Col 17/person/night. There's a notice board of things for sale, messages, maps, etc and there's a lock-up where you can leave gear (free). It is an easy walk from *TICA* bus terminal. Look for the sign: "The Backpackers' Hotel".

Hotel Salamanca Col 18/person and *Hotel Illymani* (Col 26/person) both on Avenida 2 between Calles 9 and 11, very near the *TICA* bus terminal. They're okay if you like loud televisions and hardboard partitions. The latter is overpriced for what it is.

Hotel Canadá, Avenida 5 between Calles 6 and 8. Col 10/person — hardboard partitions again.

Hotel Morazán, near Presidential Palace and Parque Morazán (see map). Col 50/person including meals or Col 20/person without meals — clean but shabby.

Pensión Americana, Calle 2 half a block from Parque Central. Col 17/person — pretty good.

Hotel Internacional, Calle 5. Col 12/person.

Hotel Musoc, Calle 16 near Avenida 1 and very convenient for the Coca Cola bus terminal. Col 19/person very clean. The management is friendly and will let you leave gear here while you go travelling elsewhere, space permitting. It can get a bit noisy.

Eats Plenty of small cafes (all much the same) where you can get cheap meals are all around Parque Morazán. Otherwise between the Parque Morazán and

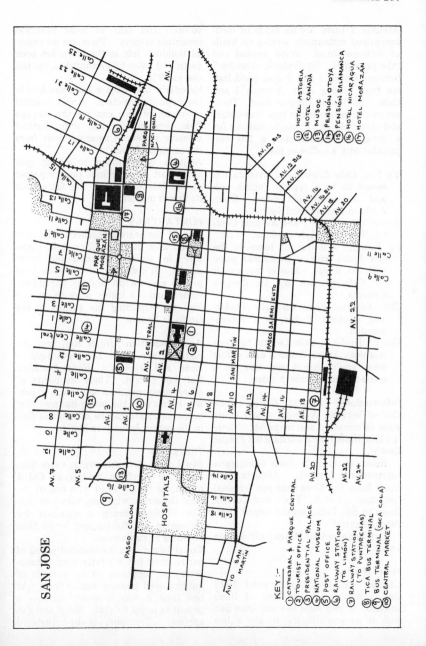

SAN JOSE

KEY:-
① CATHEDRAL & PARQUE CENTRAL
② TOURIST OFFICE
③ PRESIDENTIAL PALACE
④ NATIONAL MUSEUM
⑤ POST OFFICE
⑥ RAILWAY STATION (To LIMON)
⑦ RAILWAY STATION (To PUNTARENAS)
⑧ TICA BUS TERMINAL
⑨ BUS TERMINAL (COCA COLA)
⑩ CENTRAL MARKET

⑪ HOTEL ASTORIA
⑫ HOTEL CANADÀ
⑬ MUSOC
⑭ PENSIÓN OTOYA
⑮ PENSIÓN SALAMANCA
⑯ HOTEL NICARAGUA
⑰ HOTEL MORAZÁN

Avenida 2 there are all kinds of medium-priced restaurants serving all kinds of different food. Stroll around and take your pick. Eg *Tratoria*, Avendia 7 between Calles 7 and 9 does good Italian food. *Lung Mun*, Avenida 1 and Calle 5 does good Chinese food. There are plenty of American-type hamburger and steak places. If you're looking for a cheap snack/meal sink a few empanadas with a coffee or beer.

Ye Pub, Calle Central and Avenida 7 is meant to be a typical English pub and serves draught beer. Open 4.30 pm-2 am (closed Sundays).

Arturo's Bar, Calle 7 and Avenida Central, New York-style drinking.

La Fanega, well out of town in the San Pedro area is a student place with live music. Also in this area is *La Catedral* run by architecture students.

The *Aquarius* disco on Calle Central and Avenida 2 has been recommended.

Casey's Do-Nuts, Calle Central between Avenidas 7 and 9 has a cafe selling what you'd expect and also has a second-hand paperback store.

Information Tourist Office, Calle Central between Avenidas 4 and 6 has good information and maps, etc. There is a laundromat on Avenida 2 off Parque Carillo.

Buses to airport (Juan Santamaria International Airport): Alajuela minibuses from the Coca Cola bus terminal (see map). Col 2. Taxis cost Col 43. Buses to San Pedro suburb depart from Parque Central.

For addresses of airline offices see under *Transport*.

Places Nearby

Cartago was the capital until 1923 and is situated at the foot of Irazú volcano. A two hour bus ride from San José is an opportunity to see a live volcano and take in some beautiful mountain scenery. There are no colonial buildings left as the town has been destroyed twice by earthquakes, the last one in 1910.

Heredia is only 10 km from San José in the opposite direction. A very colonial town where you can see the volcano Poás, hot geysers and other extinct volcanic craters — amazing views from the summit of Poás.

Alajuela is a popular swimming spot and resort for Josefinos (as the people of San José are called). It's famous for its flower market.

PUNTARENAS

One of the nearest beaches to the populated area of Costa Rica it is, therefore, in season, crowded and litter-strewn. It's slightly better when local people are not on holiday (April-December) and is a handy place to use as a base for exploring the islands in the Golfo de Nicoya.

Accommodation *Hotel Rio*, near the market place. Col 13/person/night — clean and friendly. *Hotel Castalias*. Col 8.60/person. There are plenty of other cheap pensions and more expensive hotels near the beach but note that accommodation can be difficult to find in the period January to March.

The Islands

San Lucas A launch leaves every Sunday at 9 am from Puntarenas, Col 4 return, or have a word with one of the local fishermen who may take you out. The El Coro beach is excellent for swimming and fishing and better than anything in Puntarenas.

Cocos Island An uninhabited island of barren rock but it's interesting because there are supposed to be mounds of undiscovered treasure buried there. At one time it was necessary to have a permit in order to visit. See if this still applies. Transport is by chartered boat — nothing regular.

Negritos Island A regular ferry from Puntarenas departs daily, Col 9, otherwise have a word with the fishermen. Playa Naranjo is popular.

Places Nearby Some of the most popular beaches are located, north of Puntarenas, on this stretch on the Nicoya Peninsula, eg Playas Coco, Brasilito and Tamarindo. Rooms can be found in private houses for about Col 9/night though a hammock comes in very handy as if you can't find private accommodation, the other stuff ranges from the madly expensive to the very crude. Playa Coco was, at one time, a hot spot for the National Guard who did a lot of hassling young travellers. To get to these beaches first catch a bus from Puntarenas to Liberia and then take local buses from there. Further north of the beaches is the Santa Rosa National Park where many exotic animals can be seen (sloths, monkeys, peccary and birds). The bus from Puntarenas passes by the entrance to the Park and from there it's a six km walk.

South of Puntarenas, Quepos is a popular travellers' haunt though many head for the slightly more isolated Playa Manuel Antonio some six km down the coast in a National Park. Bamboo huts are for rent, Col 20/night (can be bargained down), or sleep on the beach free. The local bar and restaurant *Mary Sombra* which rents out the bamboo huts is the gringo hang-out. The beaches are excellent for swimming, skin-diving, surfing or just relaxing. The surrounding jungle can be hazardous unless you know the paths — snakes and the like. Get someone to show you the way. To get to the beach from Quepos hitch or walk, or there are buses from town to the beach at 9 am, noon, 4 pm and 10 pm. They return to Quepos at 6.30 am, 11.30 am, 1 pm and 6 pm.

PUERTO LIMÓN

Accommodation Plenty of cheap accommodation can be found by the docks and the railway station, eg *Hotel Niza*, near railway station. Col 17/person. Nearby, *Hotel Miramar*. Cheap and clean. *Hotel Wong*. Col 12.50 — basic. *Pensión Vicky*, on the waterfront, Col 19/double.

Eats The *Miramar* serves good food. There are quite a few Chinese restaurants and other cafes around the central park that are adequate and cheap. The *American Bar* near the park is a gringo hangout.

Places Nearby Puerto Limón-Moin-Colorado Bar. A jungle trip up the Caribbean coast to the border with Nicaragua. First take a bus to Moin and from there negotiate for a boat to take you up the Canal Navigable to Colorado Bar. Dense jungle scenery and amazing wild-life. From Colorado Bar you can either fly back to San José, go back the way you came in a boat or carry on up the coast in a canoe as far as the Río San Juan and San Juan del Norte. Boats are very irregular and sometimes hard to find. Avoid going in the rainy season and take insect repellant — there are plenty of mosquitoes.

Cahuita and on to the Panamanian border. Cahuita, further south on the coast, is a popular beach resort. It has one beach of black sand and another of white sand. You can skin-dive on the coral reef and there are wild-life packed jungles inland. There's only one hotel, the *Lams*, Col 15/person, otherwise ask around for rooms in private houses (a *Miss Rachel* is well known to travellers and rents out rooms as well as offering meals). Food is expensive here and there's no bank. It's possible to continue down the coast and enter Panama via the small border town of Guabito where there's one hotel, *Chinese Hotel*, Col 13/person. Transport is by banana company trucks.

TRANSPORT

Unless you specifically want to go to Panama and/or are on a tight budget, San José is one of your two choices (Panama being the other) for the cheapest flights to Colombia. Depending on your luck, initiative and the availability of transport when and where you need it, it *may* be cheaper to go to Colombia via Panama by one of the following routes:-

Boat from Colón to San Andrés Island and another boat from there to either Cartagena or Barranquilla on the mainland. Departs every 10 days or so from Colon and infrequently from San Andres Island. Total cost of transport alone is about US$30.

Infrequent and entirely at your own risk, contraband boats from Colón to Barranquila. Cost of transport alone about US$25.

Overland via the Darién Gap from Panama to Turbo. It can take 10 days in the dry season and requires a *lot* of initiative. More details are in the *Panama* section. Total cost of buses, dug-outs and boats alone about $55.

BUT you must also take the following into consideration if finance is your main consideration. (1) A US$4 tax on airline tickets bought in Panama. (2) Tourist Card for Panama or an Exit Permit (required if you stay more than 48 hours in Panama), US$2. (3) You must have an onward ticket from Panama before being allowed in. If you haven't got an airline ticket out of Panama or an MCO from an airline which operates flights to and from Panama then you're stuck with having to buy a return bus ticket. A return San José-Panama *TICA* Bus ticket will cost you US$26.50. The return half is only refundable with written permission from the Panamanian Immigration Office which costs US$10 making it

hardly worth the while. It's possible you might get away with a slightly less expensive return ticket by going to Panama on the *Panaica* bus line from San José or by going from San José to David with the *Tracopa* bus line. (4) The cost of the boat and overland trips from Panama to Colombia do *not* include food and accommodation and Panama is *not* a cheap place — reckon on US$5/day. If you're planning on the boats to San Andres it might involve hanging around for up to 10 days. If you're planning on the overland trip, allow yourself 10 days. (5) Even if you go via Panama you will still need an onward ticket before being allowed into Colombia. This also applies, of course, if you're coming from Costa Rica.

So, as far as cost goes folks, it's double Catch 22 on all sides and even if you bought one of the duty-free calculators in Panama to work out all the various permutations, by the time you'd added all the nasty little extras and the imponderables, there wouldn't be more than a dollar or two between them. One or two things, however, are clear: (1) Flights from Panama to Colombia are marginally cheaper than from San José but by the time you've added the minimum extras of US$4/ticket tax and an unusable US$13 minimum return half *TICA* bus ticket there's nothing in it. (2) The cheapest way to get to Colombia is by boat from Colón to San Andrés and from there to Cartagena by boat *if* you find a boat in Colón the same or the next day after arriving. This way you could save US$35 over the air fare or US$20 if you have to buy a return boat ticket from Colón to San Andrés to satisfy the onward ticket requirement for Colombia. The differential reduces the longer you have to wait for that boat. A seven-day wait would make it the same as the air fare. Anything over that and it's costing you more. (3) The cost of going overland through the Darién Gap will work out about the same as the air fare but of course the experience would be incomparable.

Okay back to Costa Rica.

Flights

To Colombia: The cheapest flight is San José-Cartagena via San Andres by *SAM*, Col 645, on Saturdays and Tuesdays only. But they won't sell you a ticket until you have your onward ticket out of Colombia. The same applies for all airlines serving Colombia since they don't want to have to give you a free flight back if you're refused entry for want of an onward ticket. You're allowed a stop-over on San Andrés on this flight — no extra charge. The office accepts credit cards.

Before buying an onward ticket out of Colombia make sure you know which way you'll be returning or that the airline you buy a ticket from is a member of IATA so that it's transferable to other IATA airlines. If you're going back via Miami, *Aerocondor* have flights between San Andrés and Miami for US$140 (they're IATA members). There are no student reductions any more on *SAM*.

The other cheapie from Costa Rica to Colombia is *COPA*, the Panamanian airline but it's not a member of IATA so if you buy a return ticket make sure you'll be coming back this way. They fly three times a week to Barranquilla and Medillin. *LASCA*, the national airline of Costa Rica, also do plenty of flights from Costa Rica and Panama to various places in Colombia and Venezuela but they're considerably more expensive than *SAM* or *COPA*.

A five percent tax on international airline tickets bought in Costa Rica and a US$5 airport tax on international flights are payable. Transport to Juan Santamaria International Airport in San José is by minibus from outside San Juan de Dios hospital (area marked "Hospital" on city plan), by *Alajuela*

bus from the Coca Cola bus terminal, Col 2, or taxi, Col 43 for the car.

Domestic flights are San José-Colorado Bar, daily, Col 60 and San José-Puntarenas, daily (15 minutes), Col 36.

Airline offices:

SAM (Sociedad Aeronautica de Medellin), Avenida 5 between Calles 1 and 3, tel 229794.

COPA (Compañia Panameña de Aviacion), Avenida 5 between Calles 1 and 3, tel 215596.

Aerocondor, Calle 5 between Avenidas 1 and Central.

LACSA, Calle 5, Avenida 1, tel 217315.

SAHSA, Avenida 5 between Calles 1 and 3, tel 215561.

SAS, Avenida 1 No. 348, tel 218687.

TACA, Calle 1 Avenida 3, tel 221790.

Internal Buses

San José-Quepos. Departs daily at 8.30 am, noon, 3 pm. It takes six hours — beautiful jungle and mountain scenery.

San José-Peñas Blancas (Nicaraguan border). Both *Ecatra* (Expresso Centroamericano terminal on Avenida Central and Calles 11-15) and *Sirca* (Calle Central between Avenidas 5 and 7) do this run on a daily schedule. Taking two buses in this way to Managua is cheaper than taking the through buses operated by *Sirca* and *TICA*.

San José-Puntarenas. Buses depart from behind the service station at the corner of Avenida Central and Calle 13. Sur, No 125. 2.50 colónes each — basic.

International Buses

To Nicaragua. *TICA* bus (Calle 9, Avenida 2b), usually several per day, US$6 to Managua, taking nine hours. The buses are air-conditioned (take a sweater — it gets cold) and there are long delays on the border (bureaucracy). *Sirca* Bus (Calle Central Between Avenidas 5 and 7) also do this route and are slightly cheaper than *TICA*.

To Panama. San José-Panama City. Three companies do this route, *TICA* Bus (Calle 9, Avenida 2b), *Panaica* (Avenida Central between Calles 13 and 15) and *Transportes Ferguson*, daily. The *TICA* bus departs at 8.45 am and midnight, US$13.20 and takes 15 hours. *Panaica* is cheaper than *TICA* Bus. You need an onward ticket in order to cross the Panamanian border so if you haven't got an airline ticket out of Panama you'll have to buy a return ticket (US$26.50).

San José-David. *Trapoca* (Avenida 5, Calle 14) buses depart daily at 11 am. Again, the onward ticket requirement for Panama applies.

Trains

There are two railway stations in San José: The Northern Railway Station on the north east side of the Parque Nacional for trains to Limón, Heredia and Alajuela and Ferrocarril Eléctrico al Pacífico to the south of the city (see city plan) for trains to Puntarenas. The bus there is marked "Paso ancho".

San José-Limón. Daily at 8.10 am and 12.20 pm and in the opposite direction at 6.10 am and 8.15 am. Col 27. It takes seven hours to Limon and nine hours back.

San José-Puntarenas. Daily at 6 am, 8.15 am, noon, 3 pm and 6 pm. Additional trains go on Saturdays at 12.45 pm, and at 3 am on summer Sundays only. Costs Col 11.61/single. Col 20.21/return.

Trains are clean but slow and the scenery is beautiful. Refreshments are available on the train or at stations along the way.

Panama

Although isolated geographically by the Darién Jungle, Panama was, until 1903, a province of Colombia. That was the year the Colombian Congress at Bogotá had refused to lease to the United States a strip of territory across the isthmus for the construction of a canal deemed vital to US interests by the then President, Theodore Roosevelt. So, later that year when a small revolt broke out in Panama City, US warships were sent to stop the landing of Colombian troops despatched to suppress the insurrection. An independent republic was proclaimed — immediately recognized by Washington which had financed and outfitted the revolt — and a new treaty signed in which the US was granted semi-sovereign rights over a coast-to-coast corridor in exchange for $10 million in gold and an annuity of $¼ million (later raised to $1,930,000). Colombian protests were ignored and it was not until 1921 that Bogota recognized the separation and the US paid $25 million in compensation.

This was only the most recent, if most dramatic, of a similar string of such incidents stretching back almost to the day when the Spaniard, Balboa, crossed the isthmus in 1513 and saw the Pacific. Panama City was founded a few years later and quickly became the focal point from which expeditions set out to conquer the lands north as far as Nicaragua and south as far as Chile. Because it is the shortest land route across the continent, it was also the point through which all trade between Spain and the South American colonies had to pass under the highly centralized and rigidly controlled system operated by Imperial

Spain. This system, designed to maximize tax collection and prevent the development of local industries and trade between the various colonies, was one of the major sources of discontent among the Criollos and contributed to the rise of the independence movements in the 18th and 19th centuries.

Certain ports — Veracruz (Mexico), Cartagena (Colombia) and Portobelo (Panama) — were designated as "monopoly ports" and only through these could legitimate transatlantic trade take place. For the vast Viceroyalty of Peru, which then included Peru, Bolivia, Paraguay, and Argentina, this port was Portobelo. Once a year a convoy of galleons, accompanied by a naval escort would set sail from Seville bringing European manufactures and taking back Peruvian gold, silver and agricultural products which had been transported by sea from Callao to Panama City and then by mule-back overland to Portobelo on the Caribbean. The more bulky goods such as cacao, quinine and vicuna wool were brought down the Chagres River in boats. While the Spanish fleet was in harbour the small port was packed with merchants and a whole year's business would be transacted in a few intense weeks. Once it was over, the place would be deserted until the following year due to the unhealthy climate.

Naturally, all this wealth collected in one small and vulnerable area attracted a constant stream of freebooters and pirates, mainly from Holland, France and England, who relieved them of a considerable amount of treasure over the centuries. One of the first on the scene was Sir Francis Drake who attacked twice, once capturing Nombre de Dios, another small port near Portobelo and Cruces, a town on the road between Panama City and Portobelo, carting off the accumulated treasure and burning the towns. To try and prevent this, the Spanish built large and costly forts,

some of which still stand today, but none of these deterred Henry Morgan who, in 1671, took the fort of San Lorenzo at the mouth of the Chagres River and then went upriver to Cruces and from there onto Panama City which they razed completely. A month later they were back on the Caribbean with nearly 200 mules loaded with treasure. Following this raid, Panama City was rebuilt on a new site, but the ruins of Panama Viejo (Old Panama) can still be visited a few kilometres from the present-day city.

Again in the 1730s Britain and Spain were at war and the number of attacks had increased. The most notable was Admiral Vernon's capture of Portobelo and then the fort of San Lorenzo. The fort was rebuilt and can be seen today in the Canal Zone but a few years later Spain abandoned the route and ships began trading via Cape Horn. But it was not just the buccaneers and foreign navies who made sure that the Spanish monopolists didn't have things all their own way. Because imports into the South American colonies had to take such a circuitous route with their consequent outrageous prices and lack of sufficient quantity on delivery, a lively contraband trade grew up and flourished around the fringe of the "legitimate" commerce — a tradition whihc is still very much alive today.

The next phase in Panama's history came in the late 1840s with the Californian gold rush. The quickest route from the eastern US seaboard to the Pacific coast was via Central America and thousands of adventurers made the overland trek through the Panamanian jungles to the Pacific shore and then by sea to San Francisco, as well as by the alternative route through Nicaragua. The gold rush brought into being the first railway across the isthmus from Colón to Panama City. The line took four years to build and many lives but ran successfully for many years until it was temporarily abandoned in the latter half of the century following the opening of the first trans-continental railway in the US. The rest of Panama's history centres around the canal.

Already in the 16th century the Spanish had considered the possibility of cutting a canal from coast to coast but it was not until the 1880's when Ferdinand de Lesseps arrived, fresh from the construction of the Suez Canal, that anything practical happened. A company was formed with over $100 million capital and work started in 1882, but the project was abandoned 11 years later after thousands of his workmen had died of disease. A few years later the Colombian government allowed the US to carry on where De Lesseps had stopped. But they went back on the deal which led to the declaration of Panamanian independence and the subsequent US military intervention mentioned earlier.

Since de Lesseps' attempt to cut a canal, advances had been made in medicine and it was then known that mosquitoes were responsible for transmitting the tropical fevers prevalent in that part of the world. So, before construction of the canal could begin again, measures had to be taken to protect the health of the labourers who would be working there. Under the direction of the US Colonel Gorgas, an expert in sanitation, a small fortune was spent eliminating yellow fever and almost wiping out malaria from Panama. The first ship passed through the newly-completed canal in August 1914.

Since its creation as an independent nation, Panama has existed only because of the canal, from which it earns its livelihood. But because of the growth of nationalism in the republic, the US has been obliged from time to time to increase the annual payment it makes to the Panamanian government, and provide better conditions for Panamanian workers employed in the Canal Zone.

There were riots in 1964, during which several people were killed, over Panama's right to fly its flag in the Canal Zone. Matters came to a head during 1977 and 1978 when a new treaty was negotiated between the Carter Administration and the Panamanian government of General Torrijos (who is undoubtedly a fairly typical Latin American military dictator though pursuing an issue of very real concern to Panamanians). The new treaty, which provides for return of the Canal Zone to Panama by the year 2000, provoked one of the worst rows in the US senate for years but was finally passed by a slim margin. The US has, after all, made back its original $387 million investment in the canal many times over and times have changed.

The population (one and a half million) is quite a hotch-potch of different racial mixes. Most are Mestizos but there are sizeable communities of black people, principally along the Caribbean coast, pure-bred Indians, in the San Blas archipelago, the Darién jungle and the three provinces nearest the Costa Rican border, Asians and North Americans. The black people are descended from British West Indians brought in for the construction of the Panama City-Colon railway and later for the canal — they still speak English and retain their own life-styles and customs. The largest Indian group are the Guaymí who inhabit the provinces nearest the Costa Rican border, though the group most often visited by travellers are the Cuna on the San Blas Islands off the north coast. This group still practise ancient handicrafts and are semi-autonomous, but they have got the tourist trade well sussed out so don't expect any bargains and if you have a camera expect to pay for taking pictures. If you go through the Darién jungle to Colombia you will come across the other group — the Chocó — who live in villages throughout the region. But their culture seems to be on the wane and many have been absorbed into the prevailing Mestizo culture. Only three percent of the indigenous Indians can speak Spanish, but illiteracy is no where near as glaring as it is in other Central American republics as Panama spends a quarter of its budget on education and another quarter on social security, health and other public facilities. Only some 16% of the total land area is farmed but there are a few large estates and a land reform programme is under way.

At present there is still no road through the Darién jungle — the Pan American Highway ends about 83 km beyond Panama City and does not start again until you are well inside Columbia. It is unlikely anything will be done to link the two halves for some time to come because of a law suit brought by environmentalists who are concerned about the impact of the road on the people and the wildlife in the jungle. So if you are going that way remember to make adequate preparations.

Panama is an expensive place — reckon on at least US$5 per day for a very basic existence — and the two main cities, Colon and Panama City are hustlers' havens. Mugging is common in Colon, keep your eyes wide open. But the place is worth a visit if you have the time and money.

VISAS

Visas or Tourist cards are required by all except nationals of Britain, Costa Rica, Dominican Republic, El Salvador, Honduras, Spain, Switzerland, and West Germany. If you are travelling on a visa and stay more than 48 hours in Panama you have to get an Exit Permit. So if possible, get a Tourist Card in preference to a Visa as no Exit Permit is required with a Tourist Card. Tourist Cards cost US$2, valid for 30 days, extendable to 90 days. They can be obtained from airlines, Panamanian Consuls or at the border. They are not issued to nationals of Communist countries or India or Pakistan.

You need an onward ticket to get into the country. There are a number of ways of fulfilling this requirement; one is to get a miscellaneous charges order (MCO) from an airline which operates flights to and from Panama. There is a wide choice but make sure you get one from an airline which is a member of IATA. Most are but *COPA*, the Panamanian airline is not, so their MCOs are not transferable to other airlines. Another way is with an airline ticket for a specified (though not necessarily dated) flight out of Panama but note that if the flight is to Colombia or Costa Rica you will also need an onward ticket out of those countries too before being allowed in. A return bus ticket out of the country will also do, eg a return *TICA* bus ticket from San Jose to Panama City. This will cost you US$26.50. Cheaper alternatives are available with the other bus lines operating this route eg *Panaica* and *Transportes Ferguson.*

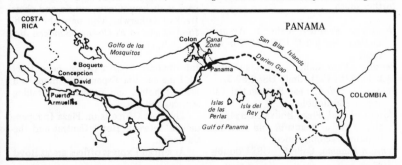

An even cheaper alternative is a return San Jose to David bus ticket with *Tracopa* (See *Transport* section under Costa Rica for further details). But note, the return half of the ticket is only refundable with written permission from Panamanian Immigration. This itself costs US$10 making it hardly worth the effort. Keep smiling.

You may also be asked to show up to US$150 or more at the border. They don't like impecunious people.

CURRENCY

US$1 = 1 Balboa

The unit of currency is the US Dollar (they don't print any notes of their own) but in Panama it is called the Balboa. Coins are exactly equivalent in size and value to their US counterparts. Banking hours are Monday-Friday, 8 am to 1 pm.

PANAMA CITY

Accommodation If you like American hamburgercocacola nightmares mixed with colonial buildings, squalid slums, and hustlers, here's Nirvana. It is also a free port packed out with consumer goodies, duty free. It's the place to buy photographic material, cassettes, calculators, etc. If you are trying to do a little wheeler-dealing as you go along you will find ready markets for this stuff further south.

Hospedaje Familiar, Calle 4, Avenida Central, No 7-10. US$2.50 for the roof.

Pensión Alfaro, Calle 8, Avenida Central behind the Cathedral. US$2.50-3.

Pensión Catedral, near Presidential Palace. US$6/double.

Hotel Colonial, Plaza Bolívar, US$4/single, it is a beautiful old colonial building, recommended.

Pensión Panama, Calle 6. US$4/double

friendly, clean and an interesting building.

Pensión America, Calle Equador. US$4-6/single — clean.

Hotel Ideal above *TICA* bus terminal. Avenida Justo Arosemena 35-51. $9/double — noisy. Avoid this place if you're a woman, the Annexe may be cheap but just isn't worth the hassle.

Pensión Mexico, Avenida Mexico between Calles 4IE and 43E, near the seafront. US$10/double.

Hotel Premier, Avenida Central 18-105. US$7-9/single, $9-12/double.

Many other cheap places are in the Santa Ana area of town. There is free camping at the Hipodromo Presidente Ramón race track.

Eats For local food there are plenty of good places in the Vista Hermosa district (eg *Piscolabis*, *El Forron* and *Via Fernando de Córdoba*) and on Avenida Balboa (eg Restaurant Boulevard). For Italian food try the *Napoli*, Calle Estudiante and Calle I, that is good and cheap. For Chinese food try the *Gran China*, Avenida Balboa between Calle 26 and 27, or the *Nueva Oriente*, near Plaza Catedral. Both are good and cheap. Get Spanish food at the *Madrid*, Via España near UK Consul. Daily comida corrida, US$2.60. The *Golden Frog*, near the Bella Vista theatre is a popular place with travellers, run by an American, with hamburgers, music and chess freaks. Otherwise you have the trash food chains of *El Coronel Sanders*, *McDonalds*, etc.

Information Tourist Office, near Hotel El Panama, Via Espana, has maps and lists of hotels and pensiones, detailing services and prices.

The Post Office is on Plaza Independencia between Hotel Central and the Cathedral.

American Express offices are at Boyd

Brothers Inc (Panama Tours), Calle 50, Edificio San Miguel 58, Telephone 64 7433.

Urban buses are plentiful with a flat rate of 20 cents.

Places Nearby Panama Viejo, the ruins of the old city of Panama, were looted and burnt by the Welsh buccaneer, Henry Morgan, in 1671. Some of the buildings were restored and it's perhaps the best part of a visit to Panama City. It is situated about eight km from the modern city. Taxi US$1.50, or a bus from the Via Espana for 10 cents.

Balboa is the Pacific end of the Panama Canal. It's not a place of any great interest unless you're in to watching ships come into and out of the Canal. But if you're looking for work on a ship going somewhere else in the world (difficult without seaman's ticket) you might find something here. It's 10 minutes from Panama City and there's a YMCA here if you need somewhere to stay.

COLÓN

The hustlers mecca and another duty-free port, but it's a lot heavier than Panama City. Watch yourself, mugging is frequent. Keep your valuables out of sight. Most people pass through quickly either on their way to the San Blas Islands or to look for a boat going to Colombia.

Accommodation

Pensión Plaza, Avenida Central, US$4/ double — clean.

Pensión Acropolis, US$4/single — clean and comfortable.

Pensión Andros Annexe. US$6/double — safe and comfortable.

Pensión Kingston. US$3/single.

Salvation Army. Free if you're low on dinero and have no demands on comfort, etc.

Eats *Tropic Bar*, Avenida Balboa and

Calle 10. The restaurant and bar are open 24 hours a day. Lunch 75 cents, dinner US$2. YMCA also provide cheap meals.

Other The Post Office is at Calle 9 and Avenida Bolivar.

Places Nearby Cristóbal is the Caribbean end of the Panama Canal. Large ocean-going liners dock here so it is another place to look for work on ships.

Portobelo is the ancient port used by the Spanish to unload European manufactures destined for the Viceroyalty of Peru and load up with Peruvian gold, silver and other products. Worth a visit to see the ruins, etc. On October 21 there is the festival of the Black Christ — processions, feasts and dancing. Buses from Colon to Portobelo leave from Calle 12 (48 km journey).

DAVID
Accommodation

Residencia Chiriqui, US$2/person.

Pensión Costa Rica, near *TICA* bus terminal, US$2/person — clean.

Pensión Fanita, used by *Transportes Ferguson International* buses for their overnight stop. US$4.50/single with air-con and bath, but there are cheaper rooms for US$3/single.

Hotel Iris, on the central square, US$9/ double.

Places Nearby Boquete can be visited from David by minibus service, 75 cents. It's a mountain village noted for camping, river fishing, swimming, riding and walking. It has some good hotels, eg *Funadores*, *Los Quetzales*, *Pensión Virginia* (US$3.10/single) that are all clean and recommended.

TRANSPORT
Flights International flights depart from Tocuman airport, 27 km from Panama City. Buses between the two go every 15 minutes from Plaza 5 de Mayo,

25 cents and take one hour. Alternatively there are colectivos which will cost US$3/person if there are five of you in the car. Ordinary taxis cost US$10 for the car. Internal flights depart from Paitilla airport nearer to Panama City. There's an airport tax of US$4.50 for all passengers and a purchase tax of US$4 on all air tickets.

The national airlines *COPA* and *ADSA* fly to all parts of Panama as well as international destinations. In addition there are a number of smaller airlines which cover specific routes: eg Transportes Aereos Interioranos SA *(Talsa)* which covers the San Blas Islands; *Chitreana* for Isla de las Perlas and *Aviones de Panama. Aerolineas Isla de las Perlas* fly from Paitilla airport to Islas de las Perlas for US$12.75 return. For further information see *Getting to Colombia.*

Trains There are two lines. The Canal Zone line is the Colón-Panama City route with seven trains per day (six on Sundays). US$3/return in first class and US$2/return in second class. This is an excellent way to see the Canal and Gatún Lake, especially if your time is limited. The station in Panama City is on Frangipani Street. In Colón it is at the junction of Calle 11 and Front Street.

The Chiriqui line is between Concepción (on the Pan American Highway) and Puerto Armuelles. The line continues onto David and Pedregal but this stretch is for goods trains only. Passenger trains depart from Concepción at 7.30 am, 2.30 pm and depart Armuelles at 6.45 am, 2 pm. The journey time is about four hours.

Buses Panama City-David. Three companies cover the route — *Utranschiriqui Transchiri* (Terminal in Panama City at Calle 7A-23) and *Transportes Ferguson.* All have daily services and take about five hours,

US$4. From David take a minibus to the border with Costa Rica and a local bus from there to San José. This works out much cheaper than taking the *TICA* bus from Panama City-San José direct. But remember that an onward ticket is required for entry into Costa Rica (arrange this before you arrive at the border).

Panama City-San José. *TICA* bus runs a daily service that takes 15 hours. US$13.20/single. Remember you need an onward ticket for Costa Rica. If you haven't got one *TICA* bus will only sell you a return ticket (US$26.50). Two other slightly cheaper lines also cover this route with a daily service: *Transportes Ferguson* and *Panaica.*

Panama City-Colón. Buses go every hour in either direction and take one hour. US$1. This is the bus you must catch if you want to watch the ships go through the Gatún and Miraflores locks on the Canal.

Getting to Colombia You need an onward ticket out of Colombia before being allowed in. Get this sorted out before you arrive. In working out the cheapest way to get from Panama to Colombia you must take into consideration the following factors. (1) If you fly there's an airport tax of US$4.50 plus a purchase tax on all air tickets of US$4 in addition to the cost of the flight. (2) The cost of the boat and overland trips mentioned below do not include food and accommodation. The longer you have to spend waiting for connections and making the journey, the less will be the cost differential between these routes and the air fare. The various adventure potentials are of course incomparable. (3) If you're relying on an MCO or a dated or undated airline ticket as your onward ticket from Colombia, make sure you get one from an airline which is a member of IATA in case you change your travel plans as they are transferable. Bear in mind in this respect that *COPA* the Panamanian airline, is not a member of IATA hence its tickets are non-transferable and there are no *COPA* offices in Colombia, so you'll have to go back to Panama City if you want a refund.

With this in mind, here are the alternatives:

Infrequent contraband boats go from Dock 5, Colón, to Barranquilla. These are entirely at your own risk. Mas o menos US$25 (bargain). This is the cheapest way. Forget about onward ticket requirements if you are planning on this. If they can get contraband through, they'll get you through (though a bottle of whisky would undoubtedly oil the wheels — bought duty-free in Panama City or Colón). "Contraband" is usually consumer goods — cameras, watches, TVs, transistor radios, etc. No one gets jailed (or "fined") for this sort of thing in Colombia unless they're tight-fisted and/or as thick as two short planks.

Boat from Colón to San Andrés Island (A Colombian Caribbean possession) and another boat from there to either Cartagena or Barranquilla on the mainland. Boats depart every 10 days or so from Colón; infrequent from San Andrés. US$15 for each leg of the journey but if you have to buy a return ticket before being allowed in this bumps the cost of transport up to US$45 in total. But then what's a return "ticket" on one of these boats? A scrap of paper with some kind of illegible rubber stamp on it and an even more illegible signature? A bottle of whisky goes a long way and the journey does, after all, take two days. Remember though, that a seven-day wait in Panama for a boat would negate any difference in price between this and the air fare (assuming a bare minimum of US$5 per day for living expenses in Panama).

A flight from Panama to Medellin by *SAM* or *COPA*, US$55, takes one hour and is *the cheapest direct flight* from Panama to Colombia. Don't buy a return *COPA* ticket unless you know for certain you're coming back this way as they're not IATA members.

Boats go from the Molle Viejo in Colón to Puerto Obladia on the Panamanian side of the border with Colombia. From there, there are boats and plane connections with Turbo on the Gulf of Urabá and from there road connection with Medellin. You may need permission from the Colombian authorities to do this trip — check this out with the Colombian Consulate in Panama. We have no more specific details as yet.

Flights from Panama to Cartagena or Barranquilla are serviced by *SAM*, *COPA* and *Avianca*. On *SAM* and *COPA* the cost is slightly more (about US$10 more) than the Panama-Medellin flight. *Avianca* is slightly more again.

Overland through the Darién Jungle is the final alternative. To make this trip you need a thick skin, a constitution of iron, at least partial immunity to just about every pathogen lurking on the face of the earth and a distinct liking for everything which slithers, slides and scratches in the night. The best time to make the trip is in the dry season — January to mid-April — when it should take about 10 days. Maps are available from the Ministro de Obras Públicas, Instituto Geográfico Nacional, Panama City. The exact route you take will, to a large extent, depend on expediency, the availability of guides and transport (usually dug-out canoes) and what you encounter on the way. One route is as follows: The first leg is from Panama to Boca de Cupe. This can be done by taking a boat from Panama to Yaviza, US$5. Walk from there to Pinogana with the aid of a guide and from Pinogana to Boca de Cupe by motor dug-out, US$2. The other way is by boat from Panama to El Real, US$6. From there a motor dug-out to Boca de Cupe, about US$3.

In Boca de Cupe you get your exit stamp and from there get a dug-out to the Cuna village of Pucuro, about US$4. Ask the village chief for permission to stay in the village. From there it's a nine hour walk through thick jungle to Paya (once the capital of the Cuna empire) with the help of a guide. Next you go on to El Esfuerzo in Colombia on the bank of the river Cacarica via Palo de las Letras. This last section is heavy going. From El Esfuerzo there are motor dug-outs to Turbo occasionally but it's usually better to go by dug-out from El Esfuerzo to Vijado, about US$18, and from there by the same means to Travesía, about US$4. From Travesía there are definite banana boats to Turbo for about US$1.5. You may have to wait a few days in both Vijado and Travesía. The Colombian entry stamp you get from DAS in Turbo.

Food is obtainable along the way (especially if you're adept at hunting) but take enough for five days. Malaria pills, mosquito netting, insect repellant and water sterilization tablets are essential baggage. Make sure you had that yellow fever jab or see a priest before you set off. The total cost of transport alone is about US$55.

OTHER PLACES IN PANAMA

San Blas Islands 365 islands off the north coast of Panama are inhabited by the Cuna Indians who are semi-autonomous and send their own representatives to the National Congress. Their culture is still very much alive and the women still practise the original weaving of Mola tapestries and wear colourful clothes with gold nose and ear rings. They're also very shrewd and have the tourist trade well sussed out. If you're thinking of taking pictures, have your money ready — they charge about 25 cents a picture.

Boats from Colon are irregular — ask around the piers. Otherwise *ADSA* flies in from Paitilla airport. There are day-trips organized by some of the large hotels in Panama City but they cost around US$20 including food. The cheapest we've heard of so far, other than sleeping on the beach for free, is the *Hotel Porvenir* on El Porvenir island, US$8/day. There are boats and flights to this island.

Pearl Islands Again these tend to be expensive. They're used as a venue for talks between the US and Panama or whoever else happens to be visiting at the time. Most people go for the fishing as the sea teems with many different species of deep-sea fish. The launch *Fiesta* goes there from Pier 18 in Balboa — enquire at the *Argonaut Steamship Agency* on Calle 55, No. 7-82 Panama City. Flights there by *Aerolineas Islas de las Perlas* go from Paitilla airport, US$12.75 return. *El Galeon* on the island Contadora has accommodation starting at US$7.50/night. The beach is free.

The Canal Zone On average, 36 ocean-going ships pass through the 67 km long Canal every day. Each ship is raised through a series of locks from sea level to a height of 28 metres, across the man-made Gatún Lake, and then lowered through another series of locks back down to sea level. Passage through the Canal takes about nine hours and the scenery is beautiful. The series of locks nearest to Panama City are at Miraflores. To get there take a *Paraiso* bus from the Canal Zone terminal near the Plaza 5 de Mayo. There is a visitors' area where you can watch the ships go through the locks. There's also a film and guide commentary and a free tour of the Canal, courtesy of the US, between 9 am and 4 pm everyday except Sundays. A lot of the Canal can be seen whilst riding on the train between Colón and Panama City. There are murals showing the construction of the Canal at the Canal Zone Administration Buildings in Balboa.

The island of Barro Colorado in the middle of Gatún Lake is now a biological reserve and scientific research station. The animals fled here when the area was flooded to create the lake. Visits can be arranged at the Smithsonian Institute in Ancón (a virtual suburb of Panama City). Visits cost US$6 including lunch and the cost of the boat.

There is free access between Panama and the Canal Zone.

GETTING A CAR TO COLOMBIA

This costs at least US$500 for the car alone plus US$90 for each passenger. The bureaucratic hassles and paperwork at either end are designed to try the patience of a saint. If you're determined, we suggest you consult one of the following for further details, since this book isn't really written for people with US$500 to throw away taking a car to South America: *Latin American Travel Guide and Pan American Highway Guide, Overland and Beyond, South American Handbook*. Further details, prices, etc, of these books can be found in the *Introduction*.

Colombia

One of the wildest, most exotic and fascinating of the Andean countries, Colombia has almost every conceivable type of geography from the largely uninhabited and jungle-covered swamps of the coastal lowlands to the cool and fertile high valleys sandwiched between the three main cordilleras which fan out across the country from the Ecuadorian border. There are beautiful old colonial towns, each with their own unique character, like Cartagena, Antioquia and Popayan, and important archaeological sites like those in the Sierra Nevada de Santa Marta (which also has the highest peaks in the country and is still largely autonomous Indian territory) and at San Agustín. The site at San Agustín is exceptionally beautiful. It is popular with travellers who are willing to go a little way off the beaten track to see something worthwhile. Many travellers bypass it in their haste to reach the old Inca heartland but you should try to get

there if at all possible.

But it's not just the geography and the cities which are so varied: along with Brazil and, to a lesser extent, Venezuela, the majority of people in Colombia are "trigueños" — a mixture of white, black and Indian. They range in type across the whole spectrum of possibilities. Many pure or almost pure Indians remain in the remoter parts of the country in places like the Pacific coast and the Amazonian jungle and it was among the latter group that William Burroughs went in search of his yage brujos. On the Caribbean coast black people predominate and the culture and atmosphere is very similar to that found in other black communities throughout the Caribbean. The people along this coast speak (Spanish) in a manner which is at first difficult to understand, dropping the s's and running their words together. They have a reputation somewhat like that which the Romans have among Northern Italians: the best thieves, dancers, carousers and lovers come from the coast and, in Bogotano eyes, they're looked on with some degree of suspicion. The mountain people by contrast are more solemn, dignified and severe and their speech is full of diminutives — "chicitico", "momentito" "gringita", etc. The different cultural and racial groups occupy quite separate dimensions in the life of Colombia and have their own religions, life-styles, standard of living, values, architecture and music — one of the facts which makes Colombia so interesting.

You might think that such a racially mixed population would have resulted in a mestizo-dominated government like that in Mexico but, in common with most other South American countries, the upper (and wealthy) classes are almost always the descendants of old Spanish families or are more recent arrivals from the USA, Canada, Germany and Switzerland. There are some 30,000 US citizens in Colombia complete with their very own secure Bogota ghetto. The Jewish population have also become a wealthy part of the upper classes and are the most often kidnapped group in the country.

Colombia has had a very stormy history and is, in many ways, the headquarters of Latin American "machismo". If you're unfamiliar with the term, it's a concept of male-to-male relationships in which one must constantly prove one's courage and endurance by playing with danger and death — in crime, war, in a car or on horseback for example. Its other face defines male-to-female relationships as one of male dominance, male potency and conquest along with chivalry, charm and attentiveness. A lot of what goes down in this country can be seen in terms of "machismo" and it lies at the base of the crime, sex repression and violence which permeates the Colom-

bian way of life. It has earned Colombia the reputation of being a nation of bandits and thieves — one not entirely undeserved. As far as travelling is concerned, this is one of the worst places on the continent for rip-offs. You must keep a constant watch over your belongings at all times and especially on the street and in buses. If you don't they'll grow legs in less time than it takes to blink.

The violence which simmers below the surface is reflected in the ubiquitous machine-gun-toting police force — a grossly underpaid and corrupt poor man's job — and in the numerous army checkpoints which dot every country road and where it's compulsory to stop and searches are carried out. Other reminders can be seen in the design of houses for the blancos and nouveau rich mestizos with their elaborate security, guards and high walls topped with broken glass. There are strong guerrilla movements in the country and certain barrios and provinces are reputed to be under their control. Except in force, the police avoid them like the plague. Bomb incidents are almost daily news at times in Bogota and the country has one of the world's highest kidnap rates. The overt repression and fear is as great here as it is in any other country notorious for such things.

Politically, the violence is rooted in the rivalry between Liberals and Conservatives which came to the surface following independence and the break-up of Simon Bolívar's short-lived dream of the Republic of Gran Colombia — an attempted Latin American United States of what is now Venezuela, Colombia and Ecuador. Partial civil wars and insurrections followed each other throughout the 19th century as each party took it in turn to impose their views on the country according to expediency and the degree of support which they could muster at any particular time. The activities of the Church which supported the Conservatives, further poisoned the issue and in 1899 things came to a head with a full-blown three-year civil war. 100,000 men died in this war and the Liberals were defeated but the defeat didn't eclipse them as a political force and the rivalry simmered on. It was in the aftermath of this war, with the country weak and in no position to put up effective resistance, that the United States encouraged a group of dissidents in Panama to declare the independence of that country in return for quasi-sovereign rights over a strip of territory through which they wanted to build a canal. Up until that time, Panama had been a province of Colombia and it was not until 1921 that Bogotá finally recognised the independence of Panama and the United States came up with a belated US$25 million in "compensation".

The struggle between Liberals and Conservatives was to break out yet again in 1948 and lead to 10 years of the worst violence Colombia has ever experienced. It began with the assassination of a progressive mayor of Bogotá and spread rapidly to the rest of the country encouraged by the major political figures in the capital. 300,000 people are estimated to have died in this civil war — known as "La Violencia" — and the memory of those terrible years which had a devastating effect on the Colombian mentality is still very much alive today.

The absurdity of "La Violencia" was that it was largely an unreal cause for which the people were fighting since there was little to choose between the party politicians of either side. The Presidents of Colombia since independence have all come from five families and these same families will continue to rule until the next revolution comes around. The fighting ended in the mid-50s with a deal between the leaders of the opposing factions whereby they agreed to swop over the administration of the country every four years until the 1974 elections and both support the same presidential candidate. But it wasn't just the lack of any clear victory in sight for either party which prompted peace negotiations. After years of guerilla-style fighting, the campesinos had developed into experienced peasant armies who became a law unto themselves, sufficiently organised to have autonomous control over their districts. At this stage there was more discernable "power to the people" spirit to the fighting and attempted occupations of haciendas owned by Bogatá barons and Medellín mafioso. This growth in the political awareness of the peasants represented a serious threat to the power of the blanco politicians and part of the rationale behind the peace negotiations was the defusing of the revolutionary potential in the countryside. After the deal was arranged, the ordinary people had to try to pick up the pieces of their peacetime lives having achieved absolutely nothing in the way of political rights or land reform during all those years of killing. The struggle is still going on today — witness the endless grafitti on every wall in any Colombian city — though these days under what passes itself off as a "democratically elected" government.

Even in the early years following the arrival of the Spanish in 1500 the country was torn by constant feuding between contending conquistadores. It was explored from three different directions, the first expedition being led by Jiménez de Quesada who landed on the Caribbean coast and pushed up the Magdalena valley where he discovered the Chibcha Indians. These people were sedentary farmers who held their land in common and had achieved a fairly high civilization by the time the Spanish arrived. They were ruled by two chiefs, one of whom had his capital near

Bogotá and the other near Tunja. Their agricultural potential remained limited since, for domestic animals, they only had the dog and their cultivated crops were confined to maize and potatoes. They were soon conquered and Bogotá founded in 1538. A year later Sebastian de Benalcázar, one of Pizarro's henchmen, mounted an expedition from Ecuador and conquered the southern half of the country, founding the cities of Pasto, Popayán and Cali along the way. His expedition arrived in Bogota in 1539. In the same year another expedition, this time led by Nicolaus de Federmann on behalf of the German Welsers who had been granted a land concession by the Spanish king, came in from Venezuela across the Andes and arrived in Bogotá almost at the same time as Benalcázar. There was immediate rivalry between these three contending factions and since the centre of power was in faraway Lima it was not sorted out until many years later when Bogotá was made into the capital of the Presidency of Nueva Granada. In 1718 it was hived off from the Viceroyalty of Peru and made into its own independent Viceroyalty, an administrative unit which also included what is today Venezuela.

The independence movement was given its head as a result of the Napoleonic Wars in Europe. When Ferdinand VII was replaced with Napoleon's brother on the Spanish throne, the colonies refused to accept the move and rival juntas were set up throughout Colombia, the main ones being at Bogotá and Tunja. A little while later Simon Bolívar ("El Libertador") landed at Cartagena and fought his way up the Magdalena valley to Bogotá and on to Cúcuta. From here he fought his way to Caracas but, being unable to hold the city, was forced to return to Cartagena. In the following year Napoleon was defeated at Waterloo and the Spanish set about re-conquering their colonies but by this time Bolívar had assembled an army of horsemen from the Venezuelan llanos and 5000 British ex-Peninsular War veterans at Angostura (Cuidad Bolívar). With this army he marched across the Andes into Colombia and joined up with Santander's liberation forces. Together they defeated the Royalists first at the battle of Vargas in the lowlands and again at the battle of Boyacá. With Colombia free, a revolutionary congress was held at Cucuta and it was here that opposing factions came to the fore. Bolívar was for a centralised and unified republic made up of Venezuela, Colombia and Ecuador whereas Santander favoured a federal republic of sovereign states. For a time Bolívar managed to impose his views and the Republic of Gran Colombia came into being. It didn't last long and even before Bolívar died it had split up into its three constituent countries. Though Bolívar is very much a cultural hero as a result of the wars for independence, the adulation which is given to him is perhaps out of proportion to what he actually did achieve. He certainly "liberated" the upper classes and the blancos from the control of the Spanish Crown but he did nothing for the Indians, the blacks and mestizos who were exploited even more than they had been under the Spanish after independence.

This long account of the violence endemic in Colombian society may make you hesitant to go there but you should remember that, as a traveller, it's very unlikely that you will come into direct contact with it, and, with at least the semblance of a democratically elected government in power, things have cooled down a lot. The only thing you need to be exceptionally careful about is drugs, if you use them. As was mentioned earlier, there are a lot of police on the streets and many army checkpoints along the country roads where searches are carried out, Travellers are not exempt from these searches and in many ways, are often "preferred customers" since, if anything is found on them, they're always good for a nice fat bribe. If you do get caught with anything, keep them talking and discreetly offer a "regalo" (gift). Don't let things get as far as the station or you'll just become another reason why the US Narcotics Bureau pours anti-drugs trafficking funds into Colombia. It's well known that two of Colombia's most valuable "invisible" exports are grass and cocaine but the issue is surrounded by an incredible amount of hypocrisy and it's common knowledge that high government officials are the biggest dealers and that diplomats and the mafia are the biggest carriers. The people who are caught and brought to "trial", with one or two notable exceptions, are not these civil servants, professionals, industrialists and mafia bosses but poor people and foreigners who are pulled with small amounts. Every few days you'll see newspaper reports about huge drug hauls, laboratories or running gun battles at an airport. The people involved in these major operations are also the ones who have sufficient money or political elbow to buy their way out of custody. There's no such thing as a "fair trial"; no pretence of "justice". If you have money or influence then you don't go to prison or you don't stay there very long. Simple as that. So if you are carrying drugs be extremely careful.

Don't be put off going there by all the stories you hear. It's a fascinating country and well worth the effort!

VISAS

Visas are not required by nationals of Western Europe, Israel, Japan or USA. Tourist Cards are required by nationals of Canada, Australia and New Zealand and are issued free from any Colombian Embassy or Consulate. You need two photographs and, depending on where you apply for the Card, may be asked to show an onward ticket before it's issued. They allow a 90 day stay.

Those not requiring visas or Tourist Cards are generally given 30 days on arrival but you can get up to 60 days if you ask (immigration officials may ask to see how much money you have if you want more than 30 days).

Onward Tickets Officially you must have an onward ticket (and sufficient money) before being allowed into Colombia, *BUT* the decision as to whether you're asked to show it/them on arrival is completely arbitrary. It has nothing to do with the length of your hair or what sort of baggage you're carrying. A very smartly-dressed Canadian woman in front of me at Cartagena Airport was hassled for both and the official wasn't satisfied with her first offering of US$500 in travellers' cheques — she had to pull out another US$500 wad of cheques before being allowed to pass on. I wasn't asked for either.

Coming in from Venezuela via Maracaibo-Maicao-Santa Marta we flashed empty *Aerocondor* ticket folders. They waved us through without even bothering to look inside. Of course your options are limited if you haven't got one and they ask to see it. Also many airlines flying into Colombia won't let you buy a ticket, let alone board the flight unless you already have an onward ticket.

Exit stamps are now obtainable at the border posts — you don't have to visit the DAS office in the nearest town to get one. There's no exit fee for land borders. Airport taxes are US$2 for internal flights and US$10 for external flights. There is an 11% tax on air tickets for flights out of the country, so, if possible, buy your tickets elsewhere.

CURRENCY

US$1 = 38 Pesos

The unit of currency is the Peso (C$) = 100 centavos. The exchange rate varies between 36 pesos and 39 pesos to the dollar. The Banco Royal Colombiano changes travellers' cheques at 36.07 = US$1 but they charge about US$1.50 (50 pesos) on each transaction. American Express change at 38.75 = US$1 if they have the money! The reason they often haven't is because everyone using their services seems to pay in US dollars or dollar travellers' cheques, because they credit you with the 38.75 pesos rate if you're buying tickets. In some places (eg Popayán), the only bank which will change travellers' cheques is the Banco de la Republica. Casas de Cambio are generally less hassle than banks and don't charge much commission (if at all). Also in some places the Tourist Office will change cheques or cash without taking commission.

There is a minor currency black-market especially in the Caribbean ports where you might be offered up to 39 pesos to the dollar, *but* the risks of being ripped-off in the exchange weigh heavily against its use — see the warning under *Money* in *On the Road*.

A WARNING!

Colombia is notorious for its rip-off artists and pickpockets, though in recent years the highest accolade for this nefarious activitiy has passed to Peru. You might even get mugged in Bogotá if you wander round in the slummy areas with sufficient gay abandon and conspicuous wealth. Buses and trains (and stations and terminals) are the favourite places. Stay awake when you're travelling. Keep your eyes and ears open and your valuables next to your skin. If your baggage is being carried on the roof or in luggage compartments get off at every stop and watch it closely. If you don't, someone else will. Don't turn your back on your baggage in a bus terminal. Unwatched, it will grow the fastest pair of legs ever known to man.

BARRANQUILLA

Accommodation A hot, seedy port with little to recommend it except perhaps a night's sleep on your way to somewhere else. There are lots of hustlers around the Plaza Bolívar, so don't let them take you to a hotel otherwise you'll end up paying their "commission" on top of what the hotel wants for a room/bed.

Hotel Selecto Anything but select, and in fact it looked thoroughly defuncto when we called, though it's reputed to be the cheapest in town at C$38/single. It's a few yards down Carrera 45 from Plaza Bolívar — give it a try if you're hard up.

Hotel Roxy, next door to the Selecto and verging on the acceptable. It is C$160/double without own bathroom — pretty busy.

Hotel Zhivago, about 20 metres down Carrera 44 from Plaza Bolívar. It is C$91/double without bath — recommended but often full.

Hotel Real, a few metres down Paseo Bolívar on the left from Plaza Bolívar. C$330/double with handbasin and fan — clean communal showers and toilets. It's a touch expensive but it's a haven of peace in comparison to those around the bus terminals and there's a friendly management. Meals are served but they're expensive compared to what's available outside.

If you don't mind doing a little walking there are other cheap hotels near the library (Biblioteca Regional) on Carrera 38 (Ave de los Estudiantes); the *Hotel Bolívar*, near the junction of Calle 33 and Carrera 38; the *Residencias Las Americas*, near the junction of Paseo Bolívar and Carrera 36. Otherwise there are plenty of other seedy and very flash hotels along the Paseo Bolívar between Carreras 40 and 44. Avoid the *Hotel Aurora*, on Paseo Bolívar opposite the

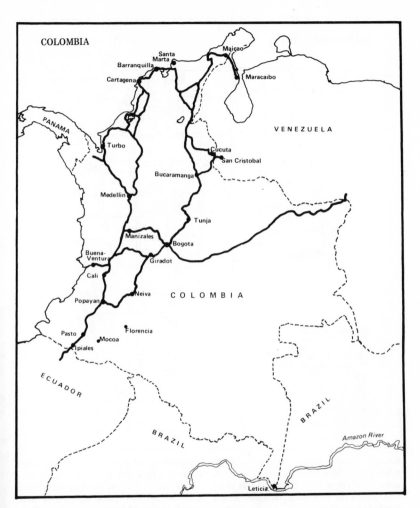

church. It's a scruffy, noisy whorehouse with a TV on constant maximum volume — probably to maintain a modicum of discretion between clients though none of them looked like the type who would care one way or the other. It's C$120/double if you're a glutton for punishment.

Eats Excellent food can be got in the cafe on the corner of Carrera 44 and Paseo Bolívar. Almuerzo and comida/cena C$50. This is more than you would pay in many smaller cafes but the food is very tasty and there's plenty of it — friendly staff and cheap ice-cold beers.

Information There's a sub-tourist office in the Biblioteca Regional on Carrera 38 but they haven't anything you wouldn't

BARRANQUILLA

① Plaza Bolivar
② Bus Terminals
③ Aerocondor
④ Post Office (Avianca)
⑤ Hotels Roxy & Selecto

Carrera 46 (Ave. Olaya Herrera)
Carrera 45
Carrera 44
Carrera 43 (Ave. 20 de Julio)
Carrera 40
Carrera 39
Carrera 38 (Ave. de los Estudiantes)

Cartagena

Calle 38
Calle 37
Calle 36
Calle 35
Paseo Bolivar (Calle 34)
Calle 33 {Calle 33 Calle 32
Calle 31
Ave. Boyaca (Calle 30)

⑥ Hotels Zhivago, California Real & Buenos Aires Bolivian Consulate.
⑦ Hotels Riviera, Magangue, Aurora. Venezuelan Consulate.
⑧ Hotel Hispano Americano
⑨ Hotels Embajada & Monaco
⑩ Hotel Bolivia
⑪ Hotel Residencias Las Americas
⑫ Biblioteca Regional & Tourist Sub-Office

Airport (Km. 9)
Santa Marta
Venezuela.

already know about: no maps, time-tables, etc. The main office is in the sub-urbs on Carrera 52 No. 72-46 but then how much do you want to know about a disaster area?

Other The Fiesta lasts for four days the week preceeding Ash Wednesday. There are parades, floats, street dancing, etc. A taxi to the airport (9km from town) is C$100-120/car, but you must bargain.

If you have anything ripped-off and need a "denunciacion" for insurance purposes go to Policia Judicial on Calle 48 at the junction with Carrera 43 (Ave 20 de Julio). There's no fuss but you must be able to speak Spanish or have an interpreter. The bus there from Plaza Bolivar is *Expreso Porvenir*.

BOGOTÁ
Once the seat of the Vice-royalty of New Granada, Bogotá was, until fairly recent times, a small city due to the lack of communications. It's now suffering from the same kind of urban blight which afflicts many other capital cities

around the world due to the sudden expansion of its population which exceeds three and a half million. Many of these people live in squalid shanty towns on the outskirts, scraping a living as best they can. There's plenty of colonial architecture left and don't miss the Gold Museum and the salt cathedral in the mines at Zipaquirá. Those in search of a legend which lured every thug in Europe during the 16th and 17th centuries should visit Lake Guatavita.

Accommodation The budget hotel area is located between Calles 13 and 17 and Carreras 15 and 17 near the various bus terminals. They vary a great deal in quality.

Picasso, Calle 17 No. 15-47. C$57/ single, C$114/double — hot water.
El Buen Amigo, Carrera 16 No. 14-45. C$61/single — hot water.
Residencias Panama, Carrera 16 No. 16-88 (also have another entrance at Calle 17 No. 15-85). C$57/single, double bed — clean. There's a complimentary coffee in the morning and the management is friendly, but the bar is noisy so make sure . you get a room well away from it.
Florian, Calle 14 No. 14-69. C$57.
Residencias Alemanes, Carrera 16, Calle 16 near to the *Panama*. C$150/ three people, C$120/double. German run. It's clean, has hot water and very good breakfasts.
Virgin del Camino, Carrera 14, Calle 8. C$114/double — hot water.

Outside this area you should try:

Hotel Carlos V, Carrera 7 No. 30—28. C$152/double, C$95/single — hot water. It's secure. The management is friendly.
Posada Kayser, Carrera 4 No. 13-18 — cheap with hot water.
Hotel Italia, Carrera 7 No. 20-40.

C$175/double — hot water.
Hotel Alcron, Calle 20 No. 5-87. C$91/ double. Plenty of hot water mitigates for its somewhat scruffy appearance.

Eats
El Rincon de Sancho, Carrera 8 No. 16-53. Full dinner C$25. Good food and atmosphere and it's close to the Gold Museum.
El Pez Dorado, Calle 22 No. 6-68. Fish specialities, Cena C$38.
Cafe Snoopy, in the lobby of the *Hotel Carlos V*. Vegetarian soy burgers and pizzas.
El Pizzaría, Carrera 8 off Calle 6. All sizes and varieties of what you would expect the place to sell.

Information Tourist Office, Calle 19 No. 6-68 in the First National City Bank Building has plenty of information, maps, etc. There's also a branch at the International Airport and another at the Sabana Railway Station.

For free vaccinations go to Carrera 15 No. 58-59. The best time to go is in the mornings. If you want a hepatitis shot go to the Clinica Bogotá on Carrera 17 No. 12-65.

Other Taxi fare to the centre from the airport is C$23 plus whatever the meter clocks up — usually an additional C$76. Collectivos cost C$6 plus luggage charge. Buses cost C$44.

Teaching English: Try the English Language Centre, Carrera 13 No. 42-35, Piso 3, Bogotá 0317, tel 245 2387; Native speakers only. Another possibility is the Anglo-Colombian School, Calle 19 No. 152-48, tel 580065. Also enquire at the British Council, Calle 11 No. 5-16, tel 438181.

Avoid getting Venezuelan visas/ Tourist Cards in Bogotá as they charge US$5 — free elsewhere except sometimes in Bucaramanga.

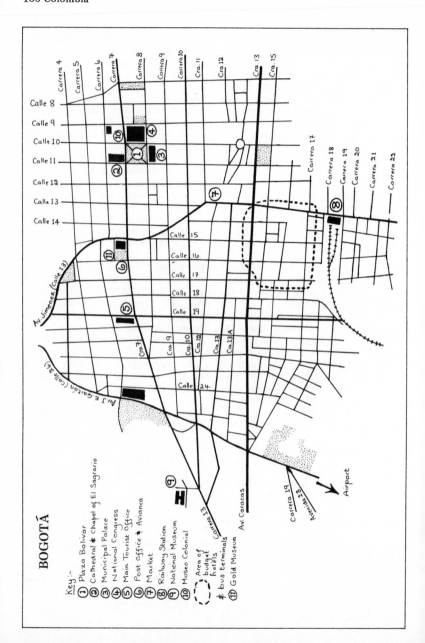

BOGOTÁ

Key:-
① Plaza Bolivar
② Cathedral ✠ chapel of El Sagrario
③ Municipal Palace
④ National Congress
⑤ Main Tourist Office
⑥ Post office ✠ Avianca
⑦ Market
⑧ Railway Station
⑨ National Museum
⑩ Museo Colonial
⑪ Gold Museum
⬭ Area of budget hotels
✠ bus terminals

Things to Do/See *The Gold Museum* (Museo del Oro), situated in the Parque de Santander on the corner of Calle 16 and Carrera 6, is a must. Thousands of pre-Colombian gold artifacts, mainly from the Chibcha civilization. Open Tuesday-Saturday, 9 am-5 pm and Sundays from 10 am-2 pm. Entry C$10 (some people say they've been given student discounts by showing an ISTC Card). Two films daily explain the legend of El Dorado.

The National Museum (Museo Nacional) Carrera 7, Calles 28-29, used to be an old prison (El Panoptico), shows the history of Colombia from pre-Spanish days to the present. The Indian artifacts are very interesting. Open Tuesday-Saturday, 10 am-12.30 pm, 3 pm-6 pm and Sunday, 9 am-noon. Entry C$20/person (free on Saturdays and every day for students).

Jardin Botánico, Carrera 66 No. 56-84. A good place to spend some time away from the noise and the cars and has a representative sample of the variety of vegetation which grows in Colombia.

Places Nearby
Zipaquirá Salt Cathedral. A cathedral carved out of solid salt half a mile beneath the surface in the vast salt mines at Zipaquira. The mines have been exploited for centuries and still contain vast resources. The cathedral has a 25 metre ceiling and is said to be capable of holding 10,000 people. There's a free concert there every Sunday morning. To get there catch a bus anywhere on Avendia Caracas (Carrera 14). They pass every 15-20 minutes. The journey takes an hour and a half, C$7.

Lake Guatavita. Discounting the rape of the Aztec, Maya and Inca civilizations, this is the nearest the gold seekers from Europe got to El Dorado though Benson and Hedges would have you believe otherwise. The legend came to life when the early Spanish explorers heard of an elaborate ceremony dedicated to the sun god which was performed each time a Chibcha leader took office. The leader-elect was rowed out into the middle of the lake at nightfall and coated from head to toe with gold dust. At sunrise the next morning he dived into the water while the nobles accompanying him threw gold objects and emeralds into the water. Others on the shore added similar offerings. The lake has yielded very little of its supposed treasures so far, though the Spanish, in their obsession, even tried (unsuccessfully) to drain it at one point. The area is now a weekend haunt for relatively affluent Bogotános and the legend lives on.

It's located about 100 km from Bogotá and about one hour's walk from the modern town of Guatavita Nueva. A bus there from Bogota, C$10 takes about three hours. There are two cheap places to stay in the town, the cheapest being at the bus agency *Valle de Tanza*, which has rooms for about C$57.

BUCARAMANGA
Accommodation
Hotel Tamana one of the cheapest and recommended, Carrera 18 No. 30-31.
Hotel Tay, Calle 33 No. 31-94. C$110/single, C$140/double. They serve excellent food.
Carolina, Carrera 18 No. 30-56. C$120/single, C$170/double.
Hotel Los Andes, C$406/single — basic.

Eats Other than the *Hotel Principe*, there's the *La Carreta* which has excellent food at reasonable prices and sometimes has live music.

Venezuelan Consulate The one here is reported to be less hassle than the one at Cúcuta but charges US$5 for a Tourist Card (Tarjeta de Ingreso) which is required by everyone. The Card is free at other consulates with the possible exception of the Embassy at

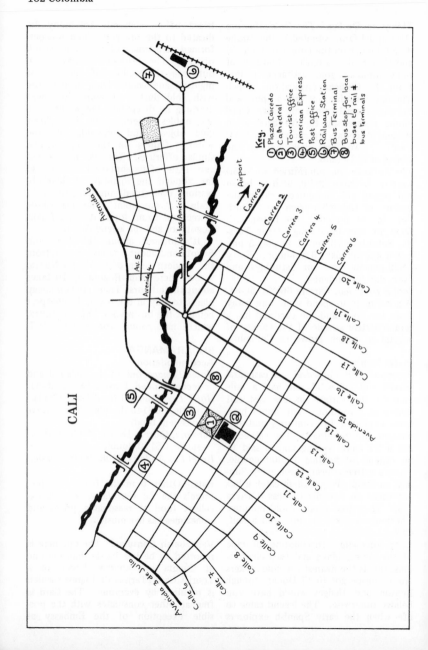

CALI

Key:
① Plaza Caicedo
② Cathedral
③ Tourist office
④ American Express
⑤ Post Office
⑥ Railway Station
⑦ Bus Terminal
⑧ Bus stop for local buses to rail # bus terminals

Bogotá which also tries to charge US$5 on occasions. Remember you may be asked to show an onward ticket before the Card is issued.

BUENAVENTURA

It's unlikely you'll come here unless you're looking for a boat along the Pacific coast either to Panama or to Ecuador.

Accommodation The three reasonably good hotels all situated in the centre along the waterfront are: *Comfort* and *Europa*, C$85/single; *Grand*, C$165/single with fans.

CALI

An agricultural boom town with little to recommend it for the traveller. You may have to stay here overnight on your way to somewhere else especially if travelling north. If going south note that there are frequent buses well into the night to Popayán. It's only a few hours away. All buses collect at the new bus terminal which is a long way from the centre. Arrivals on the ground floor; ticket offices on the 1st floor and departures on the top floor.

Accommodation

Hotel Ruisenor, Calle 15. C$70/double with private bath — clean.
Hotel Monaco, Calle 14 No. 2-13. C$40/bed, C$60/two beds — clean, cold showers.
Hotel Palmira, opposite the Monaco. C$35/two beds, C$30/bed — basic.
Casa del Viajero Nos 1 and 2. C$40/room with private bath, but they have cheaper rooms (men only!) located near the others.

Other The bus from the new Bus Terminal to centre is Ruta 1 bus to Paseo Bolívar. From there the hotels above are a three-block walk.

Information Tourist Office Carrera 3, Calle 11, has large-scale maps of the city and other information.

CARTAGENA
Accommodation

Hotel Roma, Calle San Andrés. C$7/person but the woman at the desk will try to get what she can, otherwise she's okay. They have rooms from one to four people. All have fans and clean sheets but some are rather cell-like — smelly toilets and cold showers but secure. Many travellers stay here and the owners know it which probably explains why they charge almost as much as it would cost you to get a better place. If you stay there, say "hello" to El Tortuga though he's a bit cloth-eared.
Residencias Valle, Calle San Andrés, a few metres from the *Roma* on the opposite side of the road. C$40/single.
Hotel Medellin, Calle de Avos in the other half of the old city. C$60/single — another popular travellers' hotel.
Gran Hotel, Calle de Colegio directly opposite American Express office. C$80/single. It's situated in one of the most colourful areas of the old city.

There are many other budget hotels all the way down Calle Media Luna from the Parque del Centenario (the main plaza) — see the map. They all cost around C$50-80/single. Some have rooms with beautiful overhanging balconies though you might have to wait a day or so before you get one of those.

Eats There are plenty of small cafes all of which put on a fairly standard comida corriente for between C$35-40. Try the *Cafetin Pulman*, diagonally opposite the Roma Hotel on the corner

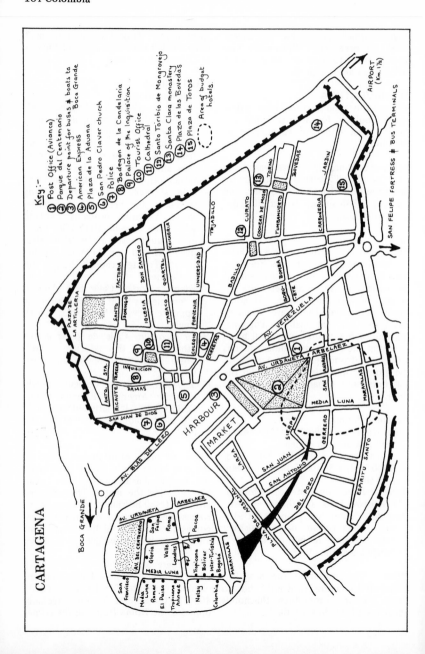

CARTAGENA

Key:-
1. Post Office (Avianca)
2. Parque del Centenario
3. Departure point for buses & boats to Boca Grande
4. American Express
5. Plaza de la Aduana
6. San Pedro Claver church
7. Police
8. Bodegon de la Candelaria
9. Palace of the Inquisition
10. Tourist Office
11. Cathedral
12. Santo Toribio de Mongrovejo
13. Santa Clara monastery
14. Plaza de las Bovedas
15. Plaza de Toros
    Area of budget hotels

of Calles Pacoa and San Andrés. They make excellent empanadas C$5 each, cafe tinto C$2/cup, a comida corriente $40 (meat, rice, fried egg, beans, salad). Also recommended is the *Cafe Venecia* on Calle del Gerro (see map).

Information Tourist Office, in the Palace of the Inquisition, Plaza Bolívar has maps and literature — friendly.

Other American Express is on Calle de Colegio 34-28 (PO Box 27-61). These people also give the best exchange rate for the dollar — if they have enough pesos (C$38.75 = US$1).

Banco Royal Colombiano only offer C$36.05 = US$1 and they charge C$50 commission on each transaction! If changing money on the street keep your wits about you — the warning given under *Money* in *On the Way* section, Cartagena is notorious. There are plenty of Casas de Cambio in the old part.

Transport from the airport to town: Taxi C$76/car and will fit up to four people. Short journey. Otherwise wait round for a bus which will cost a few pesos. Buses go to airport from Av Urdaneta Arbeláez. Long-distance bus terminals are all located on the mainland itself in Bosque about two km from the old town. Frequent buses go there from Parque del Centenario. Brasilia line runners will beseige you as soon as you get off the bus. Several buses daily to Barranquilla, Bogota, Mendellin, etc and two Pullman buses per day to Maracaibo (Venezuela). Booking in advance is recommended.

Things to Do/See A really beautiful, fascinating and lively city. Don't miss it! One of the first cities founded by Spain in the Americas, it dates back to 1533 and was originally used to store Incan plunder until the galleons could ship it back to Spain. Because it was used as a storehouse for treasure the old

city is surrounded by massive walls and protected by virtually impregnable fortresses. The city has withstood many seiges by pirates though it did fall to Sir Frances Drake in 1586 and to Baron de Pontis and Ducasse in 1697, both of whom sacked the city. Nevertheless the old part within the walls is a living museum of the architecture of 16th and 17th century Spain — narrow winding streets, churches and monasteries, large houses with overhanging balconies, patios, formal gardens and plazas, palaces, etc. The market on two sides of the harbour is chaotic and lively with plenty of bars, jukeboxes and reggae. There's little point in listing all the sights since virtually every street has something of interest though the Tourist Office will provide you with an illustrated map if you need one. Plan on spending at least several days here.

For swimming, take a bus or a boat from Parque del Centenario to Boca Grande. Round trip costs about C$70. Boca Grande is an extensive suburb of Cartagena built on a long peninsula which fronts the Caribbean Sea where the relatively affluent and affluent live. It's also a resort area for Colombians. Prices are high in comparison with the old town. If you're on the bus, just get off when you spot a suitable beach.

CÚCUTA
The border town on the road between Bogotá and Caracas (Venezuela).

Accommodation
Residencias Los Rosales, Calle 2 No.8-39, near the bus terminals. C$1.50 with fan and private bath — recommended by Peace Corps.

Residencia Mary, at the bus terminals. C$2.50/double with bath.

Hotel Central, Avenida 5 No 8-89, C$70/double.

Hotel Cinera, Carrera 5 No 10-53, C$100/double.

Venezuelan Consulate on Avenida S, Calle 15, is closed Saturdays and Sundays and is always crowded — try to get your Tourist Card (obligatory for everyone) before you get here.

Other Elsewhere in Colombia the system of having to get an Exit stamp from the DAS, before turning up at the border or an airport for an international flight has been discontinued and all this is now done at the border post itself. It may however still apply at Cucuta and you should check with DAS on Calle 17 No. 2-62, whether an Exit Permit must be obtained before going on to the border. Similarly, if coming from Venezuela, it may still be necessary to visit DAS before continuing. DAS is open daily from 8 am-12 noon and 2 pm-5.30 pm.

Buses from Cúcuta to San Cristóbal — the first large Venezuelan town — costs about C$38. Colectivos and taxis are also available. Otherwise there are frequent buses to the border for a few pesos and others which go through to the first Venezuelan town of San Antonio.

FLORENCIA
See *Transport* section later in this chapter.

IPIALES
The Colombian/Ecuadorian border town. Other than the religious sanctuary at Las Lajas which is worth a visit (you'll see plenty of postcards of this church built on a bridge over a canyon in Pasto and Ipiales), there's little here for the traveller. Unless you want to visit Las Lajas or you arrive late at night, it's best to continue on to Tulcan, the first Ecuadorian town. The budget hotels are located on the map. The Ecuadorian consulate is at Carrera 6 N0. 16-47.

DAS Exit Stamps are no longer necessary. All formalities take place at the border post. Ecuadorian customs are very easy-going — no money show-

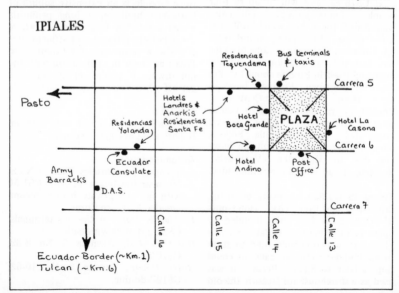

ing, no onward tickets, no appearance hassles and friendly officials. There is no exit fee for leaving Colombia.

Colectivo to Tulcan C$30-40 each depending on numbers, a taxi C$150/car, will fit six people. Taxis take you to the bus terminal in Tulcan and wait for you at the border while formalities are completed. The border at the International Bridge is only one km from Ipiales and easily walkable, but there are transport difficulties on the other side. If it's a dry day you could walk to Tulcan (about six km from Ipiales).

LETICIA
See *Transport* section later in this chapter.

MAICOA
Colombian/Venezuelan border town

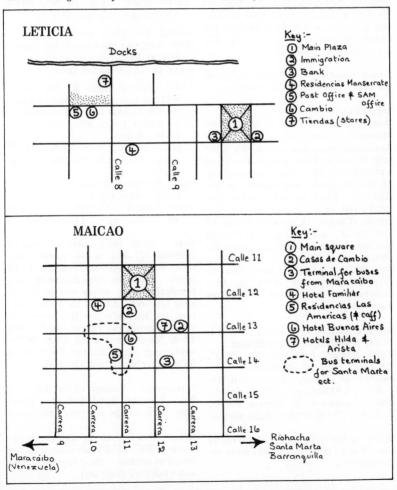

LETICIA

Docks

Key:-
① Main Plaza
② Immigration
③ Bank
④ Residencias Monserrate
⑤ Post Office & SAM office
⑥ Cambio
⑦ Tiendas (stores)

Calle 8 Calle 9

MAICAO

Key:-
① Main square
② Casas de Cambio
③ Terminal for buses from Maracaibo
④ Hotel Familiar
⑤ Residencias Las Americas (& caff)
⑥ Hotel Buenos Aires
⑦ Hotels Hilda & Arista
- - - Bus terminals for Santa Marta ect.

Calle 11
Calle 12
Calle 13
Calle 14
Calle 15
Calle 16

Carrera 9 Carrera 10 Carrera 11 Carrera 12 Carrera 13

Maracaibo (Venezuela)

Riohacha
Santa Marta
Barranquilla

along the northern route from Maracaibo to Santa Marta. It's just a hustlers' town — consumer goods, whisky, cigarettes, smuggling. Everybody is up to no good. Don't stay here if you can avoid it. Plenty of buses to Maracaibo, Santa Marta and Barranquilla which help to supplement the army's pay (they don't hassle gringos). A quick search is made of the bus — though they don't have to look too far as you can hardly move for TV sets, radios, crates of whisky, cigarettes, etc — a few back-handers are exchanged and off you go again. It's a well-established routine.

Accommodation For budget hotels see the map. You want to stay here!?

MEDELLIN
Accommodation Since there are three universities here, the University of Antioquia being the largest, it's quite easy to get to know people/be offered a place to stay by wandering around one of the campuses and talking to the students. There are quite a few one-night-stand hotels around the bus terminals (Carrera 48 between Calles 42 and 43) if you're just passing through and not intent on staying. Most are pretty basic. The drawback with this area are the hustlers — they seem to have collected here from the four corners of the earth. Some of the better places are:

Residencias Kennedy, Carrera 49 No. 44-94. C$84/single, C$120/double.
Hotel Bristol, Calle 46 No. 49-27. C$105/single, C$150/double.
Residencias Gladys, Calle 45 No. 46-64. C$130/single, C$185/double.
Hotel Casablanca 70, Carrera 45 No. 46-9. C$190/single, C$255/double.

In the market area (between Carreras 52 and 54 and Calles 45 and 50) there are the following:

Hotel Comercial on the corner of the junction between Calle 48 and Carrera 54. C240 pesos/three people, three single beds quiet with clean communal showers and toilets. The rooms are very pleasant, well decorated and spotless and the management is friendly. Restaurant on the first floor serves excellent food at reasonable prices.
Nuevo Hotel, Calle 48 No. 53-69. C$85/single, C$140/double.

Around the Plaza Bolívar there are many medium-priced hotels but expect to pay at least twice as much as you would pay in the market area:

Hotel Universo, Calle 52 No. 51-85. C$115/single without bath, C$165/double without bath. With bath the respective prices are C$175/single, C$240/double.
Residencias Plaza, Calle 54 No. 49-27, 20th floor. C$178/single, C$252/double.
Hotel Salvatore, Carrera 50 No. 53-16. C$235/single, C$345/double.
Hotel Veracruz, Carrera 50 No. 54-18. C$360/single, C$475/double.

Eats Many small cafes on Bolívar (Carrera 51) and in the market area serve comida corriente/cena for 35-40 pesos. Avoid the cafes around the bus terminals — the prices change before your very eyes. Around the Parque Bolívar, try the cafes on the pedestrian street between the Parque and Avenida 12 de Mayo (Carrera 50) where office-workers go at lunchtimes. Prices are a little higher but the food is good.

Information Tourist Office, Calle 55 No. 49-84, has hotel lists, etc. Large scale maps of the city cost 50 pesos.

Other Buses from the airport to the centre C$3. Mini-buses also wait for arrival of aircraft — more expensive than buses but they don't stop.

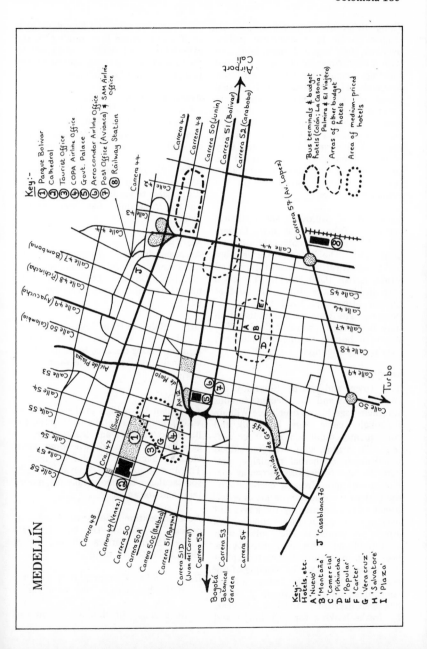

MEDELLÍN

Key:-
1. Parque Bolívar
2. Cathedral
3. Tourist Office
4. COPA Airline Office
5. Govt. Palace
6. Aerocondor Airline Office
7. Post Office (Avianca) & SAM Airline Office
8. Railway Station

Key:-
Hotels, etc.
A 'Nuevo'
B 'Montaña'
C 'Comercial'
D 'Pichincha'
E 'Popular'
F 'Carter'
G 'Vera cruz'
H 'Salvatore'
I 'Plaza'
J 'Casablanca 70'

Bus terminals & budget hotels (Colón; La Casona; Palmira & El Viajero)

Areas of other budget hotels

Area of medium-priced hotels

Airport
Cali

Turbo

Bogotá Botanical Garden

Carrera 48
Carrera 49 (Venez.)
Carrera 50
Carrera 50A
Carrera 50C (Balboa)
Carrera 51 (Popayán)
Carrera 51D (Juan del Corral)
Carrera 52
Carrera 53
Carrera 54

Cra. 47 (Sucre)

Carrera 46
Carrera 48
Carrera 50 (Junín)
Carrera 51 (Bolívar)
Carrera 52 (Carabobo)
Carrera 57 (Av. López)

Carrera 44

Calle 58
Calle 57
Calle 56
Calle 55
Calle 54
Calle 53

Av de Playa

Calle 50 (Colombia)
Calle 49 (Ayacucho)
Calle 48 (Pichincha)
Calle 47 (Bombona)

Calle 46
Calle 45

Calle 44
Calle 43

Calle 45
Calle 46
Calle 47
Calle 48
Calle 49

Av de Mayo
Avenida de Gr...

Things to Do/See A pleasant, spacious, modern town in a beautiful setting between high wooded mountains and with a very agreeable climate. Few old buildings remain though the city was founded 1675 by a somewhat unusual brand of Spanish settlers who were looking for isolation and self-sufficiency. They intermarried very little with the Indians or the blacks, divided the land into small farms which they worked themselves and refused to participate in the slave economy so prevalent in the plantations on the lowlands.

University of Antioquia and Botanical Gardens. Take any bus down Carrera 52. The huge university campus is on your right. The Botanical Gardens are really beautiful and peaceful — well worth a visit (C\$5 entry). There's a cafe inside where drinks are sold at normal prices but food is more expensive. The University administration have never seen a Student Card (ISTC) if you're hoping to find one here but they're very friendly!

MOCOA
This town and nearby Sibundoy are Indian towns and have become famous for their yage brujos ever since William Burroughs came here in 1953 and subsequently published *The Yage Letters*. The brujos, who are often skilled practitioners of herbal medicine, prepare the yage (otherwise known as ayahuasca or caapi) from a decoction of the bark of the vine *Banisteriopsis caapi*, sometimes augmented by the leaves and bark of other hallucinogenic plants. It's effects are similar to DMT mixed with an aphrodisiac. This latter property has been used by anthropologists to explain its widespread use in coming-of-age ceremonies among the Indians of the Amazonian basin. Unfortunately, Mocoa has been overrun in the last few years by freaks looking for yage brujos and

the brujos are none too happy about it so if you've come here looking for the experience tread lightly and expect to spend some time hanging around before you gain a brujos' confidence.

Accommodation *Motel El Viajero.* C\$40-50/single. *Hotel Astoria*, above the bus station. C\$30/single. *Residencias La Rivera* and *Residencias Voz del Putumayo*. Both C\$40-50/single.

Other Mocoa is on the way to Puerto Asís on the Rio Putumayo from where it's possible to get boats down to Leticia on the Amazon. See later for full details.

NEIVA
Accommodation *Hospedaje Capri.* C\$57/single. *Hotel Central*, Carrera 3 No. 7-82. C\$152/double. It's near the market and also serves meals for about C\$38.

Other Railhead from Bogota (change at Giradot) on the way down to San Agustín. Long distance buses have their terminals on Carrera 2, between Calles 5 and 6.

PASTO
An Indian town high in the mountains with a lively market Pasto is noted for its wood carvings and leatherware. It gets cold at night so have some warm clothing handy — it's at 2800 metres. The bus route from Popayán is really spectacular — enormous canyons, mountains and volcanos.

Accommodation Plenty of cheap residencias are around the bus terminals (Calle 18 and Carrera 20) and others along Calle 18 (see map).

Hotel Londres, Carrera 20 on the corner of the bus park — very basic and is a huge place. C\$50/bed whether its a single or double so you can

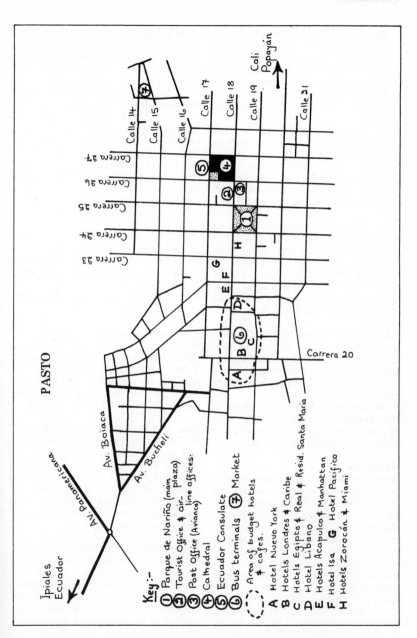

PASTO

Key:-
① Parque de Nariño (main plaza)
② Tourist Office & air- line offices.
③ Post Office (Avianca)
④ Cathedral
⑤ Ecuador Consulate
⑥ Bus terminals ⑦ Market
⌐ ¬ Area of budget hotels
⌊ _ ⌋ & cafes.

A Hotel Nuevo York
B Hotels Londres & Caribe
C Hotels Egipto & Real & Resid. Santa María
D Hotel Líbano
E Hotels Acapulco & Manhattan
F Hotel Isa   G Hotel Pacífico
H Hotels Zorocán & Miami

Av. Panamericana
Ipiales
Ecuador

Av. Boiaca
Av. Bucheli

Carrera 20

Carrera 23
Carrera 24
Carrera 25
Carrera 26
Carrera 27

Calle 14
Calle 15
Calle 16
Calle 17
Calle 18
Calle 19
Calle 21

Cali
Popayán

get a room with a single and a double bed for C$100 — it works out cheaper if there are three or four of you — "clean" sheets and hot water in the mornings. The rooms which face the street are noisy due to the juke-box in the *Hotel Caribe* opposite.

Hotel Manhattan, Calle 18 between Carreras 22 and 21. C$50/single — basic, hot water.

Hotel Pacifico, Carrera 23 No. 17-50. Somewhat more expensive but it's an old wooden hotel with balustrades and large rooms. C$300/double.

Eats Two good cheap cafes are on Carrera 20 at the junction with Calle 18 in front of the bus park, soup, meat, beans, rice, salad and coffee C$35-40. Otherwise try the *Rio Mayo*, Calle 17 No. 19-126, fruit, meat, beans, veg., salad, coffee C$35-40. They also have rooms for C$150/double — clean.

Information Tourist Office (Turismo de Nariño), Calle 18 between Carreras 25 and 26, has free large-scale maps of the town, though they're photostated on a tired machine so it fades at the edges, and other information.

Ecuadorian Consulate, 2nd floor of the Textiles Sabadell building, Calle 17 and Carrera 26 is very friendly and gives out information on Ecuador.

POPAYÁN

Accommodation Avoid the scruffy, noisy residencias and hotels around the bus terminals as they're grossly overpriced in comparison to what's available for a few pesos more in the centre of town. Around the bus terminal there are: *Hotel Roosevelt; Hotel Santa Fé; Residencias Bucareli; Hotel Huila; Residencias New York; Residencias Baraya; Residencias Neiva; Residencias Avenida; Hospedaje Londres*, etc. An example is *Hotel Santa Fe*, C$45/single, C$60/double, C$120/triple. If two people

share a bed you only pay for one. It's situated next to a disco and therefore noisy. The rooms are cell-like and very basic but clean. Showers (cold) and toilets leave much to be desired.

In the main part of town probably the best deal is the *Hotel Tunubalá* Calle 4 No. 5-78, right on the corner of the main square. (The sign is a little battered). Reception is on the first floor — shops on the ground floor. It's an old colonial house with large spacious rooms, polished floor boards, quiet patio, balconies. Clean toilets and showers and hot water. C$58/person.

Residencias Los Portales, Carrera 6 No. 4-85, right on the main square.

Hotel Colonial, Calle 3 No. 5-56, next door to Casa Mosquera (museum). C$152/double.

Hotel Los Balcones, Calle 3 No. 6-80. C$209/double.

The above three have similar prices to Hotel Tunabalá. If you want something flasher try the *Hotel Lindbergh*, Carrera 5 No. 4-08, directly opposite the entrance to the University. C$132/double with bath. If the above are full, the Tourist Office has a full list of others.

Eats Try the *La Castellana*, Carrera 6 No. 6-47, for the excellent almuerzo and comida C$42. Other, more expensive meals, a la carte. The little cafe on the corner of the main square, junction of Carrera 6 and Calle 5, is good for sitting around with a coffee and empanada watching the world go by or talking to local people.

Information Tourist Office, Carrera 6 No. 3-47, has plenty of good information and is very friendly. There's free coffee and they have bus timetables, maps, post-cards, etc. They will change travellers' cheques/cash without commission — the only other place which

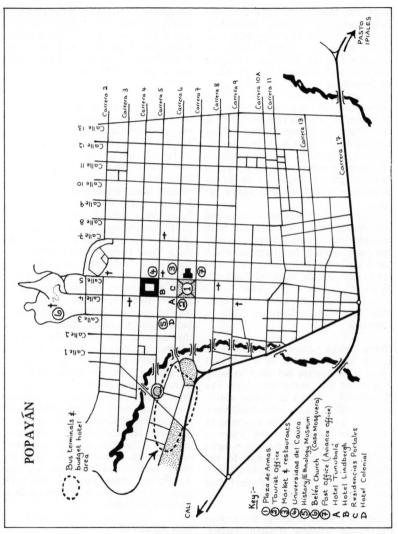

POPAYÁN

Bus terminals + budget hotel area

Key:-
① Plaza de Armas
② Tourist Office
③ Market + restaurants
④ Universidad del Cauca
⑤ History/Ethnology Museum
⑥ Belén Church (Casa Mosquera)
⑦ Post Office (Avianca office)
A Hotel Tunubalá
B Hotel Lindbergh
C Residencias Portales
D Hotel Colonial

CALI

PASTO
IPIALES

will change cheques is the Banco de la República at the bottom of the same street by the river. Office open Monday to Friday 8 am-12 noon, 2 pm-6 pm, Saturdays 8 am-12 noon, 2 pm-5 pm, Sundays 9 am-1 pm.

Things to Do/See One of the most beautiful Spanish colonial towns in the whole of Colombia. Quiet, easy-going and completely unspoilt. Many old churches and a university housed in a large old Dominican monastery. The town was founded in 1536 by Benalcazar, one of Pizarro's lieutenants, and was subject, until 1717, to the Audiencia at Quito. After that it was transferred to the Audiencia at Bogotá. The views and roofscape from the statue of Benalcazar on a hill overlooking the town are spectacular — the latter a chessboard of rich red-tiled roofs. The churches worth a visit are San Francisco (Calle 4, Carrera 9), Santo Domingo (Calle 4, Carrera 5), San Agustín (Calle 7, Carrera 6) and the Cathedral on the main square; also the Chapel of Belén (Capilla de Belén) if only for the views over the town and across the valley.

Casa Mosquera Museum (history and ethnology), Calle 3 No. 5-14, is a small museum which doesn't overwhelm with too many exhibits, but it's main attraction is the house itself. Entry C$5. Also there are: *Museo Nacional Guillermo Valencia*, Carrera 6 No. 2-69; *Museo Arte Colonial*, Calle 4 No. 9-12, entry C$5; *Museo Arte Religioso*, Calle 4, Carrera 9.

Places Nearby *Silvia* was formerly an Indian village situated in a valley at about 2500 metres but more recently is a resort for weekenders from Cali (in season). There's an Indian market once a week. Buses (Sotracauca) from Popayán go at 12.45 pm and take an hour. C$35. There are two places to stay: *La Parilla*. C$38/single — meals available. *Hotel Cali*, next to the *Hotel de Turismo*, is an old house with a craft shop. C$152/single including food — primitive and pleasant.

Puracé is a small village at the base of the Puracé volcano at 3000 metres. The sulphur mines and the waterfalls (Chorrera de las Monjas) nearby can both be visited. Beyond the village is the Puracé National Park where geysers and high altitude vegetation can be seen. The geysers are interesting in that they are different colours according to which variety of algae they support which in turn is dependent on their temperature. Buses from Popayán go at 2 am, 4 am, 7 am, 9 am, 11 am, noon, 2 pm, 5 pm, and 8 pm. C$45, taking under two hours.

San Agustín and Tierradentro are in one of the most interesting areas in Colombia — it's beautiful mountain country. The decorated underground burial caves of Tierradentro and the stone statues of San Agustín can be reached either from Popayán by crossing the Cordillera or by coming south from Bogotá via Neiva. For full details see under *San Agustin*. Buses from Popayán to San Agustín (*Autobuses Unidos del Sur*) go at 5 am (3 am on Saturdays) and 1 pm. C$244. *Taxis Verde* (a colectivo service) also do this run in both directions once a day. They take three hours less than the bus and depart when full, but booking in advance is recommended. If you want to visit the caves at Tierradentro first, before going on to San Agustín, get off the bus/colectivo at the San Andrés crossroads (Cruce San Andrés) which is about three and a half hours out of Popayán — the drivers know where it is as many travellers get off there all the time. From the crossroads it's about a half hour walk to San Andrés. On the way there you will pass the museum. The caves are situated on the mountainsides on either side, so if you're there early enough in the day you can visit them before continuing on to San Andrés (the most beautiful cave — El Aguacate — is a two-hour walk on foot from the museum).

SAN AGUSTIN
Accommodation

Hotel Los Idolos. C$25/single if you're staying for a few days otherwise slightly more. It serves good meals for C$20.

Hotel Central. C$30/single, C$60/

double — clean and friendly. They also serve good meals.

La Gatana Hotel C$20/single. It's ten minutes walk from the centre and very pleasant.

It's also possible to rent rooms in private houses for up to C$76. Small boys who wait for the arrival of buses will offer you this. Plenty of people rent horses for visiting the sites and riding around the area. About C$100/day — ask around.

Eats Other than *Los Idolos* and the *Central*, *El Mini* restaurant is recommended and the *Residencias Luis Tello* for breakfast (banana pancakes).

Places Nearby Centre of a vanished culture which flourished around the 12th and 13th centuries. Other than the stone statues and burial caves which they left, almost nothing is known about the people who lived here though archaeologists have drawn parallels with the Tiahuanaco civilization on Lake Titicaca in northern Bolivia and the Mayan

relics in the Yucatán. This area and Popayán was also the most northerly outpost of the Inca empire. The nearest sites to San Augustín are the Parque Arqueologico, where the statues have been left more or less as they were found, and the Bosque Arqueológico, where the statues have been re-arranged and linked by gravel paths. Both sites are approximately four km from the village. The area is also one of great natural beauty and very popular with travellers. Alto de los Idolos is located about 10 km by foot or horse on a hill overlooking San Agustín. It's also possible to get there by road (buses available from San Agustín) though this is a longer route (27 km). If going by foot or on horse carry straight on past the bridge for the Bosque Arqueológico and turn right across the bridge at La Chaquira (Puente de la Chaquira). At the site are located the *vigilantes* — larger statues of a different kind (often animal totems) which guard burial mounds containing large stone sarcophagi.

Alto de las Piedras, where there are

TIERRADENTRO

monoliths and tombs, is located about 5 km from San José (buses available from San Agustín). There is a museum on the site and the director there can arrange transport and guides to outlying sites if you're interested. A leaflet (in English) and free maps are available either from the Tourist Office next door to the Hotel Plaza in San Agustín or from the Hotel Yalconia outside town. If you're visiting Alto de las Piedras and want to stay overnight in San José, budget accommodation can be found at Hospedaje Nueva, C$20/single.

In the Tierradentro region, near the village of San Andrés on the road between La Plata and Inza, there are situated a number of artificial burial caves constructed by the same people who left the stone statues in the San Agustín area. The largest caves are very impressive and painted with geometric patterns. Guards are present at the three main sites. They have lights and act as guides (you will need to have your own torch (es) if you visit the smaller caves). At nearby Tablon, there are more huge stone statues. For the location of these and the burial caves see the map.

There are cheap places to stay in the village of San Andrés otherwise there is the *State Tourist Hotel* opposite the Museum at the bottom of the path to "Aguacate" cave. C$38/single with meals available for C$25-30. Also near the museum is the house of *Senora Marta de Angel* (sometimes referred to as *Dona Maria*) where you can rent a room, C$38. She also cooks excellent food at meal-times, C$30. Camping is allowed at the museum and a shower is available there. You can find horses to rent either at the museum or in nearby San Andrés.

Buses from Popayán to San Agustín go at 5 am (3 am Saturdays), 1 pm. Get off at Cruce San Andres — the bus driver knows where this is — and from there the village of San Andrés is a half-hour

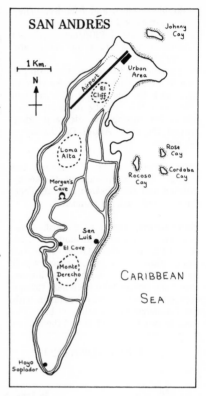

SAN ANDRÉS

walk. *Taxi Verde* colectivo from San Agustín to Cruce San Andrés goes when full. C$100. This is the same colectivo which goes to Popayán. To get from San Agustín to Tierradentro, first catch a bus to Garzon (140 km), followed by another to La Plata (60 km) and then another from there to Popayán getting off at Cruce San Andrés. The bus from La Plata to San Andrés goes at 5.30 am and returns at 4 pm. It takes three hours. The bus from La Plata to San Agustín goes at 8 am, taking seven hours.

Information The Tourist Office is next door to the *Hotel Plaza*, but the same

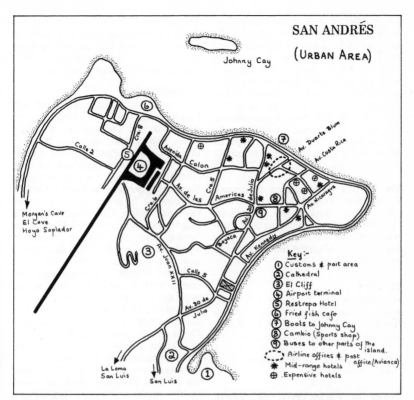

SAN ANDRÉS
(URBAN AREA)

Johnny Cay

Key:-
1. Customs & port area
2. Cathedral
3. El Cliff
4. Airport terminal
5. Restrepo Hotel
6. Fried fish cafe
7. Boats to Johnny Cay
8. Cambio (Sports shop)
9. Buses to other parts of the island.
- - - Airline offices & post office (Avianca)
* Mid-range hotels
⊕ Expensive hotels

Morgan's Cave
El Cove
Hoyo Soplador

La Loma
San Luis

San Luis

information can be got from the *Hotel Yalconia* outside town.

SANTA MARTA

Accommodation There are a few cheap hotels — most are quite expensive — but it's possible to camp/sleep out on the beaches if there's a small group of you. This is not recommended otherwise because of the danger of having your gear ripped-off during the night. *Hotel Bucanero*, Calle 22. C$76/single. *Hotel Medellin*, Calle 22 No. 280. Similar to the above.

Things to Do/See The first town on the South American mainland founded by the conquistadores in 1525 and is the place where Simon Bolívar came to die after his dream of Gran Colombia (Ecuador, Colombia and Venezuela) collapsed. The hacienda where he spent his last years — San Pedro Alejandrino — may be visited. Santa Marta is also a very popular resort town for Colombians — many beautiful beaches.

Places Nearby The Sierra Nevada mountains rise abruptly from the sea near Santa Marta, culminating in permanent snow peaks of up to 5800 metres. In this area live the Arhuaco Indians and many varieties of wild life including pumas and jaguars. The Indians are still largely autonomous and it's difficult to get permission to visit them. The nearest you're allowed to go without a safe conduct is the village of San Sebastian. To get there take a bus to Valledupar and from there a jeep (three times a day, C$30) to Puebla Bello. San Sebastían is a 28 km walk uphill from Puebla Bello: If you're interested in Arhuaco Indian culture contact Celso Domingo, a dentist in Puebla Bello who is a member of the tribe. If you want somewhere to stay in Puebla Bello try the El Hogar de Mami which costs C$84/person including three meals.

The Tairona National Park is situated 35 km from Santa Marta near Canaveral (buses from Santa Marta). It includes the "Pueblito" archeological site where relics of the ancient Tairona culture may be seen. A guided tour around the site takes 6 hours, C$228.

TUNJA

Accommodation There are few cheap places to stay. Once of the cheapest is *Hotel Dux*. The restaurant *La Fonda* serves large cheap meals.

Information The Tourist Office is on Carrera 9 No. 19-68.

Things to Do/See Very old Spanish colonial town with similarities to Cartagena except that the climate is cold. The Viceroys used it as a summer retreat. Many old buildings remain and the palace built by the Spanish noble, Casa de Don Juan de Vargas, has been restored and converted into a museum of colonial Tunja.

Places Nearby A visit to the nearby village of Villa de Leiva is recommended. It's a town which has hardly changed since the Spanish left. Plenty of old colonial buildings. Accommodation is cheapest at *Bar Roca* (C$63/single — very clean and pleasant). Other cheap accommodation places are *Posada Don Juan de Castellanos* and at the *Hotel Elvira*.

TURBO

Accommodation In case you made it across the Darien Gap on foot or came by plane from Puerto Obladia in Panama, the *Hotel Panama* is C$30/single.

TRANSPORT

The number of possible routes through Colombia are determined largely by the geography and the pattern of population. There are four mountain ranges — the Serrania de Baudo on the Pacific side; the Western Cordillera running from the Caribbean coast down to the Ecuadorian border; the Central Cordillera running from the junction of the two main rivers (Rio Cauca and Rio Magdalena) down to the Ecuadorian border; and the Eastern Cordillera which, in the north, forms the border with Venezuela and, in the south, joins with the Central Cordillera near the border with Ecuador. The bulk of the population — and therefore the communications network — is located in the southern half of the valleys of the Rio Cauca and Rio Magdalena. Because both the Central and Eastern Cordillera reach the permanent snow line, there are few cross connections. Vast areas of Columbia are very underpopulated and roads are few or absent entirely. They include the Pacific coast and the Serrania de Baudo; the Caribbean coast other than the ports of Cartagena, Barranquilla and Santa Marta; and the Llanos — the vast area of tropical grassland and forest in the basins of the Orinoco and Amazon rivers. We'll deal with the transport under headings of five main routes.

When planning your route bear in mind the following three points:

(1) Internal flights, as in most of Spanish South America, often cost only two to three times more than the bus fare over the same distance. Where roads are particularly bad and buses take all night/all day to get to their destination this might be a welcome alternative (eg from Turbo to Medellin and from Cartagena to Medell-

in). In places where there are no roads and riverboats are irregular, you may have no alternative. There are about 18 different airlines in all though many of them are small concerns which operate over limited areas. *Avianca* is the most expensive. The cheapest lines are *Satena, Aeropesca, Urraca, Tana, SAM* and *Aerocondor* in approximately that order. If you're planning on taking a flight, especially with one of the smaller concerns which may not have ticket offices in town, enquire first at the local Tourist Office or, failing that, at the airport.

(2) Where available, trains are sometimes preferable to buses especially where the roads are rough since, although they generally take longer to reach their destination, they're more comfortable and you can move around (but keep a constant watch over your belongings!).

(3) Bus transport on good roads (eg the Pan-American Highway; along the Caribbean coast; and from Bogota into Venezuela) is generally by fast Pullman-type coach. They have padded seats and there's plenty of leg room. On the rough roads they're often cramped, uncomfortable boneshakers designed for people with legs no longer than a pigmy's. In addition to buses there are "busetas" (minibuses costing slightly more than a regular bus) and "colectivos" (shared taxis which go when full and cost about half as much again as the buses).

Routes to/from Venezuela

Along the Carribean coast from Cartagena to Maracaibo and vice versa

Avianca fly from Cartagena to Caracas daily, C$3610, and Cartagena-Maracaibo daily except Mondays and Wednesdays, C$2166.

Cartagena-Barranquilla. Many buses go daily in either direction. Several companies do the run (eg *Rapido Ochoa*). C$90. It takes four hours. The bus terminals in Cartagena are all in "Bosque" outside the old city. To get there take a local bus from the Parque del Centenario (C$2) or walk — it's about one km.

Cartagena-Maracaibo. Through Pullman-type buses go twice a day. This is more expensive than doing the journey in stages.

Barranquilla-Santa Marta. Many buses go daily in either direction. Several companies do the run. C$40. It takes two hours.

Barranquilla-Maicao (Colombian border). Many buses go daily in either direction. Several companies do the run (eg *Rapido Ochoa, Expresso Brasilia*). C$180. It takes seven hours and involves a change at Santa Marta in most cases. Most of the bus terminals in Barranquilla are located around the back of the Plaza Bolívar (see the street plan).

Maicao-Maracaibo. Four buses per day go in either direction; from Maracaibo to Maicao at 7 am, 8 am, 9.30 am, 11 am. 10 Bolivars (about US$2.50). It takes three hours.

Officially you need an onward ticket to enter either Colombia or Venezuela. The Colombian customs are very easy going — they ask to see your onward ticket, but don't look closely at it so just wave any old airline ticket, stub or even a folder with no ticket in it (we did!). There's no baggage search, no money-showing, no hold-ups and no entry/exit fees. Leaving Colombia you no longer need a DAS Exit stamp from the office in Maicao — all formalities are at the border post.

If you're going to Venezuela, there's a Venezuelan Consulate in Maicao if you still need a Tourist Card (obligatory for everyone, you need to show an onward ticket before it will be issued). The Tourist Card should be free but some rip you off for US$5. If you're arriving from/going to Venezuela, the bus company (*Expresso Gran Colombia*) is on Calle 14 between Carreras 12 and 13. Buses to Barranquilla/Santa Marta are to be found on Carrera 11 between Calles 13 and 14.

Cartagena, Barranquilla, Santa Marta, Richacha and Maicao all have airports and there are connections between them all but, except for the flights to Maicoa, you'd probably spend as long waiting around at the airport for a plane as it would take to go by bus anyway.

From Bogotá to Caracas and vice versa via Tunja, Bucaramanga and Cúcuta

Bogotá-Tunja. Buses go every half hour in both directions from 4 am to 7 pm. Several companies do the run (eg *Rapido Duitama, Berliner del Fonce, Copetran, Flota del Valle de Tenza,* the latter goes on to Villa de Leiva). It takes three to four hours, C$64.

Bogotá-Bucaramanga. Several buses go daily in either direction; the same companies as above. C$150. It takes eight to nine hours.

Bogotá-Bucaramanga. Several flights leave each day (*Avancia, Satena, SAM,* etc). About C$836.

Bogotá-Cúcuta. Three to four buses leave per day (both "de lujo" and "ordinario" by *Berliner del Fonce* and *Copetran*). C$180 ("ordinario"). It takes 16-18 hours.

Bogotá-Cúcuta. Flights go daily in both directions. *Satena* costs about C$1140. There's also a twice a week plane in either direction via Villavicencio which flies over the llanos and makes many stops in small places en route. It's cheaper than the direct flight.

Bogotá-Caracas. Through bus by *Transalianza* is much more expensive than it would cost you to do the journey in stages. C$640.

Addresses of the bus companies in Bogotá are:
Berlinas del Fonce, Carrera 25 No. 16-58.
Copetran, Calle 16 No. 15-89.
Transalianza, Carrera 9 No.16-20.
Rapido Duitama, Calle 6 No. 16-08.

Bucaramanga-Cúcuta. Several buses daily by *Berlinas del Fonce* and *Copetran* go in either direction. C$70. It takes eight to nine hours.

Bucaramanga-Cúcuta. There are daily flights in either direction by *Avancia, Satena* and *SAM*. C$494.

Cucuta-San Cristóbal (Venezuela). Several buses leave daily. C$40 or Bolívars 4. It takes two hours. You can also go by colectivo for about C$50 or Bolívars 5/person. This takes one hour. It's also possible to get a bus from Cúcuta to San Antonio on the border, walk across the border and catch another bus on the other side to San Cristóbal (cheaper but takes longer).

You officially need an onward ticket before being allowed into either Colombia or Venezuela. If going to Venezuela you have to have a Tourist Card — consulates in Bucaramanga and Cucuta but they often charge US$5 whereas it's free in most other places. You need an onward ticket before the Tourist Card can be issued.

Going to Venezuela, it's no longer necessary to obtain an Exit stamp from DAS in Cúcuta — all formalities are at the border post and no exit/entry fees.

Along the Rio Cauca Valley from Cartagena to the Ecuadorian Border at Ipiales/Tulcan via Medellin, Cali, Popayán and Pasto

Cartagena-Medellin. Daily buses (Pullmans) by *Expresso Brasilia* leave at 8 am, noon and by *Rapido Ochoa* at 2.30 pm, 7 30 pm, 11 pm, 12.30 am. C$397 and takes 16-18 hours. This bus ride is notorious for rip-off artists, so stay awake, keep a constant eye on your baggage or, if it's loaded out of sight, get off at each stop and watch it.

Cartagena-Medellin. There are daily flights in either direction by several companies. *Avianca* flies at 9.35 am and 3.26 am. C$1102. *SAM* flies at 11.15 am C$1026.

Medellin-Manizales. Buses go daily. *Flota Occidental* (older buses) at 1.30 pm and takes 10 hours. C$145. *Empressa Arauca* at 6 am (express) and 9 am, 3.30 pm (Pullman buses) taking seven hours. C$165. See the Medellin street map for the location of the buses.

Medellin-Cali. Buses leave almost every hour in either direction. *Empresa Arauca* and *Flota Magdalena*, both Pullman buses. C$285 and takes 10 hours. You can go there at virtually any time of day or night but a day-time bus is to be preferred as the landscape is amazing and shouldn't be missed. Other than one or two small stretches it's a good road. Occasional army/police checks occur where you may have your baggage searched relatively thoroughly.

The railway line from Medellin to Cali was badly damaged in floods in 1974 as far as Cartago and is still not back in operation. The rest of the line escaped damage.

Cartago-Cali. The "Autoferro" goes daily in either direction. It takes three hours. C$30. The "Tren Rapido" goes daily in either direction. It takes four hours. C$35.

Armenia-Cali. The "Tren Rapido" goes daily in either direction. It takes five hours. C$35. "Exprestren con Lujos" goes daily in either direction, taking five hours. A train for those who are tired of living or who have more money than sense. It has the sorts of comfort you would expect for *this*. The price plus showers, a bar, musak and a sleeping wagon. C$200.

In Cali, tickets for the trains can be bought at the Palacio de Comunicaciones on the main square, corner of Calle 12 and Carrera 4, as well as at the station.

Cali-Popayán. Buses go every 30 minutes in either direction virtually all day and night. The following companies do the run: *Empresa Palmira, Transportes Pto. Tejada, Flota Magdelena, Cootranar, Transportes Ipiales*. C$65-72. It takes just under three hours. There are also many "busetas" doing this run (eg *Supertaxis del Sur*). They charge C$73 and do the trip in two and a half hours. In Cali all bus arrivals and departures and the ticket offices of the bus companies are grouped together in the new three-storey bus terminal near the railway station (see the street plan). You can get a bus or "buseta" from here to virtually any town or city in Colombia night or day. There is also a train from Cali to Popayan but we have no details except that it takes six hours.

Popayán-Pasto. Up to eight buses per day leave in either direction: *Transportes Ipiales, Cootranar, Flota Magdalena* and *Expreso Bolivariano*. It takes six hours. The road is good and the landscape is incredible with vast canyons with tiny settlements clinging to their almost vertical sides. C$160.

Popayán-Pasto. Daily flights are serviced by *Aeropesca*. C$380. It takes 20 minutes and departs from Popayan at 8.30 am. The drawback to this flight is that the airport at Pasto (Cano) is 40 km from town and there are no buses — only taxis and colectivos so you must add another C$76 to the cost of getting there.

Popayán-Ipiales (Ecuadorian border).

Up to seven buses leave per day in either direction. *Transportes Ipiales, Cootranar* and *Expreso Bolivariano* do the run. C$210 and it takes seven hours. For details of how to get to San Agustín and Tierradentro see under *San Agustín* or later under *Along the Rio Magdalena Valley.*

Pasto-Ipiales. Buses leave all day in both directions. Many companies do the run (eg *Flota Magdalena, Expreso Bolivariano)*. They all charge the same — C$45 — and the journey takes a little under two hours. There are Ecuadorian Consulates in both Pasto and Ipiales. It's no longer necessary to obtain an Exit Stamp from DAS in Ipiales before going on to the border — all formalities take place at the border post. It's an easy-going border, with no onward tickets needed, no money showing and no baggage searches. There are very few buses to Tulcan — the first town in Ecuador — and you'll probably have to take a colectivo. This costs C$30-40/person, depending on numbers. A taxi costs C$150 for the car (will fit six people). For this price they will take you to the new bus terminal in Tulcan and wait for you at customs. It's also possible to walk — about eight km to Tulcan.

Pasto-Tumaco. Tumaco is a small port on the Pacific coast partially built out into the sea on stilts with Caribbean-type atmosphere and archaeological finds of the Tumaco culture. *Cootranar* have one bus per day in both directions. It departs Pasto at 7 am. C$160.

Along the Rio Magdalena Valley from Santa Marta to Popayán and vice versa via Bogota, Giradot, Neiva and San Agustín.

Santa Marta-Bogotá. Buses leave three times daily in either direction by *Expreso Brasilia* ("ordinario"). Costs C$400 and it takes *30 hours.* Buses go via Valledupar and Bucaramango and take a sweater with you — it gets cold at night. It's a *rough* trip (a foretaste of Peruvian buses in the mountains!). It's recommended that you take the train if you're thinking of making this journey without a break.

There are other buses to and from Barranquilla/Cartagena and Bogotá (three times a day from each place) if you're really looking for punishment. Also there are buses from Santa Marta to Bucaramanga by *Copetran* and *Expreso Brasilia.* They take 16-20 hours.

Santa Marta-Bogotá. "Expréstren" once a day in either direction taking 24 hours. C$390. "Expréstren con Lujos". This is a luxury train with showers, bar, musak and sleeping car. It departs Santa Marta on Tuesdays and Saturdays and departs Bogotá on Mondays and Fridays. C$600 (including food) and it takes 22 hours. It's well subscribed so book in advance if possible. The name of the train is *Expreso Tayrona.*

Santa Marta-Dorado (en route to Bogotá). Ordinary trains go every day in either direction and take 20 hours. Some travellers have recommended doing this trip and then getting the bus from La Dorado to Bogotá.

Santa Marta-Barranca (en route to Bogota — full name Barrancabermeja). An "Autoferro" goes daily in either direction. C$100 and takes 10 hours. There's also a daily ordinary train in either direction for C$25 and takes seven hours.

Santa Marta-Bogotá. Many daily flights do this run by different airlines. C$1064 and takes one to two hours. You can also fly from both Cartagena and Barranquilla to Bogotá for a similar amount. Similarly there are flights from the Caribbean ports to Bucaramanga and Cúcuta.

Bogotá-Giradot. Pullman buses by many companies take three hours. C$75.

Bogotá-Giradot. Although the tracks are continuous from Bogotá to Neiva, there are no through trains and it's necessary to change at Giradot if you're going on to Neiva. There are two daily trains in either direction — a "tren rapido" and an ordinary train. The former takes seven hours, The latter nine hours.

Bogotá-Neiva. *Coomotor* buses leave three times daily in both directions taking six hours. C$160.

Addresses of the bus companies in Bogotá (terminals) are:
Expreso Brasilia, Calle 16 No. 15-34.
Copetran, Calle 16 No. 15-89.
Coomotor, Carrera 25 No. 15-36.

If you're looking for something quicker and more comfortable than a bus, check out the colectivos run by *Taxi Verde* and *Velotax*. They cost about twice the price of the buses but they're a lot quicker. They run to destinations all over Colombia. Their addresses in Bogota are:
Taxi Verde, Calle 18 No. 14-17.
Velotax, Calle 17 No. 15-07.

Giradot-Neiva. Several Pullman-type buses by many companies go everyday in either direction. C$85 and it takes three and a half hours.

Giradot-Neiva. A daily "Autoferro" train goes in either direction. C$30 and it takes four hours. This train does not generally connect with the trains from Bogota and you may have to wait until the following day for a connection. If so, and you want to keep moving, catch a bus the rest of the way.

Neiva-San Agustín. Six buses go per day in either direction by *Autobuses Unidos del Sur*. C$120 and it takes six hours. San Agustin marks the end of the Rio Magdalena valley. From here, unless you're heading for the Amazon, you must go by bus or colectivo over the mountains to Popayan and from there to the Ecuadorian border via Pasto.

San Agustín-Popayán. Buses go twice daily in either direction, one in the early morning and the other in the early afternoon, by *Autobuses Unidos del Sur*. C4244. *Taxis Verde* (colectivo service) also do this run. Advance booking is advisable.

For details of the transport to burial caves of Tierradentro see under *Popayán* and *San Agustín*.

Cross-connections Between the Cauca and Magdalena Valleys

Santa Marta-Medellin. An express train leaves twice a week in either direction. C$350 and it takes 20 hours. It departs Santa Marta Thursdays and Sundays and departs Medellin Mondays and Fridays.

Medellin-Bogotá. "Autoferro" goes three times a week in either direction C$200 and takes 16 hours. It departs Bogotá Monday, Wednesday and Friday, and departs Medellin Tuesday, Thursday and Saturday.

Medellin-Puerto Berrio. An ordinary train does the run daily in either direction. C$25 and it takes seven hours. From here you can make a connection with the trains either to Santa Marta or Bogotá.

Medellin-Bogotá. *Flota Magdalena* buses go almost every hour in either direction (first bus leaves 7.30 am, last bus leaves 11.30 pm). Less frequent services are by *Flota Occidental* and *Rapido Tolima*. C$280, 16 hours.

Medellin-Bogotá. Several daily flights are offered by different airlines in either direction. C$760.

Manizales/Pereira/Armenia-Bogotá. Approximately every two hours in either direction throughout the day there are buses by *Expreso Boli-*

variano, Flota el Ruiz, Flota Rapido Tolima and *Flota Magdalena*. C$110 taking seven hours.

Addresses of bus company terminals in Bogotá are:

Flota Magdalena, Calle 11 No. 17-10.
Rapido Tolima, Carrera 16 No. 9-42.
Expreso Bolivariano, Carrera 13 No. 8-86.
Flota el Ruiz, Carrera 16 no. 18-70.
Velotax colectivos also operate on the same routes. Their address is Calle 17 No. 15-07.

Cali-Bogotá. Over 40 buses a day go in either direction. Several different companies do the route, eg *Flota Magdalena, Empresa Palmira*. C$280 in Pullman buses. It takes 12-15 hours. Unlike most Colombian cities, Cali has a large new bus terminal where all arrivals and departures take place and where all the bus companies and colectivos services maintain ticket offices (see the city plan for its location). It's a very busy terminal and you can find transport to just about everywhere in Colombia from here throughout the day and night.

Cali-Bogotá. Many flights leave daily in either direction by many different airlines. C$760.

Routes into Peruvian and Brazilian Amazonia

This section deals with the riverboat and flight connections through the Colombian jungles to Leticia on the River Amazon via Florencia and Puerto Asis and the Rivers Putumayo and Caqueta. It also includes onward transport from Leticia and accommodation suggestions for the town en route.

If you're planning on travelling down to Leticia by riverboats and/or along the Amazon either to Peru or Brazil, you need *plenty* of time and little concern for your comfort! Riverboats are irregular (though there are plenty of

them) and you may have to wait around a few days in each place for a connection. Conditions on board are primitive — sleep in your own hammock or on the deck — the food is poor and monotonous and there are plenty of mosquitoes. But it's well worth the effort! There's an amazing variety of wild life and jungle scenery. To find a boat in one of the river ports simply walk on board and ask the captain or crew where they're heading for next and, if they're going in the direction you want to go, when they will be leaving, how much it will cost, whether the cost includes food and how long the journey will take. Don't be satisfied when you've found one. Keep asking around as prices and journey times differ considerably from one boat to the next and depend to some extent on how the captain takes to you. We made one journey completely free of charge by offering to play guitar and flute and sing songs for an hour or two every evening — something we'd have done anyway! In the larger ports it's sometimes a good idea to also visit the Jefe de la Marina (Chief Port Official) as he will have a list of all arrivals and departures and will often point out a boat or captain who's going in your direction.

If time is not in your favour or you can't find a boat for whatever reason, there are regular flights between such places as Puerto Asís, Florencia, Puerto Leguízamo and Tres Esquinas.

Via Puerto Asís and the Rio Putumayo

Pasto-Puerto Asís via Mochoa. A daily bus by *Expreso Bolivariano* takes 13 hours over rough roads. The road snakes through mountains and over a 3000 metre pass.

Satena flies to Puerto Asís from Bogotá via Neiva, San Vicent and Florencia three times a week. C$456 from Neiva. There are also more irregular (and slightly cheaper) flights along the same route by *Aeropesca* and the local airlines *Albania* and *San José* — about three times a week.

In Puerto Asís there are the following places to stay:

Residencas Nubia, C$38. You can get excellent fish in the cafe next door when it comes in from the river.

Residencias Patiño. C$38. There are plenty of other cheap and primitive places to stay down in the port area. Otherwise there's the *Residencias Nevado* near the airport with comfortable air-conditioned or non-airconditioned rooms for between C$76 and C$95.

A side-trip can be made here to San Miguel on the Ecuadorian border by local bus. It has an interesting Sunday market where the local Indians come to sell their wares. There's only one place to stay other than private rooms and that's the *Residencias Olga* — only has six rooms.

There's plenty of river traffic. For boats first enquire at the Jefe de la Marina. There's also a more or less regular steamer which goes to Leticia every Sunday, up to C$950. Otherwise negotiate your own boat. The trip to Leticia takes 10-15 days. If you don't want to go all the way to Leticia find a boat which is going to/calling at Puerto Leguízamo. At this point the Putumayo and Caqueta rivers are separated by only 25 km of low-lying land and there's a jungle track between Puerto Leguízamo and La Tagua (another port on the Caqueta). There are trucks between two ports and it's possible to hitch a ride. There's plenty of smuggling going on — naturally! From La Tagua you can find another riverboat going up the Caqueta to Tres Esquinas or even Florencia. Otherwise there are flight connections between Puerto Leguízamo or Tres Esquinas and Florencia — twice a week on average by

each company (*Satena, Aeropesca*, etc).

Via Florencia and the Rio Caqueta

The road to Florencia branches off from the main Neiva-San Agustin road at Altamira. From there and from Garzon there are regular buses to and from Florencia. The road is rough and subject to landslides but is a really beautiful journey — particularly the descent from the Eastern Cordillera.

Satena have two regular flight schedules which cover Florencia. They are:

Neiva-San Vicente-Florencia-Tres Esquinas-Puerto Leguízamo and Bogota-Neiva -San Vicente -Florencia -Puerto Asís. Flights to Florencia are daily except Sundays and the cost from Neiva is C$304. Flights to Tres Esquinas and Puerto Leguízamo are twice weekly and cost C$456 and C$532 respectively from Neiva. *Aeropesca* run a similar schedule and the local airlines, *Albania* and *San José*, run a more irregular schedule about three times a week.

Accommodation in Florencia

Prices tend to be high because most food is imported from outside. *El Dorado* C$20/single. *Residencas Turista* C$35/single with bath and toilet. This one is near the market.

For a riverboat down the Rio Caqueta, take a local bus to Puerto Rico on the Rio Guayas and try there, although a better bet would be to take a flight from Florencia to Tres Esquinas on the Rio Caqueta itself (more river traffic here). Remember that if you don't want to go all the way to Leticia, get off at La Tagua then take the 25 km dirt track through the jungle to Puerto Leguízamo and from there find a riverboat going up the Rio Putumayo to Puerto Asís, or take a flight from there to Puerto Asís or Florencia.

Leticia. Other than riverboats down the

rivers Putumayo and Caqueta, there are direct flights from Bogotá but they're no longer "cheap" as Leticia has become a popular tourist spot in the last few years.

Bogotá-Leticia. Flights by both *Avianca* and *SAM* go on Mondays, Wednesdays, and Saturdays. C$2470. *Satena* flies Tuesdays and Saturdays. C$2090. *Aerotal* and *Aeropesca* also do the flight (more irregular) both cost slightly less than *Satena*.

Leticia is no longer the quiet frontier town it used to be and now has a population of over 13,000. It's also become a popular tourist entry spot especially with the more expensive package tours. The classier end of the market is virtually controlled outright by the ubiquitous Mike Tsalickis — a Colombo-American who went there at the end of the sixties and set up the Parador Ticuna, a number of "jungle lodges", riverboat tours, etc and laid on Indian dance spectacles for the tourists. Nevertheless you can still arrange your own, cheaper tours with other local people, and it's doubtful whether you'll get closer to jungle life on the river than you will in Leticia. Accommodations include the following:

Residencias Pullman, C$39 to string up your own hammock or C$57 for a jungle hut with use of shower and toilet — clean.

Residencias Monserrate, C$57/single.

Residencias Quina and *Tacana*, C$76/single.

Residencias Amazonas, C$114/single including three meals — good food.

Hotel Alemania C$110/single, C$140/double — German run.

Pension Cano C$152/double without food.

Parador Ticuna, in case you have excess money you want to get rid of. C$570/single, C$760/double, C$190 for each additional person. There's a total of 13 rooms all with baths (hot and cold water) and each room will sleep up to six people — swimming pool, bar, restaurant. It's address is Avenida Libertador No. 6-03, tel 15.

One of the most popular places to eat is the *La Barra* (Spanish food, beer and wine). Another is *La Cabana* (reasonable food at reasonable prices). For tourist information go to either Mike Tsalickis at the Parador Ticuna, Avenida Libertador No. 6-03, or Antonio Cano at Calle 8 No. 9-53. The bank will not change travellers' cheques. Bring enough cash with you (dollars or pesos) or try the Cambio next door to the *Hotel Anaconda* where you can also get good rates for Peruvian soles. There's a local handicraft shop on Almacén de Alvaro Sierra, Calle Nueva del Puerto for such things as necklaces, drums, maracas, ceremonial masks, snake skins, bows and arrows, etc from the Yagua, Chama and Ticuna Indian tribes.

You can hire dug-outs for around C$114/day or motorboats for around C$380/day to make your own trips on the river. A small local airline (*ATA*) offers charter flights over the surrounding jungle and rivers in Cessnas at reasonable rates. You hire a boat and a guide to take you to the nearby lakes of Tarapoto, Campete or Yaguacaca. All support an amazing variety of bird life and you can find the world's largest water lily — the *Victoria Regia* — with leaves up to one and a half metres in diameter and capable of supporting the weight of an adult person. On trips to Tabatinga and Benjamin Constant — both in Brazil on the opposite side of the river from Leticia — the major attractions are the villages of the Ticuna Indians, particularly the village of Mari-Acu. A daily ferry between Leticia and Benjamin goes constantly in either direction for about C$76.

In Colombia there's a US$10 airport tax on international flights and an

11 percent tax on airline tickets for flights out of the country. In Brazil the extras are a US$2.50 airport tax on international flights or about US$0.60 for internal flights. It makes a lot of sense, therefore, to go to either Ramon Castilla or Benjamin Constant across the river from Leticia to get a flight.

Leticia/Benjamin Constant-Iquitos (Peru). Flights by Cruzeiro do Sul go in both directions on Wednesdays and Saturdays. They take one hour and cost around US$26 excluding taxes.

Ramón Castilla-Iquitos. *TANS* (the Peruvian military airline flies this route every Friday and Sunday for about US$16, but you must book in advance.

Letica/Benjamin Constant-Manaos (Brazil). *Cruzeiro do Sul* flies in both directions on Wednesdays and Sundays. It takes three hours and costs US$65 excluding taxes.

Leticia-Manaos. There's a possibility of a free or very cheap flight on Fridays with the *Petrobras* plane (*Petrobras* is the Brazilian oil company). The crew stay at the *Hotel Anaconda*. Ask to speak to them there/buy a few drinks. A letter of recommendation helps but the gift of the gab works just as well.

Leticia-La Pedrera via the Rivers Amazon and Caqueta. (1731 km). There's a steamship service on the *Vapor Nariño* or go by tugboat. It takes seven days there and nine days back.

Leticia-Iquitos (479 km). Take the steamship service on the *Vapor Nariño* or a smaller riverboat. It takes about four days there and three back.

Leticia-Manaos-Belén de Pará (total 3338 km). Take the same steamship service on the *Vapor Nariño* every seven days or so or go by tugboat or other riverboat. It takes about 12

days there and 16 days back (about half this time to Manaos). Costs up to US$25.

The Brazilian port of Benjamin Constant is possibly a better place to find a boat going to Manaos or Belén. There's a daily ferry in either direction between Leticia and Benjamin Constant. About US$2. Ferries to Rámon Castilla — the other Brazilian port on the opposite bank to Leticia are more irregular. Ask around at the port area.

COLOMBIAN CARIBBEAN ISLANDS
SAN ANDRÉS & PROVIDENCIA

These two islands, about 216 km off the coast of Nicaragua, are popular with travellers and many of the airlines connecting Central America and Miami with Colombia stop off in San Andrés. Despite the fact they're also popular with Colombian holidaymakers at certain times of the year, they're largely unspoilt. Providencia is completely so. Both islands are covered with coconut palms and the beaches and sea are second to none. The largely black, English-speaking population are very friendly and easy-going. Small animal life abounds in the palm forests and hedgerows, particularly the bird life and iridescent blue and green lizards. The islands are a custom-free zone so fags and booze are cheap and there's no shortage of other goodies. Don't miss them if they're on your route!

How to get there You can fly in from most Central American capitals — Belize, San Salvador, Tegucigalpa, San José and Panama — and from Miami. The main airlines which stop off here are *Avianca*, *SAM*, *Aerocondor*, *SAHSA* and the Costa Rican airlines, and all of them offer stop-overs (some for a small extra charge).

The cheapest flight from Central America is San José (Costa Rica)-San Andrés-Cartagena by *SAM*. US$75.

There are two flights per week on Saturdays and Tuesdays. The cheapest flight from the US is Miami-San Andrés by *Aerocondor*. US$140. Two flights go per week. If you're heading for the US on this flight confirm your booking at the *Aerocondor* office in San Andres at least several days in advance.

There are supposedly no airport taxes on international flights from San Andres (elsewhere in Colombia it's C$380), but the official must have "forgotten" this "fact" as far as we were concerned and insisted on C$190 payment. Protests in fluent Spanish were to no avail.

Flights from the Colombian mainland ports of Cartagena and Barranquilla everyday by *Aviance, Aerocondor* and *SAM*. The latter two are the cheapest at C$1216 plus C$60 Airport tax. It's a half hour flight. There are also boats to San Andrés from Colón (see the *Panama* chapter), Cartagena and Barranquilla on average about once per week which cost about US$25 and take two days, but they're not easy to find and you may have to wait around a few days. No regular ferries do these routes.

SAN ANDRÉS

Accommodation *Hotel Restrepo* is undoubtedly the cheapest, friendliest and pleasantest place to stay and very popular with travellers. C$60 each whatever you get — some rooms have their own showers and toilet, others don't. All rooms have fans and are clean. There's a common room/dining room downstairs where you can get breakfast (two fried eggs, home-made bread, coffee), lunch and dinner (rice, beans, fish/meat, salad, sweet and coffee — big helpings). All meals C$40 and, other than the fried fish cafe at the end of the road on the beach, these are the cheapest meals you'll get on the island. Some of the men who belong to the fishing cooperative also live here.

They're very friendly and will often offer you free fishing trips in their boats. In the evening people sit around in hammocks and on benches talking. Hotel location is on the town plan.

Other mid-range hotels (C$152/single upwards, C$228/double upwards) can be found in the main part of town. They include: *Hotel Las Vegas, Hotel Morgan, Kingston Hotel, Hotel Antillas, Hotel C. Eden, Hotel Europa, Hotel Miramar, Hotel Coliseo.*

Eats Other than the *Hotel Restrepo*, the cheapest place to eat is the fried fish shack on the beach at the end of Carrera 8 — same road as the Restrepo. Fried fish straight out of the sea and breadfruit chips C$25-30. Beer and mineral waters are available. For other relatively cheap cafes try the ones on Avenida 20 de Julio and Avenida Costa Rica. The largest ice-creams you've ever seen can be got from the Heladería at the corner of Avenida 29 de Julio and the sea-front drive (Avenida Colombia or Calle 1) but they're not cheap. C$20!

Other To change money, it's probably best at the sports shop (*La Opera Washington*). Cash or travellers cheques are changed at 37 pesos = US$1. The Post Office is in the *Avianca* office on Avenida Duarte Blum. Airline offices of *SAM, Aerocondor, Avianca,* etc are on Avenida Duarte Blum.

Places Nearby Johnny Cay is a small coral island (San Andrés itself is a coral island) a few hundred metres from the main beach opposite the end of the runway with beautiful sand and clear, turquoise water. You can hire snorkelling or scuba diving gear. Boats leave from the beach between Avenida 20 de Julio and Avenida Duarte Blum — or you can swim out there.

El Cliff is a high cliff alongside the runway with excellent views over the town and the rest of the island. Follow the road which winds up there from the airport terminal — a 20 minute walk.

Morgan's Cave (La Cueva de Morgan) is a natural cave supposedly used by the Welsh pirate, Henry Morgan, who often used San Andres as a base and source of supplies in the 1600s. You can either walk there (give yourself all day there and back) by following the coast road around the West side of the island and branching off at El Cove (a tiny port), or hire a cycle in town and ride there. It's also possible to hire mini-mokes but they're quite expensive. It's a beautiful coast road and there are occasional cafes/bars where you can find ice-cold beers/mineral waters.

Hoyo Soplador is at the southernmost tip of the island where the sea has carved out an underground channel through the coral with an outlet at the far end. When the wind is in the right direction the sea spurts through the outlet like a geyser. When it's really strong the jet is said to reach the same height as the tops of the coco palms!

San Luis is another beach on the East side of the island. It's perhaps worth a visit if you're into shells and sea urchins but it's heavily polluted with oil and garbage unlike the beaches along the north end of the island.

PROVIDENCIA ISLAND

This is a smaller and completely unspoilt island about 85 km to the north of San Andrés. If you're looking for peace and quiet, this is the place — very few facilities. You can either sleep on the beach, rent a room in a private house or stay at the *Hotel Aury*. There are very occasional boats from San Andrés (about eight hours) and a daily flight which costs C$456 return. Book the flight in the airport terminal concourse.

OTHER INFORMATION

To Panama Overland For further details see under *Panama* chapter. For Turbo-Medellin there's a daily flight by *Satena*. US$16 and it takes 55 minutes. There are also daily buses between the two places via Antioquia which is worth stopping off at as it's a beautiful old town.

Inflation This has been double figures for years. In 1977 it was 30 percent. In 1978 it was over 20 percent. This means that all the prices given in this book are going to go out of date fairly rapidly — bear this in mind — but it doesn't necessarily mean you'll be spending more *dollars* per day as the exchange rate will rise giving you more pesos to the dollar. The thing which will affect how much you spend per day particularly on transport, will be any further rise in OPEC's oil prices. Keep an eye on the newspapers regarding this. According to a survey in the *Chronicle*, Colombia's weekly English-language newspaper, the average monthly budget required for a working class family in Colombia now stands at C$6418 (about $200), yet 56.6 percent don't get this much. The average monthly budget required by an office worker and his family was C$11,505 (about US$400), but 75 percent don't get this. In other words Colombia is no longer a "cheap" country.

Ecuador

It often comes as a surprise to first-time travellers to South America that almost 50% of the populations of the Andean republics of Ecuador, Peru and Bolivia are pure or almost pure-blooded Indians, descendants of the people who settled these lands long before the arrival of the Spanish and who produced a number of remarkable civilizations culminating in the Inca Empire which stretched from southern Colombia to northern Argentina. Ecuador is the first of these republics where you will encounter what is effectively a dual culture. It's perhaps not strictly accurate to say that a dual culture exists since the Spaniards largely destroyed the social cohesion of Indian society in their zeal to exploit the Indians as cheap or free labour on their agricultural estates, robbed them of their precious metal artifacts and imposed an alien religion upon them. This policy of regarding them merely as a source of cheap labour has been continued by the blanco-dominated post-independence governments and so in many ways their "culture" is somewhat moribund. They nevertheless occupy quite a separate dimension in the life of Ecuador with their own villages, life styles, crafts and language. With the exception of Otavalo Indians whose crafts and weaving has attracted a great deal of tourist attention in recent years and so drawn them into the money economy, most Indians own little or no land and live a subsistence existence scratching a bare living from the soil in the highlands or working as indentured labourers on the lowland plantations. They have little interest in commerce and no sense of belonging to anything other than their own immediate tribe or group — hardly surprising after centuries of exploitation with every deck stacked against them. Things are beginning to

change in terms of land reform but progress is painfully slow and subject to reversal by military coups. The Indians are, therefore, naturally suspicious of power politics if not totally and understandably cynical.

The different groups of Indians are very distinctive in the clothes they wear and if you stay long enough in Ecuador you'll learn to recognise which village or town they come from. They're a very friendly, easy-going people and one of the great joys of any visit to this country. The quality and variety of hand-woven fabrics which they take to sell in the markets is superb and is as good as anything you will find in the markets of Mexico, Guatemala, Peru and Bolivia.

Ecuador is a country made up of three distinct geographical regions each with their own ambience, vegetation and people. The lush, tropical coastal lowlands with their endless banana plantations is the first of these regions. Much of the land in the centre and south of this region is parcelled out into huge estates and their produce — bananas, cacao, coffee and sugar — account for a large slice of Ecuador's economy. It is here that Guayaquil is situated — the country's largest city and very much a rival to the capital, Quito. Quiteños look on people from Guayaquil with much the same sort of suspicion and unease that Bogotaños regard people from the Caribbean ports. There are some beautiful beaches on this coast, particularly around Esmeraldas, and if you're into the sea it's as well to remember that this is the last chance you will have of swimming in warm water since, further south, the Humboldt current which comes up from Antarctica makes the sea very cold.

The next region is the Andean highlands with its central valley hemmed in by mountain peaks on either side — many of them extinct or still active volcanoes like Cotopaxi (the world's highest active volcano at 5896 metres) and Sangay (continuously active). Large areas of this region are very barren, partially because of over-grazing and removal of tree cover over the many centuries that it has been inhabited, and it's here that the majority of the Indians live. Some of the most spectacular scenery on the continent is to be found where the mountains drop down to the lowlands and if at all possible you should try to take the train from Quito to Guayaquil for one of the most memorable rail journeys to be had anywhere in the world. Another favourite travellers' mecca is at Baños, south-east of Quito, a lush, forested area of waterfalls and gorges on the very edge of the sierras where they drop down into the jungles of the Amazon basin. Like many travellers, you may find this area so attractive that you stay here for weeks. Quito itself — the world's second highest capital city at 2850 metres — is a beautiful place of steep, narrow cobbled streets with well-preserved colonial architecture, shady plazas and parks, impromptu Indian street markets and old churches embellished with a riotously baroque style in stone carving formed by a marriage of the arts of medieval Spain and the Inca Empire. And all this within sight of the spectacular, snow-covered peak of the sleeping volcano, Pichincha.

The other distinct region of Ecuador — the Oriente — on the eastern side of the Andes is typical Amazonian jungle with a high rainfall and few roads. Only 3½ percent of the population live in this area but it's here that oil was discovered in the early '70s. The government says, largely for the sake of appearances, that it is pinning its hopes on the income from this resource to improve the general standard of living and education and to diversify industry so that the country is less dependent on the export of bananas (Ecuador is one of the world's major suppliers of this fruit) but it's unlikely that the poor people will see much of it. Ecuador is ruled by a small oligarchy of wealthy landowners in cahoots with the military and US and European multinational companies. It has one of the lowest literacy rates on the continent and less than half of the children between the ages of six and 15 attend school.

Much of the Oriente was lost to Peru in 1941 following a dispute about the border in this region. The loss still rankles and is occasionally resurrected when government leaders need to focus national attention away from internal events. It is possible to get into Peru from the Oriente via the river system but the journey is difficult as there is little transport and is fraught with bureaucratic hassles since the Peruvian side is under military administration. If you're thinking of going this way, it's advisable to check out the situation before you set off with the Peruvian Embassy in Quito.

The Incas first arrived in the central valley around 1450 and founded a settlement where Quito stands today but, unlike Cuzco, none of it remains since the stone was used in the construction of the Spanish city. When the Sapa Inca, Huayna Capac divided the empire between his two sons, Atahualpa and Huascar, just before the arrival of the Spaniards, the former chose Quito as his capital. Atahualpa was later to defeat his half-brother in the civil war which followed this division but was himself enticed into a trap by Pizarro at Cajamarca in Peru and then strangled after he had fulfilled the ransom set by the Spaniard. After the death of Atahualpa and the collapse of much of the Inca Empire, Pizarro claimed Quito but in order to enforce his claim had to send an army north to forestall an attempt by Pedro de Alvarado to take it from him. This was the first taste of the squabbling and assassination which was to go on between rival conquistadores for the next 30 years until the Spanish throne finally established its authority in Lima. It was during this period that Pizarro's brother, Gonzalo, who had set himself up at Quito, outfitted an expedition under the leadership of Orellana to search for gold in the Amazonian lowlands. They didn't find any gold and Orellana didn't return but the expedition floated down the Amazon to the Atlantic and so became the first bunch of Europeans to cross the continent in this way. The Herzog film, *Aguirre, Wrath of God*, is based on this expedition and is worth seeing if you get the chance. It paints the conquistadores in their true colours as gold-obsessed megalomanical thugs and the church as being totally hypocritical.

For 300 years after the Conquest, Ecuador was relatively peaceful until the demand for independence from Spain gathered force at the end of the 18th century. An attempt was made at setting up an independent government in 1809 but Quito was too strongly garrisoned and it wasn't until Sucre with an army of Venezuelans and Colombians defeated the Spanish forces at the battle of Pichincha in 1822 that independence was gained. The country was induced by Bolívar to join the Republic of Gran Colombia but the union only lasted a few years and in 1830 Ecuador followed Venezuela's lead and split off. At the time this happened, the Indian provinces around Pasto in what is today southern Colombia attempted to join with Ecuador but were prevented from doing so by the Colombian army.

Until very recently, the country was governed by a succession of military juntas and an oligarchy of wealthy landowners. Elections for a civilian government were held last year but things have a long way to go before it will be truely representative. All the same, people are much easier-going than

.in neighbouring Colombia and the change in atmosphere is quite remarkable. This is one country where you can feel completely at ease.

VISAS
They're not required by anyone. 15-day or 30-day stay permits are issued at the border posts/airports (known as a "T3") that are renewable up to a total of 90 days at an Immigration Office. Before crossing a land border into a neighbouring country, you must obtain an Exit Stamp from the nearest Immigration Office, eg at Tulcan if crossing to Colombia or Huaquillas if crossing to Peru via Tumbes. If leaving by air, they're obtainable at the airport. There is no exit tax if the entry permit in your passport is marked "T3" — in practice, almost everyone, and no onward ticket required for entry or minimum funds. There's a 10 percent Government Tax on all airline tickets for flights out of the country, plus a VS\$2 Airport Tax for international flights.

If you lost your passport or have it stolen an Immigration Office will issue you with a new "T3" valid for an eight-day stay while they check with the records at the border where you entered. The Immigration Office in Quito is on Avenida Amazonas No. 3149 and 2639 (it's the same building!) between Avenida Marina de Jésus and Avenida de la Republica (off Parque El Hippodrome). Plenty of buses go from the old town. It's open 8.30 am-12 noon, 2.30 pm-6 pm and they are friendly and helpful.

Peruvian visas The Embassy is on Avenida Cristóbal Colón, Quito. It's open 10 am-12, 4 pm-6 pm. If you're hoping to get a letter from him excusing you from the obligation of having an onward ticket — forget it. He's heard it all a thousand times and knows all the answers. Fluent Spanish, a wallet full of Credit Cards, etc are all greeted with the same bored, uncompromising expression. If you need a visa for Peru (eg Australasians) they cost 60 sucres. Before issuing it he'll ask to see an onward ticket but doesn't examine it — a friend just waved an empty *Aerocondor* ticket folder!

CURRENCY

US$1 = 26.10 sucres

The unit of currency is the sucre (Suc) = 100 centavos. The sucre is a stable currency and there is no blackmarket.

Peruvian Soles There are plenty of Casas de Cambio in Quito (eg Rodrigo Paz on Avenida Amazonas in the area where all the airline offices are situated) but they'll only sell you Soles at the official bank rate and the bank rate in Peru is often higher than it is in Ecuador. Wait until you get to Huaquillas on the Ecuadorian side of the border where you'll find scores of money-changers who'll offer you rates (at least for cash) almost or as good as

what you'll find on the street in Lima — presently around 170 Soles = US$1. Inflation in Peru is like a Ferrari out of control so don't take this figure as gospel. Ask someone who's just come back from Peru what the present rate is.

Ecuador is one of the few South American countries (Venezuela, Bolivia and Uruguay being the others) where you are allowed to draw out any money sent to you from abroad entirely in US dollars (cash or cheques). So if you're having money sent to you, Ecuador is one of your possibilities.

AMBATO

The town was completely destroyed in the earthquake of 1949 so there are very few old buildings left. It's famous for its "Fiesta de frutas y flores" which takes place in February. There's a large market every Monday with smaller ones on Wednesday and Friday.

Accommodation

Pensión Americana on the main square, Suc26.10/single — hot shower extra. *Residencial Unión* Suc80/double. *Hotel Europa*, Suc32/single. *Hotel Nacional*, Suc 42/single.

Eats *El Alamo* in the centre has good meals for Suc26. Also recommended are the *Cafe Los Monjes* and the *Rondador* near the Mercado Central.

Other The main bus terminal is about two km from the centre of town.

BAÑOS

Located in one of the most beautiful settings in all of South America and surrounded by mountains, river gorges and waterfalls, Baños should not be missed. It's very popular with travellers and many spend a long time here. As its name implies, there are hot, natural sulphur springs in the vicinity.

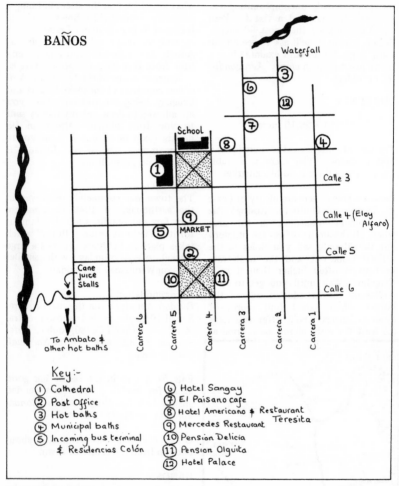

BAÑOS

Waterfall

School

Calle 3

Calle 4 (Eloy Alfaro)

Calle 5

Calle 6

Cane Juice Stalls

To Ambato & other hot baths

Carrera 6
Carrera 5
Carrera 4
Carrera 3
Carrera 2
Carrera 1

<u>Key</u>:-
1. Cathedral
2. Post Office
3. Hot baths
4. Municipal baths
5. Incoming bus terminal & Residencias Colón
6. Hotel Sangay
7. El Paisano cafe
8. Hotel Americano & Restaurant Teresita
9. Mercedes Restaurant
10. Pensión Delicia
11. Pensión Olguita
12. Hotel Palace

Accommodation

Residencias Olguita, Carrera 4 between Calles 5 and 6. Suc30/single.

Hotel Santa Clara Suc40/single.

Hotel Sangay, Carrera 3 beyond Calle 1. Suc90/single. Suc160/double without own bath. Suc140/single, Suc200/double with own bath.

Hotel Palace, Carrera 2 and Calle 1. Suc90/single. It's also the only

place in town where you can change money — no banks.

Also recommended are the *Hotel Américano* and the *Residencias Teresita* next to each other on Calle 2 between Carreras 3 and 4.

Eats The best restaurants in town and the ones most popular with travellers are:

Hotel Américano — run by Bruce and Jenny, an American couple.

Mercedes Restaurant, Calle Eloy Alfaro (Calle 4) No. 4-20 — natural home-cooked vegetarian food, also books to swop and chess. It's a very friendly place where you can sit for hours.

El Paisano Restaurant, Carrera 3 between Calles 1 and 2 — excellent vegetarian food, herb teas, etc. It's a very friendly place.

If you've grown tired of the normal bland fare in most South American cafes, this is the place to come and eat your way back to health.

Other Post Office is closed between 12 noon and 3 pm. There are no banks so the only place where you can change money is the *Hotel Palace* (Suc25 = US$1).

Things to Do/See The nearest and cleanest hot baths are the ones by the waterfall at the end of Carrera 2 beyond the *Hotel Palace*. They've got free public hot pools or private rooms with heat control on tap for Suc5. The other hot baths are out of town. Follow either Calle 5 or 6 until you get to the main road out to Ambato where there are a number of cane juice stalls. Turn left there and follow the main road until you reach the blue and white sign with a figure of a person diving. Turn left and follow the road towards the mountains. Several outdoor public pools of various heat or private rooms with heat control for Suc5. Gringas in bikinis attract gawping groups of local guys.

For walks, follow either Calles 5 or 6 to the cane-juice stalls on the main Ambato highway and then take the dirt track down to the river which is crossed by a rickety suspension bridge. The track continues on the other side over the mountains — beautiful and spectacular scenery and plantlife.

CUENCA

This interesting city, the third largest in Ecuador, is surrounded by four rivers and contains many old buildings from the Spanish colonial era. It is also a suitable base for visiting the Inca ruins of Ingapirca.

Accommodation

Hotel Hiltons, corner of Presidente Córdoba Calle and Padre Aguirre Calle. Suc60/person — very unrecommended especially for women. It's dirty, grimy, noisy and full of drunks — or it was.

Residencial El Inca, Calle General Torres between Bolívar and Sucre. Suc50/person. It's clean, has attractive decor, is friendly and serves meals. There's hot water — when the wiring doesn't catch light! A friend nearly burnt the place down but all the staff were most apologetic and spent half the night trying to get a hot shower together for her! They will wake you up for the early buses at 4.30 am if you ask.

Other hotels with the same prices as the *El Inca* are:

Hotel Pichincha near *El Inca* on Calle General Torres.

Hotel Residencial, Calle Gran Colombia No. 10-77.

Hotel Majestic, Calle P. Cordero No.11-24.

Residencias Athenas, Calle P. Cordero No. 11-87.

Eats There are few cafes in Cuenca and they tend to close early. *Fiesta* Soda Fountain (Fuente de Soda), on Calle Bolívar between Gen. Torres and Padre Aguirre has excellent breakfasts (juice, two eggs, hot buttered rolls, milk coffee) for Suc20. *High Society* restaurant, near the First National City Bank has good breakfasts (egg, toast, marmalade, juice and coffee or cocoa and air-conditioning!) for Suc30. *Hamburger Cafe*, opposite the *Hotel Pichincha* has

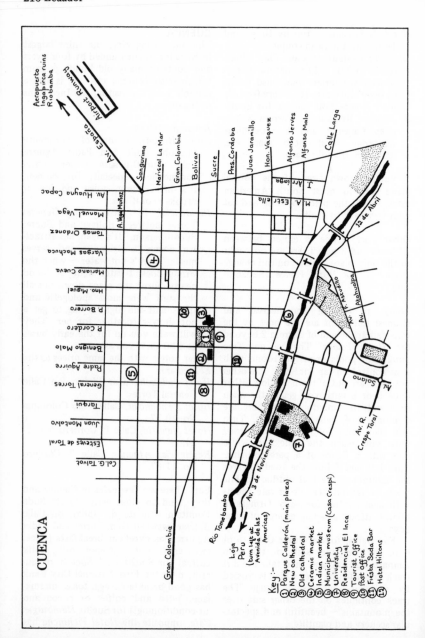

CUENCA

Key:-
1. Parque Calderón (main plaza)
2. New cathedral
3. Old cathedral
4. Ceramic market
5. Indian market
6. Municipal museum (Casa Crespi)
7. University
8. Residencial El Inca
9. Tourist Office
10. Post office
11. Fiesta Soda Bar
12. Hotel Hiltons

Aeropuerto
Ingapirca ruins
Riobamba

Airport Runway

Av. España

Sangurima
Mariscal La Mar
Gran Colombia
Bolivar
Sucre
Pres. Cordoba
Juan Jaramillo
Hno. Vasquez
Alfonso Jerves
Alfonso Malo
Calle Larga

J. Arriaga
M. A. Estrella
12 de Abril

Av. Huayna Capac
A. Vega Muñoz
Manuel Vega
Tomas Ordoñez
Vargas Machuca
Mariano Cueva
Hno. Miguel
P. Borrero
R. Cordero
Benigno Malo
Padre Aguirre
General Torres
Tarqui
Juan Montalvo
Esteves de Toral
Col. G. Talvot

Gran Colombia

Av. F. Astudillo
Av. Atahualpa

Av. Solano

Av. R. Crespo Toral

Río Tomebamba
Av. 3 de Noviembre

Loja
Peru
(turn left at
Avenida de las
Americas)

good cheap hamburgers, hot dogs and steaks.

Information Tourist Office is on the main plaza, Calle Sucre. It is helpful and has maps of the city for Suc20. To change money there are plenty of banks around the main plaza and *Cambistral* — a Casa de Cambio on the main plaza, Calle Sucre. They will change cheques (and cash).

Things to Do/See The Indian market on Thursdays, between Calles Gen. Torres, Córdoba and Padre Aguirre, has clothes and textiles. There's also a handicraft shop — *Productos Andinos* — run by an Indian Cooperative on Gran Colombia No. 6-24 between Benigno Malo and P. Cordero.

Remigio Crespo Toral Municipal Museum is on Calle Larga between P. Cordero and P. Borrero Calles. It's open Mondays-Fridays, 8 am-12 noon, 2 pm-5 pm, and divided up into four different sections. The archaeological section contains ceramics, stone and metal weapons and jewellery of the Canari and Inca periods and a golden chest shield from the Chordeleg civilization. Another section has many oil paintings about the foundation of the city and colonial times. The Hall of the Independence of Cuenca has documents and other odds and sods from Independence days as well as the predictable busts of Bolívar and Sucre. The fourth is the Historical Relics section.

Places Nearby The Incan ruins of Ingapirea, situated some 50 km north of Cuenca in Cañar Province, were constructed with the same mortarless, polished stone technique as the monuments you will find in Cuzco, Pisác and Macchu Picchu in Peru. Excavation and reconstruction work is still going on there.

To get there take the Autoferro to Ingapirea station at 4.30 am. It takes two hours and costs Suc15. It returns at 3.30 pm. The station is approximately an hour's walk to the ruins. Or you can take the Pan-American Highway north out of Cuenca and head for the town of Cañar via Azogues (you may well have to take a taxi — get a group together). A few kilometres before you get to Cañar turn right along a dirt road and head for the village of Honorato Vasquez — it's not signposted so you will have to ask local people the way unless you're in a taxi. Between this village and the ruins you pass a farm called San Pedro. Well worth a visit.

ESMERALDAS

Accommodation Though it's not recommended — it's a rough town — you might find yourself having to stay here overnight on your way to the beaches of Atacames or Súa. Don't sleep out.

Hotel Colón, cheap and nasty, but it's tolerable for a night. Suc26/single.
Hotel Bolívar Suc52/single — somewhat better.
Residencia Dominguez. This is one of the better cheaper ones. Suc45/single.
Hotel Tyrol — only if you have money to throw away!

Eats *Miramar* is a hut right on the beach with excellent views at the end of the No. 1 bus route and serves some of the best crab in South America. Suc40. *Derby*, in the main square has meals for Suc50. The *Tyrol* also serves very good food but it's expensive, Suc70!

Places Nearby The beaches of Atacames and Súa are relatively isolated and undeveloped beaches that are very popular with travellers who are willing to go out of their way to find a quiet easy-going place to relax for a while and soak up some sun, sand and sea.

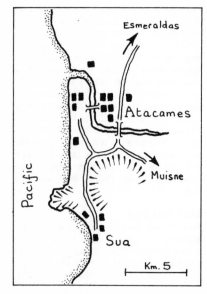

Other than the beaches of Salinas and Playas near Guayaquil, they're also the last beaches where you'll be able to enjoy a warm sea. South of Tumbes, the first town in Peru, and all the way down the rest of the Pacific coast the sea is very cold due to the Humboldt current which comes up from Antarctica. You can sleep on the beaches, sling up a hammock or take over one of the many palmhuts to be found here. But remember that it can get cold around 4 am in the morning, so take a sleeping bag with you. Also it's not wise to leave your belongings unattended — is it anywhere in the world? So keep an eye on them. There are also wooden huts to rent for about Suc20/night. They're primitive and can't really be regarded as secure. Otherwise, there are one or two hotels to stay at.

At Atacames the *Hotel Tahiti* has very pleasant rooms with bath for Suc100 or not-so-pleasant rooms without bath for Suc45. Food extra. *Cabañas del Sol* is an expensive Club Mediterranee-type place — great, if you like that sort of thing. Bamboo huts have bath, shower and idyllic views through coconut palms. It's the occasional haunt of minor diplomats from Quito. Suc160/night without food! *Hotel Las Vegas* is clean and modern with large windows. Suc110/night.

In Atacames there are quite a few wooden huts which prepare food where you can get fish or meat with rice for around Suc15. They also do "ceviche" for a little more. ("Ceviche" is a Latin American dish made out of prawns or crab tossed up with sliced raw onions, lemon juice and oil and sometimes other raw vegetables.) There are also a number of makeshift bars where you can get cold beers, etc and a sort of Wild West saloon bar, *Saloon Atacames*, which is the nearest you'll get to some action in the evenings other than sitting around a camp-fire with fellow travellers.

In Súa, *Hotel España* is on the beach and has a discotheque. Suc30 during the week; more expensive at weekends. There's also *Hotel Turismo* — by far the better of the two — a house on stilts run by a friendly black guy. His wife's an excellent cook but unfortunately does it with river water which is supposed to be contaminated with amoebic dysentery (unconfirmed). If you want to be sure, eat at the *Motel Chagra Ramos*.

To get there (Esmeraldas-Atacames-Súa) take a bus with *Transportes Súa* whose office is on the main plaza in Esmeraldas. Suc6-8 and it takes about 40 minutes. There are five buses per day and the last one leaves about 5 pm. They're often packed out so buy a ticket as soon as you can. It's possible to walk to Atacames in the evening from Esmeraldas, but not advisable except in a group as you may encounter thieves. A taxi will be about Suc25.

When the tide is out, you can walk to Súa from Atacames along the beach and around the rocky headland which separates the two. It's possible to find oysters in these rocks. There are also Micro-buses direct to Quito at weekends and direct Pullman-type buses to both Quito and Guayaquil from Esmeraldas — see under *Transport* for details.

GUAYAQUIL

Though doubtless an under-statement, it's probably true that guidebooks sometimes create or underline prejudices about certain places in travellers' minds. So after all I'd been told and read about Guayaquil before going there, I expected to be almost eaten alive by thieves and rip-off artists from the moment I got off the ferry. It wasn't like that. It turned out to be a fairly pleasant and lively city, but there's one thing they were right about — it's expensive!

Accommodation The cheapest places to stay are undoubtedly in Duran across the river where the rail terminal from Quito is situated. If you're prepared to stay there, the following are basic and all for under Suc52/single. *Pensión Sarmiento*, Esmeraldas y Cuenca. *Pensión Duran*, Esmeraldas y Loja. *Pensión Buenos Aires*, Loja y Esmeraldas. *Pensión Los Angeles*, Loja y Esmeraldas.

In Guayaquil itself, some of the cheapest places are clustered around the *Ecuatoriano* bus terminal at the junction of Chiriboga and Chimborazo. They include: *Residencias Ayacucho; Hotel El Cisme; Residencias Mar de la Plata; Hotel Florida* (Suc78/room); *Hotel Boston*, Chimborazo 711 with Sucre (Suc65/single). Another cheap place is the *Residencias Roma*, Ayacucho 415. Suc26/single — hot water.

Nearer the centre of town there are:

Residencias Pauker, Banquerizo Moreno 902 with Junín is German-run.

Suc122/person. The rooms differ in quality, some are very pleasant with windows, other more sombre — clean sheets, hot water, clean and secure. The air-conditioning is kaput but it gets cool enough to sleep at night without it anyway. They also serve good meals.

Hotel Turista, Baquerizo Moreno 903 with Junín, next door to the *Pauker*. Cheaper at Suc78/single.

Hotel Delicias, Clemente Ballen 1106. Suc52/single.

Eats Plenty of good cafes are on the main street — 9 de Octubre — where they spill out onto the pavement, and around the various bus terminals. If you're looking for the Peace Corps try the *Bar Loy*, Calle Pasaje 101 at the corner of Cuenca, in the port area. there are plenty of discotheques and nightclubs around the Parque Centenario, but drinks are expensive. At least Suc52 each.

Information At the Tourist Office, Centuris, 9 de Octubre 424, Office No. 205 at the junction with Pedro Carbo, English is spoken and they are helpful.

Other Ferries across the Rio Guayas to Durán (rail terminal for Quito/Riobamba) go every 15 minutes. 5 centavos. There's also an enormous bridge further up river but going this way will take you a lot longer and cost a lot more (eg taxi at least Suc157). If you're arriving on the train from Quito (Autoferro), the fare includes the cost of the ferry so don't throw your ticket away!

Here are some bus company addresses and terminals in Guayaquil:

Flota Imbabura (to Quito), Luque 1028 corner of P. Moncayo.

Cooperative de Transportes Patria (to Riobamba), P. Moncayo 1212 corner of Aguirre.

Transportes Esmeraldas (to Esmeraldas

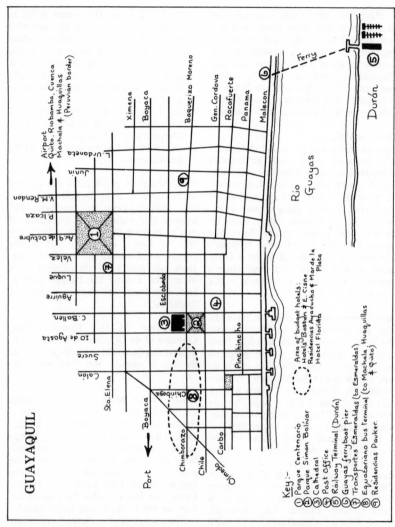

GUAYAQUIL

Airport Quito. Riobamba, Cuenca Machala & Huaquillas (Peruvian border)

Ximena
Boyaca
Baqueriza Moreno
Gen. Cordova
Rocafuerte
Panama
Malecon

Durán

Ferry

Rio Guayas

L. Urdaneta

Junin

V. M. Rendon

P. Icaza

Av. 9 de Octubre

Veléz

Luque

Aguirre

Escobedo

C. Ballen

10 de Agosta

Sucre

Colon

Sto. Elena

Chiriboga

Boyaca

Port

Chimborazo

Chile

Carbo

Olmedo

Pinchincha

Area of budget hotels:
Hotels Boston & E. Cisne
Residencias Ayacucho & Mar de la Plata
Hotel Florida

Key:—
① Parque Centenario
② Parque Simon Bolivar
③ Cathedral
④ Post Office
⑤ Railway Terminal (Durán)
⑥ Guayas ferryboat pier
⑦ Transportes Esmeraldas (to Esmeraldas)
⑧ Equatoriano bus terminal (to Machala, Huaquillas & Quito)
⑨ Residencias Pauker

via Sto Domingo los Colorados), Luque 901, corner of St Elena.

Transportes Colón (to Machala), Avenida Olmedo.

Ecuatoriano (to Quito, Machala and Huaquillas), junction of Chiriboga and Chimborazo.

Transport to the Galapagos Islands It's very difficult to get there cheaply these days if only because the Ecuadorian Government is actively discouraging the availability of cheap transport. Some travellers have managed to get a lift with the Ecuadorian navy, by having a letter on headed notepaper from a "reputable" institution (eg a university) stating that they are student of botany/zoology, etc. It's worth a try. Otherwise try *Armada del Ecuador*, corner of Avenida Canar and Vivero in Zona 1. Catch a bus there from the Malecón. Two boats do the cheap trip (and you must ask for them by name) but they seem to spend a lot of their time in dry dock — be persistent! They are called *Jambeli* and *Tarqui*. It's an 11-day trip, there and back, in flat-bottomed boats (rough!) for about Suc2610. The alternative to the above is one of the Suc7830 tours by sea (*Transnave*) or by air. It's unfortunate, but unless you have a lot of money spare, you may have to forgo a visit to Galapagos. See under *Transport* for more details.

Things to Do/See *The Municipal Museum*, 10 de Agosto, corner of Pichincha, 4th floor is open Monday-Friday, 8.30 am-12,30 pm, 3 pm-6 pm. This is the only museum in Ecuador where you can see the shrunken heads ("Tzantzas") made by certain tribes in the Oriental region. Many have been reduced to fist size without their original features being lost! There's also an archaeological section featuring objects from the various coastal cultures of Ecuador.
Casa de la Cultura Museum is at 9 de Octubre and Machala, 7th floor, on the Parque Centenario. It's open Monday to Friday 9 am-12 noon, 3 pm-6 pm, and has Pre-Columbian gold work (bracelets, ear-rings, chest shields, ceremonial masks, etc) and ceramics.
The *Barrio Las Peñas*, at the bottom of Santa Ana hill to the right of the city as you cross the river, is the place where the city was first founded with many old houses, fortifications and cobbled streets. To get there, follow the Malecón or Rocafuerte to the point where they reach the hill.

HUAQUILLAS (Ecuadorian border town with Peru).

Accommodation Probably the best place to stay is the *Hotel Continental* on the main street (Avenida de la República). Suc40/person — clean with cold showers. There are others if this one is full (see the map).

Eats Adequate meals can be got at the *Pensión Loja* restaurant for Suc25. If you want to kill a little time in the evening, try the bars down the last street on the left before the bridge (border).

Other Huaquillas is *the* place to buy Peruvian soles. There are scores of money-changers who wander around the streets and bars — identifiable by their black attache cases. The rate they offer for cash is only slightly lower than the highest rate you're likely to find on Jirón Union in the centre of Lima. When the bank rate in Peru was 130 Soles = US$1, they were offering 170 Soles = US$1. The rate for travellers' cheques, however, is not so good — around 150 Soles = US$1, so have some cash with you! Ecuador is one of the few South American countries where you can buy cash dollars in any quantity you like and at a good rate. There is officially a limit of 1000 soles (sometimes 5000) which you're allowed to take into Peru, but no one bothers as the whole money changing scene on this border is just too open for anyone to pretend otherwise.

Crossing the Border There is a set procedure to follow at the border:
(1) Go to the Ecuadorian Immigration office for an Exit Stamp. There is no Exit Tax if your Entry stamp is marked "T3".
(2) Cross the bridge calling at Ecuadorian passport control.

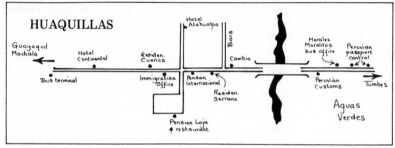

HUAQUILLAS

Guayaquil / Machala — Bus terminal — Hotel Continental — Residental Cuenca — Immigration Office — Pensión Internacional — Residen. Serrano — Pensión Loja & restaurant — Hotel Atahualpa — Bars — Cambio — Morales Moralitos bus office — Peruvian passport control — Peruvian Customs — Tumbes — Aguas Verdes

(3) Cursory baggage search by Peruvian customs — it would seem pointless for it to be other than cursory as the bridge and street are packed with stalls and street vendors and money changers.

(4) Go to Peruvian passport control. Most times the official will ask to see your onward ticket (though not always — two friends were not asked the day after I went through). He will only accept an MCO or a specific flight ticket out of the country or a Tumbes-Guayaquil bus ticket. If you haven't got any of these you'll be directed next door to the *Morales Moralitos* bus office where you're offered a choice of bus tickets at twice the price they'd cost you in Tumbes. Some of the choices are: Cuzco-Puno 1200 soles (the cheapest), Puno-La Paz 2000 soles, Lima-Tumbes 4000 soles. *Morales Moralitos* bus company have a bad reputation with travellers but if it's any consolation, I was later allowed to change my Cuzco-Puno ticket in Arequipa for the bus journey from that city to Puno and use it again for the journey from Puno to Yunguyo. So they can't be that pernicious! The tickets are open and your name is typed on them. When you have your ticket you are stamped with an automatic 90-day entry permit.

(5) Go to Peruvian passport control where they check you have your

stamp.

(6) A colectivo to Tumbes costs 85 soles each. Don't listen to the taxi drivers' bullshit about "difficulties" with buses from Tumbes. There are as many as three police checkpoints on the way to Tumbes — you merely have to show your passport.

IBARRA

This is the first major town after Tulcán which has some interesting old buildings. There's a railway line from here to San Lorenzo on the Pacific coast if you want to go that way.

Accommodation *Hotel Imbabura* near the main plaza. Suc52/double — clean, friendly, cold water. *Residencias Vaca* Suc78/single — clean, friendly, hot water. *Residencias Astoria*, one block from the railway station. Suc20/single with hot water.

Places Nearby Buses for Esperanza leave from the Mercado all day. Beautiful embroidered shirts can be bought here. San Antonio de Ibarra is famous for its wood carvings. The buses which go to Otavalo pass by this village.

LOJA

A pleasant town, surrounded by hills, is a base for visiting Vilcabamba, a town famous for its numerous centenarians. From Loja you can go to Peru via Machala, Macará or Zamora though the latter two routes are rough.

Accommodation *Residencial Cooperative Loja*, Suc15/bed in dormitory accommodation. *Paris*, Suc52/single with hot showers — new and clean. *Hosteria Casablanca*, Suc105/single — often full.

Things to Do/See Market days are on Saturdays and Sundays.

OTAVALO
Very popular with travellers for its friendly and colourful Indian population and for the Saturday market where some of the most beautiful woven fabrics and clothes in South America can be bought, many people stay here for a long time, renting rooms in private houses in town or in the surrounding hills.

Accommodation
Pensión Vaca, Calle Sucre No. 10-7. It's quiet, friendly and has plenty of atmosphere with good views of the volcanoes from a wood-wormed balcony. There's dormitory-type accommodation and the beds are hard so you'll need a sleeping bag to lie on. Suc20/single.
Mariscal Suc45 — very basic.
Pensión Otavalo One of the better hotels, a friendly manager. Suc35/double.
Residencias Colón Suc42/person — hot water, not too clean.
Riviera Suc52/person. It also serves reasonably priced food.
Pensión Los Andes Suc20/bed.

Eats *Herradura* is a typical local restaurant with good food that's inexpensive. *Ali Mieni*, on the Plaza de los Ponchos is run by an American. Banana bread and fruit pies, etc — it has vegetarian food at reasonable prices. It's a popular meeting place for travellers. *La Casa Verde*, a white house on the large marketplace, is run by a Canadian and has Vegetarian food.

Things to Do/See The principal attraction of Otavalo is the Saturday market. Many Indians come in from neighbouring villages to sell their weaving — some of the most beautiful you will find anywhere in Latin America but prices are quite high as it's become a tourist attraction. The market starts at 6 am and you must be there at that time if you want to pick anything up (relatively) cheaply. Between 7 am and 8 am the market gets packed out with tourists arriving from Quito. It might be better to find out which villages the weavers come from and go there to buy something — many of them come from Peguche, Quinchuqui and Iluman — very friendly people.

Other It's difficult to find anywhere to change travellers cheques, so have a ready supply of cash with you.

QUITO
The second highest capital city in the world (over 3000 metres), Quito is one of the pleasantest and most interesting cities you will come across in South America. The old part, dating from the 16th century, is more or less intact and consists of low adobe houses with red-tiled roofs, steep narrow and often cobbled streets and many old churches and monasteries with amazing stone-carved facades and glittering interiors. There are many Indians in traditional costume who either live in the old city or come in from neighbouring villages to sell their weavings, clothes or agricultural products. You'll find something to delight you on virtually every street.

Accommodation
Hotel Gran Casino (often known as the *Gran Gringo*), Calle García Moreno No. 330. This and the *Astoria*, are the travellers' hotels. It's a huge place with friendly management. Suc40 each — single, double, triple

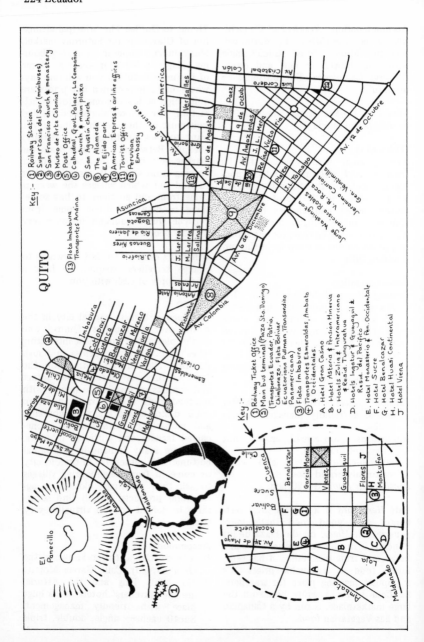

QUITO

Key :-
① Railway Station
② Supertaxis del Sur (minibuses)
③ San Francisco church & monastery
④ Museo de Arte Colonial
⑤ Post Office
⑥ Cathedral, Govt. Palace, La Compania church & main plaza
⑦ San Agustin church
⑧ The Alameda
⑨ El Ejido park
⑩ American Express & airline offices
⑪ Tourist Office
⑫ Peruvian Embassy

⑬ Flota Imbabura
   Transportes Andina

Key :-
① Railway Ticket Office
② Main bus terminal (Plaza Sto. Domingo)
   (Transportes Ecuador, Patria,
   Chimborazo, Flota Bolivar,
   Ecuatoriano Pullman, Transandino
   Panamericana)
③ Flota Imbabura
⊕ Transportes Esmeraldas, Ambato
   & Occidentales
A. Hotel Gran Casino
B. Hotel Asteria & Pension Minerva
C. Hotels Zulia & Interamericana
   & Resid Tungurahua
D. Hostls Ingatur & Guayaquil &
   Rsdal. del Pacifico
E. Hotel Monasterio & Pen. Occidentale
F. Hotel Sucre
G. Hotel Benalcazar
H. Hotel Huasi Continental
J. Hotel Viena

rooms — hot water, TV, cheap meals virtually all day and evening. Meals Suc20 (bread, soup, main course and fruit juice — but they'll cook anything you want, eg fried egg and chips!) There's a free notice board. Be careful of the wiring!

Hotel Astoria, Calle Loja, the other popular travellers' hotel. Suc40/person — hot water, good views from some of the top rooms, cafe, bar. Very security conscious at the reception desk but they're okay.

Residencias Santa Lucia, situated in a beautiful narrow street right in the centre of the old town. It's clean and light and the rooms have balconies. Suc50/person.

Hotel Viena: Calle Flores 421. Old colonial house. Costs Suc120/person without bath. Clean.

There are plenty of other hotels of a similar quality and price in the old city whose locations are marked on the city plan (if you're not keen on large gringo gatherings) as well as expensive and mid-range hotels. Other mid-range and expensive hotels are located to the north and west of El Ejido park in the new town, particularly between Ulpiano Paez, 9 de Octubre, Avenida Amazonas, Juan León Mera and Reina Victoria where many of the airline offices, banks and embassies are situated. If you want to stay in this part of town ask around among the other travellers in the restaurant *Fuente* next door to the casa de cambio *Rodriguez Paz* on Avendia Amazonas, junction with Jorge Washington. One of the cheaper ones is *Residencia Bethania*, Juan León Mera No. 870. Suc130/person. Many Peace Corps people stay here.

Eats The *Hotel Gran Casino* undoubtedly has some of the cheapest meals (bread, soup, main course, fruit juice, Suc20) you will find in the city. It's open to non-residents — just walk in. There are plenty of other local restaurants on virtually every street in the old town which offer meals like chicken, rice, beans and maybe a salad for around Suc25-35. If you have chicken, make sure it's cooked properly — a lot of restaurants tend to under-cook meat and over-cook the beans!

In the new town, one of the most popular meeting places for travellers and the Peace Corps is the *Fuente* restaurant on Avenida Amazonas, junction with Jorge Washington. You can eat a meal here for between Suc50-70 depending on what you have, but if you just want a snack, they have hamburgers for Suc18.

Flandres, 9 de Octubre No. 300 and Jorge Washington (corner). French cuisine with pleasant atmosphere but it's relatively expensive, about Suc104 for a meal. Soup Suc20, steak with trimmings Suc60. Also they have other meats, fish and pancakes. Ecuadorian musicians play here.

La Llama, on the Alameda near junction with 7 de Septiembre. This grilled chicken restaurant is one of the best in Quito. A quarter chicken with salad and potatoes costs Suc50 (as with other restaurants, ask them to cook the chicken well!). They also have steaks and sausages, again for Suc50 a meal.

Information Tourist Office is on Ceturis, Avenida 10 de Agosto No. 1239 on the north side of El Ejido park. There's also another on Reina Victoria between V. R. Roca and J. Carrion. The Post Office also has some information.

The Immigration Office, Avenida Amazonas No 3149 and 2639 (same place!) between Avenida Marina de Jésus and Avenida de la República (off Parque El Hippodrome) is open 8.30 am-12 noon, 2.30 pm-6 pm. It's quite a long way out to the west but there are plenty of buses both from the old and new towns. They deal with visa extensions and lost passports — helpful.

Peruvian Visas The embassy on Avenida Cristóbal Colón (see city plan) is open 10 am-12 noon and 4 pm-6 pm. Visas cost Suc60 and are issued on the spot. If you're hoping to get an official letter excusing you from having an onward ticket before being allowed into Peru, forget it. The consul knows all the answers, but if you're applying for a visa he doesn't actually examine the ticket he asks for so just flash any airline ticket if you haven't got one that would otherwise satisfy him.

Other The railway booking office is on Bolívar between Benalcazar and García Moreno. A Ferrocarril goes to Guayaquil on Tuesdays, Thursdays and Saturdays. Try to reserve a seat on the right hand side for the best views. The train station is one and a half km along Calle Maldonado and, as the train leaves at 6 am, you may well have to walk there as there are no buses and very very few taxis about 5.30 am. From the Gran Casino or Astoria give yourself at least 20 minutes to walk there, it's a stiff climb uphill with a pack on your back.

Buses There are three routes to know about:

No. 3 route, El Panecillo, Plaza 24 de Mayo, Calle Garcia Moreno past the Government Palace and through the embassy/business quarter (Avenida Amazonas).

No. 1 and 2 route, Plaza Santo Domingo and along Avenida 10 de Agosto.

To the airport: Bus marked *Aeropuerto* goes from Plaza Santo Domingo to the airport.

Long-distance bus company details:

terminal	bus company	destinations
Plaza 24 de Mayo	Transportes Esmeraldas	Esmeraldas, Santo Domingo, los Colorados
	Transportes Occidentales	Esmeraldas, Santo Domingo, los Colorados, Machala
	Transportes Ambato	Ambato
Plaza Santo Domingo/ Cumanda	Panamericana	Ambato, Riobamba, Cuenca, Loja, Guayaquil, Machala, Huaquillas & Colombian cities
	Transportes Ecuador	Ambato, Riobamba, Guayaquil
	Transportes Patria	Ambato, Riobamba, Milagro, Machala, Huaquillas
	Transportes Chimborazo	Ambato, Riobamba
	Santa	Ambato, Riobamba, Loja, Guayaquil, Cuenca
	Expreso Sucre Cotopaxi	Ambato, Riobamba, Cuenca
	Ecuatoriano Pullman	Santo Domingo, Portoviejo, Manta
	Cooperativa Baños	Ambato, Baños, Puyo, Tena
	Cooperativa Amazonas	Lago Agrio, Coca
Manuel Larrea/ Portoviejo*	Flota Imbabura	Otavalo, Ibarra, Tulcán
18 de Septiembre No. 801/Avenida Guerrero	Transportes Andina	Otavalo, Ibarra
	Aerotaxi (microbuses)	Otavalo, Ibarra, Tulcán

*they also have a terminal in the old city of Flores between Bolívar and Sucre.

Teaching English. Try the following places:

Colegio Americano (Principal Mr Metz), situated near the Catholic University and have a rapid turnover.

Alliance Academy — North American foundation.

Cotopaxi Academy — North American foundation.

Cardinal Spellman School — a Catholic Institute. They have two schools, boys and girls.

Instituto Benedicto, Calle Colonia, near British Embassy — a language school.

You could also try the British Council although at the moment it consists of only one guy who's in the process of setting it up (Mr. Foley). Contact him c/o British Embassy at the very end of Avenida 12 de Octubre where it turns into Avenida Gonzales Suarez.

Things to Do/See Some of the many churches worth looking at are;

La Compañia, Calle Garcia Moreno half a block from Plaza Independencia. It's probably the most interesting with amazing ornate stone-carving both outside and in, solid gold altar and gilded balconies.

San Francisco, Calle Cuenca, facing a large cobbled plaza. This is one of the oldest churches in South America.

Santo Domingo church, Plaza Santo Domingo. Another combined church and monastery that has some excellent wood-carving.

Cathedral, Plaza Independencia, the Bishop's Palace faces it across the square.

La Ronda street is one of the most photographed of all streets in Ecuador. A carefully preserved cobbled street with colonial houses, it's been re-named Morales and is a continuation of 24 de Mayo going downhill.

The daily Indian market (weavings, clothes, food, etc), on Benalcazar at the junction with 24 de Mayo, often has a better selection of weavings than the market at Otavalo and the prices are about the same.

For a relaxing place to spend a hot afternoon, try El Ejido park. There are plenty of old trees, gardens and fountains. El Panecillo is the hill at the far side of the old city. During Inca times there was a sun temple situated here. There are excellent views over Quito and of the volcano Pichincha with its snow-capped peak.

National Museum of Popular Arts and Crafts, Mejía and García Moreno, one block north of Plaza Independencia is open 9 am-12 noon, 3 pm-6 pm (free).

Municipal Art and History Museum, Calle Espejo No. 1147, just off Plaza Independencia is open Tuesday to Sunday 8.30 am-12 noon, 3.30 pm-5.30 pm. Entry Suc 5. A building which once belonged to the Jesuits before they were banished from the Spanish colonies in 1776 has paintings and sculpture.

Franciscan Museum, part of the church and monastery of San Francisco, Calle Cuenca, is open Monday to Saturday from 9 am-11.30 am, 3 pm-5 pm. Entry Suc5. Painting, sculpture and wood-carving; the bureaux made of different types of wood and studded with mother-of-pearl are particularly worth seeing.

Fray Pedro Bedon Dominican Museum, part of the Santo Domingo Convent, Plaza de Santo Domingo, Calle Flores No. 151 is open 3 pm-5 pm. Entry Suc3 — painting and sculpture.

National Museum of Colonial Art, Calles Cuenca and Mejía is open Monday to Friday 10 am-1 pm, 3 pm-6 pm — paintings.

Even if you're not into museums, many of the above are worth visiting just for the sake of the buildings themselves, as they're almost always housed in old colonial houses with beautiful peaceful, shady patios.

RIOBAMBA
Accommodation
Residencial Villa Esther, next to the train station. Suc20/person.

Pensión La Nueva, next door to the bus terminals Suc25/person. It's basic with cold water only.

Residencial Balcón de los Andes, Guayaquil No. 30-17, just opposite the railway station. Suc20/person.

Eats *Hotel Metro* serves a very good almuerzo for Suc35. *Napolitana* restaurant, Constituente No. 23-35, is cheaper and serves reasonable food for Suc20 (almuerzo and cena).

Things to Do/See As far as size and range of products go, probably only Oaxaca in Mexico and Huancayo in Peru rival the market in Riobamba. It's held every Saturday in nine separate plazas and connecting streets and up to 10,000 Indians from the neighbourhood attend. Ponchos, rope-sandals, hand-tooled leather goods, woven belts, Indian bowler hats, etc can be bought and there are plenty of food stalls, many offering roast guinea pig — something you'll find all the way through the Andes from Ecuador to Bolivia.

SAN LORENZO
This is the most northerly port in Ecuador and there's little to attract the traveller except perhaps the wooden houses which are built on stilts. You can find boats here to take you down the coast to Esmeraldas (see later under *Transport*). Take insect repellent with you — plenty of mosquitoes!

Accommodation *Imperial*, Suc25/single. This one is a large white wooden building on stilts and is quiet, peaceful and scruffy. *Pailon*, Suc30/single — basic.

Eats *Salón Ibarra*.

Boats Down the Coast There is a cargo boat which takes passengers and plies between Esmeraldas and San Lorenzo via Limones. About Suc26 and takes 7-10 hours. It departs San Lorenzo on Mondays and Fridays and Esmeraldas on Wednesdays and Saturdays. One traveller who made this trip warned not to get off at Limones as "Indians with spears demand tax!" Maybe he'd taken too much yage or unwittingly got mixed up in a local tourist attraction. There's also a daily launch from San Lorenzo to Limones. Suc10. The Pacific coast here consists of swamps and mangrove forests with plenty of rain. The population is almost 100 percent black and coconut, rice and fish are just about the only foods.

Half way between San Lorenzo and Ibarra is the town of Santo Domingo de los Colorados in the vicinity of which live the Colorado Indians. Because the women leave their breasts uncovered and both men and women paint their bodies with a red vegetable dye which is also supposed to be an insect repellant they have become a kind of voyeuristic tourist attraction. If you're into herbal medicine they are perhaps worth a visit, as they shun Western medicine and use only preparations made from the leaves of plants which grow in the area — contact the tribal chief, Abraham Calazacón, in the first instance. Otherwise there's nothing much else to do but gawp.

TULCAN
Accommodation
Residencias Avenida, opposite the bus terminal. Suc30/bed, single, double and triple rooms — clean and cozy. The sheets are clean and the management is pleasant, but they're also occasionally used as whore houses and as the rooms are only separated by a thin board partition, the noise they kick up can keep you awake half the night. Cold water only.

Residencias Española, next to Residencias Avenida — exactly the same facilities and price.

Other, generally more expensive, hotels are on the main street near the centre of town, but there's not much point in staying there if your next move is a bus to Otavalo or Quito as the bus terminal is 2 km from the centre of town. This makes the above two residencias far more convenient for the buses.

Eats *Pollo a la Brasa* cafe, four doors away from the Espanola/Avenida, serves excellent barbequed chicken Suc35 and cold beers. The Espanola also has a cafe on the ground floor but service is indifferent. The cafe in the bus terminal is expensive.

Other To change money, two casas de cambio in the centre of town near the Post Office and *Hotel Inti Huasi* stay open late (6.30 am-6.30 pm). They offer 25.50 sucres = US$1 for travellers cheques which isn't too brilliant, but the money changers at the bus station only offer 25 sucres = US$1.

Things to Do/See This Ecuadorian town is on the Colombian border. Although the town is friendly enough, there's little here for the traveller, except perhaps a visit to the cemetery which is famous for its sculptured trees and bushes.

Crossing the Border to Colombia The border here is easy-going with no searches but you must have an onward ticket for Colombia (eg a return bus ticket from Tulcán to Ipiales if you haven't got an MCO or an airline ticket). You must obtain an Exit Stamp from the Immigration Office in Tulcán before turning up at the border. It's situated in the Edificio Portuario on the 2nd floor and is closed Saturday and Sunday and lunch times (11.30 am-

2 pm). At weekends you can obtain this Exit Stamp from the police station between Tulcán and the border. There's no Exit Fee if your Entry Stamp was marked "T3". Otherwise it's US$2.

TRANSPORT

Through the highlands from Tulcán to Guayaquil and the Peruvian border, there's an excellent system of paved roads. Buses are frequent between most cities and towns and journey times are relatively short so this will probably be the preferred method of transport. The roads down to the Pacific coast are however, not up to the same standard and the ones in the lowlands of the Orient (Amazon basin) are even worse, often being impassable in the rainy season. There is one rail journey which should not be missed if you're travelling between Quito and Guayaquil or vice versa, as it's one of the most spectacular in the world — see later under *Railways*.

Buses The main route through Ecuador is Tulcán-Ibarra-Otavalo-Quito-Ambato-Riobamba. From Riobamba there are three possible routes to the Peruvian border: Riobamba-Guayaquil-Machala-Huaquillas (most popular); Riobamba-Cuenca-Machala; Riobamba-Cuenca-Loja-Macara. There are connections to San Lorenzo on the Pacific coast from Ibarra, to Esmeraldas, Atacames and Sua from Quito, and to Banos from Quito, Ambato or Riobamba.

Tulcán-Quito. Several companies cover this route (eg *Flota Imbabura, Transportes Andina, Transportes Yan Dun, Transportes Velotax, Supertaxis del Sur*). The minibuses are quicker but cost about 15 percent more than the ordinary buses. Tulcán has a new central bus terminal from which all departures and arrivals take place. It's situated about 2 km from the centre of town. In other Ecuadorian cities, the various bus companies maintain their own terminals although they're often clustered together. For their location in Quito and Guayaquil see the city plans and the address lists in each section.

Tulcán-Ibarra. There are frequent buses throughout the day by several companies. Suc20 and takes two hours.

Tulcán-Otavalo. Frequent buses go throughout the day by several companies. Suc26 and it takes three hours.

Tulcán-Quito. Frequent buses throughout the day leave between the hours of 4 am and 12.30 am (next day). Suc60 by ordinary bus and Suc70 by minibus. It takes about five to six hours and there are at least three police/army checkpoints on the way where you have to get out of the bus while they search it. But they don't bother gringos.

Ibarra-San Lorenzo. A daily bus goes in either direction. Suc40 taking eight hours.

Otavalo-Quito. Frequent buses by several companies leave throughout the day. Suc55 and it takes two hours with *Transportes Andina*.

From Quito to Esmeraldas (Pacific coast) buses by *Transportes Esmeraldas* and *Transportes Occidentales* leave daily. It takes eight to nine hours, Suc50-55. There are connections to Atacames and Súa beaches several times per day (last one leaves at 5 pm). It takes half an hour to Atacames and 40 minutes to Súa. Suc8 to Atacames and Suc10 to Súa.

Quito-Guayaquil. A total of 24 buses per day by *Panamericana*, *Transportes Ecuador*, *Santa* and *Ecuatoriano Pullman*. It takes 10 hours and costs Suc60 except *Ecuatoriano Pullman* which takes 10 hours by a different route for Suc71. It's recommended that you take the ferrocarril between Quito and Guayaquil rather than the bus (see

under *Trains*).

Guayaquil-Machala. There are frequent buses daily by *Transportes Colón*, *Ecuatoriano Pullman*, *Cooperative CIFA*, *Panamericana*, taking five hours. Suc37.

Guayaquil-Huaquillas. Buses by *Ecuatoriano Pullman* at 6.45 am, 9 pm, 11 pm, 11.45 pm and 12 midnight. Takes seven hours.

Machala-Huaquillas. Frequent buses go daily by the same companies who do the Guayaquil-Machala trip. Suc25 and it takes two hours. There are two passport check points on the road to the border, but no fuss and the bus waits for you.

Quito-Machala (direct). Two buses per day by *Transportes Occidentales* leave at 7.50 am and 10 pm and four buses per day by *Panamericana* (first bus 9.45 am, last bus 10 pm). They take 14 hours. Suc90. *Ecuatoriano Pullman* also do the same route at 7.10 pm.

Quito-Huaquillas (direct). Two buses daily by *Ecuatoriano Pullman* at 8.15 pm, 12.30 am. Three buses daily by *Panamericana* at 3 am, 11.55 am, 6 pm. These all take 16 hours. Suc100. *Transportes Patria* leaves at 4.05 am and takes 18 hours. Suc80. The addresses of Ecuatoriano Pullman are Calle 9 de Octubre, junction with Colón in Machala, and Avenida de la Republica in Huaquillas.

Quito-Ambato. Frequent buses daily by many companies do this route. (eg *Panamericana Transportes Ecuador, Transportes Patria, Transportes Chimborazo, Santa, Expreso Sucre, Cooperativa Baños*). They take two and a half hours. Suc25.

Quito-Baños. Buses go three times daily by *Cooperative Baños* (first bus 7.20 am, last bus, 8.20 am) taking six hours. Suc30. They have a tendancy to be broken down, so it's often more convenient to catch one of the frequent buses to Ambato and change there for a more frequent bus to Baños.

Ambato-Baños. Regular buses leave throughout the day. It takes one and a half hours. Suc20. It's often much easier to backtrack to Ambato and get a bus to Riobamba from there as they're much more frequent.

Baños-Riobamba. Only one through bus daily does this route. It takes two and a half hours. Suc20. It's often much easier to backtrack to Ambato and get a bus to Riobamba from there as they're much more frequent.

Quito-Riobamba. Frequent buses go daily by the same companies who do the Quito-Ambato route, taking five hours. Suc45.

Quito-Cuenca. Three buses leave per day at 3.30 am, 5.30 am, 8 15 am, by *Panamericana*, Suc65. Two buses leavé per dày at 2.45 pm, 7 pm, by *Santa*. Suc90. Two buses leave per day at 12.05 pm, and 9.20 pm, by *Expreso Sucre*. Suc 80. All take 12 hours.

Ambato-Cuenca. At 9.30 am daily, *Flota Imbabura* have a bus doing this route. It takes nine to ten hours. Suc90. The bus terminal is on the lower plaza. Also at 10.30 am, *Expreso Sucre* have a bus. Costs. less but can take up to 12 hours. The roads are in poor shape but the views are amazing. Much of the time you are well above the clouds and it's like being in a plane.

Riobamba-Cuenca. Several buses daily by different companies take eight and a half hours. Suc45. From Riobamba there are buses to Guayaquil (11½ hours); Suc50 and a once-daily bus to Huaquillas which leaves in the evening.

Cuenca-Guayaquil. This route takes nine hours. Suc70.

Cuenca-Machala. It takes eight hours. Suc70. Transportes Buenos Hermanos (terminal in Cuenca, Calle Gran Colombia 5-6) also do this trip in only six hours and then continue on to Huaquillas, a further one and

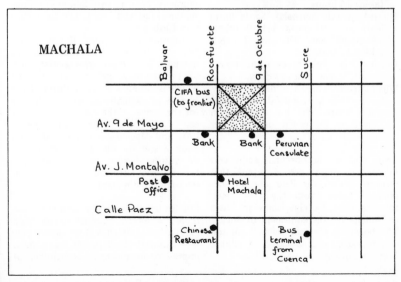

a half hours. The through trip to Huaquillas is Suc93.

Cuenca-Huaquillas (see above). Other companies doing this through trip to the border town are *Expreso Sucre* (terminal in Cuenca, Avenida 3 Novienbre) departing daily at 9 pm and *Turismo Oriental* (terminal in Cuenca on Sangurima, junction with Vargas) departing daily at 10.30 pm.

Other than the most popular route to the Peruvian border at Huaquillas via Machala, there is an alternative border crossing between Macará and La Tina via Loja. There are some hair-raising roads near the border and you generally need a little more time to go this way — though it's only measured in hours. Peruvian Tourist Cards can be obtained at the border if you need one, but if you're wanting to buy soles, get them in Macará.

Quito-Loja (via Cuenca). Once daily buses by *Panamericana* go at 5.30 am and by *Santa* at 6 pm. Both Suc100 taking 15 hours.

Quito-Loja (via Machala). *Santa* buses leave at 1.40 pm (Suc110) taking 16 hours and 5.10 pm (Suc80) taking 17 hours.

Cuenca-Loja. This takes eight hours. Suc60. Several buses go daily.

Loja-Marcará. There's a daily bus by *Cooperativa Loja*. Suc50 and it takes eight hours. The bus terminal in Loja is in the centre on the other side of the river.

From Macará, the border is about two kilometres. Many people report that onward tickets for Peru are not demanded here. From the first small town in Peru, La Tina, there are buses to Sullana for the equivalent of Suc20. The border is open between 8 am and 6 pm except for a two-hour dinner break at midday.

Trains Quito-Guayaquil (and vice versa) by Autoferro is one of the most spectacular train journeys in the world. From Quito the train first climbs over the 3800 metre Urbina Pass and then via a series of tunnels, bridges and an ingenious system of switchbacks down to sea level and banana plantations. The scenery is amazing and the mountainsides so steep where the switchbacks are located that it takes some courage to look over the side.

It departs Quito at 6 am on Tuesday, Thursday and Saturday. Book in advance at the ticket office at Bolívar No. 443 between Benalcazar and Moreno. The fare includes the cost of the ferry boat across the River Guayas to Guayaquil from Durán so hang on to your ticket when you get off the train. It leaves Guayaquil at 6.40 am on Monday, Wednesday and Friday. Take the 6 am ferry across the River Guayas to connect. Book in advance at the ticket office on the corner of Loja and Malecon on the river front. Either way the trip takes 12 hours and is Suc90. Both journeys involve two 20-minute stops for breakfast and lunch. The lunch stop is in Riobamba.

Coming from Quito, if you would like to by-pass Guayaquil without missing the most spectacular part of the journey, get off at Sibambe which is situated at the bottom of the system of switchbacks. Buses wait here for the arrival of the Autoferro and you can find connections with Cuenca, Loja and Machala. For the best views book a seat on the right-hand side of the autoferro from Quito to Guayaquil and on the left-hand side coming in the opposite direction.

For Riobamba-Guayaquil and vice versa there's a mixed passenger/goods train *(Tren Mixto)* which is much slower than the Autofero bus, pulled by a most impressive steam engine straight out of the 30s. It stops at all stations along the way.

It departs Riobamba at 6.30 am and arrives at Durán at 4 pm which has included two long stops for breakfast and lunch. It then leaves Durán (Guayaquil) at 6.20 am, arriving in Riobamba at 4 pm, same with the two meal breaks. Both journeys take nine hours. Suc35 (first class), Suc25 (second class).

The Quito-Guayaquil line branches at Riobamba and goes on to Cuenca.

There's a daily Tren Mixto between Cuenca and Riobamba (and vice versa). Suc12 and it takes 14 hours. The train is heavily used by local people taking products to and from markets. There's an Autoferro two to three times per week between Cuenca and Riobamba. It returns the same day. This is a convenient train (if you don't mind getting up at an ungodly hour!) for visiting the Inca ruins of Ingapirca from Cuenca. It departs Cuenca at 4.30 am and takes two hours to Ingapirca station. Suc15. The return train leaves at 3.30 pm from Ingapirca to Cuenca.

For the Quito-Otavalo-Ibarra-San Lorenzo route, a "Tren Mixto" departs three times per week. From Quito to Otavalo takes four and a half hours. Suc13. There's an Autocarril daily between Ibarra and San Lorenzo at 7 am. This takes six hours Suc60. The journey gives an excellent cross-section of the country from the highlands through the foothills and down onto the coastal lowlands.

THE GALAPAGOS ISLANDS

These islands — 600 km west of the Ecuadorian coast and famous for their unique wildlife, mainly reptiles and birds, need little introduction. Anyone acquainted with Darwin's theory of evolution will known of them. They are volcanic islands rising to 3000 metres and, because the sea round them is cooled by the Humboldt current from the Antarctic, desert co-exists with sub-tropical forest on many of the islands. Since they have never been connected to the mainland, all the life forms have developed independently of those found elsewhere in the world, and so completely that the majority don't even have an instinctive fear of people — the islands were uninhabited when discovered by the Spanish in the early 1500s and many of the smaller ones still are. They're undoubtedly worth a visit if you have the money and time, but there are no longer any easy or cheap ways of getting there and you'll have little change from US$300. Unless you have that sort of money and two weeks to spare then regrettably you'll probably have to give them a miss. Most of the suggested budget will go on transport to the islands from the mainland and on inter-island boat trips. Otherwise it's possible to live there cheaply especially if you have a tent and are prepared to camp.

There are five ways of getting there:

(1) Once a fortnight on Saturday there is a flight by the armed forces (*Fuerza Aerea Ecuatoriana*) from Quito and Guayaquil to the islands and back. The flights are called "vuelos logísticos" and are intended principally for the residents of the islands who can get first priority. The flight costs Suc522/single or Suc1044/return, but it's very difficult to secure a seat on the outgoing flight from Quito or Guayaquil without a letter from a scientific organization saying you're a student of biology/geography/etc, or a temporary resident's permit. Getting one of these flights back from the islands is somewhat easier if they're not booked out by residents but you must get your name on the waiting

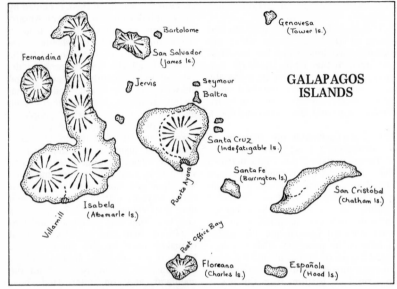

list kept by the *Capitania del Puerto* in Puerto Ayora on Santa Cruz Island as soon as you arrive. So it's *possible* to reduce costs by taking a normal commercial flight out to the islands and one of the "vuelo logistico" flights back to the mainland.

(2) Twice weekly flights by *TAME* on Tuesdays and Fridays go from Quito or Guayaquil. They are bookable either through a *TAME* office (Quito, Avenida 10 de Agosto No. 239; Guayaquil, Edificio Gran Pasaje) or from *Metropolitan Touring* (Avenida Amazonas No. 239, Quito, with another office in Guayaquil). The flight costs Suc4332 return from Guayaquil or Suc4854 return from Quito. Flying from Quito will cost you more than making your own arrangements for transport to Guayaquil and flying from there. Also, if you get your ticket through *Metropolitan Touring* they're inclined to try to palm you off with a package tour costing about Suc9600. Again,

be firm.

(3) There is the possibility of a "cheap" boat trip lasting 11 days from Guayaquil to the islands, around the islands and back again with *Armada del Ecuador* (corner of Avenida Canar and Vivero, Zona 1, telephone 34 5317). You must ask for the boats by name — the *Jambeli* and *Tarqui* — though they seem to spend a lot of their time in dry dock and you have to be insistent. It's a rough ride in flat-bottomed boats. Suc2349.

(4) *Transnave*, Malecón No. 905, junction of V E Redon, Guayaquil, run by the Ecuadorian Navy, offers 12-day cruises to Galapagos in the *Calicuchima* (five days at sea included) for about Suc7830. They're not recommended, the food is lousy and the crew indifferent.

(5) Package tours (12-14 days duration) are arranged by a travel agent which cost Suc 9650 upwards. Try *Metropolitan Touring* (address previously given), *Turismundial* (Avenida Ama-

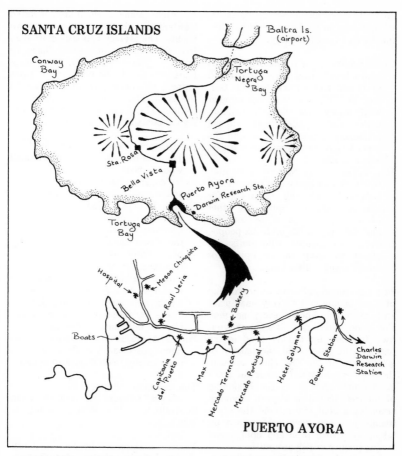

zonas 657, Quito), *Condor Tours* (Avenida Colón), *Coltur* (259 Santa Prisca and 1676 Avenida 10 de Agosto, Quito).

All planes land at Baltra airport, an old US air base just off the coast of the main island, Santa Cruz. Buses meet the planes and take passengers to the ferry for Suc10. The ferry to Santa Cruz (about 100 metres) costs Suc20. From the far side you take a truck or jeep to Puerto Ayora on the far side of the island for Suc50.

Puerto Ayora The cheapest way to stay on the islands is to camp and put your own food together, but you're only allowed to do this in certain designated areas and you must first obtain permission from the National Park Office. The camp sites are: Tortuga Bay and Charles Darwin Research Station, Santa Cruz Island: Post Office Bay, Floreana Island; James Bay, San Salvador Island; Volcan Celdo, San Salvador Island. If you have no tent, there are a few cheap places to stay (but no medium-priced hotels — they're all expensive!). Try:

Gus Angermeyer, a German immigrant who's been living here for over 40 years and speaks fluent Spanish, German and English. It's very popular with budget travellers. Accommodation is about Suc50/night. He can personally arrange tours around the other islands or put you onto others who also can.

Max, a French guy who owns a funky weatherboard house and will hire out hammocks, etc. You can arrange for him to take you round the other islands in his yacht *Mistral* for Suc2088/day. It fits up to six people.

Lucretia, an islander who rents out places to sleep in his house for Suc26/night — ultra basic.

Just ask around in Puerto Ayora for any of these people — it's a very small place and everyone knows everyone else. For food, you can either put your own together by buying food in the market, the stores and the bakery or go to one of the few cheap cafes in the town — the *Flamingo* near Lucretia's or *Meson Conchita* at the beginning of the road to Baltra Airport. If you're arranging a boat trip around the other islands you can keep costs down by taking your own food and doing some fishing (plenty of fish around!).

The Charles Darwin Research Station and the Giant Tortoise Sanctuary and Breeding Farm are situated at Academy Bay on Santa Cruz. Here you have to buy a permit for Suc156 (they stamp your passport). This entitles you to visit the Sanctuary and the other islands.

Visiting the Other Islands Before you even think of doing this, it's important to get a group together of up to eight people. Boats are Suc2000-2500/day to hire (ie about US$12/

day each). Many of them are converted trawlers though there are one or two yachts. The average trip lasts more than five days and you usually have to organize your own food. Some captains will do all the cooking for extra money, otherwise you take turns with the crew. Plan to be doing your own fishing. There are some more or less regular boats between the islands.

Puerto Ayora/Santa Cruz-San Cristóbal. The post-boat *San Pedro II* is a small wooden boat that goes once a week. It departs Puerto Ayora Tuesday afternoons, arrives Wednesday mornings. It departs San Cristóbal Wednesday afternoons. Suc100 one way. Contact: *Hermogenes Moncayo* near the Power House. The Navy supply boat *Pinta* is irregular. Contact *Capitania del Puerto.*

Puerto Ayora/Santa Cruz-Floreana. The post-boat *San Pedro II* goes every 14 days. It takes 10 hours. Suc100. There are occasional freight boats. Contact *Capitania del Puerto.*

Puerto Ayora/Santa Cruz-Isabela. The same post-boat *San Pedro II* goes occasionally. You'll have to enquire.

The cheapest charter boats — often converted trawlers — cost between Suc1000-2000. They include the following:

Normita is skippered by *Joselito* (Gustavo Villasis) who's a friendly guy that will do his best to see you have a good trip. He charges Suc1000/day.

Mistral is skippered by the Frenchman *Max* (mentioned previously under accommodation). He has scuba diving equipment on board. His wife cooks excellent food on the trip. Suc2088/day.

Cristo Rex I and *II*. This is a larger ship which takes seven or more people. Ask for *Raul Jeria* near the Capitania del Puerto.

Xavier is another larger ship with lots of room on board — clean. Ask for *Allessandro Padrana*. Suc1000/day.

Narcissa is a really beautiful ship. Ask for *Victor Lopez* who lives near the *Meson Conchita*. Best time to meet him is between 2 pm and 4 pm.

In addition to these there are a number of luxury yachts for the well-heeled but you wouldn't be reading this if you had the money to afford a trip on one of those.

Sources of Information

The Galapagos Guide can be bought in Quito, Guayaquil or at the Charles Darwin Research Station on Santa Cruz. Suc182. It's more or less essential reading if you're planning on visiting the other islands.

Galapagos: The Flow of Wildness (two volumes) is published by the Sierra Club and Ballantine Books. Suc261. It has excellent photography and well worth having a look at before you set off on your journey, as whilst you're travelling it will probably be out of range of your pocket and rucksack space.

THE ORIENTE

The lowlands and Amazon River basin on the eastern side of the country, up to the border with Peru, is the Oriente. It's possible to find boats to Nueve Rocafuerte (the most easterly Ecuadorian town on the border with Peru) to Iquitos, but because of the long-standing dispute over the border between Ecuador and Peru, you must first obtain permission for this trip from the Ministry of Defence in Quito. The other Oriente towns — Coca, Limon Cocha, Tena and Lago Agria — are easier to get to and, with the exception of Lago Agria, are beautiful. Lago Agria is just an oil town and has little of interest for the traveller.

There are three daily buses from Quito to Tena via Ambato, Puyo by *Cooperativa Banos* which takes 11 hours. Suc61. If you want to stay in Puyo, eight hours out from Quito, try the *Pension Tungarahua*, Suc35/bed. In Tena, try *Hotel Danubia*, Suc30/bed. It serves meals and has running water. Otherwise there is the *Nueva Residencial*, Suc25/bed or the *Hotel Turismo*, Suc25/bed. From Tena there are a number of daily buses to Misahualli. Suc10, taking about one and a half hours. This is a very small town and there are only two places to stay at: *Hotel la Posada*, Suc25 — interesting place with the best food in town, and the *Misahualli Hotel* which has electricity but is not as pleasant as the other place. From here, or from Tena, there are motorized dug-outs to Coca along the Rio Napo. The dug-outs take 12-15 people and cost around Suc150/person. The journey time is about 10 hours. There are several places to stay at in Coca: The *Residencia* next to bus station is basic but clean with shower and mosquito nets, Suc30; *Hotel Huasi*, Suc25, no showers or running water; others are near the barracks. From Coca there are similar boats to Limon-Cocha and from there twice weekly boats 200 km further on to Nueva Rocafuerte which take about two days. Suc100. The best time to do this trip is between September and October, and January and May. There's also a road between Coca and Lago Agria and from there to Quito. Buses go three times per day (*Cooperative Amazonas*), taking 14 hours from Quito to Coca. Suc80.

If you do manage to get permission for the overland trip to Iquitos, via Nueva Rocafuerte, you can find freight canoes in Pantoja — the first Peruvian village — for Iquitos which take about five days. The price is negotiable. There are sometimes canoes between Nueva Rocafuerte and Pantoja for about

Suc150, otherwise there is a jungle path between the two which takes a day to walk. Also, cigarettes and a bottle of spirits usually secures a lift. The whole trip from Coca to Iquitos requires a lot of initiative and scant regard for comfort. Insect repellant is a must (plenty of mosquitoes, etc). It rains a lot and you'll need some waterproof clothing and a sweater as it gets quite cold when it rains. The jungle scenery is beautiful! Indian tribes in the area are the Jivaros, Cofanes and Aucas.

OTHER INFORMATION
Indian Markets
Sunday: Cuenca, Salcedo, Machachi, Sangolgui.

Monday: Ambato.
Tuesday: Otavalo, Riobamba, Latacunga, Guano.
Wednesday: Riobamba, Pujili.
Thursday: Saquisili.
Saturday: Otavalo, Riobamba, Latacunga.

Books about Ecuador One of the best places to buy foreign language books in Quito — they stock books in English, French and German as well as Spanish — is *Libri Mundi*, Juan Leon Mera, junction with Vientimilla. It's open 9 am-7.30 am on weekdays and 9 am-1 pm, 3 pm-6 pm on Saturdays.

Peru

When the Spanish invaded South America, the theocratic Inca Empire was at its height spreading over what is today Peru, Bolivia, Ecuador, the northern parts of Chile and Argentina, and the southern parts of Colombia. The conquest shattered the foundations of this civilization but the imposition of a mining economy, an alien religion and the parcelling out of the land among the conquerors was to have even worse consequences than the collapse of the empire itself.

The Spanish, in their haste to exploit the precious metal deposits, herded millions of Indians to their deaths as forced labourers in the mines, dislocated agricultural communitites and destroyed the collective farming system which was at the base of Inca society — and of all other Indian civilizations in the Americas. Not only were they forced into the mines and onto the estates of the Spanish "encomenderos", but they were forced to surrender for nothing the lands which they had to leave or

neglect. On the Pacific coast, the Spaniards destroyed or allowed to die by neglect the huge plantations of corn, yucca, kidney bean, peanut and sweet potato which once fed a large proportion of the population and which were irrigated by a magnificent system of aqueducts and water chanels. Many of these vast public works which were constructed by the Incas have been claimed by the ravages of time and the Spanish demand for building stone but much still remains, particularly of the mountainside terraces which can still be seen all over the Andean plateau. Some of them are still in use today. All these terraces and aqueducts, not to mention temples, palaces, fortresses and roads, were made possible through a wise distribution of labour as well as a religious force which defined the people's sacred relationship to the soil. Personal liberty as we know it today did not exist. Submission to the "ayllu" (the basic earth-cell commune) was absolute and central authority in the form of the

Sapa Inca and his regional governors unchallengeable but no one went hungry and everyone had a right to the land.

These days, the descendants of the people who created that amazing civilization without any knowledge of the wheel, iron or heavy draught animals are a disenfranchised and depressed sub-culture within Peruvian society. They still comprise around 50% of the population and though the Peruvian Government concentrates heavily on promoting them and the ruined achievements of their predecessors, the vast majority are condemned to a bleak existence scratching a bare living in the harsh environment of the 3000 metre-plus Andean plateau. They have one of the lowest literacy rates on the continent. Most of them live on a diet which would bring accusations of genocide against the Peruvian Government at the UN. Only a tiny minority have any access to a supply of potable running water. Almost two million of them can speak only Quechua (the main Indian language) and it was only very recently that this became the official second language of Peru and began to be taught in schools. Other than the fortunate minority who have access to tourist markets and archaeological sites, virtually all of them are completely outside the money economy.

The destruction of this rich and admirable culture by a mindless and avaricious bunch of thugs and those who followed later to continue the plunder was an unmitigated disaster and has been a profound effect on the Peruvian psyche ever since. On the one hand the Indians cling to the crumbs of what could be salvaged in the face of Spanish oppression, and on the other, the blancos and mestizos look to Spain for their cultural roots. It seems never the twain shall meet. There's a good deal of discrimination against the Indians by the rest of society, many of

whom regard them as little more than lazy, coca leaf-chewing savages and certainly never to be taken into account in the affairs of the nation. Only where tourist-related expediency dictates otherwise is there any attempt to acknowledge and promote the various facets of Indian culture. The weakness here, of course, is that whenever a particularly colourful aspect of a culture is singled out from the whole and promoted as a tourist spectacle, it tends to lose in authenticity what it gains in the economics of entertainment. You might think that after centuries of this sort of oppression the life force which created the indigenous cultures in this part of the world might no longer be around but in fact it's alive and well though you have to try a little harder to come in contact with it. You might say it's gone into hiding.

To find it you must get off the main tourist routes or at least be there when the day-trippers have left. A fiesta in a small village might be a good place to go looking especially if there are flute or brass bands playing. Quechua music is very characteristic and quite different from the music you will hear in the cities of the lowlands. A wedding in a rural area or the outskirts of a small town might be another. Coming across one by accident it's more than likely you will be invited to take part in the festivities. "Chicha" will be thrust into your hand and you'll be drawn into the dancing — something else which is very characteristic and infused with ritual. There's often a band laid on for such occasions. You might also find it in a small cafe late at night when a few people have gathered to relax and chat after the day's work. Leave your camera at home: bring an instrument along instead and play them some songs. They'll send you home with your head full of Quechua melodies.

In other words, if you come to Peru looking for the Inca Empire as it used to be — and thousands of people do just that — the only place you will find it is in your own imagination or at the various archaeological sites. This is in no way meant to suggest that visits to these places are something of an anticlimax — quite the opposite! The time you spend in the Urubamba valley culminating in a visit to Macchu Picchu will be one of the most memorable parts of any visit to South America. But the life force which made possible all these places is, sadly, no longer a visual experience. It's still there but it's more a dimension of mind and contacting it depends on meeting and getting to know Quechua people. You can't do this in a day.

The Incas were the inheritors of a vast amalgam of cultures which had either preceeded them in this part of the world or were contemporaneous with them but the only information we have about them comes from archaeology. The main reason for this lies in the policy which the Incas adopted of purging and distorting the memory of cultural origins from the minds of the people they conquered. They did this by an effective system of selective manipulation of remembered history which was woven into the "official" Inca history. The latter had been created with the Incas cast in the role of "civilizer". Since none of these civilizations — including the Inca — had invented a system of writing and all traditions were orally transmitted from one generation to the next, this sort of manipulation was relatively easy. By the time the Inca civilization bagan to grow in the Cuzco valley in the 11th century, all the main threads of religion, agriculture, social organisation, art, pottery, weaving and building had been brought to a high degree of perfection.

The threads can be traced right back to 2000 BC and even earlier when a coastal civilization based on fishing sprang up near Supe. It was followed in time by the Chavin culture which started on the coast but spread up into the mountains and whose influence stretched from Piura to Pisco. This culture flourished from 800 BC to 200 BC and its main archaeological site is at Chavin de Huantar near Huaraz. The next major development came with the Nazca and Mochica in the south and north respectively. They both cover the period from 400 AD to 800 AD. The Nazca are, of course, famous for their gigantic animal and geometric figures cut into the stony desert near the town of the same name — a source of endless speculation as to their purpose and the subject of a long and tedious book for the gullible by von Daniken. The Mochica are notable for their exceptionally beautiful and realistic designs on pottery, examples of which you can see in almost any museum in Peru. This culture must take the prize for the high point in the development of this art.

The southern coastal cultures eventually spread into the altiplano giving rise to the Tihuanacu civilization around the southern end of Lake Titicaca between the 10th and 13th centuries. They were a religio-military group and the originators of the cult of the weeping Sun God but little else is known about them other than what can be gleaned from the ruins they left at Tihuanacu in what is today northern Bolivia. This cult of the weeping Sun God was to become the state religion of the Incas and imposed on all the peoples they subsequently conquered. It was, along with Quechua, the state language, to be one of the major factors which made for cohesion within the Empire.

What the Incas themselves contributed to this cultural evolution was not so much a further refinement of the arts — with the exception of their beautiful and unique stone work whose precision is almost unbelievable — but an efficient and centralised social and military organisation, excellent com-. munications and a vast programme of agriculturally-related public works designed to irrigate the desert, prevent soil erosion in the mountains and increase crop yields. The produce from the land was split three ways; the first part went to the people themselves; the next to the Sun religion for the maintenance of the priests and the construction of temples, and the last part to the Sapa Inca who represented the state. This last part was used to maintain the army, the administration, the engineers, the road construction crews and to build up food reserves for distribution during lean years or in case of crop failure.

By 1450 the empire had expanded as far as Quito and taken in the last of the major independent cultures in existence at the same time. This was the Chimu with their capital at Chan-Chan near present day Trujillo. The ruins of this enormous city, which covered 25 square km and included step pyramids, walled compounds, irrigated gardens and gigantic stone-lined reservoirs, is well worth visiting though the area has reverted to desert. At its height, this empire ruled over 1000 km of coast up into Ecuador and had a well-developed craft system which mass produced pots, jars, fabrics and gold artifacts. The amount of gold which had been amassed in this city was by all accounts staggering and although the Incas took the bulk of it away to Cuzco, enough remained to put a leer on the faces of the Spanish conquistadores.

The Incas might well have been able to hold the Spanish at bay when they arrived 100 years later had it not been for the fact that upon the death of Huayna Capac the empire had been divided between his two sons, Atahualpa and Huascar. These two fought each other for control of the empire and though Atahualpa was victorious the

empire was left weakened. It was at this point that Pizarro arrived and lured Atahualpa into a trap at Cajamarca where he was recovering from a war wound. An enormous ransom was set in gold and silver and although Atahualpa fulfilled his part of the bargain, he was strangled. The empire fell apart but not as abruptly as some chronicles would have it.

Under the watchful eyes of Pizarro, a puppet emperor, Manco II, was crowned in Cuzco in 1534 and for two years there was an uneasy co-existence between the Indians and the Spaniards. Disenchantment with the greed and cruelty of the conquerors grew to such a pitch that Manco II gathered an army of 50,000 warriors and besieged Cuzco. For a while they were within a hair's breadth of regaining what they had lost but they were eventually forced to retreat to Ollanaytambo and from there, being no match for the Spanish cavalry, to Vitcos. Here Manco II was surprised by a Spanish attack led by Almagro and Gonzalo Pizarro and though Manco managed to escape, large numbers of his soldiers were captured, a lot of treasure, and his son, Titu Cusi. After this set-back the remnants retreated to Vilcabamba on the edge of the sierra and a new capital founded here. All bridges into the kingdom were cut and all passes heavily guarded. From this citadel Manco attacked the Spanish at Huamanga (Ayacucho) and as far away as Lima using captured Spaniards, horses and war materials to construct a modern army. In the meantime the conquistadores were fighting among themselves for control of Peru. Pizarro was assassinated by the Almagrists but they themselves were defeated by Pizarro's brother, Gonzalo, and forced to ally themselves with Manco and take refuge in Vilcabamba. But it was merely a marriage of expediency and in 1545 after an attempt to negotiate peace with a Viceroy sent out by the Spanish king, Manco was assassinated by seven of the Spaniards who had sought refuge with him.

Titu Cusi took over Sapa Inca and though a period of peace followed he refused to leave Vilcabamba being rightfully suspicious of the Spaniards. Missionaries were sent to Vilcabamba to Christianise the Indians but they met with little success and in the end made such a nuisance of themselves that they were expelled. Titu Cusi died of pneumonia during this time and was succeeded by his son Tupac Amaru. Angered by the expulsion of the missionaries and having decided to exterminate the Inca successor state at Vilcabamba, a new Spanish Viceroy gathered a huge army together and attacked Tupac Amaru in 1572. After a number of set-backs the armies of Tupac Amaru were routed but Tupac himself escaped and Vilcabamba was left in flames, the treasure having been taken off into the jungle. Tupac later offered to return to Cuzco if he was granted an amnesty. This was agreed but as soon as he returned there a mock trial was held and he was sentenced to death along with his chieftains. All of them were tortured to death and the Viceroy then set about a witch hunt of anyone connected with the royal line, murdering them or exiling them to Chile or Darien. It was the end of the Empire.

There were further Indian revolts in 1780 under the leadership of Tupac Amaru II and again in 1814. The same fate befell Tupac Amaru II as did his Vilcabamba predecessor — he, his wife and children and chiefs were tortured to death in the Plaza de Armas at Cuzco — but the second revolt had the sympathy of many Creoles (American-born blancos) and foreshadowed the fight for independence from Spain a few years later.

In many ways, no area of Spanish America was more unready for revolt against the mother country than Peru. The colony was dominated by wealthy families, criollos and peninsulares who had been granted privileges by the Spanish Crown. They had been corrupted by easy money and the abundance of slave labour and there were fewer people of independent mind than in any other of the Spanish provinces of South America. This was well understood by San Martin who had shipped his Army of the Andes up to Peru after completing the liberation of Argentina and Chile. Much to the annoyance of his commanders, he waited a long time before advancing on Lima as he saw no point in liberating the city if its inhabitants were going to be politically hostile. Lima was entered in 1821 and the independence of Peru declared with much of the country still under the control of Royalist troops under the leadership of the Viceroy, La Serna. San Martin's army was too weak to face the Royalist troups in battle and so he went to Guayaquil to solicit military help from Bolivar and also support for his idea of setting up a monarchy in Peru. Bolivar had no sympathy with San Martin's monarchical ideas and the military aid that he offered was insufficient and so, following this meeting, San Martin retired to Europe disillusioned. Bolivar and Sucre were to complete the liberation of Ecuador, Peru and Bolivia with their victories over the Spanish at Pichincha (Ecuador), Junin (Peru) and the final one at Ayacucho (Peru).

In the late 19th century a dispute arose between Peru, Bolivia and Chile over the ownership of the Atacama desert. Previously no one had thought of this area as being of any value until nitrates began to be used as a fertilizer and though the Spanish had been aware of the existence of large nitrate deposits in this desert for a long time they had only been used for making gunpowder. Suddenly the desert became a very interesting proposition and within a year the Chilean navy had deprived the Bolivians of their Pacific littoral and taken the Peruvian part of the desert up as far as Tacna. A year later they entered Lima and occupied it for three years. The War of the Pacific, as it was called, still rankles on Peruvian and Bolivian consciousness and every so often, either in concert or individually, they threaten to attack Chile to regain the lands lost in this war. In 1978 belligerence again reached fever pitch in Bolivia over this issue.

Reform has been desperately slow in Peru and subject to the same reverses of military coups and dictators as it has elsewhere on the continent. A notable attempt at radical reform was made by Haya de la Torre who formed the Alianza Popular Revolucionaria Americana in 1924. The "Apristas", as they were known, advocated the return of the land to the Indian communities, an economic programme that would lift the Indian farmers out of purely subsistence agriculture, a campaign to eliminate illiteracy among them and progressive labour laws. The ruling oligarchy was alarmed and outraged and hounded 'la Torre for three decades, five years of which were spent in political asylum at the Colombian Embassy in Lima. He was eventually allowed to return and fight an election in 1962 after having made suitable pro-capitalist and pro-landowner noises but, though he won the election, the military leaders annulled the results.

Another attempt at land and labour reform was made in 1968 when the armed forces under the command of Gen Velasco Alvarado deposed the civilian president Belaunde whose economic programme, though well-intentioned, had proved alarmingly extravagant and likely to lead to the resurgence of the Apristas. Velasco wasn't a typical military officer, however and saw the army, not as champions

of the status quo, but as an agent for change. He nationalised Standard Oil and began a programme of radical land reform but in such a way that he avoided US retaliatory sanctions and in fact ended up being supported by them. For a while the Indians (or "campesinos" as they prefer to be known) enthusiastically took up his lead and started to set up farming collectives on land granted to them by the new government but it all came to an abrupt end several years later with another military coup. The country has, once again, been taken back to the 19th century with the wealthy landed oligarchy and the industrialists back in power. The farming collectives were starved of funds and the land given back to its former owners. Today, the Peruvian economy is perpetually on the brink of bankruptcy and inflation is running very high. Last year Peru was given a US$600 million loan by the International Monetary Fund to float it over the crisis. It's well known what such loans demand in terms of control over the economy and social reform.

Peru is undoubtedly the most popular country in South America for travellers and deservedly so. Having been the cradle of civilization in the southern half of the continent and then headquarters of the Spanish Empire it has endless fascinating and often spectacular archaeological sites, colonial towns, churches and museums. The sites themselves are too numerous to attempt a comprehensive listing in a book of this size so we've concentrated on the main cultures — Chavin, Chimu, Nazca and Inca — but if you're interested in archaeology the best thing to do is to read up about them before you go there. One of the most readable accounts is to be found in *The Ancient Sun Kingdoms of the Americas* by Victor Wolfgang von Hagen (Paladin, 1973). Also, any Peruvian Tourist Office will supply you with details and maps of

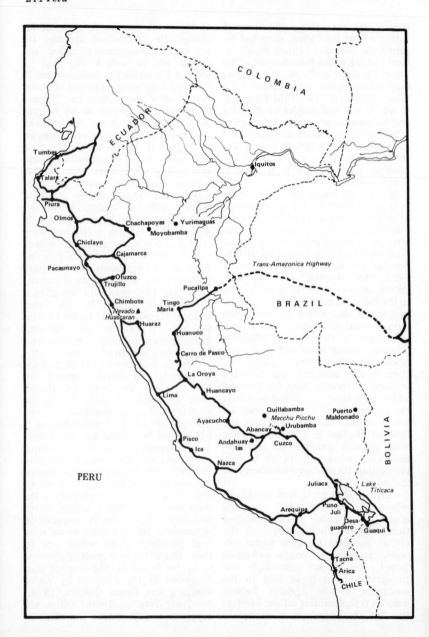

archaeological sites in their area and these, in terms of usefulness, are some of the best on the continent.

But Peru isn't just an archaeologist's dream. Its mountain people are some of the friendliest and most colourful you will find anywhere and their street markets, like the ones in Huancayo, Pisac, Juliaca and Puno, are full of interest and attract thousands of visitors. It's a country of endless variations from the strange sandy deserts of the northern coastal belt with their oasis towns to the snow-covered mountains which tower above the 3000 metre Andean plateau with their predominantly Indian villages and towns to the hot steamy Amazonian jungles on the far side of the mountains. Not a lot has changed here since colonial times — even communications are still pretty primitive and the road journeys in the mountains are an adventure into dust, rocks and punctures — much more so than in Ecuador or Colombia. So many different adventures and experiences are possible here that you could find yourself, like most travellers do, spending months trucking around in this country. It's also the cheapest place you will find on the whole continent. Have a good time! You can't fail to!

VISAS

Not required by nationals of Western Europe, USA, Canada or Japan. Required by nationals of Australia, New Zealand and South Africa.

Visas cost US$2.50 and are issued on the spot for a 90-day stay. The Peruvian Embassy in Quito is on Cristobal Colon — see the city plan. There are consulates in Guayaquil, Machala (Ecuador) and Arica (Chile).

Possession of an onward ticket is obligatory. An MCO for a minimum of US$40, a flight ticket for a destination outside Peru, or, a bus ticket for a destination outside Peru are all acceptable. If you haven't got any of these

you will be directed to a Morales Moralitos bus office where you will be offered a choice of bus tickets at approximately twice the price they'd cost you inside Peru itself. Coming from Ecuador via Huaquillas, the choices are: —

Cuzco-Puno: 1200 soles (the cheapest on offer).
Puno-La Paz (Bolivia): 2000 soles.
Lima-Tumbes: 4000 soles.

The tickets are open (ie not dated) and your name is typed on them. Once you've bought a bus ticket (if you have no MCO, etc) your passport is stamped with an automatic 90-day entry permit — everyone gets the same. Border officials don't always ask for an onward ticket. You might be lucky.

Morales Moralitos bus company have a bad reputation with travellers but to balance the record, I was allowed to change my Cuzco-Puno ticket (bought at the Huaquillas/Aguas Verdes border) in Arequipa for the bus journey from that city to Puno and use it again for the journey from Puno to Yunguyo so they can't be that pernicious!

There's generally a cursory baggage search at the border. 9% Tax on all airline tickets (domestic or international). US$5 airport tax on international flights.

MONEY

US$1 = 155 soles*
US$1 = 170-175 soles**

*official — cash or cheques
**blackmarket — cash only

The unit of currency is the sole = 100 centavos. The only bank which will change travellers' cheques is the Banco de la Nación. Don't change more than you need — you get a lousy rate for them outside Peru.

You're officially allowed to bring into Peru up to 1000 soles. If you're bringing in more, hide them, though I didn't meet anyone who was body searched and the street changing scene is so open on the borders — even inside the passport examination offices themselves! — that a blind eye must be turned to it.

Peru suffers from high inflation and the economy frequently totters on the verge of collapse. Due to this the exchange rate can vary considerably from one week to the next and there's a lively blackmarket in currency to be found in most cities with Lima giving the highest rates. Before changing any money on the blackmarket ask around among your fellow travellers to find out what the current rate is. The best place to change in Lima is on Jirón Union which links the Plaza San Martín to the Plaza de Armas. The most unusual people will approach you ranging from retired Swiss residents to local accountants. Many of them are simply trying to amass sufficient hard currency to buy US consumer goods. Just amble up Jirón Union looking like you have no particular place to go. People will approach you.

The best place to buy soles outside Peru is on the border with Ecuador at Huaquillas. The rates offered here are only slightly less than those in Lima itself. Money changers are easily identified with their black attache cases — and there are scores of them! If you enter Peru from Bolivia via Copacabana and Yunguyo, it's more than likely the border officials will offer to change money at the blackmarket rates (they'll take dollars or Bolivian pesos). If you're going the other way, they'll offer to take your soles in exchange for Bolivian pesos at a rate (100 soles = Bolivian pesos 11) which is better than that which you'll get in the bank or shops in Copacabana (100 soles = Bolivian pesos 10).

Low-denomination Peruvian notes must be some of the dirtiest, scruffiest, tattiest notes I've ever come across anywhere in the world. In fact they're a health hazard!! Spend them quickly or you might become "home" to uninvited guests!

Currency Declaration Forms are no longer issued on the border.

ABANCAY
Accommodation
Hotel Gran is next door to Morales Moralitos bus office. US$2/double with own bath.

Hotel El Misti is next door to Hidalgo bus office, similar to the Gran.

ANDAHUAYLAS
Accommodation
Gran Hotel is on the Plaza de Armas, costs 120 soles/double and is basic.

Hotel Restaurant Chifana is between Hidalgo and Andino bus offices — 120 soles/double and serves adequate meals.

Hotel Delicias is only a few rooms and they're relatively expensive at US$3/double but you might need a little comfort after that bus journey from Ayacucho!

Eats: Other than the *Restaurant Chifana* there is the *Restaurant Las Palmeras* which serves cheap food.

AREQUIPA
A beautiful, old city constructed out of white volcanic stone and sited at the foot of an immense snow-capped volcano 5500 metres high (El Misti). It has retained its colonial atmosphere and although it's the second largest city in Peru is very easy-going with plenty of interesting places to see.

Accommodation With a few exceptions, most of the budget hotels are located on San Juan de Dios between Alto de la Luna and Santo Domingo. Also located

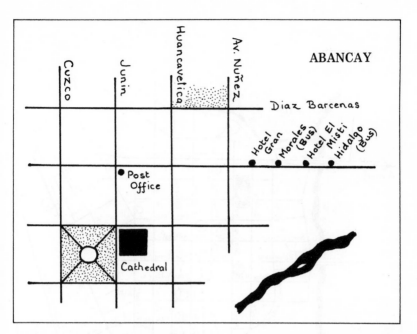

on this street are virtually all the bus company offices and terminals and many cheap restaurants though the best deal for food is to be found at the *Restaurant Chez Niño* on San Francisco just at the back of the Cathedral.

Hostal Royal at 300A San Juan de Dios. 145 soles/single; 350/double (2 beds). 450 soles/4 beds — clean but no hot water.

Hotel Corona at 316 San Juan de Dios — 180 soles/single; 230 soles/double (matrimonial); 370 soles/two beds, two people; 450 soles/two beds, four people. All these prices plus 10% taxes.

Hostal V. Lira at 209 San Juan de Dios costs 240 soles/single; 440 soles/four people in double room; 660 soles/person in triple room. Hot water. Also on this street with similar prices to the Corona are the *Hotel Tacna* (512 San Juan de Dios) and the *Hostal San Juan de Dios.*

Hostal San Roman at Tristan 100A. 180 soles/double but cold water.

Hostal El Mirador in the Plaza de Armas (Portal de Flores No. 102) at the junction of Ejericiios and Mercaderes on the first floor. 300 soles/single; 550 soles/double; 750 soles/double with private bath. Clean, hot water, secure and a roof-top snackbar with beautiful views over the city and of El Misti. Friendly staff.

Hostal Excelcior on Mercaderes between San Francisco and Jerusalen. Similar to the El Mirador and with its own cafe.

Other budget hotels at the lower end of the market are:

Hostal Comercio at 102 San Camilio, just off San Juan de Dios.

Hostal Moderno at 114 Alta de la Luna.

Hotel Pensión Colonial is opposite the Hostal Moderno.

Hotel Pacífico at 236 Alta de la Luna.

Hotel Europa at Tacna y Arica, on the

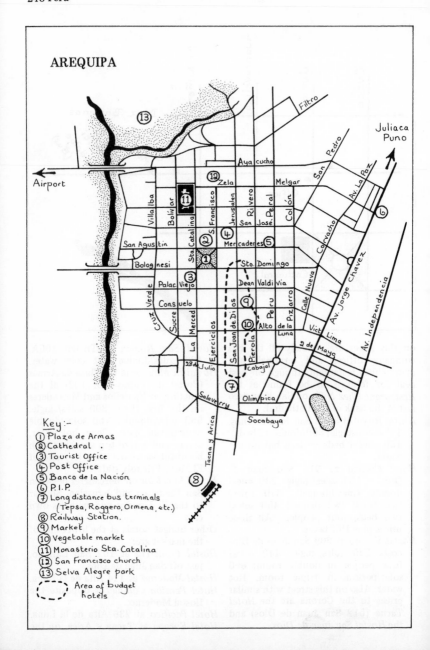

AREQUIPA

Key:-
1. Plaza de Armas
2. Cathedral
3. Tourist Office
4. Post Office
5. Banco de la Nación
6. P.I.P.
7. Long distance bus terminals (Tepsa, Roggero, Ormena, etc.)
8. Railway Station.
9. Market
10. Vegetable market
11. Monasterio Sta. Catalina
12. San Francisco church
13. Selva Alegre park
- - - Area of budget hotels

left about 50 metres from the train station.

Eats Plenty of cheap restaurants serving typical Peruvian fare on San Juan de Dios, Alta de la Luna and San Camilio. Can eat for 100 to 120 soles. There's little to choose between them.

The best deal in town for food is the *Restaurant Chez Nino*, 125-129 San Francisco, just behind the Cathedral. Starters for 60-120 soles and main meals for 150-170 soles. Amazing amount of delicous food and very popular with local people. Well worth spending the small amount extra to eat really excellent food. Add 20% taxes to all menu prices.

For sitting around and having a drink try the un-named cafe/bar run by an old Swiss lady on the Plaza de Armas near the junction of Bolognese and Santa Catalina. She also serves very good sandwiches. Good place to meet local people and rap with them.

Other Tourist Office: on La Merced No. 117 between the Plaza de Armas and Palacia Viejo has city maps but not much else.

Buses to the airport: No. 3 blue bus marked "Zamacola" or "Aeropuerto". Costs 10 soles and takes approximately 20 minutes. Doesn't go right up to the terminal so you have to walk the last 200 metres — bus driver will tell you when you're there as it isn't obvious. Catch it in town on the corner of La Merced and Palacio Viejo or at Puente Grau (the bridge at the bottom of Selva Alegre).

Market: Lively weekend market on Dean Valdivia and San Camilio. Good for general items but if you're looking for hand-crafted things get them in the mountains.

Long-distance bus terminals/ticket offices: Most are situated on San Juan de Dios between Alta de la Luna and Salaverry except for Morales Moral-

itos which is on Victor Lira just before the junction with Avenida Jorge Chavéz. Colectivos also on San Juan de Dios and Salaverry.

Arequipa is a good place to see films. Current American/British films with frequent programme changes. Cheap seat prices (about 50 soles!).

Places to see

Monasterio de Santa Catalina This is the biggest attraction in the city and well worth seeing. Costs 100 soles to get in (the Tourist Office will tell you it's 50 soles with a Student Card but the hard-faced git on the door will brusquely tell you otherwise!). It's a city within a city containing narrow cobbled streets, houses, gardens, fountains, churches, bakeries, cloisters and a graveyard and was, until fairly recently, a functioning convent. The few nuns who remain now occupy only a very small part of the walled complex and the rest has been opened up to the public. You can spend hours wandering around inside and there's a cafe where you can buy snacks and drinks if you're there that long. It's only disappointing feature is that there are very few artifacts left from the days when the nuns used to live here (perhaps they lived very frugally?) but the gardeners have made up for that with pots of flowering plants and small gardens here and there. Don't miss it!

Iglesia y Claustros del la Compañia and *San Ignacio Chapel*. An ornate Jesuit church on Santo Domingo on the corner of the Plaza de Armas. Excellent stone carving and beautiful facade. Don't miss the chapel of San Ignacio off to one side of the church (internally) where the Seminary was riotously painted with jungle scenes by the "Cuzco School of painters". Costs 10 soles entry.

San Francisco Church and Monastery Another interesting church dating from the days of the Conquest; between

Ayacucho and Zela.

Selva Alagre If you're looking for a quiet, shady afternoon under the eucalyptus trees this is the place to go. Very popular with local people on a weekend.

Archaeological Museum Situated in the University area off Avenida Independencia junction of Avenida La Salle. 15-20 minutes walk from the centre.

AYACUCHO

Peaceful, easy-going mountain city with much of its colonial buildings intact. Mountain scenery on the way there by bus is breath-taking.

Accommodation

La Colmena on Jirón Cuzco just off the Plaza de Armas. Very popular with travellers especially Germans, Swiss and French. Very clean, quiet, with friendly management. Sometimes full. 200 soles/single; 360 soles/double; 510 soles/triple; 680 soles/quadruple all without private bath. 420 soles/double with private bath and toilet. Hot water usually only in the mornings up till about 2 pm.

Hotel La Crillonesa at 165 Jirón Vivanco (also called Calle Nazereno), near market. 200 soles/single; 360 soles/double; 510 soles/triple; 640 soles/quadruple. No rooms have private bath/toilet but there's hot water all day.

Hostal Santiago is next door to the Crillonesa. Similar prices and quality.

Hostal Santa Rosa on Jirón Lima. Modern but traditionally built with shady patio, costs 437 soles /double. Has a cafe and regularly puts on folk music evenings — open to non-residents.

Eats Several cheap cafes on Vivanco and San Martín between Grau and 2 de Mayo serving local food. Eg. Omlette ("Tortilla Natural") 40-50 soles; with vegetables 60 soles. Coffee with milk 25-35 soles (large glass).

El Alamo is next door to the Colmena Hotel. Serves excellent food at very competitive prices. Eg fried fish and chips, 75 soles (just the thing for a homesick Englishman!); mixed salad (carrot, avocado, beetroot, cucumber, lettuce and onion) with dressing 45 soles. Plenty of other things at similar prices and very clean.

El Baccara on the corner of Plaza de Armas on Jiron Lima. If you like the food and prices at the Alamo you'll like this cafe too. It also has a bar which is usually pretty lively and is a good place to meet local people. It closes at 10 pm nominally but if you're having a good time with some local people they usually twist the owner's arm and he lets the laughter and beer continue until he literally isn't capable of keeping his eyes open any longer.

For snacks there's a good cafe on the top side of the Plaza de Armas opposite the Cathedral (sandwiches, coffee, etc) and a small cafe in the back of the University next to the Cathedral (meals at mealtimes, otherwise drinks) — go through the entrance, across the patio and down the corridor on the right hand side, turn left at the end. Quiet, shady patio with tables and chairs.

Other Tourist Office is situated at Asamblea. No. 138. Closed Saturdays and Sundays. Helpful, free maps of town.

Banks: Banco de la Nación, Jirón Callao, will only change travellers' cheques between 11 am and 1 pm after which it's closed. The bank clerk will tell you where to buy blackmarket soles!

Local folk music: Hostal Santa Maria and Hotel Turistico often put on local folk evenings which they advertise in all the hotels. Usually costs about 80-100 soles entrance.

Market: The market on Vivanco is very colourful and has some of the most beautiful "mantas" you will find in

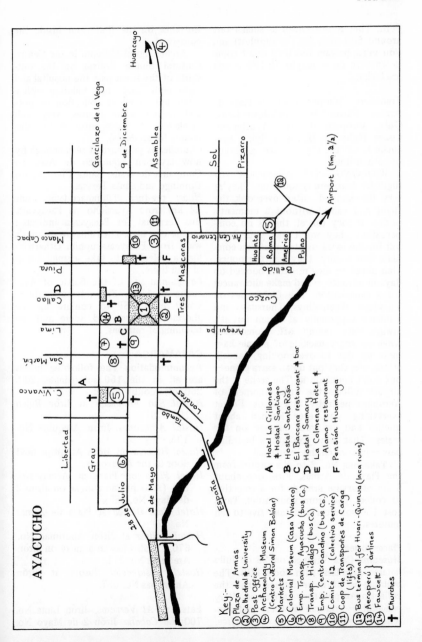

AYACUCHO

Key:-
① Plaza de Armas
② Cathedral & University
③ Post Office
④ Archaeology Museum (Centro Cultural Simón Bolívar)
⑤ Markets
⑥ Colonial Museum (Casa Vivanco)
⑦ Emp. Transp. Ayacucho (bus Co.)
⑧ Transp. Hidalgo (bus Co.)
⑨ Emp. Centroandino (bus Co.)
⑩ Comité 12 (colectivo service)
⑪ Coop de Transportes de Carga (lifts)
⑫ Bus terminal for Huari-Quinua (Inca ruins)
⑬ Aeroperú } airlines
⑭ Faucett }
✝ Churches

A Hotel La Crillonesa
✝ Hostal Santiago
B Hostal Santa Rosa
C El Baccara restaurant & bar
D Hostal Samary
E La Colmena Hotel ✝
Alamo restaurant
F Pensión Huamanga

Peru. They're not cheap as such (start around 500 soles for the simplest) and you must bargain but they don't come down very far — maybe 10-15% if you are lucky.

Transport Aeroperu is on the Plaza de Armas. Fawcett is on 196 Jirón Lima. Only Aeroperu do the Ayachucho-Cuzco flight but if you're flying Aya-cucho-Lima then you have a choice of both airlines.

WARNING! The Ayacucho-Cuzco flight by Aeroperu is notorious. They're very disorgansied, often overbook the flight and cancel without a moment's notice. If they cancel, there's no compensation, they won't pay your hotel bill for the extra nights and if you complain too loudly, they call the police. Plan ahead — they're often booked up days in advance — and make allowances for a cancellation. The flight goes on Tuesdays, Wednesdays, Thursdays and Sundays supposedly at 7 am but it's always late taking off. Sometimes, when an angry backlog of people have built up due to overbooking, cancell-ations, etc, they put on an extra plane — but don't count on it! The scene at the airport reflects the untogetherness of Aeroperu perfectly. It's chaos. Forget everything you ever learned about queues and get your luggage on the scales. That way you get a boarding pass — just watch the Peruvians!

Take bus No. 2 to the airport from the Plaza de Armas. First one about 6 am otherwise arrange for a colectivo to collect you from your hotel. Taxis cost 150 soles/car and take five to ten minutes.

Places to see

Museums Casa Vivanco on 28 de Julio (shares premises with local PIP). The building is of more interest than the collection of pots they have there. Very peaceful — you can sit there and con-template your navel all day, free.

Entrance on the first floor inside the courtyard.

Archeological Museum in the Centro Cultural Simon Bolívar on the out-skirts of the town past the hospital and night club. Large new building with a small but excellent collection of pots and carved stone figures, very well displayed. 30 soles entrance (no dis-counts for students).

Churches If you haven't séen enough by now try San Francisco de Asís, La Compañia de Jesús, Santa Clara, Santo Domingo and Santa Teresa.

Huari pre-Inca Tihuanaco-type ruins 24 km from Ayacucho via Pacaycasa. Bus terminal for Pacaycasa indicated on the city plan. The ruins are an hour's walk from Pacaycasa uphill. Otherwise hire a colectivo to take a small group of you there.

La Quinua site of the Battle of Aya-cucho in 1824. For veterans only — you'll need ESP to conjure up the ghosts of Bolívar and Sucre and the booming of cannons.

CAJAMARCA

Accommodation The following hotels are all in the 150 soles/single, 200-250 soles/double range:-

Hostal San Francisco at Jirón Belén No. 570.

Hostal Amazonas Jirón Arequipa No. 195.

Hostal Becerra on Jirón Arequipa next door to the Amazonas.

Hotel Plaza on Plaza de Armas No. 631 (Also has an annexe on Jiron 2 de Mayo No. 585).

Hotel Casa Blanca at Plaza de Armas No. 37.

Hostal Bolívar at Jirón Apurimac No. 670. It also has an annexe on Jirón Arequipa No. 211.

Hostal Residencial Jusovi at Jirón Amazonas No. 637.

Eats Try *Al Ververas*, Jirón Lima No. 700; *La Cabaña* Jirón 2 de Mayo No.

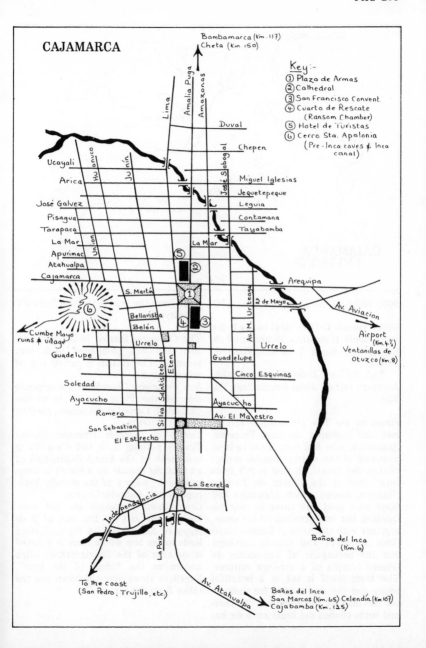

CAJAMARCA

Bambamarca (Km. 117)
Cheta (Km. 150)

Key:-
① Plaza de Armas
② Cathedral
③ San Francisco Convent
④ Cuarto de Rescate
   (Ransom Chamber)
⑤ Hotel de Turistas
⑥ Cerro Sta. Apolonia
   (Pre-Inca caves & Inca canal)

Duval
Chepen
Ucayali
Arica
Miguel Iglesias
Jequetepeque
José Galvez
Leguia
Pisagua
Contamana
Tarapaca
Tayabamba
La Mar
La Mar
Apurimac
Atahualpa
Cajamarca
Arequipa
S. Martin
2 de Mayo
Av. Aviacion
Cumbe Mayo
ruins & village
Bellavista
Belén
Airport
(Km. 4½)
Urrelo
Ventanillas de
Otuzco (Km. 8)
Guadelupe
Urrelo
Guadelupe
Cinco Esquinas
Soledad
Ayacucho
Ayacucho
Romero
Av. El Maestro
San Sebastian
El Estrecho
La Secreta
Baños del Inca
(Km. 6)
To the coast
(San Pedro, Trujillo, etc.)
Av. Atahualpa
Baños del Inca
San Marcos (Km. 65) Celendín (Km. 107)
Cajabamba (Km. 125)

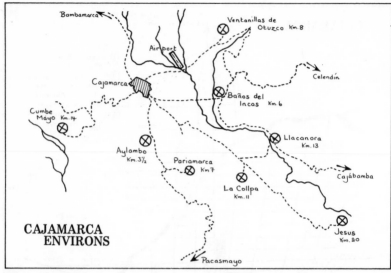

Bambamarca

Ventanillas de Otuzco Km.8

Airport

Celendín

Cajamarca

Baños del Incas Km.6

Cumbe Mayo Km.14

Llacanora Km.13

Aylambo Km.3½

Pariamarca Km 7

Cajábamba

La Collpa Km.11

CAJAMARCA ENVIRONS

Jesus Km.20

Pacasmayo

566; *Salas*, Jirón Arequipa No. 170.

Other Tourist Office: Next to the Belén monuments (Conjunto Monumental de Belén) one block from the Plaza de Armas.

Post Office: Jirón Lima No, 406.
Aeroperu Office: Jirón Amalia Puga No. 525.

Places to see The place where Pizarro met and captured the Inca Emperor, Atahualpa, who had gone there to treat a wound at the nearby thermal springs (Banos del Inca). All that is left from Inca times is the Cuarto de Rescate (Ransom Room) which Atahualpa had filled with gold and silver to buy his freedom but was garotted all the same, together with the ruins at Cumbe Mayo (Inca aqueduct and Chavín carvings) and the necropolis of Ventanillas de Otuzco (crypts of a pre-Inca culture). The town itself is set in a beautiful valley and the area is ideal for walks — see the map of the environs. The thermal baths (Baños del Inca) are a six km

walk from the centre through beautiful countryside.

The Cathedral Started in the 17th century and not completed until very recently. The facade is carved out of volcanic rock.

San Francisco Church on the opposite side of the Plaza de Armas to the Cathedral. Carved stone facade, cloisters and art museum.

Cuarto de Rescate (Ransom Room) There's nothing in it but it's a fitting testament to the brutal destruction of an amazing culture by a bunch of thugs and the hypocrisy of the morally bankrupt Roman Catholic Church.

Cerro Santa Apolonia the hill overlooking the city at the end of 2 de Mayo or San Martín. A flight of steps leads to the top where there is a carved stone altar of the Chavín culture often known as the "chair of the Inca". Excellent views over the town and the valley from the top.

Nearby Excursions

Baños del Inca Hot natural sulphur springs (about 70°C). Open air swimming pool and private baths. Six km from the centre of town — a pleasant walk or, if you're feeling geriatric, there are buses.

Ventanillas de Otuzco a necropolis left by the pre-Inca culture which thrived here between 500 AD and 1000 AD. Eight km from the centre of town.

Cumbe Mayo Here are to be found a pre-Inca (Chavín) aqueduct which was used to supply the town with water; artificial caves with petroglyph carvings of Chavín influence, and a carved sanctuary in the shape of a human head made out of a geological outcrop.

For other possible walks in the neighbourhood see the map of the environs. Choose your route and put on your boots.

CHICLAYO

You might have to stay here overnight on your way to Cajamarca but otherwise there's little incentive to stop.

Accommodation

Mediterraneo on Calle Basta, near the Plaza de Armas. 120 soles/single — clean and friendly management.

Astoria in the centre of town. 200 soles/single — one of the best mid-range hotels.

Americano on Calle Basta — 300 soles/double with bath.

Other Water is frequently in short supply in this town as it's on the edge of the desert.

Tourist Office: Las Acasias No. 305 La Victoria Suburb.

Bus terminals: Most are on Calle Basta.

CUZCO & THE URUBAMBA VALLEY

(Pisac, Urubamba, Ollantaytambo, Macchu Picchu)

CUZCO

Ancient capital of the Inca Empire and still the cultural centre of the Quechua people. According to legend it was founded by Manco Capac who, together with his wife Mama Ocllo, emerged from Lake Titicaca at the command of his father, the Sun. Historically, it was founded around 1200 AD and reached its zenith about 1438 during the reign of the Inca Pachacutec, the Tihuantisuyo peoples' greatest conqueror and organizer.

Following the Spanish Conquest it became one of the world's most remarkable monuments to the fusion of two different cultures. The unique, mortarless stone masonry of the Incas can still be seen down many streets, around the base of Spanish-style houses and even inside cafes as well as at the fortress of Sacsayhuaman overlooking the city and at numerous sites in the Urubamba valley. It is also the starting point for visiting Pisac, Ollantaytambo and the most famous archaeological site in the Americas — Macchu Picchu. Plan to spend at least several days in Cuzco itself. There's plenty to see and do.

Accommodation

All the following budget hotels (under US$2/single) are located within two to three blocks of the Plaza de Armas:

Bolívar on Calle Tecsecocha. 108 soles/single without private bath; 192 soles/double. Hot water, frequently full.

Colón at San Juan de Dios No. 142. 180 soles/single without bath: 240 soles/double.

Granada at Siete Cuartones No. 290 — 160 soles/single without bath: 240 soles/double.

Los Andes at Tullumayo No. 582 — 192 soles/single without bath; 336 soles/double.

Macchu Picchu at Calle Quera No.282 — 240 soles/single without bath; 480 soles/double.

Palermo at San Agustín No. 287 — 132 soles/single without bath; 336 soles/double.

Panamericano at San Agustín No. 331 374 soles/double without bath.

Plaza at Calle Espaderos — 180 soles/single; 288 soles/double — no bath.

Procuradores at Procuradores No. 315 — 108 soles/single, 192 soles/double, without bath. With bath — 180/300.

Espaderos on Calle Espaderos — 180 soles/single, 288 soles/double.

Argentina at Plateros No. 313 — 300 soles/single; 660 soles/double without bath.

Colonial at Matara No. 288 — 168 soles/single; 288 soles/double without bath.

Royal at San Augustín No. 256 — 120 soles/single; 240 soles/doubles without bath.

Santa Teresa at Santa Teresa No. 364 — 259 soles/single; 504 soles/double without bath; 648 soles/double with private bath.

Inca at Quera No. 251 — 108 soles/single; 216 soles/double without bath. out bath.

La Nusta at Calle del Medio — same prices as the Inca.

Cabiedo at Calle Garcilaso No. 210 — 264 soles/single with bath: 528 soles/double with bath.

Amanta at Plateros No. 368 — 330 soles/single; 450 soles/double without bath; 342 soles/single with bath.

Central at San Augustín No. 249 — 132 soles/single with bath; 264 soles/double with cold water only. Hot water showers costs 20 soles extra.

Plateros at Plateros No. 340 — 189 soles/single; 315 soles/double without bath; 342 soles/single with bath.

Puno at Tullumayo No. 115 — 108 soles/single; 192 soles/double without bath.

"C" and "Q" (and to a lesser extent "K") are inter-changed with gay abandon in the spelling of proper nouns in Cuzco and can be a source of confusion. Eg Quera may be spelt: Quera; Qquera; Ccuera. Tecseccocha may be spelt: Tecseccocha; Tecseqocha; Tecsecocha. Manco Capac may be spelt: Manco Capac; Manko Qhapaq.

If you arrive at the airport you will be besieged by runners from various hotels all of whom tell the old, old story that theirs is the best and sits virtually in the middle of the Plaza de Armas, etc, etc. Some of them offer free taxi rides to their hotel (though it's probable that you pay for it in the end by an increased hotel tariff). You can always take one for the night and, if you don't like it, go looking for another without having to lug your bags around.

If you're looking for a mid-priced hotel go first to the Tourist Office in the Plaza de Armas. They have a complete list of all hotels in the city with current prices and services available. Many of them are located on Avenida el Sol and between the Plaza de Armas and Plaza San Francisco.

Eats Plenty of small cafes and restaurants serving local food at reasonable prices particularly along Plateros, Mantas, Marquéz and the Plaza de Armas. Eg *Casa Azul* on Plateros (excellent meal — four courses! — for 60 soles); *Rick's Cafe*, Santa Catalina No. 118 (very good meals, especially steak apanado, but avoid the "American breakfasts"); *Ayllu Cafe*, top end of the Plaza de Armas (milk products especially natural yoghurt. Coffee and good for breakfast); *La Posada Cafe* on the Plaza de Armas (good food and excellent egg sandwiches and pancakes. Three-course "comidas" for 80 soles); *Govinda* on Procuradores is a Hari Krishna caff. Good clean food (vegetarian only) and excellent soups — a little expensive but then it's all good for the soul and there isn't a "Back to Godhead" in sight! Peaceful little place. *Restaurant Vegetariano*, Portal

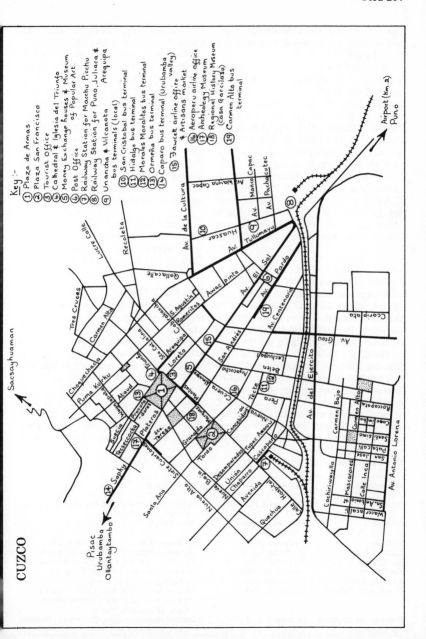

CUZCO

Key:-
1. Plaza de Armas
2. Plaza San Francisco
3. Tourist Office
4. Cathedral & Iglesia del Triunfo
5. Money Exchange houses & Museum of Popular Art.
6. Post Office
7. Railway Station for Macchu Picchu
8. Railway Station for Puno, Juliaca & Arequipa
9. Urcancha & Vilcanota bus terminals (local)
10. San Cristobal bus terminal
11. Hidalgo bus terminal
12. Morales Moralitos bus terminal
13. Ormeña bus terminal
14. Caparo bus terminal (Urubamba)
15. Bawcelt airline office (Urubamba valley) & Artisans market
16. AeroPeru airline office
17. Archeology Museum
18. Regional History Museum (Casa Garcilaso)
19. Carmen Alto bus terminal

Carvizos on the Plaza de Armas. Vegetarian food as you might expect. Open from 11 am.

If you're looking for a little action try the two gringo bars on Procuradores which have music — *El Calypso* and *El Retabillo* — latter serves mulled wine (it gets cold of an evening in Cuzco). There's also the *Chatuchay Taverna* on the Plaza de Armas which has drinks, snacks and local music and is a kind of "mestizos big night out". US$1 cover charge, often very crowded. Music starts around 8.30 pm. The Chinese restaurant on Plateros near the junction with the Plaza de Armas often has a local band playing but the food's somewhat expensive (though good).

Other Tourist Office: In the Capilla Lourdes (Lourdes Chapel) on the corner of Loreto and the Plaza de Armas next to the Iglesia de la Compania. One of the best tourist offices you will find anywhere in South America. Free maps of town; the Sacred Valley of the Incas (Urubamba Valley); Inca Trail to Macchu Picchu. Timetables and other information about museums, transport, hotels, cafes, night spots, sights pinned around the walls. Very well organised. If you're going on the Inca Trail they will store excess baggage here free until you return (it's locked up safely).

American Express agents: Lima Tours Ocona No. 160, P O Box 531.

Poste Restante: The Posta Restante at the Post Office on Avenida El Sol has a very strange method of sorting letters: they're put into separate male and female sections! From our own experience, letters do get sorted correctly though how they divine the sex of an initial when no honorifics are used remains a mystery. However, if you are expecting a letter which isn't turning up in your respective pigeon-hole, ask to sort through the other section. They're used to this!

Local bus from airport to city centre: 14 soles, frequent.

Aeroperu office; Matara No. 295. Fawcett office: Avenida El Sol No. 393.

THE INCA TRAIL

If it's at all possible for you to make this trek through the mountains from km 88 on the Cuzco-Macchu Picchu railway to Macchu Picchu then you should do it. Few experiences in South America are so worth while but you need to start making plans in Cuzco if you're not carrying a tent and cooking equipment with you or you have too much baggage to take with you over 4000 metre passes (very thin air!). Excess baggage is easy. You can either

Bus Terminals

bus company	terminal	destinations
Morales Moralitos	Calle Belén No. 451	Abancay, Arequipa, La Paz (Bolivia), Lima, Nazca, Pisco, Puno
Ormeno	Portales Harinas No. 117 (Plaza de Armas)	Abancay, Lima, Nazca, Pisco
Hidalgo	Tecte No. 361	Abancay, Ayacucho, Huancayo, Lima
Carmen Alto	Av Pardo No. 322	Abancay, Ayacucho, Huancayo, Lima
San Cristobal	Av Huascar No. 120	Arequipa, Juliaca, Lima, Puno, Sicuani
Sur Peruana	Limacpampa Chico	Arequipa, La Paz (Boliva), Puno
Expreso Juliaca	Ruinas No. 407	Arequipa, La Paz (Bolivia), Puno
Transportes Caparo	Saphy No. 700	local — Calca, Chaullay, Coya, Huayllabamba, Quillabamba, Ollantaytambo, Pisac, Urubamba, Yucay
Transportes Unancha & Vilcanota	Huascar	local — Andahuaylillas, Chinchero, Huaypo Lago, Pikillacta

leave it at the Tourist Office free of charge (it's locked up securely) or possibly with "Explorandes", Procuradores No. 372 which is run by an American and his Peruvian wife. This place doesn't store baggage on a regular basis but they do sell maps of the Trail which are superior to those put out by the Tourist Office (free) and, if you buy one and rap for a while, may agree to store your baggage.

If you have no tent or cooking equipment (latter could be dispensed with if you're willing to eat cold/dried foods) these can be hired from the place which specialises in camping equipment half way along the top side of the Plaza de Armas opposite the Tourist Office. The only snags to this are that they want a *large* (returnable) deposit, though the cost of hire itself is cheap (100 soles/day for 2-person tent), and they don't have a lot of them so you may not be able to hire at the time you want them. Plan ahead as far as possible. The deposit problem is no trouble if you have sufficient cash (soles or dollars) but if you only have cheques which you have to date and make payable to the hire firm then you have yourself a problem when it comes to paying back the deposit. This requires thought, otherwise you could end up with a massive excess of soles (poor rate outside Peru). If you can't think of any way around this, remember that a tent *isn't essential*. Plenty of people go on the trail without one.

Further details and maps in a separate section later.

In and around Cuzco

Many of the antiquities (Inca ruins), museums and churches are grouped together in "circuits" for which you have to buy a combined entrance ticket which entitles you to see each one of the places on each particular cirucuit. There are considerable reductions for holders of International Student Cards.

The two main "circuits" are:

Sacsayhuaman, Kenko, Puca Pucara, Tambomachay, Qoricancha and Museo de Santa Catalina. All except the last are Inca ruins on the hills overlooking Cuzco. The fortress of Sacsayhuaman from which the Incas made their last stand against Pizarro's invading forces is, of course, the most magnificent remaining example of Inca construction and stone masonry outside of Macchu Picchu, Pisac and Ollantaytambo. Some of the polished blocks of stone out of which it is constructed weigh tons. The site is a 20-30 minute walk uphill from the Plaza de Armas. Don't miss it! The annual Festival of the Sun — Inti Raymi — on 24th June is also held here. The other sites are all further along the road towards Pisac.

Combined tickets for all sites cost 200 soles or 50 soles with student card. Santa Catalina on Santa Catalina Calle is open Tuesday to Sunday between 9 am and noon and 2 pm to 6 pm. The other sites are open everyday but, since they are not enclosed by walls or fences, you can go there any time of day or night.

Museum of Religious Art (corner of San Andres and Hatunrumiyoc), the Cathedral and San Blas Church (in the small square of the same name on corner of San Blas and Carment Alto). The Cathedral was built over the foundations of the Palace of Wiracocha and is noted for its silver altar and paintings of the Cuzco school. The church of San Blas contains some of the world's most beautiful wood carving done by the Cuzco school in the 17th century. Don't miss the pulpit and the altar pieces.

Combined entrance ticket for these places is 150 soles or 40 soles with student card. The Museum of Religious Art (Museo de Arte Religioso) is open Monday to Saturday between 9 am and noon and 2 pm to 6 pm.

Other Museums

Archeological Museum at Calle Tigre No. 165 off Saphi. Open Monday through Sunday between 8 am and noon and 3 pm and 6 pm. Entrance is 50 soles. Ceramics, textiles, gold objects, carved pieces, etc from Inca times.

Regional History Museum on Calle Heladeros at the corner of Garcilaso. Open Monday to Saturday from 9 am to noon and 2 pm to 5 pm.

Popular Art Museum at Galerias Turisticos, Avenida El Sol. Next door to the Casa de Cambio, no fixed opening times — enquiry necessary.

Inca walls in various parts of the city. These can be found almost everywhere in the old part of the city — the Tourist Office will provide you with a map indicating them all. The principal sites are Sta Clara, Loreta (probably the best), Maruri, San Agustín, Tullumayu, Choquechaca and Hatunrumiyoc (whose wall contains the famous 12-angled stone).

Churches If you aren't sick to the back teeth of gawping at churches having got this far through Latin America there are plenty of others to see in Cuzco. One of the most visited is the Church and Monastery of La Merced on Mantas, just off the Plaza de Armas. Tour of historical objects and priceless, glittering, bejewelled monstrances — if you're into that sort of thing and can manage to contain your disgust at the enormous wealth of the Roman Catholic Church compared with the poverty of the average campesino.

FESTIVALS

March-April: Holy Week (no fixed date). Procession of the "Lord of Earthquakes" on Holy Monday.

June: Corpus Christi. (No fixed date). Procession in which the silver carriage and gold monstrance are taken out of the Cathedral as are the patron saints of the neighbouring towns and villages.

June: Festival of Raqchi in Sicuani. Folklore festival.

June 24th: Inti Raymi (Festival of the Sun). Enacted on the ground in front of the fortress of Sacsahuaman. Parades and dances — people come for miles around (including lotsa tourists). The most colourful of all the festivals in Peru. If you're around at that time, go and see it.

July 16th: Festival of the Virgen del Carmen at Paucartambo. Dancing, drinking, bands, processions. Probably best experienced in a smaller town. The same festival at Pisac is exceptionally lively and goes on for days. The tourists only come in droves for the procession on Sunday (and for the regular Sunday Market with which the procession coincides) and only in the late morning/early afternoon. When they've gone or before they arrive, local people get on with celebrating and you can get involved in some amazing scenes.

THE URUBAMBA VALLEY

The valley should not be missed and is a much more interesting way of going to/coming back from Macchu Picchu as opposed to taking the train all the way. (From Ollantaytambo to Km 88 or Macchu Picchu you have to take the train as there is no road). Spectacular mountain scenery, friendly people and beautiful Inca ruins surrounded by agricultural terraces some of which, particularly around Pisac, are still in use. Ruined terraces throughout the valley indicate that in Inca times the steep mountain sides were intensively farmed.

Transport in the Valley

Buses Transportes Caparo, Calle Saphy No. 700, Cuzco.

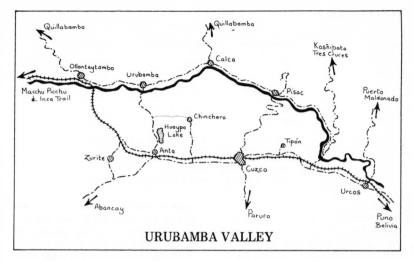

URUBAMBA VALLEY

Cuzco-Pisac-Calca-Yucay-Urubamba.
   Daily service in either direction at approximately 5.30 am, 6 am, 8 am, 10.30 am, 11.30 am, 1.30 pm, 3 pm 4 pm. ("Approximately" because departure time depends to a certain extent on demand).

Journey time, Cuzco-Urubamba: 2-2¼ hours. Pisac-Urubamba: 2-2½ hours. Fare: Cuzco to Pisac (52 soles); Calca (67 soles); Yucay (100 soles); Urubamba (105 soles). Pisac to Urubamba (70 soles).

Urubamba-Ollantaytambo
   There are supposedly four buses per day in either direction at approximately 8 am, 1.45 pm, 3 pm, and 5.30 pm. but they're very unreliable and sometimes don't turn up at all. Costs 40 soles and takes half an hour. It's probably better to hitch this stretch (easy, but you generally have to pay).

Caparo also go to Chaullya and Quillabamba — enquire in Cuzco. Fares are Chaullay (225 soles); Quillabamba (315 soles).

You can also go by truck from Ollantaytambo to Quillabamba. Several leave everyday from the plaza — just ask around. Ask 300-360 soles for the ride. Spectacular route.

Trains

Cuzco-Macchu Picchu. Daily Tourist Train is direct — no stopping. Departs Cuzco: 7 am. Arrive: 10.30 pm. Departs Macchu Picchu: 4 pm. Arrives: 7.45 pm, Cost is 2,300 soles!! An expensive way of getting to Macchu Picchu. You cannot take this train if you want to get off or on at any point between Cuzco and Macchu Picchu. If you want to get off at Ollantaytambo or Km 88 (for the Inca Trail) or get on at Aguas Calientes, you must take the local stopping train — twice daily in either direction.

Cuzco-Chaullay. Local Train. Stops at all stations including Ollantaytambo, Km 88, Aguas Calientes and Macchu Picchu. Two trains daily in either direction. Except for departure time from either Cuzco or Chaullay all times are approximate and the train is often up to two hours late.

Train Timetables

Cuzco	Ollantaytambo	Macchu Picchu	Chaullay
05.30	07.40	09.08	10.51
13.30	15.40	17.19	18.55

Chaullay	Macchu Picchu	Ollantaytambo	Cuzco
06.00	07.52	10.02	12.00
12.00	13.47	15.55	17.35

Fares: Cuzco to   Ollantaytambo (176 soles first class, 104 soles second class)
    Macchu Picchu (292 soles first class, 172 soles second class)
    Chaullay (442 soles first class, 261 soles second class)
Ollantaytambo to Km 88 (40 soles second class)
    Macchu Picchu (120 soles first class, 70 soles second class)

PISAC

Accommodation There are only three places to stay unless you can root out a private room with someone who lives there. Electricity in the town is sporadic. Take some candles or get some from a tienda, on main plaza.

Pension y Alojamiento Roma on the right-hand corner of the street just over the Urubamba bridge — see · map. Run by the re-incarnation of Mother Hubbard. Sleazy, dormitory-type accommodation for a rip-off 90 soles/bed but somehow you don't mind. Baggage safe — Mother Hubbard has hawk's eyes. Meals served downstairs but tend to be inedible. Eat elsewhere.

A few rooms for rent above the tienda on the corner of the plaza — see map.

Albergue Turistico Chongo Chica is 300 metres down the road towards Urubamba from the bridge. Bar, swimming pool, single/double/dormitory rooms available. Scruffy and run down but if you really don't fancy Mother Hubbard's place after looking at it, this is the place to stay.

Eats The best place to eat is the small cafe on the plaza — see map. Excellent clean cheap food. Otherwise there are two indifferent cafes on the street facing the Urubamba bridge.

Things to Do/See Famous for its magnigficent Inca ruins and Sunday market. Well heeled, camera-toting tourists are brought by the bus-load to the Sunday market but they don't get there until around 10.30 am so there's plenty of time to look around for bargains. Everything from lumps of iron pyrites to

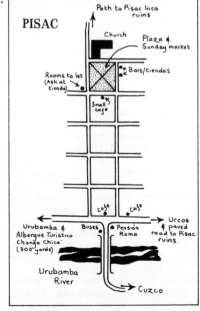

ponchos and musical instruments — small but excellent range of goods. If you're in the area around July 16th stay here for the fiesta of the Virgen del Carmen. Andean flute bands and brass bands play non-stop for three nights and three days through the streets. Everyone gets completely out of their heads and there's a procession around the plaza with the Virgen's image on Sunday about noon.

Inca Ruins You need at least four to five hours to see them. It's a stiff climb up the mountain side and they're spread out over a large area. Some beautiful stone-work, temples, forts and re-constructions complete with thatched roofs. Amazing views down the valley in either direction. Get there by taking the path which goes up-hill from the left-hand side of the church on the plaza.

Entry to ruins is 150 soles or 30 soles with Student Card. The ticket also entitles you to visit Ollantaytambo ruins without further charge so hang

onto it. The "ticket booth" is about 400 metres up the slope from town.

URUBAMBA
Sleepy town with almost nothing going on. Ideal if you want to rest up though the "Albergue" in Ollantaytambo is to be preferred. It's better to hitch from here to Ollantaytambo as the buses are unreliable. Caparo bus office will tell if they expect one to go there that day.

Accommodation
Hotel Urubamba on Jirón Bolognesi is 100 soles/single; 200 soles/double without bath.
Hotel Turista on the main road through town opposite the petrol station, relatively expensive.

OLLANTAYTAMBO
One of the most beautiful and tranquil places in the whole valley. You could stay forever — some people do!

Accommodation
Albergue is the best place to stay by far and probably without compare anywhere in the country. Run by two young couples, one American, the other Canadian. Farmhouse-type accommodation, clean sheets, comfortable beds, storm lamps, common room, large walled garden with clothes-washing facilities. Breakfasts only served. Hot water sometimes otherwise its limited and the place is often full by late afternoon though they often let you sleep on the floor if you have your own bedding or hammock. There's a dormitory (eight beds) for 200 soles/bed or 300 soles/bed if you share it. Also smaller room with two beds at the same price. If the above beds in the main building are taken there's an annexe which costs 50 soles/bed. To get there from the centre of the village take the dirt-track to

URUBAMBA

the railway station and across the log bridge on your left just before you reach the railway tracks. The sign is over the door on the other side of the log bridge.

Pensión Bahia on the plaza is often full. Very limited accommodation.

Hostal is 40 metres off the main square see map — along the Inca walls. 200 soles/double in dormitory-type accommodation. Grubby and uncomfortable beds. Not a patch on the Albergue.

Eats All three cafes on the plaza serve good and reasonably cheap food. There is little to choose between them except that the young boy who takes the orders in the caff nearest to the road to the ruins is very absent minded and you have to keep reminding him that you ordered food half an hour ago (or an hour ago, etc).

If you have an instrument take it into El Bohemio cafe and drink some beers and play. They're very friendly

OLLANTAYTAMBO

people. If the local doctor is there he'll play some Quechua folk songs which will have them all singing till early hours. One night we were there the local police inspector came banging on the door about midnight — not to break it up, but to get in on the singing and have a few beers! The station-master looked like he was nursing a hangover as well the following morning.

Things to Do/See Unlike Pisac and Macchu Picchu, the Inca ruins are rarely visited by tourists so you have the whole site to yourself most of the time. Entry to the ruins is free with the ticket you purchased in Pisac, otherwise you'll have to pay 150 soles or 30 soles with a Student Card.

In addition to the ruins themselves, the whole village has been constructed on Inca foundations and you can see typical Inca stone-work down almost any street.

Ollantaytambo is the last place where you will be able to buy food and drink for the Inca Trail — you cannot buy anything on the Trail itself. There are two tiendas on the top side of the plaza which stock most basic things (including tinned fish and meat) and the local firewater — similar to Pisco. The chocolate they have for sale however is pretty rough and you'd be advised to get in a supply in Cuzco if you're planning on taking any. Also dried packet soups are best bought in Cuzco. Fresh-baked bread for the Trail can be bought every evening from the Bakery — see map for location. No camping equipment for hire in the village.

THE INCA TRAIL TO MACCHU PICCHU FROM KM 88

A little has already been said about this under "Cuzco" in the "Accommodation" section but we'd like to emphasise once again that if it's at all possible you should make this trek. You may hear

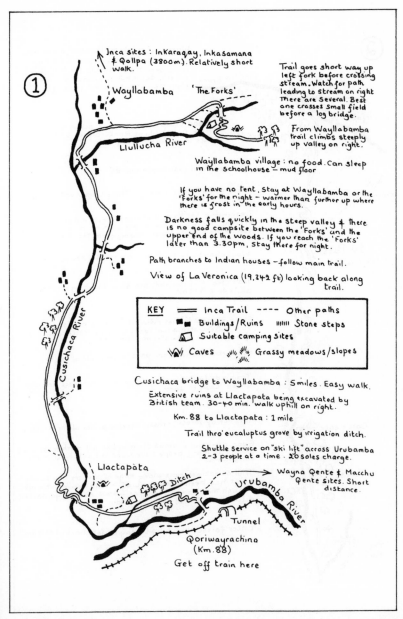

① Inca sites : Inkaraqay, Inkasamana & Qollpa (3800m). Relatively short walk.

Wayllabamba   'The Forks'

Llullucha River

Trail goes short way up left fork before crossing stream. Watch for path leading to stream on right. There are several. Best one crosses small field before a log bridge.

From Wayllabamba trail climbs steeply up valley on right.

Wayllabamba village : no food. Can sleep in the schoolhouse — mud floor.

If you have no tent, stay at Wayllabamba or the 'Forks' for the night — warmer than further up where there is frost in the early hours.

Darkness falls quickly in the steep valley & there is no good campsite between the 'Forks' and the upper end of the woods. If you reach the 'Forks' later than 3.30pm, stay there for night.

Path branches to Indian houses — follow main trail.

View of La Veronica (19,342 ft) looking back along trail.

Cusichaca River

KEY
═══ Inca Trail   - - - - Other paths
■▪ Buildings/Ruins   ﹏ Stone steps
⌂ Suitable camping sites
〰 Caves   🌿🌿 Grassy meadows/slopes

Cusichaca bridge to Wayllabamba : 5 miles. Easy walk.

Extensive ruins at Llactapata being excavated by British team. 30-40 min. walk uphill on right.

Km. 88 to Llactapata : 1 mile

Trail thro' eucalyptus grove by irrigation ditch.

Shuttle service on "ski lift" across Urubamba 2-3 people at a time. 20 soles charge.

Llactapata

Ditch

Urubamba River

Wayna Qente & Macchu Qente sites. Short distance.

Tunnel

Qoriwayrachina (Km.88)

Get off train here

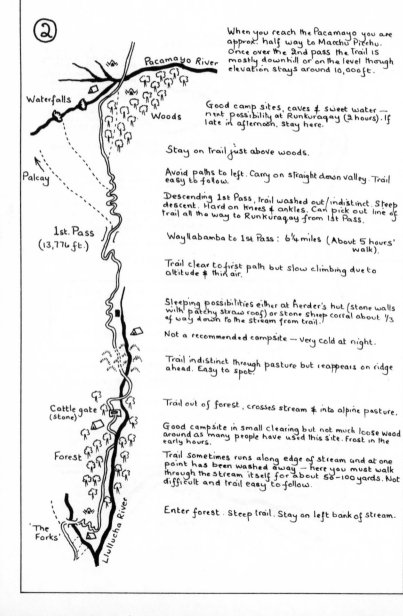

When you reach the Pacamayo you are approx. half way to Macchu Picchu. Once over the 2nd pass the Trail is mostly downhill or on the level though elevation stays around 10,000 ft.

Pacamayo River

Waterfalls

Woods

Good camp sites, caves & sweet water — next possibility at Runkuraqay (2 hours). If late in afternoon, stay here.

Stay on trail just above woods.

Palcay

Avoid paths to left. Carry on straight down valley. Trail easy to follow.

Descending 1st Pass, trail washed out/indistinct. Steep descent. Hard on knees & ankles. Can pick out line of trail all the way to Runkuraqay from 1st Pass.

1st. Pass (13,776 ft.)

Wayllabamba to 1st Pass: 6¼ miles (About 5 hours' walk).

Trail clear to first path but slow climbing due to altitude & thin air.

Sleeping possibilities either at herder's hut (stone walls with patchy straw roof) or stone sheep corral about ⅓ of way down to the stream from trail.

Not a recommended campsite — very cold at night.

Trail indistinct through pasture but reappears on ridge ahead. Easy to spot.

Cattle gate (stone)

Trail out of forest, crosses stream & into alpine pasture.

Good campsite in small clearing but not much loose wood around as many people have used this site. Frost in the early hours.

Forest

Trail sometimes runs along edge of stream and at one point has been washed away — here you must walk through the stream itself for about 50–100 yards. Not difficult and trail easy to follow.

'The Forks'

Enter forest. Steep trail. Stay on left bank of stream.

Llullucha River

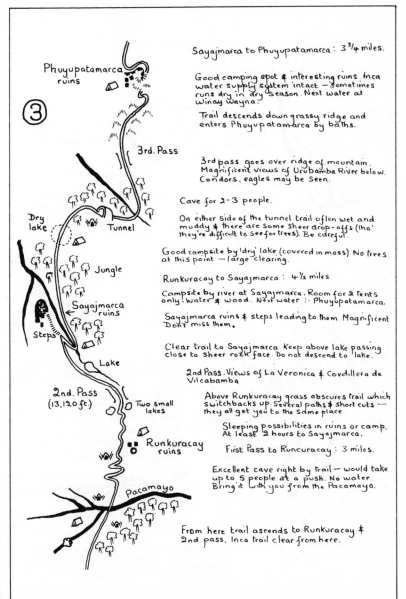

Phuyupatamarca ruins

③

3rd. Pass

Dry lake

Tunnel

Jungle

Sayajmarca ruins

Steps

Lake

2nd. Pass (13,120 ft.)

Two small lakes

Runkuracay ruins

Pacamayo

Sayajmarca to Phuyupatamarca : 3¾ miles.

Good camping spot & interesting ruins. Inca water supply system intact — sometimes runs dry in dry season. Next water at Wiñay Wayna.

Trail descends down grassy ridge and enters Phuyupatamarca by baths.

3rd pass goes over ridge of mountain. Magnificent views of Urubamba River below. Condors, eagles may be seen.

Cave for 2-3 people.

On either side of the tunnel trail often wet and muddy & there are some sheer drop-offs (tho' they're difficult to see for trees). Be careful.

Good campsite by 'dry' lake (covered in moss). No trees at this point — large clearing.

Runkuracay to Sayajmarca : 4½ miles

Campsite by river at Sayajmarca. Room for 2 tents only! Water & wood. Next water :- Phuyupatamarca.

Sayajmarca ruins & steps leading to them. Magnificent. Don't miss them.

Clear trail to Sayajmarca. Keep above lake passing close to sheer rock face. Do not descend to 'lake.

2nd Pass. Views of La Veronica & Cordillera de Vilcabamba

Above Runkuracay grass obscures trail which switchbacks up. Several paths & short cuts — they all get you to the same place.

Sleeping possibilities in ruins or camp. At least 2 hours to Sayajmarca.

First Pass to Runcuracay : 3 miles.

Excellent cave right by trail — would take up to 5 people at a push. No water. Bring it with you from the Pacamayo.

From here trail ascends to Runkuracay & 2nd pass. Inca trail clear from here.

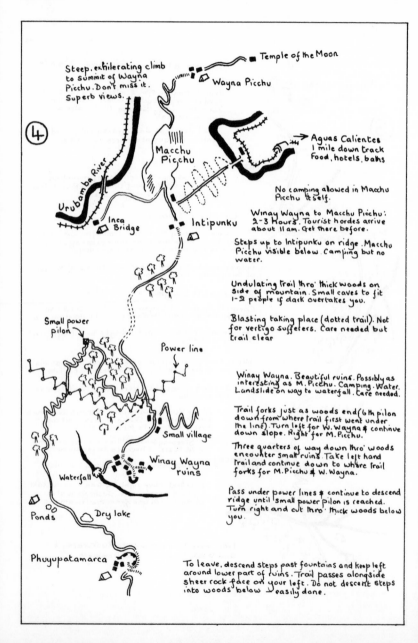

④

Temple of the Moon

Steep, exhilerating climb to summit of Wayna Picchu. Don't miss it. Superb views.

Wayna Picchu

Macchu Picchu

Urubamba River

Aguas Calientes 1 mile down track Food, hotels, baths

Inca Bridge

Intipunku

No camping allowed in Macchu Picchu itself.

Winay Wayna to Macchu Picchu: 2-3 hours. Tourist hordes arrive about 11 am. Get there before.

Steps up to Intipunku on ridge. Macchu Picchu visible below. Camping but no water.

Undulating trail thro' thick woods on side of mountain. Small caves to fit 1-2 people if dark overtakes you.

Blasting taking place (dotted trail). Not for vertigo sufferers. Care needed but trail clear

Small power pilon

Power line

Winay Wayna. Beautiful ruins. Possibly as interesting as M. Picchu. Camping. Water. Landslide on way to waterfall. Care needed.

Trail forks just as woods end (6th pilon down from where trail first went under the line). Turn left for W. Wayna & continue down slope. Right for M. Picchu.

Three quarters of way down thro' woods encounter small ruins. Take left hand trail and continue down to where trail forks for M. Picchu & W. Wayna.

Small village

Winay Wayna ruins

Waterfall

Ponds   Dry lake

Pass under power lines & continue to descend ridge until small power pilon is reached. Turn right and cut thro' thick woods below you.

Phuyupatamarca

To leave, descend steps past fountains and keep left around lower part of ruins. Trail passes alongside sheer rock face on your left. Do not descend steps into woods below ◡ easily done.

stories in Cuzco that part of the trail is "dangerous" because blasting is going on. It's true that this is happening between Winay Wayna and Macchu Picchu and that you have to scramble over rocks and boulders for 200 metres across a mountain side high above the Urubamba River but to describe it as "dangerous" is being excessive. Travellers and workmen cross this patch every day. But such is the power of rumour. Ignore it.

The trail and the ruined Inca cities along the way were "discovered" (in the sense that Columbus "discovered" America, ho, ho) by the North American explorer Hiram Bingham at the beginning of the 20th century though, of course, they were known to local campesinos and probably always had been since the Conquest. But semantic chauvinism apart, Bingham's books describing his explorations in South America and particularly his re-discovery of Macchu Picchu are worth reading — Lost City of the Incas: The Story of Macchu Picchu and its Builders (New York 1948) & Across South America (Houghton Mifflin, New York 1911).

"Lost City of the Incas" Macchu Picchu may well have been but it was certainly not the "lost City". Following the murder of Atahualpa by Pizarro's bunch of thugs in 1534 and the conquest of Cuzco, the Inca kingdom continued to exist until 1595, centred on Vilcabamba further down the Urubamba River. Bingham very nearly re-discovered Vilcabamba but dismissed the outworks which he came across as part of a minor settlement/fortification. The re-discovery of this last city of the Incas had to wait until the 1960s and the explorer Gene Savoy. He has written an excellent book which covers his re-discovery of Vilcabamba and the high jungle cities of the pre-Inca Chachapoyas civilization between Macchu Picchu and Vilcabamba, so if the Inca

Trail whets your appetite for exploration and trekking through the Andes you might like to get hold of a copy of his book and tackle more difficult trails. The book is called, Vilcabamba: Last City of the Incas (Robert Hale, London 1971).

Before setting out for the Trail you need to consider what to take with you and what to leave behind especially if you're carrying a large pack. Arrange to store anything that isn't absolutely necessary. The hardest part of the Trail is the first pass over the first pass at 13,800 metres, during which your pack will be at its heaviest. Excess gear can be stored safely at the Tourist office in Cuzco and sometimes at "Explorandes", Procuradores Na 372, Cuzco (a private travel company which sells the best maps of the Trail) though they don't offer a regular service for this — talk with them. Another possibility is to speak with the people who run the Albergue in Ollantaytambo — very friendly people from the States and Canada who run one of the best and cheapest hotels you'll find anywhere in South America. If you're staying there on your way out and way back they'd undoubtedly let you store small amounts of gear there.

Maps for the Trail are included in this book and the Tourist Office in Cuzco also issued a free map which, though less detailed, is very useful for comparison as it shows the course of the Urubamba River in relation to the Trail

Plan on taking five days to complete the walk (or longer if you want to spend a lot of time exploring the various ruins along the way) though if you're pushed for time and are in good physical shape it can be done in four days Work out your food requirements on this basis and remember that you have to take it all with you — there's nowhere you can buy food along the way. It helps to have a portable stove as this enables to take a lot of dried food and so reduces the weight of your pack. Water can be taken from virtually any of the streams and rivers along the way and except at the back end of the dry season there's no shortage except between Phuyupatamarca and Winay Wayna. The best choice of food is naturally to be found in Cuzco but you can buy virtually everything you need in the tiendas at Ollantaytambo if you're passing through there on your way, though I didn't see any dried packet soup. Many people take a bag of coca leaves and a ball of hash along with them. They can be bought for a few pence (legally) in virtually any tienda in the highlands Don't forget to take a few candles and matches with you.

At present, the only place it's possible to hire tents from is half way along the top side of the Plaza de Armas (in Cuzco) down a small alleyway but there's heavy demand for them and you may not be able to hire one when you want it. They're not essential as there are caves along the way where you can sleep. Take a sleeping bag and warm clothes as it gets cold at night particularly on the way up the first pass. After that it's okay. A water bottle is useful and a small axe or machete if you're going to be making a fire at night. Loose wood is often hard to find around the regular camping spots having been used up by many previous trekkers. And lastly, cooking equipment if you're taking a stove.

The Trail starts at Km 88 on the Cuzco-Macchu Picchu railway line. You must take the ordinary train as this is the only one which stops at all stations along the way (the tourist train is non-stop from Cuzco to Macchu Picchu). There's no station as such at Km 88 but the train always stops there — just keep an eye on the kilometer signs as you go down the valley.

MACCHU PICCHU

Probably the most famous and spectacular archeological site in the entire Americas — and rightfully so. Its setting, on the saddle of a mountain high above a U-bend in the Urubamba River against a backdrop of 6000 metres plus mountains, is superb. Few experiences anywhere in the world are comparable. If you're coming off the Inca Trail, the sight which greets you at Intipunku — especially in the very early hours of the morning when there's no one about — is one you'll never forget. It's pure magic! And if there's anything to surpass this magic it can only be the walk up to, and the view from, Winay Picchu (Huayna Picchu) — the mountain which overlooks Macchu Picchu and has yet more Inca ruins and terraces.

Naturally, being the magnet which it is, the site is overrun with well-heeled tourists from all over the world at certain times of the year but as the vast majority only come for the day on the tourist train from Cuzco you can avoid the onslaught by exploring the site from dawn till around 10.30 am and from around 3 pm till 6 pm, retiring to the quiet of Winay Picchu during the intervening period. The only way to make it during the early morning is to approach the site from the Inca Trail (if you sleep at Winay Wayna the previous evening, it's a 1½ to 2 hour walk to Macchu Picchu so you must be on your way by dawn) or to stay at Aguas Calientes, about a km or two down the railway track from Macchu Picchu station, and walk to the site from there after dawn (up to two hour's walk). If you are coming up from Aguas Calientes early in the morning there's a possibility of a lift up to the site from Macchu Picchu railway station with the workers. During the rest of the day mini-buses meet both the Tourist and ordinary trains and take you to the site via the switchback "Hiram Bingham Highway" for an outrageous 140 soles, one way. The alternative is

to walk up the old Inca Trail to the site — a stiff 1½ hour climb but only half hour or less coming down.

Entry to the site costs 650 soles (valid for two days) or 100 soles with a Student Card (valid one day). Baggage can be left securely and free of charge at the ticket gate. If you come onto the site from the Inca Trail before 8.30 am you get in free (as there's no-one on the gates) but you have a problem about where to stash your baggage whilst you explore the site. Some people stash them in the overgrown terraces. If you do this keep a periodic eye on them.

There is an expensive Tourist Hotel just outside the site whose restaurant is open to non-residents. The waiters can be pretty off-hand with backpackers though part of the reason for this may be that they are over-worked. Maybe. There's also a soft drinks hut across the road.

Macchu Picchu was discovered as recently as 1911 by the North American explorer, Hiram Bingham, and his two books are well worth reading for background information. They are: *Lost City of the Incas: The Story of Macchu Picchu and its Builders* (New York 1948) and *Across South America* (New York, Houghton Mifflin, 1911). It's also a good idea to visit the Archeological Museum in Lima on your way through Peru as there are some excellent scale models of Macchu Picchu, Winay Wayna and Pisac in there. If you've seen the, orientation is much easier when you get there.

Budget accommodation in the area for people who want to stay overnight or for a few days is at Aguas Calientes, down the railway from Macchu Picchu station. (There's no road so you have to walk alongside the track).

AGUAS CALIENTES
Accommodation
Hostal Municipal is about 100 metres back from the tracks. Green house, 100 soles/single; 200 soles/double.

Hostal Caminantes is the first one you come across and right on the tracks. 120 soles/single; 240 soles/double. Clean, warm beds.

Hospedaje Macchu Picchu; 120 soles/ dormitory; 150 soles in a room with four beds; 300 soles/double. Clean sheets on beds. Cold water and the toilets work!

The accommodation fills up quickly in the early afternoon leaving only the most expensive *Hospedaje Macchu Picchu* with vacancies by the evening.

Eats Plenty of small caffs by the tracks. All pretty funky. In some the service is atrocious; in others it's just overloaded but they do try. One of the best and friendliest is the *Cafe El Carrilano* though where you eat will probably depend on who you meet. Local tiendas stock coca leaves and a limited range of basic necessities.

Other The village is noted for its thermal springs. They're set well back from the tracks and you need to ask directions from the local people. Entry fee of 10 soles.

Note that the last train back to Cuzco (local train) officially comes through Macchu Picchu station about 3.30 pm but it's invariably late by anything up to two hours. You can also board it at Aguas Calientes.

HUANCAYO
Famous for its enormous Sunday market and generally the first town which travellers stop at in the mountains above Lima. It's cold at night so have warm clothes handy.

Accommodation
Hotel Santo Domingo at Ica No. 675. Quiet, friendly place with pleasant court yard — 150 soles/single; 200 soles/double. The beds are uncomfortable if there are two of you but hot water most of the time.

Hotel Roma at Loreto No. 447. Another friendly place but no showers, either hot or cold. Comfortable beds, clean sheets — 150 soles /single; 300 soles/double.

Hotel Real on Calle Real (the main street) — 250 soles/double without bath; 300 soles/double with bath. Quiet place, friendly, large rooms and hot water.

Hotel Ferrocarril on Giraldez just down from the railway station — 300 soles/ double. Clean, quiet, tepid water. Popular with travellers who have come by rail from Lima.

Hotel/Restaurant Huancay on Calle Giraldez, next to the Ferrocarril. 150 soles/single; 300 soles/double — no double beds.

Hotel Prince see map for location — 270 soles/single; 492 soles/double; 660 soles/triple all with private bath. Without private bath rooms are 40 soles less. Hot water, modern hotel.

Hotel Regent on Lima — see map — 365 soles/single; 730 soles/double both with private bath. New, hot water, private telephone, etc. For the slightly better heeled.

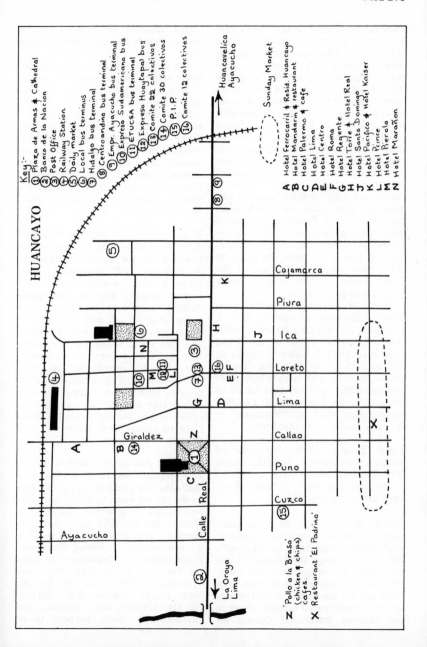

HUANCAYO

Key:-
① Plaza de Armas ✦ Cathedral
② Banco de la Nacion
③ Post Office
④ Railway Station
⑤ Daily market
⑥ Local bus terminus
⑦ Hidalgo bus terminal
⑧ Centro andino bus terminal
⑨ Empr. Ayacucho bus terminal
⑩ Expreso Sudamericano bus
⑪ ETUCSA bus terminal
⑫ Expreso Huaytapal bus
⑬ Comite 22 colectivos
⑭ Comite 30 colectivos
⑮ P.I.P.
⑯ Comite 12 colectivos

A   Hotel Ferrocarril ✦ Resid. Huancayo
B   Hotel Mandarin ✦ restaurant
C   Hotel Palermo ✦ cafe
D   Hotel Lima
E   Hotel Centro
F   Hotel Roma
G   Hotel Regente
H   Hotel Torre ✦ Hotel Real
J   Hotel Santo Domingo
K   Hotel Pacifico ✦ Hotel Kaiser
L   Hotel Prince
M   Hotel Pierola
N   Hotel Marañon

N   'Pollo a la Brasa' (chicken ✦ chips) cafes.
X   Restaurant 'El Padrino'

Eats Plenty of chicken and chips (pollo à la brasa con papas) on the Giraldez side of the Plaza de Armas. Popular with travellers. All about the same price — quarter chicken and chips for 85-100 soles. Coffee with milk is 25 soles. Tostados from 50 soles — depends what you want on them. Excellent little cafe next to the Hotel Prince. Serves lunchtime "businessmen's" meal for 100 soles: 3 courses plus an alcoholic maize beer and fruit punch. In the Sunday market area make for "El Padrino" which does the best food (pollo al horno con puré (mashed potatoes and plantain) plus salad for 70-75 soles) and often has a Peruvian harp player who plays all afternoon. He's an excellent musician — no charge, but you can tip him if he turns you on as he does most people. Also plays at the Hotel Turista in the evenings where you have to pay to get in.

Bars are nothing to write home about — the usual, all men, no women, juke box, etc, but they do sell a particularly fine beer, if you're into strong dark beer which is called "Extracto de Malto Backus" or "Cerveza Negra". Costs 85 soles and is therefore more expensive than ordinary beer for about 50 soles/bottle. It's similar to a slightly more bitter stout eg "Mackeson" — if you're familiar with that brew.

Other Tourist Office: top floor of Banco Internacional building, Calle Real. Friendly, but no maps.

Bicycles for hire: Turismo Huancayo Ltd., Calle Real 356.

Sunday Market Some beautiful craftwork — woven ponchos, blankets, wall hangings, bags, belts, carved gourds, etc but few things are "cheap". There are quite a few gringos and many tourists who come up for the day from Lima just for the market so stall owners are very unwilling to bargain. Prices in the Mexican market of Oaxaca for woven blankets are cheaper but, of course, there's no such thing as alpaca there.

It's possible you might find bargains in the nearby villages/towns of Hualhuas (woven alpaca goods), San Jeronimo (silverware) and Jauja (markets on Wednesdays and Sundays). Hualhuas is a particularly fine place — beautiful Indian village where nothing happens except llama and alpaca herding and weaving. It's a 15 minute bus ride from Huacayo, costs 20 soles there and 15 back! Buses from the Plaza Inmaculada — marked "local bus terminus" on the town plan.

If you wander off into the back-roads down the bottom end of town (in the direction of the Sunday Market and further) you will occasionally come across a local wedding where they'll make you really welcome. Live bands, dancing, maize beer (chicha), etc. Have a few 10 or 50 sole notes handy as it's the custom to stick them on the branch of a tree which is brought round from time to time to keep chicha flowing. Very friendly people but go home before sun-set if you have valuables on you otherwise you might get mugged — take this with as many pinches of salt as you like but it was the advice given by several local people who were present.

Transport Few of the colectivo services have regular cars to Ayacucho so if that's the way you want to go, you have to do the leg-work to round up sufficient people — otherwise it's the bus. Hidalgo and ETUCSA have the better buses to Ayacucho but they're often booked up days in advance. Plan ahead. Centroandino use beaten-up old buses for this run which they over-crowd excessively. "Full" on the booking form means nothing. They literally fill the corridor with anybody and anything else which happens to be around at departure time and pick up even more on the way. It's a wonder they ever get to their destination given the condition of the roads, but somehow they do. All the buses take about 14 hours in the dry season but can take up to 36 hours in the wet season.

HUARÁZ
Accommodation

Alojamiento Tabariz on Avenida Raymundi, one block from the Empresa Huaraz bus terminal — 150 soles/ single; 250 soles/double.

San Isidro costs 125 soles/single — friendly place.

Hotel Barcelona is a new hotel on Avenida Raymundi No. 612. 450 soles/double with private shower.

Hotel Residencial Raymundi at Avenida Raymundi No. 820 has similar prices to the Barcelona.

Pension Janett at Avenida Centenario No. 106 costs 150 soles/single; 250 soles/double.

Pensión Mi Casa on the corner of Palmita and Independencia — similar prices to the Janett.

Other Tourist Office was at Jirón Centenario No. 113 *but* may have moved to Pomabamba No. 415.

Things to Do/See Situated in one of the most spectacular mountain areas of Peru — the Callejon de Huaylas — and overshadowed by some of the highest mountains in South America including Huascarán which, at 6772 metres, is second only in height to Aconacagua in Argentina. Many Archaeological sites dating back to the Chavín culture and before; excellent hiking country; spectacular, hair-raising road journeys down to the coast and east to Huánuco. Many of the towns were devastated by the 1970 earthquake though reconstruction has been underway for several years. Many of the roads however, are still pretty rough.

The ruins of Wilkawain are a two hour walk into the mountains from the centre of town — well signposted. They date back to 1000 AD. You need to take a flashlamp with you. Colectivos are also possible as there's a road to the site but they're expensive and you need to get a group together.

EXCURSIONS IN THE VALLEY

Chavín de Huantar Site of the ruins of the Chavín culture dating back 2500 years. Carved stone heads and other relief carvings. There used to be seven different underground levels to explore but the 1970 earthquake closed down all but two. Guides are available, bring a torch.

Direct bus to Chavín from Huaráz on Tuesday, Thursday and Sunday (returns: Monday, Wednesday and Friday) by Empresa Huascaran. Takes six or seven hours. Otherwise, take a local bus or truck to Recuay (cheap hotel: *Hotel Santa Fe* 100 soles/single) and then on to Catac. From there trucks leave for Chavín in the early morning and late evening. In Chavín village accommodation at *Hotel El Condor, Hotel Inca* and *Hotel Gantu* — all about 150 soles/single and very basic.

Trekking over the mountains From Yungay via Lake Llanganuco and the Huascaran National Park to Piscobamba. Three to four day hike over a well-travelled route. You need to take sufficient food, a tent, sleeping bag and cooking equipment. Information on this trail from the National Park office in Huaráz at Avenida Centenario No. 912. If you're coming up from Lima information about this area can also be obtained from Cesar Morales Arnao, Hernando de Soto No. 250, Urb Salamanca, Lima 3. Tel 351746.

Basic accommodation and food in Piscobamba and transport north to Huallanca and south to Chavín. Roads

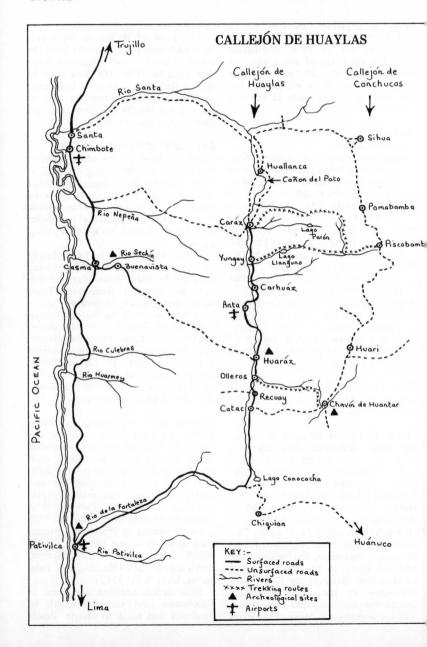

CALLEJÓN DE HUAYLAS

KEY:-
— Surfaced roads
- - - Unsurfaced roads
∼∼ Rivers
×××× Trekking routes
▲ Archeological sites
✝ Airports

are pretty rough.

Another trek is possible through the mountains (again, over a well-travelled path) from Olleros and Chavín de Huantas. Olleros is situated between Huaráz and Recuay. Enquire at the National Park office in Huaráz. The trek takes three to four days. As with the Yungay-Piscobamba trek you need a tent, cooking equipment and your own food.

Pre-Chavín ruins at Sechin near Casma If you're coming up to Huaráz from Casma on the Trujillo-Lima coast road it's worth stopping off in Casma for the day to visit the ruins which are some of the oldest monuments in South America and date back to around 1500 BC. They're situated about 7 km from Casma and it's possible to walk there — the route is well-sign-posted. Otherwise take a colectivo going to Buenavista and get off at the branch road to the site (2 km from here). The site is open from 8 am-5 pm and costs 50 soles entry. Excavation and reconstruction work was going on here up to a few years ago but the project ran out of money and little has been done since then.

Lake Paron Nestled under the snow-capped peak of Huandoy. Beautiful scenery and popular as a resort area with local people. Transport difficult at other times. Enquire in Caraz.

Caraz is a good town for relaxing in and enjoying the mountain scenery. Like all the towns and villages in this valley, it was hit by the 1970 earthquake. Places to stay there include *Hotel Caraz* (half a block from the Plaza and costing 100 soles/single; 150 soles/double. Cold water); *Hotel Herrera* (two blocks from the Plaza: 75 soles/single. Very basic), *La Suiza Peruana* (150 soles/single, hot water, the best hotel there is in town).

ICA
Centre of Peru's wine-making area and the origin of the famous "Pisco" brandy. Pleasant town with a good archaeological museum which provides maps of all ancient sites in the Department.

Accommodation
Budget hotels include *Pensión Campos; Bolívar; Imperial* and *Borjas*. If you want something a little better try the *Colon* (400 soles/double. Restaurant serves three course meals for 120 soles).

Other Tourist office is Jr Cajamarca No. 179.

IQUITOS
Capital of Peruvian Amazonia and completely cut off by land from the rest of the country. Access is by plane (Fawcett and Aeroperu) or riverboat from Yurimagua or Moyobamba on the River Marañon or Pucallpa on the River Ucayali. Like Manaos in Brazil, Iquitos took part in the rubber boom at the beginning of the century and then went into a long decline when the bottom fell out of the market. Prosperity returned (for some) when oil was discovered. It's now a fairly modern town with paved streets and plenty of cars. It's also Peru's most expensive town.

Accommodation The two cheapest hotels in town are the *Residencial Internacional* and the *Hotel Residencial*, both on Calle Lima and costing US$2/single without private bath — basic. *Hotel Anita* has rooms for US$2.50/person with shower. Also recommended are the *Peru* — US$2/person in room with shower and balcony — and the *Lima* — US$4/double with shower. Good value.

Eats *Marisco Chic* serves excellent fish. *Chifa Central* serves good Chinese good as does the *Wung Cha* on the corner of San Martín and Arica. Plenty of fruit, especially pineapples, in the market. Situated at the end of the Malecón on the waterfront.

Rivertrips Anything connected with organised tourism is extortionately expensive so if you're thinking of travelling either up- or down-river you will need to suss out your own riverboat. Plenty of smaller boats going up-river to Yurimaguas, Moyobamba and Pucallpa and down-river to Yurimaguas, Moyobamba and Pucallpa and down-river to Leticia (Colombia), Benjamin Constant (Brazil) and Manaos (Brazil) but no fixed schedules. Most of the traffic goes to and from Pucallpa from where there are direct buses to Lima. For boats along this part of the Ucayali enquire down by the Wharf and also check with the Jefe de la Marina (Calle Sargento Lores), Meneses (Jirón Lima), Bellavista (Malecón Tarapaca No. 596), Hurtado (Avenida Grau No. 1223) and Casa Pinto (Sargento Lores No. 164).

The trip between Pucallpa and Iquitos takes four to seven days. Costs between 800 and 1000 soles including poor food cooked in river water. If at all possible, cook your own food. Many people come down with intestinal infections on this trip. Take your own hammock (or pay extra for a cabin with berth) and plenty of insect repellant! Excellent jungle scenery and Indian villages. (NB Pucallpa is as expensive as Iquitos).

JULIACA

A market town 44 km from Puno on Lake Titicaca. Also a railway junction between Cuzco, Puno and Arequipa.

Accommodation
Hotel Benique is opposite the railway station — 150 soles/single. Basic. *Hotel Barreros* is also opposite the rail-

way station — US$4/double, more comfortable than the Benique.

Also recommended are the *Hotel Arce* (US$4/double, clean but cold water only); *Gran Hotel* (120 soles/single. cold water); *Alojamiento Vulvón* (80 soles/single, cold water and very basic).

Market Sunday and Monday. One of the largest markets you'll ever see. Every conceivable thing is sold here but much of the market is taken up with alpaca knitted and woven goods and hides. Bargains possible but prices are little different from those in Puno.

LIMA
Capital of the Republic and an enormous sprawling metropolis but with a compact centre containing many beautiful old colonial buildings including the Cathedral, the Church and Convent of San Francisco, the Palace of Torre Tagle and the former headquarters of the Inquisition. Plenty of interesting places to see, museums to visit, street markets, cafes, displays of folk dancing and culture from the various regions. From June to October a thick sea mist hangs over the city almost continually making the weather cool and damp. You may need warm clothes in the evenings during this period.

Accommodation
Hotel Europa at Jirón Ancash No. 376. The most popular of the gringo hotels and often full as a result — though not the pleasantest of budget hotels you could find. 270 soles/single; 370 soles/double bed for 2 people; 440 soles/2 beds; 660 soles/triple. Free notice board. If you met someone in the Gran Casino in Quito the chances are you'll meet them here too.
Hotel Richmond at Jirón Unión No. 706. Probably the pleasantest of the gringo budget hotels. 224 soles/

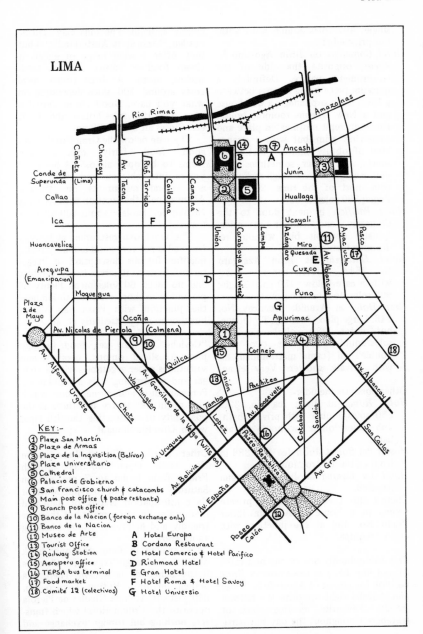

LIMA

KEY:-
1. Plaza San Martín
2. Plaza de Armas
3. Plaza de la Inquisition (Bolívar)
4. Plaza Universitario
5. Cathedral
6. Palacio de Gobierno
7. San Francisco church & catacombs
8. Main post office (& poste restante)
9. Branch post office
10. Banco de la Nacion (foreign exchange only)
11. Banco de la Nacion
12. Museo de Arte
13. Tourist Office
14. Railway Station
15. Aeroperu office
16. TEPSA bus terminal
17. Food market
18. Comité 12 (colectivos)

A. Hotel Europa
B. Cordano Restaurant
C. Hotel Comercio & Hotel Pacifico
D. Richmond Hotel
E. Gran Hotel
F. Hotel Roma & Hotel Savoy
G. Hotel Universio

single; 407 soles/double both without private bath.

Hotel Comercio on Jirón Agostino N. Wiese, opposite the side of the Government palace. Definitely a museum piece being a cross between a Dickensian orphanage, a warehouse and a New Orleans rooming house. Huge, decrepit moth-eaten place and somewhat grim but with a strange kind of obtuse charm. Quiet, clean sheets, hot water sometimes — if you can find it — though reckon on cold most of the time. 204 soles/single; 390 soles/double.

Hotel Pacifico is next door to the Comercio and similar in price. Equally decrepit but without redeeming features.

Hotel Universio at Jirón Azangaro No. 754A. Modern concrete hotel with a cafe below. 450 soles/single; 900 soles/double with private shower.

Gran Hotel at Avenida Abancay No. 546. Large place, friendly, TV lounge, hot water. 330 soles/single; 660 soles/double; 605 for two with double bed (cama matrimonial) all with private shower. Very clean.

Other possibles include:-

Hotel Roma at Jirón Ica No. 326. 550 soles/double with private bath; 495 soles/double without private bath.

Hostal del Sol at Jirón Ica No. 388 in front of the Teatro Municipal.

Hotel La Casona at Jirón Moquegua No. 289.

There's also the possibility of private rooms in a house at Avenida Javier Prado No. 456 at the junction with Jirón Arequipa.

Eats Undoubtedly one of the best cafes (if not *the* best) is the *Cordano Hnos Cafe* on the corner of Agostino N. Wiese and Ancahs right opposite the railway station. Favourite meeting place of travellers throughout the day but particularly at night. The bills may well be headed, "Ano de la Austeridad"(!!) but they offer a wide range of excellent cheap food — salads, snacks, sandwiches, meals. A three course meal costs around 100 soles depending on what you have. Good cheap Peruvian wine for 120 soles/bottle and beer, etc. Closes around 10.30 pm.

The cafe below the Gran Hotel serves good food fairly cheaply and seems to be open almost 24 hours. If you're into chicken and chips there are several restaurants on Avenida Abancay near the junction with Avenida Nicolas de Pierola — about 100 soles for a meal.

The vegetarian restaurant at Ucayali No. 133 is not very good and only really qualifies for the description of "vegetarian" because it serves two vegetables and no meat. 60 soles/meal. Plenty of pie and cake shops on Jirón Unión near the junction with Plaza San Martín but they're not particularly cheap.

"Ceviche" — raw sea food (usually prawns), sliced onions, peppers and sometimes other vegetables with a vinegar and oil dressing — is a well-known Peruvian dish and perhaps one which you might like to try but there is the possibility of contracting the fish tapeworm. Give it a thought.

Other Tourist Office at Jirón Unión No. 1066. Open Monday through Friday from 9 am to 7 pm and on Saturdays from 9 am to 1 pm. Much of their information is out of date and inaccurate. Short on maps but they are friendly and helpful if you're planning an itinerary.

As elsewhere in Peru, the only bank which will change Travellers' Cheques is the Banco de la Nación. There is a branch on Jirón Rufino Torrico No. 830 just off Avenida Nicolas de Pierola opposite the Crillon Hotel which transacts nothing but foreign exchange and gives 154.70 soles = US$1 for cheques. Often crowded at certain times of the day. There's also a branch on Avenida Abancay opposite the Gran Hotel if you're staying in that area.

The best street rates are to be found in Lima (blackmarket so cash only). Jirón Unión is the centre of this activity. Just wander up and down the street looking like you have no particular place to go and you'll be approached by several people in no time at all. It's pretty safe and all sorts of people from retired Swiss residents to local professional people will approach you. (I was actually taken back to one accountant's house and served drinks in the process!). The rate depends on how much you change and varies from 170-175 soles = US$1.

American Express: Jirón Ocona No. 160 down the side of the Hotel Gran Bolívar. If you've had your cheques ripped off they replace immediately without fuss and even with no passport (a friend had both stolen). Complicated forms to fill in but same-day replacement.

Camera repairs: reasonable rates for this kind of work with Sr Pedro Franco, Jirón Pachira No. 240 and with Frank Burdin, Jirón Lampa No. 1115.

Post Office: Poste Restante is pretty good — they hand you the pile and you find your own. Excellent selection of post-cards in the arcade. Cost 15 soles each with discount if you buy over 10.

Guide Book: Maybe worth getting hold of a copy if you're going to be spending a lot of time in the country. *Guide to Peru — Handbook for Travellers*, 3rd edition, Reparaz. In English, Spanish or French. Costs 280 soles. On sale at the Museo de Arte and at bookshops on Colmena (Nicolas de Pierola).

Buses to airport: From junction of Avendia Nicolas de Pierola and Plaza San Martin (Hotel Gran Bolivar side).

Taxis cost 400-600 soles/car. Public transport doesn't start up until about 6 am. If you're going on Fawcett airlines they'll collect you from your hotel in the early hours of the morning and take you to the airport on their own bus for 250 soles. During the rest of the day you can pick this bus up at their office.

Embassies:
Australia: Natalio Sanchez No. 220, 6th floor. Tel: 288315.
Bolivia: Avenida Orrantia No. 145, San Isidro suburb. Tel: 228231.
Brazil: Cmdt. Espinar No. 815, Miraflores suburb. Tel: 462635.
Canada: Libertad No. 130, Miraflores suburb. Tel 460935.
Chile: Avenida Javier Prado Oeste No. 790, San Isidro suburb. Tel: 407965.
Ecuador: Las Palmeras 356, San Isidro suburb. Tel; 228138.
France: Plaza Francia 234. Tel; 238618.
Eire: Carlos Porres Osores No. 410. San Isidor suburb. Tel: The leprechauns took it.
Japan: Avenida San Felipe No. 356. Jesús Maria suburb. Tel: 614041.
New Zealand: Avenida Salaverry No. 3006. San Isidro suburb. Tel: 621890.
Netherlands: Las Camelias No. 780, San Isidro suburb. Tel: 402855.
UK: Natalio Sanchez No. 125, 12th floor. Lima. Tel: 233830.
USA: Garcilaso de la Bega No. 1400, Lima. Tel 286000.
West Germany: Avenida Arequipa No. 4202, Miraflores suburb. Tel: 459997.

Bus Terminals
TEPSA: Paseo de la Republica near junction with Avenida Roosevelt. (Coastal routes only and international routes.)
Hidalgo: Avenida Bausate y Meza 1535.
Arequipa Express: Nicholas de Pierola

1249. (Arequipa and Southern Peru).

Expreso Cajamarca: Nicholas de Pierola 1163 (Trujillo, Chiclayo, Cajamarca).

Morales Moralitos: Nicholas de Pierola 1147 (Southern Peru including coast and mountain areas).

Expreso Sudamericana: Nicholas de Perola 1153. (Coastal and mountain routes throughout Peru).

Carmen Alto de Ayacucho: Jr Garcia Naranjo No. 354-366, La Victoria suburb. (Southern coastal and mountain routes).

Comité 12: Jr Montevideo 736. Colectivos to Huancayo and possibly Ayacucho.

Comité 22: Jr Ayacucho 997. Same as above.

Expreso Internacional: Avenida Carlos Zavala 145 (Pisco, Cuzco, Arequipa, Tacna).

Expreso Turismo, Victoria: Avenida N. de Pierola 1219 (Arequipa, Cuzco, Puno, La Paz, Trujillo, Cajamarca, Chiclayo).

Airlines

Aeroperu office: Plaza San Martín.

Fawcett office: Hotel Bolívar, Plaza San Martín.

Neither airline offers student reductions any more except — so I was told at the office — on the Aeroperu flight from Chiclayo to Lima(?!).

Things to Do/See In the centre the *Cathedral* and the *Torre Tagle Palace* are both worth a visit. *The Palace of Inquisition* on the Plaza of the same name (also known as Bolívar on some maps) seems to be closed indefinitely check with the Tourist Office as it may have been opened up again.

Convento de San Francisco de Jesús, on Plaza San Francisco opposite the Europa Hotel is well worth a visit — historical and religious exhibits dating back to the Conquest and extensive catacombs containing thousands of skeletons. Guided tours approximately

every half hour throughout the day. Costs 50 soles or 20 soles with Student Card.

Museum of Anthropology and Archaeology, Avenida Sucre, off Avenida Brazil in Pueblo Libre suburb. Plenty of buses down Avenida Brazil (walk from there in three minutes) from Avenida Tacna, cost 12 soles, or a colectivo from the centre for about 120 soles/car. Excellent museum and one which doesn't overwhelm you with too many exhibits. It's a must if you're at all interested in the pre-Hispanic cultures of Peru. Some very good scale models of the Inca settlements at Pisac, Winay Wayna and Macchu Picchu. Orientating yourself on the actual sites is very much easier if you've seen these models on the way through Lima. Open till 6 pm every day except Monday. Costs 130 soles entry (no student reductions unless you're Peruvian!).

Gold Museum Meseo Miguel Mujica Gallo in Monterrico suburb. Bus No. 71 from Parque Universitario. Takes an hour. Gold artifacts of the pre-Hispanic cultures of Peru contained in an underground building.

Museo de Arte Paseo Colón just at the bottom of Paseo de la Republica. Excellent collection of pottery, weaving fragments, jewellery, mummies, etc and paintings from the Spanish period. Open 10 am-12 noon and 3 pm-7 pm every day except Monday. Costs 100 soles entry or 40 soles with a Student Card. In the foyer, there's a notice board with details of cultural activities eg folklore evening every Wednesday (dances, music and costumes from the various regions of Peru) costs 80 soles, two hour show.

Museum of Natural History Avenida Arenales No. 1200. Bus No. 54A from Avenida Tacna or take a colectivo or taxi. Birds, butterflies, mammals, shells and plants from the various parts of Peru. Open 8 am-6 pm every day except in the afternoons on Saturdays and Sundays. Admission 30 soles — double that on Sundays.

Campo de Marte Plaza Jorge Chavéz and Avenida Salaverry — check out with the Tourist Office whether there are any folklore concerts being put on here. If there are, go and see them (dancing, music, costumes). Costs 100 soles entry (no student reductions).

Street Markets Probably one of the best is the daily market all the way along both sides of Avenida Nicholas de Pierola from the Plaza San Martín to Avenida Tacna. Everything from carved gourds to mantas, old coins, tarantulas, butterfly collections, pottery. Some real bargains to be found if you hunt around and especially if you have something to swop which they're interested in. Another good market on Sundays all along Avenida Abancay and spilling into Avenida Cuzco though this is more of a household domestics market but if you're into herbs, books or clothes it's well worth a visit.

Other Information South American Explorers Club at Avenida Portugal 146 (between Avenida Bolivia and Avenida España three blocks from Avenida Alfonso Ugarte). Tel: 314480; Meeting place for explorers which also puts out the magazine *South American Explorer* — an excellent publication containing articles, letters and news from all over South America. Highly recommended especially as a source of information and help if you're planning on going off the beaten track. Membership costs US$25 per annum which includes four issues of the magazine (published quarterly) or you can get the magazine for US$10 plus US$3 airmail postage (Postage address; Casilla 3714, Lima 100, Peru.)

NAZCA
Accommodation
Hotel Royal US$1.30/single, basic.

Hotel Central US$1/single, even more basic.

Hotel Oropezca is one block from the Plaza de Armas, friendly, US$1/single.

Hotel Roman on the Plaza de Armas — US$1/single, similar to the Oropezca.

Things to Do/See The big attraction here is, of course, the famous Nazca lines — huge figures, lines and geometric patterns cut into the stony desert, some of them miles long. They were carved by the Nazca people who reached the height of their civilization around 800 AD and are thought by the less eccentric to be a pre-Inca calendar, by the more eccentric of the van Daniken ilk to be a landing spot for extra-terrestrial beings. They can only be fully appreciated from the air — flights available from the local airport (cost about US$25 for half hour flight).

Visiting the Lines: Book flight from Hotel Monte Carlo. If you can't afford the flight the next best thing is to get a local bus to the site 22 km from town (twice a day, 40 soles) and see the lines from the tower which was built there in the mid-1970s.

There's a small museum just off the Plaza de Armas which is given over to the Nazca civilization. Also the Nazca valley is full of other ruins from this civilization including aqueducts which are still in use today!

PISCO
Centre of Peru's grape growing area and source of the (in)famous Pisco spirits — the local hard stuff. The town retains its colonial atmosphere.

Accommodation
Hotel Jorge Chavéz is probably the cheapest in town — cold showers and try to get a room with window.
Others include: *Humberto, Pisco* and *Grau.*

PUERTO MALDONADO

Amazonian port on the Rio Madre de Dios which flows north-east into Bolivia via Riberalta and Guayaremerin and then becomes the Rio Madeira which continues on through Brazil via Pôrto Velho. Riverboats possible all the way to Manaus.

Accommodation A number of very basic hotels in wooden houses for an average price of 100 soles/single. Most provide mosquito nets over the beds — you need them! If you've been travelling up-river from Bolivia and fancy a touch of comfort after all those nights on deck being bitten into insomnia by mosquitos go to the *Tourist Hotel*. This costs US$9.50/double and about US$1 less for a single. All rooms have their own shower and toilet — clean as you might expect for that price.

PUNO

The main town on Lake Titicaca and the rail head for Cuzco and Arequipa. It's a pleasant town but gets very cold at night (and isn't that warm during the day if it's cloudy) so have warm clothing with you. Few of the budget hotels have any form of heating in the rooms.

Accommodation

Hotel Colón on Calle Tacna. 130 soles/single; 100 soles each/cama matrimonial; 100 soles each/triple; 80 soles each/quadruple. The rooms facing the street are the best; the others round the back of the courtyard are pretty dingy. Toilets frequently unbearable; hot water sometimes for an extra 10 soles. Cafe attached but food more expensive than in the cafes on the street. A few fleas but popular place for travellers.

Hostal Torrino at Calle Libertad 126 costs 175 soles each/two beds; 150 soles each/3 beds; 118 soles each/4 beds.

Hotel Tacna at Calle Tacna 261 — dormitory for 80 soles/bed; 250 soles/double.

Hotel Venezia at Calle Tacna 255 costs 245 soles/double. No singles.

Hotel Roma at Calle Libertad 115 costs 240 soles/double, no singles.

Hotel Colonial at Calle Lima 245, 250 soles/double; 150 soles/single — no hot water.

Hotel Extra costs 200 soles/bed in rooms with up to 4 beds.

Hotel Turistas is opposite the Post Office. 700 soles/single without own bathroom; 940 soles/double. 970 soles/single with own bathroom; 1300 soles/double. Your usual carpeted tourist hotel but like other cheap hotels it was cold in there though perhaps the rooms have heating.

Eats Excellent meals at *La Isla* restaurant on Alfonso Ugarte. Trout for 85-90 soles; avocado salads for 40-50 soles; tortilla de verduras (vegetable omlette) for 40 soles. Beer and wine, etc and popular with travellers. A few greasy chicken and chip places on Calle Tacna opposite the Hotel Colon (quarter chicken and chips for around 100 soles). Somewhat more expensive cafes on Calle Libertad — good for coffee and cakes in the evenings especially if you're looking for warm places.

Other Tourist Office: Calle Duestua 342. Maps of Puno and details of how to get to the floating islands of Uros and the ruins at Tihuancaco just over the border in Bolivia. Otherwise they haven't got much.

PIP Office (in case you get anything ripped off on the Arequipa-Puno train — a favourite with rip-off merchants) is at Calle Libertad 168.

Poste Restante: Friendly little office. They give you the whole pile and let

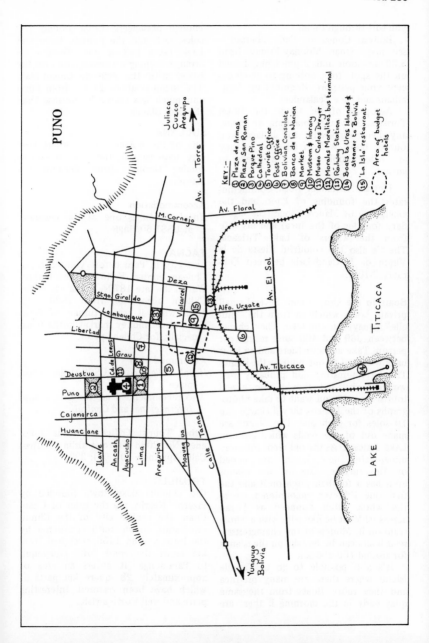

PUNO

KEY :-
1 Plaza de Armas
2 Plaza San Roman
3 Parque Pino
4 Cathedral
5 Tourist Office
6 Post Office
7 Bolivian Consulate
8 Banco de la Nacion
9 Market
10 Museum ✝ library
11 Museo Carlos Dreyer
12 Morales Moralitos bus terminal
13 Railway Station
14 Boats to Uros Islands ✝ Steamer to Bolivia
15 'La Isla' restaurant.
⸜⸝ Area of budget hotels

you sort through them.

Bolivian Consulate: Calle Libertad — see map. Open Monday-Friday from 8.30 am-noon and 2 pm-4 pm. Issued on the spot, free, nothing to show except your passport. Required by Australians and New Zealanders.

Aeroperu office: inside the Hotel Turistas. If you're planning on flying anywhere especially to Juliaca and Cuzco, book well in advance as they are often booked up 1-2 weeks in advance.

Fiestas: November 4-5th. Commemorates the founding of Puno and the emergence of Manco Capac (the legendary founder of the Inca) and his wife from the waters of Lake Titicaca. There's also the colourful Fiesta de la Virgin de la Candelaria between February 2-10th.

Boats to the Uros Islands Several small private boats which go from the "muelle" (quay) on the lake. They charge between 360 and 400 soles return per person. Take an hour there and an hour back with half to one hour on the island. They're interesting and probably well worth a visit but they're also a real tourist trap. If you want to take photographs of the Indians they'll charge you 10 soles for each one. The islands are made out of the reeds which grow in Lake Titicaca. As the old reeds rot away under-water new layers are added on the surface. One of the islands even has a football pitch on it and the first one I'd ever encountered where the whole pitch bounced as I ran across it! Must be like jelly with a whole team on it. Models of the characteristic reed boats can be bought on the islands for around 150-200 soles.

It's also possible to go to Taquile Island where there are many pre-Inca and Inca ruins. Boats from the same quay early in the morning if there are enough passengers. Costs around 750 soles each and the journey there and back takes half a day. Possible to arrange sleeping accommodation on the island with the Jefe de Comunidad. The island is about 24 km from Puno and much less visited by tourists than the Uros islands.

SULLANA
One of the northern oases where you may have to stay the night if you're coming through from Ecuador via Macara.

Accommodation
Hotel Wilson is one of the cheapest at US$1.60/single.

TACNA
Last city in Peru before you reach the Chilean border. Following the Nitrate War in the late 1870s. Tacna was under Chilean occupation from 1880 until 1929 when it was returned to Peru. Good street money market in the town especially for Chilena pesos.

Accommodation
Hotel Callao costs US$2/single, good place.

Also recommended are the *Luz, Gruta, Internacional* and *Central.*

Other Tourist Office: Avenida Bolognesi No. 2088. Fawcett airlines office: Calle Apurimac 207. Tel: 3391.

TRUJILLO
Old colonial oasis town founded by Pizarro. Nearby are the ruins of Chan-Chan, the capital city of the Chimú civilization which, until conquered by the Incas around 1450, stretched 1000 km along the coast form Guayaquil to Paramonga. It covers an area of approximately 28 square km parts of which have been restored. Interesting place and well worth a visit.

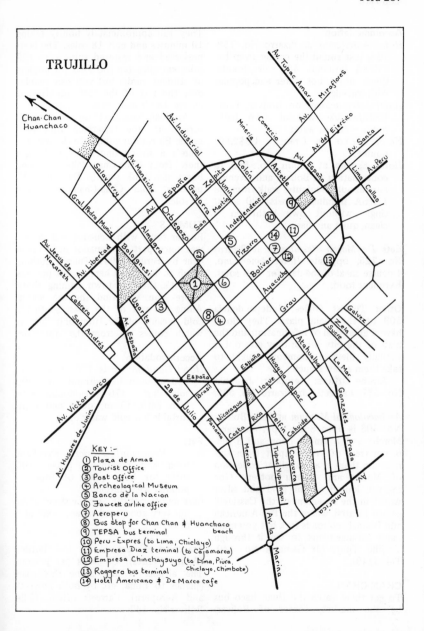

TRUJILLO

KEY:-
1. Plaza de Armas
2. Tourist Office
3. Post Office
4. Archeological Museum
5. Banco de la Nacion
6. Fawcett airline office
7. Aeroperu
8. Bus stop for Chan Chan & Huanchaco beach
9. TEPSA bus terminal
10. Peru-Expres (to Lima, Chiclayo)
11. Empresa Diaz terminal (to Cajamarca)
12. Empresa Chinchaysuyo (to Lima, Piura, Chiclayo, Chimbote)
13. Roggero bus terminal
14. Hotel Americano & De Marco cafe

Accommodation

Hotel Americano at Pizarro No. 758-768, just round the corner from the TEPSA terminal. 462 soles/double. Clean, quiet, hot water and popular with travellers.

Hotel Internacional on Bolivar. Costs US$3/double without own bathroom — no hot water.

Hotel Latino on Grau — US$2.80/double.

Hotel España at Unión No. 546 (a continuation of Bolívar and Avenida Peru about 10 minutes walk from the TEPSA terminal). Costs 190 soles/single without own bathroom — clean, quiet and basic.

Eats *De Marco Restaurant* at Pizarro No. 725, opposite *Hotel Americano*. 4-course meal-of-the-day for 140 soles. Excellent food.

Other Tourist Office: Independencia 509 on the main plaza. They don't have a great deal of information and the map of the city which they give out is virtually illegible. Someone ought to take them a new stencil.

Airline Offices: Aeroperu: Jr Junin No. 537. Fawcett: Jr Pizarro No. 532.

Archaeological Museum at Calle Bolívar No. 406 is open 8 am-1 pm (January-March) and 8 am-12 noon and 3 pm-6 pm (rest of year). Apart from this museum there is an excellent collection of Moche and Chimú pottery (the Spanish looted all the gold and silver work) in the basement of the Cassinelli garage located where the Pan-American and Huanchaco roads fork but you must make arrangements to see it through Trujillo Tours (Jr Gamarra No. 440. Tel: 3149).

CHAN-CHAN

To get there catch the Huanchaco bus by the market, corner of Bolívar. They run approximately hourly taking 10 minutes and cost 18 soles. The best-preserved and restored ruins cost 120 soles entrance fee (30 soles for holders of student cards) but you can wander over the rest of the vast ruin free of charge. Don't miss them.

At Huanchaco itself there is a superb surf beach and fishermen with reed boats. Be careful going into the water — there's a strong undercurrent. To get there from Chan-Chan take the same bus which took you to the ruins, 15 minutes from Chan-Chan and costs 22 soles.

TUMBES

Border town with Ecuador and in fact was once part of Ecuador until taken over by Peru in 1941. There's nothing much to keep you here except perhaps that it's the last town coming south where you will find the sea warm. Along the rest of the coast south it's cold because of the Humboldt Current which comes up from the Antarctic.

Accommodation

Hotel Gandolfo costs 190 soles/single; 360 soles/double without bath. 290 soles/single; 470 soles/double with own bath. Clean, quiet and comfortable but cold water only.

Eats

Hotel Restaurant Florian. Excellent food and reasonable prices. 100 soles for large plate of food — popular with travellers.

Cafe and tienda ("F" on the street plan) has very good sandwiches, cakes and desserts.

Transport Colectivo to the border (Aguas Verdes): 85 soles per person. The airport is also along this road (planes to Lima, etc by both Fawcett and Aeroperu). Fawcett office: Calle Bolívar No. 147.

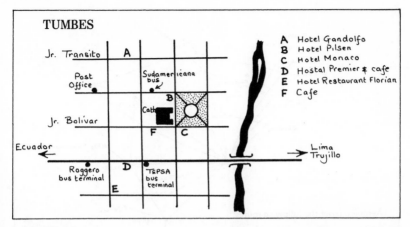

TUMBES

A Hotel Gandolfo
B Hotel Pilsen
C Hotel Monaco
D Hostal Premier & cafe
E Hotel Restaurant Florian
F Cafe

Jr. Transito

Post Office

Sudamericana bus

Cath

Jr. Bolivar

Ecuador

Lima Trujillo

Raggero bus terminal

TEPSA bus terminal

TRANSPORT

Note on Internal Flights As with other Andean countries, internal flights are relatively cheap (two to three time the price of the equivalent bus fare) and so well worth considering if your time is limited, the road is particularly rough, or you've had enough for the time being of 18-hour plus bus journeys over boulder strewn river beds. When the two airlines fly the same routes, their prices are the same and, except on major routes, they generally share the days of the week between them. There's a 9% government tax on all airline tickets bought in Peru whether for international or internal flights.

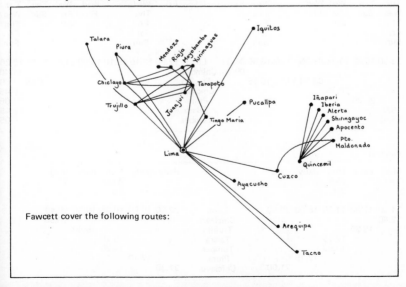

Fawcett cover the following routes:

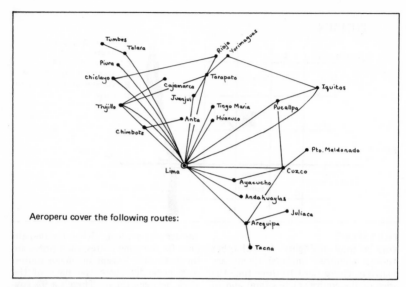

Aeroperu cover the following routes:

The Coastal Route — Flights:

Aeroperu

Mon Tue Wed Thu Fri Sun	Tue Thu Sun	Mon Wed Fri Sat	Mon Wed Fri	Mon	Mon Wed Thu Fri Sat Sun	Tue Fri		Mon Fri	Tue Wed Thu Fri Sat Sun	Mon	Mon Wed Fri Sat	Mon Wed Fri	Tue Thu Sun	Mon Tue Wed Thu Fri Sun
13.30	19.05	19.15	07.00	17.00	16.00	08.30	Lima	12.50	18.10	19.10	12.30	21.45	22.35	18.20
						09.40	Chimbote							11.40
			08.30	17.55	16.55		Trujillo					17.15	18.15	11.00
		20.15					Chiclayo							20.45
	20.35						Piura							21.05
15.00							Talara							16.45
15.45							Tumbes							16.05

Fawcett

Mon Thu	daily	Mon Wed Sat	daily	daily		daily	daily	Mon Wed Sat	daily	Mon Thu
11.30	17.30	11.30	16.00	20.00	Lima	22.30	19.00	16.35	19.30	19.40
12.40					Chiclayo					18.30
	18.20				Trujillo				18.40	
		12.55			Talara			15.10		
		13.50			Tumbes			14.20		
			17.15		Piura		17.40			
				21.00	Chiclayo	21.30				

Aeroperu

Mon Wed Sat	Tues Thu Fri Sun		Tues Thu Fri Sun	Mon Wed Sat
12.35	12.35	Lima	17.30	17.30
13.55	13.55	Arequipa	16.15	15.40
14.45	—	Tacna	—	15.10

Fawcett

daily	daily		daily	daily
12.50	11.00	Lima	15.30	14.50
13.50	—	Arequipa	14.30	—
—	12.30	Tacna	—	13.10

Buses and Colectivos

Most of the bus companies covering this route stop at all the major towns en route. You can book to any of them and get off where you want. This also applies if you want to get on at any point — just flag a bus down and pay the driver's mate.

Ecuador/Peru border (Aguas Verdes)-Tumbes. Colectivo costs 85 soles per person and takes half an hour. Very few local buses go to the border.

Tumbes-Trujillo-Lima (and vice versa).

TEPSA: Four buses daily — from Tumbes at 8.30 am, 1 pm, 5.30 pm and 7 pm. There's also another bus just to Trujillo at 11.30 am. Fares: To Trujillo 1200 soles, to Lima 2095 soles. Journey time: 14 hours to Trujillo. 23 hours to Lima.

Rogerro: Two buses daily. From Tumbes at 2 pm and 8 pm. Fares same as TEPSA. Journey time: Same as TEPSA.

Sudamericana: One bus daily. Slightly cheaper than the others but approximately same journey times.

Trujillo-Lima (and vice versa)

TEPSA: three buses daily — from Trujillo at 11 am, 9 pm, and 10 pm. Fares: 870 soles. Journey time: nine hours.

Rogerro: two buses daily — from Trujillo at 6.30 am and 10.30 pm. Fares and journey time same as TEPSA.

Sudamericana: one bus daily — slightly cheaper than the others.

Peru Exprés: one bus daily — from Trujillo at 10 pm. Fares and journey time same as TEPSA.

El Condor Exprés: one bus daily at 9 pm from Trujillo. Fares and journey time same as TEPSA.

Trujillo Exprés: two buses daily — from Trujillo at 5 am and 1 pm. Fares: 1485 soles. Journey time: seven hours.

Lima-Arequipa (and vice versa)

TEPSA: two buses daily — from Arequipa at 1.15 pm and 7.30 pm. Fares: 1650 soles. Journey time: 18 hours.

Ormeno: six buses daily — from Arequipa at 8.30 am, 10.30 am, 1 pm, 3.30 pm, 6.30 pm and 8 pm. Fares and journey time same as TEPSA.

Sudamericana. Three buses per week from Arequipa on Monday, Wednesday and Friday at 12.30 pm. Fares: 1300 soles. Journey time same as TEPSA.

Morales Moralitos: One bus daily Same fares and journey time as Sudamericana.

If you're calling off at Nazca, the fares and journey times are as follows: Arequipa-Nazca: 980 soles, 10 hours. Lima-Nazca: 715 soles, seven hours.

Lima-Tacna (and vice versa)

TEPSA: one bus daily at 1 pm from Lima. Fare: 2400 soles, journey time 24 hours.

Arequipa-Tacna (and vice versa)

Ormeño: five buses daily — from Arequipa at 6.45 am, 11 am, 4 pm, 7 pm and 9 pm. Fares: 600 soles. Journey time: six hours.

Exprés Cruz de Sur: four buses

daily. From Arequipa at 7.15 am, 10.30 am, 4.30 pm and 7 pm. Same fares and journey time as Ormeno.

Morales Moralitos; Empresa C. Liendo and Empresa de Omnibuses Angelitos Negros also have one bus daily each. Same fares and journey time as for Ormeno.

Comité 26 (Colectivo): three cars daily at 8 am, 1 pm and 5 pm. Fare: 1000 soles. Arequipa-Moquegua: 400 soles. Arequipa-Ilo: 560 soles. Arequipa-Mollendo: 250 soles. Three buses daily by Ormeno at 7 am, 2 pm and 8.15 pm.

Arequipa-Arica (Chile)

Comite 26 (Colectivo). Arranged according to demand — if there's not enough local demand you'll have to get a group together and charter a car. Fare: 2500 soles. BUT this is a very expensive way of getting to Chile. The cheapest way is to take the bus to Tacna and catch the twice daily train from there to Arica (see below).

Tacna-Chile border (26 km)

Again several colectivos. Costs 3000 soles. The Chilean passport control post is five km beyond the border. From there it's 14 km to Arica.

Train This is the cheapest way to get to Arica (Chile) from Tacna.

dep Tacna	arr Arica	dep Arica	arr Tacna
08.30	15.00	08.30	15.00
10.05	16.35	10.05	16.35

On the northern section of the route choose Rogerro rather than TEPSA if at all possible. Their buses are better and they don't stop as often to put down and pick up passengers. TEPSA buses are often dirty and frequently serve as a "milk run" along the way. If cheapness

is your priority take the Expreso Sudamericano buses. The addresses of the bus company offices are to be found under the appropriate town sections.

Buses and Riverboats

Lima-Cajamarca.

Expreso Cajamarca: One bus daily — from Lima at 8 pm, 20 hours.

This is the longer route unless you can find a bus going via San Pedro on the coast which is the quickest way.

Trujillo-Cajamarca:

Empresa Quiroz: One bus per day in the evening — takes eight to ten hours during the dry season but longer in the rainy season. It's a cold journey so take warm clothes with you.

From Cajamarca to Iquitos

The route goes to Yurimaguas on the River Marañon, a tributary of the Amazon. From here you take either a plane or a riverboat to Iquitos. Hair-raising roads along the way.

Cajamarca-Celendin:

Two buses daily — taking five hours. Go via the Abra Loma del Indio pass, 3186 metres.

Celendin-Chacapoyas:

Trucks only — no buses, takes about 14 hours. Many landslides on this road during the rainy season. Count on getting stuck at this time of year. There are direct buses from Chiclayo via Bagua and Olmoa, taking 17 hours.

Chachapoyas-Rioja:

Trucks only. If you have no luck or wish to go a different way, find a truck for Mendoza (five hours, 86 km). From here there are planes to Moyobamba.

Rioja-Moyobamba:

Truck or fly with Fawcett. From Moyobamba to Iquitos you can fly or take a riverboat. Airline

Routes to Cajamarca and transport from there to Iquitos via Mendoz, Moyobamba and Yurimaguas — Flights

Aeroperu

Tue Thu Sat	Mon Wed Fri Sun	Wed Sun	Tue Sat		Tue Sat	Wed Sun	Mon Wed Fri Sun	Tue Thu Sat
07.30	08.00	07.30	07.30	Lima	17.30	17.40	13.00	17.30
			09.20	Juanjui	15.20			
09.35	09.05	09.35	10.05	Tarapoto	14.20	15.05	11.35	14.55
		10.30		Rioja		14.20		
			12.00	Trujillo	13.00			
		12.05		Chiclayo		13.05		
10.30				Yurimaguas				14.10
12.00	10.15			Iquitos			10.45	13.00

Fawcett

Mon Thu	Tue Thu Sat	Tue Fri Sun		Tue Fri Sun	Tue Thu Sat	Mon Thu
11.30	09.30	11.30	Lima	17.55	17.00	19.40
		12.15	Tingo Mario	16.50		
14.00	10.45	13.20	Tarapoto	15.40	15.30	16.50
		14.35	Trujillo	15.00		
	11.35		Pucallpa		14.30	
15.20	13.00		Iquitos		13.30	15.50

Fawcett also cover the following routes:

Fri Sun	Mon	Thu		Thu	Mon	Fri Sun
11.00	08.30	08.30	Trujillo	17.00	17.15	17.10
12.10	09.50	09.50	Juanjui	14.30	15.30	15.30
13.40			Tingo Mario			14.30
	10.50	10.50	Tarapoto	13.40	14.00	
			Rioja		12.55	
			Moyobamba	12.50		
	12.00	12.00	Yurimaguas	12.30	12.30	

offices in Moyobamba: Fawcett: Alonso Alvarado 701. Aeroperu Alonso Alvarado 973/977.

Moyobamba-Yurimaguas:

Many buses and trucks. Difficult road especially in the rainy season when the journey can take ten hours.

Plenty of riverboats in Yurimaguas which will take you to Iquitos but the journey takes four to seven days and you need your own mosquito net and hammock. No standard fare — must haggle with the captain. Best chance of a boat in the rainy season (December-May). Both Fawcett and Aeroperu fly from here to Iquitos. Occasionally there are also military planes which are cheaper still but, as with riverboats, you need to speak with the captain.

Ruins of the Chavín and Inca civilizations are found in the jungles of this area almost weekly and are beginning to alter the traditionally-held view that the Inca were an exclusively highland and coastal people. It's possible to hire Indian guides to walk from Chachapoyas to Rioja via Moninopampa over the mountains. Takes about six days and you need to take your own food, machete, etc. It's a hard walk through creepers and thick jungle and includes wading through several rivers.

If you're interested in the archaeology of the region, the jungle, or the lives of people who inhabit this region today, one of the best accounts is to be found in *Vilcabamba — Last City of the Incas* by Gene Savoy (Robert Hale, London. 1970) who has been exploring this country for years. Some excellent maps are included in the book if you're interested in trekking around some of the more remote ruins especially the extensive ruins at Vilcabamba and Muyok Viejo.

Routes to Huaráz (Callejón de Huaylas) and Chavín

Flights Aeroperu fly: Lima-Chimbote-Anta (the nearest airport to Huaraz).

From Lima: Monday and Friday at 8.30 am. Arrive Chimbote: 9.40 am. Arrive Anta: 10.30 am.
From Anta: Monday and Friday at 10.50 am. Arrive Chimbote: 11.20 am. Arrive Lima: 12.50 pm.

Buses

Pativilca-Huaráz: Many trucks that you can hitch a ride with, takes 15 hours. There is also a direct bus from Lima; takes 10 hours.
Chimbote-Huaráz: via the Santa valley. The road follows the old railway line which was completely destroyed during the earthquake which hit this region in 1970. Expreso Moreno: One bus daily at 6.30 am, takes 10 hours. Transportes Soledad also do this run daily at 8.30 am.
Casma-Huaráz: Empresa Soledad, one bus daily — from Huaráz at 10 am, takes 6½ hours.
Huaráz-Chavín de Huantar: Three buses weekly on Tuesdays, Thursday, Sunday by Empresa Huascaran. Takes six to seven hours. Otherwise take local bus or truck to Recuay and then on to Catac. From there trucks leave for Chavin in the early morning and late evening. Costs 130 soles and takes seven hours. There are also direct Lima-Chavín de Huantar buses which take 15 hours.

The Central Highway — Lima to Iquitos via La Oroya, Cerro de Pasco, Huánuco and Pucallpa.

The all-weather road runs as far as Pucallpa and from there you must take either a flight or riverboat to Iquitos. For the first part of the journey as far as Cerro de Pasco there is a choice of train (the cheapest method) or bus. The maps show railways continuing in two directions from here as far as Yurimaguas and Pucallpa and if they weren't destroyed or have been repaired since the 1970 earthquake it may be possible to get a lift on a freight train. Enquire with railway workers on the sidings.

Trains

Lima-Cerro de Pasco via La Oroya. This is the same train which goes to Huancayo. Change at La Oroya for Cerro de Pasco. Daily train. From Lima at 7.40 am except Sundays, arriving 6.15 pm. Depart Cerro de Pasco 6 am. 1st class: 320 soles; 2nd class: 280 soles. Tickets are sold the day before the train leaves. Get to the station by 7 am. Take it steady as the train goes over the pass — you're up at nearly 5000 metres! Possibly the highest railway in the world.

Buses

Lima-Huánuco: 14 hours.
Huanuco-Tingo Mario: 4½ hours.

Flights

Aeroperu

daily	Tue Thu Sat	daily	Mon Tue Wed Thu Fri Sat	Tue Wed Thu Fri Sat Sun		Tue Wed Thu Fri Sat Sun	Mon Tue Wed Thu Fri Sat	daily	Tue Thu Sat	daily
19.00	08.00	19.10	14.45	13.00	Lima	14.40	16.35	21.30	13.00	22.30
				13.40	Huánuco	14.00				
			15.30		Tingo Mario		15.50			
	09.00	20.10			Pucallpa			20.30	11.40	
20.30	10.15				Iquitos				10.45	21.00

Fawcett

daily	daily	daily	Tue Thu Sat	Tue Fri Sun		Tue Fri Sun	Tue Thu Sat	daily	daily	daily
06.45	16.00	19.30	09.30	11.30	Lima	17.55	17.00	21.50	19.30	10.30
				12.15	Tingo Mario	16.50				
			10.45	13.20	Tarapoto	15.40	15.30			
				14.35	Trujillo	15.00				
	20.30		11.35		Pucallpa			14.30	20.50	
08.15	17.30		13.00		Iquitos		13.30		18.00	09.00

Tingo Mario-Pucallpa: 11 hours.

Lima-Pucallpa (direct): 32 hours, 847 km. Depart: 8.30 pm, costs 1650 soles.

Several bus companies cover this run. Eg Nor Oriente (office in Lima at the junction of Avenida Luna Pizarro and 28 de Julio. Also Transportes Arellano. There are considerable delays on this route during the rainy season from December to March.

Pucallpa is a busy port on the river Ucayali which runs into the Marañon just below Iquitos. Plenty of small riverboats and larger ships — they cost between US$8 and 12 and take between three and seven days to get to Iquitos. Sometimes food is thrown in (rice and beans) and a small shared cabin. Take plenty of insect repellant with you and if possible your own mosquito net and hammock. Some tinned food helps too — cooking is done with water taken from the river and unless you have a constitution of iron you may spend a large part of the trip with your rear end hanging over the side of the boat. "Hygiene" is apparently a bourgeois pre-occupation. In addition to riverboats there is a motor boat called the *Santa Rosa* which does the journey in much less time but costs around US$20.

If you have to hang around in Pucallpa waiting for a boat (no regular schedules) the cheapest hotels there are: *Hotel Peru* (US$1.20; very basic); *Hotel Los Angeles; Hotel Amazonas; Hotel Don José* and the *Hotel Europa* (US$3/double). If you're looking for something a little better, try the *Hotel Tariri* (on Calle Raymondi near Calle Frederico Basadre — US$5.50/double with own shower and air-conditioning).

Tourist information from: Enrique Mauldhardt at the *Hotel La Cabana* on nearby Lake Yarinacocha. The lake is largely a tourist trap but the water is clean and it's possible to camp. There's also a summer school here for the study of Indian languages, 30 minutes by bus from Pucallpa.

Lima to Cuzco and Puno via Huancayo, Ayacucho, Andahuaylas and Abancay.
One of the most popular Andean routes. Plenty of other travellers. the road from Huancayo to Cuzco is pretty rough except in the vicinity of Ayacucho. If you time is limited or for any other reason you want to miss out Huancayo or both Huancayo and Ayacucho, there are direct buses from Lima (and vice versa) on good paved roads. We deal with the direct buses first.
Lima-Ayacucho via Puquío, Pisco and Nazca (missing out Huancayo):

> Carmen Alto: three buses daily in either direction. From Ayacucho at 12 noon, 3 pm, and 6 pm. Fare: 1050 soles. Journey time: 18 hours. Address in Ayacucho: Avenida Centenario 165-171. Address in Lima: Jr Garcia Naranjo, La Victoria Suburb.

Lima-Cuzco via Abancay, Puquío, Nazca and Pisco (missing out both Huancayo and Ayacucho):

> Ormeno: One bus daily on Monday, Wednesday, Thursday, Saturday and Sunday. From Cuzco at 8 am. Fare: 1600 soles. (To Abancay: 400 soles. To Nazca: 1400 soles).
> Morales Moralitos: Two buses daily. From Cuzco at 8 am and 3 pm. Fare: 2000 soles. (To Abancay: 500 soles. To Nazca: 1500 soles).

Hidalgo and Carmen Alto also run through buses to Cuzco from Lima three times per week but they go via Huancayo and Ayacucho.

Lima-Huancayo: The cheapest way to do this leg of the journey is by train. The quickest way is by bus or colectivo.

Train: Daily in either direction except Sundays. Departs from either end at 7.40 am. Fares: 1st class, 320 soles; 2nd class 280 soles. Journey time: nine hours. Tickets are sold the day before departure. Get to the the station by 7 am on the morning you are going. This is one of the highest railways in the world and goes over a 4500 metre pass.

The railway continues on as far as Huancavelica but you must catch the trains from the Chilean station which is about a km from the main station in Huancayo. Departs 6.45 am and 1 pm Monday-Saturday and at 1.30 pm on Sundays. Takes 3½ hours.

Buses
Lima-Huancayo: The following bus companies cover this run:-

> Hidalgo: six buses daily in either direction (three in the morning; three in the evening).
> ETUCSA: two buses daily at 8 am and 1 pm.
> Sudamericana: one bus daily in either direction at 7.30.
> Centroandino: one bus daily in either direction.
> Empresa Ayacucho: one bus daily in either direction.

Fares: Hidalgo and ETUCSA: 600 soles. The rest: 500 soles. Journey time: seven hours (same for all). Most of the companies run excellent new buses on this leg of the journey as the road is surfaced all the way and so there's little to choose between them.

Comite 22 (colectivos). Same as above.

Addresses of bus company and colectivo company offices are in the Lima section.

Huancayo-Aracucho: Rough road for most of the way with the additional disadvantage that most of the bus companies do the run at night leaving only the dawn run into Ayacucho during the light. Buses tend to be rough and ready and though there are one or two relatively new buses doing the run there's no way of predicting whether you will get one. Book in advance. Forget about colectivos unless you can find one that's going in any case — otherwise they'll want something between 2000 and 6000 soles!

Hidalgo: depart Huancayo Monday, Wednesday Friday, Sunday at 5 pm. Costs 700 soles and takes about 13 hours.

ETUCSA: Depart Huancayo Sunday and Tuesday at 5 pm. Same price and time as Hidalgo.

Centroandino: Daily at 4.30 pm. Costs 700 soles and takes about 14 hours. Buses packed to capacity and beyond. "Full" on the booking form simply means the seats are full. After that it's the Guiness Book of Records trip with a telephone kiosk.

Empresa Ayacucho: Daily at 4.30 pm and 7 pm. Same fare and time as Centroandino.

Transportes Gutarra: Daily at 6.30 am and costs the same as Centroandino but takes a little longer. This is the only bus company which runs buses during the day.

Ayacucho-Abancaya and Cuzco: Again a rough road with long journey times (12 hours to Andahuaylas: 18 hours to Abancay and 24 hours to Cuzco). It's sometimes difficult to get on a through bus to Cuzco from Ayacucho. You have to wait and see how many people get off the bus in Ayacucho and be on their booking list as far in advance as possible. Hidalgo and Carmen Alto are the companies which do the through run. If no luck, get a bus to Abancay with one of the other bus companies and then take a bus from there to Cuzco (more choice of companies from here and the road is good to Cuzco).

Bus schedule from Ayacucho:

Company	Journey	Mon	Tue	Wed	Thu	Fri	Sat	Fare	Time
Empresa Ayacucho	Ayacucho-Huancayo-Lima	6 pm	3 pm	6 pm	3 pm	6 pm	3 pm	900 soles	18+ hrs
	Ayacucho-Andahuaylas	10 am	8 am	10 am	10 am			700 soles	12 hrs
	Ayacucho-Cangallo	2 pm				2 pm			
Centro-andino	Ayacucho-Huancayo-Lima			daily at 6 pm				900 soles	18+ hrs
	Ayacucho-Huancayo			daily at 5 pm				700 soles	14 hrs
	Ayacucho-Andahuaylas	8 am	8 am		8 am		8 am	700 soles	12+ hrs
Hidalgo	Ayacucho-Lima		6 pm		6 pm		6 pm	900 soles	18 hrs
	Ayacucho-Andahuaylas	6 am		6 am		6 am		700 soles	14 hrs
Carmen Alto	Ayacucho-Abancay-Cuzco	6 am		6 am		6 am		1100 soles	24 hrs

Empresa Gutarra also cover the same places (Jr Vivanco in Ayacucho)

Bus schedule from Cuzco:

Company	Journey	Schedule	Fare
Hidalgo	Cuzco-Abancay-Huancayo-Lima	Mon, Thu, Sat at 7.30 am	1600 soles (Lima) 1100 soles (Ayac.) 300 soles (Abanc.)
Carmen Alto	Cuzco-Abancay-Huancaya-Lima	Tue, Thu, Sat at 8 am	same as above
Morales Moralitos	Cuzco-Abancay-Puquío-Nazca-Piscio-Lima	daily at 8 am and 3 pm	2000 soles (Lima) 1500 soles (Nazca) 500 soles (Abanc.)
Ormeno	Cuzco-Abancay-Puquío-Nazca-Pisco-Lima	Mon, Wed, Thu, Sat, Sun at 8 am	1600 soles (Lima) 1400 soles (Nazca) 400 soles (Abanc.)

Cuzco-Puno: There is a choice on this leg of the journey between bus and train. Most travellers take the train since the road between Cuzco and Juliaca is rough and journey times are the same.

Train

	Cuzco-Puno Mon-Sat		Puno-Cuzco Mon-Fri	Sat
Cuzco	08.10	Puno	06.45	09.20
Juliaca	17.35	Juliaca	07.49	10.25
Puno	19.00	Cuzco	17.35	19.40

Fares: Cuzco-Puno 1204 soles first class, 650 soles second class. Cuzco-Juliaca 1103 soles first class, 596 soles second class. Book as far in advance as possible. First class is often booked up at least one or two days in advance. Booking office is open 7 am to 5 pm. Train connects at Juliaca with the line to Arequipa (see next section for details).

Warning The Cuzco-Puno train and the Arequipa-Juliaca trains are notorious for rip-offs. Keep a constant watch over your belongings. Never leave them unattended!

Buses

Morales Moralitos: Daily bus at 8 am. Goes on to La Paz (Bolivia). Cost of the Cuzco-La Paz ride: 2500 soles. This is a very expensive way of doing this leg of the journey. (See the last section for details of cheaper methods).

Sur Peruano: Daily buses at 3 am and 10 am.

Juliaca Express: Daily buses at 3 am and 10 am.

Transturin: do the Cuzco-Puno-Copacabana-La Paz run in super deluxe buses with hostess service, etc. Sunday, Tuesday and Thursday at 7 pm. US$25 to Copacabana; US$30 to La Paz. Strictly for those who are bored with life and have more money than sense.

Transport to Macchu Picchu/Urubamba Valley/Chaullay/Quillabamba.

Full details in the Cuzco and Urubamba Valley sections.

Cuzco-Puerto Maldonado. Buses and trucks to Puerto Maldonado via Urcos and Quince Mil. Also flights from both Cuzco and Quince Mil (see below). From Pto. Maldonado there are riverboats over the Peru/Bolivian border to Riberalta and Guayaramerin via the Madre de Dios River. From Guayaramerin there are riverboats to Porto Velho in Brazil. You need plenty of time to make this trip — two to three weeks. Very few travellers go this way — more details in the Bolivian section.

Flights Because of the difficulties with buses and the long journey times, many travellers take the Aeroperu flight from Ayacucho to Cuzco. This particular flight is notorious for being cancelled at a moment's notice and for Aeroperu overbooking the flight. Don't count on getting the flight on the day you booked for. You may well find yourself in the company of a muttering mass of delayed travellers who have been going down to the airport everyday for several days in the hope of finally making it. Aeroperu *sometimes* lay on another plane to clear the backlog but most of the time they adopt a couldn't-care-less attitude and don't take kindly to complaints.

Aeroperu

Mon	Mon Wed Thu Fri Sun	daily	daily	Tue Thu Fri Sun	Mon Wed Sat	Thu Sun		Thu Sun	Mon Wed Sat	Tue Fri Sun	daily	daily	Tue Wed Thu Fri Sun	Tue
06.45	09.35	06.30	07.00	07.00	07.00		Lima	10.20	08.40	10.30	09.05	12.05	11.30	
							08.30 Andahuaylas 08.50							
			07.40	07.40			Ayacucho			08.00	09.30			
	07.55	10.40	07.35	08.30			Cuzco				09.00	08.00	11.00	09.55
09.15	08.55						Pto Maldonado						09.15	08.55
09.55							Cuzco							07.30
11.35							Pucallpa							
13.00							Iquitos							05.30

Fawcett

Mon Fri Sun	Tue Fri	daily	daily	Mon Thu Sat	Wed Sun	Mon		Wed	Wed Sun	Mon Thu Sat	daily	daily	Tue Fri	Mon Fri Sun
09.30	06.00	07.00	09.50	06.00	06.00		Lima	10.30	10.30	12.10	09.30	08.30	11.05	
10.10							Ayacucho							10.30
	07.00	08.00	10.50	07.00	07.00		Cuzco		09.10	09.10	11.10	08.30	07.30	
				08.10			Arequipa			08.30				08.30
		08.10			09.00		Pto Maldonado	14.10			14.10			08.30
					09.40		Iberia	13.10						13.10
					11.00		Quincemil	12.00						12.00

Examples of fares on these routes:
Lima-Cuzco: US$41.10 (6597 soles).
Lima-Ayacucho: US$22.50 plus 9% tax (3875 soles).
Ayacucho-Cuzco: US$18 (2687 soles).

Arequipa-Cuzco & Puno
Flights — Aeroperu
Arequipa-Cuzco: Daily except Sunday at 8.15. Arrive Cuzco: 8.55 am.
Arequipa-Juliaca: Daily except Sunday at 10.35. Arrive Juliaca: 11.10.
Cuzco-Arequipa: Daily except Sunday at 9.25 am. Arrive Arequipa: 10.05.

Juliaca-Arequipa: Daily except Sunday at 11.35. Arrive Arequipa: 12.15.

Fares: Arequipa-Cuzco: US$19.60 plus 9% tax.
Arequipa-Juliaca: US$11.40 plus 9% tax.

Trains Trains from Arequipa to Juliaca connect with the trains running from Cuzco to Puno. Normally you don't have to change — just make sure you're on the correct part of the train as carriages are detached at Juliaca. The journey from Arequipa to Puno goes through some magnificent mountain scenery so you should take the day train by preference. Another factor in favour of the day train is that the one at night gets bitterly cold and none of the carriages are heated except the buffet car.

This train is notorious for rip-offs. Keep an eye on your baggage all the way. Never leave it unattended. If you do go on the night train stay awake the whole way!

If you're coming up from Arequipa and want a connecting train for Cuzco see the previous section for train times.

Fares: Arequipa-Puno: first class, 1117 soles, second class, 606 soles. Arequipa-Cuzco: first class, 2119 soles; second class, 1148 soles. Buffet: 2459 soles. (Heated).

Buses

Arequipa-Cuzco:

San Cristobal Four buses daily at 6 am, 7 am, 1 pm and 2 pm from

	Arequipa-Puno			Puno-Arequipa		
	Mon, Wed, Fri	daily		Tue, Thur	Sat	daily
Arequipa	08.45	21.30	Puno	06.55	09.20	20.30
Juliaca	17.21	06.10	Juliaca	08.00	10.25	21.30
Puno	19.00	07.45	Arequipa	16.50	19.00	06.00

Cuzco. Fares: 800 soles to Juliaca, 1100 soles to Arequipa. This company does not run buses to Puno so if you are heading there from either direction you must change companies for connections to Puno.

Sur Peruano Two buses daily from Cuzco at 3 am and 10 am. Same fares as San Cristobal. This company also runs buses to Puno.

Juliaca Express Two buses daily from Cuzco at 3 am and 10 am. Same fares as San Cristobal and also run buses to Puno.

Arequipa-Puno:

Morales Moralitos One bus daily in either direction. From Arequipa at 10 am, takes nine hours and costs 700 soles. The bus terminal is on Victor Lira in Arequipa, not on San Juan de Dios as most other companies but they do maintain a ticket office there.

Comité 3 (Colectivos) Address is Salaverry III, Arequipa. Daily car Arequipa-Puno, costs 1250 soles.

Puno-Bolivia There are three possible routes to La Paz (Bolivia) from Puno.

The first is by bus in three stages:

Puno-Yunguyo:

Morales Moralitos One bus daily except Saturday at 7 am. Takes four hours and costs 400 soles. On the way to Yunguyo they will offer to take you across the border to Copacabana for an extra 100 soles (depending on demand — there are usually a lot of travellers on this bus). This might sound cheap but it's even cheaper to get off and take either a truck or a local bus to Copacabana. The border is very, very easy-going. No hassle, even if you walk across.

Transportes La Perla One bus daily to Yunguyo. Takes four hours and costs 350 soles. Their buses are often contracted out to Morales Moralitos.

Yunguyo-Copacabana:

Plenty of local buses in the main plaza all day for 50 soles, although they try you with 100 soles first — just haggle, no one else pays that much! Even cheaper is one of the frequent trucks from the same plaza for the equivalent of Bolivian pesos

3 (US$1 = Bp20). If you happen to have walked to the border from Yunguyo (a few km) you can get a truck from there for Bolivian pesos 2.

Exit stamps are no longer required before turning up at the border. They're very easy going on both sides. No searches, no money showing, no onward tickets. On the Peruvian side the border officials will offer to buy back your Peruvian soles for Bolivan pesos at a very favourable rate (considering that Bolivian pesos are a stable currency). The offer is Bolivian pesos 11 = 100 soles. The banks and shops in Copocabana will only give you Bolivian pesos 10 = 100 soles.

Copacabana-La Paz:
 Several buses daily via the Straits of Tiquina. Eg Transportes Manco Kapac — departs 7 am, 10 am, 1 pm, 2 pm, 4 pm. Takes four to five hours and costs Bolivian pesos 27. The ferry across the lake costs Bolivian pesos 2. A beautiful journey and far preferable to the route via Desaguadero. There are also microbuses which cost Bolivian pesos 30 and trucks which cost Bolvian pesos 15-20 depending on the driver.

The second route is by bus and train via Desaguadero/Guaqui.

Puno-Desaguadero:
 Morales Moralitos One bus per day on Mondays, Tuesdays, Thursdays and Sundays. Takes 4½ hours and costs 400 soles. Morales also do the through run Puno-La Paz on the same day. Fare is an outrageous 1080 soles, journey time eight hours. At Desaguadero walk across the border to Guaqui (very short walk). Easy-going customs, no exit visa required before turning up at the border.

Guaqui-La Paz:
 Daily ordinary train taking four hours. On Fridays only there is a ferrobus which connects with the arrival and departure of the Lake Titicaca steamers. Takes two hours to La Paz but availability of space depends on how many people get off the steamers. If you don't want to catch the train or there is no space, take a local bus to La Paz.

The third route is by steamer over Lake Titicaca to Guaqui and then train or bus from there to La Paz.

Puno-Guaqui:
 Steamer — the two ships which do this lake crossing are the *Inca* and the *Ollanta*. Departs Puno on Wednesdays at 8 pm, takes 12 hours. Departs Guaqui on Fridays at 2 pm. Fare in second class is Bolivian pesos 60 (US$3) — bunk in dorm, no food, no sheets. First class is approximately double — four to eight people to a cabin.

Guaqui-La Paz:
 Ferrobus from Guaqui connects with the steamer. Takes two hours and costs Bolivian pesos 30. Not always room for everyone.

If you want to see Lake Titicaca then the steamer is no use to you as it sails during the night. There is also a hydrofoil Puno-Copacaban (and vice versa) but it's very expensive and noisy. Avoid buying combined train-steamer-train tickets from Cuzco to La Paz (or vice versa) as it works out very expensive — US$25!

ODDS & SODS
In case of rip-off Only applies if you have taken out baggage insurance or if you have your passport stolen. For passports/travellers cheques: Buy (i) papel sellado (sellosexto) from any

stationers ("papelleris") for 10 soles and (ii) forma copia certificada de Guardia Civil. The latter is only available from the Banco de la Nacion for 50 soles. Take these papers to the local branch of the PIP. Here you make a brief statement about what was lost, the circumstances, etc. which is typed out on the papers you bought. These then have to be rubber-stamped and signed by the chief ("Jehe"). As the Guardia is regional you can only report the loss at the place where it happened otherwise they will tell you to go back to the place it happened and report it there. Use your imagination if this is the case, after all if you've had something stolen what difference does it make when or where? You've still lost it.

You'll be given copies of this statement and with these you can get your passport and cheques replaced. You also need them to make a claim against the insurance company for loss so keep them in a safe place or send them to the insurance company. When you get your passport replaced (if stolen) you also have to visit Immigration to get a new Tourist "card". For this you need a photocopy of your passport and another sheet of "papel sellado".

It's a very time-consuming process and can be costly if you've had your passport stolen. (If you're British, for instance, the Embassy/Consulate will telex London for confirmation of who you say you are (costs 4000 soles) and then issue you a new passport (costs 3700 soles). This works out at around US$52 plus travelling expences. It pays to look after your gear!

Immigration in Lima is on Paseo de la Republica. New Tourist "card" issued same day. Photocopies and "papel sellado" are available in the foyer.

Bolivia

Geographically, the Tibet of the Americas and one whose mystique and remoteness attracts many travellers. The altiplano, where 75 percent of the population live, is a strange, dry, dusty, almost treeless plateau of over 3500 metres on which are situated the world's highest capital city — La Paz at over 3600 metres — and South America's highest and largest freshwater lakes — Titicaca and Poopo. It has a vast, eerie sort of beauty that you're not likely to forget in a hurry. Bolivia is the most Indian nation on the whole continent. 70 percent of the population are pure blood Indians. They are a rugged, sun-baked and severe people with a history of oppression and exploitation unequalled anywhere else on the face of the earth. It is with them that the analogy with Tibet ends. Even the voluminous skirts and bowler hats worn by the women — a characteristic which makes them a favourite photographic topic — were imposed by the Spanish King, Carlos III, at the end of the 18th century. The style was modelled on the clothes worn by the peasant women of Estremadura, Andalusia and the Basque provinces in Spain. The centre parting of the hair was the result of a decree put out by the Viceroy Toledo.

Following the collapse of the Inca Empire, the Spanish herded millions of these people to their deaths as slave labourers in the silvermines of Potosi and when the silver ran out and tin became a valuable commodity in post-independence days, the whole sad story was repeated. Today, although the mines are nationalised, the miners at the face earn a wage which is well short of covering the most basic of human needs and life expectancy is a mere 35 years. And that's if they're lucky. By that time most have died of silicosis-pneumonia, a well-known occupational disease of working in high silica dust environments. Unless they have relatives who are still capable of working and prepared, or even able, to support them, the families of the men who die are then destitute. The mining company owns the houses they live in so if there's no member of the family working in the mines, out they go. Even if they had sufficient land on which to grow food, self-sufficiency would be almost impossible in this harsh plateau where rain rarely falls and when it does often floods and where the temperature drops at night to around freezing point but can climb as high as $20^{\circ}C$ during the day. The diet of these people lacks 40% of the protein and 80% of the calcium considered necessary for the maintenance of health. Most are illiterate. A large number speak only the Indian languages of Aymara and Quechua and, until the revolution of 1952, none of these people had the vote — for what it's worth. Even today the franchise depends very much on the political colour of the incumbent military junta.

To make life bearable, especially in the mines, the Indians chew coca leaves constantly and in the evenings burn their guts out with "aguardiente" — the local fire-water which is almost pure alcohol. The use of coca goes back to Inca days when it was used for ritual purposes and by those who worked in the mines. The Spanish energetically promoted its use. It was good for business. Each year, a million kilos of coca leaves were consumed in the Potosi mines and even the Church levied a tax on these wages of misery managing to provide almost the entire budget for the Cuzco bishopric from it.

Today, much of the leaf is refined into cocaine and smuggled into the US or over the border into Brazil and refined there. As you might expect, none of this activity takes place without the knowledge of high government officials who are all taking their cut. Cocaine is one of Bolivia's major "invisible" exports.

Silver was discovered in the Cerro Rico by the town of Potosi in 1545 a few years after the Spanish had invaded this part of the world from Peru. In its heyday Potosi rivalled many a European city for its extravagant living. So rich was the vein of ore that the yield from this mine alone accounted for 99% of the mineral exports from Spanish America until other mines were opened up in Mexico. According to the records of the Casa de Contratacion in Seville, Spain, 185,000 kg of gold and 16 million kg of silver were sent to Europe between 1545 and 1660 — an amount which was 3½ times the total European reserves at the time. But these are official figures only and since a great deal of smuggling took place the actual amounts must have been considerably more. Little of this incredible amount of wealth ever saw the light of day in Spain since the monarchy was mortgaged to the hilt and shipments were spoken for before they arrived. Extravagance by the monarchy, the church, and expenses incurred in the numerous wars which Spain instigated in those days ensured that virtually all the silver was immediately passed on to German, Genoese, Flemish and Spanish bankers to cover loans they had advanced. All this easy money also stifled Spain's industrial and agricultural development and is the main reason why, today, Spain is one of Europe's poorest nations.

Tin is mined these days in Oruro and Potosi and is Bolivia's main export along with copper which is extracted from the mines at Corocoro but almost none of the wealth which these exports generate ever reaches the people who mine it, let alone anyone else. In addition, the world price of tin is determined far from the altiplano in the stock markets of North America and Europe and foreign companies are still involved in mining operations despite the fact that these have been nationalised. In 1964, Phillip's Industries, a Dutch conglomerate, were given the franchise to mine lead, silver and zinc from one of the Oruro mines. According to the terms of the contract, they paid the state 1.5% of the sale value of the crude zinc they extracted!

Exploitation, outright theft and annexation of Bolivian territory have been the lot of this unfortunate country ever since the Spanish arrived. Up until the late 19th century, Bolivia had a Pacific littoral centred on the port of Antofagasta. It was lost to Chile following the War of the Pacific from 1879 until 1883. The reason for the conflict lay in the presence of nitrates in the Atacama Desert, most of which was until this time part of Bolivia and Peru. Although the Spanish had been aware of these deposits for centuries and used them to make gunpowder, no-one thought of it as having much value until it was discovered in the 19th century to be an excellent fertilizer. Suddenly the desert became very interesting. Mining of the nitrates began in the desert around Antofagasta and further north in the Peruvian section but the actual operations were controlled more by Chilean and, to a lesser extent, Peruvian interests. When the Bolivian government proposed a tax on the mineral, the Chilean Navy attacked and took the whole of the desert up to Tacna in Peru. Bolivia was "compensated" with a railway from Antofagasta to Oruro with duty-free facilities at the port for the export of Bolivian commodities but Bolivia has never accepted the annexation and frequently threatens war with

Chile whenever internal conditions hit a low spot and national attention needs to be focused abroad. As recently as 1978 war fever rose to its highest pitch for years with Peru threatening similar action for the same reason and Argentina lending support because of dissatisfaction over the results of arbitration concerning three tiny islands in the Beagle Channel off Tierra del Fuego. The real tragedy about the loss of Antofagasta is that, after the Chilean annexation, one of the world's largest deposits of copper ore was found here but as it was British capital which had financed the war it was to be a long time before the Chileans started to reap any benefits from their acquisitions.

Bolivia's next loss was to Brazil. Up until 1903, the Acre territory in the Amazon basin up against the present borders of Peru and Bolivia was a part of Bolivia. At the end of the 19th century, the rubber boom, centred on Manaus, took off in Brazil and by 1890 accounted for one-tenth of Brazil's export income. The Bolivians participated in this boom by ransacking the forests of the Acre in a lightning military campaign. So rich was the area in rubber trees that by 1910 rubber accounted for 40% of Brazil's export earnings. Bolivia was in no position to do anything about the loss and was "compensated" with a totally useless railway running from Porto Velho to Riberalta but it was never completed and fell into disuse not long afterwards.

Then in 1932 Bolivia fought Paraguay over ownership of the Chaco. The area had previously been of little interest to either country and was inhabited by a few tribes of Indians. Trouble started when various North American and European oil companies began to speculate about the possibility of oil in the area and a quarrel was engineered with Standard Oil supporting Bolivia and Shell supporting Paraguay. Hundreds of thousands of people lost

expenses via exploitation of the resource. There was nothing in the agreement which specified how "expenses" would be calculated nor about what "expenses" would be considered reasonable. That was all left up to Gulf. Many other companies secured similar deals.

Since independence, Bolivia has had more military coups than most people have had hot dinners. Few governments last more than a year and many have only lasted a matter of weeks. Generally the coups involve no one outside the main plaza in La Paz and is essentially a reshuffling of white military officers — power is held exclusively by the tiny blanco minority which comprises a mere 5% of the population. The war with Paraguay was, however, to sow the seeds of revolution. Demand for radical reform came together under the aegis of the Movimiento Nacionalista Revolucionario (MNR) led by Victor Paz Estenssoro, a lawyer and professor of economics. Though he was forced into exile in Buenos Aires, the MNR with the help of other left-wing groups won the 1951 elections but were prevented from taking office by the military. The miners rose in armed revolt and after heavy fighting defeated the military. Paz Estenssoro was brought back from exile to lead the new government which then pressed ahead with its programme of reform. This included granting the right to vote to illiterates (the majority of adult Indians); nationalisation of the tin mines, and redistribution of land. The revolution did have the effect of making the peasants and miners feel part of the nation and that the government was trying to do something for them but, even with US support, Estenssoro's efforts to raise the standard of living produced small results. Division of the landed estates among the peasants did not result in increased food production and with primitive equipment and transport and

their lives in this war and when peace was finally negotiated with Paraguay having won, Bolivia lost a huge slice of its former territory. It didn't lose as much as it might have since an agent of Standard Oil chaired the peace negotiations and, with an eye on future concessions, secured for Bolivia continued ownership over thousands of square miles claimed by Paraguay. This was only the start of the oil companies' interference in the affairs of the two nations and some incredibly one-sided concessions were to be handed out in the years which followed. One particularly notorious concession was awarded to Gulf Oil in which it was agreed that the company would recover 100% of all capital invested in oil prospecting if no oil was found, or, if it were found, that the company could recover all a lack of trained technicians the productivity of the miners remained very low. Dissension and corruption within the MNR began to grow, forcing Estenssoro to become increasingly autocratic which in turn aroused the indignation of even his former supporter. He was overthrown in a military coup in 1964 led by Gen Rene Barrientos. Being the principal body of support behind the MNR, the miners were attacked by the army and, after much bloodshed, their leaders were arrested and deported.

The 1952 revolution was the 179th change of government since independence and the only one which produced radical results. Reform of a sorts continues to move at a snail's pace but the country is back in the hands of the military and was, until his overthrow in 1978, led by one of Bolivia's longest-lasting dictators, Hugo Banzar.

One of Bolivia's Greatest weaknesses has been the failure to settle and farm the rich lowlands on the east side of the Andes. The area is very sparsely settled and then only by blancos and mestizos. For the most part the Indians refuse to move from the altiplano despite its harshness. Their roots lie on the high plateau, they are physically adapted to it and fear that if they move they will succumb to lowland diseases. Agrarian reform to them is essentially conservative and a means of preserving or reviving the remnants of an old way of life which the Spaniards almost destroyed and which others have since treated with equal lack of respect. Nevertheless, the lowlands are slowly being colonised. Santa Cruz has become a very cosmopolitan city with a large expatriate colony made up of people drawn from many countries around the world, particularly Japan, Germany and the United States. Colonies of Mennonites also farm land in the vicinity. This hot, steamy area of jungle and scrub takes up 70% of Bolivia's total land area yet has only 25% of the population. The irony is that during colonial times parts of it became very prosperous due to the activity of Jesuit missionaries who set up reduciones as in neighbouring Paraguay. When they were expelled, the settlements fell apart and were looted. Nothing remains of them today.

VISAS

These are not required by nationals of Western European countries, Israel, Canada and USA, but they are required by nationals of Australia, New Zealand and Japan. Visas/Tourist Cards are free and issued on the spot, with nothing to show.

Bolivian Consulate in Puno, Peru (location marked on street plan) is open 8.30 am-12 noon, 2 pm-4 pm Monday-Friday. The Yunguyo-Copacabana border on Lake Titicaca is very easy-going. 90-day stay permit is given to everyone. There are no searches, no money-showing and no onward tickets are required.

There's a two percent Sales Tax on internal air tickets and a three percent Tax on international tickets.

CURRENCY

US$1 = 20 Bolivian pesos

The unit of currency is the Bolivian peso (Bp) = 100 centavos. The currency is stable and there's no blackmarket. There's also no restriction on import and export of Bolivian pesos. So if you are having money sent to you from abroad, Bolivia is one of the possible countries, since it can be paid entirely in dollars (see under *Money* in the main introduction).

Casas de Cambio are less fuss than banks and will also sell you cash dollars (no limit) but for a commission of three percent. Note that if you're coming into Bolivia from Peru via Copacabana,

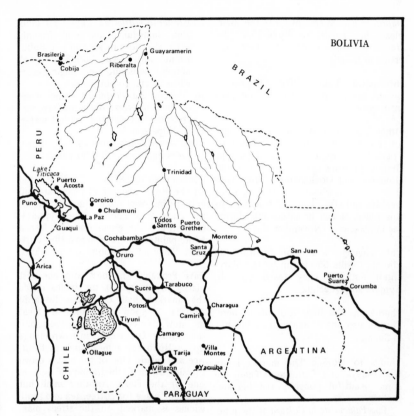

the bank there will only change a maximum of US$50 travellers' cheques per person per day. It also only opens for a short time each day.

COCHABAMBA

Accommodation A very friendly town and has an excellent climate — much warmer than on the Altiplano. There's a varied selection of good food available including dairy products.

Alojamiento Cochabamba and *Residencial Escobar*, both on Calle Nataniel Aguirre on the corner of the main Plaza — clean, hot water, share showers. Both Bp20, but showers are an extra Bp5 at the *Escobar*. You get somewhat better rooms at the Escobar.

Hotel Aroma (Bp15), *Residencial Oriental* (Bp20), *Residencial Pullman* (Bp 15), are all on Avenida Aroma.

Residencial Bolivia and *Residencial Lopez*, next to the bus terminal, both BP25.

Alojamiento Sudamerico, Calle Estoban Arce 6882. Bp25 — good place.

Residencial La Paz, near the railway station. Bp20/person — clean, hot water but make sure your room is secure.

Eats *Cafe Paula*, corner of 25 de Mayo and Bolivar, serves lunch for Bp20.

Napoli, Calle Sucre, just off the main plaza, has meals for Bp20-25. The *Heladeria Espana* has the best ice-cream in Bolivia.

Information Tourist Office, Exprinter, on the main plaza, has maps and gives information.

Other Bus terminals and ticket offices are on Avenida Aroma. The buses to Todos Santos on a tributary of the Rio Grande go from the corner of Avenida Oquendo and Oochabamba. From here there is a riverboat to Trinidad once weekly, and also plenty of trucks go to this place. It can be impossible during the rainy season (November-May).

The language school on Instituto de Idioma, Casilla 550 is run by the Maryknool Fathers. They teach Spanish, Aymará and Quechua.

There's a Brazilian Consulate here. There's also one in Santa Cruz, but not in Sucre.

Things to Do/See The market is on Wednesdays and Saturdays. There are some beautiful ponchos and blankets for sale.

The *Palacio de la Cultura* at the junction of 25 de Mayo and Perú is a group of museums all under one roof. It's worth a visit.

Places Nearby The Indian ruins of Sipi-Sipi, from before the Conquest, are rarely visited. They're a two-hour bus ride out of Cochabamba followed by a four-hour walk from there into the mountains. You can camp there.

COPACABANA

Accommodation Most alojamientos and pensiones are Bp30-50/person during the fiesta (see under *Things to Do/See)* when prices naturally drift upwards. Hotels cost from Bp50 upwards.

Alojamiento Gutierrez. Calle Gral. Gonzalo Juaregui. This good friendly place also does meals and tea. Bp90/ room with two "double" (well almost) beds and one single bed — clean sheets, no hot water.

Residencias La Porteñita, same street as the Gutierrez. It's a modern concrete hotel, clean and has hot water, Bp45/person.

Hotel Ambassador, same street as above, for comparison — Bp100/person.

Other cheap places to stay are indicated on the street plan. If all places are full enquire half-way along the top side of the Plaza 2 de Febrero (main square). Go through the green door set into a white-painted wall and across the courtyard. They let out rooms on occasions.

Eats Probably the best and cheapest places to eat are at the tables inside the market hall on Calle Eduardo Aboroa. A good filling meal of meat or stew, sauce, rice, potatoes and salad, Bp7. Other cafes in town charge up to Bp25 for a meal such as trout, rice and salad. One of the best is down the side of the Cathedral on the bottom side of the Plaza. Another small but excellent place for coffee, tea and sandwiches is marked on the street plan. It's run by a really friendly Indian woman. Beers are Bp12 on average.

Other Banks only open for a short time each day. A maximum of US$50 travellers cheques per person can be changed on any one day.

Things to Do/See This interesting little town on the shores of Lake Titicaca is a much better way of entering Bolivia from Peru than by going via Desaguadero/Carmen which also coincides with the Independence Day celebrations (August 3-10) — lantern processions, amazing firework displays, parades, brass bands, plenty of chicha. People go

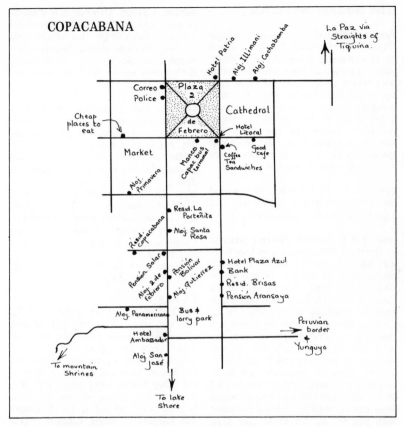

COPACABANA

La Paz via Straights of Tiquina.

Correo
Police

Plaza 2 de Febrero

Cathedral

Cheap places to eat

Hotel Patria
Aloj. Illimani
Aloj. Cochabamba

Hotel Litoral

Market

Manco Capac bus terminal

Coffee Tea Sandwiches

Good cafe

Aloj. Primavera

Resid. La Porteñita

Aloj. Santa Rosa

Resid. Copacabana

Pensión Solar

Aloj. 2 de Febrero

Pensión Bolivar

Aloj. Gutierrez

Hotel Plaza Azul
Bank

Resid. Brisas

Pensión Aransaya

Aloj. Panamericano

Bus & lorry park

Hotel Ambassador

Aloj. San José

Peruvian border

Yunguyo

To mountain Shrines

To lake Shore

really crazy all week, it's very lively and not to be missed if you're in Bolivia at this time. Just before and during this fiesta accommodation is very difficult to find so if possible you should get here before it starts. The special market during the fiesta has mountains of popcorn.

Excursions To get to the Islands of the Sun and Moon (Inca ruins), ask around among the boat owners down by the shore. Prices vary and you'll need a group of at least five people to fill a boat. Average Bp50-90. It takes up to

four hours for a round trip. Make sure they have enough petrol on board — they often run out and then you're stranded until another boat comes along.

COROICO

Coroico is very popular with travellers for its beautiful mountain scenery — snow-capped peaks surround the town. The climate is much warmer than on the Altiplano and the people are friendly. There's also an Inca highway over the mountains to the town which takes up to five days. It's similar to the Inca Trail in the Urubamba Valley in Peru.

Accommodation *Alojamiento Pijuán* (Pijoán). Bp15/person. Meals are served by arrangement. *Lluvio de Oro*, Bp30/single, is a friendly place with swimming pool which costs a wee bit extra. This one is popular with travellers. If you're going to be staying here for more than a few days, it's best to enquire about renting a house (go for Bp30-100/month), but you must stay on top of the grape-vine to get a good cheap place as they are much in demand.

Eats The bar on the main plaza is good for snacks and drinks. It's friendly and a good place to meet other travellers.

Inca Trail to Coroico The trek takes up to five days over an old paved Inca highway which is still in use by local Indians taking goods to market. To get to the start of the trail, take a bus to La Cumbre from La Paz (same bus which goes to Coroico) or a truck. At La Cumbre find the statue of Christ and then ask the local people to point the track out to you — it's well known. Most of the trail is downhill and follows a river. There are waterfalls and Incan suspension bridges. Only on the last leg of the walk will you find villages where food can be bought, so bring sufficient with you to last for about four days. The Trail is quite distinctive and there's no danger of losing it.

Other It's possible to go from Coroico to Brazil via Caranavi, Riberalta and Guayaramerin in the dry season, but virtually impossible during the rainy season (May-October).

GUAYARAMERIN
Situated in the northern tip of Bolivia on the River Mamoré by the border with Brazil, you will come through here if you're heading for Manaos via Pôrto Velho.

Accommodation There are a few places to stay. The best is probably the *Hotel Litoral*. Bp40/single including own shower and clean sheets. Nearby is the *Residencias Santa Ana*. Bp35/single. Both hotels are on the road to the airport.

Other A ferry goes across the river to the Brazilian border town of Guajara-Mirim every 10 minutes. Bp4 during the day, but Bp45 at night!

On the road to Riberalta two buses go daily, but the road is often inundated during the rainy season (May-December). There are riverboats to Puerto Villaroel (nearest river port to Trinidad) and it takes 10-15 days. Availability depends on depth of river. You need mosquito netting and your own bedding/hammock.

There is a Brazilian Consulate in town if you need a visa.

LA PAZ
The highest capital city in the world, La Paz is at over 3500 metres and situated in a deep canyon from the edges of which there are superb views over the whole city. Not a great deal of colonial building remains and the flatter parts of the valley bottom are covered with sky-scrapers. The Indian section, however, is reminiscent of old Quito (Ecuador) and consists of steep, cobbled streets which cling to the canyon walls and support numerous street markets.

Accommodation
Hotel Italia, Manco Capac 303. Bp30/person. It's a nice place, clean with hot water. This is the "Gran Gringo" hang-out of La Paz and often full.
Alojamiento Metrópoly, Tumusla 418, on the corner of Tumusla and Manco Capac. Bp35/person — clean, quiet and friendly. Hot showers are Bp5 extra. The woman who runs it spent some time in the US and speaks perfect English.

Alojamiento Central, Manco Capac 384. Bp25/person, hot shower Bp5 extra.

Hotel Los Andes, Manco Capac 364. It's similar to the *Italia*. Bp50/single, Bp100-120/double without own shower, Bp140/double with own shower. Many travellers stay here.

Hotel Capitol, Calle Murillo 413, just off America. Bp50/single, Bp90/double — hot water. It's friendly but overpriced as it's about the same standard as the *Italia*.

Residencias Rosario, Calle Illampu 704. Bp50 and 65/single, Bp90/double without own shower, Bp130/double with shower.

Residencias El Turista, Calle Chuquisaca 566, just down from the railway station. Bp33/single, Bp66/double without own shower.

Residencias Universo, Calle Inca 575, near the main bus terminals. It has the same prices as the *El Turista*.

Residencias Guadalquivir, Calle Potosí 1240. Bp40/single, Bp75/double.

Residencias Sucre, Plaza Sucre 340. Bp80/single, Bp130/double without own bath. This one is about as central as you will find at this price.

Residencias Bolívar, Tumusla 518, Bp50/single, Bp90/double, Bp120/triple without own shower.

Accommodation is often tight around Independence Day (August 4-6). If all the above places are full, the Tourist Office has a more or less complete list of all hotels/residencias/alojamientos. There's also an abridged version in the *Guía Turística*, a booklet put out by the Tourist Office but it doesn't indicate prices.

Eats The Rojo y Blanco cafe underneath the *Hotel Los Andes* probably does the cheapest cenas, Bp10, but they're small helpings. If you're very hungry, go somewhere else. The cafe on the corner of Tumusla and Manco Capac does good almuerzos and cenas, Bp18-25 (depends on what you have), and the helpings are large. Beers, Bp10. You can get an excellent "businessmen's lunch" at the cafe on Comercio between Genaro San Jines and the Plaza P. Velasco. The best salteñas (empanados) in La Paz — excellent for breakfast along with a coffee — are made at *Los Laureles* on Evaristo Valle near the Gran Hotel — very cheap. *La Creperie*, Av. 16 de Julio near the Plaza del Estudiantes, is supposed to have an excellent selection of pancakes and also to be a gringo hangout. But though we tried several times, we couldn't find it.

Plenty of other places to eat are in the central area and along the main artery (Av. Mariscal Santa Cruz/Av. 16 de Julio/Av. Villazon), but prices here are generally double and above those applying in the Tumusla/Manco Capac area.

Information Tourist Office is situated in a kiosk in the middle of the road where Avenida Mariscal Santa Cruz changes in to Avenida 16 de Julio between Loaiza and Bueno It will give maps, list of hotels with prices and the *Guía Turística* — a booklet containing hotels, cafes, night clubs, cinemas, travel agencies, banks and bus company addresses, routes and prices. Get hold of a copy.

Other The two most convenient Casas de Cambio are *Sudamer Ltda*, Colón 256, and *America Ltda*, Ayacucho 224. Both are between Mercado and Avenida Camancho. You can buy cash dollars at a three percent commission if you need to stock up. There are also good rates of Peruvian soles and Brazilian cruzieros, but the rate for soles is not as good as the blackmarket rate in either Puno or Lima. If you're going to Brazil, buy some cruzieros here as banks in Brazil are sometimes very strange about changing travellers' cheques — and even cashing dollars!

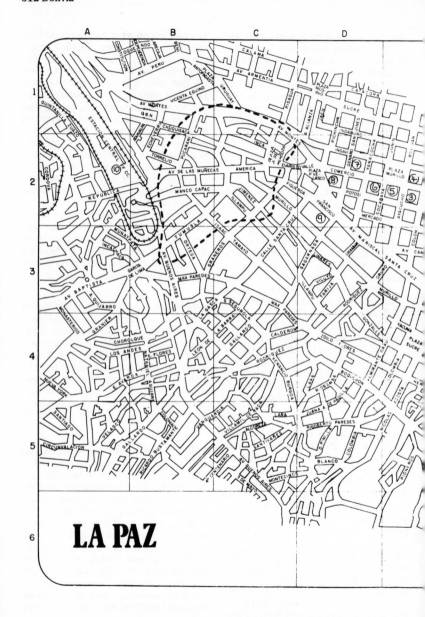

LA PAZ

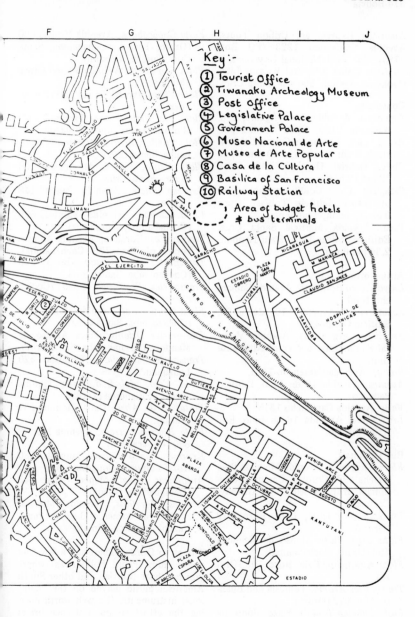

Key:-
① Tourist Office
② Tiwanaku Archeology Museum
③ Post Office
④ Legislative Palace
⑤ Government Palace
⑥ Museo Nacional de Arte
⑦ Museo de Arte Popular
⑧ Casa de la Cultura
⑨ Basilica of San Francisco
⑩ Railway Station
- - - Area of budget hotels
& bus terminals

American Express are Crillon Tours, Avenida Camancho 1223 (PO Box 4785). The First National City Bank is on Calle Colon 288, and Wagons Lits/Cooks on Avenida Mariscal Santa Cruz.

Consulates

Argentina. Avenida 6 de Agosto, Esp. Aaspiazu 2105. Open 9 am-2 pm.

Brazil. Calle Fernando Guachalla 494. Open 9 am-12 noon, 2.30 pm-4 pm.

Chile. Gabriel Gosalvez 240. Open 10 am-12 noon.

Paraguay. Calle Colón on the corner of Potosí (Edificio Tobías). Open 9 am-12 noon, 2 pm-6 pm.

Peru. Avenida Mariscal Santa Cruz, Edificio Bolívar. Open 9 am-12 noon, 2.30 pm-6 pm.

Airline offices

Lloyd Aereo Boliviano, Avenida Camancho 1460.

Ecuatoriana, Avenida 16 de Julio, Edificio Cosmos.

Aerolineas Argentinas, Avenida Mariscal Santa Cruz, corner of Almirante Grau.

Braniff, Avenida Camancho 1421.

Avianca, Avenida 16 de Julio, Edificio Petroleo.

Varig, Avenida Camancho 1315.

LAN Chile, Avenida 16 de Julio, Edificio Petroleo.

Bus Terminals

Flota Yungueña, Avenida Muñecas Psje. Viacha 497 (Coroico, Caranavi, Chulumani, Irupana, Alto Beni, Guanay, Coripata).

Transportes Avaroa, Calle Bozo 242 (Oruro).

Flota Urus, Plaza Alonso de Mendoza 194 (Oruro, Cochabamba).

Flota Kirkincho, Calle Bozo 108 (Oruro).

Transportes Aroma, Tumusla and Buenos Aires 679 (Oruro).

Flota Pullman Bolivia, Plaza Alonso de Mendoza (Oruro, Cochabamba, Santa Cruz).

Flota Copacabana, Avenida Montes 620 (Oruro, Potosi, Cochabamba, Santa Cruz, Tupiza, Villazon).

Flota San Jorge, Avenida Manco Capac 450 (Potosí).

Flota Villa Imperial, Pando 159 (Potosí, Sucre).

Cinta de Plata, Issac Tamayo 417, (Potosí, Sucre, Tupiza, Villazon).

Flota Condor, Bozo 124 (Sucre, Cochabanba, Santa Cruz).

Flota Oruro, Pje. 6 de Agosto 200 (Sucre, Santa Cruz).

Expreso Sucre, Avenida Pando 148 (Sucre).

Flota Camba, Avenida Montes 660 (Cochabamba, Santa Cruz).

Transportes Korilazo, Avenida Montes corner of Bozo 700 (Cochabamba).

Transportes El Dorado, Bozo 106 (Cochabamba, Santa Cruz).

Transportes El Cisne, Bozo (Cochabamba).

Flota Continental, Avenida Montes 521 (Cochabamba, Santa Cruz).

Transportes Oriente, Plaza Alonso de Mendoza (Cochabamba, Santa Cruz).

Transportes Bustillos, Tumusla 520 Llallagua).

Flota Veloz del Sud, Calle Tiquina corner of Figueroa (Tarija).

Flota 15 de Abril, Calle Tiquina 131 (Tarija).

Flota Riveros Herrera, Avenida Montes 660 (Copacabana).

Expreso Manco Capac, Tumusla 580 Hotel Tumusla (Copacabana).

Autolineas Ingavi, Manco Capac 445 (Desaguadero, Guaqui).

Morales Moralitos, Avenida Mariscal Santa Cruz corner of Loaiza (Puno, Cuzco, Arequipa, Lima).

Things to Do/See There are a few folk music clubs (Peñas Folklóricas) where you can hear Bolivian and other South American music played on the traditional instruments. It's well worth making the effort to go. Entrance prices vary between Bp50 and Bp100 (depends on the club). Four clubs are: Peña

Naira, Calle Sagárnaga 161; *Los Escudos*, Avenida Mariscal Santa Cruz; *Kori-Thika*, Juan de la Riva 1435; *El Internacional*, Ayacucho 206.

The Archeological Museum (*Museo Arqueologico Tiwanaku*), is largely given over to the Tiahuanacu civilization between La Paz and Lake Titicaca, but it contains relics from the rest of the country as well. Open Mondays-Fridays between 9 am and 12 noon, 2 pm-6.30 pm and Saturdays and Sundays between 10 am-12 noon. Entry Bp3.

Casa de la Cultura, Calle Potosí corner of Mariscal Santa Cruz is the national cultural museum. Open Mondays-Fridays 8 am-12 noon, 2 pm-6 pm (free).

Museo Mineralogico is the Banco Minero de Bolivia on Comercio corner of Colón with mineral specimens from the various mines of Bolivia. If you're into geology it's well worth a visit. Open Mondays-Fridays 9.30 am-1 pm, 2 pm-4.30 pm.

Museo Nacional de Arte, Casa de los Condes de Arana, Plaza Murillo on the corner of Comercio and Socabaya, is housed in an old palace which itself is worth a visit. It has paintings and sculpture from the Conquest to the present time. Open Tuesdays-Fridays 10 am-12.30 pm, 3 pm-7 pm, and Saturdays 10 am-12.30 pm. Entry Bp5.

Museo de Arte Popular, Casa de los Marqueses de Villaverde on Calle Ingavi and Jenaro Sanjunes, has craftwork, weavings, musical instruments, etc. Open Tuesdays-Saturdays 10 am-1 pm, 3 pm-7 pm.

There are plenty of small cinemas around the centre which show current American and British films with Spanish sub-titles. They use small screens and mono-sound but they're very cheap (Bp9-10).

Places Nearby The Tiwanaku (Tiahuanacu) ruins are the remains of the pre-Incan civilization which flourished here between 600 AD and 900 AD and are worth visiting. But its origins are buried in the mists of time and had been long before the Incas arrived to conquer this part of the world around 1200 AD. There are connections between it and the coastal cultures of Peru.

To get there take one of the local buses which leave daily at 7 am from the Central Station or the *Autolineas Ingavi* bus (Manco Capac 445) which leave at 7 am, 9 am, 10.30 am, 1 pm and 2 pm daily. Bp11 one way. There are two small pensiones near the site where you can stay the night if you want (both called *Ingavi* — one on Calle Bolivar and the other just off the main plaza in Tiahuanacu village).

ORURO
This tin-mining centre on the bleak, wind-swept Altiplano near the shores of Lake Poopo has little for the traveller. Jehovah's Witnesses are making a real killing here. It's largely an Indian town.

Accommodation
Residencial Pagador, Calle Ayacucho 319. Bp25/person. It's clean and friendly but there's no heating in rooms at night (you could do with it!). For a tray of two teas, bread and cheese in the morning Bp7. They will store your baggage after check-out time in the office for free — honest people.

Nearby on this same street are the *Ayacucho 339* (Bp25/person) and the *Scala* (Bp25/person). Both are about the same standard as the *Pagador*.

Alojamiento Porvenir, Calle Aldana. It's similar to the above.

Hotel Prefectural, Calle Aldana. Bp120/person!

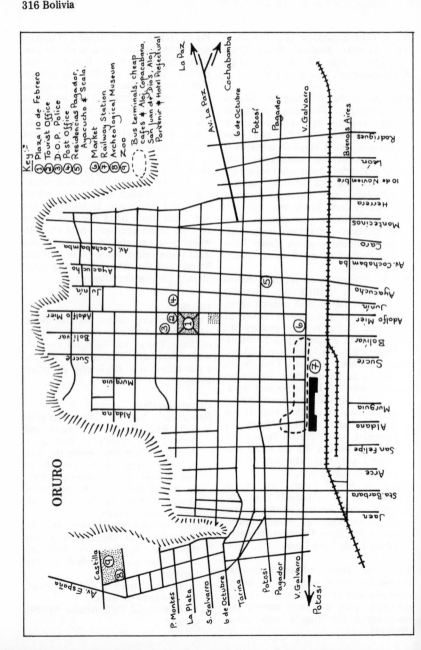

316 Bolivia

ORURO

Key:-
1. Plaza 10 de Febrero
2. Tourist Office
3. D.O.P. Police
4. Post Office
5. Residencias Pagador, Ayacucho & Scala.
6. Market
7. Railway Station
8. Archeological Museum
   Zoo

Bus terminals, cheap cafés & Aloj. Copacabana, San Juan de Dios, Aloj. Porvenir & Hotel Prefectural

La Paz
Cochabamba
Av. La Paz
6 de Octubre
Potosí
Pagador
V. Galvarro
Buenos Aires
Rodríguez
León
10 de Noviembre
Herrera
Montecinos
Caro
Av. Cochabamba
Ayacucho
Junín
Adolfo Mier
Bolívar
Sucre
Murguía
Aldana
San Felipe
Arce
Sta. Bárbara
Jaén

Av. Cochabamba
Ayacucho
Junín
Adolfo o Mier
Bolívar
Sucre
Murguía
Aldana

Av. España
Castilla
P. Montes
La Plata
S. Galvarro
6 de Octubre
Torina
Potosí
Pagador
V. Galvarro

Potosí

You need authorization from the DOP (Police), Calle Bolívar, before you can stay at any hotel, but you can book in first and then go to the police. It's just routine but probably originates from the suppression of the tin-miners' strike several years ago.

Information The Tourist Office is on the top side of the main plaza on the corner of Adolfo Mier.

Things to Do/See The Zoo (see street plan) has a moth-eaten and very sad-looking collection of Bolivian animals and birds. Entry Bp1. The museum next door to the Zoo is a pleasant little exhibition of paintings, masks, Inca stones, pre-Colombian axe heads, mummies, trepanned skulls, stuffed animals and a butterfly collection. Entry Bp1.

Other It's difficult to get out of Oruro by bus unless you have booked at least one day in advance. Many of the buses which go to Potosí are through buses which do the La Paz-Potosí run and very few people get off here. Bear this in mind if you want to spend a day or so here. The same story applies with the ferrobuses to Cochabamba.

POTOSÍ
Very soon after its foundation by the Spanish in 1545, Potosi became the richest city in the whole of America due to the vast amounts of silver which were extracted from the Cerro Rico at the back of the town. Its colonial atmosphere of rich carvings, low houses with red-tiled roofs and narrow winding streets remains intact though for a while during the 19th century it became little more than a ghost town following the exhaustion of the silver ores. Its fortunes, though not those of the miners who have to work the veins, has been partially restored due to the demand for tin. But it's a sad town and

the Indians who live here are desperately poor. A miner's pay amounts to approximately US$2 per day (though up to 40 percent of it is paid in food tokens redeemable only at the mining company's store). This wage is not even sufficient to buy the absolute basics and most are hopelessly in debt and dying slowly of silicosis-tuberculosis. The average life expectancy of a miner is 37 years. Potosí is a bitterly cold place at night, being higher than La Paz and unprotected from the Altiplano winds. Have plenty of warm clothing available.

Accommodation
Residencial Copacabana, Avenida Surrudo 319. Bp20/person. There's a cafe attached and you can get clean and hot showers for an extra Bp5.
Alojamiento Villa Imperial, Avenida Serrudo 293. Bp25/person.
Alojamiento Ferracarril, Avenida Villazon 159. Bp20/person — hot showers.
Residencial 10 de Noviembre. Bp25/person — hot showers.

Other cheapies are: *América* (Calle Cochabamba 38); *Hispano* (Calle Mattos 62); *Alojamiento San Antonio* (Calle Oruro 136); *Alojamiento Central* (Calle Bustillos 1230); *Alojamiento Tumusla* (Plaza Chuquimia 26). All are more or less of the same standard as those mentioned above. Mid-range hotels include the *Residencias Sumaj*, opposite the *Hotel IV Centenario* on Plaza del Estudiante.

Eats Restaurant *El Criollo* on Calle Bolívar 1052 has excellent food and is good value. The *El Crillon*, opposite the cinema, is also good. Others include the *La Cabana*, Avenida Serrudo, and *La Tranquita*, Calle Bolivar 975.

Information Tourist Office in the Edificio Camara de Mineria, 2nd floor, has maps and information. The same

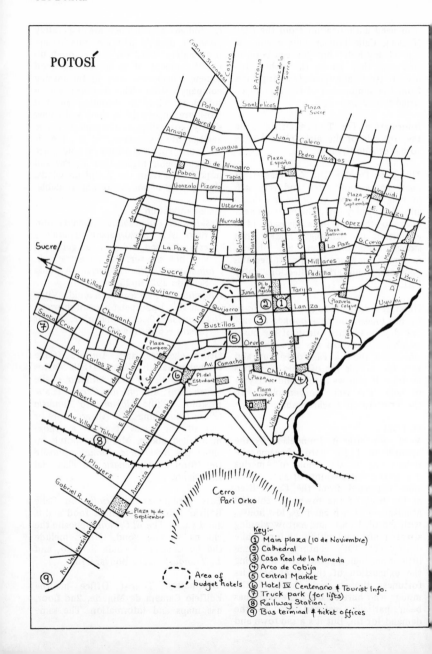

POTOSÍ

Key:-
1. Main plaza (10 de Noviembre)
2. Cathedral
3. Casa Real de la Moneda
4. Arco de Cobija
5. Central Market
6. Hotel IV Centenario & Tourist Info.
7. Truck park (for lifts)
8. Railway Station.
9. Bus terminal & ticket offices

Area of budget hotels

leaflets are available from the modern bus terminal where there is an information kiosk and from the *Hotel IV Centenario*.

Lloyd Aereo Boliviano is at Calle Lanza 19.

Other Potosí is one of the very few Bolivian towns which has a modern centralized bus terminal similar to those you will find in Mexico and Brazil, etc. It includes a restaurant which serves good food but at somewhat expensive prices.

Things to Do/See Casa Real de Moneda, just off the main plaza, originally built in 1542 and later rebuilt in 1759 is now a museum with many different sections. The wooden minting machines are still in working order after 400 years of use! (last operated in 1951). Open daily Monday-Saturday 9 am-12 noon, 2 pm-5 pm. Entry Bp5.

Places Nearby Pailaviri Tin Mines. This is the mine which made the Spanish monarchs the richest in Europe (two billion US$ in silver) and whose tin still underpins the Bolivian economy. The toll in human lives and misery has been immense and on a scale similar to Hitler's attempted extermination of the Jews. In three centuries, following the discovery of silver in the old Inca workings in 1545, eight million people died there. In their greed and because the miners died so fast in the deadly working conditions, the Spanish imported over 2500 Indian slaves with twice that number of their families and 30 000 animals *per year* from as far away as 650 km. None of this wealth has ever filtered down to the people who work the ore. The working conditions are still outrageous. A miner dies of silicosis-tuberculosis within 10 years of entering the mines. The temperature goes from the freezing cold of the altiplano surface to sauna heat in the deeper reaches of the mine. Go and experience it for yourself. You'll soon understand why Che Guevarra is a folk hero in these parts. You'll also know what the human cost of all those tin cans you've used over the years has been. It's an experience not to be missed. If it doesn't freak you out then you must have spent time in Stalin's Siberian salt mines.

To get there take the bus up to the mine with the miners at 7.30 am from the Plaza 25 de Mayo. The tour of the mines starts at 9 am Entry Bp20. Clothing is provided plus a lamp and helmet. The bus to the mines is marked *COMIBOL* — the name of the nationalized Bolivian mining company. Don't miss it.

RIBERALTA
Accommodation *Santa Rita* Bp25/ single — basic. If this is full try *Riberalta, Cochabamba* or the *Residencia*.

Eats At the *Restaurant Popular Cochabamba* you can eat for less then Bp20.

Other This is a primitive frontier town on the Beni River which you may pass through on your way to Brazil. It is connected by road to Guayaramerin on ' the Brazilian border (two buses go daily in either direction and it takes up to three hours, Bp30). The road is often inundated during the rainy season (May to December). There is no airport but flights to Cochabamba are often booked up well in advance.

SANTA CRUZ
A 1970s Spanish-American version of the "Wild West" — today it is looking decidedly settled on the edges; horses have been replaced with cars, gambling with business. There is also a large emigre population from all over the world — Menonite farmers, Japanese businessmen, English timber prospectors, American language teachers, South African cattlemen, etc. It's a relatively

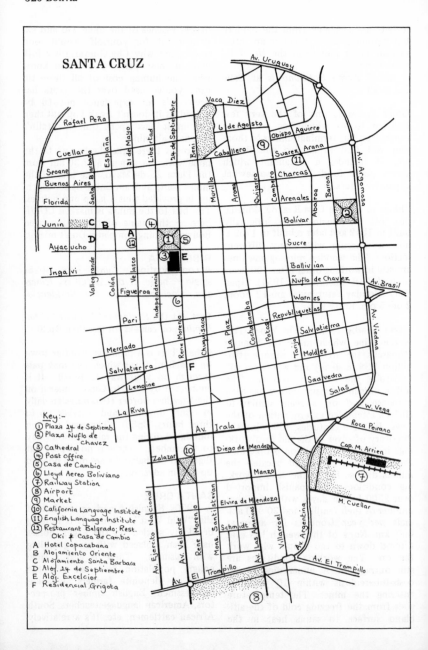

SANTA CRUZ

Key:-
1. Plaza 24 de Septiemb.
2. Plaza Ñuflo de Chavez
3. Cathedral
4. Post office
5. Casa de Cambio
6. Lloyd Aereo Boliviano
7. Railway Station
8. Airport
9. Market
10. California Language Institute
11. English Language Institute
12. Restaurant Belgrado; Rest. Oki & Casa de Cambio
A. Hotel Copacabana
B. Alojamiento Oriente
C. Alojamiento Santa Barbara
D. Aloj. 14 de Septiembre
E. Aloj. Excelcior
F. Residencial Grigota

expensive town and unless you're into some kind of trading or business, there's nothing much to hold you here. Many travellers pass through on their way to Brazil via the railway which goes from here to the border at Puerto Suarez/Corumba. From Corumba there are frequent trains to Sao Paulo and Rio.

Accommodation

Alojamiento 24 de Septiembre, Calle Santa Barbara between Junin and Ayacucho. It's the best of the budget hotels (of which there are very few). Bp40/person. It has brightly painted rooms, newly rebuilt and there's a friendly manager — very clean showers and toilets, quiet.

Alojamiento Santa Barbara, Calle Santa Barbara between Junin and Florida. Bp40/person. The rooms are somewhere on the borderline between grotty and rustic. The showers and toilets are clean. It's overpriced in comparison to the *24 de Septiembre*.

Hotel Copacabana, Junin between Espana and 21 de Mayo. Bp50/person — busy noisy, hot water. Many travellers stay here because they're not aware of the cheaper, pleasanter places a block or so away.

Other cheapies include the *Alojamiento Oriente* and *Alomjamiento Excelcior* (see the street plan for location).

Eats Plenty of cafes are in the area between Ayacucho and Florida and Santa Barbara and 24 de Septiembre but they vary greatly in price. The Restaurant *Oki* has the cheapest almuerzos and cenas — very good food. Many local people eat here and it's very popular of an evening. They also sell what are probably the best sandwiches at the cheapest prices. *Restaurant Belgrado* opposite the *Oki* (both on 21st de Mayo between Junin and Ayacucho) also serves reasonably cheap

meals, but its major attraction is that it's the chess centre of Santa Cruz. Some people (including locals) play chess here all day and half the night. They have four boards and charge a nominal Bp2/hour — good competition.

Beers are expensive in this town, Bp18-20/bottle on average though you can get one for Bp15 in the cheapest restaurants.

Information There isn't a Tourist Office but at least there is an office which is called that and two people are working there. But they have no maps and no information and don't even know the times of the trains. Large scale maps in glorious technicolour are for sale in the tourist agents *Trotamundos* on the Junin side of the main plaza (24 de Septiembre).

Other Several Casa de Cambios are marked on the street plan. None will change American Express travellers' cheques; it's cash only. They also sell Brazilian cruzieros at the rate: Cruz 0.84 = Bp1 (Cruz 16.8 = US$1). A slightly (but only) better rate than you get in Brazil, but it's as well to buy a stock here as, until you can reach San Paulo or Rio, it can be very difficult to change even *cash* dollars (this comment applies to banks as well!). Few people know the exchange rate. If you don't buy them here, the railway ticket office in Corumba will take dollars and the bus company ticket offices in Brazil will normally take them if you're buying a ticket from them (give you Cruz. 18 = US$1).

For a bus from the airport to the centre take a regular service bus, Linea No. 2 from the roundabout on Avenida Trompillo a short walk from the terminal buildings (see street plan). Otherwise taxis cost Bp10/person. To the railway station it's Linea No. 6. Bp1. A taxi costs Bp8-10/person — you may well have to take a taxi if you're catching the early ferrobus to the Brazilian border.

If you're looking for lifts in the direction of Trinidad, try asking any of the Menonite farmers who come into town to pick up supplies. Easily identifiable as they all wear identical blue overalls.

There's a Brazilian Consulate. For the address look in the phone book.

Work The main activity for travellers is teaching English. There's a heavy demand for it and so plenty of work. Try the following places:

California Language Institute, Rene Moreno corner of Diego de Mendoza on the corner of the Plaza Heroes del Chaco. See Garth who is a young American guy who's been there for two years — friendly. They can sometimes offer up to 21 hours per week teaching immediately. The wages are Bp60/hour. They teach both grammar and conversation. He also knows all about tax and residence permits if you have any problems there.

ELI (English Language Institute), corner of Suarez Arana and Abaroa (one block from the market). See the director Garrett O'Higgins. He can offer work when new courses start, otherwise he'll fix you up with private tuition in the meanwhile. It's the same rate of pay. (Bp60/hour).

Lincoln School (listed under Santa Cruz Cooperative in the phone book) sometimes has work. The director is said to be somewhat lacking in grey matter.

Centro Boliviano Americano is a normal American-style school for kids where it's possible to pick up work in a variety of subjects if you have college/university certificates.

With a combination of the above it's possible to pick up a full week's work, so that with some extra private language tuition thrown in you could be making an average of about Bp80-100/hour. Afficionados of this business say they charge Bp100+/hour for private tuition.

Flats (new and furnished) can be rented here for around Bp400/month but there are plenty of advertisements for simpler, older places nearer the centre of town for much, much less. They're unfurnished so you'd have to look around for the bits and pieces you'll need (tables, chairs, beds, cooking equipment, etc) and Santa Cruz isn't the sort of place you would find these things second-hand easily. However, you'd soon meet other expatriates who'd put you on to something. Regarding tax and residence permits see at the end of this chapter under *Other Information*.

SUCRE

A beautiful old colonial city with a mild climate, it's Bolivia's second capital city. It was founded in 1538. The Supreme Court still meets here though the other functions of government have all been lost to La Paz. It's a good place to relax in for a while.

Accommodation Almost all the budget hotels are located on Calle Ravelo (see street plan). The location of some of the others not in this street are also indicated.

Posada Victoria, Calle Junin 445. Bp25/ single, Bp50/double without own shower.

Alojamiento Potosí, Ravelo 228; *San Francisco*, Arce 191; *Residencias Bolívar*, Junin 324; *Alojamiento El Turista*, Ravelo 106; *Alojamiento La Plata*, Ravelo 28; Avaroa, Loa 111; and *Alojaimento Central*, Avenida Gutierrez, all Bp30/single,

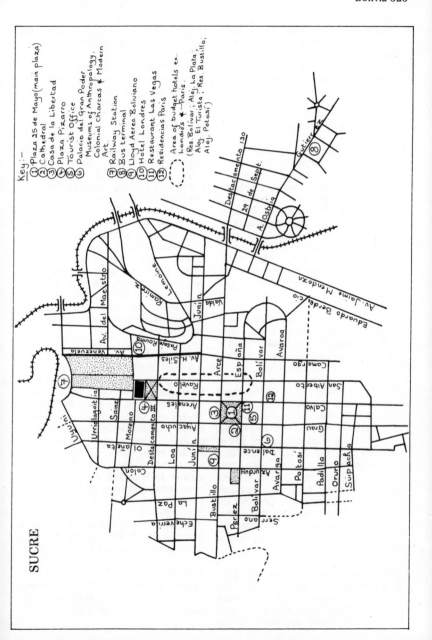

SUCRE

Key:-
1. Plaza 25 de Mayo (main plaza)
2. Cathedral
3. Casa de la Libertad
4. Plaza Pizarro
5. Tourist Office
6. Palacio del Gran Poder
   Museums of Anthropology.
   Colonial Charcas & Modern
   Art.
7. Railway Station
8. Bus terminal
9. Lloyd Aereo Boliviano
10. Hotel Londres
11. Restaurant Las Vegas
12. Residencias Paris
⊙ Area of budget hotels ex.
   Londres + Paris.
   (Res. Bolivar; Aloj. La Plata;
   Aloj. El Turista; Res. Bustillo;
   Aloj. Potosi)

Bp60/double without own bath. They are all about the same standard.

Residencias Bustillo, Ravelo 158. Bp40/single, Bp70/double without own shower.

Alojamiento Oriental, San Alberto 43. Bp40/single, Bp70/double without own shower. Bp50/single, Bp90/double with own shower.

Gran Hotel Londres, Avenida Hernando Siles 6. Bp45/single, Bp90/double — hot water, very clean. The pleasant rooms overlook a quiet courtyard. Price includes coffee, bread and butter brought round to your room first thing in the morning! It also has its own restaurant. Cena, soup, main course (excellent) and coffee, Bp18.

Residencias Paris, Calvo 144. Bp45/single, Bp90/double without own shower, Bp110/double with own bathroom.

If you're looking for something much flasher, try the *Grand Hotel*, Arce 61. Bp83/single, Bp166/double, Bp249/triple with private bathroom, Bp118/double without own bathroom.

Eats *Hotel Londres* does a good cheap evening meal for Bp18 (see above). One of the most popular restaurants with travellers, especially in the evenings is the *Las Vegas* on the España side of the main plaza (25 de Mayo). Excellent four-course meals of salad, soup, main course, ice cream, bread, all fresh, clean and well cooked. Bp25. Another cafe of a similar standard and price on the same side of the main plaza at the intersection of Perez and Grau is called the *Piso Cero*. Also try *El Solar*, Bolivar 786.

Information Tourist Office, on Calle Real Audiencia 50 (part of Grau which is renamed Audiencia in the block before the Plaza 25 de Mayo), is excellent and very well organized. It has maps, timetables and stacks of information. It's closed lunchtimes.

Things to Do/See There are plenty of old churches to see — the Tourist Office will provide you with a street plan on which they're all marked. Casa de la Libertad, bottom side of Plaza 25 de Mayo, is the building where Sucre and his generals came to work out the Constitution of newly independent country in the early years of the last century. The historical relics are worth a look, but probably the main interest is the building itself which has been beautifully restored. There are guided tours in Spanish, it's open 10 am-noon, 3 pm-5 pm and entry is Bp5.

Palacio del Gran Poder, Calle Dalence contains the *Museo Antropologico*, *Museo Colonial Charcas* and the *Museo de Arte Moderno*. Open 9 am-noon 2 pm-6 pm. San Miguel, the most famous and beautiful of the churches in Sucre is presently closed for restoration work.

Places Nearby Tarabuco has a very colourful market (ponchos and other woven garments) every Sunday. A truck from the top of Calle Calvo (Bp10) takes four hours. Go early for bargains. There's one hotel and two alojamientos if you want to stay overnight (Bp15-20/person). There's also another large market at Betanzes, on the road between Potosi and also another large market at Betanzes, on the road between Potosi and Sucre on Sundays, with hundreds of stalls and no tourists at all. Two places to stay there are the *Hotel Betanzes* and *Hotel Sucre* almost next to each other in the centre of town where all the buses and lorries stop.

TARIJA

This is another very Spanish colonial town on the way to northern Argentina — flowers, balconies, etc.

Accommodation

America, Calle Bolivar 1171. Bp25/person — clean showers.

Astoria, Calle Bolivar 533, Bp20/person. The hotel has some beautiful colonial furniture.

Vina del Mar, Calle Diego de Rojas 297 — similar to the above.

Prefectural, Avenida Las Americas on the corner of Madrid. This one is somewhat more expensive but new.

Things to Do/See There's a lively fiesta here on the first three Sundays in September — San Roque. By September 16 it's really rocking.

Other There are flights with *Transportes Areos Militares (TAM)* which is cheaper than *Lloyd Aereo Boliviano* and flies to many of the same places. Enquire at their office at Bolivar 625.

Bus Terminals

To Yacuiba via Villamontes. *Transportes 15 de Abril* buses, Bolivar 800, leave twice weekly.

To Villazon and Argentine border. Several companies operate on this route daily. Their offices are situated between Bolivar 800 and 900.

To Bermejo (the third possible crossing point into Argentina just above the town of Embarcacion from where you can catch the train to Formosa). *Transportes Tarija*, Bolivar 909, two buses go daily.

VILLAZON

It's a border town with Argentina, and a 15 minute walk to La Quaica passing through both countries' passport checkpoints along the way. If you need to stay here for the night it's probably best to cross over into Argentina.

TRANSPORT

Communications routes in Bolivia reflect its long history of concentration on the highlands and neglect of the lowlands to the East and North. Thus most of the all-weather roads and the railways run from the Peruvian border through the altiplano south towards

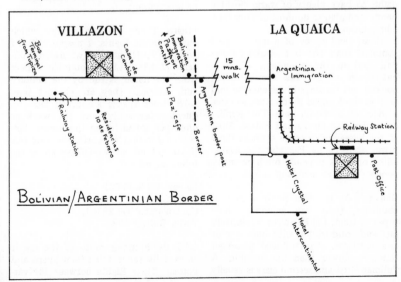

either Chile or Argentina. The only major exception to this is the railway between Santa Cruz and the Brazilian border at Puerto Suarez/Corumba. Most of the all-weather roads in the highlands are in a good state of repair but only the sections between La Paz and Oruro and between Cochabamba and Santa Cruz are asphalted. There are very few roads in the Beni lowlands and the Chaco and what few there are are generally in a poor state of repair. Travel in this area takes time and patience since you're reliant on irregular truck and riverboat connections for the most part, though there are numerous flights between the isolated towns.

Trucks are an accepted form of public transport everywhere in Bolivia and, like everyone else, you'll be expected to pay. There's usually a generally accepted "fare" over any particular route which works out at about two-thirds the cost of what the bus fare would be. Remember that in the altiplano if you are travelling on a truck it gets very cold in the evenings and at night, so have plenty of warm clothing handy and plan to do most of your travelling during the day.

Buses tend to be of a much higher standard than the bone-shaking buses you find in the mountains of Peru, but south of La Paz they're often booked out for days in advance so you have to think ahead if you want to leave a place on a certain date. This applies particularly to Oruro and Potosí. Most of the buses which come through these towns start in La Paz and the availability of seats depends on how many people get off at each stop.

Railways As in other South American countries, there are generally three types of train: (1) Ferrobus — relatively fast and comfortable with only one or two carriages. (2) Ordinary passenger trains — slower than the ferrobus. A Pullman, first and second class is usually

available with sleeping compartments on international trains (to Chile and Argentina). (3) Mixed passenger and cargo trains (Tren mixto) — much slower with generally one class of accommodation. This is the cheapest type.

As the only asphalted highways in Bolivia are between La Paz and Oruro and between Cochabamba and Santa Cruz, the ferrobus is preferable to the buses. However, except on the Santa Cruz-Puerto Suarez route to the Brazilian border, there's a heavy demand for tickets and you need to book as far in advance as possible. It's virtually impossible to get on the La Paz-Cochabamba ferrobus at Oruro for this reason. Note that although a railway is shown on the maps between Guayaramerin and Pórto Velho (Brazil), it is no longer operative. This railway was Brazil's "compensation" to Bolivia for the annexation fo the Acre territory in 1903. Although it was supposed to continue on to Riberalta it was never completed and the rest of the line proved to be uneconomic.

Flights There are two airlines which cover internal flights: *Transporte Aereo Militar (TAM)* and *Lloyd Aereo Boliviano (LAB)*. *TAM*, as you might expect from the name, is run by the military and, although they are cheaper than *LAB*, their flights are much less frequent — generally once per week or once per fortnight on the routes they cover. But they're worth checking out if you intend to fly. Offices are at the following places:

La Paz. Tel 3-25 542.
Santa Cruz. Tel 21883.
Cochobamba. Tel 28101.
Tarija, Bolivar 909.

LAB fly between most of the major cities daily (except between Sucre and Potosí). Their flights between the various frontier towns of the Beni lowlands are less frequent. The cost of their flights is about twice the price of the bus fare over the same route. Flights are sometimes delayed up to several hours. Here are some schedules and prices:

Potosí-Cochabamba (and vice versa). Mondays and Saturdays, 9.45 am from Potosi.

Cochabamba-Sucre-Tarija-Yacuiba (Argentine border). Mondays.

Cochabamba-Sucre (and vice versa). Tuesdays, 1240 pm, Wednesdays, 12.40 pm, Thursdays, 4.10 pm and Saturdays, 1.10 pm.

Sucre-Santa Cruz. Tuesdays and Thursdays.

Potosí to Cochabamba Bp245, La Paz Bp495, Oruro Bp395.

Santa Cruz to Cochabamba Bp300, La Paz Bp600, Oruro Bp450, Potosí Bp545, Puerto Suarez Bp295.

Sucre to Asuncion (Paraguay) Bp445, Cochamba Bp240, La Paz Bp 470, Oruro Bp390, Puerto Suarez Bp615, Santa Cruz Bp320.

Tarija to Asuncion (Paraguay) Bp625, Cochabamba Bp550, La Paz Bp800, Potosí Bp795, Santa Cruz Bp500, Sucre Bp350.

Trinidad to La Paz Bp365, Oruro Bp450, Potosí Bp545, Santa Cruz Bp300, Sucre Bp540, Cochabamba Bp300.

One place that is good for picking up cheap transport planes to La Paz and Cochabamba is Trinidad. Because this town is the centre of the ranching area of Bolivia, when cattle are slaughtered they have to be quickly transported to other cities before the meat goes bad. There's at least one meat plane per day — enquire at the airport. Not for squeamish vegetarians as they put you in the hold with the carcasses!

Routes to Peru

Via the Straits of Tiquina and Copa-cabana. This is the most interesting and scenic route. La Paz-Copacabana. Two bus lines serve this route: *Flota Riveros Herrera* (Avenida Montes 660, La Paz) have one bus daily in either direction going on Wednesdays and Saturdays at 7.30 am. Bp35. *Expreso Manco Capac* (Calle Tumusla 580, La Paz, same place as the *Hotel Tumusla*) go once daily at 6 am. Bp30. During the Fiesta of the Virgen del Carmen at the beginning of August they put on more buses.

A truck from La Paz to Copacabana will cost Bp15-20 depending on the driver. From Copacabana there are buses and trucks to Yunguyo — see *Peru*.

Via Guaqui and Desaguadero. La Paz-Guaqui. *Autolineas Ingavi* (Manco Capac 445, La Paz) have daily buses at 9 am, 1 pm, 2.30 pm and 6.30 pm. Bp23. From Guaqui it's a few minutes walk across the border to Desaguadero and from there take a truck to Yunguyo or Puno or a *Morales Moralitos* bus. Buses run four times per week and cost is 400 soles to Puno. If you come through on one of the days when there is no through bus to Puno, take a local bus to Yuguyo. From there daily buses run to Puno throughout the day and evening.

La Paz-Puno via the Lake Titicaca Steamers. This might initially seem like a pleasant way of covering this leg of the journey, but the boat trip takes place during the hours of darkness and so you see very little of the Lake. It's also a relatively expensive way of doing it. The journey is made by railway to Guaqui from La Paz and from there to Puno by lake steamer. The combined railway-steamer ticket is sold at the central station in La Paz. You can depart La Paz Fridays at 1.30 pm and arrive Saturday morning at 6.30 am. First class Bp490 includes cabin and food on board ship, second class Bp90, no food, no sheets and sleep in a dormitory.

Routes south from La Paz through the Highlands to Argentina

La Paz-Oruro-Potosí-Sucre-Tarija-Villazon.

La Paz-Buenos Aires (Argentina). Although cheap, it's unlikely you'd want to take this train as it's a 76 hour journey (officially) but has been known to take one week! On the other hand, if you want to get from La Paz to Villazon on the Argentinian border quickly, then it could be preferable to the bus. The train departs La Paz Thursdays, Fridays and Mondays at 11.00. It takes 26 hours to Villazon. To Buenos Aires, first class Bp460, second class Bp200.

La Paz-Oruro-Potosí-Sucre (ferrobus)

	days	arrive	depart
La Paz	Sun, Wed	–	18.45
Cruro	Sun, Wed	22.45	22.35
Potosi	Mon, Thu	05.45	06.50
Sucre	Mon, Thu	11.20	–
Sucre	Tue, Fri	–	13.45
Potosi	Tue, Fri	18.15	18.25
Oruro	Wed, Sat	01.25	01.35
La Paz	Wed, Sat	05.30	–

La Paz-Sucre Bp257 Pullman class, Bp217 first class ("Especial").
Oruro-Sucre Bp192 Pullman class, Bp161 first class.
Potosí-Sucre Bp76 Pullman class, Bp65 first class.

In addition to the above there is another ferrobus from Sucre-Potosí on Mondays and Thursdays. It departs Sucre at 16.00 and arrive Potosí at 20.30. The same prices as above apply.

Sucre-Potosí (ordinary trains), Bp64 first class, Bp38 second class.

	days	arrive	depart
Sucre	Mon, Tue, Thu, Fri	–	07.25
Potosi	Mon, Tue, Thu, Fri	12.25	–
Sucre	Sat, Wed	–	01.45
Potosi	Sat, Wed	18.15	–
Potosi	Mon, Tue, Thu, Fri	–	14.30
Sucre	Mon, Tue, Thu, Fri	19.30	–

Sucre-Villazon (Bolivian/Argentinian border) (Tren Mixto).

	days	arrive	depart
Sucre	Sun	–	06.00
Villazon	Mon	21.00	–

Fares are Bp230 first class, Bp138 second class. There's also a train from Potosí to Villazon on Mondays and Fridays at 3.40 pm. It takes 24 hours and costs Bp100 in second class.

La Paz-Oruro. Seven bus companies service this route. The journey time is three and a half hours over an asphalted road.

Transportes Avaroa, Calle Bozo 242, La Paz. Daily buses leave at 9 am, 2 pm, 5 pm and 7 pm. There's an extra bus at 8 pm on Fridays and Sundays only. Bp33.

Flota Urus, Plaza Alfonso de Mendoza 194, La Paz. Daily buses leave at 8 am, 10 am, 12.30 pm, 3 pm, 4.30 pm, 6.30 pm and 8 pm. Bp30.

Flota Kirkincho, Calle Bozo 108, La Paz. Daily buses go at 7 am, 12.30 pm, 1.30 pm and 6.30 pm. Bp30.

Transportes Aroma, Tumusla y Buenos Aires 679, La Paz. Daily buses leave at 6 am, 12 noon, 2.30 pm, 5 pm and 7 pm. Bp27.

Transportes Expreso, Tumusla 634, La Paz. Daily buses go at 7 am, 10 am, 2 pm and 5.30 pm. There's an extra bus on Tuesday at 10 pm. Bp27.

Flota Pullman Bolivia, Plaza Alonso de Mendoza, La Paz. There are daily buses at 8 am, 10.30 am,

1 pm, 4 pm, 6.30 pm and 7.30 pm. Bp33.

Flota Copacabana, Av. Montes 620, La Paz. Daily buses leave at 9 am, 3.30 pm and 8 pm. Bp30.

La Paz-Potosí. Four companies service this route with a daily bus at 6.30 pm. The journey time is approximately 11½ hours. All charge the same fare. Bp85.

Flota San Jorge, Av. Manco Capac 450, La Paz.

Flota Villa Imperial, Pando 159, La Paz.

Cinta de Plata, Isaac Tamayo 417, La Paz.

Flota Copacabana, Av. Montes 620, La Paz.

La Paz-Sucre. Five companies service this route. The journey takes 16-17 hours. Buses leave at 6.30 pm.

Flota Condor, Calle Bozo 124, La Paz. Bp150.

Flota Oruro, Pje. 6 de Agosto, La Paz. The daily bus goes at 7 pm. Bp130-150.

Cinta de Plata, Isaac Tamayo 417, La Paz. Bp120.

Expreso Sucre, Av. Pando 148, La Paz. Bp130.

Villa Imperial, Av. Pando 159, La Paz. Bp120.

La Paz-Tupiza. Two companies cover this route.

Cinta de Plata, (address above), have a daily bus at 6 pm. Bp150.

Flota Copacabana, Ave. Montes 620, La Paz. These buses are less regular. Bp140.

La Paz-Tarija. Two companies cover this route.

Flota Veloz del Sud, Calle Tiquina, corner of Figueroa, La Paz. Buses go on Tuesdays, Thursdays and Saturdays at 5 pm. Bp180.

Flota 15 de Abril, Calle Tiquina 131, La Paz. Buses leave Mondays through Saturdays at 5 pm. Bp200.

Oruro-Potosí. Three bus companies cover this route. They all run two buses per day. Bp65 and the journey time is about eight hours. There is heavy demand for seats and they're often booked up two days in advance. If you want to be sure of leaving on a certain day, book your ticket as soon as you get there. Buses are luxurious and you can sleep on them. All bus terminals/ticket offices on V. Galvarro opposite the railway station.

Potosí-Sucre. All buses arrive and depart from Potosí from the new bus terminal at the end of Av. Universitario. As with Oruro, demand for seats is heavy and they're often booked up one to two days in advance, so you must plan ahead. There is an information kiosk in the terminal with maps, information and a cafe. Three bus lines cover this route. The journey time is five hours. Bp36.

If the buses are booked up or you'd prefer to go by truck, there are plenty of trucks going to Sucre, Cochabamba, Santa Cruz, Tarija, etc, from Plaza de la Union on Santa Cruz (see street plan). They depart throughout the day. To Sucre Bp20. It takes six to seven hours depending on the number of stops. Take warm clothing with you as it gets very cold in the late afternoon and evening.

There are also daily buses from Potosí to Cochabamba, Tarija (*Flota Tarija*, journey time 10-12 hours, Bp100), Villazon (journey time 12-16 hours, Bp100), and other places.

Sucre-Camargo-Tarija. *Flota Tarija* has one bus on Tuesdays. The journey time is 16 hours. Bp160.

Sucre-Camiri. *Flota Chaqueno* buses leave on Tuesdays, Thursdays and Sundays. It takes 19 hours. Bp187.

Sucre-Santa Cruz. *Andes* have daily buses, except Mondays, at 3.30 pm. *Collita*: buses leave on Tuesdays, Wednesdays, Fridays and Sundays at 3 pm. The journey time is 18 hours. For both Bp157.

Sucre-Cochabamba. Three companies serve this route: *Oruro* (daily bus at 6.45 pm); *Minera* (daily bus at 7 pm); and *Flota Condor* (daily bus at 6.30 pm). The journey takes 11-12 hours. Bp75.

Sucre-Potosí. Four companies cover this route: *San Cristobal* (daily except Sunday at 8 am — on Sundays the bus departs at 3 pm); *Villa Imperial* (daily bus at 8.30 am); *Potosí* (daily bus at 10 am); and *Cinta de Plata* (daily bus at 11.30 am).

The Sucre-Potosí buses continue on from there to Oruro and La Paz. Journey time to La Paz is 18 hours. Bp130. It's five to six hours to Potosí. Bp30-35 depending on the company.

Tarija-Villazon. Several buses daily do this route by the bus companies located between Bolívar 800 and 900. They take up to nine hours. Bp35.

The alternative border crossings into Argentina are at Bermejo (on the river of the same name) and Yacuiba (on the Santa Cruz-Yacuiba railway line). There are two buses daily from Tarija to Bermejo by *Transportes Tarija*, Bolívar 909. They take six hours. Bp45. At Bermejo, cross the river by ferry to Agua Blanca on the Argentinian side. Two buses go weekly from Tarija to Yacuiba via Villa Montes with *Transportes 15 de Abril*, Bolívar 800. From Bermejo or Yacuiba head for Embarcacion where there are regular trains south to Buenos Aires and east to Paraguay.

La Paz-Cochabamba-Santa Cruz-Yacuiba

La Paz-Oruro-Cochabamba (ferrobus). Two ferrobuses go daily in either direction, taking nine hours. They depart La Paz at 8 am and 10 pm and depart Cochabamba at 7.30 am and 9.30 pm. There is heavy demand for this train and you need to book as far in advance as possible — at least two days. The station is on Plaza F. de Rivero.

Santa Cruz-Yacuiba (Bolivian/Argentinian border) (ferrobus). This train departs Santa Cruz on Thursdays and Saturdays at 7.30 am, Yacuiba on Mondays and Fridays at 5.15 pm. It takes nine to ten hours. Bp140 Pullman class, Bp120 first class. It's possible to book direct from Santa Cruz to Buenos Aires but the journey takes three days, and unless you're in a sleeping compartment (expensive!) you have to get off the train at Yacuiba, take a taxi to Positos on the border and then walk to the Argentinian side before re-boarding the train. If you're still into going all the way to Buenos Aries after being told that, the fares are as follows: Sleeping compartment US$50, first class US$26, second class US$19.

La Paz-Cochabamba. Ten bus companies cover this route.

Flota Copacabana, Av. Montes 620, La Paz. Daily buses depart at 7 pm, 7.30 pm and 8 pm. Bp80.

Flota Camba, Av. Montes 660, La Paz. A daily bus goes at 7 pm. Bp75.

Transportes Korilazo, Av. Montes, corner of Bozo 700. There's a daily bus at 7 pm. Bp75.

Transportes El Dorado, Bozo 106, La Paz. Daily bus leaves at 8 pm. Bp80.

Transportes El Cisne, Bozo, La Paz. Daily bus at 7.30 pm. Bp75.

Flota Continental, Av. Montes 521,

La Paz. Daily buses leave at 7.30 am, 7.15 pm. Bp80.

Flota Condor, Bozo 124, La Paz. A daily bus goes at 6.30 pm. Bp75.

Flota Pullman Bolivia, Plaza Alonso de Mendoza, La Paz. Daily bus goes at 7 pm. Bp75.

Flota Urus, Plaza Alonso de Mendoza 194, La Paz. There's a daily bus at 7.30 pm. Bp75.

Transportes Oriente, Plaza Alonso de Mendoza 278, La Paz, have daily buses at 7.30 am and 8 pm. Bp78.

La Paz-Santa Cruz. Eight bus companies serve this route. All the bus terminals are on Av. Aroma. The addresses of the bus companies except *Flota Oruro* (Pje. 6 de Agosto 200, La Paz) are to be found under the La Paz-Cochabamba section.

Flota Copacabana, daily at 7 pm, 7.30 pm, 8 pm. Bp160.

Transportes El Dorado, Daily at 8 pm. Bp160.

Flota Camba, daily at 7 pm. Bp156.

Flota Continental, daily at 7.30 pm, 7.15 pm. Bp160.

Flota Condor, daily at 6.30 pm. Bp150.

Flota Pullman Bolivia, daily at 7 pm. Bp175.

Flota Oruro, daily at 7 pm. Bp136-150.

Transportes Oriente, daily at 7.30 am and 8 pm. Bp156.

La Paz-Coroico and the Alto Beni All the various bus routes into the Alto Beni are served by *Flota Yungueña* on Avenida Muñecas Psje. Viacha 479, La Paz.

La Paz-Coroico. A daily bus goes at 9 am. Bp30, return Bp32! This is one of the most beautiful bus journeys in South America. The mountains and steep valleys are amazing. Roads cling precariously to the mountain sides and are barely wide enough for two vehicles to pass. On the way there you pass from the barren altiplano to the lush high jungle of the eastern slopes of the Andes. Coroico itself is a popular town with travellers and for a good reason. If you liked Baños in Ecuador, you'll love this place too. Try to make the journey, it's well worth it.

La Paz-Caranavi 164 km. Daily buses go at 9 am. Bp40, return Bp46!

La Paz-Chulumani 120 km. A daily bus leaves at 9 am. Bp30, return Bp36.

La Paz-Irupana 151 km. Daily bus goes at 9 am. Bp40, return Bp46.

La Paz-Coripata. Daily bus departs at 10 am. Bp30 return Bp32.

Coroico is one of the starting points for a trip through the jungle by riverboat down the Beni River to Riberalta and from there to Porto Velho (Brazil) via Guayaramerin. Riverboats run from Puerto Linares and Santa Ana. To get to these places take either a truck or bus (daily) to Caranavi and from there take a truck to Santa Ana. Remember that as an alternative to going to Coroico by bus you could walk along the old Inca trail which goes from La Cumbre to Coroico (see under *Coroico*).

Routes to Chile La Paz-Arica (Chile). A ferrobus train goes every Tuesday and Friday in either direction. It departs La Paz at 08.20 and Arica at 05.30. The journey takes 10 hours. US$16 (Bp320). This includes lunch and afternoon tea. There's also an ordinary passenger train which is much slower (about 30 hours). It departs La Paz on Tuesdays and Fridays at 10.00 and departs Arica on Wednesdays and Saturdays at 08.00. Bp130 first class and Bp100 second class. No sleeping compartments are available. Change trains at the border. Refreshments are carried on the train.

La Paz-Oruro-Uyuni-Ollague-Calama-Antofagasta (Chile) — ordinary train:

	days	arrive	depart
La Paz	Friday	—	11.00
Oruro	Friday	17.00	17.40
Rio Mulato	Friday	22.20	22.40
Uyuni	Saturday	00.56	04.30
Ollague	Saturday	08.50	09.30
Antofagasta	Saturday	22.00	—

From Antofagasta the trains depart on Tuesdays at 06.45 and arrive La Paz the following day (Wednesday) at 15.45. Take these times as approximate — the train has been known to take three days. Fares are US$15 Pullman class with sleeping accommodation, US$10 first class and US$6 second class. First class is usually very crowded and Pullman class is often booked up a long time in advance. Book your seat as early as possible.

Routes to Paraguay Going via the Chaco, the Santa Cruz-Yacuiba railway is the one to take. There are three possible routes: (1) By train from Santa Cruz to Charagua; from there to the Paraguayan border town of Fn. Coronel Eugenio Garay by truck (no buses) via Boyuibe which is 150 km from the border — Boyuibe to Eugenio Garay can take up to 14 hours (about 160 km); from Eugenio Garay to Mariscal Estigarribia by truck (again no buses) taking 10 hours; from there there are buses to Filadelfia and Asuncion. (2) By train from Santa Cruz to Villa Montes; from there by truck (no buses) to the Paraguyan border town of Fn. Canada Oruro; and from there to Mariscal Estigarribia again by truck (no buses).

Both these routes through the northern Caco area are hard going. The "roads" are unpaved and in bad condition and you can only do the trip between June and September during the dry season. In the wet season, forget it. The third is the railway.

Santa Cruz-Yacuiba ferrobus departs Santa Cruz on Thursdays and Saturdays at 7.30 am. It departs Yacuiba on Mondays and Fridays at 5.15 pm. It takes up to 10 hours. Bp140 Pullman class, Bp120 first class. There are intermediate prices and journey times to Charagua and Villa Montes.

Via northern Argentina, first go by train from Santa Cruz to Yacuiba. Cross the Argentinian border and take a train to Embarcación. From here there are trains to Formosa on the Rio Paraguay and from there a bus to Clorinda. Asuncion is an eight km bus ride from Clorinda. This is the route to take if you want to be sure of connections. If you want something more adventurous, take the route through the Chaco.

Routes to Brazil There are basically two very different routes to Brazil. If you're into the jungle and riverboat trips and have plenty of time head for Riberalta and Guayaramerin starting from Coroico, Cochabamba or Santa Cruz.

From Coroico head for Santa Ana or Puerto Linares (daily buses and trucks) via Caranavi. From there it's possible to find a riverboat all the way to Riberalta, but they don't run on any fixed schedule and you need to negotiate with the captain about the price. The journey can take two weeks or more — it depends on the state of the river.
From Cochabamba head for Todos Santos on a tributary of the Rio Grande. Daily buses go to this place from Avenida Oquendo. There are also plenty of trucks. In the rainy season (November-May) it can be impossible. From Todos Santos there is at least one boat weekly to Trinidad and sometimes others to Riberalta (latter journey can take up to

20 days). Trinidad is not actually on the river and its port — Puerto Almacen — is 12 km from the town. Moped taxis will take you there for Bp20. There's a better selection of riverboats to Riberalta and Guayaramerin from Puerto Alamacen.

From Santa Cruz head for Puerto Grether via Montero. There is a railway line from Santa Cruz to Montero but it carries freight only. It may well be possible to hitch a ride if you give the guard some beer money. From Montero there are trucks to Puerto Grether and riverboats from there to Trinidad.

The other route to Brazil and the one more commonly used is the railway from Santa Cruz to Puerto Suarez/Corumbá on the Bolivian/Brazilian border. There is no road.

Santa Cruz-Puerto Suarez (Bolivian/Brazilian border) The ferrobus leaves daily at 6 am, arriving at 6 pm. There's no need to book in advance in La Paz, just go to the station in Santa Cruz at 4 pm on the day before departure to buy a ticket (ticket office doesn't open until 4 pm). It's rarely full. Bp200 Pullman class, Bp180 second class. There's little to choose between them. Pullman has numbered and individually reclining seats, whereas second class has padded bench seats. Meals are served on the train but are relatively expensive. Wait until the train stops for a lunch break when food can be bought cheaper.

The train does not go on to Corumbá but stops at Puerto Suarez on the Bolivian side of the border. Go through Bolivian passport control (exit stamp — no fee) at the train station. There's usually a long queue. Taxis from the station to Corumbá train station cost Bp15/person but taxi drivers won't take non-Brazilians to Corumbá after 7 pm. The excuse/reason is that after that time there's no one to check baggage at Brazilian customs But this is a lot of garbage, since when you do finally go through the following morning you don't even have to show your passport, let alone your baggage. All the same, they won't take you and there's no other public transport. There's only one hotel near the station and they know it. Bp50/person or Bp100/five people to sleep on the floor in one room and sort out who gets the only bed — cold water, clean toilets. It's situated across the tracks and up the dirt road on the far side. About 300-400 metres. Eat in the shack next to the train station.

You get the Brazilian entry stamp (90-day stay) at Corumbá train station — no fuss, no money-showing, no onward tickets, no baggage search. Trains go to Campo Grande at 8 am and 8 pm. First class Cruz 100, second class Cruz 50. The second class is quite adequate, not crowded and food is served. It takes 10-11 hours.

In addition to the ferrobus from Santa Cruz to Puerto Suarez there is an ordinary train (passenger train) which leaves daily at 1 pm (officially) and takes 18-24 hours, and irregular freight trains which take even longer but which will cost you around Bp70, or less if the guard likes you. The passenger train can be a real hassle to get on. Tickets are only sold on the morning of departure and it's often hours late — sometimes a day or two! Don't count on it and in any case you won't be saving much by taking this train as opposed to the ferrobus.

Here are some odds and ends regarding transport in the Beni lowlands.

Riverboats from Puerto Villaroel to Guayaramerin take 4-7 days depending on the depth of the river. About Bp100. From Puerto Villaroel to Guayaramerin they take 10-15 days.

Buses from Puerto Villaroel to Villa

Tunari leave twice weekly, but plenty of trucks go throughout the week.

There are daily buses in either direction between Villa Tunari and Cochabamba.

Daily buses from Guayaramerin to Riberalta leave at 9.30 am and 4 pm, taking under three hours and costing Bp30. The road is often inundated during the rainy season.

LAB have daily flights from Guayaramerin to Trinidad and back, weekly flights to La Paz.

As an alternative to entering Brazil via Guayaramerin, it's also possible to go via Cobija on the south side of the River Acre which forms the border between Bolivia and Brazil. There is an airport with regular connections to the rest of the country. Get a motor canoe across the river to Brasilea, the first Brazilian town. From here there are road connections with Manaos via Rio Branco (dirt road as far as Humaite and tarmac after that) and with Porto Velho (dirt track, 800 km. There are daily buses on both these roads. Cobija is a coke-smuggling town — be careful.

OTHER INFORMATION
Working Most of what's immediately available is teaching English. There is a fairly heavy demand for it and possible schools and institutes have been included under the appropriate town earlier. Wages are not as high as they are in Mexico or Brazil but they're about adequate — average Bp60 per hour and more for private tuition.

The authorities are fairly easy going about work permits. First of all, get the institute or school to give you a letter on headed notepaper saying they've offered you a job. Take this to Immigration for an application form. They will initially send you to the DOP (Investigative Police) for another letter saying you're not wanted by them. Take this letter and the one you were given by the school back to Immigration. After that it's just a rubber stamp proceedure. A temporary work permit costs Bp900 (US$40). A permanent work permit (which, among other things, allows you to own land, etc) costs US$150. The taxation system is very lax and openly so. Very few people pay it but as a newcomer and as a gesture of your willingness, etc you might end up paying about three percent US$20 as you leave at the border if they know you've been working — ie if you had to get a work permit.

Chile

Sandwiched between the Pacific Ocean and the high peaks of the Andes, Chile must be one of the world's most unusual countries. Though it's never more than 180 km wide, it has a coastline of over 4500 km and encompasses five distinct climatic regions. In the north is the Atacama Desert — one of the world's driest areas where the only water available comes from the rivers which flow down from the Andes. It's in this desert that the rich nitrate and copper deposits are found which are the mainstay of the Chilean economy. The area used to belong to Bolivia and Peru until annexed by Chile following the War of the Pacific in the latter half of last century and those countries still cherish the idea of regaining their lost possessions — a frequent source of friction and sabre-rattling between these neighbours. Further south the desert turns into scrub and then into the fertile heartland which is well watered and intensively cultivated. The bulk of the population live in this area and it's here that Santiago and Valparaiso are situated. The Chilean Lake District — one of the world's most outstanding areas of natural beauty — forms the next zone which stretches from Concepcion to Puerto Montt. It's contiguous with the Argentinean Lake District on the opposite side of the high peaks and is a favourite travellers' haunt. Many people of German and Swiss extraction live here and because of their building styles the town is reminiscent of the Bavarian and Swiss Alps. This is ideal trekking country with beautiful forests and numerous lakes and a Mediterranean/central European climate. The last zone which stretches as far as Cape Horn at the tip of the continent encompasses the Chilean archipelago. It's a wild and largely unpopulated area of virgin forests, mountains, glaciers and islands and is home to the few remaining tribes of Araucanian Indians who populated much of Chile before the arrival of the Spanish.

Few travellers go to Chile these days though numbers have been picking up in recent years. The overthrow of Salvador Allende's government in 1973 by a military junta headed by General Augostino Pinochet and the bloodbath, widespread use of torture, judicial murders and repression which followed — and is still going on to a lesser degree — outraged and disgusted large numbers of individuals and governments throughout the world. Large scale boycotts of anything connected with the military regime were organised, often by trade unions in other countres, and thousands of Chileans sought refuge abroad. Events like this are not forgotten in a hurry and for many years Chile was give a wide berth by travellers — for good reasons. The shower of protest which descended

on the heads of the military junta initially had little effect and they continued in their brutal purge of anyone connected with the former regime though, of late, it seems they're cooling down somewhat and it's most unlikely you'll be in any real physical danger anymore so long as you're not intent on running round Santiago shouting Marxist slogans.

Although there were liberal regimes as early as the 1920s, efforts to create a socialist state didn't really get going until Aguirre Cerda was elected President in 1938. He was the first President to come from the working classes and encouraged the development of education and health programmes as well as agrarian reform. Up until then Chile was cursed (or, if you were a landowner, blessed) with the colonial legacy of enormous estates to which the abysmally paid workers were, to all intents and purposes, tied. In theory they had been "freed" during the 17th century due mainly to pressure from the priesthood who were frequently at loggerheads with the landowners over their treatment of the workers but this freedom remained illusory and still is today in some parts of the country. One event which gave it momentum was the War of the Pacific from 1879 to 1883 in which Chile fought Bolivia and Peru for possession of the mineral-rich Atacama Desert. Chile won the war and extended its territory as far as Tacna thus depriving Bolivia of its outlet to the sea at Antofagasta and Peru of its slice of the desert from Iquique north to the present border. Many of the ex-servicemen returning from this war were very unwilling to return to their wretched lives on the estates and headed for the cities looking for work. These people gradually formed an urban working class and it was their descendents who put Cerda in power.

A further step in this direction was taken by Eduardo Frei who was elected president in 1964. He attempted to make radical across-the-board reforms but generally only succeeded in raising hopes that couldn't be satisfied. The real work was left to what was dubbed the "Marxist coalition" led by Dr Salvador Allende in 1970. He was the leader of the Unidad Popular, a coalition made up of the Chilean Communist Party (Marxist-Leninist, pro-Moscow and committed to the idea of "revolution in stages"), the socialist parties, the Accion Popular Independiente (radical social democrats), and MAPU (a left-wing splinter group from the Christian Democrats). In order to govern effectively, the UP formed an alliance with the Christian Democrats by agreeing to the nationalisation of foreign-held resources, an extension of the state sector of the economy and a radical agrarian reform, but the leaders of the Christian Democrats were entirely pro-capitalist and pro-imperialist and quite incapable of actually carrying out any of these programmes. The constant attempt to keep this dithering and unreliable party happy was one of the main weaknesses of the UP Government. The other main weakness lay squarely on the shoulders of the leaders of the UP themselves. They were firmly committed to the idea of "revolution in stages" and via legal methods according to the Constitution and so often found themselves at odds with the advances which the workers themselves had made. The motivation behind this restraint lay in their determination to retain leadership over the workers and their fear of a military coup.

In September 1972, the truck drivers, encouraged by the Christian Democrats, came out on strike in an attempt to overthrow the UP Government and were shortly joined by doctors, lawyers, shop keepers, bank employees, qualified technicians and upper-class school pupils. In response to this the factory and agricultural workers formed self-defence committes, occupied factories and kept a constant watch on these installations. Trucks were commandeered to keep goods moving and shops forcibly opened to ensure that people were fed. Factories and estates which locked-out their workers were taken over and made part of the public sector of the economy. The strikers were encouraged by the activities of the right wing in cahoots with North American financial interests and Kennecot Copper Corporation which owned the Atacama mines, announced it would seize exported copper in order to "defend its rights". Meanwhile, 700,000 people demonstrated in support of the Government in Santiago and it was estimated that over the country as a whole, over two million people were mobilised in their support.

In response to this concerted effort by the workers the strike disintegrated some three months later but because the Communist element within the Unidad Popular wanted to maintain an alliance with the middle classes, three generals were brought into the government to appease them. Many of the factions within the UP were very unhappy about this.

In March the following year the country again went to the polls but not before the Communists, worried that the UP would lose the elections unless they appeased the middle classes, attempted to have all property taken over during the strike returned to its former owners. This caused internal dissension within the UP and the workers again spontaneously mobilised. The proposed measure had to be dropped.

In the elections the Unidad Popular scooped up 44% of the votes thus giving it a mandate for a further term in office but its weaknesses remained and it was still incapable of relying on the revolutionary mobilisation and organisation of its own popular base — the miners, factory workers, urban poor and the agricultural workers. Allende, the right wing of the socialist party and the Communists, remained obsessed with alliances with the Christian Democrats, who continued to be the force behind the offensive against the UP and attempts to overthrow it. Unfortunately, these were no longer the only problems which beset the UP. National debts which had been run up in the past, old machinery, the low price of copper on the international market and the drying up of foreign aid and investment caused inflation to hit record levels which in turn affected food supplies and caused imbalances between the different sectors of the economy. Six months later the army coup occurred. The rest has been well publicised.

As far as Chile's early history is concerned it was once part of the Inca Empire. These people reached as far as the Rio Maule in the Chilean heartland but were unable to expand further due to the hostile resistance put up by the Araucanian Indians — something the Spanish would come up against at a later date. The Spanish first got here in 1535 in an expedition led by Almagro, one of Pizarro's henchmen, from Peru following the conquest of the Inca heartland. They found no gold to whet their avarice and returned bitter and disappointed to Peru. Some while later, Pedro de Valdivia in another expedition pushed as far south as the city which is named after him but was captured by the Araucanians and killed. A treaty was eventually arranged with the Indians whereby they retained the land south of the Bio-Bio river but it didn't bring peace and it was only after 1877 that the Indians would allow immigrants to settle in their lands. The Indians who had been taken over and made into serfs on the estates further north were frequently in rebellion and became a cause celebre of the priesthood.

Throughout the colonial period,

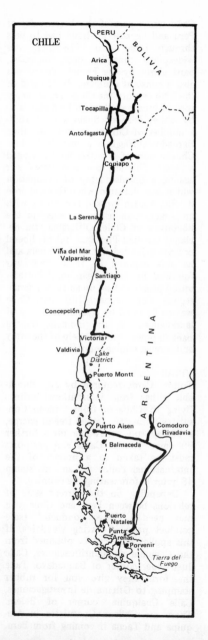

Chile was a part of the Viceroyalty of Peru and because all trade had to pass through Lima until 1778 there was widespread smuggling along the coast, particularly by the French. Piracy was also a constant problem. By the end of the 18th century the Chilean aristocracy was no longer content to be dictated to by either Peru or Spain and in 1810 a number of Chilean leaders, including Bernado O'Higgins, a half Irish, half Chilean son of a settler family, staged a revolt. This led to a seven years' war against a Spanish army of occupation which was defeated when General Jose de San Martin crossed the Andes with an Argentinian army to assist in the liberation of Chile. O'Higgins was declared the first President but his liberal policies offended the estate owners and he was deposed in 1823. Civil war followed for seven years until Portales seized power and set up an authoritarian regime. For the next 100 years Chile was to be ruled by a small oligarchy of landowners. At the moment they're back in power with the help of the army and foreign mining interests.

VISAS

Tourist Cards required by all. Obtainable either from international airlines flying to Chile or from Chilean Consulates/Embassies. Issued free of charge, a 90-day stay renewable for a further 90 days. Tourist Cards and passports must be taken to a branch of the International Police for an exit stamp 48 hours before leaving the country.

Depending on the current state of relations between Peru and Chile you may need a "salvo conducto" (safe conduct pass) if leaving via Arica. If this applies they can be obtained from the Cabinete de Identificaciones, Calle Juan Noe, corner of Baquedavo. Take the form they give you for rubber stamping to Oficina de Investigaciones, Calle Chaiquina, corner of Belem. There are Chilean Consulates in Arequipa and Tacna if coming from Peru.

Argentinian Embassy in Santiago: Calle Moneda 1123. For visas/tourist cards — eg Australians and New Zealanders. Visas costs US$6.

CURRENCY

US$1 = Ch$36

The unit of currency is the Chilean Peso (Ch$) = 100 centavos. The Peso has replaced the Escudo as the unit of currency but some of the old coins are still in circulation. If you're given them as change their value is 1 Peso = 1000 Escudos. There is no blackmarket but inflation runs fairly high and the exchange rate will, therefore, drift upwards against the dollar. Check what the current rate is with fellow travellers before changing money. No restriction on import or export of local currency.

ACCOMMODATION

There is a Chilean Youth Hostels Association with its HQ in Viña del Mar (Estadio Sausalito, Viña del Mar. Postal address: Casilla No. 159). There are three hostels:

Viña del Mar: Estadio Sausalito, 2 km from the centre of Vina.
Rio Blanco: "Riosillo", Río Blanco (Los Andes, 28 km).
Valparaiso: Cerro Concepción (Colegio Alemán), Calle Picomaya, Valparaiso.

Accommodation in the small towns of the Lake District east of Valdivia has been included under transport.

ARICA

Situated on the edge of the Atacama desert and a Peruvian town until annexed by Chile following the War of the Pacific in 1879-83. It never rains in Arica and the town is entirely dependent on the Rio Lluta for its water supply.

Accommodation
Residencia Madrid Calle Baquedano 658

near the terminal of the Chile Bus line. Ch$36/single. Hot water, clean.

Residencial Edison Calle Maipú 235. Ch$36/single. Basic.

Residencial El Cobre Calle General Lagos — Ch$36/single, clean, basic.

Other cheap places on Calles Maipú and General Lagos.

Eats Plenty of cheap cafes on the above two streets. Cheap sea-food cafes down by the harbour.

Other If you're going to Peru, take advantage of the blackmarket in Peruvian soles here. Good rate but check with travellers coming through from Peru as to the current street rate (fairly high inflation in Peru).

Bolivian Consulate on Calle Bolognesi. If you're going to La Paz on the railway, you may need to have your passport stamped by the consul before being allowed to buy a ticket.

There are some fine beaches which are only a short bus ride from the Plaza de Armas (Balneario bus line) but note that Arica is a resort town for Bolivian and, to a limited extent, Peruvian high society so prices tend to high. The sea is cold, as it is all the way up this coast as far as Ecuador.

A colectivo to the airport costs US$3 per person. A taxi costs US$9.

ANTOFAGASTA

In the centre of the Atacama desert and a Bolivian town until annexed by Chile following the War of the Pacific in 1879-83. Bolivia has never accepted this annexation and there is frequent sabre-rattling centred on the return of Antofagasta and the Atacama desert. Little here for the traveller. Plenty of heavy industry.

Accommodation

Hotel Chile-España Calle Condell 2417. Ch$54/single. Clean and friendly, meals available.

Residencial Riojanita Calle Baquedano.

Ch$40/single. Popular with travellers and frequently full.

Residencial Paola Calle Prat 766. Ch$36/single. Good place.

Splendid-Gran Calle Baquedano 534. A mid-range hotel with constant hot water. Ch$140/single.

Other cheap hotels in the US$1-1.50 range include the *Plaza* (Calle Baquedano 461); *Residencial Colon* (Baquedano 329); *Residencial O'Higgins* (Sucre 665) and others around the train station.

Eats Cheap restaurants on Calle Prat such as *Delicias de Mar; La Coquimbana; La Mil Delicias* and *Espanol.*

Other Bolivian Consulate here if going that way on the railway. Need stamp in passport before buying ticket. Another Consulate at Calama on the way to the Chile/Bolivian border. Railway passes through here.

The Post Office is on Calle Washington on the corner of Calle Prat.

Places Nearby If you'd like to visit the desert towns of Baquedano, Calama and San Pedro de Atacames there are daily buses from Antofagasta (eg Flecha del Norte bus line from Antofagasta to Calama at 8 am. Takes three hours and costs Ch$54). Near to Calama are the world's largest open-cut copper mines at Chuquicamata which are open to visitors. Bus from Calama to Chuquicamata costs Ch$10. Go by colectivo from there to the mines, Ch$10.

CONCEPCIÓN

Industrial town with its port of Talcahuanu situated between Santiago and Valdivia.

Accommodation

Residencia Turismo, Calle Cauplican 67. Ch$50/single. Basic.

Another place to stay which has the same name is located at Calle Freire 552. Ch$50/single.

PORVENIR

The only Chilean town of any size on Tierra del Fuego.

Accommodation

Hotel Tierra del Fuego costs Ch$100/ single.

Residencial Cameron costs Ch$80/ single. Good meals available.

Eats The *Yugoslav Club* serves good cheap lunches (most of the population is Yugoslav). Otherwise *Hotel Bella Vista* has a good but more expensive restaurant.

IQUIQUE

Another Atacama desert town between Arica and Antofagasta.

Accommodation The budget hotel area is located on Avenida Amunategui between 700 and 800.

PUERTO MONTT

The end of the Pan-American Highway and the railhead for Santiago. There is a strong community of German settlers who came here in the mid-1800s and have remained an important section of the population. Good place to start a trip into the Lake District or go by boat via the Chilean Pacific Archipelago to Tierra del Fuego.

Accommodation The two pensiones on Calle Vial 754 and Anibal Pinto 328 are excellent value and have hot water. Both offer bed and breakfast for Ch$100. It's often cheaper to find private accommodation with a family.

Hotel Ramwiller on Calle Quillota near the railway station costs Ch$80/ single. Basic.

Hospedaje Teresa Felmer on Calle San Felipe near the railway station costs Ch$100 for bed and breakfast. Clean and friendly management.

Hotel Sur is also near the railway station and Ch$100/single. Quiet and clean. It's often cheaper to find private accommodation with a family.

Dora Pineda, Calle San Martín 233 — bed and breakfast for around Ch$80.

Eats Plenty of cheap fish cafes on the quay side and in the market. Can eat for around Ch$90.

Other Tourist Office: Edificio Diego Rivera, Calle Quillota 124 next to the theatre. Maps and information.

El Tepual airport is 16 km from the centre of town. LAN-Chile have a bus service which costs Ch$50. Taxis cost US$4.

PUERTO NATALES

Last Chilean town of any size on the mainland before Punta Arenas on the Straits of Magellan. Popular with travellers in summer because of the nearby Parque Nacional Torres del Paine in the Andes. Fantastically beautiful area — lakes, glaciers and high, steep mountains.

Accommodation

Pensión Busca on Calle Valdivia. Ch$70. Hot water, friendly bar. Supper costs Ch$60; breakfast Ch$30. Both good meals.

Parque Nacional Torres del Paine. Entrance fee: Ch$40. Many "refugios" (where you can stay the night — or, take a tent) and well-marked trails. If you're coming in from Argentina, the Forestry Department runs a bus during the summer months (last bus: 16th March) from Calafate for Ch$80 at 8 am on Friday mornings. Returns in the afternoon. The rest of the time it's easy to hitch with forestry trucks which go up and back everyday. They pick up all hitch-hikers. Take your own food with you (1-2 days is not enough) and a good sleeping bag — a tent is preferable. The weather can change rapidly — like Baden Powell, be prepared.

Other There is an airport at Puerto Natales and road links with Punta Arenas and Rio Gallegos (Argentina).

PUNTA ARENAS
Last Chilean town on the mainland opposite Porvenir on the island of Tierra del Fuego.

Accommodation
Posia on Calle Boliviana 238, four blocks from the main plaza. Ch$100 for bed and breakfast. Evening meals for Ch$50. Good food.

The Pensión at Calle Boliviana 284 is very similar. Ch$100 for bed and breakfast.

Others in this price range (bed and breakfast) include: *Hotel Monte Carlo*; *Hotel Savoy* (Calle Valdivia); *Hotel France* (Calle Valdivia); *Pensión Paris; Residencial Roca* (Calle Roca near the main plaza); *La Selecta* (Ch$160 bed and breakfast).

Eats One of the cheapest places to eat is the *American Service Restaurant*, Ch$50 for a meal.

SANTIAGO DE CHILE
Capital city of Chile and although the fourth largest city in South America a pleasant place with many plazas and parks including the Cerro Santa Lucía almost in the centre of the city and from the top of which there are magnificent views over the city and the Andes which rise abruptly from the plain. Founded in 1541 by Pedro de Valdivia.

Accommodation
Hotel Valparaiso Calle San Pablo 1182, corner of Calle Morande. Ch$200 per person or Ch$100 per person for four people in room with two beds. Convenient for Northern Bus Terminal and popular with travellers.
Hotel Caribe Calle San Martín 851. Ch$100/single — clean, quiet and convenient for the Northern Bus Terminal. Many travellers.
Hotel Continental Avenida General McKenna 1262. Ch$100/single — meals available. Convenient for the Mapocho railway station.
Hotel Florida Avenida General McKenna. Ch$100/single — similar to the Continental.
Hotel Mundial, Calle La Bolsa 87. Ch$100/single; Ch$180/double — clean and good value.

Plenty of other cheap places around the railway stations and a YMCA if you like those kind of places. 10% service change in many hotels and a 20% tax on all hotel bills in Santiago.

Eats Some of the cheapest restaurants are located in the Mapocho market area (NB. Service charge of 20% if you sit down at a table, so if you're short on schekels you'll have to do a stand up and beg job). Some excellent food especially if you're bored out of your brain with carne, frijoles and arroz. Also cheap places on Calle Bandera eg *El Ray del Pescado*; *El Pollo al Conac*.

Other Tourist Office: corner of Morande and Catedral — maps, info, friendly and helpful people.

American Express: Turismo Cocha, Agustinas 1122 (PO Box 1001), tel 82764/83487.

Transport State Railways' booking offices for the Antofagasta-La Paz line are at Huérfanos 972, office 408. For the Santiago-Buenos Aires line book at Alameda 853. For the remaining internal lines book at Estado 33 (corner of Alameda). Santiago has an underground rail system.

Bus terminals — for the north buses leave from Calle Morande. For the south buses leave from Plaza Almagro near

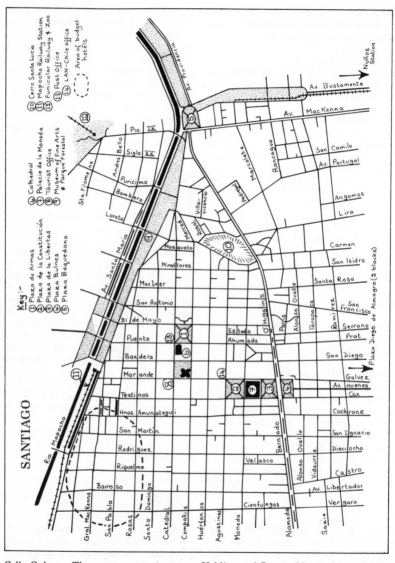

SANTIAGO

Key:-
① Plaza de Armas
② Plaza de la Constitución
③ Plaza de la Libertad
④ Plaza Bulnes
⑤ Plaza Baquedano

⑥ Cathedral
⑦ Palacio de la Moneda
⑧ Tourist Office
⑨ Museum of Fine Arts & Parque Forestal

⑩ Cerro Santa Lucia
⑪ Mapocho Railway Station
   Funicular Railway & Zoo
⑬ Post Office
⑭ LAN-Chile office
   Area of budget hotels

Calle Galvez. There are one or two exceptions to this rule — Flota Barrios leaves from Av Garcia MacKenna for example. If you want to hitch south to Valdiva and Puerto Montt, Linea 2 city buses will put you on the right road — three stops, Ch$4.

Shipping enquiries: Empresa Marítima del Estado on Calle Agustinas for boats south from Puerto Montt. They're sometimes very vague about their boats unless you are booking a first class passage. Perseverance and a little Spanish helps.

Airport: there are two airports — one for international flights (Pudahuel) and another for internal flights (Los Carrillos). Local service buses run to Pudahuel (26 km) every half hour from Plaza de Bulnes and from Mapocho railway station — they costs Ch$12. There is also a Pullman bus service by Aerobuses Tour Expres from Hotel Carrera on a regular schedule for CH$36. There are also special airport taxis if you can find them for Ch$80. Local buses to Los Cerrillos airport (marked "Cerrillos") leave regularly from Alameda and take 20 minutes.

The funicular railway to the top of San Cristóbal costs Ch$20 return.

Places Nearby The ski resort of Portillo has been taken over by the jet set and unless you have US$20 a night to spare just for a room then forget about it and head for the Lake District where the scenery is some of the most beautiful in the world.

VALDIVIA
Like Puerto Montt, this is a good place from which to start a trip into the Lake District. Strong German influence.

Accommodation There is a camp site in Saval Park. Many cheap hotels are located on Calle Chacabuco such as *Hotel Pelz* (Ch$250/double). The *Residencia Plaza*, three blocks from the plaza is another cheap hotel (Ch$100/ single with breakfast). If you'd like a hotel with plenty of character but slightly more expensive, try the *Schuster* — an old German hotel.

Other Tourist Office: Calle Maipú.

VALPARAISO
The principal port and second largest city after Santiago. It's a modern business and commercial city and little remains of the old colonial part as this has been wrecked several times over the centuries by earthquakes. Not much here for the traveller.

Accommodation
Hotel Salcido Calle Esmeralda 1107. Ch$100 per person.
Hotel Herzog Calle Blanco 395. Ch$80 per person without breakfast.
Hotel Cecil Calle Serrano 591. Ch$100/ single. Good place.

Many other cheap hotels on Calles Cochrane and Blanco Encalda near Sotomayor. Also a Youth Hostel — see beginning of "Accommodation" section.

Eats Cheap restaurants are located on Calle Prat.

Other Tourist Office on Calle Esmeralda. Information service for the State Railways and Empresa Marítima del Estado (boats south from Puerto Montt) at the port railway station near the landing pier on Plaza Sotomayor.

Long distance bus terminals are mainly located on Plaza Sotomayor. To get there from Plaza Aduana go via Plaza Echaurren and Calle Serrano.

VIÑA DEL MAR
A few minutes away from Valparaiso by express bus. This is the resort town for moneyed Chileans — expensive hotels and restaurants, casinos.

Accommodation *Youth Hostel* (Albergue), Estadio Sausalito, 2 km from the centre. This is the cheapest place you will find at Ch$30 per person. Hot showers.

There are one or two relatively

cheap places on Calle Valparaiso but don't expect miracles as it is a fashionable resort.

Other Tourist Office: Opposite the main post office.

TRANSPORT

Flights LAN-Chile runs scheduled services between Santiago and Iquique, Arica, Puerto Montt, Balmaceda and Punta Arenas. Cheaper flights can sometimes be found either with Ladeco (a private airline) or with the military airline, especially in the south beyond Valdivia. They take a considerable amount of hunting down.

LAN-Chile also fly once weekly to Easter Island from Santiago and they have standby fares on flights to and from Santiago. The LAN-Chile flight Puerto Montt-Puerto Arenas (and the Ladeco flight) are often booked up two weeks in advance. Cost of the fare is US$85.

There is a 5% tax on all forms of transport in Chile plus a 2% tax on one-way air tickets and 1% tax on all round trip air tickets. Also US$6.50 exit tax payable on international flights only.

LAN-Chile Domestic Timetable

	Mon Wed	Tues	Fri	Thur	Sat	Mon Fri	Sat	Tues Sun	Wed	Tues Sat	Thur
Santiago	08.00	16.00	08.00	15.00	16.00	15.15	08.00	09.00	15.15	08.00	08.00
Iquique		18.00	10.00								
		18.40	10.40								
Arica	10.20	19.10	11.10	17.20	18.20						
Pto Montt								10.30	16.45	09.30	
								11.10	17.25	10.10	
Balmaceda										11.10	10.00
Pta Arenas						18.15	11.00	13.10	19.25		

	Mon Wed	Tues	Fri	Thur	Sat	Mon Wed	Sat	Tues Sun	Fri	Tues	Thur	Sat
Pta Arenas						19.15	12.00	14.00	19.15			
Balmaceda										12.00	11.00	12.00
Pto Montt								16.00	21.15	13.00	12.00	
								16.40	21.55	13.40	12.40	
Arica	11.05	19.55	12.00	20.45	21.45							
Iquique	11.35											
	12.15											
Santiago	14.15	22.10	14.15	23.00	23.59	22.15	15.00	18.10	23.25	15.10	14.10	14.00

Railways Railways are very slow but cheap. Book well ahead as there's heavy demand for tickets. Information on all trains except the Antofagasta-La Paz train can be obtained at Calle Estado 33, Santiago. For info on that service go to Calle Huérfanos 972.

International Trains
To Peru
Arica-Tacna:

dep Arica	arr Tacna	dep Tacna	arr Arica
08.30	15.00	08.30	15.00
10.05	16.35	10.05	16.35

This is the cheapest way to get from Arica to Tacna but takes longer than the buses.

To Boliva
Arica-La Paz ferrobus

Every Tuesday and Friday in either

direction. Departs Arica at 5.30 am. Departs La Paz at 8.20 am. It takes 10 hours, costs US$16 (Ch$ 576) and the fare includes lunch and afternoon tea.

There's also an ordinary passenger train which is much slower (about 30 hours). Departs Arica on Wednesday and Saturdays at 8 am. Departs La Paz on Tuesdays and Fridays at 10 am. Fares are US$ 6.50 (Ch$234) in first class; US$5 (Ch$180) in second. Change trains at the border. Refreshments are available on the train but there are no sleeping compartments.

Antofagasta-La Paz

Departs Antofagasta on Tuesdays at 6.45 am, arrives La Paz on Wednesday at 3.45 pm. Departs La Paz on Fridays at 11 am, arrives Antofagasta on Saturdays at 10 pm. These times are approximate and the train has been known to take three days. You can also catch the train at Calama but don't count on a reserved seat. There is a Bolivian Consulate in Calama if you need a visa/tourist card. Fares are US$15 in Pullman class with sleeping accommodation, US$10 in first class and US$6 in second class. First class is usually very crowded and Pullman class is often booked up a long time in advance. Book as far ahead as possible. Before you book your ticket on either train to La Paz you need your passport stamped by the Bolivian Consulate in Arica, Antofagasta or Calama.

To Argentina
Antofagasta-Buenos Aires

Departs Antofagasta on Tuesdays at 12 midnight and arrives Salta on Friday at 2.55 pm. It stays here until 11.30 pm when it leaves for Buenos Aires. Arrives Buenos Aires Retiro Station at 8.50 am on Sunday. The fare is US$29 including sleeping accommodation, dining car included. Snow often disrupts the service during the winter (May-October).

Valparaiso/Santiago-Buenos Aires

The Transandine Railway runs between Los Andes, north of Santiago to Mendoza in Argentina. Part of the line is electrified — between the Chilean frontier at Las Cuevas and Uspallata in Argentina. This is one of the most spectacular railways in the world and goes through a tunnel under the high Andes and over 4000 metres. Aconcagua, the highest mountain in the western hemisphere at 6960 metres can be seen from the Chilean side of the border. It is only one of the many magnificent mountains that can be seen along this route. Best time to travel is between November and May when there are generally clear skies.

The train departs Santiago (Mapocha station) on Mondays, Wednesdays, Fridays and Saturdays. It takes 25 hours to Buenos Aires and nine hours to Mendoza. Cost is US$10 to Mendoza and US$13 to Buenos Aires. Sleeping compartments are available from Mendoza to Buenos Aires. Change trains at Los Andes either way.

From Buenos Aires it departs Sundays, Thursdays and Fridays at 6 pm and arrives Mendoza at 8.40 am. It departs Mendoza at 9.20 am and arrives Los Andes at 4.40 pm. You change trains there then depart Los Andes at 5.30 pm and arrive Santiago (Mapocho station) at 7 pm. In Santiago tickets can be bought at Calle Estado 33. The line is sometimes blocked with snow between May and November.

Internal Trains It's probable that the only trains you'll find of use are the ones between Santiago and Valparaiso and the line between Santiago and Puerto Montt via Valdivia.

Santiago-Valparaiso: three express trains daily in either direction (seven on certain days). First class costs Ch$36 and the journey takes three hours. There is also a "Rapido" on Mondays through Saturdays which takes slightly less time and costs Ch$45.

Santiago-Valdivia & Puerto Montt: daily at 7 pm and 9 pm, takes 18 hours and fares to Puerto Montt are Ch$410 Pullman or Ch$250 second class. To Valdivia costs Ch$230 second class. From Valdivia to Santiago the ordinary train departs at 8.15 am daily and the express at 5.15 pm daily. A Pullman express also leaves Valdivia three times per week at 6.15 pm.

Santiago-Antofagasta: local train departs Thursdays and Sundays and takes forever. The express departs 2 pm on Tuesdays and takes 2½ days! Cost is Ch$430. The return trains depart on Mondays and Thursdays at 6.35 pm. Sleeping compartments are available.

Santiago-Iquique: Departs Thursdays and Sundays, coming the other way it departs on Thursdays at 10.35 am. The train is principally a freight train with one passenger carriage tacked onto the end. Takes 6½ days! Just the thing if you're writing a budget travel guide and have a portable typewriter handy.

Buses Buses in Chile are modern, comfortable and fast — a welcome change after all the bone-shakers you experienced in Peru BUT they're more expensive.

Arica-Antofagasta: Several daily by different companies. Eg Norte Sur at 8.45 pm. Cost Ch$400 — takes 12 hours.

Santiago-Arica: Several daily by different companies. Costs Ch$720 — takes 32 hours.

Santiago-Valparaiso: Many daily in either direction. Eg Turbus and Condor bus lines. Takes two hours and costs Ch$40.

Santiago-Puerto Montt: Several daily in either direction. Eg Via Sur (depart from Plaza Diego de Almagro). Takes 16 hours and costs Ch$900.

Santiago-Mendoza (Argentina). Minibuses depart frequently in either direction on a daily basis throughout the summer taking nine hours and costing Ch$650 (about US$17).

Cheaper coming the other way from Argentina. This stretch is easy to hitch. During the winter months the route is often blocked by snow.

Hitching As in Argentina, hitching in Chile is relatively easy especially south from Santiago to Puerto Montt and in Tierra del Fuego so if you want to save some money/meet local people this is the country to do it. Another easy hitching route is the road from Santiago to Mendoza in Argentina — during the summer months only.

Public transport in the Lake District (buses and ferries) and in Tierra del Fuego is dealt with separately below.

Boats The road and the railway south from Santiago end at Puerto Montt so if you are heading for the Chilean archipelago or Tierra del Fuego you must either fly or take a boat from here.

Puerto Montt-Punta Arenas The old boat which used to do this run — *El Navarino* — is now out of service and the route is covered by the *Rio Baker*. The agents are Empresa Marítima del Estado (Address in Santiago: Calle Agustinas. Address in Valparaiso: Port Railway Station near the landing pier on Plaza Sotomayor. There's also an office in Puerto Montt). Fortnightly sailings taking four days to Punta Arenas. Fares: First class US$60 includes meals and a berth in a 4-6 person cabin; third class US$27 (Ch$900). There is no second class. Third class fare does not include meals but does include a berth in a dormitory.

You can only book first class in Santiago or Valparaiso and it's often booked up two to three weeks in advance. The agents in Santiago and Valparaiso can be very vague about the availability of places in third class so, in practice, if that's the class you're thinking of travelling in, you might as well head for Puerto Montt and try your luck there. If third class is "officially" full when you get to Puerto Montt the agents will tell you to hang around the gangplank until the ship is ready to sail when there's a very strong possibility that the captain will take you on. This is a fairly common occurence and well worth trying if the ship is full. Meals on board ship (if travelling third class) cost Ch$75 each.

Quellen (Chiloé Island)-Puerto Chacabuco (near Puerto Aisén). You can use this as a partial alternative to getting down to Tierra del Fuego if you can't get on the Puerto Montt-Punta Arenas ferry or if you haven't the time to wait around for the next ferry. From Puerto Aisén you go by road to Comodoro Rivadavia (Argentina) via Coihaique and Paso Río Mayo. From there a road runs south to Río Gallegos and Punta Arenas with a choice of two ferries across the Straits of Magellan.

Overnight ferries in either direction by different companies on different days. Fares are Puerto Chacabuco-Quellen: Ch$310 and Puerto Chacabuco-Puerto Montt: Ch$600.

There are buses between Quellen and Castro (another town on Chiloé Island), Puerto Montt and Santiago

daily. Fares from Quellen: to Castro (Ch$100) to Puerto Montt (Ch$300); to Santiago (Ch$1200). Buses cross from Puerto Montt to Chiloé Island by ferry. Also possible to hitch.

In addition to the above regular ferries and boats there are cargo boats from Puerto Montt to Puerto Aisén (about US$12; take two and a half days) and others from Castro on Chiloé Island to Punta Renas. Enquire at the docks.

If you get to Puerto Aisén and don't want to go via Argentina by road to Tierra del Fuego, there is an airport from which Ladeco flies regularly to Punta Arenas.

THE LAKE DISTRICT
One of the most beautiful areas in the world and not to be missed. Many travellers spend weeks down here and are reluctant to leave. High snow-capped mountains, crystal clear lakes, forests, glaciers and a northern Mediterranean climate. If you plan on doing some walking in the mountains have a good sleeping bag with you and preferably a tent. The area straddles the Andes and is shared by Chile and Argentina.

Routes through the Lake District
Puerto Montt-Bariloche (via Lago Todos Santos & Lago Nahuel Huapí)

Puerto Montt-Puerto Varas: Bus takes half an hour and costs Ch$15. Also possible to go by train.

Puerto Varas-Ensanada across Lake Llanquihue: Boat, takes two hours and costs Ch$35

Ensanada-Petrohué: Bus, takes half an hour and costs Ch$15.

Petrohué-Puella across Lago Todos Santos: Boat, the *Esmeralda*. Departs 9 am, takes 2½-3 hours and costs Ch$240.

Puella-Puerto Frías: Bus, takes one and a half hours and costs Ch$435. Goes over a steep pass. The bus is

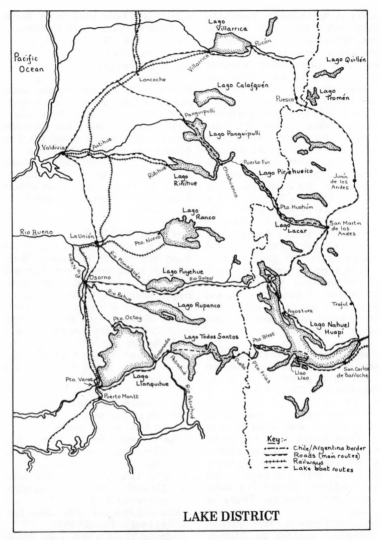

LAKE DISTRICT

an expensive 26 km hop and if you want to save money and have a pleasant walk you could skip the bus. Clear Argentinian customs in Puerto Frías.

Puerto Frías-Puerto Alegre: Boat, takes half an hour and costs Ch$100. From here it's a very short bus hop to Puerto Blest.

Puerto Blest-Llao Llao across Lago Nahuel Huapí: Boat, takes one and a half hours and costs Ch$325.

Beautiful scenery.

Llao Llao-San Carlos de Bariloche: Frequent buses, take 30 minutes.

As an alternative to starting from Puerto Montt, you may start from Osorno on the Santiago-Puerto Montt railway. Buses from there four times daily to Puerto Octay on Lago Llanquihue — takes one and a half hours. Buses from there to Ensanada, from Ensanada follow the above route.

Accommodation & other Information

Puerto Varas: Tourist Office at San Jose 325 has hotel and restaurant brochure for the whole areas. Recommended accommodation:

Hosteria Loreley: Ch$300/each including evening meal and breakfast, own shower and toilet, very clean.

Bellavista on the edge of the lake. Ch$125 per person, basic.

Ensanada: No food shops but several hotels.

Petrohue: No food shops and only one hostel — *Hosteria Petrohue*. Also a camp site with facilities.

Puella: No food shops and only one hotel. Chilean customs and passport control.

Osorno-Barriloche (via Lago Puyehue & Angostura)

The route is paved on the Chilean side but not on the Argentinian side. Through bus two or three times weekly (daily in summer) — total costs is approximately US$30.

Valdivia-Bariloche (via Antihue, Riñihue, Puerto Fuí & San Martín)

Valdivia-Choshuenco: Daily buses or come by combination of rail and bus.

Choshuenco-Puerto Fuí: Daily buses at 6.30 pm — takes an hour.

Puerto Fuí-Pirehueico: Boat, daily at 8 pm — takes one and a half hours.

Pirehueico-Puerto Huahum: Buses, daily on Monday, Wednesday and Friday (and sometimes on Tuesdays and Sundays) in the morning. Chile/Argentine border is located here.

Puerto Huahum-San Martin de los Andes across Lago Lacar: Launch on the same days as the bus to Puerto Huahúm.

San Martín-Bariloche: The most direct route is via Traful but the alternative route via Angostura and Lago Nahuel Huapí is the most scenic (not possible in winter). The latter route takes about 10 hours.

Validivia-Bariloche (via Villarrica, Pucón, Puesco, Junín de los Andes & San Martín)

The route goes via the Tromen Pass and is not possible in winter due to snow falls. Chilean customs are located at Puesco, Argentinian customs at the pass.

Valdivia-Loncoche: Train on the main Valdivia-Santiago line. Change here for train to Villarrica.

Lancoche-Villarrica: Train.

Villarrica-Pucón: Bus to the far side of Lago Villarrica. From here excursions are possible to the active volcano of Villarrica.

Pucón-San Martín de los Andes: Direct bus then another bus from there to Bariloche.

Instead of going over the Tromen Pass it is possible to branch off at Villarrica and take a bus to Panguipulli on Lago Panguipulli. There is a launch service across this lake to Choshuenco on Mondays, Tuesdays, Thursdays and Saturdays. Takes two and a half hours. From there by bus to Puerto Fui. Onward transport from here to San Martín — see Valdivia-Bariloche.

Other Accommodation

San Martín de los Andes

Lacar at Ch$100/single is a centrally

located, old pension. Good value.

Casa Alba at Ch$100/single including breakfast.

Mi Ranchita, Ch. 80/single without breakfast.

Bariloche: One of the cheapest places to stay is the *Club Andino* hostel opposite the railway station — take your own bedding, costs Ch$35 per night. Very friendly and serves good cheap food. Many of the other cheap hotels are located on Calle Moreno. Note that in the summer high season hotel prices tend to rise as it is a popular Argentinian resort.

El Retalito, Ch$70/single.

Hotel El Mirador, Moreno 500 — Ch$140/double with breakfast, hot water.

Los Andes, Calle Moreno — Ch$140/double without own shower.

Residencial Candeago, Calle Moreno, up the hill from the main plaza — also Ch$140/double.

Residencial Los Brothers, Calle Albarracin 427, Ch$140/double.

Villarrica

Vista Hermosa at Ch$100/single. Beautiful views and a North American proprietor.

Parque Unión costs Ch$100/single.

For transport from Bariloche (buses, trains and planes) to the rest of Argentina see the *Argentina* section.

TIERRA DEL FUEGO
Ferries across the Straits of Magellan
Punta Arenas-Porvenir

From 1 December to 30 April: departs Punta Arenas 8.30 am and 3 pm, Mondays to Saturdays. Departs Porvenir 12 noon and 6 pm.

From 1 May to 30 November: departs Punta Arenas 9 am Mondays to Saturdays. Departs Porvenir 1 pm.

On Sundays throughout the year the ferry departs Punta Arenas at 9 am and Porvenir at 1 pm. The above times are approximate and are altered according to the tides.

Punta Delgada-Mainland

Several ferries daily in either direction, costs Ch$45. This is the best ferry to catch if you are hitching north into Argentina as all the oil traffic between Rio Grande (Argentinian Tierra del Fuego) and Rio Gallegos, etc, goes on this ferry. The road on the mainland side also goes down to Punta Arenas.

Buses
Punta Arenas-Rio Gallegos

Bus costs Ch$400. There is an Argentinian Consul in Punta Arenas at Calle Valdivia 961 (tel 22887).

Porvenir-Rio Grande

Buses to this town in Argentinian Tierra del Fuego are operated on Wednesdays and Sundays by one company, Mondays and Thursdays by another. Departure time is 1.30 pm and cost is Ch$400.

Rio Grande-Porvenir

Coming into Chilean Tierra del Fuego buses operate on Mondays and Thursdays by one company, Wednesdays and Saturdays by another. Departure time is 6 am, cost is Ch$400.

Rio Grande-Ushuaia

Costs US$15 but hitching is relatively easy as is hitching north from Rio Grande to Rio Gallegos and Comodoro Rivadavia. Plenty of oil traffic.

Argentina

If you went entirely on the mass media's portrayal of events in Argentina over the last few years, you'd probably give it a wide berth thinking it was a dangerous miasma of political intrigue, assassination, violent strikes and street battles. These things do go on and are part of the continuing struggle, particularly by the urban workers, to force a more equitable distribution of wealth and power but, without wanting to belittle this struggle, it's unlikely that you as a traveller will come into contact with any of it unless you're involved in political activities. Most of it takes place in the industrial suburbs of Buenos Aires and occasionally in one or other of the larger cities. Don't let it put you off going there.

The roots of the struggle go way back to the beginning of the 19th century and the rivalry between Buenos Aires and the provinces. When Buenos Aires became the capital of the new Viceroyalty of the Río de la Plata in 1776, which included what is today Argentina, Bolivia, Paraguay and Uruguay, it was a small unimportant town which served merely as a military outpost to rival its Portuguese counterpart across the river at Colonia. Spanish colonial emphasis remained on Lima through which all trade originating in both the Viceroyalty of Peru and that of La Plata had to pass. Buenos Aires only started to trade directly with other countries in 1778. Also at this time, the Pampa and Patagonia had not been conquered and were still controlled by the Indian tribes who had settled this area before the Spanish arrived. Asunción, in what is now Paraguay, remained the most important settlement and the place from which much of the southern half of the continent had been explored and conquered. Attempts to settle what is now the site of Buenos Aires took place as early as 1516 after Juan de Solís first explored the Río de la Plata delta but it had to be abandoned because of the hostility of the Indians and was not re-founded until 1580. Meanwhile other expeditions had sailed up the Paraná and Paraguay rivers and, finding the Guaraní Indians friendly, had founded Asunción. The eastern slopes of the southern Andes were explored and conquered mainly by expeditions from the other side of the Andes.

The development of a national consciousness came about largely as a result of British military and commercial activities in the Río de la Plata during the Napoleonic Wars when the Spanish king was a prisoner of the French. In 1806, a British naval force, which had just taken part in the annexation of the Cape of Good Hope, South Africa, sailed for Buenos Aires and took the city. The occupation didn't last long and several months later the porteños (as the local inhabitants of Buenos Aires are frequently known) managed to retake their city. British reinforcements which arrived shortly after this event were too weak to attempt a recapture and had to content themselves with taking Montevideo until their forces were augmented. This happened the following year with a force of over 10,000 men. The attempt was unsuccessful and the British forces were defeated yet again — a string of events which gave the porteños a great deal of confidence in their own abilities to rule themselves. The Spanish Viceroy had fled during the first capture of Buenos Aires and was in disgrace. He was deposed and replaced by a junta of local notables who, in 1816, declared the independence of Argentina and successfully countered a bockade of the La Plata by the Spanish navy and an attempted army invasion from Peru. One of the principal leaders of the fight for independence was General José de San Martín who, along with Bolívar and Sucre, have become folk heroes of Latin American culture. San Martín was, only a short while later, to lead an Argentinian army over the Andes from Mendoza to help in the liberation of Chile and then of Peru.

Following the declaration of independence, there was a long period of internal conflict between, on the one hand, the Unitarist party representing central control and dominated by Buenos Aires, and, on the other, the Federalist party representing local automony which was supported by the caudillos, the large landowners, and the gauchos. The latter group were suspicious of the power of the cities. One of the Federalists, Juan Manuel de Rosas, took control of the country in 1829 and almost immediately, as far as his policies are concerned, turned Unitarist and a reign of terror followed. He was deposed in 1851 by Urquiza, the Governor of Entre Rios Province, with Brazilian army support. But this was not before the tariff restrictions he had imposed on the import of foreign manufactures had given Argentinian factories and workshops the chance to prove they were capable of producing goods of a similar quality or even better than those which had previously been imported. With Rosas' fall from power, Argentina's nascent industrialization collapsed as foreign goods once more poured into the country. A period of civil war followed in which Buenos Aires fought for control against the provinces. They were initially defeated and the capital moved to Paraná, but two years later they fought the provinces again and this time were successful. The capital was moved back to

Buenos Aires and Bartolomé Mitre became president.

Later in the 19th century, the economic and social picture of Argentina was drastically changed by immigration from Europe — six million, mainly Italian and Spanish, in 60 years — and the demand for cheap food from that part of the world. The pressure for space and grazing land led to the Indian Wars of 1878-83 in which the tribes who occupied the pampa and Patagonia were virtually exterminated and their lands taken over by the officers who had led the campaign. Pedigree cattle were imported from Britain and, following the introduction of refrigerator ships in 1877, the export of fresh beef began in earnest. The meat trade made Argentina into one of the richest countries in South America. But by 1943 there were more workers employed in industry than in cattle-raising and agriculture, and these urban workers were largely ignored by the conservative regime then in power. It was obviously time for a change.

Among the group of young officers who staged the coup d'etat in 1943, was Colonel Juan D. Perón. He had had experience of Mussolini's Italy as military attache and saw, probably more clearly than anyone else, that a new type of leader was required who based his power and support on trade unions, industrialization and nationalization. He chose for himself the then unimportant post as head of the Secretariat of Labour — a job no one else wanted. From there he encouraged the development of trade unions, Secretariat-supervised collective bargaining between workers and employers, and the construction of housing for the working class. The widest possible publicity was given to these developments with the help of Eva Duarte, a glamorous radio actress whom he was later to marry. His growing political influence was looked on with envy and jealousy by his fellow officers who arrested him two years later. Mass demonstrations were immediately organized by trade union leaders, ably assisted by Eva Duarte, and, it being obvious they were virtually in control of the capital, Perón was released. In the elections held a little while later — by common consent, the cleanest that had ever been held in Argentina — Perón swept to victory with almost two-thirds of the seats in the Chamber of Deputies and all but two of the seats in the Senate. In the space of a few years, Argentina has been taken from the era of the land-owning oligarchy into that of the urban proletariat and the "welfare state".

The euphoria turned sour following the death of Eva in 1952. The rising cost of living caused widespread discontent and corruption in government circles and the state-owned industries and agencies began to approach levels not exceeded even under the regime of Rosas. When it was rumoured that Perón intended to distribute arms to the trade unions, the armed forced marched against Buenos Aires and Perón was forced to take refuge on board a Paraguayan gunboat which was in Buenos Aires harbour. A fortnight later he was granted political asylum and allowed to travel into exile in Spain. A massive purge of Perónistas followed from the armed forces, the federal and provincial administrations, the judiciary and the universities, and the military was placed in charge of the trade unions. But Perón's political force was not fully spent and, after a period of dithering civilian government under Illia, who was deposed by a right-wing military coup d'etat, the 1973 elections were won by the Perónista candidate. He promptly resigned and paved the way for Perón to return from exile, to successfully fight another election and become once again the President of Argentina. Perón died the following year and left the Presidency in the hands of his second wife,

Maria Estela Martinez de Perón. Two years of violence, kidnapping and assassination followed, until the army, under General Jorge Videla, took over once again. The army are still in power but the struggle between the urban workers and the army and land-owning conservatives continues and is unlikely to be resolved for quite some time.

If you're wondering of what relevance all this is to a traveller, it has as much relevance to Argentina as the history of the Inca Empire has to Peru. Argentina and Chile are the only two South American countries in which the industrial workers have fought to wrest power from the entrenched land-owning oligarchy and succeeded — for a while. At the present time both countries are back in the hands of right-wing military regimes but the seeds have been sown and things will never be quite the same again for the oligarchy. If it's any indication of the military's ability to govern, inflation in Argentina is presently running at around 300 percent per year! As relevant as the history of the Inca Empire to Peru? Well, the passage of time has that magical quality of bestowing romanticism to history. Argentina's recorded history is relatively modern and, along with Uruguay and Chile, it is untypical of most Latin American countries in being almost exclusively European in composition. Most of the others are Mestizo nations or dual cultures of Mestizo and pure Indian.

Aside from politics, Argentina has some of the continent's most spectacular natural beauty sites. These include the Andean Lake District (contiguous with its Chilean counterpart on the western slopes of the Andes) centred around Bariloche; the Moreno Glacier near Calafate; half of the island of Tierra del Fuego, and the Iguazú Falls shared with Brazil on their common border. They are all the favourite haunts of travellers as well as Argentinian holidaymakers and are all highly recommended if you want to see Nature at her best. If you're Welsh, you might like to head for the Welsh colonies of Puerto Madryn and Trelew (as well as other settlements further inland) where some of the descendants of those who came here in the 19th and early 20th century still speak Welsh. But gradual assimilation has made large inroads on their culture which they came here in an attempt to preserve.

VISAS

Not required by nationals of Western Europe (except Portugal), Canada, USA or Japan. They are required by nationals of Australia, New Zealand, Israel and South Africa and cost US$6. The Argentinian Embassy in Santiago (Chile) is at Calle Moneda 1123. Visas are issued on the spot.

CURRENCY

US$1 = 1250 Argentinian Pesos

The unit of currency is the Argentinian Peso (Ar$) = 100 centavos. Inflation in Argentina is terrific and the rate changes by a factor of at least 10 percent per month. Before you buy any pesos, ask fellow travellers what the current rate is or check with a casa de cambio. Get rid of all your pesos before leaving the country — no one wants them outside. The above rate was at the time of writing.

All prices quoted in this section in Ar$ will obviously be way out of date within a matter of months but the cost is US$ will stay much the same. To get the cost in US$ work on the basis of the exchange rate which applies when you're there. Panama has cheap pocket calculators for sale, so buy one if you pass through!

Airport Taxes are Ar$1000 for domestic flights, Ar$2000 for flights to Uruguay and Ar$5000 for other international flights.

ACCOMMODATION

As with neighbouring Uruguay, Argentina has a number of Youth Hostels. Most of these are in areas of scenic beauty and outside actual towns, though there are one or two very useful hostels inside the cities — especially Buenos Aires. Other than camping, you won't find anything cheaper. The hostel in Buenos Aires is an excellent bargain at Ar$2200/night and almost next door to Avenida La Plata underground station (subway station if you're North American). The YH HQ is at Corrientes 1373, Buenos Aires, (tel 40 7134). The office is open from 12 noon till 8 pm. You need an International YH Card in order to make use of these hostels — can be bought at the Argentinian HQ. Following is a list of hostels:

Buenos Aires. Calle Mármol 1555, (tel 92 0774). To get there take the underground Linea "E" to Estacion Avenida La Plata or take any one of the following colectivos: 2, 5, 7, 15, 26, 52, 56, 65, 69, 84, 85, 86, 96, 103, 105.

Delta. Situated on an island between the rivers Abra Vieja and Luján. To get there take a train from Retiro station, BA, to San Fernando (hopefully not the last one), then take colectivo No. 710 to the river station and there catch a launch to the island. It's open all year and has 40 beds.

Pinamar (Buenos Aires province). The bus companies *Rio de la Plata* or *Anton* will take you there. It's open all year and has 80 beds. It's suggested you book in advance for this hostel at the HQ in BA — no cooking facilities.

Steinhause (Valle Hermosa — Córdoba). Get there on bus lines *Compañia*

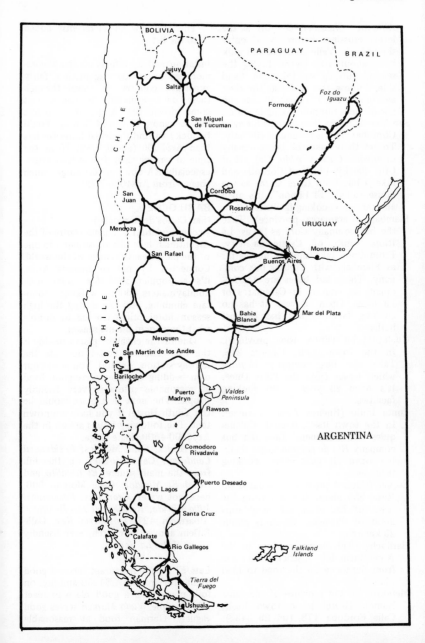

Ablo or *Chevalier*. Get off at the level crossing before you enter the town of Valle Hermosa and walk back about 100 metres taking the second turning on the right hand side. Follow this as far as the river and cross over. It's open all year and has 30 beds but no cooking facilities.

San Marcos Sierra (San Marcos Sierra — Córdoba). This is a camping site only. To get there take the bus company *Compañía Cotil y Ablo*. Get off at Cruz del Eje north of Córdoba and take a bus from there as far as the house called "El Limon". It's open all year — no cooking facilities.

Fiambala (Catamarca province). Take the bus company *Cotil* as far as La Rioja south of Catamarca city. From there take another bus as far as Fiambala with *Cóndor* bus company. These last buses are not frequent, so enquire in Catamarca or La Rioja. Open all year, it has no cooking facilities but has thermal baths.

Gualeguaychu (Entre Rios province). In the town itself, Caseros 218. Take the bus company *Urquiza* which leaves from the Plaza Once. It's open all year — no cooking facilities.

Punta Indio (Buenos Aires province). In the town itself, Avenida Calchaquies and Costanera. Take the bus company *Rio de la Plata* to get there. It's open all year — no cooking facilities.

Esquel (Chubut province). Situated on Ruta 259 about five km from the town of Esquel in the neighbourhood of Trevelin, which is about 25 km away.

Bariloche (Río Negro province in the Argentinian lake district). Five km from Bariloche on the road to Llao Llao.

Mendoza (in the province of the same Name). Hostel is in town itself, Calle Cordoba 478, (tel 25 3438).

This is a new hostel recently added to the list.

Inflation and its effects on staple commodities has made Argentina a fairly expensive country to travel through these days, especially if you've just come down the Andes from places like Ecuador, Peru and Bolivia. You'll be lucky to find a normal hotel for less than Ar$3000 (about US$2.70 at the time of writing this). In the large cities, especially BA don't expect to get much change from Ar$4000-5000.

BARILOCHE
(San Carlos de Bariloche)
Accommodation The main centre of the Argentinian lake district situated in one of the most beautiful areas of the world. Connected by rail to Buenos Aires, it's a popular spot for Argentinian holidaymakers (skiing, walking, mountain climbing, etc). So during the high season hotel prices rise up to double what they are in the off season.

One of the cheapest places to stay is the *Club Andino* hostel opposite the railway station. Ar$100. You need your own bedding but they serve good food at reasonable prices — very friendly people. The next best place would be the Youth Hostel if you have your own tent. The following hotels are all in the Ar$3000-4500/single range:

Los Andes, Calle Morales; *Residencial Candeago*, Calle Morales up the hill from the main square; *El Retalito* and *Hotel El Mirador*, Calle Moreno 500, have hot water; *Gran Luz; Residencial Villa Elfrida; Residencial Los Brothers*, Albarracin 427; *Hosteleria Rex*, Calle Elflein above the church, very friendly place; *Hotel La Veneta*.

Eats *El Fortin* restaurant serves a good dinner for around Ar$1250 and lays on folk music. It's a good place to meet other people. *Viejo Munich* serves good vaguely German food at reasonable prices and *Abo Elflein* also serves good, reasonably cheap food.

BUENOS AIRES

Buenos Aires is a huge modern city of over three and a half million people with some of the widest boulevards of any city in the world (Avenida de Mayo and Avenida 9 de Julio). Little remains of the colonial period except around the Boca alongside the River Riachuelo where it enters the Río de la Plata — a lively area of bars, restaurants and clubs. Nevertheless, it's a pleasant city and easy to get around, especially to the underground railway (subway) which local people call the "subte"

Accommodation One of the best and cheapest deals in BA is the Youth Hostel at Ar$2200/night — address under the list of hostels. As far as hotels go, there are literally thousands of budget hotels and which area you choose to stay in will depend largely on what you want to be close to — the centre, railway stations or bus terminals, etc. There are plenty of budget hotels around the two main railway stations of Constitucion and Retiro. In the central area, try anywhere along Suipacha or between Florida and 25 de Mayo. The following are all in the Ar$3000-5000/ single range: *Hotel Ocean*, Maipú 907; *Petit Hotel Goya*, Suipacha 748, rooms have their own showers and toilets; *Fenix*, San Martín 780; *Cambridge*, Suipacha between Lavalle and Corrientes, friendly place; *Hotel Principe de Gales*, San Martín 794; *Hotel Varela*, Estados Unidos 342; *Hotel Viena*, Lavalle 368, good cafe downstairs; *Internacional*, Mexico 950; *Victoria*, Chacabuco 726, can use the kitchens if you want; *Hotel Torino*, 25 de Mayo 724 — basic; *Aguila*, Cangallo 1554; *Micromar*, Calle Dr Finochetti near the Plaza Constitution, English owned, meals available; *Central Argentino*, next to Retiro Station.

Eats If you want local colour, music and a cheap meal, head for the Boca area and take your pick. Many are open till the early hours of the morning. There are plenty of laughs here.

Many cheap cafes are around both Retiro and Constitución stations and are open all hours. In the central area, try along Florida which is a pedestrian street very popular with travellers and local people. Hundreds of cafes along this street range from the very flash to the stand-up-and-get-indigestion type.

Information Tourist Office, Santa Fé 883, will give you armfuls of maps and glossy leaflets in glorious technicolour — very helpful people. It's open 8 am-8 pm.

Airports The main international airport is Ezieza, 34 km from the centre. The cheapest way to get there is to take bus No. 86 from the corner of Peru and Avenida de Mayo for Ar$150. Make sure the bus is marked "Aeropuerto", otherwise it will stop short of the airport. A taxi costs Ar$12,500 — US$10.

Internal flights and also flights to Asunción, Santiago de Chile and Montevideo depart from Aeroparque about four km from the centre just past the Puerto Nuevo area. The bus to this airport from Retiro Station is No. 56. Costs Ar$60.

Airline Offices: *Líneas Aereas del Estado (LADE)*, Calle Peru 710; *Austral Líneas Aéreas* Avenida R S Pena 701; *Aerolineas Argeninas*, Calle Peru 22.

Railway Stations Information connected with anything about the railways can be obtained from the information centre in Galerías Pacífico at Florida 753. If you want to leave luggage safely Retiro Station has good left-luggage facilities. Here are the stations:

Retiro Station. Ferrocarril Nacional

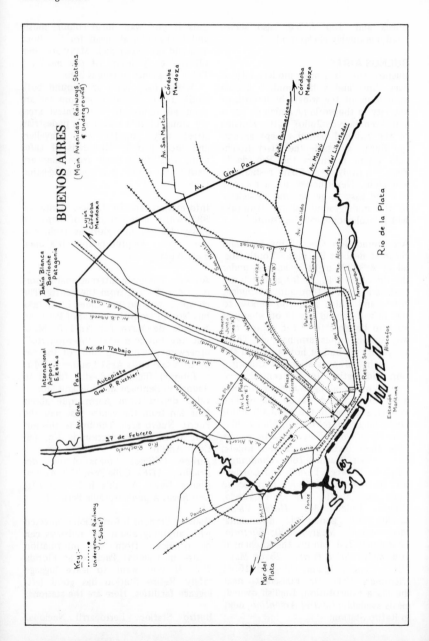

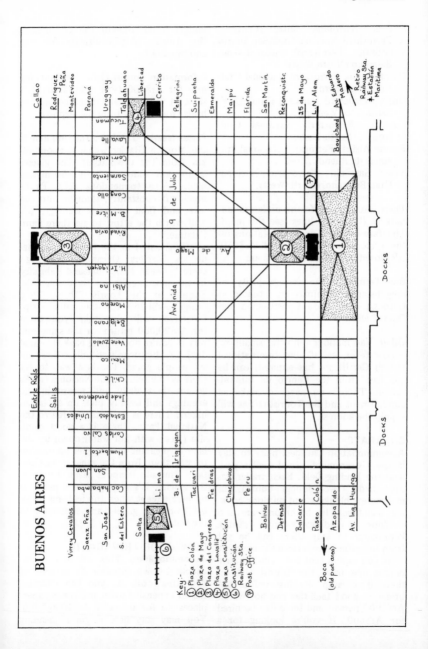

BUENOS AIRES

Key:-
① Plaza Colón
② Plaza de Mayo
③ Plaza del Congreso
④ Plaza Lavalle
⑤ Plaza Constitución
⑥ Constitución Railway Sta.
⑦ Post Office

Gral. Bartolomé Mitre (Central). Ferrocarril Nacional Gral. San Martín (Pacific). Ferrocarril Nacional Gral. Belgrano (North West).

Constitución. Ferrocarril Nacional Gral. Roca (Southern).

Once. Ferrocarril Nacional Domingo F. Sarmiento (Western).

Lacroze. Ferrocarril Nacional Gral. Irquiza (North Eastern).

Puente Alsina. Ferrocarril Nacional Provincia de Buenos Aires.

Vélez Sarsfield. Ferrocarril Nacional Gral. Belgrano. (North West).

There are five different underground-railway ("Subte") lines (see the map). The fare between any two stations on the system is a flat rate of Ar$150. It's closed between 1 am and 5 am.

Bus Terminals The vast majority of long-distance terminals are situated at Córdoba 416, Plaza Constitución and Once Station.

Other Vaccinations (cholera, smallpox, yellow fever, etc if your International Health Certificate has expired) can be got free from the Centro de Inmunizacion. There's no need to make an appointment and the Tourist Office will supply the address.

CALAFATE

Accommodation Cheapest place to stay is the Government-owned trailer park near the landing field. Each trailer has four beds (two double bunks), air mattresses, blankets and outdoor cooking facilities. The bathrooms are also outdoors — cold water only. Ar$500. Permission to stay there can be got from the office across from the church.

If you have a tent with you (or have rented one from the Tourist Office), there is a camp site just before the bridge — good facilities and hot water. Ar$1000/person and tents can be hired for Ar$500. If you're looking for a budget hotel, one of the cheapest is the *Amado*. Ar$3700/single for bed and breakfast.

Information Tourist Office has tents for hire for Ar$500 (will sleep four). It's situated on the main street before the bridge on the way from the airport.

Places Nearby The big attraction here is the Moreno Glacier which is about 80 km from the town itself. The glacier is one km wide and about 50 metres high. It's a tremendous sight. Pieces break off constantly, thunder into the lake and float away as icebergs. It's well worth the effort to get there from Calafate.

It's situated in the Parque Nacional de los Glaciers. Occasional buses go there between November and February in the mornings — no fixed schedule. Enquire at the Tourist Office. They charge Ar$6250 for the round trip. Colectivos will also take you there for Ar$20,000 return (or the same one way if you're not coming back the same day) but they won't go unless there are six people going. The best way to get there is to hitch. Parque Nacional trucks go up there daily and return in the evenings and usually pick up all hitchhikers. There is no entrance fee to the National Park. There is a good camp site (free) with hot water down by the lake in pleasant woods. Get permission to stay there from the rangers in Calafate. The site is about seven km from the glacier. It's very quiet and peaceful up here except when the icebergs break off from the glacier and thunder into the water.

COMMODORO RIVADAVIA

Accommodation This oil and petro-chemical town supplies 28 percent of Argentina's oil. As you can imagine, it's an expensive town and the cheapest places go for between Ar$4000-5000. You may stay here if you're heading for Puerto Aisen in Chile.

Some of the budget hotels are: *España; Hospedaje Hamburgo*, Calle B. Mitre, good restaurant attached; *Colón; Hotel Central*, (also has good restaurant attached). Other cheapies are near the bus terminal.

CORDOBA

Accommodation This is Argentina's third largest city, situated in a beautiful area with some excellent places to stay in the nearby mountains. Much of the colonial atmosphere of the place remains.

Pensión Susy Entre Rios. Ar$6250/ double.

Residencial Plaza, 150 metres from the bus terminal. Ar$3750/single — clean and friendly. Quiet.

Hotel Lady, near the bus terminal. Ar$6250/double with own shower — friendly.

Hotel Central 100 metres from the bus terminal. Ar$6250/double — hot water. A good restaurant is attached with food at reasonable prices.

Eats *Mendel,* San Jeronimo near the railway station, has good food at reasonable prices. *Palacio de Pasta* sells the sort of food you would expect with a name like that. The meals are cheap.

Information The Tourist Office, in the bus terminal has maps and information. The long-distance bus terminal is a new place with ticket offices, shops and cafes, etc as well.

Things to Do/See The Viceroy's House (Casa del Virrey), Calle Rosario east of the Plaza San Martín, houses the Historical and Colonial Museums, but is worth visiting for its own sake. It's open Tuesday-Friday 9 am-6 pm and Saturday-Sunday 9 am-12 noon.

JUJUY

This city and Salta a little further south are two beautiful cities surrounded by mountains and forests, and with their colonial atmosphere and buildings intact. New buildings continue to be put up in the old style. Many travellers come here on their way down from Bolivia.

Accommodation

Bristol opposite the railway station. Ar$5625/double — hot water.

Cleveland, Alvear 782. Ar$3125/single, clean and basic.

Hotel del Norte near the railway station. Ar$3125/single — clean and friendly. Other cheapies include: *Residencial San Remo* Ar$5625/double; *Residencial Lavalle*, Ar$5625/double.

Information Tourist Office on Güemes 1632 and Avenida Belgrano has helpful people, maps and information.

Airport is 40 km from the town. Local buses run there — enquire at the Tourist Office.

Places Nearby Termas de Reyes, hot springs, are 24 km from town. Camping is allowed free of charge below the expensive *Gran Hotel Termas de Reyes.* The springs are 45 minutes away from Jujuy by local bus.

MENDOZA

It's the centre of the vineyard area of Argentina and a pleasant city with many trees. Although founded in 1561, it was destroyed by earthquake and fire in the middle of the last century and is now a fairly modern city of low houses. This is the town from which General San Martín set out with his Army of the Andes to liberate Chile and Peru from the Spanish. There is a huge monument to him on the Cerro de la Gloria in the Parque San Martín.

Accommodation

El Descanso, Gral. Paz 463. Ar$6250/

double. It's a nice place.

Margat, Juan B. Justo 75. Ar$3125/
single — clean.

Zamara, Peru 1156. Ar$6875/double.
It's friendly and situated in a converted house.

Pensión Janni, junction of 9 de Julio
and Infanta Mercedes San Martín.
Ar$3125/single.

Namuncua, Chile 829. Ar$6875/double
with own shower.

Pension at Catamarca 371, Ar$3000
with cooking facilities.

Eats *Piccolini* Sarmiento 234, is an
Italian restaurant with good cheap food
and friendly atmosphere. *El Rey de la
Milanesa* has good cheap meals. *Hotel
Nevada*, Las Heras 691. Ar$1800-
2200 for a four course meal. *Taberna
la Tapita* on 25 de Mayo 1529 has good
cheap meals.

Information The Tourist Offices in
the main bus station on Avenida Zapata
and also on San Martín are very helpful.
They have maps, literature, etc.

Things to Do/See Wine Bodegas — there
are many of these in the nearby area.
Most are only too pleased to entertain
visitors and they're very generous with
the vino collapso at the end of the visit
(free!). One of the largest is the *Bodega
de Arizu* which is 10 minutes by bus
from town. You can visit anytime. The
annual wine festival in Mendoza is in
mid-February; a good time to be there.
There's also a grape harvest festival in
March.

The Historical Museum on Calle
Montevideo near Calle Chile has all
manner of bits and pieces from the life
and times of General San Martin as well
as of the history of Mendoza.

Other The Chilean Tourist Office on
9 de Julio 1022 is worth a visit if you're
heading in that direction either by train
or bus. Maps, information, etc can be
got here.

PUERTO MADRYN

If you're Welsh, this is home away from
home for you. The first batch of Welsh
colonists arrived here in 1865 and were
re-inforced over the years by many
more immigrants both from Wales and
from the US. The last group arrived in
1911. The original idea was to create
a Wales beyond Wales and to keep the
language alive. They've only been partially successful at this since only about
10 percent of the people in the many
towns and settlements they founded
can speak the language. The other major
Welsh settlements are at Chubut and
Treflen (Tevelen) at the food of the
Andes.

Accommodation

Hotel Paris, Ar$4000/single.

Vasconia, 25 de Mayo 43, Ar$4000/
single, hot water.

Petit Residencial, Ar$7500/double —
serves good meals for Ar$2000

Eats *Ranchao Grande* has excellent sea
food at reasonable prices.

Places Nearby The Valdés Peninsula
neaby is a wildlife sanctuary — sea
lions, sea elephants, penguin colonies.
The best time to visit is in the spring-
time. The biggest penguin colonies outside Antarctica are to be found further
south 30 km from the town of Cama-
rones between Puerto Madryn and
Comodoro Rivadavia. If you're into
wildlife it's well worth a visit.

RÍO GALLEGOS

Accommodation Not a particularly
interesting town, but one you may have
to stay overnight in on your way to
or from Tierra del Fuego. It's an expensive town. Don't expect too much
change from Ar$4000/single in a
hotel. If you're there in summer during
the school holidays, the Catholic
School in the centre of town allows
backpackers to sleep in the classrooms
free of charge.

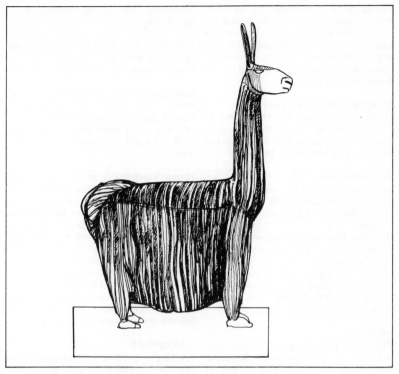

The following hotels are the cheapest available but still cost Ar$3000-4000/ single: *Hotel Asturiano*, diagonally opposite the Post Office and *LADE* office (there's no name sign — just a Pepsi sign) — hot water, heating, very clean; *Residencial Mariol*, Calle Avellaneras; *Punta Arenas; Plaza; Colón; Victoria*, end of main street — basic and friendly; *Internacional* — hot water.

Eats The cheapest cafe you'll find in this town is the *Al Fondo*, Calle San Martín 933. The "menu completo" here costs Ar$2000-2500 depending on what you have to eat.

Information The Tourist Office is on Calle 9 de Julio.

SALTA

Accommodation The following hotels are in the Ar$3000-4000 range (the cheapest available): *Residencial Artur*, Rivadavia 752 — no hot water; *Cepmer*, Yrigoyen 1195, good place; *Pensión Madrid*, Calle B. Mitre; *Residencial España*, corner of Balcarce and Necochea. Other cheapies include *Residencial Siena; La Florida* and *Mendoza*.

Eats *Los Dos Chinos*, Alberdi 187, has good cheap Chinese food. *La Pergola* has local Argentinian food.

Information Tourist Office on Calle Buenos Aires 61 near the main plaza, has maps and information.

Things to Do/See Sister city to Jujuy and an intact gem of colonial Argentina. It's popular with travellers. You can get excellent views over the city from the top of Cerro San Bernardo. Follow the steep path which goes to the top via the Stations of the Cross.

SAN MARTIN DE LOS ANDES
North of Bariloche on the shores of Lago Lacar in the Parque Nacional Lanin, this beautiful little town is not as over-run with tourists as Bariloche.

Accommodation
Lácar, old house in the centre of town. Ar$5625/double. Meals are available.
Casa Alba. Ar$3125/single — pleasant hotel.
If you'd like to stay outside town on the shores of the lake try the *Hosteria Arrayan*, three km from San Martin, which has self-contained cabins all with excellent views over the lake. The proprietor is English. Ar$6250/person including meals.

USHUAIA
This is the world's most southerly community, if you discount scientific settlements on South Geogia and in Antarctica, and capital of the Argentinian half of Tierra del Fuego. The setting is beautiful amid snow-capped mountains, pine forests, glaciers and waterfalls.

Accommodation *Castelar*, San Martín 845, Ar$4000/single. It has a restaurant attached with good food. *Ona*, Ar$3750/single in the unheated rooms, Ar$5625/single in the heated rooms.

During the summer months, backpackers are allowed to sleep free in the school gymnasium. Have a sleeping bag handy to lie on. If you'd prefer to stay in a private house, ask at the Tourist Office. There's a Youth Hostel about 15 minutes out of town (Albergue). Ar$1875/person in dormitory accommodation. One of the cheapest deals you'll find.

Eats The *Tanta Nina* has good German food and also serves the best fish in town. Otherwise eat at the *Castelar.*

Information The Tourist Office, next door to the Hotel Albatros, helps in finding private rented accommodation and also has a small map showing possible treks and excursions in the nearby area.

Places Nearby Parque Nacional Tierra del Fuego. Entrance fee Ar$500. You can camp here but there are no facilities (they're in the process of being built). The glacier in the Parque north of Ushuaia can be reached by a two to three hour walk.

Other If you're thinking of flying out of Ushuaia with *LADE*, book a seat as far ahead as possible, as there's a heavy demand for tickets and it's often booked up for two weeks in advance.

TRANSPORT
Hitching is good in Argentina and you can cover distances in little more time than it would take on the bus. This applies as much to Patagonia and Tierra del Fuego as to the more developed northern half of the country. In the various National Parks, take advantage of the workers'/rangers' trucks which go between the Parks and the nearest towns virtually every day. They generally pick up all hitch-hikers. This applies particularly to the Moreno National Park which is 80 km from the town of Calafate. Buses to the park are rare and colectivos charge Ar$10,000 and won't go unless they have a full car.

As for the other transport possibilities, second class railway fares work out at approximately half the cost of a bus, though they are slower. One of the best deals available are the *Lineas Aéreas del Estado (LADE)* and *Austral Líneas* flights which are often the same or even less — no exaggeration! — than the equivalent bus fares. There are also night flights ("vuelos nocturnos") which are even cheaper than day flights. They're very useful in the Lake District, Patagonia and Tierra del Fuego, though, as you can imagine, there's heavy demand for tickets and you must book ahead as far as possible. Some routes are booked up for two weeks in advance, though it's possible to get on at a day's notice if there are cancellations.

In Buenos Aires, information about the railways can be got from the information centre in Galerías Pacífico on Florida 753. The BA offices of the domestic airlines are: *LADE*, Calle Peru 710, and *Austral Líneas Aéreas*, Avenida R. S. Peña. You can book ahead here for flights in other parts of the country.

Flights *LADE* connect all the main towns and cities in southern Argentina on a regular schedule — Ushuaia, Río Grande, Río Gallegos, Calafate, Perito Moreno, Comodoro Rivadavia, Puerto Madryn, Bariloche, Buenos Aires and the Falkland Islands (Islas Malvinas). Book as far ahead as possible. The following are some examples of their flights.

Comodoro Rivadavia-Falkland Islands. This flight is on Mondays only for Ar$52,500 return. You do not have to pay the normal International Airport Tax on this flight, since the Argentinian Government consider the islands to be part of Argentina and this is therefore an internal flight.

Comodoro Rivadavia-Bariloche. This flight is Ar$45,000. This is one of the flights that costs less than the bus which is Ar$51,000.

Comodoro Rivadavia-Ushuaia. This is

Ar$27,500. Buy the tickets in advance in BA if possible as there's heavy demand. It goes via Lago Argentino (Calafate), Río Gallegos and Río Grande.

Río Gallegos-Ushuaia. Ar$9000.

Ushuaia-Calafate. Ar$29,900.

Río Gallegos-Calafate. Ar$8750.

Río Gallegos-Perito Moreno. Ar$18,760.

Río Gallegos-Trelew. Ar$25,000.

Río Gallegos-Bariloche. Ar$55,000. It takes seven hours with seven stops.

Rio Gallegos-Buenos Aires. Ar$50,000.

Mendoza-Buenos Aires. Ar$61,000. This is on a vuelo nocturno with *Austral*.

Railways There's an excellent system of railways throughout northern and central Argentina which connect with the Chilean, Bolivian and Paraguayan systems.

To/From Chile

Salta-Antofagasta. One train does this route weekly on Wednesdays at 4.40 pm (often late) but does not operate during the winter months. Ar$11,250 first class, Ar$6250 second class. The seats are not numbered, so you must get there at least an hour before departure if you want to be sure of a seat, as it's chock-a-block by then. Buy the ticket at Villalonga Furlong, Calle Alvarado, Salta, anytime up to 10 am on the day of departure. There's no heating on the train and it gets very cold at night — goes up to 4453 metres via the Chorillas Pass. It takes 15 hours. Coming the other way, the train departs Antofagasta on Thursdays at 12 midnight and arrives in Salta at 2.55 pm on the Friday (next day).

Buenos Aires-Santiago de Chile. This one departs from Retiro Station on Sundays, Tuesdays, Thursdays and Fridays at 6 pm, arriving at Mendoza at 8.40 am the next day. It departs Mendoza at 9.20 am and arrives at Los Andes (Chile) at 4.40 pm. Change trains here for Santiago and Valparaiso.

You leave Los Andes at 5.30 pm and arrive at Santiago Mapocho Station at 7 pm. Coming the other way, trains depart Santiago on Mondays, Wednesdays, Fridays and Saturdays. US$13 second class.

The line may be blocked on occasions during the winter months. This is one of the most spectacular railways in the world and goes through a tunnel at over 4300 metres. Aconcagua, the highest mountain in the Western Hemisphere (over 7600 metres) can be seen from the Chilean side of the border along with many other snow-capped peaks. The best time to travel this route is between November and May when there's a good chance of clear skies.

It's also possible to get to Chile via the railway to Bariloche and bus through the lake district from there to Puerto Montt or Valdivia (see below).

To/From Bolivia

Salta-La Quiaca/Villazon (Bolivian Border). Local trains depart at 6 am on Mondays, Wednesdays and Saturdays. It takes 15 hours. Ar$10,150 first class, Ar$7850 Tourist class. The train goes through Jujuy at 10.45 am.

There are also four international trains per week from Buenos Aires to La Paz, but it's unlikely you'll want to use them as the journey takes at least 70 hours and has been known to take up to a week! If you're interested, they depart BA Retiro Station on Sundays and Thursdays at 5.20 pm and on Mondays and Wednesdays at 8.30 pm. It costs Ar$37,500 first class, a sleeper costs double that. These trains stop in Salta and can be used to get to the border at La Quiaca for the same fares as

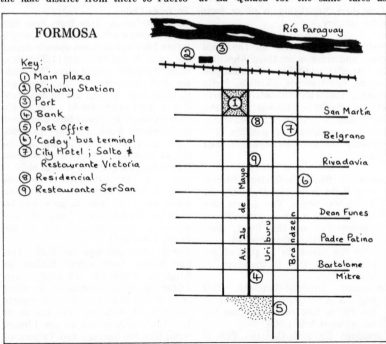

the local trains. The Thursday and Sunday trains from BA come through Salta at around 9.30 pm on Fridays and Mondays respectively.

Jujuy-Buenos Aires (Retiro Station). This train goes on Tuesdays, Wednesdays and Sundays. Ar$50,000 first class, Ar$41,000 Turista class.

Salta-Yacuiba (Bolivian border). Local trains via Güemes and Embarcación connect with the trains from there to Santa Cruz. There's also one train per week from BA Retiro Station to Santa Cruz (Bolivia) via Güemes and Yacuiba. But, as with the through train to La Paz, it's unlikely you'll want to take this train as it takes three days. It's better to do the journey in stages.

To/From Paraguay If you're coming from Bolivia and want to head straight for Paraguay, there are local trains from Salta/Juyjuy/Güemes both to Formosa via Embarcación and also to Resistencia. The route to Formosa is the more direct one. From Formosa take a bus to Clorinda (eg *Empresa Godoy*) and then the ferry across the Río Paraguay (costs Guaraníes 280) to Ita Enramada. From here Asunción is an eight km bus ride (costs Guaraníes 15). If you take the route to Resistencia on the railway, then catch a similar bus to Clorinda as if going direct to Formosa.

Salta-Resistencia. This goes on Tuesdays, Thursdays and Saturdays. You change at Güemes and Metan and it takes 30 hours. Ar$12,500 first class, Ar$8750 tourist class. It has been reported that it's no longer operative.

Buenos Aires-Asunción. Two trains go weekly from Lacroze Station on Monday and Wednesday. US$20 first class, US$16 second class. It takes about 52 hours. The line goes via Posadas and is ferried across the Rio Paraná to Encarnación on the Paraguayan side of the river. Coming in the opposite direction the train departs Asunción on Mondays, Wednesdays and Fridays at 4.30 pm.

If you don't want to make the journey in one leap, take the train to Posadas, stay there the night and then catch either the bus or train from Encarnacion to Asunción (both forms of transport daily). The ferry across river Paraná costs Ar$1300 plus Minicipal Tax of Ar$250.

Internal Trains For short hops inside Argentina, trains are ideal and considerably cheaper than the buses. For example the train from Buenos Aires to Córdoba costs Ar$6900, whereas the bus costs Ar$21,000. Here are the principal internal routes used by travellers.

Buenos Aires-Bariloche. They depart BA Constitución Station daily during the summer months. In the winter months they depart only on Tuesdays, Thursdays and Sundays. They take 40 hours. Buffet car and sleeping accommodation is available. If you want to get there quicker and in more comfort "Los Arrayanes" departs weekly and takes 27-29 hours. Ar$5000 first class. It's got sleeping cars, restaurant, a movie car and air-conditioning and even hostesses and a doctor in case you expire from all this high living.

There is an alternative route to the lake district via Zapala north of San Martín de los Andes and Junín. Daily trains go from Constitucion Station at 1.40 pm. Ar$10,000 (all one class). It takes 35 hours. From here there are buses south through the Lanin National Park.

Buenos Aires-Foz do Iguaçu (Iguazu Falls). This train departs thrice weekly from Lacroze Station at 5.30 pm as far as Posadas, taking 27-32 hours. Ar$15,000 first class, Ar$12,500 second class. The train is divided at Concorida, four hours from BA, so make sure you get into the correct half. From Posadas to the Falls by bus takes seven hours. Ar$6500. Details of the Falls are in a later section.

Jujuy-Buenos Aires Retiro Station.
Trains leave Tuesdays, Wednesdays and
Sundays. Ar$50,000 first class, and
Ar$41,000 tourist class.

Buses Buses are modern, comfortable
and fast, but none too cheap. In the
north and central parts of the country,
if you're doing short hops it might be
preferable to use the railways. You'll
certainly save a lot of money this way.
Remember that in Patagonia and Tierra
del Fuego *LADE* and *Austral* flights are
often cheaper than the buses, BUT
there's heavy demand for tickets and
they're often booked out for up to two
weeks in advance.

Most large towns have a central bus
terminal from which all arrivals and
departures take place. The bus network
is excellent with daily departures between all the major centres of population. In BA there's no central terminal
but most of the bus companies are located either at Plaza Constitución or at
Once Railway Station. There's also another terminal at Córdoba 416. Here are
some examples of fares and journey
times:

Buenos Aires-Mendoza. Ar$33,000.

Buenos Aires-Córdoba. Ar$21,000.

Buenos Aires-Bariloche. Ar$20,000 tak-
ing 24 hours.

Buenos Aires-Río Gallegos. This takes
about 50 hours. Ar$58,000. The
ticket office is at Gral. Hornos 255
near Plaza Constitucion.

Buenos Aires-Comodoro Rivadavia. Cost
is Ar$37,500. It takes 32 hours and
goes daily.

Puerto Iquazu-Posadas, Ar$15,000.

Foz do Iguaçu (Brazil)-Asuncion (Paraguay). Cz$170. It's slightly cheaper
to Asuncion from Foz rather than
Pte. Stroessner if you buy Cz$ on
black market.

Posadas-San Ignacio. Ar$2750.

Posadas-Corrientes. Ar$10,750.

Resistencia-Salta. Ar$33,500, daily at
5 pm. It takes 17 hours and is
best to go only as far as Guemes if
heading north.

Güemes-Jujuy. Ar$2600.

Güemes-La Quiaca (Bolivian border).
Ar$14,500.

**Transport in Patagonia and Tierra del
Fuego** Buses tend to be less regular in
this area (few people live here in comparison to the rest of the country),
so you need to do some planning if
you don't want to get stuck somewhere for days on end. Here are some
examples.

Comodoro Rivadavia-Bariloche. Three
times weekly costs Ar$51,000.

Comodoro Rivadavia-Coihaique (Chile).
Ar$27,000. Twice weekly.

Comodora Rivadavia-Rio Gallegos. Four
times weekly. Ar$22,500.

Río Turbio-Chile border. Ar$700. There
is a bus from here to Puerto Natales
in Chile for Ch$50.

Río Gallegos-Calafate. Ar$7500, once
weekly (the *LADE* flight is cheaper).

Río Gallegos-Punta Arenas (Chile). Cost
is Ar$13,750.

Río Grande (Tierra del Fuego)-Ush-
uaia. Ar$18,750 once weekly. This
route is easy to hitch with the
Vialidad Nacional road-workers truck.
There's also plenty of oil traffic
north of Río Grande as far as Comodoro Rivadavia, so save your money
and hitch a ride.

Río Grande-Porvenir (Chile). This route
is done on Wednesdays and Saturdays by one bus company and on
Mondays and Thursdays by another.
Departure time is 6 am (same for
each day). Costs US$11 (Ch$400).
Coming in the opposite direction the
departures are on Mondays, Wednesdays, Thursdays and Sundays (same
price). It takes six hours.

Ferries across the Straits of Magellan
Punta Delgada-Punta Espora. This is the
ferry which takes all the oil traffic across

the Straits from Río Grande to Río Gallegos. It's a 40 minute crossing for Ar$1250. The ferries are owned by the Argentinian oil company *ENAP*. The road from Río Gallegos runs through Chilean territory to Punta Delgada then, on the other side of the Straits, again through Chilean territory to the Argentinian border at San Sebastián. From there it continues to Río Grande and Ushuaia. If you're coming from Argentina, have some Chilean pesos handy for the ferry — easy to buy in Río Gallegos.

Punta Arenas — Porvenir. The departure times of this ferry are approximate and are affected by the tides.

December 1-April 30: Departs Punta Arenas on Monday through Saturday at 8.30 am and 3 pm. It departs Porvenir on Monday through Saturday at 12 noon and 6 pm.

May 1-November 30: Departs Punta Arenas on Monday through Saturday at 9 am and departs Porvenir on Monday through Saturday at 1 pm. The ferry runs throughout the year on Sundays at 9 am from Punta Arenas and from Porvenir at 1 pm.

THE IGUAZÚ FALLS

These falls are a travellers' Mecca and one of the most superb natural sights on the whole Continent. Don't miss them! They're at least as spectacular as Niagara Falls or Victoria Falls, if not

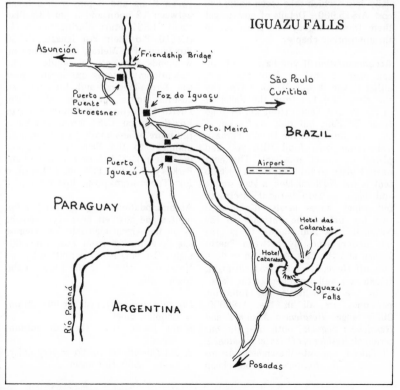

more so. The Brazilian side is best for overall views, but on the Argentinian side there are a series of catwalks which weave their way through the thick jungle and over the river as far as the "Garganta del Diablo" (Devil's Throat) — an incredible experience. The surrounding jungle is full of wild life.

To get there from Buenos Aires take the three times weekly train from Lacroze Station as far as Posadas opposite the Paraguayan town of Encarnación. It takes 27-29 hours. Ar$15,000 first class, Ar$12,000 second class. Make sure you get into the right carriages since the train is divided at Concordia, four hours out of BA. From Posadas to Puerto Iguazú, there are daily buses which take seven hours and cost Ar$15,000. Details of how to get there from Paraguay and Brazil are in the appropriate chapter.

Accommodation If you have a tent you can camp almost next to the Falls, either in the Parque Nacional Opé (by the river, two km from the Falls) or in the Parque Nandú (four km by road from the Falls but only half a km as the crow flies from the Devil's Throat). Take your own food with you and plenty of insect repellant. The next nearest place to the Falls if you have no tent is the *Hosteria Opé*, a very simple and basic pension without electricity but which serves meals. It's located two km before the entrance to the National Park and known to all the bus drivers who ply between Puerto Iguazú and the falls. Ask them to drop you off there. It costs Ar$1000/night. It's an easy walk from here to the Falls.

In the town itself, the following pensiones are all in the Ar$2000-3000 range: *Residencia Misiones* and *Residencia Segovia*, both near the bus terminal; *Residencia Oriente*; *Residencia El Tulcan*, opposite the cinema; *Alvaro Nuñez*; *Vivi*; *Jupiter* — good cheap

restaurant attached; *El Pilincho de Don Antonia*.

Eats Try the *Jupiter* or the *Restaurant Churrasquería* on Avenida Cordoba. Both serve good, inexpensive food.

Other For transport from Puerto Iguazú to the Falls, buses throughout the day for Ar$1000/one way. The Falls are 23 km from town. There's no entrance fee to the park if you're on a bus.

Transport to the Brazilian Side. From Puerto Iguazú, walk down to the river (10 minutes) and catch the ferry to Puerto Meira on the other side. Ferries are frequent throughout the day between 8 am and 6 pm, with a break between 12 noon and 2 pm (Brazilian time). US$1/return during the week, (Cz$10 Pto Meira-Pto Iguazu, Cz$30 Pto Iguazu-Pto Meira), US$2/return on weekends and national holidays. The Argentinian customs are located near the ferry landing and the Brazilian customs across the other side. From Puerto Meira there are hourly buses to Foz do Iguaçu. Cz$4. From here buses run more or less hourly from 7 am until midnight to the Falls (less frequent in winter). Cz$11. Entrance to the Falls Park is Cz$70. The Falls are 32 km from Foz. The customs posts close at 6 pm.

Accommodation Camping facilities are limited and nowhere near as convenient as on the Argentinian side. The nearest site is eight km from Foz, US$1.60/ night. Camping is not permitted by the *Hotel das Cataras* or the Falls. In the town itself:

Dormitorio Estrela, near the bus station, Cz$60 — quiet.

Hotel Brasil, near the bus station. Cz$100.

Avoid *Dormitorio Apolo* — very noisy. Costs Cz$60. Hot water.

Hotel Colibri, Avenida Republica Argentina. US$2.50/person.

Residencia Nobel, Avenida 25 de Mayo. US$2.50/single — clean.

Cisne Hotel, Avenida Brasil. US$3/ single. It's more expensive during the summer.

Hotel Excelsior, opposite the bus terminal, US$3 including breakfast.

Hotel Americano, US$4/single with breakfast — hot showers.

Eats Two places near the bus terminal which serve reasonably good food fairly cheaply are *Buffet Rafaib* and *Charlie Brown's*.

The Argentinian Lake District
The main routes through the Lake District, which is shared between Chile and Argentina, are described in the Chilean chapter.

Uruguay

For an otherwise unremarkable country of precious little else but huge cattle ranches and sheep farms, Uruguay was once the world's most advanced nation as far as social welfare goes and well ahead of those who these days pride themselves on such programmes.

By 1915 legislation had already been passed providing for an eight hour working day, holidays with pay, old-age pensions, unemployment benefits, free medical treatment, legalized divorce, the nationalisation of important industrial installations and services such as electricity, telephones, transport, banks, insurance, port facilities and chemical products, and the abolition of capital punishment and bullfighting. The Church was also disestablished. These reforms, remarkable considering the times, were largely the work of one man — Jose Batlle y Ordonez — an extremely energetic political journalist who, until he became the leader of one of the principal political parties, the Colorados, edited his own newspaper. He was twice elected to the Presidency and upon the expiry of his first term of office announced that he would observe the habitually ignored clause of the Constitution which prohibited a president from succeeding himself — an action unpreced-

ented at that time in South American politics.

Naturally, Batlle's innovations outraged the conservatives (whose political party was known as the Blancos) and some even went as far as branding him insane but it could never be said of him that he acted out of any motive other than sincere conviction. Batlle believed that the disorders of the 19th century were largely due to corrupt elections and excessive presidential power and so he persuaded the Colorado party that they must make themselves worthy of popular support by securing honest elections. Had he not altered the whole climate of government in this way, Batlle's reforms would never have been practical. His influence was felt for a long time after his death though Uruguay's experiment in social welfare has now turned distinctly sour following the military coup of 1973.

Since that time there has been massive emigration to other South American countries so that today Uruguay has a population of only three and a half million but with over 10 million head of cattle and 23 million sheep! There are many reasons for this emigration and they are not all connected with the existence of the military government.

One of the main reasons is the lack of any meaningful land reform and the backwardness of livestock production and management methods. Five hundred families monopolize over half the land and these same families also control three-quarters of the capital invested in industry and banking. Despite low yields, profits remain high because of the low costs — the biggest latifundios provide work for barely two people per 1000 hectares, and then not for the whole year. Livestock is still dependent for food on periodic rains and natural soil fertility. Meat production per animal is not half that of France or Germany and wool production is well down on Australian standards. It's the same old story of big landowners sending their profits abroad, frittering their time away at beach resorts and playing the absentee landlord. It adds up to high unemployment and a depopulated countryside. The "gaucho" of folklore with his leather boots, gold and silver adorned belt, diet of barbecued beef or mutton and rarely off his horse is dying out and is more often found these days in miserable hut settlements between the ranches hoping some work will turn up somewhere soon.

The gauchos were once important in making Uruguay (or the "banda oriental" as it was known) into one of the meat meccas of South America. For 200 years after their arrival, the Spanish largely ignored the east bank of the La Plata river, other than to build a fort at Montevideo, and it remained a kind of no-man's land between the Spanish and Portuguese empires. Cattle were introduced and multiplied rapidly and were followed by nomadic bands of gauchos who killed them for food and to sell their hides, though not on any organised commercial basis. This came later with the arrival of Argentinian ranchers who found it profitable to employ the gauchos to look after their herds. As more and more ranchers arrived, the land was gradually staked out into large "estacias" and has remained so ever since. The gauchos, who laid no claims to the land, naturally got no change out of this division of spoils.

Uruguayan nationalism was late in developing and until 1800 the "banda oriental" was merely part of the Viceroyalty of La Plata. A national conscience and the subsequent demand for independence came about partly as a result of the British capture of Buenos Aires in 1806. The occupation didn't last long, but long enough for over US$1 million of loot to be sent back to London and paraded around the streets. The sight of all this treasure excited the avarice of British businessmen and with the reinforcements which were sent out by the Government went many merchant ships with their holds stuffed full of British manufactures. By the time they reached their destination the Argentinians had retaken Buenos Aires and the reinforcements, being too weak to attempt to recapture the city, had to be content with taking Montevideo. It was here that the merchantmen unloaded their goods. When yet more reinforcements arrived several months later, the British attempted to retake Buenos Aires but were resoundingly thrashed and forced to agree to the evacuation of both Buenos Aires and Montevideo. However, during the seven months that Montevideo was occupied, the city enjoyed an activity and prosperity previously unheard of and when the troops were evacuated the Uruguayans were increasingly reluctant to revert to their status as poor dependants of the Viceroyalty of La Plata, dominated by Buenos Aires.

But independence for Uruguay didn't just involve a simple political separation of the east and west banks of the La Plata. Brazil had for a long time cherished the idea of extending its borders to the east bank of the La Plata and not long after the British left invaded and annexed the "banda". A long and bloody war of attrition began under the leadership of the Uruguayan patriot, Artigas, but he was forced to flee to Paraguay in 1820. Five years later another band of patriots took up the struggle with Argentinian backing and eventually defeated the Brazilian forces at Ituzaingo in 1827. The British were none too happy about these hostilities since throughout them the Brazilian navy blockaded Buenos Aires and so disrupted trade that in 1828 they intervened and arranged a treaty whereby Brazil and Argentina formally recognized Uruguay as an independent buffer state between them.

It was a fragile arrangement and marked neither the beginning of internal peace in Uruguay nor the end of foreign intervention. The Uruguayans were now divided into two factions, the Argentinian dictator Rosas supporting one party and the Brazilians the other. Following the overthrow of Rosas by an army which contained some 3000 Brazilian troops in 1852, Brazilian paramountcy was again re-established in Montevideo but the constant interference in Uruguayan affairs precipitated the greatest international war in Latin American history — the War of the Triple Alliance (described in the Paraguayan chapter).

In the present century following the gradual withering away of Batlle's idealism, the continued reliance upon one industry and the total lack of any land reform, Uruguay again came to the fore through the activities of the Tupamaros. This group, founded by Raul Sendic, a former member of the Uruguayan Communist Party, were the first Latin American urban guerrilla organisation and for a time were very successful in their armed resistance to the tottering and corrupt government of Jorge Areco and later to that of Gen Bordaberry after the military coup of 1973. They gained a lot of sympathy amongst the working people by their Robin Hood-type actions which included distributing money which had been robbed from banks and casinos; seizing food trucks and driving them into poor neighbourhoods in order to distribute the food; pilfering government documents which exposed the truth about official corruption, tax evasion and fraud, and many others.

When it became obvious in the early '70s that regular police and military tactics were ineffective against them — they were organised on a cellular basis and so infiltration was extremely difficult — the government panicked and invited the USA to help them. They received help in the form of CIA and even FBI agents. Dan Mitrione, a former US police chief, was one example — sent to instruct the Uruguayan police in the latest methods of interrogation and riot control, his actions against Tupamaros prisoners forced the guerrillas to escalate the conflict. They managed to kidnap Mitrione and he was offered to the government in exchange for imprisoned Tupamaros but they refused to accede to the deal and Mitrione was shot. A short while later the government declared a state of seige and suspended almost all civil liberties. When the military took over a year later they continued along this path by closing Congress, outlawing labour and student organizations and imprisoning some 5000 opponents of the regime — one political prisoner for every 500 citizens. Nothing much has changed since that time except that the military government has become increasingly entrenched, corrupt and paranoid. One of these days it's going to have to wake up.

Few travellers visit Uruguay, not because of its politics, but because it's not on the way to anywhere else and the Iguazu Falls act as a huge magnet drawing most people into Brazil directly from Argentina. Montevideo, where about half the population live, is, however, worth a visit if you're thinking of

going through Uruguay and there are excellent opportunities for camping around Lake Negro.

VISAS
Not required by nationals of Western European countries (except Portugal), Canada, USA, Israel and Japan. Required by nationals of Australia, New Zealand and South Africa. 90-day stay permits are issued at the border.

CURRENCY

US$1 = 6.10 Pesos

The unit of currency is the new Uruguayan Peso (U$) = 100 centimos. There are no restrictions on import or export of local currency and there is no blackmarket. There is a three percent ticket tax on all flight tickets bought in Uruguay, a US$2 airport tax for destinations outside South America and Mexico and a US$1 airport tax for other destinations.

ACCOMMODATION
As in Chile, Mexico and Argentina, Uruguay has a Youth Hostels Association where you can find cheap, dormitory-type accommodation but some of them are in out-of-the-way places and so of limited use if you're just passing through. A full list of them follows:

Albergue Carmelo Zagarzazú: 260.5 km, Ruta 21, Colonia, Parador Zagarzazú.
Albergue Colonia Suiza: Hotel del Prado, Nueva Helvecia, Colonia (tel 169).
Albergue Montevideo: Canelones 935, corner of Río Branco, Montevideo.
Albergue Paysandú: Gran Bretaña 872, Paysandú (tel 4247).
Albergue Piriápolis: Simon del Pino 1136, Piriápolis, Maldonado.
Albergue Villa Serrana: 148 km, Ruta 8, Chalet "Los Chotas". Llaverreja.
Camping El Suazal, Durazno.
Camping Los Titanes, Colonia Evángelica Arménica, 64.5 km, Ruta Interbalneario, Canelones.
Albergue Valisas: Rocha, above the castle on the beach.

COLONIA
Departure point for the ferries to Buenos Aires.

Accommodation   *Buenos Aires*, Calle Artigas, U$9 per person. Other cheapies include the *El Mirador*, *Colonial* and the *Italiano*. All in the U$9 to 12 range, there is also a camp site if you have a tent.

FRAY BENTOS
If you thought this was another name for corned beef you wouldn't be too far wrong. This is where it all started and the town is centred around the huge meat processing plant.

There's a bridge over the Rio Uruguay here to the Argentine on the other bank which you can cross on foot. Otherwise there's a launch four times per week.

MONTEVIDEO
Capital of Uruguay and a city well-known for its many beautiful squares and parks of which El Prado and the Parque Rodo are perhaps the best — a busy, modern city.

Accommodation
Youth Hostel HQ (Asociacion de Alberguistas de Uruguay), Calle Canelones

No 935 on the corner of Río Branco. They have a list of hostels and other associated information.

Hotel Triglau Palace, Avenida 18 de Julio near the Onda bus terminal — U$12/single, clean and recommended.

Pensión Porvenir, Calle Canelones — U$6/single, clean.

Hotel Río Tom, junction of Calle Canelones and Paraguay — U$15/double.

Residencial Suevia, Calle Uruguay 1242, U$14/double — hot water.

Hotel Libertad, Plaza Zabala — U$6/single, basic.

Hotel Niza, Calle Maldonado — U$9/single, basic.

Hotel Continental, Avenida 18 de Juilo 1253 — U$20/single, good.

Many other hotels near the Plaza Libertad and along Avenida 18 de Juilo. There is a 7% tax on hotel bills in Montevideo.

Eats

El Pinar, Calle San José 148, good cheap food.

Hispano, Calle Río Negro, good place for pizzas and snacks.

La Gloria, Calle Yaguaron, good cheap food and large helpings.

YMCA, Calle Colonia, the restaurant on the 6th floor does good cheap meals.

Aloha, near the Onda bus terminal on Av 18 de Julio — good cheap meals.

Ora del Rhin, Convencion 1403 — a good European-style bakery.

Vegetarians will have a hard time in Uruguay as, in common with Argentina, the national dish is beef, steaks, chops and stews — in fact anything that contains plenty of meat. Pizzas are popular so it may be possible to live on cheese pizzas and the like.

Information Tourist Office, Plaza Cagancha at 18 de Julio No 845 — friendly people, maps of the city and travel information. Their headquarters is at Avenida Agraciada 1409 (fifth floor). There is also a telephone number you can ring (214) for information on buses, trains and the location of hotels, etc.

American Express, Turisport Ltda, Bartolomé Mitre 1318, (tel 86 300).

Banking hours are 12 noon to 4 pm, Mondays to Fridays. There are no casas de cambio and all money changing is done in the banks and hotels.

Post Office is on Calle Buenos Aires, corner of Misiones.

Brazilian Tourist Office is on Calle Convencion between Mercedes and Colonia. Useful if you want to pick up maps and information about Brazil before going there.

Transport The airport is at Carrasco which is about 50 minutes by the bus which leaves from Avenida 18 de Julio, cost is 55 centimos. Taxis are expensive and charge 20 cents for the first 600 metres plus 10 cents for each succeeding 170 metres. There's also a charge for each piece of luggage and a 20% extra charge between midnight and 6 am.

Places to Visit If you're looking for somewhere green and peaceful to relax in try El Prado park about three km from Avenida 18 de Julio on Avenida Agraciada. It has woods, lakes, rose gardens and also contains the Museums of Fine Art and History. The Parque Rodó on Rambla Presidente Wilson has an open-air theatre, artificial lake, amusement park, etc. Also contains the National Museum of Fine Art. The Zoological Gardens are also worth a visit.

Museums

Natural History, Buenos Aires 562.

Botanical, 19 de Abril 1179.

Historical: Zabala 1464 and Rincón 437.

Oceanography and Fish. Rambla Republica de Chile 4215 on the sea front at Puerto Buceo.

Others mentioned previously. They're all open Tuesday to Sunday and there is no entrance fee.

There is an extensive stretch of excellent beach along the whole length of the city's frontage with the sea. Bus numbers 15 and 125 from Calle San José will take you there. All the beaches are sandy and clean.

PAYSANDU
Bridge to Argentina and a popular crossing point. You can stay at the *Hotel Internacional* for U$25 for a double — clean and centrally situated. There are daily ferries to Colón and Concepción on the Argentinian side of the Río Uruguay.

PUNTA DEL ESTE
A popular resort town with good beaches, surfing, swimming and boating but not the best place for a budget traveller as there are plenty of luxury hotels, casinos, flashy restaurants and expensive holiday homes.

Accommodation Relatively cheap hotels can be found around the railway station.
Tourbillon: Calle 9 and 12 — U$15/ single.
Colombia: U$20/single.

Eats Cheap places to eat, as you might expect in a place like this, are hard to find.

Other Tourist Office: Liga de Fomento, Parada 1, near the railway station. May be able to help with finding a cheap place to stay in the off-season.

SALTO
Another river crossing port from Argentina on the Rio Uruguay.

Accommodation The *Plaza* near the bus terminal — U$10/single. Clean and basic, good food available if ordered in advance. Others in the U$10 and

less range include the *Magnolias, Uruguay* and *Español*. There's also a campsite if you have a tent.

Transport Ferry to Concordia in Argentina runs six times per week Monday to Friday; three times per day on Saturdays and twice per day on Sundays. Takes 15 minutes and costs 20 centimos.

SANTA TERESA
North of Rocha and La Paloma and located in a national park. It's a fortress town which was built to ward off possible Brazilian incursions. If you're looking for unspoilt beaches where you can live fairly cheaply this is the place to come as opposed to Punta del Este where you will have to mingle with the rich. Cottages can be rented for a week/month/season or there are hotels for shorter stays. Excellent beaches, fresh water pools, bird sanctuaries and, nearby, the largest lake in Uruguay — Lake Negro.

TRANSPORT
Flights
International flights:
Montevideo-Buenos Aires: Aerolineas Argentinas US$30. By *PLUNA* or *AUSTRAL* (Uruguayan domestic airlines) it costs US$20. Daily flights.
Montevideo-Rio de Janeiro: Three flights weekly by *Varig* — US$150.
Montevideo-Asuncion: Iberia Airlines (once weekly); *PLUNA* (twice weekly): *LAP* (three times weekly).
Colonia-Buenos Aires: Three times per day by Aerolineas Argentinas — US$18. Cheaper by the domestic airlines. There is only a few dollars difference between a flight from Colonia to Buenos Aires on one of the cheaper airlines and the total cost of the bus fare from Montevideo followed by the cost of the ferry from Colonia to Buenos Aires.

Internal flights:

PLUNA and *TAMU* (the military airline) link Montevideo with most towns of any size on a daily basis.

Railways There is an excellent system of railways and they are cheaper than the buses even in first class but much slower. The railway station in Montevideo is on Calle Río Negro at the junction with Paraguay.

Montevideo-Salto: two trains per week, 17 hours, costs U$25.

Montevideo-Paysandú: two trains per week.

Buses Buses are comfortable, even luxurious, fast and have extensive services domestically and internationally to Brazil, Paraguay and Argentina. Onda is the largest line but COT and TTL are just as good and marginally cheaper. Onda bus terminal in Montevideo is at Plaza Libertad. Buses for Brazil leave Montevideo from COIT, Calle Paraguay 1473.

Montevideo-Pôrto Alegre (Brazil). Daily, 11 hours and costs US$15.

Montevideo-Asunción (Paraguay). One bus per week, 29 hours, costs US$20.

Montevideo-São Paulo (Brazil). Daily, US$17.

Also daily buses to the Argentinian towns of Santa Fé, La Falda and Cordoba.

If you don't want to travel via the old route to Pôrto Alegre, it's now possible to take the new coast road through Chuy. Change buses at Chuy for Pelotas and again there for Pôrto Alegre. This is a much more scenic route than the old road.

Internal routes:

Montevideo-Punta del Este: several buses daily by Onda and COT lines, U$12.

Montevideo-Colonia: By ordinary bus takes four hours and costs U$12. By express coach it takes two hours and costs U$21.

Montevideo-Salto: Daily buses, U$40.

Montevideo-Paysandú: Daily buses, take seven hours and cost U$30.

Boats

Montevideo-Buenos Aires One ferry per day. Departs at 9 pm; arrives BA at 7 am next morning. Costs US$23 in first class: US$15 in second class. Includes sleeping accommodation though you may find this almost impossible due to the row from the discotheque. Tickets from Cia de Navigacion Fluvial Argentina.

Montevideo-Colonia Twice daily in summer, once daily in winter. Takes two and a half hours. Same company as the above. There's also a more expensive hydrofoil on this route which takes 50 minutes. Three crossings daily. Company is Aliscafos.

Colonia-Buenos Aires Car ferry (takes foot passengers) once daily at 1.30 pm and costs US$6. It takes three hours. Company is Cia de Navigacion Fluvial Argentina. There's also a more expensive hydrofoil three times per day by Aliscafos. The cost is US$10 and the passage must be paid in US dollars. Make sure you get the ticket from the company offices rather than from a travel agent as they take a hefty commission. Hydrofoil takes 45 minutes to an hour. The cost of the bus from Montevideo plus the hydrofoil passage works out almost the same as a flight from Montevideo to BA.

Carmelo-Tigre Daily launch at 11 am, costs US$10 and takes four hours. Train from Tigre to Buenos Aires takes 35 minutes and costs 30 cents.

Paraguay

Of all the countries in South America, Paraguay is perhaps the one about which least is known and which is least visited by travellers other than those taking a short cut from northern Argentina to the Iguazú Falls. Its political system and civil rights record must be one of the worst on the continent and this may be one reason why it's bypassed by many travellers but it doesn't really deserve this kind of isolation. It's an interesting country of friendly bilingual people (who speak Spanish and the indigenous Indian language, Guarani) and a music all of its own which can be heard in the bars and cafes of Asuncion and other cities. Along with Bolivia, it is Latin America's poorest and most backward country yet only 100 years ago it was its most advanced. the reversal of fortunes goes back to the War of the Triple Alliance in 1865.

Unlike the rest of Spanish America, Paraguay declared its independence from Spain without having to fight a war of liberation in 1811 and from 1814 until 1840 was ruled by the dictator Gaspar Rodriguez de Francia. Under his regime the power of the oligarchy — the latifundista and merchants — was destroyed and the country put on the road of autonomous self-sustained development in isolation to the rest of the world. Carlos Antonio Lopez, who succeeded Francia as dictator, continued this policy, much to the chagrin of British merchants who were making large inroads into the economies of the neighbouring republics and the Brazilian Empire at the time. Politically it wasn't exactly a pretty place but by the time the invaders appeared on the horizon Paraguay had telegraphs, railroads, numerous factories making construction materials, textiles, paper, crockery and gunpowder, and the highest literacy rate in the Latin half of the continent. The steel industry, like other essential economic activities, belonged to the state and there was even a merchant navy fleet with a shipyard at Asuncion. Almost all the land was held as public property and holdings granted to peasants in return for permanent occupation and cultivation without the right to sell. This move away from the latifundios had benefited agriculture a great deal and even the pre-Conquest practice of raising two crops per year instead of one had been revived. Paraguay had accomplished all this without owing a penny to foreign creditors.

As development proceeded however and more and more goods were exported they became increasingly subject to arbitrary taxes and hold-ups by both Brazil and Argentina, in this way exposing Paraguay's traditional weakness — no direct access to the sea. The last straw came with the invasion of Argentina by Brazil to overthrow the dictator, Rosas, and extend Brazilian influence over Uruguay thereby making Paraguayan exports entirely dependent on the good will of two huge, hostile neighbours both of whom were dependent on British capital. A treaty was drawn up between Argentina, Brazil and Uruguay which detailed in advance the spoils to be gained from any war with Paraguay — Argentina was to take the Chaco and Misiones provinces and Brazil large slices of eastern Paraguay. Though history books will tell you that the Paraguayan dictator Lopez was a "proud and wilful man" and that it was the Paraguayan armed forces which made the first move, it was obvious that some conflict was in the offing given the support they were getting in their belligerence from British merchant banks.

The War of the Triple Alliance broke out in 1865 and was financed by large loans at exorbitant interest rates from the Bank of London, Baring Brothers, and Rothschilds. When it ended five years later 250,000 Paraguayans — half the total population — had been wiped out and only 10% of those left were male. Paraguayan prisoners were marched off to work as slaves on the coffee plantations of Sao Paulo and the country opened to "free trade". The land was parcelled out in latifundios and thoroughly looted of everything that was of any value. Paraguay has never recovered from this disaster and indeed had to fight yet another war between 1929 and 1935 this time with Bolivia over ownership of the Chaco though in this war they were the victors and increased their territory in this area. About this time, large American and British oil companies were interested in the possibilities of finding oil in this region — since shown to be unfounded.

Following the war of the Triple Alliance, successive puppet dictators were installed by the victors in Asuncion and this has been continued ever since. The present dictator, Alfredo Stroessner — whose regime is the longest-running of any dictatorship in the world at the moment — did his training under Brazilian generals and has turned Paraguay into an enormous concentration camp held together by US and Brazilian financial and political interests. Even the land along the borders with Brazil has been sold to Brazilian coffee latifundistas which partially explains why 1.5% of the population owns 90% of the cultivated land but that less than 2% of the total land area is cultivated! Hundred of thousands of Paraguayans have been forced to emigrate to Argentina and Brazil to look for work. The regime is thoroughly

corrupt and appears to exist purely to serve the interests of the tiny ruling elite whose major activity is smuggling. Consumer goods, luxury items, etc, are smuggled from areas with low tariffs to those with high tariffs and illicit drugs (cocaine and heroin) to North America. What industry there is is totally moribund.

The only agricultural progress which is being made centres around the Mennonite communities in the Chaco. These people, originally from Germany and other central European countries, are a Protestant sect who set up self-sufficient and self-contained agricultural communities most of which reject the world at large — though some have since opted for co-existence with the modern world. The only place you will see them unless you visit their communities around Filadelfia is in the market places selling their produce to wholesalers. They came to Paraguay in the 1920s and were given quite remarkable rights by the Government which included: freedom of religion; freedom from conscription; freedom to use their own language (a German dialect) and operate their own schools. in other words, they are virtually autonomous. Paraguay was only one of the places which they set up communities in. You can also find them in Mexico, Belize, Colombia, Bolivia, Brazil, Argentina and Uruguay.

The idea of self-sufficient, socialistically-organized communities goes back a long way in Paraguayan history to the time when the Jesuit missionaries arrived here around 1600. These agents fo the Catholic Church, over whom the civil authorities had little or no control, used music to draw the Guarani Indians out of the forest where they had taken refuge rather than become virtual slaves on the estates of the Spanish conquerors. In this way, over 150,000 Guaranis were able to move back into their primitive community organization and revive their traditional crafts. There was no Latifundio system in these "reduciones" as they were called: the soil was cultivated partly to satisfy individual needs and partly to develop projects of common concern and to acquire the necessary work tools, which were common property. The Indians' lives were paternalistically though intelligently organized: musicians and artisans, farmers, weavers, actors and painters and builders gathered together in workshops and schools. Money was unknown and traders were barred from entering. Any business had to be conducted at an appropriate distance from the reduciones. Because of slave-raiding parties from Brazil, the communities in the north had to be abandoned and they became concentrated in the province of Misiones — now a part of Argentina.

It was one of the most successful experiments ever carried out with an indigenous population in the Americas and was looked on with alarm and envy by the large estate owners. 158 years later it came to an abrupt end when the Spanish crown finally succumbed to criollo landlord pressure and expelled the Jesuits from Latin America. As soon as this happened the missions fell apart and were looted for everything of value. Whole communities were sold in the slave markets of Brazil. Others were taken forcibly to work plantations in Paraguay but many fled back to the relative safety of the forest. The Jesuits' records of the missions and their books were all burnt or used to make gunpowder cartridges.

This long catalogue of periods of progress and relative prosperity followed by disaster you'll find reflected in the atmosphere of this country and even in its geography. It's the country which is perhaps in most need of an urgent shake-up. By going there you might just help this process along a little. Don't let the politics frighten you off. Peoplewise, it's a very friendly country.

VISAS

Tourist Cards or visas required by everyone. Obtainable from airline offices, large travel agents if you are booking transport through them, or from Para-

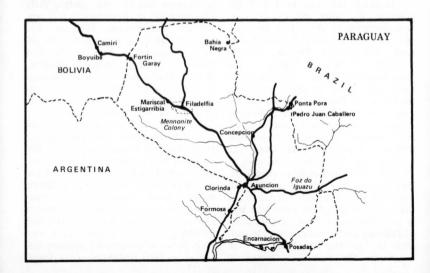

guayan Consulates. Cost is US$1, no photographs are required and it's valid for a 90-day stay.

CURRENCY

US$1 = G140 (official rate)

The unit of currency is the Guaraní (G) (G) = 100 centimos.

There is a small blackmarket though you won't necessarily be offered a better rate on the street than you are offered in a Casa de Cambio. There are no restrictions on export or import of local currency. Only Casas de Cambio will change travellers' cheques, banks will not change them. Get rid of any excess Guaraníes before you leave the country. It's difficult to change them outside the country.

American Express Agents are on the corner of Gral Diaz and Chile.

ASUNCIÓN

Easy-going city with many folk music bars where local people play the traditional harp and guitar music so characteristic of Paraguay. There are few tourists but cheap accommodation may be hard to find between May and September. One out of every five Paraguayans live here and it's the only town of any size in the country. Because Asunción is built on the banks of the Río Paraguay there are plenty of mosquitoes at night.

Accommodation

Pensión Asunción at Calle Eligio Ayala 376. Popular with travellers as it's one of the cheapest, centrally located places you will find. G400/double.

Hotel de Mayo at Calle 25 de Mayo 350. Also has an annexe at Calle 25 de Mayo 336 where the cheapest rooms are to be found. G250-500/single depending on the room.

Residencia Royal at Calle Herrera 838, corner of Tacuari. G350-400/double

depending on the room. Small hotel.

Residencia Chaco on Calle Eligio Ayala on the corner of Yegros 168. G350/person in room with own bath; G600/double. Hot water, pleasant rooms.

Pensión Santa Rosa at Azara 664. G350/single. Good restaurant.

Residencial Ñandutí at 14 de Mayo 662. G490/single with own shower and including breakfast.

Hotel America near Itá Enramada bus terminal. G250-300/person. Clean, hot water and mosquito nets.

Hotel Savoy is near the railway station. G200/single including breakfast.

Eats

Lido on Plaza de los Heroes. A lunch counter popular with travellers and Peace Corps Volunteers, excellent empanadas.

Rotisería on Calle Azara near the junction with Iturbe. Roast chicken for around G140.

Cafe Rosendal on Estados Unidos and Figueroa. Good cafe with local harp and guitar music.

Some of the cheapest cafes and bars, many with local music are located on Benjamin Constant.

Information Tourist Office is on the corner of Alberdi and Oliva. Maps and information. Another excellent source of information and maps, particularly of the Chaco area, is the International Federation of Auto Clubs on the corner of Brasil and 25 de Mayo. Also the United States Information Office (USAID) has a good booklet on Paraguay.

Bus terminals: Long distance terminals are located on the streets surrounding the Plaza Uruguay particularly on Eligio Ayala and Paraguari. Up the hill from the Plaza on Paraguari is the local bus terminal. There is another local bus terminal on the corner of Luis

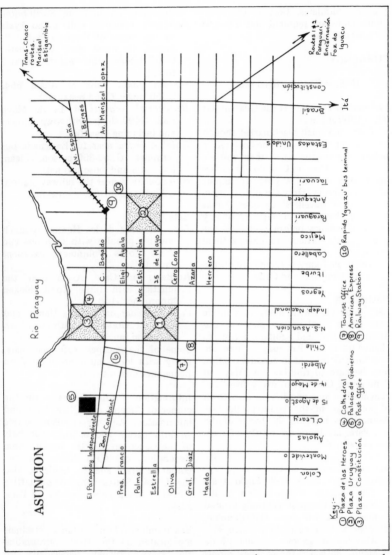

ASUNCION

Rio Paraguay

Key:-
① Plaza de los Heroes
②Ⓡ Plaza Uruguay
③Ⓒ Plaza Constitución

④ Cathedral
⑤ Palacio de Gobierno
⑥ Post Office

⑦ Tourist Office
⑧ American Express
⑨ Railway Station

⑩ Rápido Yguazú bus terminal

Trans-Chaco routes, Mariscal Estigarribia

Routes 1 #2 Paraguari Encarnación Foz do Iguacu

Herrera and Constitucion (known as "Litoral"). Buses to Puerto Stroessner and Foz do Iguacu with Rápido Yguazú bus line on Antequeria — see street plan. Others which go there are Flota San Agustín, Nuestra Sra de Asunción and Pluma.

Shipping enquiries/scheduled riverboat services: Compañía Marítima on Benjamin Constant.

Peace Corps offices: Brasil 293. Might be worth paying a visit if you're thinking of travelling around Paraguay as you may be given the addresses of Peace Corps who are living in the sticks or in remote towns and villages.

Casas de Cambio: most are located on Calle Palma.

Airport: President Gral Stroessner airport is located 15 km north-east of the city. Bus No. 139 from there to the centre cost G40. A taxi to the centre cost US$9.

What to see/excursions Museum in the Botanical Gardens has a collection of Indian handicrafts and historical exhibits and the house itself is well worth seeing.

Casa de la Independencia, 14 de Mayo and Franco, is an interesting historical museum and it's free.

ITAUGUÁ

30 km from Asunción, this is the town where the famous "ñandutí" lace is made. You can see examples of the craftspeoples' work hanging outside their houses. Prices here are somewhat lower than those in Asunción so if you're thinking of buying some of their work, spend a day visiting this town. Buses from the Litoral bus terminal corner of Herrera and Constitucion take one hour.

The Maca Indian reservation on an island a km out in the Río Paraguay opposite the Botanical Gardens has become a tourist trap. Tourists are obliged to take a special launch out to the island (expensive) plus a fee of G60 to enter the reservation.

CONCEPCION

On the way to the Paraguay/Brazil border at Pedro Juan Caballero.

Accommodation Very few places to stay. One of the cheapest is the hotel above the *Bar Victoria*. The *Francés*

costs G600/double without bath in the high season (May-September) but approximately half that in the low season. It also has more expensive rooms with their own shower.

Transport Two daily buses to Pedro Juan Caballero, six hours.

ENCARNACIÓN

Wide dusty streets, bullock carts and gauchos. Most of the town is old and rural though it also has a busy port. Situated on the banks of the Río Paraná opposite the Argentinian town of Posadas.

Accommodation Most of the cheap places are around the railway station. They include the *Suizo*, *Colon* and *Hospedaje Comercio*. All priced around G150 to 200/single. A better place, if you're looking for something with character, is the *Retka*. A small pink house in beautiful garden. Excellent home cooking — bed and breakfast costs G550 with own shower.

Transport Ferries all day across the Río Paraná to Posadas.

Places Nearby Try to visit the nearby village of Quindy where wooden rings inlaid with mother-of-pearl (anillas de coca) are made. Take a horse-drawn carriage there — they're very cheap.

TRANSPORT

Flights Internal flights are covered by Transportes Aéreos Militares (TAM) and Líneas Aéreos de Transportes Nacional (LATN). International flights are covered by the Paraguayan national airline, LAP, and the national airlines of neighbouring republics.

Airport tax on international flights to Brazil, Argentina, Bolivia and Uruguay is G500. On all other international flights the airport tax is G700.

Railways Other than a few, generally private, lines linking ranching or forestry estates with the nearest town, there is only one railway in Paraguay. This is the Asuncion-Encarnacion line linking Paraguay with Argentina on the Río Parana opposite Posadas. Trains take three times as long as the buses but cost half as much.

Asunción-Encarnación: one train daily in either direction. Takes 15 hours and costs G520 first class; G390 second class.

Asunción-Buenos Aires: "Express" train on Monday, Wednesday and Friday at 4.30pm. Takes 34 hours and costs US$15 in second class (pleasant enough and probably not worth the extra for first class). The train is ferried across the Río Paraná from Encarnación to Posadas.

Buses There are plenty of international bus connections between Asunción and various major towns and the neighbouring republics of Brazil, Argentina and Uruguay as well as to the Iguazú Falls but as is the case elsewhere, it's much cheaper to take a local Paraguayan bus to the border, cross the border on foot, and take another local bus from the far side.

To Argentina Asunción-Buenos Aires: There are two main routes: (1) via Encarnación and Posadas on the Río Paraná and (2) via Clorinda and Formosa across the Río Paraguay.

Asunción-Encarnación: Daily buses by several companies. Takes 6 hours and costs G750. Frequent ferries throughout the day across the Río Parana from Encarnación to Posadas. Daily connections from Posadas north to Iguazú Falls and south to Buenos Aires.

Asunción-Buenos Aires: Direct bus. Twice daily at 6.30 am and 3 pm by Río Paraná company (US$15) and Pluma company (US$21.50). Takes 24 hours.

Via Clorinda and Formosa: Local bus from Asunción to Itá Enramada on the Paraguayan side of the Río Paraguay, costs G15, eight km. From there take the ferry across the river to Clorinda on the Argentinian side. Costs G280. From Clorinda there are frequent daily buses to Buenos Aires via Formosa on a good paved highway eg Empresa Godoy.

As an alternative to this crossing it's also possible to take the ferry across the river in Asunción itself (Chaco E ferry) and from there head for the border at Puente Pilcomayo.

To Brazil Two possible routes:

Asunción-Foz de Iguaçu (Iguazú Falls). The falls are seven km beyond the Paraguayan border. Take a bus to the border at Puerto Puente Stroessner on the Paraguayan side of the International Bridge. Frequent daily buses by Flota San Agustín (G490); Rápido Yguazú (G630); Pluma and Nuestra Sra de Asunción — takes six hours. Clear Paraguayan customs at the International Bridge and walk across to the Brazilian side. Clear Brazilian customs on the far side and take a local bus to Foz do Iguacu (seven km). All the above mentioned buses go through to Foz do Iguacu but cost US$2 more just for taking you across the border. From Foz you can either go to the Brazilian side of the Falls direct (about 35 km) or the Argentinian side of the Falls by bus from Foz to Pôrto Meira, ferry across the Río Iguaçu to Puerto Iguazú (Argentina) and from there by bus to the Falls (Puerto Iguazú to the Falls, about 23 km).

There are regular daily buses from Foz do Iguacu to Curitiba and São Paulo. Eg Autobuses Sudamericanos (19 hours, US$10). Good paved road.

The bus departs 10 am.

Asunción-Pedro Juan Caballero/Ponta Pora. Direct buses from Asuncion to Pedro Juan Caballero, twice daily. Takes 12 hours and costs G840. Alternatively, take the bus to Concepcion initially and from there by bus to Pedro Juan Caballero at a later date — again two buses daily, take six hours and cost G560. To cross the border in P. J. Caballero go first to the Delegación de Gobierno for exit stamp, then to the Brazilian consulate and then walk down the road to the Brazilian customs post in Ponta Porã. From Ponta Porã there are rail and bus connections with Sao Paulo and Campo Grande.

There's also another route via riverboat along the Rio Paraguai to Bahia Negra — see below under "Boats".

To Bolivia The only way to go there directly is via the Chaco. The road is rough as hell and you should plan for at least two days to get from Asuncion to Camiri (the first Bolivian town with bus connections to the rest of the country). The journey can only be done between June and September if you want to be sure of transport. During the rainy season it's virtually impossible.

Asunción-Filadelfia (a Mennonite settlement). Daily bus by Nuevo Asunción Co on Calle Paragaui near Plaza Uruguay. Takes 10 hours and costs G1400. If you want to stay here for the night try *Hotel Florida*, US$4.

Filadelfia-Mariscal Estigarribia. Daily bus. Takes three hours and costs G280. There are one or two very basic pensiones here which will accept both Bolivian and Paraguayan money.

From Mariscal Estigarribia to the border post at Fortin Eugenio Garay and from there via the Bolivian border town of Boyuibe to Camiri there are no buses and you must rely on infrequent petrol trucks though it's likely that any lift you arrange in Mariscal Estigarribia will take you all the way to Camiri. Estimate on at least seven hours from Mariscal Estigarribia to Fortin Garay and another 12 to 14 hours from there to Boyuibe. Take your own food and water, cost of a lift with a truck is approximately US$5. Paraguayan customs/passport control at Fortin Garay and Bolivian equivalent at Boyuibe.

Another way to enter Bolivia indirectly is by riverboat from Concepción to Corumbá, cross the river to Puerto Suarez on the Bolivian side and from there take the ferrobus to Santa Cruz (no road).

Boats Asunción-Concepción: Regular service up to Río Paraguai every Tuesday (returns on Wednesdays) with Flota Mercantil del Estado (Office in Asunción: Estrella 672-682). Takes 24 hours and costs G1190 in second class without food, good modern boats with restaurant on board.

From Concepción there are Riverboats (irregular schedule) to Corumbá. Also there's a once monthly boat from Concepción to Bahia Negra at the point where the Paraguayan, Bolivian and Brazilian borders meet. It's possible to take this boat as far as Pórto Murtinho on the Brazilian side of the Río Paraguai. From this place there are regular bus connections with Campo Grande.

Asunción-Buenos Aires: The scheduled service (every 10 days) is often cancelled and in any case is expensive in comparison with the alternatives. Only possible when the river is high enough. If you're that interested in going down river to Buenos Aires, negotiate for a cargo boat — it's a two to three day journey.

Enquiries about the scheduled boats: Compañía Marítima on Benjamin Constant, Asunción.

Books *Green Hill Far Away* by Peter Upton (W H Allen, London, 1977) is an excellent novel — very accurate in its portrayal of Paraguay.

Brazil

Coming from Spanish America, the change in attitudes, tempo of life and building styles will be immediately apparent. Suddenly you know you're in a different sort of country and it all seems to happen in just the time it takes to cross the border. Having become accustomed to the slow and stoical plod of life in the Andean countries, whose nature seems to have changed little from colonial days, you're suddenly in the middle of a vibrant land whose people are going hell-for-leather to make it as one of the world's most powerful industrialized nations. Except for one or two gems of the colonial legacy, such as Ouro Preto and Olinda which have been left behind intact in the scramble to make it into the 20th century, here is a country of sprawling modern cities, wide boulevards and a pace to life somehow quite alien to that of Spanish America outside of such cities as Caracas or Mexico City. Nowhere is this more apparent than in such cities as São Paulo, Belo Horizonte, Campo Grande and the many pioneer towns which are springing up throughout Amazonia.

This energy finds its most explosive and spontaneous outlet in the annual Carnival, celebrated in every Brazilian town and city. It's an amazing weeklong display of music, dance costume, excitement and laughter (as well as street crime!) and displays the various cultural threads which have gone into making the Brazilian people what they are today. Unlike the more controlled Spanish American fiestas with their high content of religious ritual which tends to leave many of the participants as mere spectators, here everyone joins in. Even the most dour individual would be hard-pressed not to be drawn into the intense excitement worked up by the bands of percussionists and the electric guitar trios. Everyone goes crazy and when it's over collapses in a fit of satisfaction. Nothing quite like it exists anywhere else in the world (with the possible exception of Trinidad) but then no other country in the world has such a homogenous mix of different races with their various cultural traditions.

African, Portuguese and Amerindian have intermarried freely here since the Portuguese first discovered the coast of Brazil in 1500 and, although there is some racial discrimination, no other country on this continent has such a complete three-way mix which goes right across the spectrum. Aside from the few remaining Indian tribes who inhabit the Amazonian forest, there is no parallel in Brazil to the dual culture society which exists in the Spanish American countries with large pure Indian populations such as Guatemala, Ecuador, Peru and Bolivia. Black people are still predominant in the coastal region north of Rio de Janeiro — which explains why the best Carnivals are found here — and white people in the provinces south of Sao Paulo but immigration from Europe and Asia has considerably altered the picture from what it was around the time of independence. In the 70 years up to 1954, Brazil took in over four and a half million immigrants from Europe — mainly from Italy, Portugal, Spain and Germany — and has averaged 50,000 a year since then. There is also a sizeable Japanese community which owns a large chunk of the coffee and market gardening industry.

You'll undoubtedly find the pace of life exciting but it's perhaps well to remember that it isn't all Carnivals and other innocuous explosions of natural energy. It does have its negative aspects and is a pace which has little time for consideration of the effects which it might and does have on the people and the environment they live in. In this respect it's fairly accurately described as reckless. Behind the glitter of the city centres, the skyscrapers and the super-highways, there are millions and millions of industrial and agricultural workers whose wages won't even cover the basic necessities of life and who are condemned to live in the "favelas" (shanty-towns) which ring every Brazilian city. These are without any of the amenities (water, sanitation, power, medical facilities, etc) which other industrialized nations take for granted. Trade unions are prohibited. Political expression is rigidly controlled by the military government. Torture and the "disappearance" of opponents of the regime is commonplace and, until recently, there were even "death squads" of off-duty police who methodically gunned down "subversives" in the cities under the pretext of putting a squeeze on drug, gambling and prostitution rackets.

The most dramatic example of this recklessness in recent years has been the rape of the Amazon forest. It's true that much of the responsibility for the destruction lies squarely on the shoulders of multinational companies and foreign individuals, but without the collusion of the government and its agents this couldn't have happened. The Amazon forest is enormous but it's also the last of its size in the world. It contains one third of the world's trees and covers an area of five million

square kilometres — an area larger than Europe. Previously unknown Indian tribes each with their own completely self-sufficient culture are still occasionally found by explorers and road-construction teams. However, of the thousands who lived there more or less undisturbed until the middle of the last century, only 100 remain with a total population of no more than 40,000. They've been reduced to their present levels by outright murder (by planters, tappers, ranchers, road-construction teams and the army), by European diseases to which they have no immunity and by the destructive effects of new highways and loss of forest cover. Their cultures are completely integrated into and totally dependent on the forest. If it's destroyed, their culture and tribal society dies with it.

By a strange, ironic twist, this forest though one of the world's most abundant natural resources, is also potentially a desert — something which is very hard to believe when you're in the middle of it. Left alone the forest is self perpetuating. The trees live almost entirely on recycling whatever drops to the forest floor. They also recycle about 50 percent of the rain which falls. It's weakness lies in the fact that the forest is rooted in only the thinnest of soils covering a laterite bed. If the tree cover is removed there's nothing to soak up the rain so flooding, erosion and leaching of nutrients takes place. Within two years what little soil there was has been washed away and the sun has started to oxidize the laterite subsoil. Unless this process is reversed (very difficult) then within another two years you have a desert. You'll see patches of this desert and others well on their way to it if you take the route through the jungle from Porto Velho to Manaus. Quite a few of the plots date back to the attempt to re-settle destitute Sertao peasants in Amazonia. It failed miserably since they found, as everyone else has, that after raising up to four sets of crops the land is exhausted and rain has washed away the better part of it.

Even selective forestry has been found to be virtually impossible or, at best, uneconomic because there's a high degree of biological cooperation between all the various plants and between the plants and animals which live in the forest. If this balance is seriously disturbed or one or more elements of it removed, then the rest suffers. Many trees, valued for their wood, will not grow if there are too many or too few of the same type growing in a certain area. Others will not grow unless there are certain insects or vertebrates present. Only in recent years have researchers begun to discover the extremely complex pattern of inter-relationships which holds the forest together but, because there's still a lingering belief that this area can be made into the larder of Brazil, millions of hectares of forest are burnt down every year in the vain hope that it can be made productive. In the last 60 years, one quarter of the forest has been destroyed — mainly by foreign enterprises such as Jari Forestry and Ranching, Liquigas, Volkswagen and King Ranch of Texas. But this has been with the connivance of the government, which is desperate to reduce its enormous foreign debt and find some way of feeding or re-settling its millions of starving "favela" dwellers. It's even well known by now among these entrepreneurs that, once the forest cover has been removed, the land has a life of no more than three years; but in that time they can raise huge herds of cattle, collect their largely tax-free profits and head off somewhere else leaving the country to sort out the devastation they've wreaked.

Every year another four percent of the forest is burnt down, which means that by the year 2000 it will have gone. It's difficult to appreciate the amount of burning which is going on without being there, but in the 2400 km journey from Campo Grande to Manaus I was rarely out of sight of huge forest fires on either side of the road or the charred remains of a previous one. From the air it's even more catastrophic. It's not going unnoticed entirely and Brazil has a very active conservation movement. There are laws governing forest clearance, but with only 100 inspectors to cover an area in which 20,000 would be too few these are evaded or ignored entirely. Even the Government department set up to manage and protect this asset has been known to set in motion semi-secret deals which involve the selling off and clearance of areas of the forest as large as some European countries to foreign entrepreneurs. The latest threat to this forest has come as a result of diminishing oil reserves and the possibility — now industrially feasible — of producing a petrol substitute from vegetable matter.

You may think this is all Sunday afternoon doomsday gossip from middle-class liberals but it's been calculated that this forest supplies 50 percent of the earth's oxygen supply. If it goes, watch out. Even breathing is going to be hazardous if we haven't been fried by then. Already major climatic changes are being reported from Peru which is loosing permanent snow cover on its ice peaks and from Bolivia which has had a series of bad droughts and searing winds. The level of the Amazon River has risen signigicantly over the last 10 years and annually threatens to inundate Manaus and other river ports.

This obsession with making a fast buck at the expense of a "limitless" amount of land instead of diversifying agriculture and industry has dogged Brazil's progress, almost from the time it was discovered by the Portuguese in 1500 AD. For many years the "New World" was neglected in favour of the lucrative profits to be made in the trade of spices from the East but gradually it came to be settled by two quite different groups from Portugal. They were both after the same thing — instant wealth — but differed in that the North-East was settled by aristocratic families with adequate capital resources, who set up huge estates worked by slave labour or very poorly-paid serfs and on which they played the role of absentee landlord. The land to the south was settled by much poorer but more energetic settlers from northern Portugal who, until the discovery of gold at the end of the 17th century in the central Minas Gerais and diamonds 25 years later in Goias, could do little but scratch a bare living from the soil.

The huge northern estates concentrated almost entirely on sugar cane. They became the world's major source of sugar during the second half of the 16th century and for the whole of the 17th. After this there was a rapid decline as a result of competition from the Caribbean islands and an unwillingness to plough back profits to reduce costs and improve yields. The discovery of gold further south led to a gold rush. Ouro Preto is a lasting monument to this period of history. The gold petered out a hundred years later and the next massive speculative venture came with coffee, which is still the major commodity exported from the Sao Paulo/Rio de Janeiro area. For a time the coffee boom ran contiguously with a rubber boom in Amazonia which stemmed the years between 1870 and 1910. The forest were ransacked for rubber trees, fortunes were made and lost and Manaus turned into a glittering European cultural centre which rivalled those anywhere in the world. It came to an abrupt end after seeds had been smuggled out and planted in Malaya which then became the world's main supplier.

As far as its political history goes, Brazil never experienced to the same degree the rigid centralized control exercised by the Spanish crown over its American colonies. Like his counterpart in Spain, the King of Portugal expected both a personal and a state revenue from the colony, but tax evasion, corruption and smuggling were widespread and the bounty could never equal that received by the Spanish monarchs from the plunder of the various Indian empires and kingdoms. The break with the mother country came relatively easily and without the long wars of liberation the Spanish colonies had to go through. The Napoleonic Wars in Europe provided the occasion. Following the conquest of Portugal by the French, the Portuguese Royal Family were taken to Brazil by the British navy in 1808, along with a British Ambassador who was charged with the task of opening up Brazil for British manufactures and as a source of raw materials. British capital had already made inroads into the Brazilian economy even by this time and was to be hugely successful over the next century or so until replaced by American, German and Japanese capital. King Joao VI returned to Portugal in 1821 leaving his son, Pedro, in charge of the colony. Less than one year later, Brazil was an independent empire after the Cortés (the Portuguese parliament), mistrusting this arrangement, had demanded Pedro's return but had been rebuffed by the colonists who crowned him emperor in December of that year. No blood was shed.

Dom Pedro I had a bad time of it. There were secessionist movements in the north, he lost what is now Uruguay, he had marital "problems" and finally, after a military revolt in 1831, abdicated in favour of his five-year-old son. He became emperor as Dom Pedro II in 1840 at the age of 15 and ruled until the royal family was abolished in 1889 and the Republic declared, after he had lost the support of the plantation owners by demanding that slavery be outlawed (this became law in 1888, one year before he was toppled). He died a pauper's death two years later in a seedy Paris hotel but his reign had given Brazil a period of relative prosperity and stability and one which hasn't been improved on since. It was also during his reign that Brazil brought down the Argentinian dictator Lopez in that country. Also Brazil expanded its territory at the expense of Bolivia. A railway was started between Porto Velho and Riberalta to compensate Bolivia for the loss but it never reached its destination and proved to be of little use.

Later in this century, Getulio Vargas succeeded by revolution in deposing the then president. Although Vargas assumed the powers of a dictator, his 15-year stint in power saw the introduction of a number of social measures. He was deposed in 1945 and a liberal republic restored the following year. Eighteen years later a military coup followed increasing government instability, corruption and the machinations of foreign capital. The military have ruled ever since then.

Brazil, like many of the ex-Spanish colonies, is still haunted by the legacy of its colonial past. Unlike the *Mayflower* pilgrims who crossed to North America as settlers and free workers on their own farms, Spain and Portugal always had an abundance of subjugated labour in Latin America. Enslavement of the Indians was followed by the wholesale transportation of Africans. Through the centuries a legion of unemployed peasants has always been available to be moved to production centres as precious metal or sugar exports rose and fell. This structure persists today and means low wages due to the pressure of the unemployed and the frustration of a growth in the internal consumer market. In North America from the outset the centre of gravity was the farms and workshops of New England, but in Latin America the internal economic development of the colonies was never the goal of the ruling class. These people came here to fulfill the role of supplying Europe with gold, silver and food. Goods moved in one direction only: to the ports and overseas markets. The profits from them were squandered in high living and on far-away wars rather than re-invested in the place of their origin. It remains to be seen whether Brazil will achieve this transformation before it destroys the assets it still has.

VISAS

Visas are not required by nationals of Western Europe, Canada or USA, but are required by nationals of Australia, New Zealand, Israel, Japan and South Africa. Visas issued free of charge. An initial 90-day stay is given to everyone either by visa or at the border. It can be extended.

There are no money or onward ticket hassles, no hair hassles except occasionally at the Foz do Iguaçu crossing. An Exit Stamp from the Federal Police prior to arriving at the border is no longer required. All bureaucracy can be completed at the border.

CURRENCY

US$1 = 24 Cruzeiros

The unit of currency is the Cruzeiro (Cz$) = 100 centavos. The rate of exchange varies from 24-25 Cruzeiros. There's a desultory black market where you might get up to five percent more than in the banks but it's very difficult to find except in Sao Paulo and Rio de Janeiro. Better rates can be got outside the country (especially in Bolivia and Venezuela), so stock up before you get there. (Cz$29-30 = US$1 at Chuy on the Uruguayan side of the border, only Cz$28 at the Iguazú Falls).

This story takes some believing —

but it's true! There are some cities in Brazil where the banks — including the Banco do Brasil — will change neither travellers' cheques nor cash dollars into Cruzeiros. Cuiaba in Mato Grosso with a population of over 150,000 is one such place. Moreover, it can be difficult to find anyone on the street who knows what the exchange rate is. Luckily you can usually find someone in a travel agents who will change for you and usually at a better rate than what you would get in the banks. If you're changing money at a travel agents ask them whether they want cheques dated or not — often they don't as they

have to clear the cheques through banks in Sao Paulo or Rio de Janeiro. Bear this possible hassle in mind, as if you arrive in Brazil on a weekend or run out of Curzeiros at this time you could be in a real fix. Brazilian railway ticket offices will usually accept payment for tickets in cash dollars (US$) and may change more if you need them. They'll generally try you on first with a poor rate but if you just stand there with a look of pure disbelief on your face the rate rises to within two percent of what it should be.

Brazil is not a good place to have money sent to you as you are only allowed up to 50 percent of it in hard currency (US$, £, etc). The rest has to be taken in Cruzeiros. This applies too if you're thinking of buying dollar travellers' cheques against a Credit Card whilst in the country. You are allowed to re-convert up to 50 percent of the Cruzeiros you orignally bought back into hard currency before leaving the country. Obviously, try to avoid buying excess but, if for some reason or another you're caught in this situation, hang onto those bank slips.

There's a 13 percent tax on all airline tickets and MCOs for *domestic flights only* irrespective of where you buy the ticket. There's a Cz$84 airport tax for international flights either from Manaur or Rio de Janeiro (Galeao Airport), or Cz$70 from all other Brazilian airports. For domestic flights the tax is Cz$22 from Manaus or Rio de Janeiro or Cz$18 from other airports.

Brazil is an expensive country. You'll be very lucky to get by on less than US$10 per day (cheap pension and two meals), but hitching is pretty good between the main cities and this is one way to reduce expenditure if you're on a tight budget.

BELÉM
Built on the Amazon delta, it's a hot, funky Atlantic port and entrepot for all the products which come out of the jungle for hundred of km around. But there are no longer many bargains to be found — too many well-heeled tourist come through here. Its early history was one of chop and change between the Portuguese, Dutch and French as these nations wrestled for control of the Guianas and the Amazon delta. There are plenty of old colonial buildings and an old fort, though you can't visit the latter as it's now the Governor's Palace.

Accommodation The cheapest pensiones are near the waterfront and especially on Rua Gaspar Viana.

Hotel Rondônia, Rua Gaspar Viana. Cz$72/single.
Hotel Hylea, 15 de Novembro 228. Cz$72/single.
Hotel Fortaleza, Travessa Frutuoso Guimaraes 276. Cz$60-72/single.
Hotel São Braz, Avenida Governador Jose Malcher 2979, near the bus station. Cz$72/single.
Hotel Transamazônica, Travessa Industria 17, near the Ver-o-Peso market and *ENASA* riverboat booking office. Cz$72/single. It's clean and popular with travellers.

Eats *Miako*, Rua Caetano Rufino, is a Japanese restaurant with good cheap food. *Churrascaría Real*, Avenida Pedro Miranda behind the garage and filling station. All-you-can-eat for Cz$48. *Pato de Ouro* is on Rua Diogo Moia next to Sorveteria Sta. Martha. There are plenty of food stalls in the Ver-o-Peso market for stand-up snacks.

Information Tourist Office on Rua Gaspar Viana has maps and information.

Bus Terminal This is some way from the waterfront on Praça do Operário. Take a local bus either to the Praça da Republica or to the waterfront if you prefer to stay in that area rather than around the bus terminal.

Riverboats Along the Amazon Enquire around amongst the captains and crews of the small riverboats tied up along the port. How much you pay for the trip depends to a large extent on how well you speak Portuguese and on what footing you hit it off with the captain. Most of them fancy themselves as super-cool reincarnations of Humphrey Bogart. Just play the game, the trip to Manaus takes up to 12 days depending on the number of stops. It's about half that to Santarem.

If you want something more definite, *ENASA* have large boats which go to

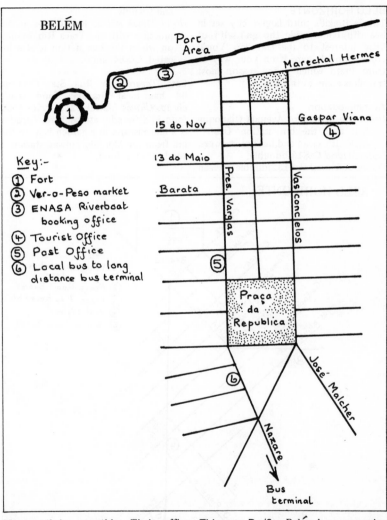

BELÉM

Port Area

Marechal Hermes

Gaspar Viana

15 do Nov

13 do Maio

Barata

Pres. Vargas

Vasconcelos

José Malcher

Nazaré

Praça da Republica

Bus terminal

Key:-
1. Fort
2. Ver-o-Peso market
3. ENASA Riverboat booking office
4. Tourist Office
5. Post Office
6. Local bus to long distance bus terminal

Manaus thrice monthly. Their office is at Avenida Pres. Vargas 41. The one-week journey is Cz$1200 first class (four bunks per cabin, dining room, bar, deck chairs, etc) and Cz$528 second class (space for a hammock, shitty toilets and your own crockery — though even in second class, food is included).

Things to Do/See Belém has an amazing carnival — the Festival of the Candles. It's one of the best and most colourful in all Brazil. Enquire at the Tourist Office or any Brazilian tourist office for details.

BELO HORIZONTE

This is Brazil's third largest city set in beautiful countryside, though itself is of little interest to the traveller. You'll come through here if on your way to Ouro Preto which is the reason most travellers come to this area.

Accommodation

Hotel São Cristovão, Avenida Oiapoque 284, near the bus station. Cz$84/single. It's clean and has hot showers.
Hotel Madrid Cz$132/double.
Pensão Nacional Cz$132/double — clean and friendly.
Hotel Minas Bahia, Rua Caetes at the junction with the Praca Rio Branco on which the bus station is also located. Cz$84/single.

Eats *Tavares* on Rua Sta. Catarina 64 has local Brazilian food that's cheap. *Chinês* Maciel 1217 serves good food in a friendly atmosphere. *Lacador* is a churrascaria in a garden just up the hill from the Monjolo railway station — good for local food.

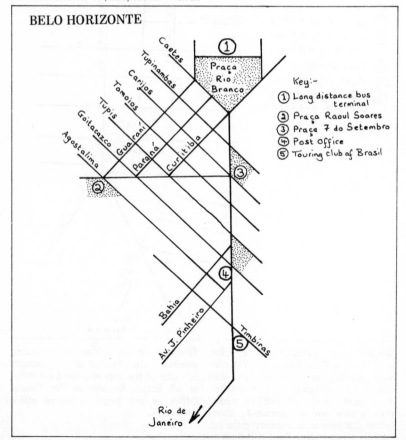

BELO HORIZONTE

Key:-
1. Long distance bus terminal
2. Praça Raoul Soares
3. Praça 7 do Setembro
4. Post Office
5. Touring club of Brasil

Praça Rio Branco

Rio de Janeiro

Information The best place to get maps etc from (free) is the Touring Club do Brasil which is located next to the filling station on Rua Timbiras at the junction with Alfonso Pena.

Bus Terminal The terminal is on the top side of the Praça Rio Branco. Frequent buses go to Ouro Preto so if you get there early enough in the day you can continue your journey rather than stay in Belo Horizonte for the night.

BOA VISTA
Capital of Roraima province in the extreme north of Brazil, most of which is natural grassland and therefore cattle-raising country, Boa Vista is a pleasant, fairly sleepy town with wide avenues reminiscent of Brasilia but on a much smaller scale. It's also a Jehovah's Witnesses stronghold — there isn't exactly a great deal more to do in the

evenings here except take it in turns to go crazy in front of a microphone to the accompaniment of choruses of "alleluia" in hoarse 300-part harmony.

Accommodation
Hotel Brasil Just about the cheapest at Cz$120/double bed for two people, Cz$50/single — good value. Rooms have fan and own bathroom (shower and toilet) and clean sheets. If you're an unmarried couple or mixed group, it's likely you'll come up against an initial vagueness about rooms talking to the manager (bible in hand and one of the local Jehovahs), but his business sense quickly overcomes any reservations he might have picked up chanting slogans about hell fire and damnation, fornication and other wholesome obsessions. After that they're a friendly bunch of people. They

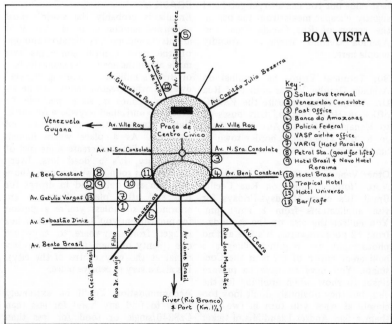

BOA VISTA

Key :-
1. Soltur bus terminal
2. Venezuelan Consulate
3. Post Office
4. Banco do Amazonas
5. Policia Federal
6. VASP airline office
7. VARIG (Hotel Paraiso)
8. Petrol Sta. (good for lifts)
9. Hotel Brasil & Novo Hotel Roraima
10. Hotel Brasa
11. Tropical Hotel
12. Hotel Universo
13. Bar/cafe

also serve excellent meals for Cz$35 — plenty of food. The guy who fills in the register is so short-sighted he can't even see his own hand-writing but you see him bombing up and down on the boulevard outside on his motorbike.

Nova Hotel Roraima, round the corner and next door to the *Hotel Brasil*. It's a slightly flasher place at Cz$180/double, Cz$80/single, but no better facilities than the Brasil. It serves meals.

Hotel Brasa, further down the street (Benjamin Constant) than the *Brasil* and *Nova Roraima*, towards the Praca do Centro Civico (main plaza). Somewhat cheaper than the Brasil but it's more basic with shared toilets and showers. There's a pool table just inside the door.

Eats The *Hotel Brasil* is probably the best value but you can also get good and slightly cheaper meals from the bar on the corner of Rua Cecilia Brasil and Avenida Getulio Vargas — friendly people here.

Bus Terminal From the terminal on Avenida Getulio Vargas corner of Rua Dr. Araujo Filho opposite the *VARIG* office in *Hotel Paraiso*, daily buses go to Manaus by *Soltur*. Also daily buses go to the Venezuelan border town of Santa Elena.

Other Venezuelan Consulate is opposite *Nova Hotel Roraima* on Rua Cecilia Brasil. It's open Mondays-Fridays for visa applications from 8 am-1 pm. You collect the visa on the same day from 12 noon onwards. It's free and no photographs are required. They're a belligerent crowd of cruds at the Consulate. You have to have an onward ticket to show when applying for the visa, but they obviously don't look too closely at what you turn in (we gave them a San Andrés Island-Miami ticket and had no trouble). The Consul is well-known locally to get drunk all the time so things get processed SLOWLY. If you're planning on a lift by truck to either Venezuela or Guiana, it's probably best to get your visa first and then look for a lift.

For lifts to Venezuela and Guyana, one of the best places to look is at the filling station opposite the *Hotel Brasil*. They don't come in that frequently, so it's best to sit around on the patio of the hotel and every time one comes in walk across to the garage and ask. The lifts are often free. It's a very rough road into Guyana and a somewhat better one to Venezuela. Note that exit stamps from the Federal Police in Boa Vista are no longer required before turning up at the border. Everything is done at the border.

BRASILIA

Brasilia is probably the world's most expensive monument to the vanity of architects and military dictators and one of the most cynical comments ever made about the needs — let alone rights — of Brazil's millions of starving "favela" dwellers who created the wealth necessary to finance it. As a spectacle it's probably unrivalled anywhere on earth. Hence its attraction to tourists and travellers. As a place where human beings can live and create some sort of community, it's a dead loss. Every weekend, as soon as work is over, those who can afford it head in droves for Rio and other places. Distances are enormous, so unless you're a glutton for punishment you'll have to take a bus to get from anywhere to anywhere else (plenty of them from the bus terminal at the very centre of the city). It's also a very expensive place.

Accommodation You'll be extremely lucky to find any hotel for less than Cz$240/single or food for less than

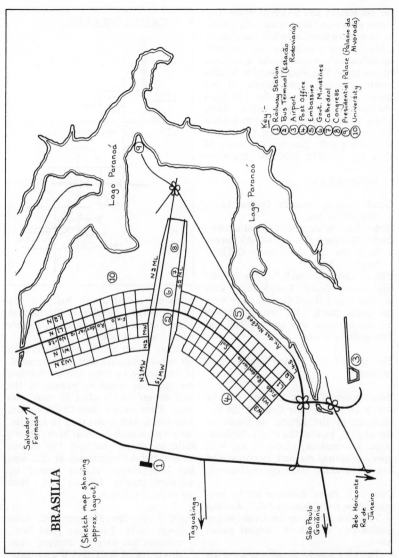

BRASILIA
(Sketch map showing approx. layout)

Key:-
① Railway Station
② Bus Terminal (Estação Rodoviana)
③ Airport
④ Post Office
⑤ Embassies
⑥ Govt. Ministries
⑦ Cathedral
⑧ Congress
⑨ Presidential Palace (Palacio da Alvorada)
⑩ University

Lago Paranoá

Lago Paranoá

Salvador Formosa

Taguatinga

São Paulo Goiânia

Belo Horizonte Rio de Janeiro

Av. das Nações

Cz$84 a meal. The best thing to do when you get there is to enquire at the Tourist Office on the middle floor of the bus terminal (*Rodoviaria*) about the possibility of a free place to stay for three nights maximum at a hotel — a scheme which was introduced at one time for students and other budget travellers. If it's still in operation, they'll send you to the Palacio de Buriti for permission and details of where it is. Other than this, the only way of avoiding an expensive hotel is to ask the Tourist Office about possibilities of bed and breakfast with a family who lives there or, to go to Taguatinga outside Brasilia where there are cheap hotels. If you decide on this, take bus No. 127 from the *Rodoviaria*. It takes half an hour. There is also a youth hostel in Brasilia for those with International Youth Hostel cards (A W Quadra 704, Bloco M Casa 35, tel 0612 259229). It's often full.

In Taguatinga:

Hotel Jurema, Avenida Central 1390, Cz$120/double.
Hotel Rio de Janeiro Cz$120/double.
Hotel Ypacarai, just round the corner from the *Rio de Janeiro*. Cz$108/double — basic.
Other cheapies include the *Hotel São Judas Tadea*, Cz$96/single with breakfast and *Hotel Central*, very near the main plaza with the clocktower on the opposite side to the *Shell* and *Esso* petrol stations.

The rest of this section applies again to Brasilia.

Information Tourist Offices can be found on the middle floor of the bus terminal; at the Palacio de Buriti; at the airport; and at the *Hotel Nacional*. Maps, information, places to see with opening hours, etc and recommended bed and breakfast places can be obtained.

Other All Poste Restante letters addressed here go to Agencia No. 7, Avenida W-3 Quadra 508, four km from the bus station (the bus to the airport passes here).

There's a bus to the airport from the bus terminal every quarter of an hour It takes half an hour, costs 15 centavos.

CAMPO GRANDE
Accommodation A typical bustling,

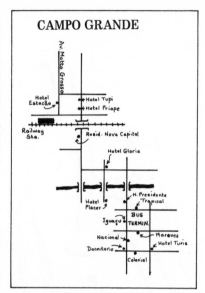

CAMPO GRANDE

sprawling industrialized Brazilian city and if you're heading north through Mato Grosso and Amazonia, it's likely you'll come via here.

Many cheap hotels are around both the railway station and the bus terminal. If you arrive by train and are heading for the bus terminal, beware of the taxi drivers who'll offer to ferry you there. They want at least Cz$10/person. You could walk in less than 15 minutes, even with a pack on your back. There's little to choose between the various budget hotels/dormitorios in this area but your choice will be limited by whether they're full or not. Here are some of the best:

Hotle Turis. Cz$195/room with three single beds. There are good beds, constant hot water in showers, clean sheets (or at least they'll unprotestingly change dirty ones) and it's quiet and friendly.
Hotel Colonial. Cz$180/room with three single beds.
Hotel Nacional. Cz$200/room with

three single beds.

Hotel Tropical Cz$215/room with three single beds — scruffier than the rest.

Hotel Presidente. Cz$240/room with three single beds.

Hotel Iguaçu. Cz$570/room with three beds. It's a mid-range hotel with the facilities you'd expect for this price.

The price per single and per double for the above hotels can be worked out on the basis that a hotel costing Cz$200/room for three would be about Cz$120/double and Cz$70/single. If you're looking for a really cheap room and don't mind dormitory accommodation, try the *Dormitorio Marques* at Cz$180/three people or the dormitório (no name), marked on the map, above the *Hotel Nacional* which costs Cz$100/person.

Bus Terminal A huge modern building on three stories from which buses go to virtually everywhere in Brazil throughout the night and day. Most of the ticket offices are on the top floor. There's little to choose in price between the various companies. What you pay for is the quality of the bus (as elsewhere in Brazil). If you've run out of Cruzeiros, the *Andorhina* ticket office will accept cash dollars at US$1 = Cz$18 if you buy a ticket with them.

CORUMBÁ
Accommodation Most of the cheap places to stay are more or less opposite the railway station, which is where you must get your entry stamp if coming from Bolivia. Hassles about getting from Puerto Suarez on the other side of the river to Corumbá after 8 pm at night are covered in the Bolivian section under *Transport* and the Santa Cruz-Puerto Suarez/Brazilian border rail link.

Pensão Esplanada, opposite railway station. Cz$72/single — cold showers.

Espinola and *Internacional*, both oppo-

site the station. Both Cz$60/single.

Pensão Marabo, Rua 13 de Junho 776, Cz$60/single. You can get meals for Cz$48.

Schabib, Rua Frei Mariano 1153. Cz$48/single — clean, basic and friendly.

Other A border town with Bolivia at the end of the rail line between Santa Cruz and the Brazilian border it's a busy river port and possible to get riverboats south from here to Paraguay.

Two trains go daily to Campo Grande and São Paulo at 8 am and 8 pm.

CUIABÁ
This pleasant town with friendly people and plenty of trees has a mixture of old colonial buildings and modern stuff, but not too many skyscrapers so the city is still human-scale. It's the capital of Mato Grosso.

Accommodation The cheapest hotels are all located on the same street as the bus terminal.

Hotel Santa Luzia Cz$180/room with three single beds (also have doubles and singles for proportionately less). It's clean, tidy, and has singing cleaners, TV and a fridge for use of patrons.

Hotel Miranda Cz$150/three people (also singles and doubles). This place is scruffy and dirty, has no clean sheets and gas masks are obligatory for toilet visits. Security for your belongings is dubious but it is one of the cheapest.

Lisboa Hotel Cz$100/person — clean, air-conditioning, etc. This is the flashest of the lot.

Other cheapies on this street and on Avenida Gal. Valle round the back of the bus terminal are: *Ideal Dormitorio; Hotel São Francisco; Dormitorio Recife; Hotel Cristal; Dormitorio Cezar; Alvorada Motel; Dormitorio Ideal.* The last

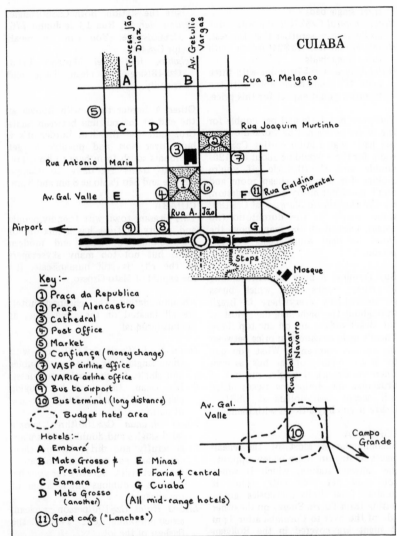

CUIABÁ

Key:-
① Praça da Republica
② Praça Alencastro
③ Cathedral
④ Post Office
⑤ Market
⑥ Confiança (money change)
⑦ VASP airline office
⑧ VARIG airline office
⑨ Bus to airport
⑩ Bus terminal (long distance)
- - - Budget hotel area

Hotels:-
A Embaré
B Mato Grosso & Presidente   E Minas
C Samara   F Faria & Central
D Mato Grosso (another)   G Cuiabá
                                (All mid-range hotels)
⑪ Good cafe ("Lanches")

two are on Avenida Gal. Valle.

There are a number of mid-range hotels in the main part of town which are marked on the map. The best are the *Hotel Mato Groso* (there are two hotels of this name — take your pick; they're both about the same standard) and the *Minas Hotel*. The *Hotel Cuiabá*, in front of the river, is located on a very busy road and would be as noisy as hell most of the time, but for this reason no-doubt cheap.

Eats Several cheap places are opposite the bus terminal. If you want something a little less indifferent, though obviously more expensive, go into the centre of town and try any of the "lanches" places along Avenida Gal. Valle. There's a very cheap and good cafe which does "lanches" (businessmen's lunches) just round the corner from *Hotel Central* (on Rua Galdino Pimentel) as you walk away from the Praca da Republica (marked on the map). Otherwise put your food together from stuff bought from the market. A wide range of food is available here.

Information There's no Tourist Office.

Bus Terminal This is located on the hill above the main part of town but you can't see this part until you get to the mosque or the steps leading down to the river. Frequent buses go to the main cities in the area, eg Sao Paulo, Porto Velho, Rondonopolis, Campo Grande, etc.

Other Cuiabá must surely be one of the few places in Brazil where the Banco do Brasil (the state bank) will not only not change travellers' cheques but won't change cash dollars either! If you need money changing here go to *Confianca* on the Praca da Republica, almost next door to the *Centro America Hotel*. It's a travel agents and will change cheques or dollars at the rate of US$1 = Cz$18.68. Ask for Joel. Their telephone number is 4309. Don't date the cheques as they have to be taken to Sao Paulo.

Free Flights into Amazonia You've heard it all before and everyone you meet will have a tale to tell BUT it is possible. The Armed Forces planes go from here to Porto Velho every 15 days (*FAB*). If you're there on the day they go, they will take you for free. Ideally you need the gift of the gab to get through to the man (who speaks perfect English) who works in the control room and will make arrangements for you. Otherwise say you're a student of botany, zoology, geography — preferably with some headed notepaper "proof" (though none of us had any and it didn't make any difference). Get the bus to the airport (bus stop marked on street plan) go into the central terminal building and take the glass-sided corridor on the far right-hand side of the ticket hall (it's partially screened off and not immediately visible). At the end of the corridor you'll find yourself at the entrance to the communications room (filled with electronic gear, etc). Speak to anyone there. By the time they discover you can't speak very good Portuguese, the guy who speaks English will have introduced himself. From then on it's up to you and how many days separate the day you get there from the day of their next flight.

CURITIBA
Accommodation
Hotel Revil, opposite the bus station. Cz$50. There's hot water — scruffy.

FLORIANOPOLIS
Accommodation
Hotel Felipe, Rua João 26. Cz$100. There's hot water, and it's clean and good value.

Other There are no casas de cambio here.

MANAUS
Capital of Amazonia and built at the junction where the Rio Negro and Rio Solimões meet to form the Amazonas. It saw its heyday during the brief rubber boom of the late 19th and early 20th century after which it went into decline. But it is again becoming important as Amazonia is opened up for other purposes. It's building styles are an amazing mixture ranging from the English-built Customs House (the stone for

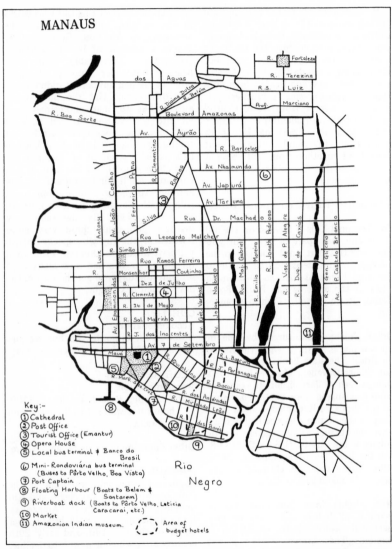

MANAUS

Key:-
① Cathedral
② Post Office
③ Tourist Office (Emantur)
④ Opera House
⑤ Local bus terminal & Banco do Brasil
⑥ Mini-Rondoviária bus terminal (Buses to Pôrto Velho, Boa Vista)
⑦ Port Captain
⑧ Floating Harbour (Boats to Belém & Santarem)
⑨ Riverboat dock (Boats to Pôrto Velho, Leticia Caracarai, etc.)
⑩ Market
⑪ Amazonian Indian museum.

⌐ ¬ Area of
L _ ⌐ budget hotels

which was imported from Britain) through Portuguese town houses to the Italiante Opera House which is world famous. The city itself is interesting and there's plenty going on. Many travellers pass through and quite a few stay to get into something or another (often connected with import/export of one thing or another but often Indian handicrafts). These people are often very helpful if you're looking for a riverboat and will put you in touch immediately with the captain you need to speak to without all the leg-work and rap you would otherwise have to go through.

Accommodation The great bulk of the budget hotels are located on Avenida Joaquim Nabuco between Avenida 7 de Setembro and the waterfront — see the detailed map of this area for locations.

Pensão Tropical, Joaquim Nabuco 508. This is the gringo hotel. Cz$45/ single, Cz$35/person in a shared room — they have doubles, triples and rooms for four people. Rooms have fans, but many are only divided from the others by hardboard partitions about three metres high which means they can be noisy and your gear only marginally safe. Some rooms are very dingy and stuffy. A good cafe is attached at street level (fairly cheap and reasonably good food). If you want to meet other travellers this is the place to hang out.

Hotel Vidal, Josquim Nabuco 681. Cz$50/person in shared room — they have singles, doubles and triples. All rooms have a fan, clean sheets but, like many in this area, many rooms are only partially divided by hardboard partitions so it can be noisy depending on your neighbours' proclivities. The management is friendly. The toilets are clean but crumbling at the edges. Price of room includes coffee. In the basement there's a bar which always has cold beers and a pool table; a good place to meet local people.

Hotel Paris, Joaquim Nabuco 765. Cz$80/person for a room with fan but without coffee, Cz$100/person for a room with fan and coffee (that's an expensive cup of coffee!).

The other budget hotels on this street and in the immediate vicinity range between Cz$50 and Cz$100/person depending on quality. Another hotel popular with travellers is the *Hotel Lar* on Rua Dos Andrados.

The other hotels nearer the centre of town marked on the detailed street plan are all mid-range to high-price hotels in comparison: eg *Minas Hotel*, Avenida Eduardo Ribeiro, Cz$198/person in a room with own bath and central heating.

Eats *Pensão Tropical* has food (mentioned previously). There are some good fish restaurants on the waterfront either side of Joaquim Nabuco (take your pick). If you want a change and like pizza, there's a huge "pizza palace" on the right-hand side going up the central Avenida Eduardo Ribeiro from the Cathedral — reasonable prices for what they serve and the area and excellent pizzas.

Information The main Tourist Office is a fair way out at the junction of Avenida Taruma and Rua Silva Ramos, but you needn't go that far for the sort of information they carry. Go to the huge flash *Hotel Amazonas* at the junction of Peixoto and Rua Marques de Santa Cruz. Make out you're a well-heeled tourist and they'll give you the lot. There are also information stands at the airport and the floating harbour.

Bus Terminal For buses to Porto Velho and Boa Vista, the terminal ("Mini-Rondoviária") is on Avenida Nhamunda just by the junction with Rua Emilio Moreira. It's a 20-minute walk from the centre though and there are buses there on Avenida Taruma.

Buses to the airport are Cz$2.50, taxis are Cz$100. Note that travel agents in Manaus won't sell you air tickets to or from any place which doesn't include Manaus as the starting

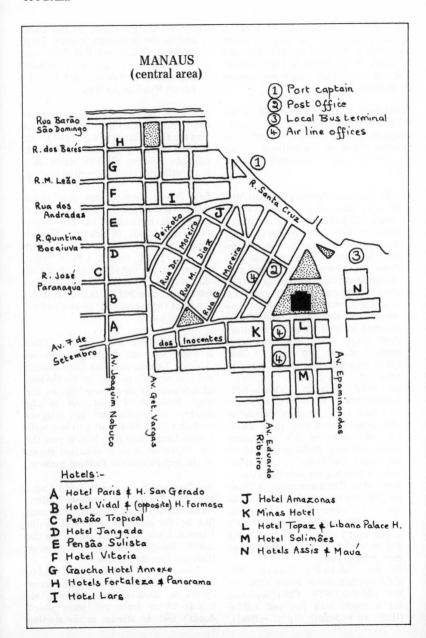

MANAUS
(central area)

1. Port captain
2. Post Office
3. Local Bus terminal
4. Air line offices

Rua Barão São Domingo
R. dos Barés
R.M. Leão
Rua dos Andradas
R. Quintina Bocaiuva
R. José Paranaguá
Av. 7 de Setembro

R. Santa Cruz

Peixoto
Rua Dr. Moreira
Rua M. Diaz
Rua G. Moreira

dos Inocentes

Av. Joaquim Nabuco
Av. Get. Vargas
Av. Eduardo Ribeiro
Av. Epaminondas

Hotels:-

A Hotel Paris & H. San Gerado
B Hotel Vidal & (opposite) H. Formosa
C Pensão Tropical
D Hotel Jangada
E Pensão Sulista
F Hotel Vitoria
G Gaucho Hotel Annexe
H Hotels Fortaleza & Panorama
I Hotel Lars

J Hotel Amazonas
K Minas Hotel
L Hotel Topaz & Libano Palace H.
M Hotel Solimões
N Hotels Assis & Mauá

point unless you also purchase an MCO for a minimum of US$50 (this is a bit of a sod if you're thinking of picking up an onward ticket for Venezuela).

Riverboats This is a very busy port and you can find riverboats to just about anywhere on the Amazonian river system. Ask around the gringos in the *Pensão Tropical* first — it might save you some leg-work. After that, go down to the Port Captain's offices. Before any boat can leave the harbour, the captains of the boats have to come here and register their journey. It's a good place to meet the man you want. Many of the captains know each other and their patches and so will point out the one you need. Otherwise tour every one of the boats tied up down by the waterfront. If no luck you'll have to take the *ENASA* boat at least as far as Santarem from where there are buses to Brasilia. The *ENASA* offices are on Rua Marechal Deodoro 61.

Lloyd Brasileiro also run scheduled boats down the Amazon. Their address is Avenida Eduardo Ribeiro 355.

Other To change money it's best to ask around on Joaquim Nabuco, as many travellers have excess Cruzeiros. You can get up to Cz$22-23 — US$1 depending on who you meet and how badly they need dollars. The Banco do Brasil will change travellers' cheques here.

Consulate addresses are as follows:
Colombian Consulate, Avenida Eduardo Albeiro 436, Sala 31.
Peruvian Consulate, Rua Rocha dos Santos 85.
Bolivian Consulate, Rua Fortaleza 80.
Ecuadorian Consulate, Conj Belo Horizonte, Casa 6. Parque 10.

Things to Do/See Meeting of the rivers Río Negro and Solimões. If you're coming by bus from Pôrto Velho, you'll see this remarkable sight on the ferry across the river without having to go to the trouble of taking a boat out from Manaus. At the point where the rivers meet there's a sharply defined colour change from the muddy yellow of the Solimões to the clearer dark brown/black of the Negro. The river is so wide at this point (eight km) that the two separate streams of water don't fully mix for another eight km downriver. The river is a magnificent sight on its own and is still over 1600 km from the sea at this point. Huge logs float past supporting their own mini-jungles on the surface, while ocean-going ships tie up in mid-stream. It's a beautiful sight.

The Salesian Indian Museum's location is marked on the street map. It's well worth seeing. There are exhibits from many of the jungle tribes of the Amazon and it's totally different stuff from what you see in the Andean highlands. Entry Cz$10. It is open Monday-Saturday 8 am-11 am, 2 pm-5 pm.

The dome of the Opera House (Teatro Amazonas) can be seen from almost any part of Manaus. Built in 1896 and rebuilt in 1929, restoration has been going on for a number of years. Entry Cz$10. It's open Monday-Saturday 11 am-5 pm.

Ethnological Museum on Rua Bernado Ramos 117 has weapons, pottery and ritual objects from the Amazon area. It's open every morning 9 am-11 am.

OURO PRETO
Accommodation *Tófolo*, Rua São José 76, near the Contas fountain. US$8/double with own shower — clean sheets. It serves some of the cheapest meals in town. *N.S. Aparecida* Cz$144/double — basic.

Eats One of the cheapest places is the restaurant at the *Hotel Tófolo* (open to non-residents). If you're looking to meet local young people try the *Cala-bouço*, Conde Bobadela — a bar-cum-cafe.

Information Tourist Office, Praça Tiradentes, has maps, opening times of the monuments and churches, etc.

Things to Do/See Don't miss this place if you're anywhere near it. At one time Ouro Preto was the state capital of Minas Gerais during the gold-rush days. It is the most beautiful and well-preserved old colonial city in Brazil set in equally beautiful countryside. Here lived the most famous of Brazilian sculptors — Antonio Francisco Aleijadinho — whose work graces many of the churches in this city particularly the Nossa Senhora do Carmo and São Francisco de Assis.

Mineralogical Museum is in part of the old Governor's Palace that is now the University of Mining. It has one of the world's most complete collections of mineral specimens.

PÔRTO VELHO

This is a sleepy riverport on the Rio Madeira which you'll almost certainly come through if you're heading north or south through the Amazon Jungle. It was once the rail head of the Pôrto Velho-Riberalta railway built by Brazil to "compensate" Bolivia for the annexation of the Acre territory in 1903 but which never reached its destination at Riberalta. It ended at Guajara Mirim and proved to be of little use to Bolivia.

Accommodation Almost all the hotels are located on Avenida 7 de Setembro between the bus terminal and Rua Goncalves Dias.

Iara Hotel, Avenida Osorio at the junction with Avenida 7 de Setembro. Cz$60/single without own bathroom, Cz$150/single with own bathroom and fan. Cz$200/three people, one double and one single bed, in room with own shower and fan — clean sheets. It's a good place.

Kennedy Hotel Cz$60/single, Cz$120/double, — share showers. It's basic but clean and there's a TV lounge. A restaurant is attached which serves the coldest beers in town (night or day) and you need them!

Hotel Nunes, next door to the *Kennedy*, both on Avenida 7 de Setembro. Cz$70-120/single for room without shower, toilet, Cz$100-180/single for room with own shower and toilet, Cz$150-250/single for room with airconditioning, shower and toilet. All rooms have fans. They also have double and triple rooms. Room prices include coffee.

If you want something cheaper you'll have to take one of the hotels nearer the bus station — *Rondônia Hotel* (wood building), *Hotel NS Nazare*, or the *Hotel Ajuricaba* (wood again). The *Villa Hotel* is nearer the town and very cheap but often full as they have only a few rooms.

Eats The restaurant next door to the *Nunes Hotel* serves some of the best and cheapest "Super-Lanches" Cz$25. They also have large cheeseburgers Cz$12-16, sandwiches for the same and the best "limãos" (lime drinks) in town Cz$6. There's an excellent pizza restaurant on the corner of Avenida 7 de Setembro and Avenida Rogério Weber. Good Japanese and local food can be got at the *Tokio* Restaurant on Rua Goncalves Dias near *Villas Hotel*.

Bus Terminal This is a fair way from town on Avenida 7 de Setembro. Daily buses go to Manaus, Guajara Mirim and Cuiabá. Book in advance if possible.

Riverboats Plenty of boats go to Manaus. You will never have to wait more than a few days and often you can find one the same day you ask. The smaller boats taking passengers only take four days to get there. The mixed passenger/

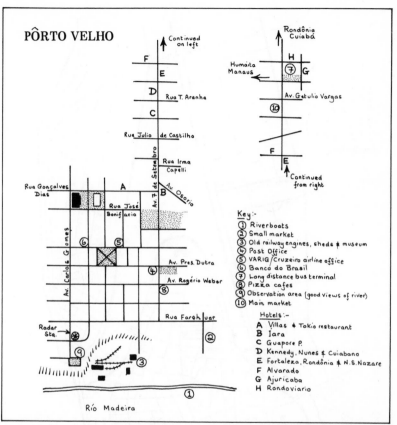

PÔRTO VELHO

Continued on left

Rondônia
Cuiabá

Humaita
Manaus

Rua T. Aranha

Rua Julio de Castilho

Rua Irma Capelli

Av. Getulio Vargas

Continued from right

Rua Gonçalves Dias

Av. Osorio

Rua José Bonifacia

Rua Carlos Gomes

Av. 7 de Setembro

Av. Pres. Dutra

Av. Rogério Weber

Rua Farqh Juar

Radar Sta.

Río Madeira

Key:-
① Riverboats
② Small market
③ Old railway engines, sheds & museum
④ Post Office
⑤ VARIG/Cruzeiro airline office
⑥ Banco do Brasil
⑦ Long distance bus terminal
⑧ Pizza cafes
⑨ Observation area (good views of river)
⑩ Main market

Hotels:-
A Villas & Tokio restaurant
B Iara
C Guapore P.
D Kennedy, Nunes & Cuiabano
E Fortaleza, Rondônia & N.S.Nazare
F Alvarado
G Ajuricaba
H Rondoviario

cargo boats can take seven days. It can be expensive and you need to do a lot of bargaining. Try the following Pôrto Velho-registered boats: *San Benedito; São Geraldo; Cicade de Rondônia.* You need your own hammock, etc. There's also the *C de Eirunepe* which runs on a regular schedule to Manaus taking 50 passengers and charging Cz$300 for first class and Cz$250 for second class. It's also possible to go deck class if you speak with the captain. This one also takes four days to Manaus.

Things to Do/See Down by the river are the old engines and carriages, etc

which used to work the railway from here to Guajara Mirim. The engines — one from Germany (built 1936) and one from the US (built 1941) — are slowly rusting away but still substantially intact. The old railway station has been well preserved and turned into a museum of railway memorabilia. There's no indication of opening times however. It's likely you will have to make personal arrangements to see inside as Pôrto Velho is hardly a tourist spot.

RECIFE
Accommodation
Hotel do Parque Rua dos Hospicios

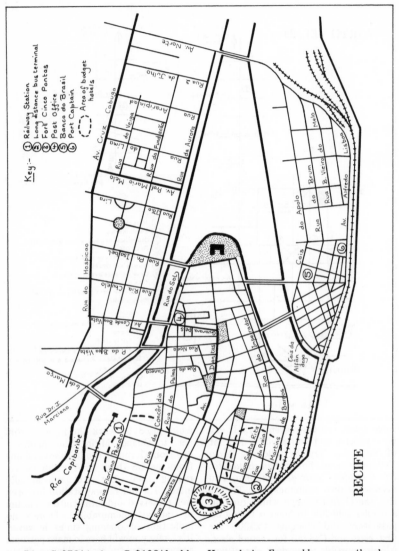

Key:-
① Railway Station
② Long distance bus terminal
③ Fort Cinco Pontas
④ Post Office
⑤ Banco do Brasil
⑥ Port Captain
⟋‾⟍ Area of budget hotels

RECIFE

51. Cz$72/single, Cz$108/double. Many travellers stay here.

Hospedaria São Marcos, Rua Padre Muniz 180. Cz$60/single. It's near the São José market.

Hospedaria Esmeralda, near the bus station. Cz$60/single — clean.

Information There's a Tourist Office at *Empetur* on Avenida Conselheiro

Rosa e Silva 773, and also at Rua Martins de Barros 593, Avenida Conde de Boa Vista 149 and Rua 7 de Setembro 10, loja 1. You can get maps, museum opening times, etc.

Things to Do/See Recife is a hotbed of what the Government would probably call "left-wing" radicals. Many of the best opposition politicians come from this town — when they're allowed to oppose. The intellectual life of the city centres around Sao Pedro dos Clerigos church (one street below Avenida Dantas). It's a city of old buildings and churches divided into three sections by canals and waterways. It stages one of the best and most lively Carnivals in Brazil.

Places Nearby Olinda, six km to the north, used to be the old capital of the state. Like Ouro Preto, it's a beautifully preserved colonial town which you may well prefer to Recife. The cheapest place to stay is near the beach to the north of town where there are many cheap hotels. Olinda has become an artists' colony and there's an excellent choice of woodcarvings and crafts available from the daily street market in the square next to the Cathedral on the hill top.

RIO DE JANEIRO

Looking down on Rio from the Corcovado or Pão de Açúcar (Sugar Loaf), it's easy to see what attracts people here and why it's considered to be the world's most beautiful city. Certainly its setting is just that and few people would dispute it. Perhaps you'll even leave still thinking that, if you manage to maintain the high you get from the top of either of those two vantage points. Down at sea-level it's not quite the same story unless you wallet is straining at the seams and you have a fistful of credit cards. But it's not just expensive. It's also overcrowded, noisy, polluted and congested with traffic. Favelas (shantytowns) ring the suburbs. As a budget traveller, you'll come into contact with a lot of the unpleasanter side of Rio. Nevertheless I wouldn't recommend you to miss it. How could you go to Brazil and miss Rio?

Accommodation The cheapest places to stay are undoubtedly the Youth Hostels/ Student Houses. There are three of them:

Casa do Estudiante Praca Anna Amelia 9, 10 and 11, ZC 39 Castelo.
Residencia Feminina Casa do Estudiante Rua Almirante Gomes Pereira 86.
Albergue Rua Diomedes Trotta 332, Ramos.

All these places cost Cz$15/person/ night and at that price they're well subscribed and may be full. Watch your belongings. The first listed is open all year; the rest only in the months of January, February and July.

If you can't get in at any of these hostels or want a hotel anyway by preference, expect to be paying from Cz$120 upwards for just the most basic of facilities. Obviously, there are thousands of hotels in Rio and they're spread right across the city, so our intention here is to direct you to a few fruitful areas in the centre where you'll find a cheap place to stay. If you don't like the area or would prefer to stay somewhere else, check into one of these places for a day or two so you have somewhere to leave your baggage and then scout around in the area you'd prefer to be. In the area covered by our street plan the budget hotels are located in and around the following streets (a few examples are listed):

(1) Praça Mauá; Avenida Rod. Alves; Rua Sacadura Cabral; Rua Senador Pompeu.
(2) Praça Tiradentes.

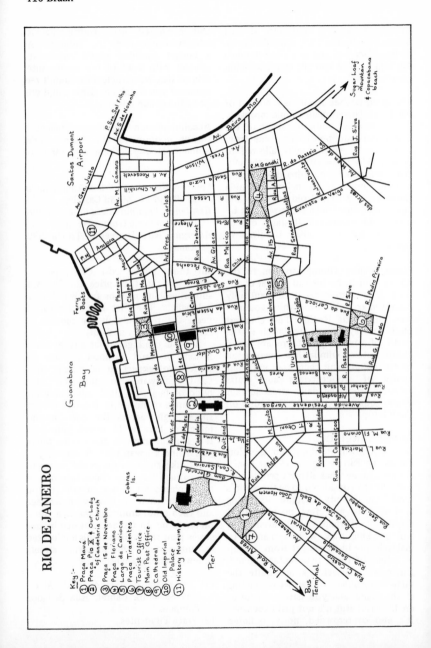

RIO DE JANEIRO

Key:-
1. Praça Mauá
2. Praça Pio X ✝ Our Lady of Candelaria Church
3. Praça 15 de Novembro
4. Praça Floriano
5. Largo da Carioca
6. Praça Tiradentes
7. Tourist Office
8. Main Post Office
9. Cathedral
10. Old Imperial Palace
11. History Museum

(3) Avenida Mem de Sá.

Hotel Cruzeiro Tefe, Rua Sacadura Cabral 169A. Cz$96/single.

Santista, Rua Sacadura Cabral 45. Cz$72/single. It's clean and very simple but with hot showers.

Rio Grande Rua Senador Pompeu near the Central Station. Cz$108/single — friendly management. To get there from the bus terminal catch service bus No. 355 about 100 metres from the terminal on Avenida Rod. Alves. Get off the bus at the junction of Avenida Baraode and Rua Senador Pompeu (takes a few minutes). From where you get off, the hotel is a few minutes walk. It's popular with travellers.

Pensão Lisboa, Avenida Mem de Sa 158. Cz$72/single. It's a nice place and also serves cheap meals for around Cz$24.

Hotel Mundo Nova, Avenida Mem de Sa 85. Cz$240/double with own shower. They serve meals.

Other cheapies on this street include the *Hotel Braganca*. Cz$144/single with own bath. Breakfasts are available.

In the Flamengo beach area, the best street to try is Rua Ferreira Viana.

Hotel Grão Pará, Cz$144/double without own shower. It's a clean, pleasant place.

Hotel Florida. Cheapest in the annexe at Cz$96/single, share showers — basic and simple.

Hotel Alameda, Rua Candido Mendes 112. Cz$120/single. Nearby is the slightly more expensive *Hotel Monte Castelo*.

If you'd like a small, self-catering flatlet to let for a minimum of two weeks, enquire at Rua Barata Ribeiro 90, first floor. These people let out flatlets on the same street at No. 194, near Copacabana beach.

Eats Restaurants are expensive but you can eat for under Cz$48 at more or less any of the hundreds of small businessmen's lunch cafes which bear the sign "lonchenette" or "lanches". They vary in price dending on the quality of food they serve but are all relatively cheap.

Information There are several Tourist Offices in various parts of the city.

Embratur, Praça Mauá 7, 11th and 14th floor.

Touring Club do Brasil, Praça Mauá. This is probably the best place for information and maps. They speak English.

Brazilian Tourist Information Centre, Rua Barata Ribeiro 272, Copacabana. They have excellent maps and a library.

There's also an information kiosk at the main bus terminal.

Guides to Rio: *Guia Quatro Rodas do Rio*, Cz$36, is in English and Portuguese and has an excellent large-scale map of the city. *Guia Schaeffer Rio de Janeiro* contains the most extensive map of the city of any guide.

Bus Terminal The terminal is on Avenida Rod. Alves at the junction with Avenida F. Bicalho. Local service buses (No.171) to the centre run along Avenida Rod. Alves. Note that buses have turnstiles and are always crowded. Have change handy!

Other Most domestic flights leave from Santos Dumont Airport very close to the centre (see street plan). International flights leave from Galeão Airport on Governador Island which is linked to the mainland by a bridge. 16 km from the centre. Local buses Nos. 322 and 328 will take you there. There's also a half-hourly bus shuttle between the two airports which costs Cz$20.

To hitch out of Rio take bus No. 392 or 394 from Praça São Francisco to the motorway entrances going south or north. It's easy to get a lift from there.

To change money, if you don't get offered a private deal on the street or in a cafe (most unlikely), Exprinter Travel Agency, Avenida Rio Branco 57A (junction with Avendia Pres. Vargas) gives the best straight deal — better than the banks.

The Peace Corps HQ is at Rua Barao de Lucena 81, Botafogo.

The British Council, Avenida Portugal 360, Urca, is a good place for checking out possibilities of teaching English if you're thinking of staying. There's also the possibility of meeting someone who already works in Rio and might offer to put you up for a few days.

Things to Do/See Ferries to the islands in Guanabara Bay depart from the waterfront close to Praca 15 de Novembro. They go to Niterói every 10 minutes and the journey takes 20-30 minutes. Cz$4. To Paqueta Island the journey takes 70-90 minutes. Cz$10. There are also hovercraft and hydrofoil ferries to Niteroi for four times the price of the ferryboats.

Pão de Açúcar (Sugar Loaf mountain). Fantastic views of the city from the top of this and from the top of Corcovado. There is a cable car to the top composed of two stages: first from the base station at Avenida Pasteur 520 to Urca, half way up, and second from Urca to the summit. Cars run all day and it's rarely necessary to queue. First car departs 8 am, last car gets back from the summit at 10 pm. Return fare Cz$168. To get to the base station take bus No. 442 from the centre of town or bus No. 511 or 512 from Copacabana.

Corcovado is twice as high as the Sugar Loaf and has the Statue of Christ on the summit with even more fantastic views of the city. There are several ways to get to the top: (1) take bus No 422 or 498 from Avenida Pres. Vargas as far as it goes up the mountain, hitch or walk the rest of the way (plenty of shade if you're walking). (2) Take bus No. 206 from Largo Carioca just off Avenida Rio Branco which goes to one of the stations on the cogwheel railway which goes to the summit. Take the cogwheel railway from here. (3) Take bus Nos. 106, 422, 497, 498, 583 or 584 to the cogwheel railway station at Rua Cosme Velho 513. Take the cogwheel railway from there to the summit. Cz$120 return. Trains go every half hour which take one and a half hours for the round trip. The first train goes at 8 am, the last at 6 pm. There's a cafe at the summit.

There are too many museums to list. Any Tourist Office or Travel Agency will provide a full list with opening times and entrance fees, etc. Two of the best are:

The National Museum, Quinta da Boa Vista, was once the palace of the Emperors of Brazil. In addition to such things as the Throne Room and Ambassadors' Room, there are collections of Indian weapons, dresses and everyday objects; mineral specimens, historical documents, etc; birds, butterflies, fishes, etc. Well worth a visit. It's open 12 noon-5 pm daily except Mondays.

The National Historical Museum, Praça Marechal Âncora, has all manner of historical objects, armour, furniture, silver, etc. The building was once the Arsenal in Empire days. It's open Tuesdays-Fridays 12 noon-5.30 pm and Saturdays-Sundays 2.30 pm-5.30 pm.

The beaches will undoubtedly be one of the reasons you've come to Rio but don't get too excited; most of the beaches anywhere near the centre of town (and including Copacabana and

Ipanema) are very polluted. If you're really looking for a good, unpolluted beach to hang around on for a while, go to Parati further down the coast.

SALVADOR (Bahia)

This is Brazil's most interesting city and, for atmosphere and culture, it beats hell out of Rio de Janeiro. Give Rio's over-commercialized Carnival a miss and come here for it instead. This easy-going city with beautiful, unpolluted beaches, has a culture steeped in a mixture of African, Portuguese and Indian folklore and religion. You'll love it. Many travellers stay for a long time. If you come here by bus, the terminal is a long way (five km) from the centre of town. Catch a bus to the centre — Praça de Sé.

Accommodation One of the cheapest places to stay is the Youth Hostel (*Albergue*), Avenida 7 de Setembro 3513, Praia da Barra. Cz$15.

Hotel Ameides, Cipriano Barata 73. Cz$40/single. The very friendly management will lock up your excess baggage if you go off to the beaches for a few days. It's popular with travellers.

Hotel Granada, São José and *Roma*, all on Avenida 7 de Setembro. Cz$72/single. The latter two are used by Peace Corps volunteers who may well put you in touch with fellow workers out in the sticks.

Tourist Motel, Praça Anchieta 16. Cz$72/single.

Hotel Benfica, Praça da Sé. Cz$168/double. Meals are available.

If you're going to stay for a while it's much better to rent a house. One of the best ways of finding one is to choose the area you want to live in and then go looking for empty houses. When you find a suitable one, ask the people who live on either side if you can rent it. Many Bahians who leave houses empty give the keys to their neighbours with instructions to let it out if anyone enquires. The same goes for the beach communities. Somewhat more expensive lets (expensive, that is, unless you're sharing with others) can be found at Joia Imobiliaria, Avenida 7 de Setembro 53 on the first floor of the Edificio Brasilgas. This is an accommodation agency.

Eats Bahian food is really excellent — hot and spicy. If you spent any amount of time in the Andean countries bored out of your skull on bland lomo saltadas, arroz y frijoles, this is the place to come. Try "vatapá" which is made from fish, rice, cashew nuts, ginger, mint and parsley garnished with palm oil.

There are many cheap, good restaurants serving local food around the Praça da Sé. If you want to splash out a little try the *Coco e Dênde*, on the corner of Avenida Princesa Isabel and Alameda Antunes in the Barra district, or the *Nova Continental* near the start of the Lacerda lift in the lower city. Excellent meat pies can be got from the *Teng Lonchenette*, Rua da Cabeça on the corner of Carlos Gomes (ask for "esfiha de carne").

Information A Tourist Office is on the corner of Mercado Modelo, Praca Cairu in the lower city. There's also an information kiosk at the bus terminal.

Other The airport is 32 km from the city. Bus No. 101 goes from the centre of town. Taxis are expensive as you might expect for that distance.

Things to Do/See Carnival starts on the Sunday before Lent and ends at midnight before Ash Wednesday. Everyone goes crazy for days and nights on end singing, dancing, drinking or just rolling around. There are floats, marching and dancing groups all in the most amazing costumes, musicians, often amplified, and thousands of people who jam the streets bopping away completely out of their boxes. There's just no way you won't become a part of it. And in Bahia, it's still largely a spontaneous explosion of the people's energy and spirit, whereas in Rio it's become very much a rich person's spectacle and big business venture.

Carnival isn't the only festival — there are many others though few quite as wild. In the first week in February is the Festas de Yemanjá — a pagan festival honouring the Goddess of the Sea. Bahians take gifts down to the beach at Rio Vermelho where they are floated out to sea amid much ritual, music and dancing. Another festival is São João in the third week of June, when bonfires are lit in the streets and people entertain each other in their homes with food and "ginepapo" — a traditional local liqueur.

The following beaches are all superb and can be reached by local service buses which depart from the Praça da Sé: Largo de Abaté, Jardim de Alá, Boca do Rio and Itapoan. If you're looking for fellow travellers, the beach which has been most colonised by them is Arembepe.

Teaching English If you fancy staying here for a while and would like to support yourself by teaching English, this is one of the best places to find work. Try YES (Your English School), Ladeira da Barra. These people will hire you without a work permit and pay Cz$48-72/hourly session. Another is the ACBEU (Asociação Brasil-Estados Unidos), Avenida 7 de Setembro, but they generally demand a work permit. Plenty of private work is available.

SÃO PAULO

This, the industrial centre of South America has a population of over nine

million and is contending hard for the title of World's Largest City. It already covers over more than 1600 square km (three times the size of Paris) and is the world's fastest growing city. Nothing of the past remains. It's a city of tall shining skyscrapers as far as the eye can see and the place to which millions of desperately poor Brazilians flock in search of the elusive American dream. Most of them end up — if they're lucky and many aren't — as abysmally-paid industrial labourers. Their wages don't even cover the very most basic of human needs and they are condemned forever to scratch out a mean existence in one of the many "favelas" (shantytowns), without sanitation, water, electricity, health services or any of the other amenities which other industrial societies take for granted. If you come away from this place with anything other than a massive feeling of shock, then you are either a complete cynic, filthy rich, or you've gone around with your eyes closed. But don't take my word for it: go and see for yourself.

Accommodation

Hotel Chaves, Rua Dos Andrados, very close to the bus terminal and the Sorocabana railway station. It's popular with travellers passing through. Cz$84/single.

Monaco, Rua das Timbiras 143. Cz$84/single.

Noreste, Rua de Triúnfo, very close to the bus terminal. Cz$144/double.

Hotel Planeta, Alameda Dino Bueno, close to the bus station. Cz$196/double.

Hospedaria Familiar, Rua dos Gusmões 218. Cz$60/single. It's very basic but one of the cheapest.

Hotel do Comercio, Ria Mauá 512. Cz$156/double.

Hotel Queluz, corner of Rua Mauá and Washington Luís. Cz$108/double.

Hotel Lima, Rua Ifigênia. Cz$96/single with breakfast.

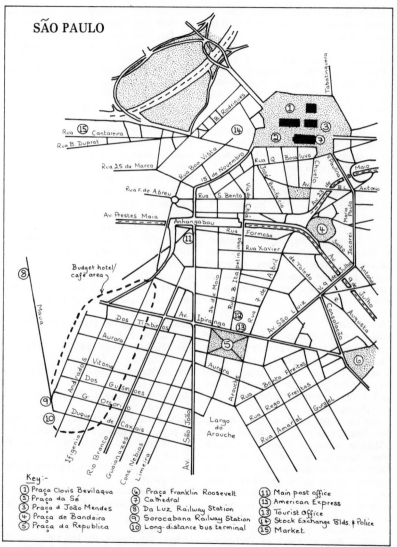

SÃO PAULO

Key:-
① Praça Clovis Bevilaqua
② Praça da Sé
③ Praça d João Mendes
④ Praça de Bandeira
⑤ Praça da Republica
⑥ Praça Franklin Roosevelt
⑦ Cathedral
⑧ Da Luz Railway Station
⑨ Sorocabana Railway Station
⑩ Long-distance bus terminal
⑪ Main post office
⑫ American Express
⑬ Tourist Office
⑭ Stock Exchange Blds. ₊ Police
⑮ Market

Eats With a high immigrant population of Japanese, Italian, Spanish and German, there's a very varied choice of food available but, as with most restaurants of this type in large Brazilian cities, they're not cheap. So, unless you have money to spare, it's back to the "lonchonette". There are plenty of these places doing set meals around the centre of town and particularly around the bus terminal and train stations. They all charge similar prices and there's little to choose between them.

Information There are several Tourist Offices: Praça da Republica, — see street plan for location. Praça Roosevelt, Viaducto Jacareí 100, Rua São Luís 125 (see street plan).

Larger scale maps of São Paulo are included in the train timetable booklet which you can get free from the larger hotels and from *H. Stern* (Jewellers), Praça da Republica 242.

Other American Express is at Kontik-Franstur SA (R), Rua Marconi 71, second floor.

The international airport is an amazing 95 km from the city at Viracopos near Campinas. Even the local domestic airport is 14 km from the city centre at Congonhas. Regular bus services to the latter.

TRANSPORT
Flights Short plane hops in Brazil are nowhere near as cheap as they are in the Andean countries so if you're on a budget, you can safely forget about them unless you're in a hurry to get back home or you don't fancy the long haul through Amazonia.

On the other hand, it is possible to find free flights with the armed forces (*FAB*) on occasions. There are as many tales floating around about these flights as there are people who have tried to get on them. The main reason for this is that success depends largely on how you hit it off with the people in charge. Qualities which auger well for success are: persistence; the ability to put a few sentences of Portuguese together; some knowledge of the present state of play of Brazilian football; the luck of the Irish. If you can make it as far as a conversation about anything *other than* the possibility of a flight

with the guy in charge, then you'll be on their next flight. And if you make it this far, don't forget to ask the guy who put you on it if he has any friends at the other place you're going to. This way you'll make lots of friends and see the insides of quite a few military transport planes. We got our first break at Cuiabá airport, though it took us a whole afternoon to get past the various minions who wanted to know why we were wandering around in the military communications area and were (unsuccessfully) intent on escorting us back to the civilian terminal building.

If you're unlucky with the above, the main airlines are *VARIG*, *VASP*, *Cruzeiro do Sol* and *Rio-Sul* which have an extensive service between all the main cities in Brazil. In addition to these, in Amazonia, there are many different "Aero-Taxi" companies who do short hops between many of the smaller places, though they're none too cheap. Here are a few examples.

Foz do Iguaçu-São Paulo. Cz$1980 by *Cruzeiro do Sol*.

São Paulo-Rio de Janeiro. Cz$931, by *Cruzeiro do Sol.*

Brasilia-Manaus. Cz$4889 by *Cruzeiro do Sol.*

Manaus-Boa Vista Cz$1558, by *Cruzeiro do Sol.*

Cuibá-Pörto Velho. Cz$2712, on Tuesdays, Thursdays, Fridays, Saturdays, Sundays at 10.10 am by *VASP* and *TABA.*

Cuibá-Manaus. Cz$4176, the same flight as above.

Cuiabá-Boa Vista. Cz$5868, on Tuesdays, Thursdays, Fridays at 10 am by *Cruzeiro.*

One of the reasons for the high cost of internal flights in Brazil is the 13 percent tax on airline tickets for domestic flights. Here are some examples of international flights.

Manaus-Bogotá (Colombia): US$153 on Fridays and Saturdays at 1.15 pm by *Varig* and *Cruzeiro*.

Manaus-Miami: US$328 on Wednesdays at 2 am by *Varig* and *Cruzeiro*, Mondays and Saturdays at 8 am by *Braniff.*

Manaus-Los Angeles: US$505 on Saturdays by *Varig*, *Cruzeiro* and *Braniff* at 8 am.

Railways South of a line stretching from Corumbá through Brasilia to Recife — the Atlantic litoral and the more developed southern states of Brazil — there's an excellent network of railways. They're considerably cheaper than buses, though slower, and second class is more than adequate and rarely crowded. Trains are kept clean and meals can be bought either in a dining car or brought to you at your seat (cost Cz$36-48/meal). Refreshments are brought round periodically — coffee, mineral waters and beer or wine. Sleeping cars are available on the routes between São Paulo, Rio de Janeiro and Belo Horizonte.

The most popular rail route used by travellers coming from the Andean countries is the Corumbá-Campo Grande São Paulo-Rio de Janeiro route. Another is the link from Buenos Aires through Paso de los Libres (Argentine/Brazil border) to Pôrto Alegre.

Corumbá-Campo Grande. Two trains leave daily at 8 am and 8 pm. Cz$100 first class and Cz$50 second class. The journey takes 10-11 hours. Second class is quite adequate and not crowded. It's a very pleasant journey. This train goes on to São Paulo. The journey from Campo Grande to São Paulo takes 23 hours. Cz$220 first class, Cz$110 second class.

São Paulo-Rio de Janeiro. Several trains do this route daily, including night trains and sleeping accommodation (recommended). The journey takes up to nine hours. Cz$100 first class, Cz$50 second class.

Railway timetables are available free of charge at Tourist Offices and larger hotels in São Paulo and from the jewellers *H. Stern*, Praça da Republica, São Paulo.

Meals on trains Cz$30 (excellent food), fizzy drinks Cz$6 and sandwiches Cz$10. If you're short of Cruzeiros on arrival in Brazil, railway ticket offices will generally accept cash US Dollars at Cz$18 = US$1.

Road transport/Buses In the more populated parts of Brazil, hitching is relatively easy as there are many private cars and transport trucks and the roads are metalled and in good condition. It's unlikely you'll be expected or asked to pay for a ride. In the Amazon basin, you'll be reliant on roadworkers' transport and logging trucks, and you need to be pretty rough and ready if you're going to take advantage of these. Logging camps and frontier towns are not the ideal places for mystics, romantics or cocktail party goers. Roads anywhere north of a line stretching from Cuiabá to Brasilia (other than the road from Manaus to Boa Vista which, although being an all-weather dirt road, is in excellent condition) are characterized by vast seas of red dust or yawning oceans of thick mud after rain. By the time you get out at the other end you'll be covered in the stuff. Your baggage will end up in the same condition. If you want to prevent this happening to your gear, get hold of a large fertilizer bag or other suitable plastic bag and put your pack inside it before you stow it away in the luggage compartment. If hitching on top of a lumber truck, be prepared for mile after mile of dust-storm as your truck jockeys to overtake the bus or truck in front. Neither will be prepared to give an inch, in conditions where visibility rarely exceeds a few feet and with trucks carrying hundreds of tonnes of lumber coming (invisibly) in the opposite direction. If you think danger's fun: try this for a laugh. I had my moments of doubt though it might be more accurate to call them panic.

Much of the Transamazonia Highway system has been completed but it's not what you might call three-lane superhighway. Very little of it has a metalled surface and so everytime it rains half the bank gets washed away and pot-holes appear. Add to this the fact that the forest on either side of the road for hundreds and hundreds of kilometres has been burnt to the ground, so there's nothing to absorb and hold the water which comes down in sheets. So the quality of the highway on any particular stretch depends very largely on how long ago it was constructed.

The bus system is very well developed and, other than planes, is the principal form of transport within Brazil. Buses are modern and comfortable and much faster than the trains but a good deal more expensive than their counterparts in the Andean countries. In addition to the ordinary buses which generally go by day, there are the "leito" buses which go by night and have reclining seats, foot rests, a toilet and on-board refreshments, etc. They cost about double the ordinary buses.

All the main cities of Brazil, much like those of Venezuela and Mexico, have modern centralized bus terminals with cafes, washrooms, toilets, etc from which all arrivals and departures take place. All the various bus companies maintain ticket offices here with notice boards detailing the routes they cover and the prices of tickets. It's generally advisable to book ahead on main routes (a few hours in advance is often sufficient), though you'll rarely encounter any difficulty in getting a seat on a day you want to move — if one company's buses are full, try

another. There's little to choose in quality between them. With this in mind, there's little point in attempting a comprehensive schedule of bus times and prices, since it wouldn't make your journey any easier to plan or give you any information which wasn't immediately visible at any bus terminal. Ordinary buses cost, on average, Cz$36 per 100 km.

Routes Through Amazonia At present there are only two direct road routes through this region, though there will soon be three (the link between Cuiaba and Santarem on the Amazon River is not yet complete). These two routes are Brasilia-Belém and Campo Grande-Cuiabá-Pôrto Velho-Manaus. The transverse road link between Belem and Cruzeiro do Sul in the far west up against the Peruvian border is complete, so this is another possibility if you're not just going from north to south or vice versa. This road crosses the Cuiabá-Manaus road at Humaitá, north east of Porto Velho.

As far as road conditions go, the Humaitá-Manaus-Boa Vista stretch is in excellent condition (all-weather dirt road) and not too dusty. Short sections of it are metalled. The stretch from Cuiabá to Pôrto Velho, however, is pretty rough and extremely dusty so be prepared for a long haul (about 52 hours!). Here's the schedule for this route:

Campo Grande-Cuiabá. There are daily buses by several companies (eg *Andorhina*). Cz$214. It's officially supposed to take eight hours, but can take 13 hours if the bus isn't fully booked and so stops frequently to pick up and put down part-way passengers. There are several meal stops, the main one at Rondonópolis. It's an excellent metalled road.

Cuiabá-Pôrto Velho. There are daily buses by *Andorhina*. Cz$620. The journey is supposed to take 44 hours, but is is more likely to take nearer 52 hours. This is because they are rarely fully booked and drivers make little allowance for the state of the road, so there are delays due to punctures and mechanical faults. Don't be surprised if the bus driver takes your bus away at one stage or another and returns with a different one (luggage is transferred). It's an extremely dusty route. Drinks and meals vary in price and quality along the route. Mineral waters are between Cz$6-10 and meals between Cz$30-50. Some of the meals are excellent in quality and variety, though the places often don't look capable of turning out meals of this standard. The route goes via Vilhena, Pimenta Bueno, Cacoal, Pres. Medice, Rondônia, Jaru and Ariquemes.

Here are some other possibilities from Cuiabá:

Cuiabá-São Paulo. Daily buses by *Andorhina* take 27 hours on the excellent road. Cz$515.
Cuiabá-Rondonópolis. There are daily buses by *Motta*. Cz$66. Connections can be got from here to Brasilia.

Pôrto Velho-Manaus. Several different bus companies do this route daily (most are about the size of a mini-bus). All of them depart at 4.30 pm. Cz$260, and take 18-20 hours. The road is sealed all the way. The reason for all the buses departing at the same time is that there are six rivers to be crossed by ferry, so they must all get there at the same time. The first ferry is across the Rio Madeiro at Pôrto Velho. The next takes place about midnight and the rest between then and dawn. The last ferry is the one across the Amazon which is also naturally the longest (about three quarters of an hour). All ferries are free but you don't get much chance to sleep as the passengers have to get

out of the bus at each ferry crossing. Some beautiful countryside and rivers are along the way, with millions of butterflies everywhere.

There are also buses from Pôrto Belho going west to Rio Branco and Guajara Mirim. This latter is one of the popular travellers routes (for the somewhat more intrepid!) between Bolivia and Brazil.

Porto Velho-Guajará Mirim. There are daily buses by *Viação Rondônia* and another company. The ordinary bus departs at 10 pm. Cz$200. The semi-leito bus departs at 10.30 pm. Cz$231. The leito departs at 11 pm. Cz$400. The journey takes 10 hours.

Riverboats between Pôrto Velho and Guajará Mirim are also possible if you're a river lover. There are also riverboats between here and Manaus (see under *Pôrto Velho* for further details).

Manaus-Boa Vista. Daily buses by *Soltur* and *Motte* go at 12 midnight. Cz$303, and take 18 hours, including a three hour stop about two hours out of Manaus where the driver gets some sleep. There are three ferry crossings — two short hops and a longer one across the Rio Branco. It's an excellent road. The bus terminal in Manaus is known as the "Estação Mini-Rondôviaria".
Boa Vista-Venezuelan Border/Santa Elena. Daily buses by *Soltur* go at 6 am. Cz$112. It takes up to six hours The road is fairly rough but not that bad. The bus takes you through both customs posts (easy-going borders — no problems) and onto the Venezuelan border town of Santa Elena. It's also possible to hitch this stretch easily as there are quite a few trucks which cover this route.
Boa Vista-Guyana. There are no buses and you must hitch a truck. The road, which is pretty rough, goes first to

Bom Fin where the Brazilian border post/passport control is situated. If this is as far as your lift is going, it's a 45 minute walk from here to Lethen, the first Guyanese town. If the truck is going further then you're in luck and may well take you all the way to Georgetown. The short stretch between Bom Fin and Lethen involves crossing two small rivers by canoe (about 50 cents). At Lethin, you must get your passport stamped at the police station. If you can't find a lift out of Lethin, there are regular flights to Georgetown in somewhat decrepit Dakotas for Guy$52 one way. There's only one hotel at Lethin.

If you're going into Venezuela from Boa Vista, it makes sense to try to arrange a lift rather than go by bus to Santa Elena. There are no buses from here to the rest of Venezuela, though there are four flights per week to Cuidad Bolívar with *Aeropostal* (see under *Santa Elena* in the *Venezuela* section for details).

Riverboats Until the advent of the roads through the Amazon jungle, riverboats were the only means of transport between most places (other than planes). They are still a very important means of communication and if you're a river fan you can spend weeks (or months if you're really into it) going from Belém to Manaus and from there to Leticia (Colombia), Iquitos and Pucallpa (Peru) or to Cobija and Riberalta (Bolovia). The main route along the Amazon (Solimões) into Peru is no problem and it won't take you more than a few days to track down a boat in Manaus. Going down to Bolivia on the Rio Madeira is a little harder and may well involve a few changes of boat plus the inevitable waiting around in small jungle towns for a connection.

Going by boat isn't necessarily cheaper and much depends on who you

go with and how you hit it off with the captain and crew. You need to take your own hammock, mosquito net and repellent, and it's a good idea to have water purification tablets with you as all water is taken from the river and may well give your guts a hard time. Food is generally included in the price you pay for a passage but it's very monotonous and standards of hygeine are lax. None of these boats can run on any regular schedule (they go when they have sufficient cargo or passengers), so it's up to you to get down to the waterfront and suss one out. It helps a great deal to speak Portuguese since few of the captains will speak anything else. Spanish is okay but creates as many problems as it solves. Details of specific boats are included under the relevant towns before.

In addition to these smaller riverboats, there are larger boats catering solely for passengers which run on a regular schedule between Manaus and Belém. These boats are operated by *ENASA* and *Lloyd Brasiliro*.

OTHER INFORMATION

Work There's a heavy demand for English teachers in many of the large cities but, if you're hoping to save some money, it might be a good idea to choose a place other than São Paulo or Rio where the cost of living is high and flats very hard to find. Wages are generally good, especially if you can gather together a full week's private tuition — this will take several weeks even with contacts.

Some language schools will take you on without a work permit but others won't. If they demand one, there are agencies in both São Paulo and Rio which will arrange one in six weeks for Cz$4800 (!). You can do it yourself much cheaper but allow up to four months. Enquire at a British Council or USIAD office. You may meet helpful people here who know the system well.

Guyana

The Guianas are a legacy of the British, Dutch and French attempts to get a slice of the colonial action in South America. Neither the Spanish nor the Portuguese ever really accepted these "incursions" on what they regarded as their divine right to partition out the whole continent between them but they were in no position to do anything effective about it because of the nature of the land — lowland swamps and jungle highlands — and the ease with which military expeditions could be mounted from the heavily fortified British, Dutch and French West Indies. As a result, disputes simmer on even today over land boundaries. Venezuela claims almost the whole of Guyana and Brazil occasionally makes noises about the borders of Surinam (formerly Dutch Guiana) and French Guiana though belligerence rarely reaches a pitch comparable to Guatemalan claims over Belize.

Guayana has a unique population mix for this part of the world consisting of approximately equal parts of people of Asian Indian and African origin, both of whom manage to retain their own, largely separate, cultures. In addition there are a small proportion of pure-blood Amerindians (about five percent) who, until very recently, lived an undisturbed tribal life in the forests of the interior, and a small northern European community (about one percent). The Asian Indian element are here as a result of a system of indentured labour introduced by the British following the abolition of slavery in 1834. Until that time the plantations of cotton, coffee, sugar and tobacco had been worked by slaves brought from Africa. When they were "freed" most of them deserted the plantations and set up their own smallholdings forcing the plantation owners to look elsewhere for a source of labour. By the first decade of the 20th century, a quarter of a million Asian Indian labourers had served their time in the colony. Most of them returned home at the end of their indenture but others settled giving rise to the present population mix. Most people live on the coastal belt, a good quarter of them in Georgetown itself.

The first northern European settlements in what is now Guyana were made by the Dutch in the early 1600s. The British set up colonies in what is now Surinam and French Guiana. Their early history was turbulent and subject to the varying military fortunes of the Dutch, British and French navies in the Caribbean and to the outcome of various wars fought in Europe. At one point, the British colony in Surinam was traded for the Dutch colony at New York. In this way Dutch influence remained paramount in the Guianas until the French Revolution and the advent of the Napoleonic Wars in Europe at the end of which Britain gained Guyana, the French, Guyane, and the Dutch confirmed in their possession of Surinam. Independence from Britain came in 1966 and since that time there's been a lot of heavy political activity centred around the tension between black and Asian Indian interests.

Guyana hit the news in 1979 following the mass "suicide" of thousands of members of a secretive and rigidly-controlled North American evangelical religious sect which had set up a huge farming commune in the interior of the country under the leadership of a Rev Jones. Though undoubtedly much of the story remains to be told, he apparantly decided that the holocaust was on its way and commanded his followers to commit suicide by drinking cyanide, though the use of the word "suicide" is, from all accounts, stretching a point since many did so only at gunpoint. The scandal rocked the Guyanese government and destroyed much of the credibility of the Prime Minister who, it was alleged, accepted bribes from the sect in return for land concessions at their "Jonestown" settlement.

Other than a few tribes of Amerindians, the interior of the country is largely unpopulated and consists of virgin jungle and barren highlands. Roads are few and far between and travel rough and time-consuming. An all-weather road is being constructed from Georgetown to the Brazilian border at Bom Fin but is not yet finished. Other than this, the only road connections are along the coast to Surinam. Bauxite is mined in the interior.

VISAS
Not required by nationals of Western Europe (except West Germany and Portugal), Australia, Canada, New Zealand or USA. Required by nationals of Israel, South Africa and Japan.

Length of stay given on arrival is arbitrary and not dependant on how much money you have. If you're a journalist or photographer then tell them you are something else. They're very wary of such people and especially the British Press whom they've never forgiven for doing an expose of their elections.

CURRENCY

US$1 = Guy$2.40

The unit of currency is the Guyanese Dollar (Guy$) = 100 cents. Import/Export of local currency permitted up to maximum of Guy$15. Anything more than this will be confiscated. Your money is counted out carefully on arrival and again on departure. You are required to prove that you've changed the difference at the official rate — look after those bank slips and/or keep some money hidden.

Don't leave the country with excess Guy$ — it's very difficult, if not impossible, to change them in the neighbouring countries except Surinam and French Guiana.

WARNING
Georgetown is a friendly city but it also

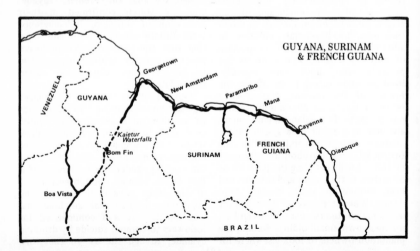

GUYANA, SURINAM & FRENCH GUIANA

has its violent side. Watch out for "choke and rob" merchants on the back streets — the Caribbean version of mugging. Many stores have grilles over the counters and security guards. Keep your valuables (watches, cameras, etc) out of sight and know who's walking behind you. The countryside itself is much more peaceful.

GEORGETOWN
Accommodation
Bill's Guesthouse: 46 High Street opposite Radio Demerara. If you arrive in Georgetown by air, taxi drivers will tell you it's a brothel — it isn't. Very friendly place run by a hospitable family. Costs Guy$3/single and Guy$5/double.

Eats Most of the restaurants are Chinese and meals cost an average of Guy$2-3. Plenty of cheap fruit in the market especially bananas (US$0.50 would buy you about 80 bananas!). You may well be invited for meals with local people — their food is much more interesting and reflects the varied African, Indian and Amerindian cultures. Tap water is drinkable.

Things to Do/See Tours around the Demerara Sugar factory are organized if you're interested.

If you're interested in visiting an Amerindian reservation contact the Chief Interior Development Officer at the Georgetown museum for a Permit. They weave beautiful hammocks which would be very useful if you're heading for Amazonia. There are also two inconspicuous Amerindian handicraft shops near the ferry and fire station. The museum where you must apply for a Permit is worth a visit (free).

Other Georgetown local buses are all wooden affairs (other than the engines of course) and have quaint names like *Hamlet*, *Queen Elizabeth*, etc. A bus to the airport takes two hours (35 km). Guy$0.75. A collective taxi there is Guy$4 (price fixed by the Government).

TRANSPORT
The only roads are along the coast towards Surinam and into the interior as far as Mackenzie, though a road is being built to the Brazilian border at Bom Fin and is used by trucks taking/bringing goods to/from Boa Vista. If you want to head for Brazil ask around for a lift in Georgetown or further south in the interior. The Guyanese border town is at Lethin (exit stamp necessary from the police here). From Lethin to Bom Fin hitch or walk. The walk will take you about 45 minutes and involves crossing two small rivers in dug-outs, Guy$0.50 each. A lift on a lorry from Bom Fin to Boa Vista is approximately Cz$30 (US$1.70), but you can pay in Guyanese money if you have no Cruzeiros. There's one hotel only in Lethin and none at Bom Fin.

There's no direct land connection between Guyana and Venezuela (and there's still an unresolved dispute about who owns the land — Venezuela claims nearly all of Guyana). It may still be necessary to obtain permission to travel inland — enquire with the police in Georgetown.

Flights
Georgetown-Lethin. There are daily flights by aged Dakotas held together by faith and sticky tape. Guy$52 one way.
Georgetown-Kaietur Falls. This is Guyana's big tourist attraction. Guy$96 return.

WORK
Work permits are unpredictable, wages are low but skilled people (teachers, office staff) should have little problem in Georgetown. Ask around or try the Demerara Sugar Company — a huge company which often needs staff.

Venezuela

Wild, vast, beautiful and empty. That's a good description of the highlands south and south-east of the Orinoco river up to the borders with Brazil and Guyana. Much of it is natural grassland with fantastic views for miles of strange mountain formations and, on the edge of the massif, over the almost impenetrable jungle which covers the llanos (plains) below. It's in this area that Angel Falls are located — the world's highest at 979 metres which is 17 times higher than Niagara Falls! — though it's unlikely that, as a budget traveller, you'll be able to spare the US$300 to go and see them. There are a few remaining tribes of Indians in this area but for the most part it's empty and, other than the occasional army post, you'll see very few people until you reach Cuidad Bolívar on the Orinoco.

This area and the Sierra Nevada in the west with its intact colonial towns like Mérida and San Cristóbal has changed little since the Spanish first arrived here in 1500 AD. Coming through them ill-prepares you for the onslaught of elevated motorways, vast skyscraper complexes and the endless torrents of traffic which oil money has made out of Caracas and, to a lesser extent, Maracaibo and some of the coastal towns. The graffiti artist has it in a nutshell: "El capitalismo convirto a Caracas en un inferno". A pretty accurate description of this city, unless you're rich or lobotomized. The setting of the city in a fertile valley against the massive green wall of the Parque Avila is one of the most beautiful in the world and the suburbs of the affluent on the slopes of the mountains with their acres of landscaped gardens and flowering trees are pleasant and peaceful but down in the valley bottom it's bedlam. The pace of life is so fast that it's a wonder anyone has the time of day to exchange a greeting let alone be friendly or helpful. Yet people are. As with São Paulo, hundreds of thousands of people flock to Caracas in search of the illusive dream of wealth or even just a job. They come mainly from the rurual areas of Venezuela but also from the other Spanish-American republics. Many of them have to spend years living in budget hotels while they hold down jobs since housing is incredibly expensive and flats very difficult to find. This is the reason why many of the budget hotels around the centre are full most of the time, though another reason is that many hotel rooms are permanantly kept for whoring purposes — if you're a woman and can't find a job, this is one of the very few alternatives. All in all, Caracas is very much the archetypal human ant-hill.

During the whole of the colonial period and for much of the post-colonial period, Venezuela was a relatively unimportant agricultural back-water with a small population. The Spanish who came here initially went panning for gold with the slaves they had made of the Carib and Arawak Indians who inhabited this area. But yields were so small that they soon gave this up in favour of agriculture along the coast and in the central highlands. Not until at least a hundred years later did they begin to spread further afield and settle the llanos — and then only patchily. This pattern of settlement is reflected today in the vast empty spaces of jungle and highland to the south and south-east of the country.

Other than three rebellions against the iron hand of Spanish colonial rule during the 1700s, Venezuela had an uneventful history until the demand for independence took on the same determination as it did in the other Spanish colonies. In 1806 and again in 1811, Francisco Miranda attempted to set up an independent administration at Caracas but eventually capitulated to the Spanish and was handed over to them by his fellow conspirators who considered him to be a traitor. He was shipped to Spain and died shortly after in a Cadiz jail. The leadership was taken over by Simon Bolívar, undoubtedly the greatest cult figure in Spanish-speaking South America. He is known as "El Libertador" and has innumerable parks and plazas named after him. Museums of his relics, and those of his ablest general, Sucre, are to be found all over the southern half of the continent. Bolívar made little headway until he decided to take the sleepy trading town of Angostura (later re-named in his honour Cuidad Bolívar), set up a provisional revolutionary government there and declared the independence of the Republic of Gran Colombia. The times were propitious for this kind of venture since the Napoleonic Wars in Europe had just ended and Bolívar's agent in London was able to raise loans, arms and recruit over 5000 ex-Peninsular War veterans who were being demobbed from the armies which had been raised to fight Napoleon. With this British force and an army of horsemen from the llanos, Bolívar was able to march over the Andes and rout the Spanish forces at the battles of Vargas and Boyaca. Shortly after this Bogotá was taken and Bolívar returned to Angostura to complete the liberation of Venezuela. The Spanish were finally defeated at the battle of Carabobo in 1821 though they continued to put up a desultory rear-guard fight from Puerto Cabello for two years. Bolívar and Sucre were to go on from here to complete the liberation of Ecuador, Peru and Bolivia.

Though in terms of economic resources and population the least im-portant of the areas which made up the Viceroyalty of New Granada, Venezuela nevertheless bore the brunt of sacrifice for independence. Not only did her patriots — and on the other side, the Venezuelan supporters of Spanish rule — fight on their own territory but they also fought in the armies which Bolívar led into Colombia and down the Pacific coast. It's estimated that over one quarter of the population died in these wars.

Bolívar's dream of a unified Republic of Gran Colombia consisting of what is today Venezuela, Colombia, Panama and Ecuador, fell apart even before he died and despotism and anarchy alternated for decades in what became Venezuela. The economy was in ruins and corruption existed on a scale never exceeded anywhere else in Latin America. In addition there was a long dispute with Britain over the frontier with British Guiana and, at the beginning of the 20th century, a blockade of Venezuelan ports by the navies of Britain, Germany and Italy in an attempt to press their financial claims. Not long after this, oil was discovered in Lake Maracaibo and within a few years Venezuela was to pass from being a penniless debtor nation into the richest on the continent. It still is the richest with the highest per capita income of US$1400 a year, but wealth still remains in a few hands though politics have become less refractory and there has been relative peace for years.

Just before oil was discovered, a "caudillo" who saw the advantages of being allied to foreign big business, like Díaz in Mexico, took over as a dictator. He was Juan Vicente Gómez, an Andean Mestizo with almost no formal education who had worked as a cattle hand before becoming a successful landowner and entering politics. He was a shrewd negotiator and considered by many to be a "brujo". His regime lasted 27 years and was even more savage than that of Porfiro Díaz in Mexico but, though he collected his own personal share of all government transactions, he saw to it that Venezuela paid off the whole of her foreign debt and thus became an attractive country for investment. Naturally little of the wealth which oil brought filtered down to the people and the vast majority continued to live in poverty with little educational or health facilities. The discovery of oil too was a mixed blessing since it resulted in the neglect of agriculture and stock raising. Food had to be imported in increasing amounts and prices rose. When Gómez died, the Caracas mob went crazy burning down the houses of his relatives and supporters and even threatened to set fire to the oil installations on Lake Maracaibo.

An oligarchy of military officers and landowners took over, but were overthrown in 1945 in a coup d'état staged by junior army officers aware of the popular discontent with military rule and determined to end the ascendancy of the elderly generals who had survived from Gómez' regime. They put a civilian government in power headed by Betancourt, the founder of the left-wing Acción Democratica. Given the forces then competing for influence, Betancourt acted too hastily in trying to convert Venezuela into a welfare state, even trying to exclude from the government the very same army officers who had put him there, and three years later the junior army officers took over again. By 1950, Colonel Perez Jiménez had surfaced as their leader and once in control began to crush all opposition ruthlessly. His regime was undoubtedly as brutal as that of Gómez but during his time the revenue from oil, which had increased tremendously, was ploughed back into public works and industries, which would help diversify the economy, and workers' flats in Caracas. Foreign investment also increased to the

point where the US owned three-fifths of the oil, all new iron mining operations, and a large share of local manufacturing industries, commerce, banking, public utilities and insurance. Opposition to his rule developed. The spectacular buildings in Caracas were a poor substitute for a better standard of living and political freedoms and he was overthrown and forced into exile in 1958 by a group of junior military officers (particularly from the navy and airforce) and civilians. An election was held and Betancourt was again elected President. Though he discontinued the former dictator's solicitous policy towards big business, he was careful this time not to act too impetuously and since that time there has been an orderly transfer of power.

Because it's an oil state and a lot of food still has to be imported, Venezuela is a very expensive country. If you're on a budget, a long stay here will mean a shorter stay elsewhere on the continent. It's also the country most culturally influenced by the US but I wouldn't recommend you to miss it if only for comparison with the other republics to the south and west. Caracas, though the largest, is only one of the cities in Venezuela and there are many, much more peaceful, places in the Sierra Nevada de Mérida further west toward the Colombian border. Venezuela also has some of the most superb beaches in the Caribbean and many beautiful islands off the ,oast. If you avoid the main resort areas, life on one of these beaches could be as cheap as anywhere else.

VISAS

Tourist Cards (Tarjeta de Ingreso) are required by all. They are issued free of charge by Venezuelan Consulates and airlines serving Venezuela. No photographs are required. They're valid for 90-day stay if issued by a Consulate and for a 30-day stay if issued by an

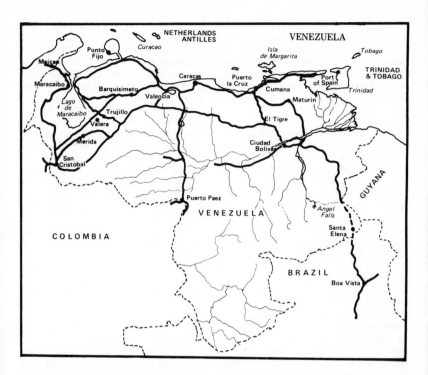

airline. An onward ticket is obligatory before a Tourist Card can be issued, but Consulates vary as to whether they want to see it and about what is an "acceptable" onward ticket. In our own case, they accepted a San Andres (Colombia)-Miami air ticket without fuss. Other people got through with Barbados-London air tickets. You're also supposed to have "sufficient" funds but they rarely ask to see.

Coming overland from Brazil, the last Consulate is in Boa Vista. The Consul here is known locally to be drunk all the time, so things go slowly but it also works in your favour if you're not sure about whether you will pass the onward ticket/money test. They're a belligerent crowd of cruds at the Consulate there but no problems getting the Tourist

Card. It's closed on Saturdays and Sundays. There's a cursory baggage search both entering and leaving but they're principally interested in girlie books and the consumer goods which Venezuelans are bringing into the country — plenty of arguments about these so expect to be at the border for up to an hour at least.

CURRENCY

US$1 = 4.28 Bolívars

The unit of currency is the Bolívar (B$) = 100 centimos. The currency is rock hard (you're in an oil state) and there's no blackmarket. The Banco Royal Venezolana doesn't charge commission for changing travellers' cheques.

Venezuela is an expensive country. You need at least US$10 per day just to provide you with the very basic of pensiones and two meals. There's very little difference in the cost of living between the large cities and the country-side.

CARACAS

"El capitalismo convirto a Caracas en un inferno" says the graffiti artist on a wall opposite the Nuevo Circo bus terminal, and, unless you're stinking rich, that's a pretty good description of the place. The setting of the city against the green backdrop of the Parque Nacional Avila is superb and almost as beautiful as Rio de Janiero (though undoubtedly I'll collect a lot of flack for saying that!). But for the rest it's a motorway city where the quality of life has been entirely sacrificed to the gods of wealth and speed. Down at street level the people who have to service this sprawling monster which promises so much and delivers so little are so spun out it's a wonder they don't collectively and spontaneously go insane. You better prepare yourself in advance if you want to survive unscathed. The city sprawls for miles and miles down the valley and almost nothing, other than the bus terminal and budget hotel area, is within easy reach of anywhere else unless you understand the intricacies of the local bus and colectivo system — and that's another story! You're sitting on top of an oil capital and because of this it's one of the most expensive places you'll come across in South America. Good luck!

Accommodation The old part of the city — though you'd be hard pressed to recognize it as such any more — is El Silencio (a name which mocks the reality). Here is located the Nuevo Circo bus terminal from which all long-distance and many local buses depart. The budget hotel area and many cheap cafes are located in the surrounding streets. It's a fairly tough area — though not dangerous — and is "home" to many thousands of people who have flocked in from the countryside looking for the American dream.

Probably one of the best budget hotels is the *Pensión San Biagio* on Avenida Lecuna (see street map). The management is friendly and it's one of the quietest whore-houses you'll find (all the budget hotels double as whore-houses). B$15/single, B$30/double — clean sheets, clean showers and toilets, secure and with space to hang your washing. There are no fans though it's cool enough at night to do without. The other cheap places are all marked on the detailed map of this area and all cost approximately the same. The *Hotel San Roque* is popular with travellers passing through but, because it's situated right outside the Nuevo Circo bus terminal, it's often full. This goes for the *Pensión Española* and the *Hotel Mar* as well.

If you can't find anything in this immediate area go a little further west to the Plaza La Concordia between Hospital and Manzon blocks. There are more cheap hotels here. Anywhere else in the city expect to pay at the very least double what you pay in this area.

Eats Two of the cheapest cafes are on Pichincha just opposite the bus terminal. They are the Restaurant *Rilz* and the *Trolebus*. Fish fillet, chips and bread, B$8, soup B$4, beers B$3. There are plenty of other things on the menu. Also one or two "pollo a la brasa" places but the chicken tends to be very greasy.

Information There is an information kiosk inside the Nuevo Circo bus terminal but they have no maps, in-different staff and stacks of leaflets in glorious technicolour which tell you

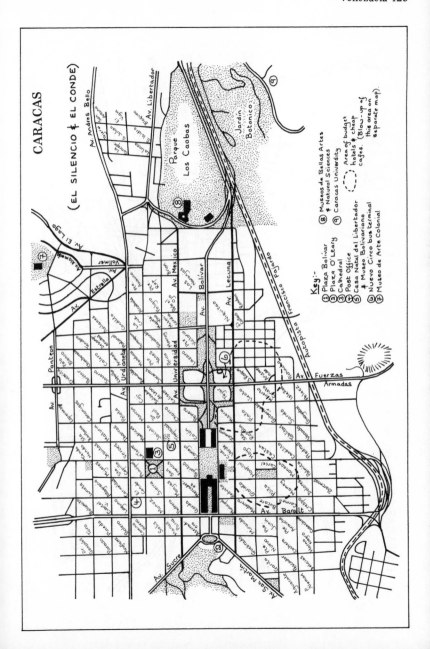

CARACAS
(EL SILENCIO & EL CONDE)

Key:-
① Plaza Bolívar
② Plaza O'Leary
③ Cathedral
④ Post Office
⑤ Casa Natal del Libertador
⑥ Museo Bolivariano
⑦ Nuevo Circo bus terminal
⑧ Museos de Bellas Artes
✚ Natural Sciences
✚ Caracas University
Ⓣ Museo de Arte Colonial

(------) Area of budget hotels & cheap cafes. (Blow-up of this area on separate map).

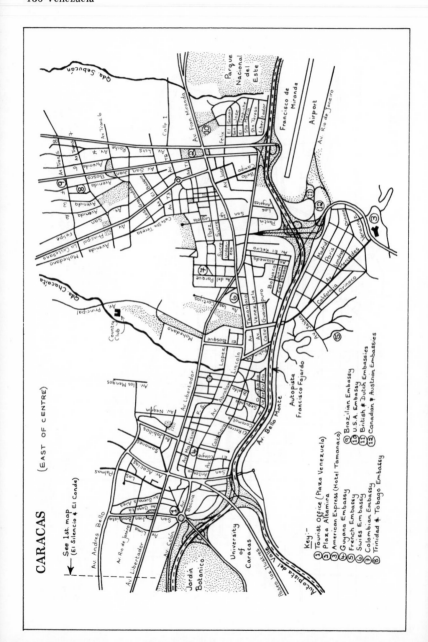

CARACAS (EAST OF CENTRE)

See 1st. map
(El Silencio ← El Conde)

Key:-
① Tourist Office (Plaza Venezuela)
② Plaza Altamira
③ American Express (Hotel Tamanaco)
④ Guyana Embassy
⑤ French Embassy
⑥ Swiss Embassy
⑦ Colombian Embassy
⑧ Trinidad ← Tobago Embassy
⑨ Brazilian Embassy
⑩ U.S.A. Embassy
⑪ British ← Dutch Embassies
⑫ Canadian ← Austrian Embassies

nothing at all. The Tourist Office itself is on the 7th floor of the Conference Centre in the Plaza Venezuela just past the *Hilton Hotel*. They give out an excellent map of Caracas backed by a road map of the whole country free of charge — as well as the Aviasa Guide to Venezuela (*Las Llaves de Venezuela)*. This is full of useful addresses, maps, restaurants, hotels, airlines, etc, though much of the information is of little concern for a budget traveller watching his/her Bolívars very carefully. They also give out another similar guide (again free) called *El Turista en la Cuidad de Caracas* by Manuel García García which is less than useless.

Avoid buying inferior maps of Caracas from local bookshops. They cost B$4 and are nowhere near as good as the free map from the Tourist Office.

Other The Banco Royal Venezolana charge no commission for changing travellers' cheques.

American Express is located in the lobby of the *Tamanaco Hotel* which is

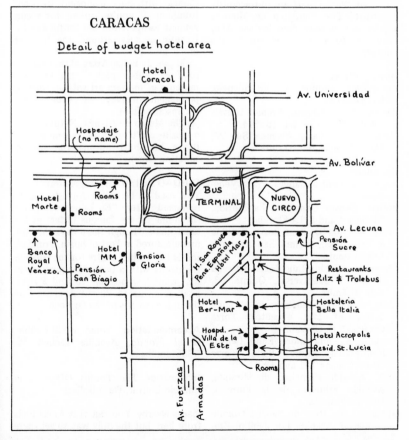

CARACAS

Detail of budget hotel area

also a good place to go to see how the other half live. Get a bus to Avenido rio de Janeiro just below the hotel from Avenida Lecuna outside Nuevo Circo.

Local buses round the city have a fixed rate of either B$1 or B$0.50 depending on the route. Plenty of colectivos go along the same routes. Local people are usually pretty helpful about putting you on the right bus.

The international airport is on the coast at Maiquetía near to La Guaira — the port for Caracas. Frequent local buses go there. Taxis are outrageously expensive. The Francisco de Miranda airport is now only used for the Aero Club and to a certain extent by the military.

Airline Offices

Aeropostal, Bloque 1, El Silencio, tel: 4834144.

Avensa, Esq. El Chorro, Avenida Universidad, Edificio 29, tel: 455244.

Viasa, Torre Viasa, Avenida Sur 25, Plaza Morelos, tel: 5729522.

Consulates

Argentina. Centro Capiles, Plaza Venezuela.

Bolivia. Centro Comercial La Florida, Oficinas 4 and 5, La Florida.

Brazil. Avenida San Juan Bosco, Esquina 8 Transversal, Quinta San Antonia, Urb. Altamira.

Colomiba. Avenida Luis Roche between 6 and 7 Transversal, Quinta 53, Urb. Altamira.

Chile. Avenida Francisco de Miranda corner of Mis Encantos, Torre Cemica, P.H. Chacao.

Ecuador. Avenida Andrés Bello, Centro Empresarial Andrés Bello, Torre Oeste, Oficina 131 and 132.

USA. Avenida Francisco de Miranda, Avenida Principal de la Floresta, Urb. La Floresta.

Guyans. Calle Real de Sabana Grande corner of Avenida Los Jabillo, Edificio Continental, 17th Floor.

Paraguay. Calle Los Angeles, Qta. Neembucu, Prado del Este.

Peru. Avenida Andrés Bello, Centro Andrés Bello, Torre Oeste, Oficina 11.0.

Trinidad and Tobago. 4a Avenida between 7 and 8 Transversal, Qta. Serrana, Urb. Altamira.

Uruguay. Avenida Urdaneta, Marron a Pelota, Edificio Yonekuru, 5th floor.

Things to Do/See Parque Los Caobas is a beautiful park right in the centre of Caracas with huge mahogany trees and fountains. If you're looking for a convenient escape from the traffic and the frenetic activity around the bus terminal, go there.

Museo de Bellas Artes, at the entrance to Los Caobas park, is an excellent museum of modern art with an amazing permanent display of cyber-kinetic art upstairs (free).

The Museo de Ciencas Naturales just opposite can't really be recommended. It's a bit short on material and inspiration (free).

CUIDAD BOLÍVAR (Angostura)

This used to be called Angostura until re-named after "El Libertador". It's the home of the famous bitters of the same name, though these days they are manufactured in Port of Spain, Trinidad, and is the trading centre for the Guyana Highlands with a busy river port where it's sometimes possible to find a riverboat going up to Puerto Ayacucho on the upper reaches of the Orinoco.

Accommodation *Roma* B$20/double. *Hotel Florida*, Avenida Tachira 30. B$35/doulbe.

Information The Tourist Office is in Edificio Bolívar, Plaza Bolívar.

Places Nearby You can visit Angel Falls from here but the only way to get there is to fly in. *Aerotaxis Tanca* do the cheapest trips: the one-day excursion from Cuidad Bolívar which includes a boat tour of the lagoon and falls from the airport at Canaima costs over B$400. Longer, more expensive tours are arranged by *Avensa*: two-day excursion from Caracas costs B$600. A five-day excursion costs nearly B$2140 and must be booked in advance. At those prices you have to be keen to see them.

MARACAIBO

Maracaibo is the centre of Venezuela's oil industry but also an important coffee and cattle centre. It's a very hot and humid town and unless you're into touring oil derricks in Lake Maracaibo there's little here to keep you.

Accommodation *Hotel Londres*, Calle 94, Avenida 6. B$20/double. Other cheapies include the *Carrazal*, *Venecia*, *San José* and *Vesuvio*.

Other The bus terminal is about one km from the centre of town. Buses throughout the day and evening go to other Venezuelan towns. There are also buses to Maicao, the first Colombian town on the Guajira Peninsula, four times daily. The buses take you across both borders and into the centre of Maicao. It's an easy-going border.

MATURIN

If you're heading for Trinidad and Barbados or coming in from there, this is the last place where you can get a cheap flight with *Aeropostal* to Port of Spain.

Accommodation One of the cheapest places to stay (though still not cheap) is the *Bella Vista*, Avenida Santiago Marino. B$32. Another on the same Avenida is the *Calibri*, B$35/single.

MÉRIDA

One of the most pleasant cities in Venezuela, it's situated in the Parque Nacional Simon Bolívar containing some of the highest peaks in the country. It still retains a lot of its colonial atmosphere and is a city noted for its many plazas and parks.

Accommodation *Hotel Mucabají*, Avenida Universidad. It's probably one of the best deals you'll find in Mérida. B$16/single — clean, pleasant and friendly staff. Other cheapies include: *Tinjaca*, B$16; *Luxemburgo*, B$20/single; *La Sierra*, B$20/single.

Places Nearby If you have a head for heights and want some superb views stretching for hundreds of kilometres (or so it seems), try to make it on the cable railway — the world's highest — to Pico Espejo. There are three trips per day on Wednesdays, Thursdays, Saturdays, Sundays and also on public holidays. The trip takes about three hours, B$25. You must book in advance as there's a quota of 600 people per day. The best time to go is between November and June when there's less chance of cloud cover at the top. A side trip can be made to Venezuela's highest village (Los Nevados) from the next-to-last stop. The village is three hours' walk over a rough trail from the station, but take your own food as there's no cafe at the village.

PUERTO LA CRUZ

Places Nearby Between this town and the port of Cumaná further east are some of the best beaches in Venezuela and on most there's no one on them. Use the town as a base from which to find a spot where you'd like to stay for a while then suss out a house or shack for rent and move there.

Puerto La Cruz is also the ferry terminal for the island of Margarita — one of Venezuela's favourite resort islands. Much of the island has been developed for the benefit of moneyed Caraqueños but there are still plenty of relatively untouched beaches and fishing villages on the north coast away from Palomar and Altagracia. The ferry-boat line is Paseo Colón, Los Cocos point, Puerto Santa Cruz, tel 24084. This is the address of *Turismo Margarita CA* who also have an address in Caracas (Avenida Este 2, Los Caobas, tel 571 3897). There are two other companies which run ferries, Their Caracas addresses are:

Conferry, Gran Avenida Sabana Grande, Torre Lincoln PB, tel 7823122.

Ferrys del Caribe, Avenida Urdaneta, Edificio Riera, tel 812170.

SAN CRISTÓBAL

The last town of any size before you get to the Colombian border, if you're heading for Bogota via Cucuta. It's a pleasant town with many plazas. There's a good road with excellent views to San Antonia on the border. A Colombian consulate is in San Cristóbal if you need a visa.

Accommodation Most of the cheap places to stay are located around the bus terminal. One of the cheapest is the *Hotel del Sur*. B$10/single. If you're looking for something a little better, try the *Horizonte*, B$30/single.

SANTA ELENA

This is the border town on the way between Boa Vista (Brazil) and Cuidad Bolívar. For a border town it's very pleasant and laid-back and the climate is excellent but it has one BIG problem — there is no public transport from here to the rest of Venezuela other than an *Aeropostal* flight to Cuidad Bolívar four times a week. Lifts are few and far between and you need one at least as far as El Dorado before you come across any public buses. Most of the traffic is only going a few kilometres down the road and so is pretty useless. It took us two days to get a lift and we only got that because the South Ameri-

can car rally was on at the time and (miraculously!) one of the rally cars broke down right where we were standing and had to be hoisted onto the back of a lorry and taken to Caracas for repairs. The power of thought works wonders.

Accommodation

Hotel Mac-King. B$25/single, B$35/double — basic. The restaurant next door serves good food but it's expensive after Brazil. Meat stew, potatoes and rice B$12, liver, onions, potatoes and rice B$10, eggs a la criollo (two fried eggs, beans and rice) B$7, an excellent filling soup made of meat, beans, potatoes, barley, etc B$5.

Hotel Brasilia. B$25/single, B$30/cama matrimonial. It's simple, clean but there's no fan.

Hospedaje Roraima B$15/single, B$30/double. The cheapest but the "rooms" are just semi-partitioned hardboard which makes for a lot of racket.

One problem here is to find a place which isn't full or reserved for whoring which to some extent explains the relatively high prices. We slept outside the garage on the road out of town about one and a half km from the centre. There was running water from a tap on the forecourt. It's also a good place to hitch from.

Other The supermarket/tienda opposite the *Mac-King* will change money if you have no Bolívars. They give US$1 = B$4 — in other words you lose about 7 percent on the transaction.

The *Aeropostal* office is next to the *Hotel Brasilia* on the main street where the *Soltur* buses from Boa Vista stop. Flights four times a week go to Cuidad Bolívar for B$120. This might be your only way out of the town if you don't strike lucky with a lift to El Dorado or

Tumeremo where you hit the public transport system.

There are daily buses from here by *Soltur* to Boa Vista in Brazil. It's an easy-going border with no hassles.

It's possible to hire transport to Tumeremo in Land-Rovers and the like. But the owners want around B$450/car/jeep, though they take six people so that works out at B$55/person, which is half the price of the *Aeropostal* flight. There are often many Venezuelans waiting here to hire transport but they may not have a sufficiently large party together — so ask around in the cafes and hotels.

TRANSPORT

Because oil has brought wealth — to some — there are a lot of private cars on the roads in Venezuela and hitching is easy. This is one very good way of keeping your expenditure down. Generally, you won't have to pay for lifts. Much of the country south of the highlands on which the main cities are built is undeveloped and you have to go via the only road into Brazil (Cuidad Bolívar-Tumeremo-El Dorado-Sta Elena-Boa Vista).

You must have an onward ticket before a Tourist Card will be issued but they don't want to see it at the borders on the assumption that the Consulate issuing the Tourist Card will have checked that out already. This gives scope for manoeuvre. See under *Visas* for further details.

Roads are generally in excellent condition (other than the road into Brazil) and buses are modern, comfortable and fast.

Flights The cheapest local airline which covers many small places all over the country is *Linea Aeropostal Venezolana (LAV)*. They also do the cheapest flights between Caracas and Curacao (Netherlands Antilles) and between Maturin and Port of Spain (Trinidad). Their office in Caracas is Bloque 1, El Silencio, tel 4834144.

Santa Elena-Cuidad Bolívar and vice versa. There are flights four times weekly in either direction. B$120 one way.

Maturin-Port of Spain (Trinidad). Flights go on Wednesday, Friday and Sunday at 2.45 pm, arriving 3.15 pm, B$124 one-way. Note that an onward ticket is obligatory before you can enter Trinidad, so plan ahead. If you're heading for Barbados your onward ticket could be a British West Indian Airlines ticket from Port of Spain to Barbados (daily flights at 7 am and 8.30 am, taking 45 minutes for about US$50 one way) but note that you also need an onward ticket before they will let you into Barbados. This you can arrange in Port of Spain. If you just want to visit Trinidad and then return to Venezuela, then a return *Aeropostal* ticket from Maturin would be the cheapest way of doing it by air (but see under *Boats* below). Coming back into Venezuela, however, you will need an onward ticket before the Venezuelan Tourist Card is issued. There are times when you need the mind of a computer!

Caracas-Curaçao (Netherlands Antilles). A daily flight at 2.30 pm goes from Maiquetía airport, arriving 3.05 pm. Approximately US$42 one way. There are also more expensive flights by *KLM* (the Dutch airline). Flights between Aruba, Curacao and Bonaire are by *Netherlands Antilles Airways*.

Buses All long-distance buses arrive and depart from Caracas at the Nuevo Circo bus terminal. All the bus companies have ticket offices here with full lists and prices of the routes they cover. There are frequent buses to all major centres of population throughout the day and evening, so there's no problem finding a bus going in the direction you want to go, but book in advance on the day you want to leave. Be at the terminal at least half an hour before your bus is due to leave and get in the queue. Seats are not numbered, so when the bus arrives there's chaos. Frequently people with tickets for a later bus will try to muscle-in on the earlier ones so you've got to be pretty aggressive. Caraquenos have it all organized beforehand — one or two get in the queue and then "reserve" loads of seats on the bus while their friends deal with the luggage outside. If there are two or more of you then do as the Caraquenos do. If there's only one of you, sharpen up your elbows. Avoid *Aerobus* if possible. Their buses are the same price as other companies and of the same quality but they're the meanest, sour-faced set of uncooperative fuckers on the face of the earth. Here are some examples of prices from Caracas:

San Cristóbal	B$40	Barquisimeto	B$20
Valera	B$35	Cumaná	B$35
Cuidad Bolívar	B$40	Puerto La Cruz	B$30
Maturin	B$35	Trujillo	B$35
Punta Fijo	B$30	Coro	B$25
Merida	B$40	Maracaibo	B$35

From Maracaibo to the Colombian border at Maicao there are four buses daily at 7 am, 8 am, 9.30 am and 11 am. It takes about three hours. B$10. The bus takes you through both borders and waits while passport formalities are completed. It's a very easy-going border. The Colombians may ask to see an onward ticket but don't want to examine it, so just flash any old airline ticket folder or the stub of a used ticket. There is no money showing and no delays. It's a major smuggling route for consumer goods, whisky, cigarettes, etc and this is their major pre-occu-pation, as well as income supplement.

Boats Puerto La Cruz-Margarita Island ferries depart four times daily in either direction, B$12 second class. *Aeropostal* also have a cheap flight from Maquetía airport (Caracas) but this will cost you around B$110.

From Venezuela to Port of Spain (Trinidad). Head for the small port of Guiria on the Peninsula de Paria (daily buses from Caracas for B$45). You have a choice here of getting a legal or contraband boat to Port of Spain but don't count on either. The name of the legal boat is *Maria Gabriela* which takes 30 passengers but it only goes when the captain has sold enough round-trip tickets. These cost B$200 which is almost the same as the *Aeropostal* return fare from Maturín and the captain will usually insist on you buying a return ticket, unless you already have an onward ticket from Trinidad. If you want to go this way, get your name down on the passenger list immediately on arrival at Immigration. They will take your passport off you and give it back to you before the boat departs complete with exit stamp. The journey takes about five hours. For a contrabandista boat you will have to ask around down by the dock, in the bars, etc. They obviously don't go on any regular schedule and you'll have to be ready to leave with a few hours notice at the most. They don't leave from Guiria itself but from La Salina (a beach area several kilometres out of town) or from Rio Salado. They'll want to be sure that your passport is in order and that you're covered as far as onward tickets for Trinidad is concerned (otherwise they might have to bring you back after you've been refused entry). The one way "fare" on one of these boats varies between B$50 and B$100 and depends to some extent on how well you bargain.

Cuba

Cuba was discovered by Christopher Columbus in 1492 on his first journey to America. The original Indian inhabitants were soon wiped out by the Spaniards who instituted a brutal system of forced labour. Already in the 16th century large numbers of slaves were being brought from Africa and today their descendents account for over 25% of the total population.

After the conquest of Mexico and Peru the main attention of the Spaniards shifted away from Cuba but it retained its importance as a communications link with the colonies. Twice a year Spanish galleons laden with the treasures of America would gather in Havana harbour and form an armada to carry the booty back to Cadiz or Seville in Spain. The Spaniards spent vast sums to defend Havana from pirates and enemy nations and the castles, fortresses and walls are still a prominent feature today.

In 1762 the British captured Havana and held it for a year before returning it in exchange for Florida. Spain held onto Cuba while the rest of South America was geing liberated in the early 19th century. The first major War of Independence did not begin until 1868. For 10 long years the Cubans struggled with a huge Spanish army to win their independence but the war ended in a stalemate although slavery was effectively abolished and the Spaniards promised to grant some form of autonomy.

The promises were not kept and in 1865 the second War of Independence began. Its leaders were the poet and writer José Martí (now revered as Cubas' national hero) and the black general Antonio Maceo. Both Martí and Maceo were killed early in the war but the struggle continued under leaders such as General Máximo Gómez and contemporary Cuban historians affirm that they would surely have been victorious but for the intervention of the United States who declared war on Spain in 1898 and stole the glory from the Cuban patriots. Instead of handing power over to those who had fought so long and hard for the freedom of their nation the Spaniards surrendered to the Americans and Cuba found itself under an American military government which lasted four years.

When the Americans finally withdrew in 1902 they retained the right to intervene militarily in Cubas' internal affairs and repeatedly did so right up to the '30s. Dictators such as Machado and Batista furthered American interests and much of the economy fell under their control. Cuban institutions were modelled on those of the United States but poverty, corruption, and illiteracy prevented them from working properly.

In 1952 Batista staged a military coup which did away with the pretence of democracy. At this time many Cuban intellectuals and labour leaders realized that reforms could only be won through armed rebellion and that Batists would never relinquish power through elections or peaceful means. The attack on the Moncada barracks in 1953 led by Fidel Castro was the most dramatic of the early actions but there were others such as the attempt to assassinate Batista in his palace in Havana in 1957. These failed and Fidel, who had been captured and imprisoned after Moncada, returned from exile in Mexico to organize a revolution in the Sierra Maestra mountains of eastern Cuba. A parallel struggle was carried on in the cities by underground worker and student groups and by January 1st, 1959, Batistas' power had been eroded to such an extent that he was forced to flee the country with his principal aides, taking with them vast sums of ill gotten wealth.

The new revolutionary government was left with tremendous problems: an economy dependent and controlled from outside, massive poverty, unemployment, and illiteracy. As they tried to find solutions they came into conflict with powerful vested interests such as wealthy landlords who refused to share their land with an impoverished peasantry, industrialists who grew rich on keeping prices high while they paid their workers as little as possible and only employed them half the year during the sugar harvest (December-July), foreign capitalists who refused to give up their investments or even deal with the new government. Counter-revolutionary groups were formed and the hopes and ideals of the revolution seemed endangered. To counter-balance this Cuba drifted further and further to the left as the US stepped up its aid and encouragement to the old reactionary interests.

The turning point came with the Bay of Pigs invasion in 1961 when the counter-revolutionaries suffered a crushing defeat and one year later during the Cuban missile crisis the United States government was forced to make a secret promise to Cuba never again to invade. Since that time Cuba has never turned back and today one finds an all-embracing socialist system modelled somewhat on that of the Soviet Union, but also a softer, humanized communism with a smile where the people have hope in the future. Although material hardships and problems continue the Cubans are fiercely proud of their revolution and would never wish to return to the uncertainties and injustices of the past.

Cuba has a population of 9.5 million of whom 2.5 million live in the city of Havana. Santiago de Cuba is the second city with about 300,000 inhabitants. There are 14 provinces. Cuba has a planned economy and the means of production are all in the hands of the state. The exploitation of labour is a thing of the past since any business or endeavor with more than one participant is government owned. Small private farms of under 67 hectares still exist and although the owners are encouraged to sell their land to the governin exchange for homes and jobs on state farms, no coercion is used and in fact mass organizaitons of small farmers exist to help them with their problems. Other individuals such as some taxi drivers or private doctors are permitted to work for themselves with a licence from the government but their efforts are vastly overshadowed by those of the public enterprises. Every Cuban is guaranteed the right to work, receive free education and medical treatment, and obtain rationed food and clothing. Housing is provided with a rent ceiling set at 10% of the wage of the highest wage earner in the family. No rent at all is paid for old apartments formerly owned by slum landlords. Public transportation is subsidized and there are no taxes of any kind.

The island of Cuba is shaped like a crocodile 150 km long floating between the finger and thumb of Florida and Yucatan. The first Europeans to smoke tobacco smoked it here and Cuban cigars are still the best in the world. Sugar is the main crop although dairy cattle and citrus fruits are of increasing importance. The Isle of Pines to the south of the main island is famous for its oranges. Cuba has always been an agricultural country and will continue to be for the forseeable future although attempts at industrialization have been made. Since the revolution much of Cubas' trade has been with the other socialist countries although ties with Western Europe, Canada and Mexico were never broken and Havana is a busy, bustling port. Today Cuba has an importance in world affairs beyond that of any other Latin American country — as events in Africa in recent years have proved all too well.

VISAS

Canadians, Danish, French, Italians, Norwegians, Swedish and Swiss need only a passport to enter Cuba but just about everybody else must apply to a Cuban embassy or consulate for a visa. In the USA contact the Czechoslovakian Embassy. A Cuban stamp in your passport could give you trouble when you try to enter countries with rightist regimes so plan accordingly. Those staying over two weeks will need an exit permit.

CURRENCY

US$1 = 0.74 pesos (official)

Only Cuban pesos can be spent in Cuba and when you change your money you'll be given a white exchange slip. Keep this paper in a safe place together with the money and present it upon request when making purchases in tourist boutiques, booking tours, etc, or when changing back excess pesos at the airport upon departure. The slip will also entitle you to a discount at certain bars meant especially for tourists and will help you get into crowded Havana nightclubs without a reservation (show it to the fellow in the black suit at the door). Otherwise you'll never be asked for the slip and you won't have to account for your money or even declare how much you had with you on entry. On the black market cash dollars buy up to two pesos in big, clean bills. You can also sell jeans, sunglasses, perfume, etc to guys around the Parque Central or in front of the flash hotels but talk to them a while before you deal.

ACCOMMODATION

The very cheapest hotels are reserved for Cubans and won't take you even if you try. Foreigners are expected to stay in the expensive first class hotels. There are a range of middle level hotels whose prices vary from 3 to 11 pesos/single and 5 to 14 pesos/double and you can try for these although they'll often claim to be full. Indeed, with the influx of Cuban expatriates from Miami recently many Havana hotels are fully booked although these visitors usually stay with their relatives and the rooms are seldom used. To get into a hotel you'll usually need a reservation from Cubatur and this can be made at the airport upon arrival. Otherwise go to their main office in Vedado but they're not overly sympathetic with poor students and workers travelling on the cheap. Camping is not allowed. The best plan if you're on your own is to have them book you into the cheapest hotel available then try to move to something else a few days later if you're finding it too expensive.

EATS

Cuba's traditional national dish is barbecued pork with white rice and black bean soup accompanied by plenty of yuca (cassava, manioc, tapioco). Fruit and salads (green tomatoes anybody?) are served when available. Since the revolution seafoods have become more readily available. The highest quality fish are cherna (grouper) and pargo (red snapper) with merluza (hake) a poor second. Lobster and shrimp are also common. Chicken is often served but good quality beef is sometimes harder to find. Any good meal is topped off with a demi-tasse of that super-strong pre-sweetened Cuban coffee. Dairy products such as ice cream and yoghurt are now common.

HAVANA

At first Havana strikes visitors as something out of the past. Cars and fashions are those of the '50s, even the nightclub acts are like something out of an old movie. New buildings are rare inside the city and the people friendly and unsophisticated, quite unlike those in the rest of Latin America. Notice how they accept you and leave you alone. They don't want or need anything from you.

Accommodation The *Seville Hotel*, right beside the National Museum, is about the best as far as price and location go, 11 pesos/single, 14/double. Nearby, the *Packard, Caribbean,* and *Regis Hotels* are cheaper, only about 4 pesos/single, 6/double, but you may have trouble getting in. Try also the *Plaza Hotel* near the Parque Central. In Vedado the *Saint Johns Hotel* near the Cubatur office is a good bet but expensive at 14 pesos/singel, 18/double. The *Deauville* and *Victoria Hotels* cost about the same as the Saint Johns. Further out, the *Hotel Presidente* is 4-6 pesos. If Cubatur insists that none of the above are available you could ask for the *New York* or the *Alamac* but Cuba isn't the place to come for cheap hotels.

Eats Food is somewhat easier, they won't try to keep you out of the grubby places. Fill up on soft ice cream (15 centavos — count your change) while you're touring or eat at one of the many small cafeterias or lunch counters with the Cuban masses. A large menu is always posted which tells you what's available but there probably won't be much selection. You can get soup and fish with rice at the lunch counter at the corner of Neptuno and Consulado near the Parque Central or eat at the *Caracas Restaurant* nearby, much better. Right across the street from the *Saint Johns Hotel* in Vedado is *Wakamba Cafeteria* which is popular with the lunch crowd or *Milan Pizzeria* around the corner. The expensive hotel restaurants and cafeterias are usually reserved for hotel guests.

Places to See Havana is different: One doesn't find the sharp contrasts of rich and poor, luxury and squalor, although one can still notice differing degrees of

affluence (or the lack of it). Havana is also the capital of the first socialist republic in America and vast new housing projects, schools, and highways can be seen outside the city.

Havana was founded in 1515 and is today the largest city in the West Indies. The old city lies west of the harbour and was once completely enclosed by a high city wall, a part of which remains near the central railway station. The Spaniards built six major fortresses to defend the city and three of these can now be visited (El Morro, La Punta, and La Fuerza). Two old colonial squares (Plaza de la Catedral and Plaza de Armas) are perfectly maintained and many of the large palaces facing onto them have been converted into museums and first class restaurants.

Flanking the old city is the Paseo del Prado which leads into the Parque Central, focal points during the 19th century. To reach the shopping district one walks along San Rafael from the Parque Central to Galiano where most of the large department stores stand. It's a fascinating lesson in economics and society to browse through the former Woolworths which still throngs with Cuban shoppers.

The Vedado hotel district is much further west on a low hill with Calle 23 (known to residents as La Rampa) at its heart. Most of the best restaurants, airline offices, cinemas, and hotels are here. Continuing west are Miramar and Marianao, the former exclusive residential neighbourhoods now devoted to schools, embassies, and offices. South of Vedado past the University is the Plaza de la Revolución with all the principle ministries of the Cuban government. Fidel makes his speeches from the podium just in front of the gigantic marble statue of José Martí.

El Morro Castle Take any bus through the tunnel then walk back from the former toll gates. They've still got a lot of work to go fixing up El Morro but the view of Havana from here is superb. Sir Francis Drake appeared before El Morro in the 16th century but it was only captured by the British in 1762. A chain used to stretch across the harbour mouth from El Morro to La Punta to control the comings and goings of ships but all traces of the chain have now been lost.

Plaza de la Catedral Visit the cathedral (but not if you're wearing shorts!) which is open for visitors in the morning and mass in the late afternoon. The building directly opposite is now the Colonial Museum. Just up from the cathedral is La Bodeguita del Medio, a bohemian style bar and restaurant once frequented by such notables as Ernest Hemingway and Salvador Allende.

Plaza de Armas Only two blocks from the above, this lovely old square housed the Spanish Captain General whose palace is now the Museum of the City of Havana. The chapel on the other side of the square was the site of the first mass and a painting inside depicts the event. La Fuerza castle which adjoins is the second oldest in the Americas (the oldest is in Santo Domingo).

Capitolio This huge building near the Parque Central was modelled on the US Congress and opened in 1926. American influence was all deciding in those days. Now the Capitolio houses the Museum of Natural Science. La Floridita where Hemingway drank 22 frozen daquiris at one sitting is nearby.

Museo de la Revolución This museum is well worth a visit even if one can't read the captions in Spanish on the exhibits. Once the palace of Batista the dictator barely escaped assassination here in 1957. The yacht *Granma* which brought Fidel and his supporters from Mexico to Cuba has been set up behind the museum and the various things to see will interest anyone who has taken the trouble to come to Cuba. The National Museum just beyond has a good collection of Cuba paintings.

Havana Harbour To see the harbour take the public launch from Muelle Luz to Regla, only 5 centavos, the cheapest harbour cruise in the world.

Other There are many other places to visit such as the Napoleonic Museum, Columbus Cemetery, the Zoo, the National Aquarium, Tropicana Nightclub, Lenin Park, and Hemingway's House, to name only a few. Two weeks would be enough to see everything at a leisurely pace.

AROUND CUBA

If you've got the money Cubatur offers a six night, seven day trip around the country from Havana to Santiago by bus. The cost is 185 pesos but that includes everything from hotels, to meals, to the flight back to Havana. This tour is heavily booked so if you're interested you should make a reservation soon after you arrive. Until Cuba opens up a little more it's easier to see the country by making day trips out of Havana (get a map and go anywhere) and that'll give you a fairly accurate impression of what's happening at the other end. Backpackers are a rare breed in Cuba so don't make rash judgements if things aren't especially geared to suit you. Remember that those cheap enchiladas you enjoyed in Mexico were cheap because the woman making them slept in a hut and her kids had to stay home and help with the work. Think about it.

TRANSPORT

The shortest flights into Cuba are from Kingston (Jamaica) and Mérida (Mexico). You can also fly directly to Havana from Lima, Panama City and San José (Costa Rica). There are frequent flights from Toronto and Montreal in Canada. As of yet only charter flights arrive from the USA. Madrid is the best departure point out of Europe.

Getting Around

Bus The Havana city bus service charges

a flat 5 centavos, exact change necessary. The routes are numbered and you soon get to know which bus will take you where.

Train To see the countryside take an early morning train from Casablanca station (just across the harbour mouth by launch from La Fuerza castle) to Matanzas, a two and a half hour trip for about a peso. Come back in the evening on another train.

Hitching Outside the city they'll be so surprised to see you that you'll probably be able to flag down almost any car. Use your hand not your thumb.

Taxi Taxis are hard to get. It's almost impossible to flag them down on the street but you can try for one at a big hotel. The new cabs have meters and the fares are relatively cheap.

Other Information Cubatur, the government tourist agency, has its office at Calle 23 (No. 156) not far from the National Hotel in Vedado. They can reserve hotels and sightseeing tours and also handle general inquiries.

Climate The rainy season is from May to October and this is when the Cubans go to the beach. The humidity can be high at this time of year but it isn't necessarily going to rain all day, usually just a heavy shower in the afternoon, and the evenings are warm and calm. October sometimes sees huricanes. The winter season is probably the best for foreigners although it does get fairly cold at times and rain is not unknown.

Things to Buy Cuba is not a place for shopping since there are serious shortages of consumer goods but you may want to pick up some T-shirts, cigars, and perhaps a bottle of Havana Club rum (used to be called Bacardi). Books and posters are cheap and plentiful. They are sold in the shops along Calle Obispo between the Plaza de Armas and the Parque Central and also in the big stores near the corner of San Rafael and Galiano (open in the afternoon). Handicrafts can be obtained in the boutique at Calle Cuba No. 64. There are tourists shops in all the major hotels but you'll probably do more looking that buying.